ENGLAND'S PIANO SAGE

THE LIFE AND TEACHINGS OF TOBIAS MATTHAY

STEPHEN SIEK

Revised Edition

THE H. W. MARSTON PRESS
WEST CHESTER, PENNSYLVANIA

England's Piano Sage, The Life and Teachings of Tobias Matthay
was originally published in 2012 by Scarecrow Press,
an imprint of Rowman & Littlefield

www.pianosage.net

Copyright © 2020
All rights reserved.
ISBN: 978-0-578-72848-3

The H. W. Marston Press is a division of Marston Records
www.marstonrecords.com

CONTENTS

List of Photographs	v
List of Figures	vii
List of Musical Examples	ix
Table of Abbreviations	xi
Preface	xiii
Foreword to the Revised Edition	xix
Introduction: The Fading Legacy	1
1. Two Lands—One Music	29
2. "Our national musical seminary"	65
3. "Lord-High-Everything-Else"	103
4. *The Overture* . . .	155
5. . . . Scottish Interlude . . .	189
6. . . . and the First "Act"	239
7. Building an Empire	279
8. Life at the Summit	325
9. Storm Clouds	381
10. The Aftermath	431
11. "Whether he is writing real music"	483
12. Final Days	533
Postlude	595
Appendix I: Selected Writings of Tobias Matthay	611
Appendix II: Selected Published Compositions of Tobias Matthay	615
Appendix III: Tobias Matthay: "The Nine Steps towards Finger Individualization through forearm rotation"	619

Appendix IV: Historical Reissues of Recordings by Tobias Matthay and his Pupils	625
Bibliography	633
Index	643
About the Author	655

LIST OF PHOTOGRAPHS

Photo 1	Portrait of Sir William Sterndale Bennett	64
	Copyright of the Royal Academy of Music	
Photo 2	Sir George Macfarren about 1882	81
	Copyright of the Royal Academy of Music	
Photo 3	Walter Macfarren about 1900	82
	Copyright of the Royal Academy of Music	
Photo 4	Tobias Matthay with family in 1880	85
	Courtesy of the Matthay Estate	
Photo 5	London's Royal Academy of Music on Tenterden Street	86
	Copyright of the Royal Academy of Music	
Photo 6	Sir Alexander Mackenzie about 1912	154
	Copyright of the Royal Academy of Music	
Photo 7	John McEwen in 1924	237
	Copyright of the Royal Academy of Music	
Photo 8	Portrait of Tobias Matthay	237
	Copyright of the Royal Academy of Music	
Photo 9	Charcoal sketch of Jessie Matthay	238
	Copyright of the Royal Academy of Music	
Photo 10	Frederick Corder about 1910	238
	Copyright of the Royal Academy of Music	
Photo 11	Arnold Bax about 1922	321
	Copyright of the Royal Academy of Music	
Photo 12	York Bowen about 1905	321
	Copyright of the Royal Academy of Music	
Photo 13	Benjamin Dale about 1914	322
	Copyright of the Royal Academy of Music	
Photo 14	Irene Scharrer about 1925	322
	Copyright of the Royal Academy of Music	

List of Photographs

Photo 15	The Royal Academy of Music building on Marylebone Road at the time of its opening in 1911	323
	Copyright of the Royal Academy of Music	
Photo 16	High Marley seen from the south	378
	Courtesy Matthay Archives	
Photo 17	The Matthay School	379
	Courtesy Matthay Archives	
Photo 18	Tobias Matthay in his studio	380
	Courtesy Matthay Archives	
Photo 19	Matthay at High Marley with Myra Hess	380
	Courtesy Matthay Archives	
Photo 20	Some Americans on the steps of the TMPS in 1924	427
	Courtesy Matthay Archives	
Photo 21	Matthay and Denise Lassimonne about 1930	428
	Courtesy Matthay Archives	
Photo 22	Tea at Marley in the summer of 1928	429
	Courtesy Matthay Archives	
Photo 23	Three Americans at Marley in the summer of 1928	430
	Courtesy Matthay Archives	
Photo 24	The concert room at the TMPS	430
	Courtesy Matthay Archives	
Photo 25	Harriet Cohen about 1930	481
	Copyright of the Royal Academy of Music	
Photo 26	Photo of Matthay taken about 1935	481
	Courtesy Matthay Archives	
Photo 27	Page from the TMPS prospectus	530
	Courtesy Matthay Archives	
Photo 28	Moura Lympany about 1940	531
	Courtesy Estate of Dame Moura Lympany	
Photo 29	Denise and Myra at Lake Como, Italy	531
	Courtesy Matthay Estate	
Photo 30	Matthay rowing on Lake Como	532
	Copyright of the Royal Academy of Music	

LIST OF FIGURES

6.1	"Thrusting" Finger illustration from *The Act of Touch*	258
6.2	"Clinging" Finger illustration from *The Act of Touch*	258
9.1	John McEwen's first graph from *The Music Teacher*	394
9.2	John McEwen's second graph from *The Music Teacher*	394

LIST OF MUSICAL EXAMPLES

2.1	Beethoven: Sonata in C minor, op. 10, no. 1, 2/mm.17-18	83
3.1	Matthay: Nocturne, Op. 3, mm. 1-7	107
3.2	Matthay: Nocturne, Op. 3, mm. 28-31	107
3.3	Matthay: MS Cadenza to Beethoven's Concerto No. 1 in C, Op. 15	108
3.4	Matthay: Motto from "In May"	109
3.5	Matthay: "In May," mm. 1-8	112
3.6	Anton Rubinstein: Etude in C, Op. 23, no. 2, mm. 1-3	127
3.7	Beethoven: Sonata in F minor, Op. 57, 3/ mm. 36-39.	133
3.8	Beethoven: Sonata in F minor, Op. 57, 3/ mm. 158-62.	134
4.1	Matthay: "Doubts" from *Love Phases,* Op. 12, mm. 4-7.	183
5.1	Matthay: "There's nae Lark," mm. 38-39	206
5.2	Matthay: "There's nae Lark," mm 1-4	206
5.3	Matthay, *"Des Mädchens Klage,"* mm. 16-19	207
5.4	Matthay: *Scottish Dances and Melodies,* Op. 15, 1/ mm. 10-11	210
5.5	Matthay: *Scottish Dances and Melodies,* Op. 15, 2/ mm. 17-20	210
5.6	Matthay, *Scottish Dances and Melodies,* Op. 15, 2/ mm. 35-39	211
5.7	Matthay: *Scottish Dances and Melodies,* Op. 15, 2/ mm. 100-103	211
5.8	Benjamin Dale: Sonata in D minor, 1/ mm. 1-15	225
6.1	Beethoven: Sonata, op. 57 1/ mm. 52-53	260
6.2	Matthay: from *Relaxation Studies,* p. 14	271
6.3	Matthay: from *Relaxation Studies,* p. 26.	271
6.4	Matthay: from *Relaxation Studies,* p. 49.	272
6.5	Matthay: from *Relaxation Studies,* p. 81	273

List of Musical Examples

6.6	Matthay: from *Relaxation Studies*, p. 84	273
6.7	Matthay: from *Relaxation Studies*, p. 115.	274
7.1	Matthay: *Concert Piece in A minor,* mm. 304-305.	314
8.1	Schumann: Novelette in F, Op. 21, no. 1, mm 1-4	335
8.2	Schumann: Novelette in F, Op. 21, no. 1, mm 1-4,	335
8.3	Beethoven: Sonata in B-flat, Op. 22, mm 30-33	336
8.4	Chopin: soprano F-sharp, Op. 15, no. 2, mm. 1-2	338
8.5	Chopin: Third Ballade in A-flat, Op. 38, mm. 1-4	340
8.6	Chopin: Mazurka in F-sharp minor, Op. 59, no. 3, mm 65-74	341
8.7	Chopin: Sonata in B-flat minor, Op. 35, 3/mm 31-34	342
8.8	Schumann: *Marche des "Davidsbündler"*, Op. 9, mm 1-4	342
8.9	John B. McEwen: Sonatina in G minor, 2/mm. 17-24	355
8.10	Denise Lassimonne: "Les longs cheveux de Mélisande," mm. 1-4	356
8.11	Matthay: "May Morning," Op. 24, mm. 1-3,	359
11.1	Edwin Gerschefski: Dance, Op. 11, no. 2, mm. 29-31	485
11.2	Matthay: Prelude Op. 16, mm. 1-4	496
11.3	Matthay: "Bravura" Op. 16, mm. 1-2	497
11.4	Matthay: "Bravura" Op. 16, mm. 18-20	497
12.1	Matthay: "A Rainy Holiday" mm. 1-8	570
12.2	Matthay: "The Fool-proof Five-finger Exercise" mm. 1-10	571
12.3	Matthay: "Shades of Czerny" Op. 44	572
12.4	*Matthay: 31 Variations & Derivations,* from an Original Theme, mm. 8-23 (Theme)	577
12.5	Matthay: *31 Variations & Derivations,* Var. 1, mm. 9-16	578
12.6	Matthay: *31 Variations & Derivations,* Var. 8, mm. 1-8	578
12.7	Matthay: *31 Variations & Derivations,* Var. 21, mm. 9-18	579

TABLE OF ABBREVIATIONS

AMAJ	*Journal of the American Matthay Association*, 1925-1949
AMAEM	*Enjoy the Music*, published by the AMA in 1975
AOT	Tobias Matthay, *The Act of Touch*
BBCWA	BBC Written Archives, at Caversham Park near Reading
BL	British Library
BLPS	Philharmonic Society papers and correspondence at the BL
BNL	British Newspaper Library at Colindale
COMM	Committee of Management Minutes from the Royal Academy of Music, London
FC	Frederick Corder, *A History of the Royal Academy of Music, 1822-1922*
FL	Tobias Matthay, *First Lights on Piano Playing*
FP	Tobias Matthay, *First Principles of Pianoforte Playing*
FRO	Family Records Office, London
HDWEA	Howard de Walden Estate Archives
JHM	Jessie Henderson Matthay, *Life and Works of Tobias Matthay*
MKF	Marjory Kennedy-Fraser, *A Life of Song*
LI	Denise Lassimonne Interviews, conducted in Hampshire, England, in August 1988
LRO	Land Registry Office, Chancery Lane, London
MA	Archives of the American Matthay Association, housed (at this writing) in Dayton, Ohio
MI	Tobias Matthay, *Musical Interpretation*
MFD	Matthay Family Documents housed in the Matthay Archives

Table of Abbreviations

MN	*The Matthay News* (American Matthay Association journal after 1960)
MRS	Tobias Matthay, *Muscular Relaxation Studies*
MT	*The Musical Times*
NA	The National Archives, Richmond, Surrey
NRG	*New Revised Grove Dictionary of Music and Musicians*
NYT	The *New York Times*
POA	Tobias Matthay, *Problems of Agility*
RAMA	Royal Academy of Music Archives
RAMCM	*Royal Academy of Music Club Magazine*
RAMDM	Royal Academy of Music Directors Minutes
RAMR	Royal Academy of Music Student Register
RAMRBC	Royal Academy of Music Rare Book Collection
TO	*The Overture*, published by the Royal Academy of Music, 1890-94
TT	*The Times*, London
VIPT	Tobias Matthay, *The Visible and Invisible in Pianoforte Technique*

PREFACE

Late in the afternoon of 2 August 1963, I stood in the lobby of the Andover Inn, some 25 miles north of Boston, to register for the sixth annual piano festival sponsored by the American Matthay Association. It was the first of nearly 40 such events I attended in subsequent years, and undoubtedly one of the last where most of the presenters had actually studied with Tobias Matthay. All are now deceased, and I have often regretted that I had not yet formulated all the questions that can no longer be asked of them. I was then a teenager, and understandably had had limited contact with people in their sixties and seventies, but I did know enough to ask one question that I have often re-asked over the years: What secret of living had these people absorbed, and what kind of a man could melt away their years by inspiring such unbridled joy and enthusiasm?

A decade later I began studying with Matthay's adopted daughter, Denise Lassimonne, but by then I was seeking more than piano instruction, since she represented a link to an earlier age—an age that had always fascinated me. That era had all but vanished, and it was becoming increasingly difficult to resurrect, as evidenced by the fact that all of Matthay's books were rapidly fading from print. I had long wanted to counter this trend by making a modest contribution to Matthay scholarship, but by the mid 'eighties the landscape had become so barren—both in Britain and America—that nothing short of a full-scale biography seemed a reasonable starting point. I often discussed this with Denise, who was uniquely qualified to serve as a resource, and through much of August 1988 I interviewed her at her home in Hampshire, England. The project was still tentative in my mind, because apart from some heirlooms, she had kept surprisingly few documents, records, or photos chronicling her life in the Matthay household. Nor did she possess any correspondence that I ever saw, and I was unsure to what extent such material even existed. I only

Preface

knew that the book could not be written without her remembrances, and within a year I had emerged with nearly 100 typewritten pages of notes. But although I found these recollections fascinating—even indispensable—they were often laced more with sentiment than substance, and I saw little prospect of fashioning a scholarly biography from such an anecdotal tapestry. At the time I was also committed to other projects, so I abandoned—at least temporarily—any plans of embarking on a Matthay biography.

After yet another decade had passed, I became president of the American Matthay Association, and although I was grateful that my background had given me some heightened insight into its mission, it became increasingly apparent that "Matthayism" had now reached a dead end. For the most part, the organization's younger members had little awareness of Matthay's accomplishments, a fact that was scarcely their fault, since the only extant chronicle of his work was a brief, long out-of-print biography by his wife. After my presidential term concluded in June of 2002, I made a silent vow to revisit my long proposed biography, but I had no idea where to begin, and I even feared that after culling all available resources, I might emerge with little more than a pamphlet. I knew only that the research had to be centered in London, where Matthay had lived for most of his 87 years, and I gradually began to refocus my American training toward the *terra incognita* of the British Library, the National Archives, the Land Registry Office, the Family Records Office, and many other institutions which provided invaluable support. But the most indispensable resource was the Royal Academy of Music, where Matthay had taught for nearly 50 years, and whose archival documents serve as the virtual backbone for much of this work.

Because this volume has been authored by an American, American spellings and grammatical preferences have been used in the narrative sections, while British quoted material is always presented in its original form. Inasmuch as the finances of the Tobias Matthay Pianoforte School, which existed from 1905 until 1945, are often discussed, it may be helpful to recall the subdivisions of British money before decimalization occurred in 1971: a pound then contained 20

Preface

shillings (20s), while one shilling was equivalent to 12 pence (12d). The guinea, often considered a more "gentlemanly" expression of payment in the Victorian era, represented the value of £1, 1s—thus the sum of 20 guineas was equal to £21. After the American Matthay Association was founded in 1925, many of Matthay's students calculated their payments and donations in American dollars, so it may also be helpful to note that in the last week of May 1925, the *New York Times* gave the exchange rate as £1 = $4.85. Ten years later, on 31 May 1935, the rate was closer to $4.95, and as the War in Europe was nearing its end on 1 June 1945, the *Times* affirmed that the pound's value had declined to approximately $4.02.

Some defense should also be offered for what may be perceived as shortcomings to this work, since although excerpts from Matthay's important writings have been included, space limitations have not allowed for an exhaustive survey. Though the essentials of his most important theories have been presented, the pages that follow should not be taken as a definitive summary of his publications, and several significant works are not even discussed. This is especially regrettable since scarcely any of his pedagogical writings are still in print, but the problem will be better addressed by modern, annotated editions, and happily, plans are now afoot to reissue many of these works. His compositions also merit a fuller examination than they receive here, even though Matthay's rightful place as a composer may prove to be minor when ranked against the major lights of the "long nineteenth century." But his music still deserves a modern assessment informed by newer editions and recordings, and I hope that the discussions which follow will encourage some additional scholarship and performances. It should also be said that this book contains no diagram of Matthay's pupils, since a comprehensive chart would not only extend to hundreds of names, but might prove misleading. Like Liszt, Matthay had pupils who absorbed his message only partially, and hence the students mentioned in these pages—whether prominent or obscure—have been included only within the context of discussions clarifying their relationship to their teacher.

Preface

On my own side of the Atlantic, many people—perhaps unknowingly—have nurtured this project for decades, but special acknowledgment must be paid to Donald Hageman, who remains not only a friend and mentor, but arguably the most knowledgeable expert today on the technical aspects of Matthay's teachings. I am also indebted to Stewart Gordon, another of my teachers, who offered support for this project and who has provided repeated inspiration by demonstrating that an outstanding musician can also be an outstanding scholar. Gregor Benko, the co-founder of the International Piano Archives, read the entire manuscript and provided invaluable support and suggestions. I must also thank the capable staff of the Music Division of the Library of Congress, who pointed me toward many essential resources within the Library's collections. The Reference Librarians of Thomas Library at Wittenberg University provided willing assistance with a number of highly esoteric requests, and I also express my gratitude to Wittenberg for assisting with several grants, including travel funds which helped me to conduct necessary research in Britain. Thanks are also offered to Professor James Croson, who created the book's musical examples, and to my research assistants, Emily McClay, Joyce Partyka, and Kathryn McNeal, who engaged in indispensable research, typing, and proofreading. For the past several years, the officers, members, and friends of the American Matthay Association (after 2003, the American Matthay Association for Piano) have provided heartfelt encouragement, and the extent to which this work relies on support from that organization's Archives will be obvious. Nigel Coxe and Robin Harrison, both graduates of the Royal Academy of Music, provided further encouragement and helpful assistance, as did my friend Mary Pendleton, a long-time student of Denise Lassimonne, who offered indispensable information about her father, Samuel, which appears in Chapter 12. I also acknowledge the contributions of my friend, the late Francis Burkle-Young, who always placed his encyclopedic knowledge of European culture at my disposal so that (I hope) the many gaps in my own knowledge may seem less apparent.

Many British institutions made their resources available to me, but none deserves greater thanks than the Royal Academy of

Music. Under the leadership of Sir Curtis Price, and more recently of Professor Jonathan Freeman-Attwood, its staff members repeatedly went above and beyond the call, and special acknowledgement must be paid to Kathy Adamson, Bridget Palmer, and Janet Snowman, who gave unstintingly of their time and energy. Peter Horton, Oliver Davis, and other staff members of the Royal College of Music also led me to valuable resources within that institution's substantial collections. Special thanks must also be given to the Howard de Walden Estate, and to its Archivist, Richard Bowden, who was willing to clarify the often confusing labyrinth of Marylebone real estate in the 1920s. Although this list is not exhaustive, the dedicated staff members of many other institutions provided incalculable assistance, including the British Library (both at the main building and at Colindale), the City of Westminster Archives, the BBC Written Archives at Caversham Park, the National Archives in Richmond, the Land Registry Office in Chancery Lane, and the Probate Department in Holborn.

But one of the greatest rewards for me was the support I received from so many British musicians and scholars, most of whom I would not have met had this project not been undertaken. Giles Brightwell generously shared his immense knowledge of the National Training School, and Christopher Fifield allowed me to examine archival items from his personal collection, as did Michael Craxton, Jean Long, Joseph Shaw, Barry Sterndale-Bennett, and John Watson—all of whom provided warm encouragement. I am also profoundly indebted to Lewis Foreman, the leading authority on Arnold Bax, who read portions of the manuscript and provided incomparable guidance as he repeatedly steered me to resources I would not otherwise have found. Monica Watson Chard, a pupil of York Bowen, and the late David Squibb, a pupil of Gertrude Peppercorn, were both exceedingly generous with their time and insights. I am deeply grateful to Ruth Harte Langrish for making available countless resources which belonged to her late husband—one of Tobias Matthay's most favored pupils. And words can scarcely express the gratitude I feel to Oscar Yerburgh and to the late Professor Guy Jonson, both of whom repeatedly opened their homes and their hearts to me, while sharing their memories of studying with Tobias Matthay.

And as all of them are aware, I am especially indebted to Alan Walker for his inspiring scholarship and unfailing support, to my editor, Bennett Graff, for his continued insights and enlightened guidance, and most of all to my wife, Maryanne, who has faithfully supported this project for the past several years, and offered only encouragement.

Springfield, Ohio
February 2011

FOREWORD TO THE REVISED EDITION

Although the original hardbound edition of *England's Piano Sage* is no longer easily found, I hope that both the trade paperback and e-book versions will make its contents even more accessible to students, teachers, and general readers. Since this book was first published eight years ago, interest in Tobias Matthay and his teachings has only intensified throughout the world, and one of the most rewarding pieces of evidence for this growth is that over 50 beautifully engineered CDs of Matthay pupils are now available on major labels. For that reason, I thought it only fitting to chronicle this development in a fourth appendix which appears near the end of this volume. All of these titles have been accompanied by carefully researched liner notes, some by me and some by other eminent scholars, and links to all the uploaded booklets have been included. My heartfelt thanks to the individuals who made this discography possible has also been expressed in Appendix IV.

Tempe, Arizona
July 2020

INTRODUCTION
THE FADING LEGACY

On 3 November 2000, the Society for American Music presented a Lifetime Achievement Award to jazz artist Billy Taylor in Toronto. On that evening, Taylor spoke at length about his early training, noting that when he first arrived in New York in the 1940s, he so idolized pianist Teddy Wilson that he even sought to study with him. He was not alone in his admiration, for over the years Wilson's graceful approach to the instrument has been well documented. In Ken Burns's highly acclaimed *Jazz* film series, author and critic Gary Giddins offered an eloquent encapsulation of his style:

> There's never been a piano player like Teddy Wilson. I think one of the things that distinguishes him from all of the [jazz] players who precede him—Waller, Duke Ellington—is they had a very percussive attack. Teddy Wilson had a light, lyrical attack. It's an exquisite sound. He makes every key sound like a chime or a bell. And he's very fast. And you realize that no one has ever made the piano sound quite like that. After two measures you know it can't be anybody else but Teddy Wilson.[1]

Since Wilson lacked the time to teach the young Taylor, he referred him to his teacher, Richard McClanahan (1893-1981), a pupil of Tobias Matthay and a past president of the American Matthay Association. After acknowledging that McClanahan "taught me everything I know about how to move a piano key," Taylor sat down at the Steinway B provided him that evening and made the piano sing in his own inimitable way. The style and the harmonic vocabulary were his, but the elegance and polish suggested—to borrow Giddins's simile—the splendor of "a chime or a bell." Whatever role McClanahan may have played in helping his students master such effects, similar terms were once used to describe a "Matthay Sound" at the piano—an insignia devoid of harshness, and characterized by extraordinary beauty, resonance, and range of tonal color.

When Matthay's pupils first began to appear in America, that "sound" was recognized as so distinctive that in 1932 the *New York Times* heralded Myra Hess as an artist who "stands alone in the beauty and personal quality of her performance."[2] And over a decade later, his imprint had become so identifiable that historian Jacques Barzun thought it uncontroversial to note that Matthay's pupils could be recognized "even in a dark room by the sound they make."[3] This accolade was offered at a time when teachers were still acknowledged as decisive in shaping their students' achievements, and the greatest homage was often bestowed on those who bequeathed a "legacy," or in other words, their pupils communicated their ideals through a lineage. But the faithful transmission of a message to subsequent generations is difficult without reference to the printed word, and today fewer prominent teachers record their insights for posterity. Some have even argued against teaching "principles" at all, on the grounds that since every artist is unique, intelligent guidance can never be standardized. But this attitude stands in sharp relief to the convictions held a century ago that teaching principles should be universally applicable to all and even verifiable by the dictates of science.

From the late nineteenth century until just before World War II, an explosion of books and pamphlets appeared in Germany, Britain, and America claiming to unlock the secrets of the greatest pianists, and nearly all invoked science as their credo. Before World War I, terms such as "weight" and "relaxation" became the watchwords of an entire generation, not only because their applications seemed to produce results, but because they fascinated theorists who had become enamored with the bounty of scientific discovery. While few doubted that the greatest talents of the nineteenth century— Liszt, Rubinstein, and Bülow among them—possessed natural gifts, increasing numbers of serious musicians began to embrace science as a means of improving performance and ease of execution at the instrument, and few questioned that it could create a brighter future for all who cared to grasp its principles. Indeed, a *leitmotif* of the entire period was that artistry—even virtuosity—was accessible to all who obeyed natural laws, and conversely, that performance could be made effortless, forever devoid of tension and pain.

At the forefront of this movement was England's Tobias Matthay, who eventually filled over a thousand pages advocating what he regarded as compliance with those laws—most of which were produced at his idyllic retreat, "High Marley," overlooking the Sussex Downs near Haslemere. But he was more than a theorist, and for a brief time, no artist-teacher in the world enjoyed such a large following. At London's Royal Academy of Music, at his own school on Wimpole Street, and at Marley—where he was happiest—he played host to hundreds of students, teachers, and admirers who eagerly absorbed his message. And while some may have perceived his pronouncements as divinely inspired, he always insisted that his advice rested purely on the scientific tools of observation and deductive reasoning.

But after World War I, through a transformation that has never been fully explained, the "science" of later commentators began to promise less to performing artists. Newer books—some invoking the authority of laboratory experimentation—undertook a mission which was largely, if not exclusively, polemical. The badge of science now cloaked entire tracts of refutation which served primarily to discredit the theories of the previous generation. Thus it is no coincidence to find Arnold Schultz's 1936 work *The Riddle of the Pianist's Finger*—written "to promote a certain way of playing the piano"—devoting nearly a third of its 310 pages to the discrediting of earlier theorists.[4] It is also scarcely surprising that one of the writers Schultz takes to task is Matthay, who at the time was perceived by most as the leader of the "weight and relaxation" school. But what is startling is the astonishing degree to which, in less than a decade, a handful of commentators displaced—and largely erased—any memory of the theories which had preceded them.

Schultz's work was at least partially inspired by Otto Ortmann's 1929 book *The Physiological Mechanics of Piano Technique*, which set the tone for virtually every theoretical work that followed—although fewer such works appeared in the ensuing years. In an earlier era, Matthay and his contemporaries, such as the German Rudolf Breithaupt, had frequently invoked the term "muscular relaxation" as axiomatic to effective performance, but Ortmann believed he had proven—with the help of a specially constructed mechanical arm—the fallaciousness of such a concept. Instead, he sought to introduce the term "muscular fixation" into the pianist's vocabulary, a quality he claimed was inevitably linked to all muscular actions, but which was undetectable through the performer's sensory experience:

> The direct dependence of force at the finger-tip upon the rigidity of the joints of finger, hand, and arm is then clearly seen. With each increase in force the "break" at the joint of least fixation, other things equal, becomes more noticeable; and this can be overcome only by tightening the set-screws or increasing the pull of the cords representing the muscles. Such facts have become so well-known in mechanics that their re-statement here becomes a truism; yet their absence in the doctrine of relaxation in piano-playing shows clearly that they have escaped detection. This is not surprising, because all such fixation is a necessary coördination; being constantly present in, and varying in a fixed way with each movement. The fixation itself, following a fundamental law of sensation and perception, is not present to consciousness.[5]

Remarkably, Ortmann, who taught at the Peabody Institute in Baltimore, and Schultz, who taught privately in Chicago, trained virtually no internationally prominent pianists. But their theories—which freely challenged the training of virtually every noted pianist of their era—were perceived as sufficiently authoritative to extinguish any interest in the philosophies which had shaped those careers. At one time, Matthay had trained the majority of the piano professors at London's Royal Academy of Music, and in America, his ideas had once been taken seriously at Yale and Juilliard. But after World War II, pianists who invoked his name were largely marginalized, and by the early 1960s few objected when one of America's most distinguished teachers, William Newman of the University of North Carolina, wrote that only Ortmann and Schultz possessed "enough understanding of allied sciences like acoustics and anatomy to permit of scientific conclusions."[6] But exactly what fresh "understanding" had been imparted from these sciences, and precisely how such information had advanced the art of piano playing was less than clear. The new "science" was being used primarily to negate earlier theories, and the content of the ideas advanced to replace them was, at best, ambiguous. In fact, scarcely any pianist from the post-War era could concisely state the pedagogical principles Ortmann advocated—and few seemed to care. But at the same time his stature had become so unassailable that by 1963 Harold Schonberg, the senior music critic for the *New York Times,* could offer him an unqualified endorsement:

> Most modern theorists ridicule the ideas of Matthay, Breithaupt, and the other nineteenth-century weight-and-relaxation specialists. In the 1920s, Otto Ortmann cast the stern eye of science (backed by dispassionate laboratory readings) on the subject, and demonstrated that it is physically impossible to play even a moderately rapid scale without a tightening, in one degree or another, of wrist, elbow, even shoulder. Ortmann's conclusions included "the need for a partial return to the older school" of Reinecke and Clementi; and he wrote that "undue stress on relaxation has seriously restricted velocity and technical brilliance."[7]

And by the century's end, Matthay was no longer even ridiculed: he had simply vanished. A telling example of this obscurity occurred in July of 1992 when five world-renowned pianists performed recitals at the University of Maryland's William Kapell International Competition and Festival. Given their eminence, it was not surprising that the University issued an elaborate program booklet detailing highlights of their careers, and four of the five biographical sketches paid appropriate homage to the artists' teachers. Several brief paragraphs announced that Seymour Lipkin was taught by Rudolf Serkin, Miecyslaw Horszowski, and David Saperton; that Paul Badura-Skoda credited Edwin Fischer with much of his musical development; and that Gary Graffman had worked with both Isabel Vengerova and Vladimir Horowitz. Even the lesser known Russian pedagogue Lea Zelikhman was mentioned as the teacher of Soviet pianist Grigory Sokolov. All of the performances were well received, but the fifth recital brought the audience to its feet and evoked no less than six encores. The pianist was Dame Moura Lympany, but nowhere in the accompanying publicity were any of her teachers even mentioned. The irony of this omission was underscored by a panel discussion on the previous morning in which the artists discussed their early training. Judging from audience reaction, Dame Moura's anecdotes concerning her work with Matthay were one of the highlights of the session, but many who attended only the concert might well have regarded her teacher—the only pedagogue of the group who left a substantial body of writings—as not worth mentioning.[8]

Today, Ortmann's legacy contravenes the view that science can make pianism accessible—and painless—to anyone who simply obeys natural laws. In fact, for most theoreticians muscular tension has become so inextricably linked to performance that the "science" of pedagogy is now focused largely on pathology, with physicians becoming the principal voice of authority to help pianists develop strategies and techniques for the avoidance and treatment of injuries. To be sure, for at least as long as pedagogical theorizing can be documented, muscular tension has concerned keyboardists, and Matthay and his contemporaries posited their views on relaxation—which they believed reflected the practices of the most accomplished performers—precisely as an antidote to the difficulties which they found common to many pupils. But as most of today's physicians are quick to acknowledge, there is a broad continuum between mere tension and physical injury, and excessive tightness or faulty practicing cannot incapacitate a limb overnight. At the very least, the fact that muscular injury is so prominently discussed today raises questions concerning many pianists' long-standing habits, or to put it more bluntly: is it possible that Ortmann was wrong and that tension is not only undesirable, but unnecessary?

But today that question is rarely addressed. "Focal dystonia," a physical ailment from which growing numbers of pianists suffer, has no known cause, and its prevalence has failed to dislodge Ortmann's influence, which still largely sets the terms for the profession as a whole. Tension, and even injury, have become almost the expectations for today's teachers, as shown for example, by the October 2002 meeting of the World Piano Pedagogy Conference in Las Vegas, which was dedicated to "Technique, Movement, and Wellness at the Piano." On the first day of the event, a Juilliard professor offered a talk entitled "A Pianist's Tools: Maintaining the Health of Your Hands," before yielding the podium to a neurosurgeon from Stanford, the Director of the Focal Hand Dystonia Laboratory at the University of Alabama, and an Australian surgeon described in the conference's promotional literature as "perhaps the leading authority of repetitive motion injuries among musicians."[9] And a few months earlier in July of 2002, the international meeting of the World Piano Conference in Portoroz, Slovenia, prominently featured Dr. Eckart Altenmüller, the Director of the Institute for Musical Physiology and Music Medicine at the Hochschule für Musik und Theater in Hannover.[10]

Curiously, while many fields pride themselves on understanding the history of their profession, relatively few pianists and teachers seem interested in revisiting the pre-Ortmann world. This neglect is sometimes explained by the observation that the pianist's art has evolved over the past century, so that today any wisdom once brought forth in an earlier era—from Matthay onward—has been successfully absorbed into the pedagogical climate, making more detailed analysis superfluous. But this merely begs the question of the means by which such absorption has occurred. Of the nearly 1500 pages penned by Matthay and Breithaupt—and the 500 spent by Ortmann refuting their views—virtually all are out of print, so most of the arguments for either side exist only in libraries. Understandably, in today's conservatories and universities their works are rarely read by serious piano students, most of whom could neither summarize nor even express an informed dismissal of their ideas.

Ironically, the science which surfaced as an antidote to tension in the late nineteenth century was later discredited by theorists in the early twentieth century who argued that tension was essential to successful technique. And for all intents and purposes, the "science" that once characterized the field has now been ceded to doctors—professionals who specialize in the treatment of pain and injury. But if Ortmann was correct, should not today's teachers be *more*, rather than less, informed about the methodology behind his conclusions? And if, as some will argue, physicians lend greater scientific credibility to modern pedagogy, what degree of confidence can be bestowed on "scientists" who have studied neither the theories they accept—nor those they reject? At this point, a brief overview of the field prior to Matthay's appearance is essential.

As the nineteenth century drew to a close, German pianism was embracing two opposing philosophies. The first was a reactionary movement advocated by—among others—the influential Carl Reinecke (1824-1910), who taught at the Leipzig Conservatory from 1860 until his death. Reinecke, who became director of the Conservatory in 1897, had been intimate with Mendelssohn, Liszt, and the Schumanns, and he made a profound impact as the guardian of "tradition" in both composition and performance.[11] Rarely a proponent of new ideas, he was frequently criticized for his excessive conservatism, and the Baden-born Oscar Beringer (1844-1922), later a colleague of Matthay at the Royal Academy, left Reinecke's studio after he discovered that "the teaching of touch and technique was entirely ignored by the Professors at the Conservatoire."[12] In a similar vein, the Stuttgart Conservatory was training pianists according to the dictates of its founder and director, Sigismund Lebert (1822-84), who, with his colleague Ludwig Stark, had authored a method of study in 1856 which was later expanded to four volumes. Their approach was acclaimed by some of the leading musicians of the day, including Liszt, who praised it for training "real artists, not parasitical dabblers."[13] But despite a rich corpus of repertoire, the Lebert-Stark offered little in the way of fresh pedagogical insights, as may be inferred by this excerpt from its foreword: "At first, play every piece slowly and forte throughout; in the beginning observe only the principal shadings, the *legato* and *staccato* in their different forms, and not until the piece can be executed without a mistake notice the lesser signs of expression. By a study of this kind a firm style of playing will be obtained."[14]

As the piano grew in size and power, that "firm style" became an obsession to many, an ideal which only increased the Lebert-Stark's dissemination and influence. The books were popular even in Russia, and years later the pianist and teacher Maria Levinskaya, who had encountered them in her youth, expressed disapproval of the outmoded philosophy they promoted: "From such teaching little more than a parody on correct finger work could arise, the essence of which was endless finger grinding, striking with force, stiffening the wrist, producing a jar of the hand, the tone getting sharp and hard, without any possibility of the true binding or any mellow sound connection."[15]

The American pianist Amy Fay, who arrived in Germany in 1869 for study with Tausig and Liszt, once remarked that Stuttgart was the place "to get the machine in working order." And not surprisingly, when she reached Tausig's conservatory in Berlin—as she confided to her sister—she was subjected to a similar regimen by her first teacher, Louis Ehlert:

> You have no idea how hard they make Cramer's Studies here. Ehlert makes me play them tremendously *forte*, and as fast as I can go. My hand gets so tired that it is ready to break, and then I say that I cannot go on. "But you *must* go on," he will say. It is the same with the scales. It seems to me that I play them so loud that I make the welkin [heavens] ring, and he will say, "But you play always *piano*." And with all this rapidity he does not allow a note to be missed, and if you happen to strike a wrong one he looks so shocked that you feel ready to sink to the floor.[16]

However, even at the height of their influence, many contemporaries of Reinecke and Lebert were beginning to sense that repetitive, rigorous drills with stiffly held fingers—however effectively they might have served the harpsichordist—were unsuitable for extracting artistic effects from the modern piano. For one thing, harpsichord technique had been almost exclusively focused on the fingers, and the increased resistance of the piano's keys required more power. Several decades earlier, even Carl Czerny, the teacher of Liszt and Leschetizky, had begun to stress the necessity for involving the entire body in tone production, and in the late 1830s, he wrote a series of letters underscoring these precepts to a fictitious pupil named "Cecilia:"

> Before any thing else, I earnestly entreat you, Miss Cecilia, to acquire a graceful and appropriate position, when sitting at the piano-forte. The seat which you use must be just so high that the elbows, when hanging down freely, may be a very little less elevated than the upper surface of the keys; and if your feet should not reach the ground, have a dwarf stool or ottoman made, of a proper height, to place them upon. You must always seat yourself exactly facing the middle of the key-board, and at such a distance from it that the tips of the elbows may be a little nearer to the keys than the shoulders.
>
> Equally important is a graceful position and carriage of the head and upper part of the chest; it must neither be stiff nor bent. Some of my former little pupils, whom I used to teaze [sic] with the reproach of *making a cat's back*—that is, sitting with their backs bent and oblique—have, in later days, thanked me for the strictness which I shewed in this particular.
>
> It is not merely that an awkward position is disagreeable and ridiculous, but it also impedes, if not prevents, the development of a free and elegant style of playing.[17]

If Czerny had advocated a greater freedom and ease at the instrument, the philosophical underpinning for a new pedagogical science was soon laid by Adolph Bernhard Marx (1795-1866), perhaps the leading musical theorist of his generation. Trained as a lawyer and later active as a professor of musicology at the University of Berlin, Marx rejected the proposition that musical training could benefit only the naturally gifted, and in 1845 he even met with Prussia's King Friedrich Wilhelm IV to promote a national system of comprehensive music education.[18] His competence in theory and composition was unexcelled, but he also offered many insightful observations about the contemporary state of piano teaching, and he was among the first to insist that technical proficiency could not be separated from artistic effects, leading him to covet musical sensitivity above all other traits, even in passages demanding extreme power:

> Each finger must be able to seize the emotional tone by itself, with the requisite degree of tenderness and accentuation, of individualization, or of melting into the next tone—must, as it were, have a soul and independent life of its own, to conduct through its nerve the soul of the player to the key. Far as the pianoforte is inferior to bowed and wind instruments in melodic power, as regards the blending of tones and their gradation in volume, much more may be achieved than one usually hears or believes, if the key be touched gently and caressingly, not dabbed at or struck; if the finger lay hold of it with intelligence so to speak; if even extreme power be not expressed in rough blows, but issue from the native power of the musical conception. The key must be felt, not pushed or struck.[19]

Marx's humanistic message was soon absorbed by one of his pupils, Adolph Kullak (1823-62), the younger brother of Theodor, a famous, but (ironically) a fairly uninspired teacher. Described by one commentator as "a rather dry technician," Theodor published a well-known method of instructional etudes called *Schule des Oktavenspiels* (School of Octave Playing) in 1848, and in 1850, with Marx and Julius Stern he founded the Berliner Musikschule, which later became the Berlin Conservatory.[20] However, in 1860, Adolph—whose pupils included Hans Bischoff—offered *Die Ästhetik des Klavierspiels* (The Esthetics of Piano Playing), a highly original work which echoes many of Marx's precepts. He pays special attention to the correct functioning of the arm, a limb that was then all but ignored by most of his German colleagues:

> As long as the fingers execute a pearling legato, the cooperation of the arm is not allowable. Should it take place, the evenness and independence of the finger-strokes would be lost. It is, however, a different

matter with separate long-sustained series of singing tones or accents not gliding on in unbroken flow. Here the weight of the arm aids the pressure of the fingers and augments the singing tone. . . . Externally and internally a co-operation of the whole nervous playing apparatus is involved, which exercises a delicate influence on the production of tone. A series of tones thus played will be distinguished by softness, fulness [sic], and melting melody. . . .

Such is the influence of the arm on the finger-stroke, the chief agent. Its working, though sensible, was still invisible.[21]

Kullak closes his work by advancing a philosophic credo which soon guided the most prominent teachers of the coming generation. He urges artists to be led by more than just their emotions, and to become in effect, thinkers guided by scientific observation and reasoning:

May this brief exposition of the subject-matter of general musical aesthetics stimulate the student to penetrate in *thought* no less than in *feeling* into the essence of pianoforte compositions. Feeling will be lovelier, the more it is spiritualized by thought.—Let the player not be content, to leave everything to his blind emotional instinct; in all there dwells a law of beauty, which would be discovered by meditation. . . .

Meditation and research—the study of the work in its least detail— the establishment of all elements of beauty on intelligent, scientific knowledge—this is the task.[22]

And soon it fell to another of Marx's pupils, Ludwig Deppe (1828-90), to develop these ideas even more emphatically in the teaching studio. Active in both Hamburg and Berlin, Deppe was more famous in his lifetime as a conductor than as a pianist, but his pedagogical influence extended as far as Leschetitzky and Tovey, and he personally trained Emil von Sauer, Elisabeth Caland (who later chronicled his principles), and Amy Fay, whose frustration with traditional teaching methods eventually led her to join his class.[23] After she returned to America, she became one of his most devoted disciples, and some fourteen years later, she recalled her first meeting with him:

> At the first conversation I had with Deppe in Berlin [in 1873], he told me that it was his object to establish a school of piano-playing, and surprised me very much by saying that up to the present day no school of piano-playing has existed. What he meant to say was, that in piano-playing no particular way of doing anything had ever been decided upon and recognized as the true method, as has been the case in singing, and in playing the violin. Everybody knows, that in singing, the Italian method is universally conceded to be the true one, because the Italians have a natural instinct, strengthened by years of experience, for tone production. There is also a school of violin-playing, and all good teachers of the violin teach the principles of its *technique* in a particular way. But when it comes to the piano, there are no fixed laws, and each teacher goes his own way. Now there is no reason why there should not be a logically developed system for forming a fine piano *technique*, which, if rightly followed out, will enable the player to obtain the results at which he aims. Deppe claims to have produced such a system, and fourteen years of constant teachings of his ideas has only increased their value in my opinion, and I wish that all teachers would examine them. I think they would find, as I have, that it makes all the difference in the world, knowing how to teach from a conscientiously artistic standpoint and getting to the bottom of things.[24]

By 1873, Fay was certainly no stranger to artistic piano playing, having studied with both Liszt and Theodor Kullak. But as teachers, neither provided her with any technical guidance save trial and error, and she was elated when Deppe offered her principles informed by a science that seemed to make immediate solutions possible:

> In my study with Kullak when I had any special difficulties, he only said, "Practice always, Fräulein. *Time* will do it for you some day. Hold your hand any way that is easiest for you. You can do it in *this* way—or in *this* way"—showing me different positions of the hand in playing the

troublesome passage—"or you can play it with the *back* of the hand if that will help you any!" But Deppe, instead of saying, "Oh, you'll get this after years of practice," shows me how to conquer the difficulty *now*. He takes a piece, and while he plays it with the most wonderful *fineness* of conception, he cold-bloodedly dissects the mechanical elements of it, separates them, and tells you how to use your hand so as to grasp them one after the other. In short, he makes the technique and the conception *identical*, as of course they ought to be, but I never had any other master who trained his pupils to attempt it.[25]

Echoing postulates of Marx and Adolph Kullak, Deppe insisted on physical ease, that is, muscular relaxation, a state that could not be observed visually, but experienced only through the executant's experience. Concurrent with this was his insistence on the release of "weight," a condition which was equally "invisible" (to borrow a term first used by Kullak and later by Matthay) to the eye. In 1885 he elaborated these concepts for a German periodical in his article "Arm-leiden des Klavierspielers" (Problems of the Arm among Pianists):

> My tone production does not develop through striking, but solely through the weight of the hand, through simple movements of lifting and falling, with quiet, relaxed fingers. The tone produced in this way is not only more refined, but also more intense in character, resulting in a more penetrating sound than the one which is struck. The former tone does not come about through more or less forced, nerve-irritating muscle action; it forms itself much more in complete repose, without any inner or outer excitement—so to speak—"conscious unconsciousness."[26]

Deppe's article was meant as a prelude to a more extensive treatise—complete with muscular conditioning exercises for the arm and shoulder—but he died before it was begun. However, despite the fact that his legacy is documented only by this short piece and by several additional offerings from adoring students, he began a revolution in piano teaching.[27] Matthay believed that Deppe was the greatest teacher of the nineteenth century, and credited him with inaugurating a new, scientific era of instruction.[28] This period was soon characterized not only by a belief in ease and muscular relaxation, but by an important Marxian corollary: the conviction that artistic success was no longer limited only to the innately gifted, but open to all who cared to grasp the relevant scientific principles. It was therefore the task of the teacher not simply to monitor endless drill sessions for the student, but to identify and explain the relevant principles governing successful execution, so that faults could be immediately and permanently corrected.

Although Marx, and to a lesser extent, Kullak, had laid the philosophical foundations for such a pedagogical revolution, Deppe had served as its principal catalyst, and he opened a floodgate which brought forth a spate of commentary in Germany, forging a movement that was aptly characterized by scholar Reginald Gerig:

> After Deppe's death in 1890, a continuous stream of publications on piano technique with an emphasis on physiology, especially on the functions of the arm, came from the press. In the years after the turn of the century, it became virtually a torrent—particularly in Germany. Besides the Deppe pupils, there were Eugen Tetzel, Alexander Ritschl, Paul Stoye, Tony Bandmann, Friedrich Adolf Steinhausen and the most influential of them all, Rudolf Maria Breithaupt (1873-1945).[29]

Rudolf Breithaupt had studied in Leipzig, where he undoubtedly encountered the reactionary influence of Reinecke, and he later taught at the Berlin Conservatory, long after Theodor Kullak's spirit had evaporated and Deppe's name was now on everyone's lips. But oddly, he always credited the Venezuelan pianist Teresa Carreño (1853-1917) with introducing him to the concept of arm weight. Born in Caracas, Carreño, whose background was profoundly eclectic, was taken at the age of eight to New York, where she studied with Gottschalk. At twelve, she relocated to Paris where she played for Anton Rubinstein, who also counseled her third husband, Eugen d'Albert (1864-1932). D'Albert, whose mentors also included Liszt, Brahms, and Bülow, was largely self taught as a pianist, but during their three-year union, it was said that he made a profound impact on Carreño's playing, and that following their divorce in 1895 she became a far more thoughtful interpreter.[30] Breithaupt never studied with Carreño, but he invited her to play for his students and presented her as a model of muscular ease and freedom: "The present writer's first suggestions of weight were received from Teresa Carreño and her 'School,' but especially from the highly-gifted technic of the artist herself. The weight-feeling had become second nature to her. She had 'taught and rolled' the weight long before the subject was systematized in my writings, which made the attempt at a complete, unified representation."[31]

The first volume of Breithaupt's major work, *Die natürliche Klaviertechnik* (Natural Piano Technique), appeared in 1905, and volume two followed in 1907, subtitled *Schule des Gewichtspiels*. This volume re-appeared two years later in English translation as *Natural Piano Technic. Vol. II: School of Weight-Touch*.[32] Replete with musical exercises and photos of hand positions, it was undertaken reluctantly at first, since Breithaupt maintained that he understood "from practical experience how difficult it is to formulate these apparently simple fundamental principles of technic without the aid of practical demonstrations [lessons]."[33] However, he relented when it became apparent to him that his first volume was insufficiently clear:

> The Fundamental Principles of weight-produced touch having . . . been laid down theoretically, it became more and more necessary to develop those principles in a gradual manner from practical experience for practical use. Also, yielding to the repeatedly expressed wish to have the substance of my work divested of its scientific encumbrance and reduced to its simplest form, in order to render the ideas clear to all, and the *"new theories"* universal, I have now condensed the work to the present volume, which contains all that is essential and important for the elementary development of a natural method of playing.[34]

The aura of "genius" seems to permeate the entire work, since many of his photos are even accompanied with captions implying that the hand-movements pictured are identical to those employed by Carreño and d'Albert.[35] The *School* also confirms that of all the weight-relaxation theorists, Breithaupt was the most extreme in his insistence that the full weight of the arm be continuously relaxed. His American pupil Florence Leonard reported that, even away from the keyboard, he seemed obsessed with the concept of weight relaxation:

> His handshake must not be taken as a test of cordiality. For hands, to a player, are a most precious possession, and since "all the actions of the hand in daily life, grasping, lifting, carrying, and the like, are active (the opposite of actions useful in playing) and fatigue the hand," Breithaupt avoids these actions of the muscles, and gives the most relaxed of handshakes. One notices too, that all his movements are relaxed. If, by chance, in illustrating a point, his hand once falls on the arm or shoulder of his interlocutor, at the next approach, it falls only on thin air,—it has been avoided,—for of all heavy hands, it seems the heaviest. "My friends always draw back when I begin to gesture," he says, laughing. "They are afraid of my arm."[36]

For scientific garnish, Breithaupt quoted a physiologist and amateur pianist, Friedrich Adolph Steinhausen (1859-1910), whose *Die physiolgischen Fehler und die Umgestaltung der Klavier-technik* (Physiological Faults and the Reshaping of Piano Technique) was published by Breitkopf and Härtel in 1905. Breithaupt later maintained that this work provided a scientific validation of several of his principles, although he continued to credit himself with their initial identifications. He claims to have originated the idea of "the fore-arm roll; but Steinhausen was the first to explain and demonstrate it." He adds that the concept of relaxation was, "as taught by Steinhausen and myself *entirely new*. Steinhausen supported the idea of weight-playing through his brilliant and destructive criticism of the finger-methods. In its essentials this was correct, though too far reaching in its form."[37]

However, when it came to favoring the arm over the finger, it seems difficult to believe that anyone could have been more "far reaching" than Breithaupt, because even while he was developing his theories, many were dismissing him as a mere caricature of the new "science." In the first decade of the twentieth century, after completing five years of study with Vassily Safonov at the Moscow Conservatory, Maria Levinskaya arrived in Berlin in quest of "finishing lessons" with an artist-teacher, and nearly 25 years later, she recalled her first meeting with Breithaupt:

> I paid a visit, amongst others, to Mr. Breithaupt, who at our first interview, whilst developing his theories, approached the piano and showed a few passages. I am sure he will forgive me when I say that on hearing his version of correct passage playing it was so far removed from my own ideal that at once I decided to study with Godowsky. It is only now, in the light of my analysis of Breithaupt's theories in print, that I can fully understand why such an impression was inevitable, for in playing he evidently tried to follow his own precepts, and avoid all precise finger articulation. Possibly he was never actually a master of it, for having once realized the sense of control it creates, it seems too great a sacrifice even for the purpose of proving one's theories to voluntarily renounce so wonderful an asset.[38]

Although notable pianists aided by Breithaupt's teachings are difficult to document, he was quite insistent that the most successful artists of the day adhered closely to his principles.[39] In addition to Carreño and d'Albert, he made frequent reference to Leopold Godowsky—then living in Berlin—and before long he had become virtually fixated on Artur Schnabel, who, though initially cordial, soon complained that he was being hounded by an unbridled eccentric:

> In those first years in Berlin I saw him very often and he would always have me play for him alone. I did not see why. Years later he published, with far-reaching effect, a book on piano-playing. In the private seances on which he so toughly insisted, I had served him, as I knew now, as one of his guinea-pigs. Once, also before the book was out, he came to the artists' room after

a concert and announced with excitement and jubilance: "Schnabel, you play with shoulder-participation." I and the people around me thought he was crazy. What did he mean? He had come only to watch and, as he hoped, to establish that I played with shoulder-participation. I had never speculated how much shoulder-participation is required, how much "fall," "weight," wrist-rolling, what elbow angles—and endlessly on.[40]

And some years later, Claudio Arrau, who was then studying in Berlin with Martin Krause, reported similar experiences:

I remember he once asked me to play for him, and while I was playing he began saying, "Yes, yes, yes! Exactly right!" There was one fundamental problem in his teaching—he only taught arm weight. His pupils didn't develop their finger technique at all. Not Carreño, of course—she knew better. But the playing of the others was always messy. Breithaupt neglected absolutely the development of the finger muscles.[41]

But Breithaupt's theorizing was also vulnerable to attack even by those who agreed with his fundamentals. For one thing, he promoted his views with a messianic zeal, insisting that he had originated all worthwhile alternatives to the older German high-finger school. While he allowed that the "much-despised Hofkapellmeister Deppe" had a glimmering of weight theory when he "came upon the idea of letting the arm fall from the shoulder through correct observation of Rubinstein's playing,"[42] he insisted that Deppe's pupils played with stiff, unrelaxed fingers. He also insisted (absurdly) that he had "invented" forearm rotation, despite the fact that Matthay had discussed this sensation extensively in *The Act of Touch*, published a full two years before the first volume of *Die natürliche Klaviertechnik* appeared. Matthay also felt that Breithaupt had overstepped himself by deifying the concept of arm weight, an obsession that he thought had done much damage to the profession:

And when, after a time some better ideas began to dawn upon the minds of a few rare teachers, such as a vague notion of "Weight" for instance, such ideas, even though on the right path, often led to the most disastrous results. The full weight of the arm was, for instance, allowed to be carried from key to key, thus actually laming and often permanently disabling many of the talented but unfortunate aspirants who worked only too well on the "systems" evolved from such half-truths.[43]

You cannot realize that each and every tone in a *musical* passage must have a *separate* musical and technical entity, and at the same time believe in the "full weight of the arm" (Breithaupt's "schwere Tastenbelastung") carried from key-*bed* to key-*bed*—to the utter destruction of Music-sense, and risk to limb and Piano! . . . Is not "cramp" (or Neuritis) so often induced precisely by such fallacious and clumsy *full-weight-carrying* process?[44]

Tobias Matthay (1858-1945), English by birth, shared at least one important trait with Deppe and Breithaupt because he was closer to German culture than many of his countrymen. Like many German immigrants, his parents retained their native language in the home, and he had no need to wait for translations of Marx, Kullak, and their descendants. But in his own writings, his Germanic background may have been a double-edged sword, since some have argued that his English was hampered by unwieldy sentence lengths, excessive capitalizations, and other encumbrances stemming from German syntax. However, his schoolmaster father had also communicated a respect for science and the scientific method, so that when the time came for organizing and systematizing a subject as complex as piano playing, the task no doubt seemed for him a natural endeavor. As he once told the *Musical Times*, he maintained a "dual interest" in music and science throughout his life, which "enabled him to bring the methods of science to bear upon the technical and musical problems of pianoforte playing."[45] Matthay's earliest writings date from about 1890, and they demonstrate that he then viewed himself as a member of a small community of forward-looking teachers who shared similar ideas. With the passage of time he began to grant himself the status of innovator, but even then he never believed he had achieved anything more significant than the identification of certain natural laws.

Like Deppe and Breithaupt, he shared a rejection of what he termed "empiric" piano teaching, or in other words, the attempt to solve problems purely through blind experimentation. Instead, he believed that appropriate physical actions could only be understood by reference to principles reached through observation and induction—principles which could never be grasped or developed purely through trial and error. With Deppe and Breithaupt he also shared a commitment to weight and relaxation, and although he disagreed emphatically with many of Breithaupt's conclusions, he shared his commitment to the printed word, leading him eventually to fill many volumes with explanations of his theories. And to Matthay's advantage, the climate was ripe for such offerings, since in the two decades preceding World War I, Europe and America were eager to devour alternatives to the long-revered finger methods. And if many of the newer, scientific solutions seemed like "quick fixes" to some, so much the better, for many musicians felt that such fixes were long overdue.

Matthay's first book, *The Act of Touch*, appeared in 1903, and though it seemed to some as a *magnum opus*, he always expected to follow it with subsequent writings. It had long been apparent to him that musicianship was also a science, and that many long-established canons of musical interpretation needed elaboration. First at the Royal Academy, and then throughout Britain, he began giving lectures on the interpretation of music, eventually identifying principles in the aesthetic realm that were no less original than those he had identified in the realm of piano technique. In this sense, he also differed radically from Deppe, Breithaupt, and their forebears, for scarcely any pianist had ever codified a principled guide to musicianship. In 1913, he distilled his lectures into a short book of less than 200 pages titled *Musical Interpretation: Its Laws and Principles, and their Application in Teaching and Performing*, which, despite its brevity, was far reaching in its influence. Some have argued that it was his most significant work, since its scope extended well beyond the boundaries of pianism, and over the years it found its way onto the bookshelves of countless instrumentalists and conductors.

Introduction

A few years before *Musical Interpretation* appeared, he opened a school which flourished for forty years, offering instruction shaped entirely around the principles he outlined in his books. At its height, the enrollment in London alone (not counting its many branches) approached 500, and while it thrived, there was no comparable institution anywhere in the world. As one of his former pupils once remarked, "It is a matter of common knowledge that, for at least twenty-five years (from say 1910 to 1935) nearly all the most promising English students of the piano gravitated at some stage of their student life, towards the Matthay School."[46] And after World War I, its constituency had expanded to all corners of the globe, as exemplified for example, by the American Matthay Association, which—at this writing—has flourished nearly continuously for over 80 years.

The School's uniqueness was attributable to the universality of the principles he adduced, for while it welcomed children of all ages, it also served as a second home to many eminent pianists from Britain and throughout the world. Rarely has any teacher been so committed to both ends of the pedagogical spectrum, for Matthay believed that no one should ignore the necessity for laying a proper foundation, and he worked tirelessly—until his final days—to create teaching materials for the young. That he could nurture artistry scarcely seemed in question, but he also brought heightened accomplishments to those of limited talent. His adopted daughter, Denise Lassimonne, once teased him with a mock-rebuke: "You're a menace! You enable people with no artistic vision at all to become successful performers!"[47] "Vision," as he freely admitted, was a quality he could not teach, but merely nurture, and he understood that he may have released a genie from a bottle. Once when an admirer asked him to what he attributed his success, he replied, "I think the answer is 'Through making "duds" play well.'"[48]

Yet a strange and ironic twist transformed an important chapter in Britain's musical history into a poignant melodrama. By the mid-1920s, just as his influence was rapidly expanding throughout the world, Tobias Matthay was suddenly attacked by one of Britain's most prominent musicians—a former pupil and once cherished friend—who denounced his teachings in print and forced him to end a half-century relationship with the institution which had once revered him. The methods of one of the world's most admired teachers were now subjected to unrelenting attack, and Matthay's eminence was clearly fading, especially in his own country. By the late 1980s, a telling confirmation of that erosion was offered by a staff member at the Royal Academy who enthusiastically supported a Matthay biography, but who counseled that "Unfortunately, most of our students would know the name 'Matthay' only because of a classroom in our building which bears his name."

Given that a man's monuments should rest upon his achievements, the pages that follow are designed to chronicle both.

Notes

1. *Jazz*, A Film by Ken Burns, Episode 5, "Pure Pleasure," Florentine Films [2000].
2. "Music in Review: Myra Hess, Pianist, Gives Her Farewell Concert—Iturbi Plays With Philharmonic-Symphony," *NYT*, 25 April 1932, 18.
3. Jacques Barzun, *Teacher in America* (Boston, 1945), 21. The complete quote is: "The pupils of Leopold Auer or Tobias Matthay can be recognized at forty paces by their posture and even in a dark room by the sound they make."
4. See Arnold Schultz, *The Riddle of the Pianist's Finger and its Relationship to a Touch-Scheme* (Chicago, 1936; reprint ed., 1959), ix. In turn, Schultz (pp. 218-310) examines the teachings of Leschetizky, Matthay, Breithaupt, and Ortmann.
5. Otto Ortmann, *The Physiological Mechanics of Piano Technique: An experimental study of the nature of muscular action as used in piano playing, and of the effects thereof upon the piano key and the piano tone* (New York, 1929; reprint ed., New York, 1981), 130. Ortmann's book is discussed in more detail in Ch. 10.
6. William S. Newman, "On the Special Problems of High-Speed Playing," *Clavier* 2 (May-June 1963): 3, 11.

Introduction

7. Harold C. Schonberg, *The Great Pianists from Mozart to the Present* (New York, 1963), 277.
8. At one time the University of Maryland sold a video tape of this panel discussion, a copy of which is now in the Matthay Archives. Somewhat ironically, the William Kapell Competition and Festival grew from an earlier series of piano festivals on the College Park campus, including those sponsored by the American Matthay Association, which were held there from 1965 to 1972.
9. On 27 October 2002, Juilliard's Yoheved Kaplinsky was followed by Frank Wilson, M.D., speaking on "Performing Arts Medicine: Looking Back and Looking Ahead," Hunter Fry, M.D., on "Repetition in Practice," and the University of Alabama's Robert Poczatek, M.D., on "Using Basic Anatomy to Solve Musical Problems at the Keyboard."
10. On 2 July 2002, Dr. Altenmüller gave a lecture entitled "The Pianistic Miracle: From Neurons to the Beethoven Sonata," and on 3 July he gave a "hands-on" session titled, "Hands and Brain—Muscles, Tendons, and Joints: Anatomy and Physiology of Piano Playing."
11. See Reinhold Sietz, "Reinecke, Carl (Heinrich Carsten)," *The Revised New Grove Dictionary of Music and Musicians* (Hereafter cited as *RNG),* ed. S. Sadie and J. Tyrrell (London, 2001).
12. Oscar Beringer, *Fifty Years' Experience of Pianoforte Teaching and Playing* (London, 1907), 26. Beringer left the Conservatory, but remained in Leipzig to study with Louis Plaidy, for whom he had high praise. Ironically, while he was still teaching at the Conservatory, Plaidy had also taught the teenaged Grieg, who left him because he found his "pedantic methods of instruction so irksome and his teaching repertory of Czerny, Kuhlau and Clementi so sterile." See John Horton and Nils Grinde, "Grieg, Edward (Hagerup)," *RNG.*
13. At least this was an endorsement that Lebert and Stark perpetuated. In America, Schirmer's edition of the method books was extremely popular. See Sigismund Lebert and Louis Stark, *Theoretical and Practical Piano School for Systematic Instruction in all Branches of Piano-Playing from the First Elements to the Highest Perfection*, 3 vols. (New York, [1899]), iii.
14. Lebert-Stark, xvii.
15. Maria Levinskaya, *The Levinskaya System of Pianoforte Technique and Tone-Colour through Mental and Muscular Control* (London, 1930), 58.

16. Amy Fay, *Music-Study in Germany from the Home Correspondence of Amy Fay*, ed. by Fay Pierce (New York, 1908; reprint ed., New York, 1979), 21-22. Hereafter cited as Fay, *Music-Study*.
17. Charles [Karl] Czerny, *Letters to a Young Lady, on the Art of Playing the Pianoforte, from the Earliest Rudiments to the Highest Stage of Cultivation*, trans. by J. A. Hamilton (New York, 1837[?]; reprint ed., New York,, 1982), 3-4.
18. See Sanna Pederson, "Marx, (Friedrich Heinrich) Adolf Bernhard [Samuel Moses]," *RNG*.
19. Quoted in Adolph Kullak, *The Aesthetics of Pianoforte-Playing*, trans. by Theodore Baker (New York, 1893; reprint ed., New York, 1972), 85. Kullak does not indicate the source from which the Marx quote was drawn. Hereafter cited as Kullak, *Aesthetics*.
20. See Reginald R. Gerig, *Famous Pianists & Their Technique* (Washington, D.C, 1974), 248. See also Horst Leuchtmann, "Kullak; (1) Theodor Kullak," *RNG*.
21. Kullak, *Aesthetics*,190-91.
22. Kullak, 328.
23. See John Warrack, "Deppe, Ludwig," *RNG*.
24. Amy Fay, *The Deppe Finger Exercises for Rapidly Developing an Artistic Touch in Piano Playing* (London, [1900]), preface.
25. Fay, *Music-Study,*318-19.
26. Quoted in Gerig, 253.
27. In addition to Amy Fay's book of Deppe exercises (first published in Chicago in 1890), see C. A. Ehrenfechter, *Technical Study in the Art of Pianoforte Playing (Deppe's Principles)*, (London, 1895). Also, in 1903 G. Schirmer offered *Artistic piano playing as taught by Ludwig Deppe together with practical advice on questions of technique,* a translation of Elisabeth Caland's *Die Deppe'sche Lehre des Klavierspiels,* first published in 1893.
28. Matthay was critical of Caland's presentation of Deppe's theories, writing in *The Act of Touch* (326), "We find the same fallacy—of relying mostly on the phenomena of Position and Movement—exhibited by those who profess to teach the methods of another of the last century's really great teachers—LUDWIG DEPPE, who indeed was probably the most advanced of all the well known nineteenth-century teachers."

29. Gerig, 329.
30. See Norman Fraser, "Carreño, (Maria) Teresa," *RNG*.
31. R. M. Breithaupt, "The Idea of Weight-Playing—its Value and Practical Application," Pt. I, *The Musician* 26 (January 1911):1, 12. Hereafter cited as Breithaupt, "Idea."
32. See Rudolf M. Breithaupt, *Natural Piano Technic. Vol II: School of Weight-Touch*, trans. by John Bernhoff (Leipzig, 1909). Hereafter cited as Breithaupt, *Weight-Touch*.
33. Breithaupt, *Weight-Touch*, 5.
34. Breithaupt, *Weight-Touch*, 5.
35. One such photo occurs on p. 37 with a caption which reads in part: "It is very easy to observe in a practical manner this rotary function, by watching the hands of a pianist (playing in a natural manner) from below. For this purpose we would draw attention to the elegant rotary curves executed by d'Albert or Teresa Carreño when playing."
36. Florence Leonard, "How Breithaupt Teaches," *The Musician* 30 (April 1915):4, 225.
37. Breithaupt, "Idea," 12.
38. Levinskaya, 56.
39. Interestingly, at the Berlin Hochschule in the late 1930s, Breithaupt taught a very young André Previn from the ages of six through nine. He regarded the youngster as gifted, but he was finally forced to tell his father that he could no longer afford to have a Jewish boy in his class. See Martin Bookspan and Ross Yockey, *André Previn: A Biography* (Garden City, N. J., 1981), 14-15.
40. Artur Schnabel, *My Life and Music, with an Introduction by Edward Crankshaw* (New York, 1964), 161.
41. Quoted in Joseph Horowitz, *Conversations with Arrau* (New York, 1982), 109.
42. Breithaupt, "Idea," 12
43. Tobias Matthay, *Some Commentaries on the Teaching of Pianoforte Technique* (London, 1911), 45.
44. Tobias Matthay, *The Visible and Invisible in Pianoforte Technique* (London, 1932; reprint ed., 1964), 166.
45. *MT*, 54 (1 Oct. 1913), 641.

46. James Ching, *Piano Playing: A Practical Method* (London, 1946), 358.
47. In August of 1988, I interviewed Denise Lassimonne extensively at her home near Petersfield, Hampshire. Hereafter cited as LI (Lassimonne Interviews).
48. Quoted in Ambrose Coviello, *What Matthay Meant: His Musical and Technical Teachings clearly explained and self-indexed* (London., [1947]), 10.

CHAPTER 1

TWO LANDS—ONE MUSIC

On the evening of 3 August 1914, German forces began invading Belgium, and the following day Britain, which was committed to its defense, declared war on Germany. Although most believed the conflict would be brief, many also knew that it demarcated a profound turning point in British cultural life, since what remained of England's two-hundred-year love affair with the music and culture of Germany had been dealt a serious blow. Within a month, *The Times* published a lengthy letter from one "Fides" extolling Tolstoy, and denouncing Nietzsche as "a sinister philosopher."[1] One week later on 14 September, the same editorial pages featured a three-column letter from a Russian-born Oxford law professor urging England to form an alliance with Russia against the "cold-blooded barbarity" of the Germans.[2] The following week, as his institution began another school year, Sir C. Hubert Parry gave his annual opening address to the students and staff of London's Royal College of Music. He began by complimenting those in attendance for their refusal to be "overwhelmed by the dreadful topic which discomposes most people's nerves," and for remaining "undaunted," with "the same bright-eyed keenness as on ordinary occasions."[3] Parry, like most enlightened observers, recognized the frenzied anti-German hysteria for what it was, and he sought to defuse it by reminding his audience that individuals of any nation might one day create priceless art:

> Think for yourselves what it would have meant if Wagner had happened to lose his life in the Dresden disturbances of 1849, and the world had never had *Tristan* or *Meistersinger*, or the *Ring* or *Parsifal*. We hear of Kreisler being in the Austrian Army, and Rachmaninoff with the Russians, and we honour them for their devotion, even if we think such beings should be set apart for other purposes. And we may have the

Chapter 1

feeling, parenthetically, that if they happened to meet in hostile squadrons the murderous frenzy of war would be stilled and they would fall on one another's necks instead of trying to kill one another. The claims of art would vindicate themselves as of higher cogency.[4]

But Parry also accepted the possibility that over the last century the pendulum had swung too far, and that for too long England had immersed itself in the shadow of German music—a phenomenon he thought it wise to acknowledge:

> I have my own confession to make. For I have been a quarter of a century and more a pro-Teuton. I owed too much to their music and their philosophers and authors of former times to believe it possible that the nation at large could be imbued with the teaching of a few advocates of mere brutal violence and material aggression; with the extravagance of those who talked about super-morality; with the ruthless implications of their insistence that the State is power, and nothing but power, and has no concern with honour, right, justice, or fair play.[5]

Parry's *mea culpa* was not unique, for although the climate was indeed changing, virtually every serious English musician from his youth had been a "pro-Teuton." At least since Hanoverian times, German composers and musicians had dominated English musical life without a trace of apology from the leading practitioners of either land. Handel was buried in Westminster Abbey, and Haydn's visits to London in the 1790s were the musical events of the decade. In 1823 the Philharmonic Society of London offered Beethoven £50 to write a new symphony—his ninth. Mendelssohn, who revered Shakespeare as much as he adored Goethe, gave the first performance of the "Italian" Symphony in London, and nine years later, he dedicated his "Scottish" Symphony to Queen Victoria, who invited him to accompany her as she sang one of his songs at Buckingham Palace.[6] The German-born Prince Albert, an accomplished musician, had already sought to expand England's awareness of Bach and Schubert, and now he openly declared Mendelssohn to be the greatest living composer, a sentiment later shared by an English music journal which announced the composer's death in 1847 as the "eclipse" of music.[7]

A natural concomitant of this reverence was the migration of German musicians to Britain, at times for economic reasons and at times—especially as civil conflicts began to escalate into a full-scale revolution in March of 1848—to escape political unrest. Even Wagner had been driven out of Dresden by Prussian troops in 1849, arriving in London several years later to assume the conductorship of the Philharmonic Society, and he was far from the only victim of his nation's internal strife. Of the 85,000 *Achtundvierziger* ("forty-eighters") who had left Germany a year earlier, a large percentage settled in Britain, although not all were driven away by life-threatening circumstances, and many continued to come well into the next decade. Tobias Matthay, born on 5 July 1826 at Lennep near Düsseldorf, in the North German Province of Bergische, was unusually self-possessed, and a bright future might have awaited him in the Prussian army, where he functioned as a surgeon. But his idealism propelled him to leave his native land since, as recounted years after his death by his daughter-in-law, Jessie Henderson (Kennedy) Matthay, he despised "military customs and tyrannies, which spread into civilian life, and determined him to seek a freer country."[8]

The Matthay family had lived in Lennep for several generations. Johann Arnold Matthay (1743-1817) had eight children, and the youngest of these, Peter Caspar (1785-1858), married Maria Elisabeth Römmerscheid (1784-1870) in 1807. Peter Caspar's profession is unknown, but he and Maria had fourteen children. A son named Tobias, born in 1823, was their ninth, and when he died just after his third birthday, they honored him by christening their next son—their eleventh child—with his forename.[9] Whatever schooling Tobias may have had, he seems to have been skilled with his hands. Jessie reports that while still in his teens he relocated to Paris with an older brother—perhaps Richard or Jonas—where he became a skilled jeweler and goldsmith, "at the same time acquiring a practical knowledge of French."[10] In 1844 when he returned to Germany to fulfill his military service obligation, he also learned "to carry himself well, and to endure long marches." While in the military he may have apprenticed to a surgeon, because his skills, at least by the standards of his day, were soon regarded as "most useful by his comrades and his commanding officer." But the army was also strengthening his disdain for authority-flaunting, and following his discharge, at some point he decided that the trait had become so endemic to his homeland that he chose to return to Paris, where he found only "more rebellion, more musketry, more barricades."[11]

By this time he had become engaged to Dorothea Eleonora Wittich, born 7 April 1827 in the neighboring village of Mettmann. As he was contemplating a return to the jewelry profession, he was struck by a parallel he drew with one of her ancestors, who had served as Court Jeweler to the Elector of Hanover, and then followed him to England after he became George I. The Elector system was long since dead, and Tobias had no royal prospects in mind, but his interest in England was intensified by his immersion in Dumas's *The Three Musketeers*, where D'Artagnan's journey in pursuit of the "adventure of the diamond studs" greatly fascinated him. But he was also enthused at the prospect of learning yet another language and, for whatever reason, he soon abandoned jewelry and made languages his stock and trade. In January of 1853, at the age of 27, he arrived in England and soon he was teaching both German and French at a boy's school in Kenilworth. In Jessie's words, "England did not disappoint him; his resolve to remain became sure."[12]

But Tobias never became totally anglicized. For his entire life, he retained the spelling, as well as the German pronunciation (Mă′-tāy) of his surname, and German was always the preferred language spoken in his home. He planned to defer his marriage until he had established himself financially in his new country, but he and Dorothea both found the separation too difficult and soon she was working considerably north of London as a language governess at a school in Saffron Waldon in Essex. Before long, Tobias relocated to Clapham, where he found a position of some permanence as a resident master at Clapham Grammar School, but as long as he remained there he was forbidden to marry. After weighing the security of his post against the hazards of striking out on his own as a private language tutor, he chose to take the risk, and he and Dorothea were married in Clapham on 23 December 1856.[13] Jessie does not indicate the nature of the wedding, but it may have been performed by a rabbi, as Tobias always retained some of his family's Jewish traditions in his home, as did his children. Perhaps Dorothea, the daughter of a Lutheran pastor, was reared in her father's faith, but since her mother was a Roman Catholic, her religious background seems a bit less certain. Jessie provides a brief portrait of the two personalities as they began their married life, and no doubt she selected characteristics from both which she found reminiscent of her husband's qualities. She wrote that Tobias was "spartan, resolute, self-reliant, incredibly patient and tenacious of purpose." He had a "horror of debt and an overwhelming sense of justice. To all his occupations he brought a tremendous zest, whether it was writing his own grammars, digging in his garden, or engraving the Lord's prayer on a sixpence."

Although Dorothea came from a nearby town, Jessie maintains that she shared none of her husband's features or temperament, appearing more Polish than German. In fact, "she might have belonged to another race:"

> She had many strains in her nature. Her great-great-grand-father, who had come over with George I, married an English wife, and their son, returning to Germany to study either at Göttingen or Heidelberg, re-entered the family strain by choosing a German wife. . . . Dorothea had a passionate love of birds and flowers and animals; full of *joie de vivre* and strongly temperamental, she had much of the minstrel spirit which might have shown itself more strongly had it been developed. The customs of the period, however, demanded that she should curb such fairy gifts, and aspire to be the domestic paragon of Victorian times. One was reminded of a lively buoy, bobbing up and down among the waves, yet securely roped to the shelter of the harbour.[14]

At 3:40 in the afternoon on Friday, 19 February 1858, their first child, Tobias Augustus, was born in their flat at No. 1 Turret Place in

Larkhall Rise.[15] Following the family tradition of naming the eldest son after the father, Tobias christened his son after himself, with the more Christian "Augustus" probably coming from Dorothea's side—perhaps it was her father's name.[16] Shortly there-after the new parents purchased a house a few blocks south of Larkhall Rise at 40 Clapham Manor Street, where they lived for the rest of their lives, and where young Tobias grew to maturity. Years later, Dorothea loved sharing her earliest memories of her son who, almost from the time he was born, seemed to share his father's streak of independence. She noted that he "sat bolt upright in her lap, looking all round him and taking in his little world, before he was many days old."[17] His father was "impatient to show him the big world," and there was much to see. Young Tobias—"Tobs" as he was soon called—was born at a propitious juncture in his country's history, for although its musical achievements were still largely overshadowed by Germany, just seven years earlier the Great Exhibition of 1851 had established Britain, at least to most observers, as the world's leader in scientific and industrial progress.[18]

In 1850 Queen Victoria had chartered the formation of a Royal Commission which approved the construction of the Exhibition's home, the massive Crystal Palace in Hyde Park. When the Exhibition was over, the building, a mammoth structure of iron and glass which comprised over 770,000 square feet of floor space, was dismantled and moved to Sydenham in the south of London, where it reopened in 1854. For the rest of the century it was home to a wide variety of exhibits, amusements, concerts, and various forms of entertainment.[19] The Exhibition itself, which attracted over six million people, lasted only 140 days, and the original plan had called for the dissolution of the Royal Commission at its completion. But with Prince Albert at the helm, the Queen soon made a decision to extend its existence in perpetuity, and its first order of business was to develop the 86 acres of land in South Kensington which it had purchased for the furtherance of scientific and artistic education. From this grew the South Kensington Museum in 1857, an institution which a few years later fostered the Science Museum and the Victoria and Albert Museum. A decade later, the Royal Albert Hall opened as part of the same complex.

The success of the Great Exhibition had been so pronounced that it netted over £186,000, and another was planned to open on its tenth anniversary, 1 May 1861. But the Franco-Austrian War of 1859 and a cotton shortage wrought by the American War Between the States delayed it until 1862. Its building of brick, glass, and iron was designed by Francis Fowke (who also drew preliminary plans for the Albert Hall a few years later), and it was situated where the Natural History Museum now stands. Replete with the distinctive furniture designs of a young William Morris, it was even larger than the Crystal Palace, and although the 1862 Exhibition made less of a cultural impact than its predecessor, it attracted even more visitors.[20] Tobias was only four years old, but his father was determined to take him "to see the wheels go round." The family finances were tight and did not allow for public transportation, so father and son walked the several miles from Clapham to South Kensington, spent the day at the Exhibition, and then returned on foot again that evening. The child was so thrilled with what he saw that he soon tried to forge some "scraps of iron and odd pieces of metal from his father's treasure box" into a rudimentary model of a steam engine. In the era of Faraday and Maxwell, the climate was ripe for scientific adulation, and like so many English schoolboys, Tobias was building a reverence for the wonders of technology. By the time he was six, he had become a tireless experimenter, and even into his adult life he retained the fruits of some of his labors:

> Tobias's pieces of metal were very precious, and eventually did take on the form of a steam-engine. There followed in the course of years a similar experiment with electricity. Both models are here to-day [in 1937] to bear witness to his resourcefulness. In chemistry, too, he was an adventurer, alarming his cautious father by keeping a powder magazine under his bed, in preparation for an astonishing exhibition of fireworks.[21]

Like his father, Tobias was always adept at manual tasks, and Jessie indicates that from both parents he inherited "long elegant fingers" juxtaposed against "two obstinate thumbs." Like his father, he could also draw with demanding precision and "architectural exactitude," and he was careful to sketch out his designs before building them. But just as often these early drawings also displayed, in Jessie's words, a "riot of romantic imagination. Again and again one finds the Pirate, so beloved of the average boy, in top boots, sword, and three-cornered hat, with cannon in the background. Although he was a gentle, home-loving boy, there remains a very vivid pencil drawing entitled 'A vagabond.'"[22]

Tobias senior engaged in a variety of pursuits to support his family through this period. In an advertisement carried by *The Times* in October 1879, he identifies himself as "22 years Head German Master at the Wimbledon School," indicating that he joined the staff a year before Tobias's birth, but it was undoubtedly a part-time appointment which necessitated a good deal of moonlighting. On 29 May 1862, *The Times* advertised his duodecimo-sized, modestly priced edition of *Schiller's Wilhelm Tell* which, with its accompanying set of English vocabulary words, was no doubt targeted at students attending grammar schools in both England and Scotland:

> Price 2s. 6d., 12mo., cloth,
> SCHILLER's WILHELM TELL, in German, the genuine edition, with an English Vocabulary by TH. [sic] MATTHAY. Williams and Norgate, 14, Henrietta-street, Covent-garden, London; and 20, South Frederick-street, Edinburgh.[23]

The Schiller play was merely one of a series of attractive, cloth-bound offerings he issued, for two months earlier on 1 April he had completed an octavo-sized German grammar primer, soon published by David Nutt. Somewhat curiously, the initials M. R. C. P. appear after his name on the title page, indicating that he had successfully completed the exam for membership in the Royal College of Physicians, first given in London in 1859. Since his naturalization papers make no mention of his earlier training as a physician's apprentice, it can be presumed that he sat for the exam sometime after August 1860, but despite occasional financial setbacks, there is no evidence that he ever practiced medicine in England. Understandably, most of his grammar school teaching was directed at male students, and he published several sets of boys' stories by Johann Christopher Schmid, including *Le Jeune Henri*, which he translated from the German into French in 1863. A year later on 19 July 1864, he sought to expand his clientele by advertising a ladies' language class, scheduled to begin in his home in late August, or as he called it, "THE CLAPHAM GERMAN CONVERSATION and TRANSLATION CLASSES for LADIES."[24] By November, the classes were running twice weekly and Dorothea ("Frau Matthay") was also offering tutorials.[25]

Two years later, it appears that Herr Matthay was also doing some teaching at the Oakley House School on King's Road in Clapham Park, since an advertisement which appeared in *The Times* on 15 October 1866 lists an "L. [sic] Matthay" as one of its professors.[26] Jessie reports that the family finances improved considerably when he was asked to return to the Clapham Grammar School as a visiting master by the new Principal—probably the Reverend Alfred Wrigley, who had formerly taught mathematics and classics at the Military College in Addiscombe before it closed in 1863.[27] Jessie provides no date but she mentions that Tobias senior also received an appointment as language tutor for the "Military College at Wimbledon," but this was probably just her way of describing the Wimbledon School, since the appointment rosters for Sandhurst frequently credit Wimbledon with preparing its candidates.[28] It was most likely an elite grammar school, since as part of his duties, Tobias was often asked to supervise student excursions to the Continent, and on more than one occasion he welcomed the opportunity to return to Germany with Dorothea and Tobs at his side. Tobias senior's father, Peter Caspar, had died in the year of Tobs's birth, so he was thrilled when he was able to arrange a visit to England for his mother, Maria Elisabeth—probably in 1863, since Jessie mentions that she was "nearly eighty." At the time, Tobias was especially proud to show her the new country of which he was now a citizen.[29]

When it came time to educate his son, Herr Matthay sought out one of his old friends, a Miss Brown, formerly Matron of Clapham

Chapter 1

Grammar School, who had now started her own preparatory school, and who also gave her young pupil his first piano lessons. On "a veritable antique" of an upright piano which "rattled aggressively," and was missing most of its ivories, young Tobias used to ask her to repeat a tune which had a "mysterious allure." He soon discovered that the source of his fascination was a harmony she termed a "dominant seventh"—his first encounter with "a musical discord." Jessie indicates that the Matthays' family piano—a mahogany upright "grand" which "soared to the ceiling"—was little better than Miss Brown's: "Its keys were nearly, though not quite, as devoid of ivory, and had the same cheerful rattle. Nevertheless they served well his first music-making."[30]

Tobias's progress was rapid and he soon outdistanced any help Miss Brown could provide, so she suggested the family retain C. Edwin Hirst, a graduate of the Royal Academy of Music who had studied with Ignaz Moscheles.[31] By April of 1869, shortly after Tobias's eleventh birthday, Hirst had relocated to 4 Abingdon Terrace in Kensington, but he was aggressively advertising his availability to "all parts of London"—including Putney, Brixton, and Clapham—and he probably gave at least some lessons in the Matthay home.[32] On 1 June he advertised a "matinee musicale" at his residence to which he sold tickets at seven shillings, a price suggesting that he featured himself rather than his students.[33] But he also gave student programs in his home, and Jessie reports that on 22 December he hosted a recital featuring "Master Matthay" performing the second and third movements of Beethoven's "Pathétique" Sonata, perhaps the eleven-year-old's first public appearance. Tobias remained with Hirst for two years, until his parents—who at least privately envisioned him as "ein kleiner Mozart"—thought he should branch out to composition.[34]

On Wednesday evening, 21 April 1869, about a year after Tobias began his study with Hirst, the family welcomed their only daughter, Dorothea Eleonora.[35] In keeping with the family tradition, she was christened after her mother, who gave birth exactly two weeks after her forty-second birthday.[36] To avoid confusion, the child's forename was soon shortened to "Dora," a nickname used so frequently throughout her life that most thought it was her given name. The eleven-year age gap between Tobias and Dora was so pronounced that he saw himself more as an uncle than a sibling, often retaining the role of protective guardian even into her adult life.

By 1870, any number of accomplished London musicians were willing to offer tutorial instruction in composition, but because the Matthays sought a more structured musical education for their son, their options were more limited. At the time, England had only one real conservatory, the Royal Academy of Music. Founded in 1822 by John Fane, Lord Burghersh (1784-1859)—he later became the eleventh Earl of Westmorland—and chartered eight years later under George IV, most of England's prominent musicians had spent at least some time there. Burghersh served as its president until his death 37 years later, but his political connections wrought so many governmental appointments and responsibilities that he was often required to function more like an absentee landlord. But he was passionate about the institution which—as he once confessed to Prince Albert—was "like my very own Child," and his prodigious fund raising kept the Academy afloat through many troubled times. But when he died in 1859 the well dried up, and the next decade was a very turbulent period for the RAM. It had never had suitable facilities, and its landlords kept increasing the rent on the rundown Tenterden Street townhouses it occupied off Hanover Square—by 1861 they were demanding £260 a year. Each year Queen Victoria faithfully donated £100 to the institution, and by the late 1860s Parliament was even contributing another £500 annually, but its income was still insufficient to offset the expenses, and in 1868 the staff was asked to take a collective salary reduction of over £600.[37] Scholarship assistance was minimal, and the Academy was beginning to acquire a reputation as a cash-and-carry institution—that is, the door was open only to those who could pay the bills.

One of its piano professors, Henry Wylde (1822-90), was determined to make quality music instruction more affordable to Londoners, and in 1861 he unveiled his own school, the London Academy of Music. Wylde had studied piano at the RAM and like Hirst, he had

Chapter 1

also studied with Moscheles. An unbridled Wagnerian and a true intellectual, he received a doctorate from Cambridge in 1851, and the following year he was instrumental in forming the New Philharmonic Society, designed to promote newer music far more aggressively than its rival, the Philharmonic Society. He brought Berlioz to London to conduct the orchestra's first six concerts, and he soon acquired a reputation as a leading-edge promoter of the most radical, modern currents. Though his conducting was often criticized, he gave London its first performance of *Lohengrin* in concert version, and in 1870 he conducted the London premiere of Liszt's *Die Legende von der heiligen Elisabeth*. On 11 November 1861, *The Times* advertised the opening of his new conservatory, located in the recently opened St. James's Hall in Piccadilly,[38] which also housed the New Philharmonic. The notice was elaborate, and it stressed affordability, since it was charging half of the RAM's thirty-guinea-per-annum fee. It read in part:

> This academy is designed for vocal and instrumental students desirous of receiving a complete musical education in this country, from the best London professors, on the moderate fees of the Continental institutions.
> Students of all ages are eligible, but only those having a decided talent, or showing an aptitude for learning, will be admitted.
> The year is divided into three terms, the fees of which are five guineas each, or 15 guineas per annum.[39]

Although Wylde's venture was somewhat unprecedented, it must have been successful, for in 1867 he relocated to St. George's Hall, which he built largely at his own expense. Situated in Langham Place, it was a concert facility designed to house both the New Philharmonic and the London Academy, and with characteristic flourish, he celebrated its opening with a series of concerts under his own baton. Not surprisingly, the first program—framed around Beethoven's Fifth—was almost exclusively German, and it was reviewed enthusiastically by *The Times* on 20 May:

> Dr. Wylde has opened his new hall in Langham-place with brilliant success. Although, we believe, St. George's-hall was not built expressly for

the New Philharmonic Conceits [sic], it was built expressly for the New Philharmonic Society, which, in conjunction with the London Academy of Music, of which Dr. Wylde is founder and "principal," does other things besides giving concerts. With so much on his hands, it was natural enough that the learned doctor should wish for a house of his own, and St. George's-hall seems likely to answer his purpose thoroughly. A more majestic "consecration of the house" than the C minor symphony of Beethoven could hardly have been selected.[40]

Hirst may have suggested Tobias enter Wylde's Academy, but however his matriculation came about, he was soon commuting regularly from Clapham to the West End. Wylde quickly took him under his wing and personally supervised both his piano instruction and "a rigorous course of harmony-exercise writing," which, according to Jessie, was conducted—oddly—without benefit of ear training. In spite of this, Tobias managed to create a few early compositions, and he found himself becoming more obsessive about the repertoire he most admired. Jessie claims that he cried when Wylde refused to let him study Beethoven's "Waldstein" Sonata—which seems unlikely, given that Matthay was at least twelve—but he acquiesced to the composer's Rondo in C as consolation, which he "dutifully studied." Determined not to let anyone stand in his way, he privately saved his three-pence-a-week allowance for fifteen weeks until he could afford his own copy of the "Waldstein." When Wylde gave him a ticket to a New Philharmonic Concert, he was ecstatic at hearing the orchestra perform Schumann's "Spring" Symphony, and he went through a similar routine until he acquired that score as well.[41]

Wylde frequently rented out St. George's Hall to various performing groups and soloists and it seems likely that Tobias heard at least some of the piano recitals occurring there and at other nearby halls. Jessie asserts that "England was playing the pianoforte very placidly at that time, under the high priesthood of Charles Hallé."[42] Another German immigrant, Hallé (1819-95), born Carl Halle in Hagen, Westphalia, gave his first piano recital at the age of nine. At 16, he went to study in Paris, where he became friendly with Chopin, Liszt, Berlioz, and Wagner. From an early age, he was attracted to the Sonatas of Beethoven, and

Chapter 1

he was the first pianist to perform the complete set of 32 in Paris and in London. He was also one of the *Achtundvierziger,* reaching England exactly in 1848. But finding London too competitive, he settled instead in Manchester, founding first a symphony orchestra, and decades later—a mere two years before his death—the Royal Manchester College of Music, which had been a lifelong dream. Whether or not he qualified for "priesthood," Hallé was revered throughout England and he continued to perform in London until his last days, giving annual programs at St. James's Hall which he termed "Beethoven Recitals," although they often featured works of other composers.

By 1867, these events had become eagerly anticipated, and in that year alone he presented eight programs in close succession, pairing his efforts with esteemed cellist Alfredo Piatti. Predictably, his repertoire was almost exclusively German, and, interspersed with a number of shorter works by Bach and Heller, the first program included Beethoven's Sonata in D, Op. 10, no. 3, Schubert's Sonata in A minor (probably D. 784), and the Beethoven cello Sonata in F, Op. 5, no. 1 (all five Beethoven cello sonatas were promised in the series, as were both of Mendelssohn's). In its 20 May review, *The Times* was euphoric, praising not only Hallé's playing, but his exemplary attempts to educate younger audiences:

> These "recitals" are not only interesting to musicians and connoisseurs, but valuable to those amateurs who wish to become acquainted with the perfect models of art. To young students they are as good as a "lesson" on the pianoforte; and we are glad to find that, by a certain modification in the charge for entry to certain parts of the hall, Mr. Hallé has thrown them open to a larger class than was hitherto able to profit by them. Good music is at present making way, and Mr. Hallé has played no unimportant part in the revolution that has for some years been slowly though surely progressing.[43]

Whatever impression the adolescent Matthay may have formed of Hallé's playing, he remembered it years later as "tending to cold perfection." But as he matured he certainly concurred with *The Times*'s critic regarding Hallé's repertoire, which Jessie adds was "of great service to the musical England of his time, for Society pianists had been wallowing in a cheap, shallow, perfunctory sentimentality."[44] Although the British love for German composers had been present for generations, there were few notable pianists residing in the country before the first major wave of immigration in the early 1850s, and there was little canon of established repertoire. Many commentators today recognize a "London School" of piano composers active from about 1770 to 1860, but however well they played or composed, Clementi and Dussek, the first luminaries from this group, were foreign born, and the music of their best English successors—even by the most generous estimates— paled beside the works of Mozart and Beethoven.[45] If anything, Jessie may have understated the banality present during her husband's youth, an era which scarcely any serious musician from the next generation remembered with fondness. The German-born Oscar Beringer, later one of Matthay's colleagues at the Royal Academy, recalled that as late as the 1860s, the English market was driven by amateur enthusiasts whose tastes were blight on the musical landscape:

> Amateur ambition had hitherto not soared above the playing of such wishy-washy stuff as Badarzewska's *Maiden's Prayer* ... Ascher's *Alice, Where Art Thou?*, *La Pluie des Perles*, by G. A. Osborne, and *Warblings at Eve* by Brinley Richards, who was also responsible for *Warblings at Dawn*: for the rest of the twenty-four hours he was dumb. The melodies of all these pieces were of a childishly sentimental description, and were harmonised almost entirely in the tonic, dominant, and sub-dominant, while their modulations were bald and obvious in the extreme.[46]

Understandably, by the later nineteenth century, pianists from the Continent who brought European repertoire with them were garnering the most acclaim in Britain, and years later, Matthay remembered artists such as Edward Dannreuther (1844-1905) and Walter Bache (1842-88) as constructive influences. Dannreuther's background was highly eclectic. Born in Strasbourg to German parents, at the age of four he moved with his family to Cincinnati, where his father founded a piano factory. At 16, he entered the Leipzig Conservatory, where he studied with Moscheles, and in 1863 he gave the first London performance of Chopin's F minor Concerto at the Crystal Palace. After a successful American tour in 1865, he enjoyed remarkable success in Britain, giving the first London performances of Liszt's Concerto in A, the Grieg Concerto, and Tchaikovsky's Concerto No. 1. Bache, a native Englishman, enjoyed a career that was also somewhat unconventional. Born in Birmingham, he studied in Leipzig for several years before entering Liszt's class in Rome in 1862. Returning to London three years later, he spent the rest of his life promoting his teacher's music, and in 1865 he even performed a two-piano version of *Les Préludes* with Dannreuther. After he became a professor at the Royal Academy, he was instrumental in creating the Liszt Scholarship for aspiring pianists, and he played host to the aging composer when he visited London for the last time in 1886 (See Chapter 3). In Jessie's words, Dannreuther and Bache were both "fine pioneers" and the best of the "vanguard from Frankfurt and Weimar," but as yet, none of the artists Tobias heard had evoked anything close to a pianistic epiphany.

Whatever aspirations he may have entertained toward becoming a touring pianist, his ideal of musical completeness could only be fulfilled by the role of composer-pianist, a model which Wylde was only too happy to nurture, even though his own compositions were few. It was a role which Tobias revered—and occasionally obsessed over—for the rest of his life, perhaps partially because of England's greatest native-born musician, Sir William Sterndale Bennett (1816-75), who was by now Principal of the Royal Academy. Born in Sheffield, Bennett had been orphaned at the age of three, and at seven he joined the choir at King's College, Cambridge, where his grandfather still sang with distinction. Two years later, he was admitted as a boarding student at the newly formed Academy, thanks to the King's College Vice-Provost, who touted him as a "prodigy." At first he studied violin and some piano, and his compositional studies were directed by Charles Lucas, but as Nicholas Temperley notes, after five years the Academy examiners "rebuked" him for "his failure to achieve anything substantial in composition."[47] He was briefly promoted to the composition class of the Academy's Principal, William Crotch, but as no further progress was seen, in the fall of 1832 Cipriani Potter (1792-1871), who had replaced Crotch as Principal, assumed direction of the sixteen-year-old's compositional efforts.

Potter was also a gifted pianist, and this proved to be a dramatic turning point for Bennett, who soon gave up the violin and began to concentrate on the piano—in his words, *"con amore."* He quickly developed a virtuosic brilliance that he employed to great effect in his own compositions, and in November he played his First Piano Concerto at Cambridge, repeating it at the Academy the following March. From that point forward, Bennett seemed an unstoppable *Wunderkind.* Lord Burghersh, President of the (now) Royal Academy, was so impressed that he insisted the institution underwrite the concerto's publication, and he then dispatched the young scholar off to Windsor so that he could perform it for the King and Queen. It was the featured work at the RAM Midsummer Concert on 26 June 1833, where it was heard and greatly admired by Mendelssohn, himself no stranger to adolescent genius. The famed composer immediately struck up a friendship with the seventeen-year-old Bennett, and invited him to Germany, not as a pupil, but "to be my friend."[48]

The promotion of Bennett's music by Burghersh and others was not exclusively motivated by aesthetic considerations, because all Academy students at that time had encountered practical difficulties that were unknown to Matthay's generation. Although Potter tended to encourage the Viennese classical masters, years later Bennett remembered "a divergence of interests" among the RAM professors which created a climate "of some perplexity." Many were guilty of perpetuating the worst elements of the sentimental salon styles, and often even the requisite scores from better composers could not be easily obtained. In fact, Bennett's son recalled that his father once had difficulty locating a copy of Beethoven's "Hammerklavier" Sonata:

> [Potter] wished to introduce his pupil to a certain composition by Beethoven, now very generally known as Opus 106. The purchase of

Chapter 1

any Sonata in those days was beset with difficulty. Academy boys had to exercise patience, until the longest ladder in the shop could be found, and until an avalanche of dust and cobwebs had fallen from the topmost shelf. On this occasion, Bennett started with little faith in the success of his errand; for Potter's sole direction had been, "Go and ask for the Sonata that nobody plays." That description, however, proved sufficient for the music-seller, and he brought down the work.[49]

Both as composer and performer, Bennett was now entering his most prodigious creative period. In May 1835 he performed his Second Piano Concerto for the Philharmonic Society, and was asked to return with the Third the following year. He then went to Düsseldorf to hear Mendelssohn conduct the first performance of *St. Paul*, and there he began his most popular orchestral work, *The Naiads*. When the two men reconnected briefly, Mendelssohn was moved to offer this unrestrained endorsement to an English colleague: "I think him the most promising young musician I know, not only in your country but also here."[50] By late October, Bennett was finished with his Academy studies and journeyed to Leipzig to pay the composer a more extended visit. Soon the nineteen-year-old was being lionized by the city's musical establishment, an honor never before conferred on an Englishman. Schumann formed a lasting friendship with Bennett, dedicating his *Symphonic Etudes*, Op. 13, to him and celebrating him in the *Neue Zeitschrift*: "Yes, were there only many artists like W. Bennett, all fears for the future of our art would be silenced!"[51] This accolade appeared in February of 1837, shortly after Bennett had performed his Third Concerto with the Leipzig Gewandhaus Orchestra under Mendelssohn's baton, and soon some of his orchestral works were heard there as well to glowing acclaim.

To a country which revered German music above its own, William Sterndale Bennett appeared to have been sanctified at the source, a mantle which none of his peers could match. But the parochialism of his native country was painfully exposed when he returned to England in July 1837, for the charisma he had enjoyed in Germany was sensed only by a small band of devotees, and his Leipzig credentials guaranteed him little in the way of professional advancement. By September he was teaching a few pupils at the Academy, but nearly a decade passed before he developed a sizeable class, and he spent most of his twenties in relative idleness. He rarely performed, and he produced such a small number of compositions that he was often pressed to explain himself to friends and associates, blaming his fallow periods on his extraordinarily severe self-criticism, and maintaining that "a composer should never allow himself to write below his proper level."[52]

He remained active as a pianist for a time, and especially as a conductor. In 1853 he was even offered the conductorship of the Leipzig Gewandhaus Orchestra, which he claimed he was forced to turn down because he was given only a month's notice.[53] In November 1855 he succeeded Wagner as conductor of the Philharmonic Society and the following year he was appointed professor of music at Cambridge, a position he took very seriously. He would have remained at the RAM had it not been for mounting conflicts with his one-time mentor, the former Lord Burghersh—now the Earl of Westmorland—which forced his resignation in May 1858.[54] For the next several years he had no formal relationship with the Academy, until in June 1866 he was appointed Principal. His administrative duties were now extensive and his teaching was restricted to composition, which he pursued by meeting all of his students in a single class twice a week.

Naturally, Bennett's knighthood in March 1871 was greeted with admiration by friends and colleagues, and an RAM committee was quickly formed to raise funds for a scholarship in his name. Composed of "amateurs mingling with musicians in its ranks," within a year it had raised £1,080 from 634 subscribers, and on 19 April 1872, a testimonial in his honor was staged at St. James Hall—moderated by Sir John Coleridge, the Crown's Attorney-General—announcing the creation of two separate awards. The lesser honor, restricted to women and simply called the Sterndale Bennett Prize, offered a year's free tuition to a female pianist. The more prestigious award was to be named the Sterndale Bennett Scholarship, offered biannually to male students "from any part of Her Majesty's dominions," to pursue studies "in three branches of music." From the beginning, the understanding was clear that young men who showed high expertise in both piano and composition—Bennett's specialties—would have a competitive edge. It guaranteed full tuition for two years, but it was subject to review at the end of the first year to assure that the student maintained the necessary qualifications. As first articulated that afternoon by Bennett's colleague, George Macfarren, these were to go beyond purely musical aptitude, since candidates would be required "to give evidence of their general literary culture," confirming that "musicians ought to have the qualifications of gentlemen."[55]

It is unknown whether he emerged as a dark horse or had already reached the status of favored candidate, but in April of 1872 fourteen-year-old Tobias Augustus Matthay was awarded the first Sterndale Bennett Scholarship. Although Jessie makes it appear that Tobias left Wylde's Academy as a result of his winning the prize—suggesting that Wylde may even have encouraged his entry—the RAM Candidates Foundation Register tells a different story. These records, entered when students first auditioned, were kept until 1874, and they reveal that Matthay auditioned for the Royal Academy at the age of 13 on 18 September 1871, suggesting that he had been studying at the RAM for a full six months before he received the scholarship.[56] He also submitted some figured bass realizations prepared under Wylde on which an RAM examiner wrote "<u>Did it himself</u>."[57] Although his piano skills are noted as "advanced," he was initially awarded no scholarship, his fees being guaranteed entirely by "Herr T. Matthay." The records also indicate that young Tobias was interested in studying composition, and one detects the possible intervention of a determined stage-door parent, one even willing to pay double the amount Wylde was asking— the RAM charged 30 guineas a year plus a five-guinea entrance fee—to insure the highest quality instruction. Also conspicuously absent is any evidence that Matthay entered on the recommendation of an established teacher, which was highly unusual at the time, particularly for advanced students. There can be little question that the Matthays withdrew their son from the London Academy against Wylde's wishes, or he would have been happy to show his support—at the very least as a form of advertising. It is unknown who Tobias's teachers were when he first entered the RAM, but given his youth, it is possible he was assigned only sub-professors for both piano and composition.

Years later, playwright and musician Louis Napoleon Parker, one of Matthay's early classmates, vividly recalled the Academy's building in the early 1870s as a "sober and stately mansion:"

> An old porter stood on guard in the hall. If my memory serves, his name was Ben. A younger one in livery, who was called—again I speak under correction—Arthur, and had oiled and curly hair like a tenor, helped Ben to stand in the hall. Both accepted tips with dignity and condescension. Farther in one came to the grand staircase, on the walls of which were memorials of the young geniuses who had achieved distinctions out of reach of mere human beings. . . .
>
> But the male student in his first year seldom ventured into the splendour of the inner hall. For him the backstairs were good enough. Narrow stairs, and a great many of them; and the class-rooms they led to fusty, musty, and dusty, and devoid of ventilation; so that it was a wonder that the professors kept awake. Nor did they. . . .
>
> The spirit of romance pervaded every room in that old house. How could it be otherwise, when every room was all day long, from eight o'clock in the morning till I know not what hour at night, sonorous with every sort of music? The walls were soaked in music, and the floors quivered to it. Long after the doors were closed at the end of the day the rooms must have vibrated to the passion, the pathos, and the beauty that had filled them.[58]

Jessie provides little information concerning Matthay's audition for the Sterndale Bennett Scholarship, but she mentions that the examiners were favorably impressed by the compositions he brought—two sonatas and a rondo—and that Bennett immediately

Chapter 1

accepted him into his class.[59] Not surprisingly, most of his composition students were upperclassmen but as Parker later remembered, not all of them gained admission to the inner circle in their first year:

> There was a door labeled "Committee Room" on the first landing of the Academy House, which in the early days of my sojourn there, I, in common with the other junior students, regarded with profound veneration. Through it we saw our seniors passing twice a week on their way to evolve masterpieces under the eye of the Principal, and the sight was one which aroused feelings of bitterest envy. To this day I have no idea how I ultimately got into the class. . . . Now you must imagine a long table covered with an official green baize; at the head sits Sir Sterndale; on each side his pupils: Joseph Parry, Eaton Faning . . . Arthur Jackson . . . Stephen Kemp, Tobias Matthay, and last but not least, Thomas Wingham, who, by reason of his undoubted genius of the authority he exerted and the noble example he set, was regarded as the doyen of the students at the time. Over this group Sir Sterndale presided with a certain indefinable grace and dignity which marked him as a being set apart, as, in short, a great man. . . . The influence of his mere external personality over the impressionable young artists who surrounded him is indescribable. I believe there was not one of us who would not gladly have died for him. . . .
>
> How did he teach? I think he taught chiefly by personal influence, by the outflow of his exquisite mind. You lost certain things when you came before Bennett by the mere fact of being in the same room with him. Vulgarity, for instance, and roughness. . . . His memory was a storehouse of all music, and the range of his knowledge embraced every composer from Palestrina to Weber and Spohr. If a student brought him something which touched a responsive chord in his imagination, which was good enough to be considered actual music, as distinguished from a mere exercise, he shirked no trouble in analyzing it, in pointing out its merits to us others, who had brought up our club-footed sonatas and wooden-legged fugues. . . . "Play me," he would say to one of us, "such and such a passage from Weber," or "show me what Beethoven would

have done in such a case"; and we were expected to remember the points in question. If we did not, then he himself would go to the piano and play them, and one led to another in a wonderful series of illustrations until the possibilities of that particular modulation, imitation or enharmonic change were completely exhausted.[60]

Parker remembered Tobias then as "a small boy: something of an infant prodigy,"[61] suggesting that his gifts were readily apparent to his classmates. The most senior of these was Thomas Wingham (1846-93), who at 26 was highly charismatic to the fourteen-year-old Matthay. Wingham was already a sub-professor at the Academy, and after he became Director of Music at the Brompton Oratory, he did much to further his teacher's music there, even overseeing an 1885 performance of a long-forgotten string quartet Bennett had composed over 50 years earlier.[62] Parker writes that Wingham was "much troubled about religion," and that his conversion to Catholicism actually cost him his organist's post and all of his private pupils, while his own vicar, the Dean of Wells, denounced him from the pulpit with "incredible ferocity."[63] Jessie notes that Wingham soon became "a strong influence in Matthay's life—the ardent, converted Roman Catholic and the young agnostic," suggesting that even as a young teen, Tobias's personal views were only partially malleable. Parker indicates that Wingham also "took his art with profound seriousness," and had already completed a number of large works which were performed in major venues, such as a Mass, which was "a favourite in the Cathedral at Antwerp."[64] Wingham adored Bennett, and shortly after his death he even composed an Elegy in his memory. Years later, he confirmed Parker's remembrance of his teacher's reverence for the classics, and in a letter to Bennett's son, he provided an even more detailed record of the classes where Tobias took his early compositional training:

> As far as I can state them, Sir Sterndale Bennett's methods were as follows: Careful study & analysis of the works of the great masters. He recommended pupils always to take some work as a <u>model</u> till they had

a complete mastery of the subject of "form." He would frequently send them down to the library for some work & make one of the pupils play it & then explain its plan & what points of interest were specially worth noticing. When pupils were sufficiently advanced he would allow them more freedom but even then would recommend them to study & even copy out & <u>learn</u> from <u>memory</u> large portions of the scores of great composers. He once required me to learn an intricate portion of Mozart's Symphony in G minor & to write it out from memory in his presence. There were several other things he used to impress upon us. One was the beginning of a composition. He used to say a work ought to be known by its very first chord & would give any number of instances from Mozart[,] Beethoven etc.

Another thing he was particular about was, points of imitation[,] canon etc. And again <u>inversion</u>. "Remember" he used to say "that by inversion you not only greatly add to the interest of your composition but you double its length." Then he gave us great assistance on the choice of "subjects," pointing out what would make effective contrasts, what could be "worked" & what could not, what could be "combined" etc. etc. He used to say that no one could be original who had not a more extensive knowledge of the works of other composers & would prove this in many ways such as comparing works by different authors written about the same time in different countries, but he used to cite Bach & Handel as remarkable exceptions to this rule. As you know, he only taught us advanced composition, we were supposed to have mastered harmony, counterpoint etc before we came to him.[65]

Parker also provided a colorful description of Bennett's humanity toward his students, traits which seem remarkably similar to those for which Matthay was later admired. One suspects that on some level Tobias was already beginning to shape his own ideals of effective pedagogy, and that Bennett was a highly influential model:

He was kind and courteous with the most ignorant; patient with the most stupid. *Experto crede*. His sharpest rebuke took the form of a delicate sarcasm, which, however gently spoken, one never forgot. Taking a passage in some dreadful sonata I was laboriously compounding for him, he would say, "Do you really like this? Don't you think that perhaps Mozart put it better?" and then, at the piano, shew me how Mozart had put it, and how I had stolen it, mutilated and disfigured it. But, once at the piano, my miserable attempt was soon forgotten, as out of the storehouse of an inexhaustible memory he poured treasure after treasure; while we crowded round him, hushed, scarcely daring to breathe, lest we should interrupt the spell.[66]

In all probability, Matthay shared in this adulation, since Bennett's influence, in Jessie's words, "proved of the highest value," and "laid the foundation of a true musical culture."[67] However, despite the praise conferred by his pupils, it could still be argued that Bennett was not teaching so much as holding court, and that the admiration he evoked was due more to charm than to substance. C. Hubert Parry, who studied piano with him as a boy, remembered him years later as a "kind and sympathetic" teacher, but added that he was "too sensitive to criticize."[68] But regardless of the skills Bennett may have imparted to Tobias—then his youngest pupil—one can imagine a marked affinity between teacher and student, since both held a reverence for German culture, and in all probability, even conversed in German when they chose.[69] It also seems likely that Tobias would have felt a heady intoxication in the presence of a cherished confidante of Mendelssohn and Schumann. Within time, all of his classmates either graduated or withdrew, and Jessie indicates that his last session with Bennett was a tutorial, in which "he had his beloved master all to himself."[70]

Matthay appears to have kept all the compositions he created during this period, and whatever Bennett's expectations, it may be inferred that his assignments were systematic and thorough. Tobias was in his class for about six months before he completed anything, suggesting that his teacher disapproved of creative efforts without significant preparatory training. He also kept some of his counterpoint exercises, although these may have been directed by organist Charles Steggall (1826-1905), who taught many of the RAM's entering students. One surviving example is taken from Volume II of Albrechtsberger's

Collected Writings on Thorough-Bass, Harmony, and Composition, for Self-Instruction, which was translated by Sibilla Novello and published in London in 1855. Matthay's assignment (which dates from October of 1872) spans four pages, and required him to provide various harmonizations for the soprano line given in Albrechtsberger's Example 608, a four-part, first-species exercise appearing on page 93 of the Novello publication.[71] His first full-scale composition under Bennett was a piano sonata completed about four months later on 27 February 1873. He titled it "Sonata No. 3 in G major," so he probably viewed the student works he had presented to the scholarship committee in the previous year as his Sonatas 1 and 2. He assigned the G major the opus number of "5," and with very few exceptions he continued to chronicle his student works consecutively, although his published opus numbers later superseded these early designations. Two more sonatas followed—completed on 31 March and sometime in May, respectively—and his first two orchestral works are transcriptions of piano pieces. His "1st Score," a transcription of Hummel's "Indian Rondo," was begun in July of 1873, so he may have worked at it over the summer holidays.[72] He followed this with a violin sonata, his opus 9, which he completed on 23 October, before orchestrating a brief, seventy-five-measure piano study by Cipriani Potter, completed on 10 December 1873.[73] It is tempting to speculate that Bennett may have assigned this piece, perhaps having studied it with Potter years earlier. Tobias copied parts for both transcriptions, but it is unknown whether the Academy orchestra ever performed them.

His subsequent orchestral works—all notated in exacting, "fair copy" draftsmanship—exist in score only. His "3rd score," which he designated opus 10, is a brief symphony in A minor,[74] begun a few weeks before he completed his Potter transcription, and the "4th score" was a more substantial multi-movement symphony in F, begun on 3 February 1874.[75] His small wind section includes horns in C, clarinets in B-flat, and a trumpet in F, and he completed the first movement on 18 March. On the same day he began his first Piano Concerto—in D minor—which added three trombones and tympani to the orchestral texture.[76] With three (projected) movements, this appears to be his most ambitious effort to date, and the piano writing shows a mixture of Mendelssohnian and Lisztian influence. He completed the first movement on 25 May 1874 and the second movement in October, but he left only four measures of the finale, which was evidently intended to be an explosive presto. His next score, also begun in October, is an "Ouverture" in D, but he completed only about 180 measures.[77] While he was working on the Concerto, he also wrote two brief piano pieces: "Reverie," completed in June, and "Sketch," completed in August,[78] while his last surviving Bennett score, "Scherzo for Orchestra," was begun on 6 January 1875.[79] With a brisk, almost naïve theme in G, the "A" section is a mere 25 measures, followed by a thirty-three-measure Trio in D, and ending with a seventeen-measure Coda. It is unclear why several of the larger projects were left unfinished—nor precisely how Bennett may have evaluated the efforts of his youngest student.

Bennett had also been instrumental in shaping the finer details of the Academy's governance system, which at the time Tobias entered, could be broken down into three distinct levels—at least on paper. After Westmorland's death in 1859 the office of President had been left vacant, and since the four Vice-Presidents who completed the top tier served purely as sinecures, the highest executive rung played little role in the institution's management. The next level consisted of a group of over 20 Directors—titled nobility, bankers, accountants, and a few professors among them—who met yearly and effectively controlled the institution's financial matters. Day-to-day practical issues were decided by the Academy's Committee of Management, which for many years assured the students that it was responsible for "all orders whatever for the government and regulation of the Academy."[80] It formed the most important level of governance, meeting at least monthly, and sometimes more often depending on circumstances, before expanding to a weekly pattern by the mid-1880s. When Tobias entered, Bennett presided over the Committee, and one of his achievements had been to re-structure its make-up so that at least half of its fifteen members were Academy professors. As time passed, that proportion increased, so that by the end of Matthay's student days, most were professors—although some were retired.

Chapter 1

The Academy's calendar closely paralleled that of the leading British public schools, in that there were three thirteen-week terms per year. The Michaelmas (fall) term began on the third Monday in September before Michaelmas (29 September) and extended nearly to Christmas. After a four-week break, the Lent term began on the third Monday in January and extended to mid-April. After a week's break, the Easter term commenced on the fourth Monday of April and ran till late July. This was followed by an eight-week summer holiday which extended through August and much of September. All students were expected to pursue a concentration, termed a "first study," analogous to the "majors" pursued in today's colleges and conservatories. Most often this was a concentration in voice or a specific instrument—although occasionally subjects such as harmony and counterpoint were permitted—tutored by a professor for 60 minutes a week and usually divided into two 30-minute segments on different days. A long-standing Academy custom also permitted students to attend the lessons of other students within their principal area, and this was a practice Matthay maintained long after he opened his own school years later. Students were also expected to pursue "second studies," and when Matthay entered there was some concern that professors were padding their teaching loads by devoting too much time to these pupils. So eventually a firm decision was reached that a "second study" should receive no more than 30 minutes per week unless additional fees were advanced. At the time Tobias arrived, multiple "first studies" were also permitted for an extra three guineas per term, and that fee escalated considerably over the years. Fortunately, his scholarship allowed him to "major" in both composition (then generally known as "harmony" in British academies) and piano at no cost, although a high level of keyboard proficiency was expected for serious composers, and all students were required to study piano unless they were exempted by virtue of their competence. Although a "first study" was possible on any instrument, voice, keyboard, and strings were the favored areas during Matthay's student years.

There was an expectation that students would remain in residence for at least three years (by the mid-1880s students were required to attend for no less than three consecutive terms), and many stayed longer, depending on their interests and circumstances. After completing certain required courses, they were then permitted to take exams to determine if they merited the coveted Academy Certificate. In "special cases" the title of Associate of the Royal Academy of Music (A.R.A.M.) was conferred, and the Committee also reserved the right to grant this title as an honor to accomplished musicians who had not taken the exams. The highest honor was to be named a Member of the Royal Academy, which the Committee of Management granted only to former students "who distinguish themselves in the Musical profession after quitting the Institution." (The designation "Member" was later changed to "Fellow," and its awarding required a vote by two-thirds of the Directors.) There was also an Honorary Member category, which could be extended either to graduates or non-graduates, and over the years the Academy paid tribute to famous musicians such as Charles Hallé and Anton Rubinstein by adding their names to its ranks.

In the fall of 1872, Frederick Corder was admitted as a student, and although he was older than Tobias, they eventually became close friends. On the occasion of the institution's one-hundredth birthday in 1922, after many years' service as an RAM composition professor, Corder published a history of the Academy, in which he graphically offered his own version of the atmosphere on Tenterden Street some fifty years earlier:

> What a queer place it was! The concert room and the whole of the first floor of two ordinary London houses thrown into one, and looking therefore strangely low for its size. A nine-inch platform occupied the rear, backed by a fair-sized organ in a perfectly hideous case. Behind this were large windows looking into what had been a pleasant double garden, but was now a chaotic timber yard. [This was undoubtedly a remnant of the serious fire in 1866 which destroyed a carriage maker's factory. Miraculously, no permanent damage was done to the Academy.] The front portion of the drawing room was filled with rows of common wooden school benches, gradually in process of exchange for iron stuffed seats, as funds permitted. On these sat intermittently, while waiting for their individual lessons,

Chapter 1

a hundred or so of remarkably good-looking young ladies (the Academy standard of female beauty has always been high), while a few similar benches placed sideways right and left of the orchestral platform were occupied by some half a dozen male students, looking painfully shy and self-conscious at having to sustain the battery of so many pairs of fair eyes. Of course it was very wholesome training for them.[81]

Corder fails to mention that male and female students were forbidden to speak to one another except at rehearsals—a rule that was not changed until 1888 when Alexander Mackenzie became Principal. He continues:

How ludicrously bad were those orchestral and choral practices compared with those of today! Yet the material was quite good. The orchestra, led by Weist Hill and other professors, contained many students who afterwards reached to eminence. . . . We were usually engaged in rehearsing some choral work . . . such as Bennett's "Woman of Samaria", which we got to know by heart, and the choir contained such singers as . . . the dazzling Clara Samuel, Miss Reimar, Grace Bolton, and many others. Even among the boys were Henry Guy and Walter Wadmore, with a fair sprinkling of composers and pianists, such as Tobias Matthay and myself, who could at least read, if our voices were not up to much.[82]

By the time Corder arrived, Tobias Matthay was entering his second year at the institution he would call home for the next 53 years. And soon, he was about to do more than sing in the choir.

Notes

1. *TT*, 7 Sept. 1914, 4, col. A.
2. *TT*, 14 Sept. 1914, 10, col. E.
3. C. Hubert Parry, *College Addresses delivered to Pupils of the Royal College of Music*, ed. H. C. Colles (London, 1920), 215. Parry's address was given on

24 September 1914, according to the *RCM Magazine* (v. 11/1, 1914). Hereafter cited as Parry.
4. Parry, 217. The phrase "Rachmaninoff with the Russians," is a bit ambiguous. Whether Parry knew it or not, Rachmaninoff never served in the Russian army, though both of his grandfathers had been generals.
5. Parry, 222.
6. See R. Larry Todd, *Mendelssohn[:] A Life in Music* (Oxford, 2003), 439.
7. See R. Larry Todd, "Mendelssohn, Felix," *RNG*.
8. JHM, 1.
9. MFD.
10. MFD; JHM, 1.
11. JHM, 1.
12. JHM, 2. Although Jessie makes it appear that Tobias Matthay senior arrived in England in 1848, the term *Achtundvierziger* was also used by German expatriates who fled in later years. On 2 August 1860, Matthay became a British citizen, citing continual disturbances "by military summons in his professional vocation" as his reason for leaving. His date of emigration is given in his naturalization papers on file at the National Archives in Richmond. In 1854 he applied to a state office in Düsseldorf to be released as a Prussian subject and his petition was granted, so for over six years he was a man without a country. A copy of his release certificate is included with his citizenship application.
13. MFD.
14. JHM, 2-3.
15. MFD. The handwritten family record reads: "Tobias Augustus./geboren Freitag den 19te Februar, 1858 Nachmittags/ 20 Minuten vor 4 Uhr in Turret Place,/ Larkhall Rise, Clapham, London."
16. MFD. The Naturalization papers state that Dorothea was also the granddaughter of a clergyman, Daniel Friederich Wittich, of Mettman.
17. JHM, 3
18. See John R. Davis, *The Great Exhibition* (Stroud, 1999).
19. The Crystal Palace was destroyed by fire on 30 November 1936. See Michael Leapman, *The World for a Shilling[:] The Story of the Great Exhibition of 1851* (London, 2001), 230. See also Michael Musgrave, *The Musical Life of the Crystal Palace* (Cambridge, 1993).
20. See "The International Exhibition," *TT*, 3 Mar. 1862, 6, col. A, and Leapman, 283.

Chapter 1

21. JHM, 3.
22. JHM, 3-4.
23. *TT*, 29 May 1862, 15, col. A.
24. *TT*, 19 Jul. 1864, 15, col. A.
25. *TT*, 3 Nov. 1864, 3, col. A.
26. *TT*, 15 Oct. 1866, 2, col. A.
27. On 27 June 1863, *The Times* (p. 16, col. D) carried a notice regarding the sale of the Addiscombe College properties, and on 17 July 1866 (p. 4, col. A), the Clapham Grammar School announced Wrigley's appointment as Headmaster, noting that he was formerly "Professor of Mathematics and Classics in the late Military College, Addiscombe."
28. *TT*, 15 Jan. 1861, 7, col. B.
29. JHM, 6.
30. JHM, 4.
31. The name of the Prague-born Ignaz Moscheles (1794-1870) is omnipresent in histories of nineteenth-century British musicians, since he taught in London from 1825 through 1846. Even after he returned to Leipzig, he continued to teach numerous English pianists, including Arthur Sullivan.
32. For example, see *TT*, 1 Apr. 1869, 15, col. B, and 22 April 1869, 12, col. B.
33. *TT*, 1 Jun. 1869, 1, col. C.
34. JHM, 5.
35. MFD. The family record reads: "Dorothea Eleonora/ geboren Mittwoch den 21ste April, 1869 Abends/ 20 Minuten vor 11 Uhr in 40 Manor Street, Clapham,/ Surrey."
36. MFD.
37. Frederick Corder, *A History of the Royal Academy of Music, from 1822 to 1922* (London, 1922), 68-75. Hereafter cited as FC.
38. St. James Hall was opened in 1858 by the publishers Cramer, Beale, & Chappell "for concerts on a large scale and for public meetings." See Simon McVeigh, "London (i), §VI: Musical life: 1800–1945", *RNG*. Pianist Oscar Beringer notes that John Ella presented many of his Musical Union chamber concerts in the hall, where he "insisted on having a low platform placed in the centre of the room for the performers, with the audience seated in a circle all round." As a performer, Beringer found this "a most uncomfortable arrangement." See Oscar Beringer, *Fifty Years' Experience of Pianoforte Teaching and Playing* (London, 1907), 7.

39. *TT*, 11 Nov. 1861, 1, col. B.
40. *TT*, 20 May 1867, 12, col. D.
41. JHM, 5.
42. JHM, 16.
43. *TT*, 20 May 1867, 12, col. D. The most recent, comprehensive study of Hallé's career also includes the dates of all his London concerts. See Robert Beale, *Charles Hallé: A Musical Life* (Aldershot, 2007), 240.
44. JHM, 16.
45. See Nicholas Temperley, ed., *The London Pianoforte Piano School*, 20 vols. (New York and London, 1985).
46. Beringer, 8.
47. See Nicholas Temperley, "Bennett, William Sterndale," *RNG*.
48. J. R. Sterndale Bennett, *The Life of William Sterndale Bennett* (Cambridge, 1907), 21-30. Hereafter cited as Sterndale Bennett. Peter Horton has an outstanding discussion of Bennett's three youthful concertos in "William Sterndale Bennett, Composer and Pianist," Ch. 6 in Therese Ellsworth and Susan Wollenberg, eds., *The Piano in Nineteenth-Century British Culture*, (Aldershot, 2007), 120-25.
49. Sterndale Bennett, 33. Although William Sterndale Bennett never hyphenated his surname, his sons and descendants altered it to "Sterndale Bennett," or more commonly, "Sterndale-Bennett."
50. Mendelssohn to Thomas Attwood, 28 May 1836, cited in Sterndale Bennett, 41.
51. Robert Schumann, "William Sterndale Bennett, Drittes Konzert," *Neue Zeitschrift für Musik*, 9:(21 Feb. 1837), 65. "Ja, gäb' es nur noch viele Künstler, die in dem Sinne wie W. Bennett wirkten—und niemandem dürfte mehr vor der Zukunft unserer Kunst bange sein!"
52. Sterndale Bennett, 103.
53. Sterndale Bennett, 228-232.
54. FC (68-69) describes a growing series of conflicts between Westmorland and the RAM faculty by the summer of 1856. He had grown so increasingly meddlesome in Academy affairs that he even insisted on assigning pupils to specific teachers. So many of his teachers resigned, that for the 1858-59 year Westmorland was the only remaining member of the Committee of Management. Corder wryly observes that the minutes of their meetings for that year are "very scanty."

55. "Sir Sterndale Bennett," *TT*, 20 Apr. 1872, 5, col. F.
56. RAM Candidates Foundation records for Michaelmas term 1871, 117.
57. RAMRBC. The exercises, dated May 1871, have not yet been catalogued at this writing.
58. Louis N. Parker, *Several of My Lives* (London, 1928), 60-61.
59. These three youthful works survive in the Archives of the Royal Academy of Music. Matthay called his first Sonata in C his "opus 1" (RAMRBC MS 2009). The A-flat Rondo, his "opus 2" (RAMRBC MS 2010), bears a striking similarity to Beethoven's Rondo in C—which supposedly Wylde forced him to study. The other Sonata, in G minor, he termed "opus 4" (RAMRBC MS 2007).
60. Louis N. Parker, cited in Sterndale Bennett, 403-405.
61. Parker, *Several of My Lives*, 71.
62. See Rosemary Williamson, *Sterndale-Bennett: A Descriptive Thematic Catalogue* (Oxford, 1996), 325-26.
63. Parker, 66.
64. JHM, 8.
65. Letter from Wingham to James Sterndale Bennett, 2 Mar. 1887, from the Sterndale-Bennett Private Collection.
66. Parker, 72.
67. JHM, 7.
68. Quoted in Sterndale Bennett, 399.
69. Fluency in German was by no means an expectation, even for Bennett's most favored students. Parker, who was reared partially in Germany, recalled (p. 74) that he was required to act as Wingham's interpreter when they visited Cologne in 1871. In Wingham's presence, he was always "careful to reverse the compliments" he received from their German acquaintances who singled him out as a "distinguished English composer" because of his bi-linguality.
70. JHM, 8.
71. RAMRBC (not catalogued at this writing).
72. RAMRBC MS1943.
73. RAMRBC MS 1942.
74. RAMRBC MS 1940.
75. RAMRBC MS 1941.
76. RAMRBC MS 1952.

77. RAMRBC MS 1936.
78. The "Reverie" is RAMRBC MS 2022, while the "Sketch" is RAMRBC MS 2023.
79. RAMRBC MS 1938.
80. This phrase appeared annually in RAM catalogues throughout Tobias's student days and well into the 1900s.
81. FC, 76-77.
82. FC, 77.

Portrait of Sir William Sterndale Bennett by Thomas Oldham Barlow, after a portrait in oils by John Everett Millais (1873)

CHAPTER 2

"OUR NATIONAL MUSICAL SEMINARY"

On 29 July 1873 *The Times* devoted nearly an entire column to the annual year-end public concert of the Royal Academy of Music, which it dubbed a "useful and well-conducted institution." The generous press coverage may be partially explained by the presence of Catherine Gladstone, wife of the often controversial Prime Minister, who spent her Saturday morning personally conferring dozens of prizes "with a kind word or look for each favored recipient." Among others, she presented honors to a fifteen-year-old Tobias Matthay, who received a book award, and whose Sterndale Bennett Scholarship had been renewed the previous April. By now there were over 200 pupils at the RAM, and the program was immense. Six symphonic movements by students were performed, plus the first movement of Beethoven's "Emperor" Concerto, the first movement of Schumann's Piano Concerto, two movements from Mendelssohn's D minor Concerto, Sterndale Bennett's *Caprice* in E (according to *The Times*, "one of the most finished and original pieces ever written for pianoforte with orchestral accompaniments"), an organ fugue by Bach, and an assortment of chamber offerings by Ludwig Spohr. The songs and arias which followed were so numerous that *The Times* conceded, "a mere glance at the vocal music will suffice." Nonetheless, no fewer than twenty singers were cited, performing repertoire as ambitious as the complete finale—"ingeniously contrived and dramatically effective"—to George Macfarren's *Robin Hood*. The occasion also served as the conducting debut of Matthay's future piano teacher and Macfarren's younger brother, Walter, whom the newspaper lauded by observing that, "one more thoroughly fitted for the task could hardly have been selected."[1]

The article also suggests that the Academy had faced significant problems in recent years, and at times it reads as nothing so much as a glowing progress report. For example, the vocal selections "afforded unequivocal satisfaction, as guarantees of the progress made by the pupils now being educated at our national musical seminary, which since its institution in 1822, and its incorporation by Royal Charter, has done so much for the legitimate progress of music in this country." Predictably, the Principal, Sir William Sterndale Bennett, gave a short address before the concert began thanking Mrs. Gladstone, which *The Times* reprinted in its entirety. His tone suggests that enrollment figures may have offered some recent concerns, as well as the Tenterden Street facilities, which long ago had begun to show their age:

> Madame,—As Principal of this Institution, allow me again to return you my sincere thanks for the honor you have done to the directors and the committee in consenting to attend here this morning. I feel great pleasure, in which I am sure you will participate, in telling you that the number of students has considerably increased, more than 40 having entered this year, and the total at present being over 200. In an artistic sense the standard of excellence has also been raised, and I have no hesitation in stating that we have found talent so remarkable and so greatly in excess of former years that it is a pleasure for us to increase those rewards which you have so kindly undertaken to distribute. I cannot let this opportunity pass without referring to the kind interest taken in the welfare of the Royal Academy of Music, and the advancement of the art of music in this country, by his Royal Highness the Duke of Edinburgh and the authorities of the Royal Albert Hall. The propositions made to us from time to time have been seriously considered; but it was found that we should not be justified in incurring the expenditure attendant on the removal of the institution, and as the new accommodation offered presented but slight advantages over the premises we now occupy, we felt compelled to decline. In conclusion, I beg to tender my sincere thanks to the committee, professors, sub-professors, and officers of the institution for their untiring zeal and activity in each of their departments. The success which has followed their efforts you, Mrs. Gladstone, will now have the opportunity of estimating.

The full context leading to Bennett's speech can scarcely be gleaned from *The Times* piece alone. By the early 1850s, the RAM had outgrown its surroundings on Hanover Square, resulting in an application in 1854 to the Commissioners of the Exhibition of 1851 "to lend room upon their estate for a building in which the Academy could carry on its labours."[2] Their negotiations proved unsuccessful, and by the early 1860s the Academy's financial woes had become so pronounced that only Parliament's guarantee of an annual £500 grant, supported by William Gladstone, then Chancellor of the Exchequer, saved it from ruin. On 22 June 1866, Bennett was appointed Principal and the future seemed brighter, but the following year Disraeli rescinded the grant and sought to close the institution. By November 1867, the RAM Directors felt the situation hopeless enough that they began devising a plan to dissolve the Academy, which was thwarted only when they were advised by Queen Victoria that absent the consent of the faculty, neither she nor they had the authority to revoke its Royal Charter—forcing the school to limp along for a while longer.[3] More than one commentator has labeled this the Academy's "crisis" period, and Corder indicates that by December 1868 the RAM had only 66 pupils, a meager number that still strained its existing facilities, compounding Bennett's problems.[4] Thus both the Academy and its Principal owed their lifeblood to the collapse of Disraeli's government in 1868, which brought Gladstone to power and resulted in an immediate restoration of funding.[5] In March 1871 Bennett's knighthood was conferred on Gladstone's recommendation, and the scholarship which Matthay now held had been created to honor this distinction. Hence, any cordiality shown to Mrs. Gladstone at the awards ceremony transcended mere formality.

Bennett also briefly commends the "authorities" of Royal Albert Hall, a false compliment which was no doubt offered for diplomatic reasons. According to Corder, a few months earlier in 1873 (the immediate discussions actually began in July of 1872 and had been preceded by earlier exchanges for nearly a decade), the RAM had been approached by the Society of Arts with a new proposal to remove its facilities to "rooms in the labyrinthine corridors of the Albert Hall," with "alterations, furnishing and other expenses" to be borne entirely by the Academy. To compound the burden, in lieu of rent, the proposal recommended withholding the Academy's government grant in perpetuity, a scheme that was flatly rejected by its Management Committee.[6] Although Bennett's remarks indicate that relocation plans had been considered at some point, *The Times* also suggests that pressure may have been placed on the school to merge or affiliate with another institution, a proposition that it happily dismisses:

> Altogether the proceedings augured well for the future progress of the Royal Academy of Music, which we think has acted wisely in preserving its independent position. If it cannot continue to exist as it has existed for so long a period, it has really no pretence to exist at all. We believe sincerely that it can—more especially with such a musician for its chief director and pilot as Sir W. Sterndale Bennett.[7]

But eighteen months later, Sir William Sterndale Bennett, Britain's most prominent musician, was dead at the age of 59—and his aura passed with him. On the morning of 6 February 1875, a solemn cortege of over 30 carriages wound its way to Westminster Abbey, where he was soon laid to rest in the North aisle alongside Purcell and Handel. Lauding him as "the first musician of our day," *The Times* devoted an entire column to his funeral, an event without parallel among nineteenth-century British musicians, as this brief excerpt suggests: "There were members from all the Societies of Music, not only from those of our own country, but of France, Italy, and Germany, and with the carriages of those who desired to do honour to the memory of the man who has been laid in Westminster Abbey it was pleasant to see those of the Queen and of her two elder sons."[8]

Whatever his degree of admiration for Bennett, Matthay never capitalized on—and rarely even referenced—his connection to him in his later writings, and a small amount of evidence suggests that their relationship may have been clouded by less positive elements. Though he entered the Academy only a year later, Corder was six years Matthay's senior, and he seems to have been unimpressed with its Principal. He made no effort to join his class, and writing five decades later in 1922, his tone is almost one of dismissal—both for Bennett and his successor, George Macfarren:

> I only conversed with [Bennett] on the occasion of my admission as a student and found him a worn and weary man, whose life-experience seemed to have been a bitter one. . . . It is melancholy to record the non-fruition of high hopes, which is the story of so very many English musicians; it is still sadder to read of such a fine generous character fading into weakness, but with all this it is surprising to learn what a vigorous and admirable part Bennett took in the Academy's severe crisis of 1866. His music indicates a beautiful talent ill developed through deficient intellectual power. Exactly the reverse was it with his friend and rival, George Macfarren, whose compositions shew little natural spontaneity and owe their equally brief fame to the robust mentality of the composer. The two together would have made one great man; separately they have left little trace on musical art.[9]

Corder's portrait scarcely consists with the popular sentiments of Bennett's myriad admirers, and although by the time he penned these remarks he and Matthay were the closest of friends, there is no reason to presume that Matthay was ever in total agreement with this estimate. However, Bennett's music never reached the popularity—even among the English—that his early promise and later charisma might have suggested, and there is no evidence that Matthay in his maturity held any special affection for his works, so perhaps he would have concurred to some extent with Corder's views.[10] But whatever opinion he eventually formed of Bennett's accomplishments, he was understandably crestfallen at his passing, which occurred a few weeks before his seventeenth birthday. Within a month, George Macfarren (1813-87), one of the most senior RAM professors—and by far the most conservative—was chosen to succeed Bennett and he delivered his inaugural address on 25 September 1875, the most salient points of which were summarized two days later by *The Times*. He stressed that students should not attend the RAM for "amusement," but to pursue "a particular course in life," and he hoped they were "all actuated by seriousness of purpose."[11]

Like Bennett, Macfarren had been associated with the RAM for most of his life, and though many remembered him as kindly, at times he could be less than tactful in his dealings with colleagues. Wagner, who once conducted one of his overtures, dismissed him as "Mr. MacFarrinc, a pompous, melancholy Scotsman"—evidently unaware that he had been born in London.[12] With only limited success, Macfarren struggled for years to achieve fame as an opera composer, and he retained a puritanical zeal well into his seventies, confiding to friends that he "worked hard, not for the sake of work, but for the love of work."[13] He had suffered vision problems since childhood, and before he was 50 he became totally blind—remarkably—with no demonstrable ebb in his productivity. He continued to compose with the assistance of copyists, and even though he was not elected Principal until the age of 62, he served that office with distinction for the last twelve years of his life. Corder acknowledges that Macfarren's obstinate, uncompromising manner ruffled many feathers, but insists that those who knew him well "could not but revere him," and he found it disturbing that so many "spoke ill or slightingly of him."[14] But his bluntness was conjoined to an inflexible sense of principle which the Academy sorely needed, and his first order of business was to improve its dilapidated facilities by overseeing major structural alterations:

> In 1876, after vain attempts to acquire a better site, a 35 years' lease [it was actually drawn for 36½ years[15]] of Nos 4 and 5 Tenterden St. was obtained and the premises re-modelled. The 1st and 2nd floors were knocked into one, giving a concert hall of almost cubic dimensions, and the heavy expenses thus entailed quickly justified themselves by the rapidly increasing studentship. This was 286 in 1876 and 341 in 1877. Ten years later it reached 500 and remained at about that figure for the ensuing twenty years.[16]

Macfarren also permanently put to rest any future merger schemes, even when pressure emanated from so high a source as the

Prince of Wales. On 15 June 1875, Prince Edward, president of the Society of Arts, held a highly conspicuous press conference to publicize the new "National Training School for Music," which—firmly backed by the Commissioners of the Exhibition of 1851—was being erected next to the newly opened Royal Albert Hall. Every dignitary in London had been invited, including the Lord Mayor, as well as the Archbishops of Canterbury and York. The Prince's younger brother, the Duke of Edinburgh, did most of the talking, briefly summarizing the circumstances leading to the need for the National Training School, and occasionally referencing the Royal Academy. Ten years earlier, Edward had consented to chair a committee of "16 gentlemen, to consider and report on the state of the musical education of the country," resulting in a firm decision that Britain's finest musical talent was being denied scholarship assistance. Through means largely unspecified, this was to be remedied by the Academy's relocation to the Albert Hall ("as was originally intended"), and the optimistic scheme of creating 300 new competitive awards to be funded by business and civic leaders. All were apparently disturbed by Bennett's refusal to leave Tenterden Street, so plans were carried forward for a separate institution, whose structure was now nearing completion. A year later the school was ready to open, and the Academy was again asked to merge with it, becoming—in the words of Charles Freake, its principal benefactor—a part of "the cultivation and development of the art of music,"

> in which both the Prince of Wales and the Duke of Edinburgh were known to feel so much interest, as had also been the case with the late Prince Consort, whose name would always be remembered with gratitude for the powerful influence he had exercised on the intellectual advancement of the country, and to whose efforts might be traced in great measure the important place which music now held in the estimation of all classes.[17]

But in less flowery terms, if the proposal had been accepted, the Royal Academy would have ceased to exist, because a prime condition of the merger was the forfeiture of its Royal Charter. Corder indicates that the negotiations were "protracted," and in fact they continued for four more years. The Training School had fallen short of its financial goals, and the Royal Family, in consort with Sir Henry Cole, one of the principal organizers of the Great Exhibition, were being prodded by the Society of Arts to effect a merger with the RAM.[18] On 20 July 1878, the Academy Directors met to discuss a letter from Prince Christian, the German-born son-in-law of Queen Victoria, which revealed that the proposed composite institution now even had a name—"The Royal National College of Music." Christian advised that its charter had been roughed out a week earlier by its "Execution Committee," overseen by the Prince of Wales.[19] The discussions continued for another 18 months, and the Academy Directors, who usually met only once a year in the spring, convened an "Extraordinary Meeting" on 13 December 1879, to discuss yet another letter from Christian, which promised the RAM a grant of £3,000 per annum if it would surrender its Charter. But Macfarren was intractable, and though at the time he was harshly criticized for what many regarded as short-sightedness, he eventually forced support for a resolution which no doubt saved the Academy from extinction: "The Royal Academy of Music is willing to be placed on a more solid basis than that upon which it is now constituted, and to be enabled to enlarge its sphere of operation, but it cannot surrender its present Charter on any conditions, whatever."[20]

But whatever his virtues as an executive, by many accounts Macfarren was exceedingly conservative and didactic as a teacher, and it was probably fortunate for Matthay that his administrative duties prevented him from taking over Bennett's remaining students. Instead, the nation's most prominent composer was quickly brought in, and Jessie recounts that shortly after Arthur Sullivan was hired to assume the instruction of the Academy's most promising pupils, they were using adjectives such as "miraculous." Although by the fall of 1875, Sullivan had already collaborated once with W. S. Gilbert to create *Trial by Jury*, a successful curtain-raiser, he was still seen primarily as a symphonic composer—in fact many thought he was already scaling the heights that his former teacher had failed to reach. Born in Lambeth in 1842, he had entered the RAM in his mid-teens, where—as the holder of the Academy's first Mendelssohn Scholarship—he was also a pupil of Bennett. In addition, his Scholarship underwrote three years of study at the Leipzig Conservatory, where he studied piano with Moscheles and composition with Julius Rietz. His first major success was his incidental music to *The Tempest* (the first of five such Shakespearean offerings), which was begun in Leipzig and performed at the Crystal Palace under August Manns in 1862 to marked acclaim. This was followed by works such as his overture *In Memoriam* (1867) and his cantata *The Prodigal Son* (1869), which helped establish him as Britain's leading composer, and soon gave him entrée into an exalted social circle. He traveled with Dickens, Tennyson, and the painter John Millais, but Jessie insists that he never exuded a trace of pretension:

> Arthur Sullivan might well be called, both bodily and spiritually, a military bandmaster's son. He sensed his instruments as passionately as a painter senses his colours. He preached the gospel of work, work, work, exhorting his students to "take off their coats to their job," sparing themselves no drudgery. He himself was their best example; for he could point to rows of books on the top shelf of his library, and say, "Do you see all these? They are my counterpoint exercises." And, not content with these, he continued to keep himself in working trim by utilizing his spare moments for further contrapuntal training, just as an instrumentalist would practise exercises to keep his fingers in order.[21]

For several years, the Academy had tried to engage Sullivan to teach composition, and six years earlier in 1869—perhaps out of loyalty to Bennett—he had agreed to become Professor of Score Reading and Figured Bass, "receiving Four Pupils in one hour."[22] This was the extent of the commitment he was willing to make at the time, and he even tried to decline his five-shilling-per-hour compensation, until the Committee of Management advised him that "gratuitous services, however cordially rendered, are not accepted by the institution."[23]

Whether he was concentrating on his own career or simply trying to avoid competition with his former teacher, Sullivan accepted no additional responsibilities until the Committee met to choose Bennett's successor on 8 February 1875—two days after he had been laid to rest. The first recorded words of their resolution are almost obscured by Macfarren's largely illegible signature (he had been picked to chair the meeting and evidently insisted—despite his blindness—on adding the customary signature at the end of the minutes). But in the "emergency" Sullivan was clearly requested to "waive his objections to undertaking a class & kindly to accept that of the late Sir Sterndale Bennett."[24] Sullivan responded immediately, and the Committee met five days later to acknowledge his letter of acceptance.[25]

Matthay identified with Sullivan even more closely than he had related to Bennett: both had decidedly middle-class backgrounds which had instilled them with strong work ethics, both aspired to intensive training as pianists as well as composers, both were enamored with German music and its surrounding culture, and both had entered the Academy on substantial scholarships as pupils of William Sterndale Bennett. But whereas Bennett often inspired through his mere presence, Sullivan was a demanding taskmaster. In Jessie's words, "nothing in the shape of padding or redundancy escaped his eagle eye, and for clumsy use of the orchestra no allowance could be made." Bennett could afford to treat composition largely as a theoretical science, but it was Sullivan's livelihood, and he knew all too well about the tyranny of performance deadlines. There was little immersion in historical perspective, but he instilled a reverence for mechanics and practicalities with caveats such as, "Don't depend upon expression marks, score everything, score your colours, score your accents."[26]

Perhaps because he had been Bennett's last pupil, Matthay grew increasingly confident during his time with Sullivan and found his composition classes to be the most exciting time of his week. Most of his surviving works from this period are larger than those he produced for Bennett, so Sullivan probably viewed him as already somewhat accomplished when he entered his class. On 1 August 1875, he completed an "Intermezzo" for orchestra in G,[27] with a brass section that included horns in both D and C, and a month later he completed what is probably his longest and most serious transcription: the first movement of Schubert's Piano Sonata in A minor, Op. 42 (D. 845).[28] He assigned Schubert's haunting, monophonic opening theme to the oboe, before admitting the strings to render the harmonies. One of his most significant works under Sullivan was a "Concert-Ouverture" in C, completed on 17 November 1877, and extending to nearly 400 measures.[29] At some point, Matthay had the score bound in leather, so it may be presumed he regarded the work with some esteem, although over 60 years later, he wrote on the title page: "Very <u>primitive</u> indeed—yet a point or two of promise of things quite different!" An even larger "Sullivan" work was a one-movement Symphony in C, which he completed the following March, and whose performance time he noted was 12 minutes, "<u>including</u> repeat."[30] However, in his maturity, Matthay could be a stern critic of his early work, and in May of 1940 he wrote on the title page: "<u>This is of no musical value whatever</u>—a mere exercise[.] It must not be compared with another later symphonic movement in C—which is far better!"

Although it can be little verified by studying his compositions from this period, some remembered that he often experimented with unorthodox harmonies, and on one occasion his offerings met with disapproval from his classmates. Jessie notes that Sullivan was developing "a warm corner in his heart" for Matthay, and he immediately took up his cause with, "There's no telling how far he'll get, if he manages to write out all the bad!"[31] Though not then a member of Sullivan's class, violinist Alfred Walker was a first-year student from Cambridge whom Matthay befriended, and years later he provided a colorful portrait of the budding composer-pianist. At the time, the Academy reserved the right to assign secondary instruments to students as required, and evidently it felt that several of its pianists were needed in the orchestra's percussion section:

> I took violin as my first study and so played in the orchestra two days a week. The orchestral playing brought me in contact with a number

Chapter 2

of advanced students—pianists—who liked to take turns at the kettle drums. Eaton Faning, Bampfyled [F. W. Bampfylde], and Matthay.

We all liked Matthay very much, but there was a feeling that he was—well—a little bit crazy, some of his ideas being quite revolutionary. I remember his pointing out some 5ths in my harmony exercises. "But," said he, "I don't mind; in fact I like them."[32]

The Academy prospectuses list Sullivan's name through April 1878, but the exact amount of time he spent on Tenterden Street is difficult to document. Jessie indicates that he served as Bennett's successor for three years, departing only after *H.M.S. Pinafore* opened in 1878, because "there was no more time left for his young composers."[33] While this may be true, she never mentions the most important reason for his departure, and the true facts may have been so objectionable that the Academy staff had virtually pledged never to speak of them publicly. In the Committee of Management minutes no mention is made of the events provoking his resignation, and additional evidence for a covenant of silence is supported by Sullivan's obituary in the January 1901 issue of the *R.A.M. Club Magazine*, which lavishes praise on his achievements as a student and composer but—incredibly—makes no mention of the nine years he spent there as a professor.[34] A similar and even more conspicuous omission is made in Corder's detailed history of the RAM, which appeared 21 years later, since he includes a full-page photo of Sullivan at the age of 12 in his Chapel Royal uniform, but indicates no relationship to the Academy past his teens.[35] Even more remarkably, the circumstances surrounding Sullivan's situation were not only widely known, but one of the most heavily publicized musical events of 1876. It appears that the Academy was so disturbed by those circumstances that it sought to gloss over, or even rewrite, history wherever possible.

In point of fact, the Royal Family had actively sought Sullivan to head the newly founded National Training School, which was slated to open in May of 1876, and he eventually accepted. Once the School opened, to remain at the RAM at all may have been a Spartan endeavor, since whatever he might have been accomplishing in his new post, he was clearly industrious as a composer, throwing himself into his work with extreme alacrity. In July 1877 he wrote to Cole that he was "hard at work from morning till night," and he was already expressing alarm over the Training School's diminishing endowments.[36] Jessie also reports that as Sullivan's work with Gilbert increased on *Pinafore*, he was compelled to be away from the RAM for weeks at a time, but his students were only more enchanted when he returned "with little consciousness of his own supreme genius," unpretentiously offering quips such as: "It's all very well, you know, but you have to find the tunes, and do all the scoring!"[37] Exactly where he gave his classes is also less than certain, since it seems unlikely that he would have kept his personal notebooks at the RAM, and if Matthay and his other pupils saw them on a bookshelf, they were probably in his home at Albert Mansions on Victoria Street, which also served as his studio.[38]

After the summer break of 1878, Sullivan returned to the RAM for the Michaelmas term, but he suddenly withdrew in mid-October. Since *Pinafore* had already opened in May, it seems unlikely that his involvement with the production played much of a role in his departure. Perhaps by then Macfarren had made it clear that there was no hope left for a merger with the Training School, and it is also possible that the two men had a confrontation. On 25 October, the Committee of Management read Sullivan's letter of resignation, accepting it "with very great regret," and immediately appointing Ebenezer Prout (1835-1909) as Professor of Harmony and Composition "for Mr Sullivan[']s place."[39] Sullivan may have recommended Prout—who was to receive seven shillings per hour—since he had taught at the Training School from its inception. Though largely self taught, Prout held an unassailable reputation as a theorist and teacher, and he quickly endeared himself to Academy students and staff, even though he retained a connection to the Training School until it closed in 1882. On 5 May 1880, the Management Committee even voted unanimously to elect him an Honorary Member of the RAM, a status not lightly conferred.[40] Arguably a true eccentric, Prout was the son of a Congregationalist minister and he was rarely seen in public without both volumes of the *Well-Tempered Clavier* under his arm. In Jessie's words, he effected the air of "an Old Testament Prophet, going about with the Kingdom of Heaven in his bosom, in the shape of Bach's 48 Preludes and Fugues."[41]

On 3 October 1877, at the age of 19, Matthay was elected an Academy sub-professor of pianoforte, the rough equivalent of a graduate teaching assistant in today's universities.[42] He taught piano to students for whom this was merely a functional or secondary skill, under the supervision of Walter Macfarren. He was not inexperienced, since Jessie reports that he had been teaching piano in his parents' home since he was 16, and the extra income he earned in Clapham was no doubt helpful, as his scholarship had by then expired, and at the time sub-professors were not paid—their sole compensation was a reduction to half tuition after two years of service.[43] According to Matthay's own recollection, the following year he was made a sub-professor of harmony under Prout's supervision while he also worked in an advanced composition class under his master's critical eye.[44] On 22 February 1879 he completed a quartet for piano and strings that earned him first place (out of two) in what was evidently the only awarding of a £25 Academy prize given by J. F. H. Read.[45]

Prout counseled him in theoretical analysis as well, enthusiastically leading him through the intricacies of Wagner's scores, and nurturing a flame first ignited in June 1877 when Matthay heard the aging composer's music performed under Hans Richter's baton at Royal Albert Hall. Six London concerts exclusively devoted to the master conducting his own works—later expanded to eight—had been scheduled with Dannreuther's help to offset the deficits incurred by the Bayreuth Festival in the previous year. But Wagner's health was failing, and Richter was on hand to assist him while the composer watched from an armchair prominently positioned on stage. Alfred Walker provided Matthay with a ticket to one of the concerts, and years later, he recalled the excitement they both felt on that evening:

> So when Wagner came to London and gave his historical concerts in the Albert Hall it happened that I had two tickets in my pocket given me by a

friend who was playing in the orchestra. With these I ran across Matthay and invited him to come with me. He was only too eager to avail himself of the opportunity.

So off we set together and tramped across Hyde Park to hear and see the great and wondrous Wagner. I remember how full Matthay was then of the Wagnerian lore. He knew all the motifs and other peculiarities that were such novelties in those days. I remember how interested he was when Richter took over the conducting from Wagner.[46]

Obviously, when Matthay first entered the Academy in the fall of 1871, he was expected to study piano as well as composition, and although he may have initially studied with a subordinate, he was soon working with William Dorrell, one of Bennett's closest friends. Like Bennett, Dorrell had a lifelong relationship to the RAM, having studied under both Potter and his pupil W. H. Holmes (1812-85), but by 1870 he was tiring of his duties, and only Bennett's urgent appeal to their friendship kept him from resigning.[47] Dorrell evidently felt Matthay to be gifted, for it appears that he sought to challenge him wherever possible. Jessie reports that in July 1872—a few months after the Sterndale Bennett Scholarship was awarded—he thought his pupil ready to play Bennett's charming Theme and Variations, Op. 31, for the honored guests present at Wood's Rooms for the Academy's Jubilee Dinner.[48] Dorrell also assigned him the composer's substantial Sonata in F minor, Op. 13, and soon after it was completed, Matthay began work on Bennett's large programmatic Sonata, *Die Jungfrau von Orleans*—all of which undoubtedly intensified the bond between the RAM Principal and his youngest student.[49]

Pleased with Matthay's work on a Hummel concerto—which shortly after his arrival he performed with John Hullah and the Academy orchestra—Dorrell decided to stretch his horizons, and after some deliberation, he announced, "Now I am going to give you something modern—but I don't know that I ought to, as it is so revolutionary." The work in question was Mendelssohn's D minor Concerto, suggesting that Dorrell's tastes were conservative even by Victorian standards, but Matthay took to it well, and he may have been the soloist who performed it before Mrs. Gladstone at the July 1873 graduation ceremonies.[50] Dorrell's repertoire expectations must have been substantial, and Jessie reports that within the three years or less they worked together, he also assigned the Mendelssohn G minor Concerto, the Beethoven first and third Concertos (which Tobias was thrilled to receive) and several shorter works with orchestra.[51] After he left the Academy, Dorrell remained close to his pupil, and probably felt a tinge of pride when Matthay eventually became a well-established RAM professor. When Dorrell died in 1896, Matthay attended his funeral, and he was touched to learn that his former teacher had bequeathed him £200.[52]

Walter Macfarren (1826-1905), George's younger brother, became Matthay's teacher after Dorrell's retirement in December of 1874, and soon they performed Beethoven's "Emperor" Concerto together, since Macfarren was fond of Beethoven and was now also conducting the Academy orchestra.[53] Like Dorrell, Macfarren had also studied under Potter and Holmes, and as a teacher he had inspired such steadfast loyalty that during the Academy's "crisis" period the Committee of Management was forced to retrench when they sought to re-assign his pupils.[54] Though less conservative than Dorrell, Macfarren regarded Matthay as "rather a wild horse, requiring to be ridden on the curb, for he imagined him always ready to bolt after the alluring 'moderns.'" For example, Macfarren was annoyed when his pupil brought him the Liszt E-flat Concerto, advising that to pursue such repertoire was the equivalent of "going to the dogs."[55] But Matthay did convince him to allow Schumann's rarely played Introduction and Allegro, Op. 134, and however the engagement came about, in August 1876 he performed it at the Crystal Palace under August Manns, "who from the first proved a real friend."[56] Manns must have been impressed with his young artist, because in November he invited him back to the Palace to perform Schumann's more familiar Concerto in A minor. Matthay was not yet prominent enough to appear on one of Manns's Saturday Concerts, and most likely he performed on a weekday program, where the artists' names were rarely mentioned in published advertisements. About the same time, he also gave a performance of the work at the Academy under

Macfarren's baton, and Walker, then a member of the violin section, recalled an afternoon rehearsal:

> I . . . have a vivid recollection of Matthay playing the A minor Concerto of Schumann with the orchestra at an afternoon practice. We students talked his playing over, as we usually did after such performances, and I remember it was conceded that his phrasing, especially in the melodic passages, was most effective,—and this, not withstanding [sic] the fact that his memory failed him at one point, and Walter Macfarren, the conductor, had to grant him a fresh start. I can see Matthay now as he took his hand from the keyboard and despairingly clasped it to his forehead. . . . But I can also hear in memory the notes of that turn rolling out in that little melody as it occurs in the middle register of the piano, early in the movement [Walker is probably referring to bar 65 of the first movement]. His power of tonal control was, even in those days, quite remarkable.[57]

Sir George Macfarren about 1882

Chapter 2

Walter Macfarren about 1900

Undoubtedly, Matthay viewed the mere presence of Bennett, Sullivan, and Prout as educational and inspirational, but it seems he saw much less value in his piano instruction. According to Macfarren, Matthay remained with him for three years, probably continuing his piano studies until he was appointed a sub-professor of harmony in 1878. But Macfarren also reported that Charlton Speer, who followed Matthay as the second holder of the Sterndale Bennett Scholarship in 1874, studied with him for eight years,[58] so it might be inferred that Matthay ceased his piano studies somewhat sooner than many of his classmates. Like most serious students, he occasionally encountered technical and musical problems in the practice room, but these were routinely addressed simply by assigning additional repertoire or studies, and Jessie writes that from an early age he was required to become his own pedagogical analyst. For example, at one point he was foundering over a passage in the second movement of Beethoven's Sonata, Op. 10, no. 1, and despite repeated attempts he found that he was still timing the second beat in bar 17 too late:

> He was vainly struggling in time to get the little arpeggio to finish on the beat, until at last it occurred to him to seek to arrange the timing of it so as to *finish on the beat ahead.* It was the success that attended this effort which opened his eyes to the fact that all sense of rhythm in music resolves into this sense of looking ahead TOWARDS something. Thus came about his teaching of phrase-sense, group-sense, key-sense, and sense of the Whole as always being Progression, or purposed movement.[59]

Example 2.1 Beethoven: Sonata in C minor, op. 10, no. 1, second movement, mm. 17-18

Like many musicians, Matthay was beginning to acquire a catalogue of devices and techniques which he found helpful in his own playing and teaching, and from all reports he enjoyed his piano students. After he began teaching harmony classes, he had also endeared himself as a lucid clarifier of limitless patience, totally dedicated to his students' understanding and well being. Jessie cites numerous examples from his sub-professorship days demonstrating his warmth and benevolence, including an occasion when a class of harmony pupils was forced to sit on the floor owing to the inadequacy of the Tenterden Street facilities.

Chapter 2

Matthay immediately left the room and "disappeared into some remote corner of the building." When he returned, he was "lugging with him a heavy oak form on which he got them comfortably seated." On another occasion a female student who studied both piano and harmony with him felt embarrassed when she understood nothing of his lengthy explanation. Without missing a beat, Matthay simply said, "All right, I will start and explain it all over again." His manner was always positive and nurturing, and he let nothing stand in the way of drawing the best from his students, even when he dealt with one who was "panic-stricken at having to play a concerto at an orchestral practice:"

> Said Matthay: "Would it make you feel less nervous if I turned the pages for you?" This help was accepted with joy, but on getting ready for the occasion Matthay had the misfortune to break his spectacles. This did not put him out in the least. He got the break mended with some handy sealing wax and turned the pages, blissfully unconscious that the red blob was providing great amusement to the audience of students.[60]

Matthay may have regarded his sub-professor status as a potent drawing card for outside pupils in both piano and harmony, because he soon began advertising in *The Times*. This notice ran on 28 April 1879, and again on 1 May:

> PIANOFORTE, Harmony—Mr. TOBIAS A. MATTHAY, R.A.M., will have a few hours DISENGAGED after Easter. Address 40, Manor-street, Clapham.[61]

As he was approaching the end of his student days, Tobias Matthay's slender, six-foot frame towered over many of his classmates. He was powerfully built with long limbs, and even though period photographs do not always show him with the spectacles for which he was later so well known, his receding hairline already suggested a mantle of intellectualism, rather than athleticism. As he began to contemplate his future, he was well aware that his nine years of study at the Academy had been, in Jessie's words, "far more

Tobias Matthay in 1880 as he began his teaching at the RAM; his sister, Dora, is at left, his mother, Dorothea, is at right; his father, Tobias senior, is seated

London's Royal Academy of Music on Tenterden Street as it appeared in Matthay's student days and as he began his teaching there

preoccupied with composition than with piano."[62] Thus, by the spring of 1880, he was hopeful that the RAM would offer him a permanent appointment in harmony, and no doubt he made his desire known to Prout as well. But whatever Prout's reaction, his recommendation would probably have had little impact since as yet he enjoyed no seniority. It is also tempting to speculate that George Macfarren—who undoubtedly influenced the Committee of Management's final decision—was antagonistic to Matthay's Wagner worship, because he was so violently hostile to the composer that he actually hoped an earthquake would devour Bayreuth, swallowing "the spot and everybody on it."[63] He advised C. Hubert Parry, his former pupil, that "every presence there gives countenance to monstrous self inflation," and he added that Wagner should have been great, but that "everything he has put down is wrong."[64] Corder, also Macfarren's pupil, harbored pronounced Wagnerian sympathies, and after he won the Mendelssohn Scholarship in 1875, his planned trip to Bayreuth caused "a regrettable breach" with Macfarren.[65]

But if Macfarren's musical views were reactionary, ironically, his administrative competence also played a role in sealing Matthay's fate, and in fact, the expectation of a compositional appointment was probably unrealistic on logistical grounds. When Matthay entered the RAM in 1871 it had just over 200 students, and now—less than a decade later and thanks largely to Macfarren's persistence—that number had almost doubled. Unbridled growth in any institution usually creates staffing concerns, but conservatories tend to limit composition concentrations to students who show a specialized aptitude. By contrast, they require everyone to study piano, and sharp enrollment increases nearly always necessitate staffing expansions in keyboard. By April 1878 the Academy Prospectus was listing only five Professors of Harmony and Composition—including Macfarren and Sullivan, who had relatively few students—but 15 Professors of Pianoforte. In addition, the catalogue cites a number of sub-professors whose main instrument was piano, such as Matthay, F. W. Bampfylde, and Charlton Speer.[66] Although these men taught the required harmony courses

Chapter 2

as well, they taught them in classes, rather than privately, allowing for a larger student-teacher proportion than the one-to-one ratio necessary for piano.

Perhaps Matthay should have also learned from the experiences of his senior classmates who had studied under Bennett. For example, Eaton Faning entered the RAM in April 1870 at the age of 19, and unlike Matthay, he even had the recommendation of an Academy examiner, R. Lindley Nunn of Ipswich.[67] Walker remembered that Faning was perceived by many as "the most talented" composer in Bennett's class,[68] and he easily won the Mendelssohn Scholarship in 1873. But notwithstanding such impressive credentials, in October 1877 his Assistant Professorship still came in piano. Moreover, even though the Committee voted unanimously in his favor, it mandated that his first year be supervised by his former teacher, F. B. Jewson, suggesting that Faning's piano accomplishments were less impressive than those of Matthay and his colleagues.[69] Thomas Wingham, another of Matthay's close friends and also one of Bennett's star pupils, was a brilliant choral and symphonic composer, but he too was given only a piano professorship.[70] So perhaps it should have come as no surprise when, on 24 July 1880, the Committee voted to give Matthay a year's appointment as an Assistant Professor of Pianoforte. By the fall of 1880, although the number of composition professors had increased by two (including Prout), they were far more seasoned than those recently appointed to teach piano—a number which had now (with Matthay) risen to 17.[71]

Although he enjoyed teaching motivated piano students, Matthay often remarked that the Committee's decision to deny him a composition post had been a bitter disappointment and—at least on some level—one that he never got over. But nonetheless, at the age of 22, he was happy to have been offered the equivalent of a full-time job, a status that his father (at least after he married) had never reached with any educational institution. No doubt both of his parents and his eleven-year-old sister attended the recital he gave at Clapham Hall on 14 May, where the heavily Germanic program included Beethoven's 32 Variations in C minor—a work that Matthay frequently revisited throughout his career. Jessie indicates that the concert was scheduled to celebrate his new standing, so perhaps by mid-term he knew the decision was imminent, even though it was not made official till July. Joined by several of his RAM colleagues, he also featured chamber works, including some or all of the Mendelssohn D minor Trio, Op. 49, Schubert's Nocturne in E-flat for piano trio, D. 897, his own Piano Quartet prepared under Prout (which had won the Read Prize in the previous year), several of his smaller works for piano and strings, and three of his songs. From his parents' home in Clapham, he sold tickets to the event at one, two, and three shillings.[72] He also went to the trouble and expense to advertise the concert on three separate occasions in *The Times*, and no doubt the proceeds barely covered his expenses, if he even managed to break even.[73] The program also indicates that the piano was supplied by Broadwood, Matthay's instrument of choice for the next several years.

Beginning in the fall of 1880, the Academy compensated Matthay at the standard assistant-professor rate of three shillings and sixpence per hour, issuing his payment three times a year—in December, March, and May. Until about 1886, each term the Committee of Management devoted part of one meeting to approve the entire run of checks, recording all Academy expenses in registers that were unusually complete. For example, it can be seen that Macfarren was paid £100 a term—or £300 a year—for his work as Principal, and that in the Michaelmas term of 1876 he was also paid £62, 14s, 9d for his composition instruction. In the same term, his brother Walter was paid £136, 10s for his piano instruction, while he received another £50 each term for conducting the Academy Orchestra.[74] Understandably, Assistant Professors received far less for their efforts, and in December 1881 Matthay was paid only £23, 16s for the thirteen-week term, indicating that he taught 136 hours.[75] Although it is possible he was assigned ten "first-study" students per week, this is unlikely, since junior professors nearly always taught a large complement of "second studies" who studied for only 30 minutes per week. In all probability, he taught a combination of hour and half-hour lessons, as well as an additional pupil or two who entered at mid-term, which was very common at the time. But it may not always be possible to infer a teaching load purely from compensation, since adjudication or other occasional responsibilities may have carried some additional remuneration. That would explain the £27, 7s, 9d Matthay earned the following May, suggesting perhaps that he taught either 12 "first studies" or 24 "second studies," or a combination thereof, plus several fractional lessons—but more likely that his piano duties were mingled with other tasks.[76]

After his new appointment, he continued briefly to advertise for private students, and now he evidently felt he could afford to hire a studio at the Stanley Lucas music shop on New Bond Street. Matthay's connection to Lucas may have been brought about through Dorrell, since the two men were so close that after Dorrell passed, Lucas even served as one of the executors of his estate.[77] On 26 February 1881 Matthay placed a notice in *The Times*, but since it may have appeared only once, the additional pupils might not have justified the added expense of advertising:

> MR. TOBIAS A. MATTHAY begs to inform his pupils and friends that he will in future give his PRIVATE PIANOFORTE LESSONS in town at Messrs. Stanley Lucas, Weber, and Co.'s, 84, New Bond-street, W. For terms, &c., address Mr. Matthay, 40, Manor-street, Clapham, S.W.[78]

Financial concerns seemed to wear heavily on the Matthay family through the entire decade. As early as 1879—perhaps motivated by the necessity for educating Dora—Tobias senior began to place a series of advertisements in *The Times* which, despite Jessie's claims to the contrary, suggest that the family's finances were precarious and that he was grabbing at any opportunity which came his way. On 6 September he was again advertising for a ladies' class, but volunteering now to be present in Croydon as well as Clapham, and by 29 October he was offering to expand his orbit to Wimbledon.[79] However successful these ventures may have been, a year later on 4 December, he was again advertising his publications, offering an entire catalogue of grammar methods—complete with accolades:

> MATTHAY'S METHOD OF LEARNING GERMAN in the SHORTEST POSSIBLE TIME.—Opinions of the Press:—"We do not know where we could get better guides than those Herr Matthay has given us for the attainment of German. Herr Matthay has shown in his works that he is a thorough student and a successful teacher of his mother tongue." Complete Grammatical Course of the German Language, 6s.; German Grammar, 2s. 6d,; Deutsche Litratur und Lesebuch (invaluable to those who prepare for Civil Service for India, and for the higher Oxford and Cambridge Exams), 7s.; Questions for Examination on the German Grammar Vocabulary, 2s. 6d. Dulau and Co., Soho, London; or of Herr Matthay, 40, Manor-street, Clapham, S.W.[80]

By April, Matthay was either paying or sharing the rent for his father's studio space at Lucas's shop: "GERMAN LANGUAGE AND LITERATURE.—PRIVATE CLASSES for LADIES, at Messrs. Stanley Lucas, Weber, and Co.'s 84, New Bond-street, W. For terms, &c., address Herr Matthay, 40, Manor-street, Clapham, S.W."[81] Whatever their financial situation, Tobias senior and Dorothea planned to celebrate their silver wedding anniversary with a party on 23 December and perhaps their son may even have helped fund the notice that appeared on 8 December in *The Times* to reach their "distant relatives" (*Verwandten*). Judging from the rough grammar, it was probably typeset by a *Times* copy editor who lacked fluency in German, but the ad can roughly be translated as: "For our Silver Wedding [anniversary], taking place on the 23rd of December, we would like to invite distant relatives."[82]

But even before the party occurred, Tobias senior began to advertise for a position in the public schools in anticipation of the coming winter term. He composed two ads with similar, gender-specific copy,

Chapter 2

and the following military school notice, aimed at boys, appeared in *The Times* on 19 and 22 December:

> GERMAN LANGUAGE and LITERATURE at MILITARY TUTORS and SCHOOLS.—For terms and PROPESCTUSES of MILITARY TUTORS where Herr Matthay (Author of "German Literature," "Grammatical Course," "Grammar," "Questions for Examination," &c.) teaches, address Herr Matthay, No. 40, Manor-street, Clapham, S.W.[83]

On 21 and 24 December, he placed a very similar notice which substituted "LADIES' SCHOOLS" for "MILITARY TUTORS and SCHOOLS," suggesting that he was leaving no stone unturned.[84] In May, June, and later in August, on New Bond Street and in his home, he was again advertising classes targeted at young men, since he references their usefulness in passing the examinations at Sandhurst and Woolwich.[85] By the fall, he was even advertising correspondence courses with a modest ad which ran on 4 November—and a more extensive notice which appeared on 8 January 1883:

> GERMAN LANGUAGE by CORRESPONDENCE.—A Complete Grammatical Course of the German Language, consisting of 152 exercises on all the different parts of the German grammar; terms five guineas. A Complete Course of Acquiring the German Grammar, consisting of 212 questions on all the different parts of the grammar; terms three guineas. Address Herr Matthay, no. 40, Manor-street, Clapham, London, S.W. Hundreds of Herr Matthay's pupils have gained high marks in German at the examinations for Sandhurst, Woolwich, India and Home Civil Service, Staff College, Matriculation, Higher Oxford and Cambridge Examinations, &c.[86]

Although it could be argued that Herr Matthay was merely enterprising, additional evidence suggests that these various pursuits were motivated by financial concerns. For example, on 18 September 1886, Dora performed a piano audition at the RAM, but not before her brother had petitioned to get her fees reduced. Two months earlier on 26 July—before she had even appeared—the Committee of Management voted to reduce her tuition from the normal 11 guineas per term (£11, 11s) to eight guineas (£8, 8s) and to waive her five-guinea entrance fee, "in consideration of Mr Matthay[']s Services & Position in the Academy."[87] If his parents' financial state was precarious, one wonders if Matthay may even have borne some of the remaining expenses, although his funds were also tight. Two years later, on 6 June 1888, he placed a letter before the Committee of Management asking to have his father considered for the position of German professor at the RAM, but they declined on the grounds that there was no "prospective vacancy."[88] Separately, these events prove little, but when taken as a whole, they suggest an aging professor scrambling for whatever work could be had. To make matters worse, by the mid-1880s Tobias senior was facing substantial competition from other German tutors with similar credentials. For example, one Fraülein Perger, who boasted a "Government Diploma," advertised weekly in the *Clapham Observer* for several years.[89]

In addition, the younger Matthay clearly had his own financial problems, and although he seems to have been respected by his Academy colleagues, his first two decades of service were marked by meager compensation. Pay scales were dictated somewhat by custom, but more often by favoritism, and virtually never were wages increased as a matter of policy. Thus, professors were accustomed to submitting formal requests to the Committee of Management whenever increases were sought, and not infrequently those requests were postponed for future consideration—sometimes for years. Although the account ledgers show some general increase in Matthay's earnings for the first several years, this was due purely to his class size, since his pay rate of 3s, 6d per hour remained constant. Thus, in the spring of 1884, he was paid £42, 5s, 3d, indicating he now taught the equivalent of 483 thirty-minute lessons over the thirteen-week term (about 35 lessons per week), and almost certainly that a number of his students were still "second studies," for whom the compensation was only half of the hourly rate. Although he was certainly teaching at least one "first study" by the spring of 1884, because the Academy

Register records that Edward Cuthbert Nunn, who studied composition with George Macfarren, elected to pursue two principal studies, arriving in that term with Matthay as his piano teacher.[90]

There was evidently an enrollment decline in the fall of 1884, and the Committee may have seen it coming. Not infrequently, titles and promotions were used to pacify staff in lieu of salary increases, and almost certainly this logic was behind Matthay's rather contradictory appointment to the rank of Professor on 26 July 1884—barely three weeks after the Committee members had voted "unanimously" to re-appoint him to the rank of Assistant Professor.[91] Matthay wrote a gracious letter thanking them for the promotion, which was read at the 1 October meeting, but his salary was still frozen, and ironically the fall term was one of his worst yet: his compensation fell to £31, 6s, 6d. Since this figure is evenly divisible by two, he could have taught as many as 13 "first study" students that term, but as the breakdown of "first-" versus "second-studies" cannot be inferred from these numbers alone, he could just as easily have taught say, six "first studies" and fourteen "second studies." He also offered ten additional hours of instruction, which could be explained either by attrition or by students who entered at half term.[92] Obviously, enrollment fluctuations were an unpleasant fact of life, and despite his promotion, Matthay's income had suddenly dropped by over £10 in a single term—back to a level only slightly above where it began four years earlier. That winter, he wrote a letter asking for an increase in his fee which the Committee read on 4 February, but after some discussion, "no proposition was made."[93] Not until it read his second letter on 24 July 1885—a year after his promotion—was his rate raised to five shillings per hour.[94]

Although the Committee minutes occasionally make reference to a policy of rewarding teachers whose efforts have increased Academy enrollment, such a practice can rarely be verified by studying the account ledgers. In the fall of 1885, Matthay's outside teaching began to pay off—at least for the Academy—because he brought in another "first study," Nina Maynard, 19, of Wandsworth Common. However, it should be noted that his students were not always unswervingly loyal, because within two years she was studying with C. H. Eyers, a more senior professor.[95] However, in the Lent term which followed, he brought Maud Samuel, whose entire family was musical and eventually became some of his strongest supporters.[96] Dora—whom Jessie describes as his first "really serious pupil"—entered the following fall. According to the Academy Candidates Foundation Register, she also studied voice with J. T. Hutchinson, and from the number of solo appearances she made it can be inferred that she was an accomplished singer as well. Also in the fall of 1886, Matthay brought Emily "May" Christie, 17, of Brixton, and Elizabeth Agent, 20, of Belham.[97] Jessie indicates that Christie had begun her piano studies with Matthay while attending a girl's school in Camberwell, where she began addressing him as "Mr. Tobs," thus paving the way for the nickname by which he was later best known.[98] Fifteen-year-old Melanie Hall of Briston entered on 22 September 1888, and a year later he brought Ellen Horncastle, 16, from North Kensington, but there was no inclination to raise his pay, and he had now been at the five-shilling rate for four years.[99] Finally, after five years, on 25 September 1890, the Committee voted unanimously to raise his rate to seven shillings an hour.[100]

It should be noted that Matthay's compensation was not that far out of line with what some of his colleagues were paid, but many clearly had additional pursuits which helped sustain them professionally. For example, beginning in October 1877 Eaton Faning was also paid the modest sum of 3s, 6d per hour, and in the early 1880s he earned even less than Matthay, averaging around £11 per term.[101] But this was due to his choosing a reduced teaching load, since in 1883 he was appointed to the staff of the Royal College of Music, and in the fall of 1885, after also taking a job at Harrow, he requested that the Committee assign him no students at all for the next two terms.[102] Still, Matthay probably felt some disappointment that a full year before he had even reached the seven-shilling rate, his friend Thomas Wingham—whose reputation rested more with composition than piano—had been granted an unusually generous rise to 10s, 6d an hour, the maximum fee the Academy then paid, and a compensation which eluded Matthay for another decade.[103]

Chapter 2

Not surprisingly, he was still living at home, since housing expenses in the metropolitan area were escalating. By 1887, new houses in Clapham were being advertised at rates of between £300 and £350 per annum, and then only if long-term leases were signed. Even modest, unimpressive dwellings in Clapham could not be had for less than £100 to £150 a year, which was nearly Matthay's entire annual salary.[104] The situation worsened for him early in 1893, as he was now contemplating marriage and financial security was no doubt a paramount consideration. He submitted a request for an increase on 19 January which the Committee considered collectively with those of three other professors, but he was told that his request could not "be acceded to," since "no more than two years had elapsed since Mr Matthay's rate of fee had been raised."[105] On 16 February the Committee considered his request to be placed on the Metropolitan Examination Board, an organization which evaluated candidates twice a year throughout the city for their suitability as "Licentiates" of the Royal Academy, a status entitling them to use the "L.R.A.M." initials after their names. No action was taken at that meeting and Matthay's application was reconsidered on 11 March, after which he was advised that it would be "kept on file in the event there is a vacancy."[106]

A year later, he again requested a salary increase, but it was "deferred" at the 1 March 1894 meeting, and on 8 March the Committee officially decided that no fees could be raised that year.[107] Perhaps as consolation, a week later he was placed on an "Auxiliary" Metropolitan Examination Committee, chaired by Walter Macfarren.[108] By January of 1895, opportunity had knocked, since Matthay, Corder, and Alfred Walker were now listed as professors at Trinity College. Founded as a church music school in 1872, Trinity had branched out to other areas of music within several years, and the notice which it placed in *The Times* on 3 January boasted a faculty of over 40.[109] Although he remained on the school's roster for nearly a decade, he probably did little teaching there. However, when he was first appointed, the Academy's Committee of Management may have feared an impending exodus, because on 21 February 1895 his hourly rate of compensation was raised from seven to eight shillings, and

Corder—who by then was a member of the Committee—was given the same raise.[110] His rate was increased to nine shillings per hour on 2 March 1898, and on 8 February 1899, less than two weeks before his forty-first birthday—and a full ten years after Wingham had reached the same level—Matthay and Corder were both advanced to the maximum rate of ten shillings and sixpence an hour.[111]

But if Matthay's compensation was not fully commensurate with his worth to the RAM through this period, the artistic experiences to which he had been exposed were about to change his life profoundly. And whether he knew it or not, he was soon to conduct pioneering research in a laboratory where little science had yet been performed.

Notes

1. *TT,* 29 July 1873, 10, col. F. The article appeared on a Monday, two days after the ceremony occurred. All references to this ceremony are taken from the same article.
2. *TT,* 16 June 1875, 7, col. F.
3. See RAMDM, 20 Nov. 1867, and 13 Dec. 1879.
4. FC, 75.
5. See Sterndale Bennett, 371-75.
6. FC, 75.
7. *TT,* 29 July 1873.
8. *TT,* 8 February 1875, 5, col. F.
9. FC, 77-78.
10. Matthay's *Musical Interpretation,* discussed in Ch. 8, offers dozens of musical examples from repertoire he often taught to his students, including a passage from Alexander Mackenzie's *Scottish Concerto,* but no Bennett works are excerpted. And although he wrote a substantial number of piano works, Bennett's compositions rarely appeared on recitals given by Matthay pupils.
11. *TT,* 27 September 1875, 5, col. C.
12. See Richard Wagner, *My Life,* (New York, 1927) 318.
13. Nicholas Temperley, "Macfarren, Sir George (Alexander)," *RNG.*

14. FC, 78.
15. See COMM, 9 Dec. 1876, 392. The rent was to be fixed at £600 a year.
16. FC, 78.
17. *TT* 16 June 1875, 7, col. F.
18. Cole was knighted in 1875. Twenty-five years earlier he had felt slighted when Colonel William Reid, a war hero, was chosen to chair the Royal Commission's Executive Committee, and he submitted his resignation. However, he was persuaded to stay after he received a personal appeal from Prince Albert—and the offer of an £800-per-annum salary. See Davis, *The Great Exhibition*, 57-59. Some of the best modern scholarship on the brief existence of the National Training School is contained in G. W. E. Brightwell's "In Search of a Nation's Music[:] The Role of the Society of Arts and the Royal Academy of Music in the Establishment of the Royal College of Music in 1883," in Peter Horton and Bennett Zon, eds., *Nineteenth-Century British Music Studies*, vol. 3 (Aldershot, 2005), 251-72. See also David Wright, who argues that Sullivan was highly ineffectual as the school's director in "Grove's Role in the Founding of the RCM," Michael McClelland, ed., *George Grove, Music and Victorian Culture*, (London, 2003), 219-44. Hereafter cited as "Wright."
19. RAMDM, 20 July 1878.
20. RAMDM, 13 Dec. 1879.
21. JHM, 12.
22. COMM, 8 April 1869, 12.
23. COMM, 22 May 1869, 14.
24. COMM, 8 Feb. 1875, 264.
25. COMM, 13 Feb. 1875, 269.
26. JHM, 12.
27. RAMRBC MS 1937.
28. RAMRBC MS 1944.
29. RAMRBC MS 1935.
30. RAMRBC MS 1945.
31. RAMRBC MS 1945.
32. Alfred Walker, "Student Days with Matthay," *AMAJ*, (Summer 1932), 12. Here-after cited as Walker.
33. JHM, 12.

34. See "Sir Arthur Sullivan," *RAMCM*, No. 2 (Jan. 1901), 18-19. Not surprisingly, the obituary also makes no mention of his tenure as Principal at the National Training School.
35. FC, opposite 68.
36. See Arthur Jacobs, *Arthur Sullivan, a Victorian musician* (Oxford,1984), 107.
37. JHM, 8.
38. In June 1877, Sullivan moved from no. 8 Albert Mansions to no. 9. See Jacobs, 105.
39. COMM, 25 Oct. 1878, 81.
40. COMM, 5 May 1880, 162.
41. JHM, 9.
42. COMM, 3 Oct. 1877, 24.
43. See JHM, 15, and COMM, 6 Feb. 1878, 37.
44. See "Tobias Augustus Matthay," in the *MT* (54, no. 848): 1 Oct. 1913, 642. In the same article Matthay claims that he was made a sub-professor of piano in 1876, but this is contradicted by the Committee records, which undoubtedly are more reliable. The article contains other errors regarding dates, such as the assertion (p. 642) that he was made a "full professor of the pianoforte" in 1880, four years before that status was actually conferred. The article possibly used the term informally to distinguish it from the status of sub-professor.
45. The autograph is MS 1957 in the RAMRBC. See also JHM, 9.
46. Walker, 13.
47. Sterndale Bennett, 395.
48. By chance, Matthay was present at a rather ominous event in the Academy's history, for Henry Cole, who had wangled an invitation to the dinner, proceeded to regale Bennett and the other dignitaries with the promise of a £5,000 grant if the RAM "remodeled its administration," his euphemistic way of referencing the Albert Hall relocation scheme. Bennett's son later wrote, "The present administrators of the Institution, who were Mr Cole's hosts, did not understand their guest's remark, nor was it subsequently explained to them." See Sterndale Bennett, 418-19.
49. Bennett's most important solo piano works are contained in Nicholas Temperley, ed., *Works for Pianoforte Solo by William Sterndale Bennett: from 1834 to 1840*, vols. 17-18 of *LPFS*.

50. Unfortunately, no record can be located at the RAM which identifies the specific soloists for this event, but it seems very likely that the Academy would have asked its first Sterndale-Bennett scholar to perform.
51. JHM, 11.
52. Jessie (JHM, 7) incorrectly states that Dorrell died in 1895 and that he left Matthay only £100. Dorrell actually died on 13 December 1896, and his will, on file at the London Probate Office, lists many bequests of £200 or more to relatives, friends, and associates, which no doubt his substantial estate of £26,328, 13s, 2d easily fulfilled. The Committee of Management Minutes of 17 Dec. 1896 indicate that Matthay attended Dorrell's funeral with the Academy's secretary [F. W. Renaut].
53. Macfarren conducted the RAM Orchestra for five years, from 1873-78, assuming the post, according to Corder, after the normally unflappable John Hullah left "in a fit of temper" (FC, 79). Macfarren's official RAM obituary indicates that, like his brother, he was afflicted with vision problems which forced him to resign his conductorship in 1878 (*RAMCM*, Oct. 1905, 3), but Corder suggests it was rather a female student's complaints that drove him out. He was replaced by a much beloved professor with the unlikely name of William Shakespeare.
54. See Macfarren's obituary in the *RAMCM*, No. 16 (Oct. 1905), 2-5.
55. JHM, 11.
56. JHM, 12.
57. Walker, 12-13.
58. Walter Macfarren, *Memories: An Autobiography* (London, 1905), 132.
59. JHM, 13.
60. JHM, 13-14.
61. *TT*, 28 April 1879, 3, col. C, and 1 May 1879, 3, col. D.
62. JHM 91.
63. Quoted in Jeremy Dibble, *C. Hubert Parry: His Life and Music* (Oxford, 1992), 141.
64. Dibble, 207.
65. FC, 69.
66. See RAM Prospectus for October 1880.
67. See RAM Candidates Foundation [1822-74], 186.
68. Walker, 12.

69. See COMM, 3 Oct. 1877, 86.
70. JHM, 8.
71. COMM, 24 July 1880.
72. *TT*, 1 May 1880, 1, col. C.
73. The ads ran on 29 April, 1 May, and 12 May 1880.
74. COMM, 9 Dec. 1876. It should be noted that after 1875, no checks are recorded to Sullivan, suggesting that after Bennett's death, he may have donated his services. Perhaps Macfarren felt that the £400 per year he was receiving as Principal of the National Training School was compensation enough, and did not insist on paying him. And as Wright notes (p. 228), Sullivan's NTSM salary was actually a very small part of his annual income, which in 1880 came to a total of £9,998, 12s, 6d.
75. COMM, 17 Dec. 1881.
76. COMM, 3 May 1882.
77. See the last Will and Testament of William Dorrell, dated 14 Jan. 1897, 1, FRO.
78. *TT*, 26 Feb. 1881, 3, col. D.
79. *TT*, 6 Sept. 1879, 3, col. B and 29 Oct. 1879, 13, col. B.
80. *TT*, 4 Dec. 1880, 2, col. F.
81. *TT*, 6 Apr. 1881, 18, col. B.
82. *TT*, 8 Dec. 1881, 1, col. B. "MATTHAY.—Zu unserer am 23 December statt findenden SILBERNEN HOCHZEIT ladet entfernte Verwanten [sic] ein.— T. MATTHAY, 40, Manor-street, Clapham, London."
83. *TT*, 19 Dec. 1881, 14, col. E, and 22 Dec. 1881, 12, col. B.
84. *TT*, 21 Dec. 1881, 14, col. E, and 24 Dec. 1881, 15, col. C.
85. *TT*, 13 May 1882, 15, col. C, 3 June 1882, 3, col. D, and 5 Aug. 1882, 3, col. E.
86. *TT*, 8 Jan. 1883, 1, col. D.
87. COMM, 26 July 1886.
88. COMM, 6 June 1888.
89. See, for example, her ad in the *Clapham Observer, Tooting & Balham Times, and Surrey County Observer* on 8. Jan. 1887, 8, col. 2. Similar notices appeared on a weekly basis for several years.
90. RAMR for 1887, the first year Registers were kept. The Registers also provide the dates that presently enrolled students first entered and usually the names of their teachers.

Chapter 2

91. COMM, 2 July 1884 and 26 July 1884.
92. COMM, 20 Dec. 1884.
93. COMM, 4 Feb. 1885.
94. COMM, 24 July 1885.
95. The Candidates Foundation Registry records Nina's entry circumstances, including the fact that she entered on Matthay's recommendation. By 1887, these records had been replaced by the Academy Register, which records only Eyers as her teacher.
96. See Chs. 5 and 7.
97. RAM Auditions Register for Michaelmas term, 1885 and 1886.
98. RAMR, Fall 1886.
99. RAM Auditions Register for Michaelmas term, 1888 and 1889.
100. COMM, 25 Sept. 1890.
101. In December 1881, for example, Faning was paid £11, 7s, 6d, compared with Matthay's £23, 6s. Wingham was paid £40, 19s, which was the same amount paid to Prout. COMM, 17 Dec. 1881.
102. See COMM, 7 Oct. 1885.
103. Wingham wrote the Committee of Management a letter of thanks which it read on 12 Oct. 1889. COMM.
104. See various ads in the *Clapham Observer*, 23 July 1887.
105. COMM, 19 Jan. 1893. All four requests were denied.
106. COMM, 11 Mar. 1893.
107. COMM, 1 Mar. and 8 Mar. 1894.
108. COMM, 15 Mar. 1894.
109. *TT*, 3 Jan. 1895, 1, col. C.
110. COMM, 21 Feb. 1895.
111. COMM, 2 Mar. 1898 and 8 Feb. 1899.

CHAPTER 3

"LORD-HIGH-EVERYTHING-ELSE"

By the late 1880s, Wagner was beginning to be viewed by many in England as the epitome of German romanticism, but that eminence had taken decades to reach. Commenting on Matthay's reverence for the composer, Jessie references a London pioneering group known as "The Working Men's Society," and suggests that "had young Matthay been born twenty years earlier, he would doubtless have been an enthusiastic member."[1] The Society had been the brainchild of the German-born Karl Klindworth (1830-1916), who brought a new wave of Germanic thought to England which challenged the long accepted dominance of the traditional German masters. While studying with Liszt at Weimar, Klindworth had joined with Hans von Bülow, Joachim Raff, and an American, William Mason, to form an earlier society dedicated to the promulgation of what Wagner termed "the music of the future"—the view that programmatic, literary concerns should amplify or even override purely musical designs. In 1854 he relocated to London, where over the next 14 years he performed with limited success as a pianist and conductor, since his chosen repertoire—especially the orchestral works of Liszt and Berlioz—was often several steps ahead of what his audiences were willing to accept.

Klindworth was thrilled when Wagner arrived in London in 1855 to replace the Italian-born Michael Costa as conductor of the Philharmonic Society, but his vision was not, at least initially, shared by all. Although Wagner's operas had yet to be performed in London, J. W. Davison, *The Times*'s critic, had already rejected the composer's doctrine of *Gesamtkunstwerk*, and in fact was ready to condemn it without reservation. Although he had not yet heard *Tannhäuser* or *Lohengrin*, he announced authoritatively that these operas "fully revealed and illustrated" the "Wagnerian system:"

Chapter 3

The "system" however, failing to be understood, the inventor was resolved to become his own apologist, and, in a work entitled *Kunstwerk der Tukunft* [sic], he set forth at large his views and opinions to the world. . . . Since, however, Herr Wagner only came forward last night as a conductor, this is not the place to examine his doctrine. It will serve for the moment to say that his assumed mission is to elevate poetry in the lyric drama to its ancient place by the side of music—in short to make it of equal importance. His notion of tune is "melody spoken," and in all respects that the words and the music should go hand in hand. Of Greek music nothing positive is known, beyond the fact that it bore no resemblance to what is called music in the present day; and as the art now exists—in the state of perfection which it has gradually reached through the hands of successive great masters and men of genius—the theory of Herr Wagner is philosophically false and practically impossible.[2]

Not surprisingly, Wagner's year with the Philharmonic was not altogether successful, and his baton soon passed to William Sterndale Bennett, but Bennett's appointment in no way signaled the end of German dominance at home. In his first year, his intimacy with the Schumanns enabled him to engage Clara to perform Beethoven's "Emperor" Concerto for her London debut—a wise choice since her husband's music was still considered too radical by many.[3] In the ensuing ten seasons, Bennett was generally successful by adhering to largely traditional—that is, less programmatic—repertoire and he never attempted anything so ambitious as Anton Rubinstein's "Ocean" Symphony, which Klindworth conducted in 1861 to nearly universal disapproval.[4] But the advocates of the "new" aesthetic persevered. During his stay in London, Wagner was so impressed with Klindworth that he entrusted him with the piano-score adaptations of his *Ring* cycle, a project which occupied him well into the next decade. In 1867, Klindworth was instrumental in creating "The Working Men's Society"—avowed Wagnerites who met weekly to study his operas act by act—and the following year he performed many of his *Ring* transcriptions for them.

When Klindworth left London in 1868, the Society was taken over by yet another transplanted German, pianist Edward Dannreuther, who had been elated six years earlier when he first heard Wagner conduct the Prelude to *Die Meistersinger* at the Leipzig Gewandhaus. His success as a pianist made him something of a matinee idol in London, where he soon befriended literary figures such as Dickens, Browning, George Eliot, and Matthew Arnold, as well as William Morris and George Grove. But even though he moved in prestigious circles, his militant endorsement of Wagner's music lost him the support of Henry Fothergill Chorley as well as many other admirers.[5] In 1872 he re-organized the Working Men's Society into the London Wagner Society, and he also began to write and lecture extensively. Matthay became a member of the Wagner Society in the early 1880s, and with his two friends Charles and Walter Dowdeswell, amateur musicians who maintained an art gallery on New Bond Street, as Jessie recounts, he contributed many programs for the benefit of its members: "Matthay found that he also could be a good 'working man.' Charles lectured and Walter sang, and at the piano Matthay was 'Lord-High-Everything-Else.' They gave many evenings together, not only at the Wagner Society but also at Clapham and elsewhere."[6]

Parker was also a member and later wrote that he found the organization a useful vehicle to "getting known in London."[7] Its other members included Ferdinand Praeger (1815-91), a Leipzig-born musician who settled in London in 1834, and scandalized Society members 50 years later by publishing the controversial *Wagner as I Knew Him*, a personal memoir so wrought with fallacies that his German publisher soon withdrew it from circulation. Another member was Ashton Ellis (1852-1919), who gave up medicine to devote his life to Wagner scholarship, and according to Parker, was "the fiercest in denouncing the book."[8] But amid these clashes, Wagnerism in England could also boast artistic accomplishments from outstanding musicians. Dannreuther's cause was aided immeasurably by Wagner's friend and associate, the Austrian conductor Hans Richter (1843-1916), who began appearing regularly in England in 1879, and who set new performance standards both for Wagner and for the entire German repertory. In 1882, following London's first complete performance of *The Ring* at Covent Garden under the baton of Wagner's friend Anton Seidl, Richter conducted *Tristan und Isölde* and *Die Meistersinger*, and Jessie notes that even the Matthays' limited finances did not deter them from attending each production in turn:

> To these memorable performances Matthay went with his father. They were memorable indeed, for anything more luxurious than gallery seats was not to be thought of, and as the performances rarely finished before 1 a.m., father and son were obliged to walk home [from Covent Garden to Clapham] some four miles. Nevertheless these were days of enchantment: the outcome of which had of course to be the intensive study of the scores.[9]

When Matthay began his teaching career at the RAM, he was eager to serve the dual masters of piano and composition, but he clearly would have preferred the title "composer-pianist." Though piano miniatures form the bulk of his published output, he left a sufficient number of large, unpublished works to confirm that his ambitions extended well beyond the realm of the character piece. Many of his shorter pieces were dashed off quickly—often in a few hours—and inspired to some extent by a desire to provide his students with playable material. For example, on the evening of 24 January 1884, he completed his (unpublished) "Tale of the Olden Days" in less than three hours, and he wrote his Toccatina in G on the evening of 6 December 1887.[10] But there can be little question that "Wagnerism" was a defining influence in many of these shorter compositions, and it can surely be seen in the plaintive 1882 Nocturne published as his Opus 3, and dedicated to Mrs. Sutton Sharpe. Her husband was from a well-known publishing family, and she had studied composition with H. C. Banister at the Academy, where Matthay may have taught her piano.[11] The Nocturne's opening chorale-like passages (Example 3.1) soon merge into a more Chopinesque texture (Example 3.2), and while the work is not always harmonically advanced, Matthay opens it with a variety of major-minor modal alterations (for example, measures 2-3) suggesting an English folk idiom—one of many excursions he made into this realm:

Example 3.1 Matthay: Nocturne, Op. 3, mm. 1-7

But soon, the Nocturne's chromaticism and enharmonic spellings suggest a more pronounced Wagnerian influence:

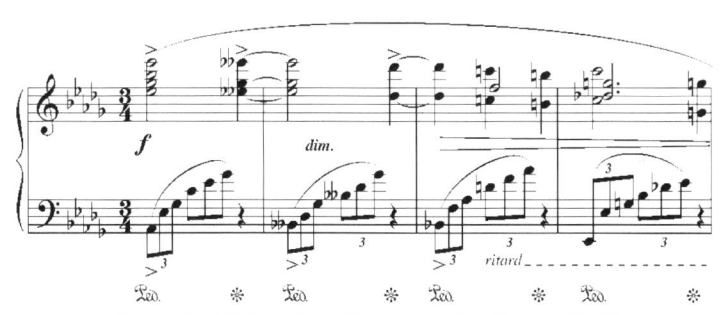

Example 3.2 Matthay: Nocturne, Op. 3, mm. 28-31

But rarely was the Wagner element so pronounced as in his cadenza to the first movement of Beethoven's Concerto No. 1 in C, Op. 15. On 27 May 1881, he completed a fairly conventional, if somewhat Lisztian, cadenza "expressly for Miss Werge"—perhaps Esther Emily Werge, who had just entered the Academy as a violinist. Since Matthay had few, if any, "first studies" at the time, he would have had every incentive to encourage a "second study" sufficiently accomplished to play a Beethoven concerto.[12] And for whatever reason, five months later, he began another cadenza for the same movement, this one an imaginative *tour de force* which filters Beethoven's familiar themes through several *Tristan*-like episodes:

Example 3.3 Matthay: MS Cadenza to Beethoven's Concerto No. 1 in C, Op. 15 (completed 16 October 1881), mm. 32-39

While his festive 1883 overture "In May"—arguably his most significant orchestral work—had decidedly Wagnerian overtones, this was by no means characteristic of all his larger works. Four years earlier, under Prout's guidance, he completed another overture, "Country Life," which Jessie indicates was conducted by Frederick Cowen at Covent Garden in 1880, the year Cowen succeeded Sullivan as conductor of the Promenade Concerts.[13] Completed on 27 October 1879, the full title was "Concert Overture[:] Reminiscences of Country Life for Full Orchestra," and its folk-like theme, planted firmly in F for the first 18 measures, shows little harmonic innovation.[14] Armed with the hindsight of nearly two decades in September of 1898, Matthay wrote on the title page: "Was done at a Prom Concert/ Not good enough to perform now." In September of 1881, his student days now behind him, he completed a piano concerto in D minor which was far more substantial than the work he had produced under Bennett in the same key. A single movement filled with Lisztian fire, it was titled "Concert-Piece for Pianoforte and Full Orchestra," and

Matthay noted that it extended to 672 bars, or 703 bars including the composed cadenza. In 1940, on the last page of the autograph of his bound score, he wrote "<u>Believed</u> to take between 20 and 25 minutes," suggesting that it was never performed.[15] But since he also arranged the work for four hands in April of 1882, it seems likely that he heard it at least once in this form, perhaps even assigning it to his students.[16]

Matthay often created piano arrangements of his orchestral works, and he completed a two-piano version of "In May" (sometimes known as "In May-Time") on 25 July 1883,[17] about five months after he had finished the orchestral score.[18] He may have heard it performed in this manner, but though he often insisted that "In May" was his finest composition, he had to wait nearly 20 years before a conductor was willing to embrace it. The work is dedicated to "Sir Arthur Sullivan by his old pupil," and though Jessie mentions that it won "second place" in a competition organized by the Philharmonic Society,[19] Matthay was never successful at placing it in one of their concerts. In 1882 the Philharmonic invited younger composers to submit overtures for a contest (they received 46 scores), and Oliver King's "The Prize Overture"—the only title provided in the Society's printed program—was performed on 25 April 1883 at the fourth concert of the season.[20] A few motives from King's work were offered in the program notes, as was the (anonymous) motto of Matthay's "honorably mentioned" score—identifiable by a handwritten letter he sent the Society on 21 April asking for a return of "the score with [this] motto:"[21]

Example 3.4 Matthay: Motto from "In May" [mm. 4-7 in the score]

Matthay's long struggle to become established as a composer began in earnest two months later, when he made his first request to the Society in a letter which read in part:

> On my applying for the return of my score, the assistant secretary also alluded in gratifying terms to the Umpires' opinion of my work. Now

bearing this in mind, I thought if I applied to you, you might perhaps possibly grant my Overture the honour of a hearing at one of your next season's Concerts.

Hoping you will do me this honour and give me this encouragement.[22]

He also encloses a list of his other "unproduced" works, including an Introduction and Allegro dedicated to the RAM, which he completed on 30 December 1880.[23] He later titled it "In Summer," re-labeling it first a "Symphonic Overture" and then—over 20 years later in April of 1904—a "Symphonic Poem" to "call it as one does now-a-days." Matthay may have seen it as an even larger, more substantial cousin of "In May," and years later in February of 1932, he acknowledged that if some of the "padding" were removed, "it might be quite a strong work!"[24] He also lists an "Interlude"—perhaps the Andante (or "Romance") for full orchestra he completed on 29 May 1881—which he dedicated to Prout.[25] In addition, he mentions a Concert Etude in D minor for piano and orchestra, two additional piano concertos (perhaps he was including the earlier concerto he had begun under Bennett) and a "Scena" for contralto and orchestra. Undoubtedly, this was his setting of George Macfarren's poem "Hero and Leander," a ten-minute "Scena and Aria" he completed on 21 June 1879, complete with parts.[26] But no encouragement was forthcoming, and in November of 1885 he even invoked Sullivan's assistance before writing to Francesco Berger, the Honorary Secretary of the Philharmonic's Directorate:

Dear Mr. Berger,

Sir Arthur Sullivan informs me that to obtain a hearing at the Philharmonic Society's Concerts I must apply to the Directors through you. Will you kindly therefore lay before them my petition to be heard either as <u>composer</u> or as a <u>pianist</u>: I should especially like to have performed an Overture in E (which Sir Arthur has seen) but of course have other scores ready for performance.[27]

But once again, the Society was unresponsive, and two years passed before Matthay was able to elicit any interest in his work. And although the German-born August Manns (1825-1907)—who conducted orchestral concerts at the Crystal Palace for 42 years—gave "In May" a rehearsal, he elected not to perform it. Jessie writes glowingly of Manns's warmth and concern for younger composers, and she even reproduces a letter he sent Matthay on 8 September 1887, offering his first impression:

Dear Mr. Matthay,

I have just had a superficial look at the work. It seems to be very complicated and will require a great deal of rehearsing before an ordinarily clear reproduction can be obtained. Bayreuthian Polyphony will send many a conscientious Conductor to a premature grave. "Wagner! Wagner! Immortal thy life work will be; but yet we thy caretakers are strongly induced to wish that thou hadst never lived." I will give your work a first reading on Saturday between twelve and one.

Yours faithfully,
August Manns[28]

But three years later, he lamented to the Society that the overture "still lies 'unproduced.'" Feeling that he had been the victim of a technicality, he again reminded the Directors that "In May"

was mentioned in the <u>Philharmonic</u> program as the work <u>second</u> to the one that received the <u>Society's prize</u>. The Society did however not see fit to produce any of the unsuccessful works. And last year when I did apply to have <u>this Overture</u> or <u>some other of my Orchestral compositions</u> produced my application it seems arrived too late.[29]

But by the century's end, "In May" still had not received a public performance. However "Bayreuthian" the work may be, Manns's discomfort with Wagnerian traits is well documented,[30] and his reaction to Matthay's work may be understood more clearly when the simple horn call motto cited above is placed in context:

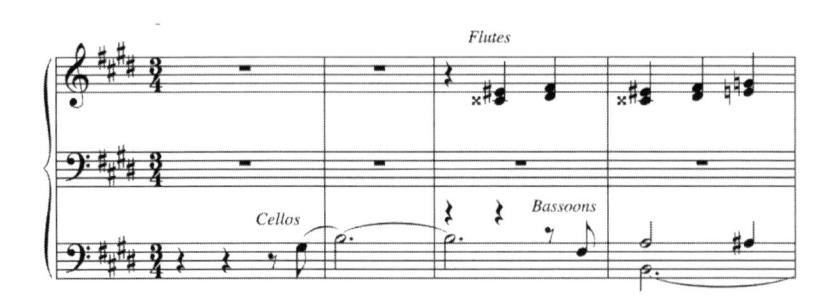

Example 3.5 Matthay: "In May," mm. 1-8

Matthay had seen his Academy friend Frederick Corder only intermittently through the later 1870s, since in 1875 after winning the Mendelssohn Scholarship, Corder had spent the next three years in Cologne. After that he went to Milan for two years, before becoming the director of concerts at the Brighton Aquarium, a position he kept until 1882. Matthay and Corder not only shared a German-Jewish heritage but a profound commitment to nurturing the best in their students, and they soon formed a close friendship that traversed many decades. Corder was also a devoted Wagnerite, and in 1879 he published a highly popular translation of *Parsifal* with his wife, Henrietta. This was followed three years later by their complete translation of *The Ring*, which for many years was deemed the standard throughout the world whenever those operas were performed in English. In 1888 after Corder returned to the RAM as a composition professor, he joined with Matthay to help form the Excelsior Society, the joint inspiration of several Academy professors and students, including composer Granville Bantock (1868-1946), who at the time was Corder's pupil. Jessie reports that although the Society's scope was broader than Wagnerism, its "most valuable work was done in the form of lecture-performances of some of the Wagner Music-Dramas, generally recited by Corder and 'orchestrated' by Matthay at the piano; his sister Dora Matthay helped when the occasion demanded. The cast was supplemented by the singing members of the Excelsior Society."[31]

By the late 1880s, few were bold enough to claim they thoroughly understood Wagner's work, but musicians and intellectuals no longer needed to defend their advocacy, and by the century's end—despite the genesis of an "English Musical Renaissance"—Wagner had become so fascinating to the concert-going public that a Germanic domination of British musical taste seemed even more assured to many. But this transformation could not have been brought about by music partisans alone, and "Wagnerism" was furthered by scientific, as much as artistic, conviction. The "music of the future" had been promoted by Wagner as scientifically inevitable, and in England the writings of Darwin and others added fuel to the flames. Whatever the Victorians may have believed about art, they were just as passionate about the science which they believed legitimized it, and by now Wagner was seen by many as the apex of an evolutionary chain. Matthay had not had the advantage of a university education, but he was reared in a highly disciplined environment where literature and intellectual inquiry were revered, and—while not purely an autodidact—he was accustomed to poring through volumes of his own choosing to expand his knowledge. Clearly, he was well aware of the underlying intellectual currents which shaped the artistic beliefs of his day, and Jessie cites a veritable pantheon of authors whom he studied, his readings often interspersed with composition and practicing on summer seaside holidays.

He visited a variety of coastal cities, summering for example, at Bexhill in 1882, and Hunstanton several years later, and during one of his holidays he became acquainted with Eugene Candler and his family. Jessie identifies Candler only as "a retired business man with ample leisure,"[32] but he was probably the same Candler whose wife gave birth to triplets—two daughters and a son—at their home in St. John's Wood on 5 May 1864.[33] If so, his children were only six years younger than Matthay, and by the mid-1880s, both of his daughters were of marriageable age. Matthay probably encountered the family sometime before 1885, since his charming miniature "A Summer Day-Dream" was dedicated to Mrs. Candler about this time.[34] She may have played the piece, since it is far simpler than most of the music he produced through this period, although the hypnotic 10/8 time signature creates some unusual metrical effects. Jessie describes the entire family as intellectuals inspired by Candler's immersion in "wide reading and deep philosophical thought," and she names Darwin, Thomas Huxley, John Tyndall, and Matthew Arnold as guiding influences, as well as many lesser-known writers caught up in the Darwinism of the age. For example, Matthay and the Candlers read the banker-turned-amateur-anthropologist Edward Clodd (1840-1930), whose child's primer, *The Childhood of the World* (1872), sought to reconcile science with religion. But despite his religious convictions, Clodd's *The Story of Creation* (1887) was a veritable paean to Darwin, with detailed charts and diagrams effortlessly traversing the fields of geology, zoology, botany, and paleontology.[35] Another favored author was Clodd's intimate friend and Darwin's biographer, the Canadian-born atheist Grant Allen (1848-99), who tried to unite science and aesthetics to the point of writing poetry about the theory of evolution. They also read the biographies of James Cotter Morison (1832-88), a devout Roman Catholic who brought fresh insights to figures as diverse as Gibbon and Macaulay.

Conspicuously absent from this canon is any suggestion of German philosophic thought, and even though he could have pursued their writings without benefit of translation, there is little evidence that Matthay had more than a passing acquaintance with Kant, Hegel, or the German Romanticists. Despite his love for German culture, his quest after the meaning of life led him almost exclusively to the Victorian thinkers who offered a rational, secular view of the universe—a view which promised to unite art and science into a comprehensive unity. Although the ideas expressed by these writers were all encompassing and often radical, it remained for a philosopher to capture his imagination by uniting their diverse views into an integrated system. Jessie indicates that Candler and his family were all "ardent disciples" of Herbert Spencer (1820-1903), and Spencer's ideas were clearly the most defining influence in Matthay's intellectual development, even to the point of inspiring his ideas about piano playing.[36] By his own account, his interest in Spencer began at the age of 16 when he attended one of his lectures, although Walker, who did not meet Matthay until two years later, suggests that his own devotion to both Spencer and John Stuart Mill may have led Matthay to read their works.[37]

Though he lived to be 83, Spencer spent most of his life in poor health, and was known for a variety of eccentricities, such as the wearing of earmuffs to avoid over-excitement when he argued with others.[38] Although he had little formal education, he developed an astonishing grasp of disparate areas of knowledge, and at the age of 16 he even became a civil engineer for the railways. At 28 he began working as an editor for *The Economist*, which enabled him to meet Huxley, Tyndall, and other leading intellectuals of the period. An earnest student of economics and an admirer of Adam Smith, Spencer began to publish numerous articles—regarded as radical in their day—urging an extremely limited role for government. He called for the abolition of the Poor Laws, national education, the central Church, and virtually all regulations governing commerce and trade. At times he published in *The Westminster Review*, where he met Marian Evans (soon to write as George Eliot), who worked there as an associate editor. They spoke briefly of marriage, and though nothing came of it they remained lifelong friends. In 1852 Spencer published an article called "The Developmental Hypothesis," which was not well received because it was not yet supported by scientific evidence. Nonetheless, it anticipated many of Darwin's theories which were not expressed until *The Origin of Species* appeared seven years later. Spencer was actually the first to popularize the term "evolution," and he even coined the catchphrase "the survival of the fittest."[39]

Naturally, after Darwin became a household word, Spencer was seen as one of his staunchest advocates, but he also used Darwinian science to support a broader framework of psychological, ethical, and political theory. When his book *The Principles of Psychology* first appeared in 1855, it had met with criticism, but he gained a broader audience in 1862 when he published *First Principles*, which united all of his earlier biological and psychological ideas into a sweeping, scientific theory which was later—albeit improperly—identified as the source of a heterogeneous movement known as "Social Darwinism."[40] For better or for worse, he had unleashed a floodgate of controversy and debate, and his ideas inaugurated a movement in Britain, and especially America, which flourished for several decades—influencing scientific and industrial leaders as diverse as William James and Andrew Carnegie. Darwin even paid a nod to him in the sixth edition of *The Origin of Species* when he predicted that "Psychology will be securely based on the foundation already laid by Mr. Herbert Spencer, that of the necessary acquirement of each mental power and capacity by gradation."[41]

Spencer also directed his attention to education and aesthetics, and Matthay was intimately familiar with his most widely read and translated work, *Education: Intellectual, Moral and Physical* (1861).[42] Spencer's book is a hymn both to science and to the science of psychology, and many of its passages foretold Matthay's later conviction that "valid" art demanded obedience to the laws of science:

> Not only is it that the artist, of whatever kind, cannot produce a truthful work without he understands the laws of phenomena he represents; but it is that he must also understand how the minds of spectators or listeners will be affected by the several peculiarities of his work—a question in psychology. What impression any given art-product generates, manifestly depends upon the mental natures of those to whom it is presented; and as all mental natures have certain general principles in common,

there must result certain corresponding general principles on which alone art-products can be successfully framed. These general principles cannot be fully understood and applied, unless the artist sees how they follow from the laws of the mind. . . . And only when the artist rationally understands these psychological principles and their various corollaries, can he work in harmony with them.[43]

Undoubtedly, Matthay was also familiar with Spencer's essay "The Origin and Function of Music," first published in 1857 and reprinted several times during the author's lifetime with additional comments to answer those who attacked his views.[44] Spencer argues convincingly that music originated with human language and speech patterns, and although Darwin and others disagreed, Matthay made similar analogies between speech and music in his later writings, so it seems unlikely that he rejected Spencer's arguments.

The broader philosophic ideas that Matthay found most attractive in Spencer's vast output are difficult to determine with certainty, but it may be safely assumed that, his financial problems notwithstanding, the young Matthay saw himself as largely self reliant, and the convictions which characterized his behavior over the next six decades—particularly his commercial practices—were not incompatible with the *laissez-faire* capitalism that Spencer espoused. A life-long student of psychology, he also believed that human nature required a scientific explanation, and he shared Spencer's rejection of the concept of innate ideas. Although such a belief was not at odds with many prevailing views in his time, it challenged long-established convictions concerning musical ability, and Matthay rejected the view that "talent" was purely endowed. This can be easily documented by surveying his entire career as a teacher, inasmuch as he later wrote that given the requisite intelligence, virtually any skill could be acquired—or taught—and he explained "genius" merely as the ability to concentrate on a problem with greater ease. But although Spencer believed that human beings were born *tabula rasa*, he also subscribed to the theory of "associationism," which was prominent in the nineteenth century and argued that acquired skills—if repeated and practiced often enough—could be transmitted to successive generations. Spencer's critics later denounced this as a form of racism, since it implied that given the acquired capabilities of their ancestors, certain groups would by nature be innately superior. While the best evidence suggests that Matthay remained agnostic on this question, no instances can be cited where Spencer's views in this realm colored his daily conduct in any meaningful sense.

Jessie mentions several other close friends from the 'eighties with whom Matthay shared intellectual camaraderie. She describes William Teetgen only as "a leisured business man," but he must have enjoyed a degree of affluence since over the years *The Times* frequently cited his philanthropic gifts to the poor.[45] In May 1881 he was elected to the Common Council in Bishopsgate Ward, and for many years he was also an active supporter of his church in St. Botolph's Parish, Bishopsgate. On 25 November 1894, he was one of the honored guests at the ceremony to open the Bishopsgate Institute, which began as a public library to serve as a bridge between the City and the East End, opening for business on New Year's Day, 1895.[46] Jessie indicates that although Matthay and Teetgen often spoke, they most often corresponded: "Their purpose seemed to be to see how far the human mind might travel in pursuit of truth; and although they tilted at one another through reams of foolscap, the letters that remain rather amusingly go to prove Teetgen as a Mystic-Rationalist, and Matthay a Rationalist-Mystic!"[47]

She does not elaborate on the limits which Matthay may have placed on reason, nor precisely in what areas he felt "mysticism" to be a superior form of cognition. However, inasmuch as religion seemed to be a more significant value to Teetgen, one can imagine some intellectual parrying, which—to Teetgen's credit—never seemed to place him on the defensive or caused him to evade an argument. Another of Matthay's close friends was Sir Montagu Frederick Montagu-Pollock (1864-1938), a dedicated intellectual educated at Harrow and Cambridge, who loved the English countryside and later became an accomplished landscape painter. Like Teetgen, he was also a philanthropist of some prominence, and the biographical sketch which appeared in his *Times* obituary undoubtedly captured some of the qualities which Matthay most admired:

> An indulgent parent and a great lover of children, he was perhaps seen at his best when absorbed in their entertainment. He possessed in marked degree a simplicity of outlook combined with keenness of intellect, which rendered him as much at home in a discussion with a crofter in a remote Highland glen as when immersed in the abstrusities of paleontology with his friend the Abbé Breuil.[48]

If Matthay held his own with such minds, they must have regarded him as a formidable intellect, and Jessie indicates that he was sent "forward into music greatly enriched by their companionship."[49] Perhaps it seemed a natural extension for him to try his hand at writing, and by the mid-1880s he was contributing concert reviews to a community newspaper. She reports that the Matthay family had faithfully attended Manns's Saturday afternoon concerts at the Crystal Palace for years, and eventually,

> he began to write as a critic, sending his effusions weekly to the *Clapham Observer*. This he enjoyed greatly, letting himself go both in praise and in blame. In this way he became friends with his pen, getting into the habit of setting down, no matter how lengthily, what he afterwards called his "Thoughts and Reflections." It was fine discipline for him.[50]

But since most *Observer* reviews at this time are quite brief and none are signed, it is difficult to track Matthay's contributions. The paper's full title was the *Clapham Observer[,] Tooting & Balham Times, and Surrey County Observer*, and it was a community weekly published on Saturdays, containing items of interest to the local residents. Unfortunately, the copies which survive in the British Library only imperfectly document the 1880s,[51] although the paper's advertisements frequently indicate that connections to the Crystal Palace were easily made by rail from Clapham.[52] Despite Jessie's assertion, as might be expected from many community newspapers, the numerous concert reviews are full of "praise," but contain relatively little "blame." For example, this review of a Clapham voice recital—which Matthay may or may not have written—appeared on 15 October 1887:

> Concert at the Wesleyan Chapel—A very successful concert was given in the hall, behind the above chapel last Monday evening. The audience, which was very large and most enthusiastic, thoroughly appreciated the very entertaining programme which was presented. Miss Maud Leslie sang tastefully, as also did Miss Hayter, while Mr. Maude was heard to advantage in "Tom Bowling." His first song "S. tu Savais," was rather out of his compass.[53]

Matthay was also the subject of several *Observer* reviews, and he most assuredly did not contribute the piece which appeared in the paper on 28 November 1885, praising him in glowing terms for the opening recital he gave at the newly opened Surrey Conservatoire of Music. The school proudly boasted the participation of many RAM and Royal College personnel, including the recently knighted Sir George Macfarren, who acted as its Principal.[54] Oddly, Matthay, a Clapham resident, seems to have taught there little, if at all, perhaps because the school only existed for about three years. The Conservatoire took over the facilities of the Clapham Grammar School, which had recently closed—undoubtedly an unwelcome development for Herr Matthay and his family. A committee of subscribers—including Matthay's friend Walter Dowdeswell—had been formed to raise funds for instruments and the building's needed renovations, and in a ceremony overseen by the Lord Mayor of London, the cornerstone was laid about two weeks after Matthay's recital.[55] His program, before a largely feminine audience, took place in the newly refurbished concert hall, converted from what had once served as the Grammar School's chapel. The *Observer*'s reviewer, if lacking somewhat in musical (and literary) expertise, was exceedingly complimentary:

> The new concert hall of the Conservatoire (formerly the private chapel of Clapham Grammar School, and then, till recently, known as St.

Luke's Church) was formally inaugurated on Monday evening with a pianoforte recital by Mr. T. A. Matthay, a Professor at the Royal Academy of Music, a neighbour among Claphamites, and a performer of such exceptional ability as to entitle him to a foremost position in the front rank of pianists. There was a large attendance of members and students of the Conservatoire, as well as of the local musical public, and under its new condition, in the presence of much womanly beauty, adorned with conventional taste, with here and there a graceful foliage plant, the interior of the building looked quite picturesque and comfortable. Mr. Matthay played with astounding brilliancy, and seemed not to tire, but rather to gather strength as he proceeded. His programme—from start to finish—was one that demanded the nicest combination of head, heart, and hand; its due interpretation else were [sic] impossible. Brahms [probably the B minor Rhapsody from Opus 79], Schumann [the *Nachtstücke* and a Novelette], Chopin [the G minor Ballade, the C-sharp minor Scherzo, and three Preludes], Henselt, were selected in turn, and a few masterly examples of the player's own supplied a *finale* of acknowledged fitness. [Matthay concluded with one of his own compositions simply advertised in *The Times* as "Etude" —probably the demanding study in E later published under the title "Bravura."] There were perhaps among the audience those who would have given ear more readily to something different—even though it were a mere tickling of the sense rather than an appeal to the understanding—but they could have none than a favorable opinion of the player, while the really cultured were simply delighted with the rare treat put before them. At suitable intervals songs were acceptably given by Miss Kate McKrill and Mr. Walter Mackway [an accomplished singer and the director of the Clapham Philharmonic Concerts], the latter accepting, at a moment's notice, the task of Mr. [J. T.] Hutchinson [Hutchinson taught voice at the RAM, and a year later became Dora's teacher], who was kept away by indisposition. Miss Amy McKrill accompanied.[56]

Matthay and his associates repeated the concert three days later at Prince's Hall in Piccadilly, which Jessie describes as "the precursor of the Wigmore and Aeolian Halls."⁵⁷ It was the second program he had given there, and she reports that his London recitals were annual events each fall for a number of years. Although he was always careful to include some of his own music, he performed a substantial amount of repertoire during this period, and scarcely ever seemed to recycle works from season to season. For example, on the afternoon of 28 November 1884, his first concert included—in addition to his own recently composed *Seventeen Variations* in C on an original theme—the Brahms *Variations and Fugue on a Theme of Handel* and the first four of Schumann's eight *Fantasiestücke*. He also offered three Chopin works: the Berceuse, the Scherzo in B-flat minor, and "Etude in G flat" (probably the "Black Key"), two Liszt Etudes—the Consolation No. 6 in E and *La Campanella*—and the second movement (*il moto perpetuo*) from Weber's Rondo in C. Hutchinson, this time with Ernest Ford at the piano, also contributed three songs, including Matthay's unpublished setting of Byron's "There be none of Beauty's daughters."⁵⁸ Although he was still years away from his first *Times* review, *The Musical World* was quite impressed, noting that he was "equally at home in passages demanding the utmost delicacy as well as in those which encourage the drawing out of the instrument's full-tone capacity." The reviewer found his Brahms Variations "intellectual," the Chopin Scherzo "appropriately impulsive," and hoped that "Mr. Matthay will soon give us another recital."⁵⁹ But the London press could be ruthlessly critical, as shown from the highly mixed reaction Matthay received a few years later from the *Musical Times* for his recital on 17 March 1887:

> As an executant he is clever but unequal. Some of his selections were beautifully played while others were rendered in an eccentric and even slipshod manner. In Chopin's familiar Nocturne in D flat, his memory failed him; but immediately afterwards he gave a splendid rendering of the composer's far more difficult Etude in A minor (Op. 25, No. 11) [the "Winter Wind"].⁶⁰

No doubt Matthay was grateful that the *Clapham Observer*'s critic ventured up to the West End a year later for his fifth annual program on 15 November 1888:

> Mr. Tobias A. Matthay's Pianoforte Recital.—The annual recital of this gifted musician took place on Thursday afternoon at Prince's Hall, Piccadilly, which, we are glad to say, was well filled. We have often commented on the brilliant and versatile qualities of this performer, and we must add that upon this occasion, in the presence of a highly sympathetic and appreciative audience, Mr. Matthay once again acquitted himself of an arduous task in a manner calculated to add to the number of his already numerous admirers. The interesting program consisted of Beethoven's Sonata in D minor (op. 31, no. 2), his rendering of the allegretto movement being especially fine; pieces by Brahms, Schumann, and Grieg, in all of which his admirable power of execution and delicacy of touch were both displayed to good effect; Rubinstein's Etude in E (op. 23, no. 2) [The key is actually C], also a brilliant achievement; Scherzo in B minor, Op. 20 (Chopin), in which the clever pianist was altogether in his element, equally a success; six movements by Mr. Matthay himself [probably his *Monothemes*, later published as Op. 13], loudly applauded; Etudes from Henselt, Goetz, and Raff; Valse Caprice in A flat (E. Cuthbert Nunn), all equally well handled; and last, but not least, "Rhapsodie Hongroise," by Liszt [probably the second Rhapsody in C-sharp minor], splendidly played, brought the recital to an effective termination.[61]

No one considered it pretentious that Matthay or any of his colleagues should hire a London hall each year rather than perform their annual programs at the Academy, since an appearance on RAM premises would have required permission from the Committee of Management, and such permission was rarely granted. By November of 1892 Matthay was in his twelfth year of teaching at the Academy, but the Committee still allowed him to present a concert of his own works only after he agreed to issue private invitations so that it would not be seen as an Academy event.[62] And eighteen months later, on

10 May 1894, even after he had agreed to issue invitations for a June program featuring his RAM students, his request was denied, "after some discussion," on the grounds that "it would be inexpedient to create a precedent for such use of the Room."[63] Obviously, Matthay was also required to advance his own fees for hall rental, which necessitated charging admission, but he was probably able to keep costs down by scheduling many of his Prince's Hall programs on Thursdays at three o'clock, which was a time reserved for less prestigious events. He began by charging seven shillings and sixpence for the stalls and one shilling for the balcony, but by 1887 he had lowered the stall price to five shillings, which perhaps increased attendance.[64] No doubt he performed in as many venues as he could, and on 16 September 1885, a full two months before he played at the Conservatoire and at Prince's Hall, he gave an hour's program at the Crystal Palace. He was scheduled at five o'clock on a Wednesday afternoon—sandwiched between two organ recitals and in direct competition with the Grenadier Guards and a "Siamese Band"—and he was probably allowed to keep little, if any, of the 2s, 6d admission the Palace charged for each of its events.[65]

Although—perhaps out of necessity—Matthay's interest in the piano had been growing to an extent, in the spring of 1886 his entire perspective on the instrument was changed forever. Jessie speaks of three great pianistic influences—in her words, "his great initiates"—and arguably the most important of these, Anton Rubinstein (1829-94), served as an inspirational beacon for the rest of his life. Given his reactions to London's leading practitioners in his day, Matthay's interest in his own instrument had been rather lukewarm, but when Rubinstein appeared, Jessie writes that it was as if he had found "an angel:"

> For Matthay to hear Rubinstein was to pass into a changed world. Here was a Titan, a Michelangelo, a Dante! Was this really still the pianoforte, with its supposed limitations? Henceforward one might think of it as an orchestra. In this he would find consolation. It was a wonder that must be recaptured, must be reconstructed; and to this end his life should be devoted.[66]

"Lord-High-Everything-Else"

It is unknown why Matthay had not heard the Russian-born Rubinstein's earlier London recitals, but conceivably he may have been unsuccessful in procuring tickets, which generally disappeared quickly at highly inflated prices. By the spring of 1876, Liszt was no longer touring and many considered Rubinstein the greatest pianist in the world. At that time he gave a highly successful series of recitals at St. James's Hall, returning the following spring to give another series and to conduct and perform his own works at the Crystal Palace. He toured England again in the spring of 1881, and in June performed three London recitals before capacity audiences, while he oversaw the British premiere of his opera *Il Demonio* at Covent Garden. By the mid-1880s, Rubinstein was almost as well known in England as a composer as he was as a pianist, and *The Times* marveled at his stamina:

> Taking into account what Rubinstein has produced, from oratorio, opera, and cantata to symphony, concerto, and chamber music, instrumental and vocal in almost every shape, it is difficult to understand how, with so much incessant brainwork, he can find leisure for that assiduous practice without which it would seem impossible to keep in perfect order such manipulative skill as his playing invariably exhibits.[67]

In the 1885-86 season, he toured Europe with his set of seven "historical" recitals for which he had become famous: unprecedented journeys through the keyboard repertoire from Byrd to Balakirev, in which he presented their works more or less in chronological order. He turned his Herculean powers to programs of such immense length that he actually performed the modern equivalent of about 16 separate recitals within a two-week span. By November he had reached Vienna, but despite the ambitiousness of his scheduled programs, *The Times*'s correspondent seemed less than awed:

> Anton Rubinstein is now giving in Vienna his *Cyclus*, or series of seven concerts, illustrating the whole history of piano music. Selections from the works of 31 composers are to be performed. The first concert opened

Chapter 3

with selections from early English composers—namely, "The Carman's Whistle," by William Bird, and "The King's Hunting Jig," by Dr. John Bull. Beethoven, Schumann, and Chopin are each to have one whole evening devoted to them; but the Beethoven programme is rather trying, for it comprises eight sonatas. Eight sonatas in one evening is a great deal, even for an enthusiast.[68]

But few who heard him were ever bored, and on 7 April when he first appeared in Paris, *The Times*'s French correspondent wrote that his opening recital, in which he played 36 compositions from the Virginalists through Mozart virtually without pause, "transformed the instrument," and sent his audience into "transports."[69] But the fifth concert on 19 April offered excitement of a more histrionic nature:

> Tonight Rubinstein gave his fifth concert at the Salle Erard, in presence of an immensely-crowded house, amid outbursts of the greatest enthusiasm, excited by the unparalleled interpretation of Schubert and Chopin. The illustrious artist suddenly fainted in the middle of the entertainment. A great uproar arose, everyone hurrying through the house to get information. After an interval of 10 minutes the public was informed that Rubinstein was ready to recommence, but the whole audience protested against the proposal. The fainting was a natural consequence of the superhuman efforts of the great artist.
>
> I have just heard that Rubinstein, although rather exhausted, is improving.[70]

Each of Rubinstein's seven London recitals—from 18 May through 8 June—was scheduled at 2:30 in the afternoon in St. James's Hall. Nonetheless, he still found the time and endurance to perform in outlying cities on the days he was not appearing in London. At St. James's Hall a "limited number" of reserved seats in the orchestra could be had at the staggering price of one guinea (£1, 1s), and the series was so successful that an eighth concert had to be added on 11 June. Dedicated to the "Slavonic school of modern music," it featured elaborate works by Glinka, Balakirev (including

Islamey), Rimsky-Korsakov, Cui, Liadov, Tchaikovsky, and both Rubinsteins—the performer and his brother Nicolas—and it opened with no fewer than eleven Chopin Etudes.[71] Whether or not Matthay was able to attend each concert, he was definitely in the audience for the final program, because he was entranced by Rubinstein's performance of his own C major "Staccato" Etude, Op. 23, no. 2, which he evidently offered as an encore.[72] Despite the fact that while the concerts were running, Rubinstein endorsed both Challen and Becker pianos,[73] he performed only on the Erard, and Jessie reports that Matthay was soon at the company's London showrooms on Great Marlborough Street, making arrangements to renounce his commitment to Broadwood—at least for a season:

> He was told by the manager: "Ah, you will find it much easier to play this Etude on the Erard." However, Matthay found to his surprise, when he began practicing on the Erard, that the new action, so far from helping him, entirely baulked him, and that the C Major went from bad to worse!
>
> The fact is that in those days, practically the full weight of the Erard action was left against the player, and was not disguised (as it usually is to-day), by leaden weights inserted in the fronts of the keys. Obviously, Matthay had been indulging in *key-hitting*; and when this full key resistance was met it caused him to miss sounding the notes! He therefore had to readjust his technical notions until he could successfully cope with this heavy surface resistance.[74]

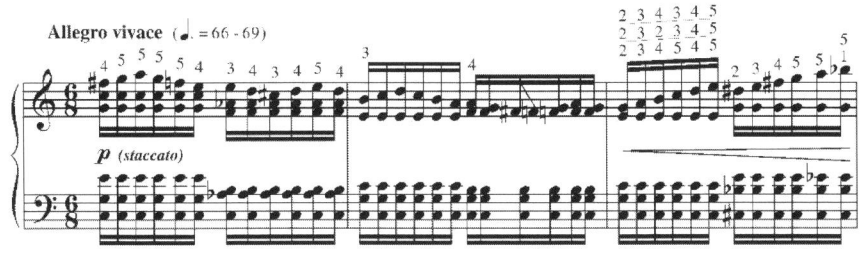

Example 3.6 Anton Rubinstein: Etude in C, Op. 23, no. 2, mm. 1-3

Matthay no doubt experienced a substantial change when he switched from the Broadwood to the Erard, but Jessie's explanation implies that the Erard had a stiffer action, and this is highly unlikely. Playable, well-conditioned instruments from both manufacturers survive from this period, and it is clear that the Broadwood, which used heavier hammers than the Erard, tended to offer greater key resistance.[75] Both instruments contained rear key weights, customary for all concert grands, and in the 1880s the Erard—which was built both in Paris and Kensington to identical specifications—had one of the lightest, most responsive actions in Europe. Thanks to his receding hair line, the twenty-eight-year-old Matthay might have been taken more often as a schoolmaster than an athlete, but his hands were large, and his powerful, six-foot frame could have easily mustered the strength to overcome a stiff, even sluggish, piano action. In all probability the Erard was too finely adjusted to tolerate such over-compensation and—in other words—its action was not too "heavy," but too responsive. Jessie is probably correct that Matthay had been "indulging in key-hitting," that is, he was making little effort to sense the key's resistance as he depressed it—a precept that later formed a cardinal element of his teaching—and this miscalculation threw off his timing and accuracy. And she is almost certainly correct that a door had been opened in his thinking:

> The Erard, in fact, taught him the valuable lesson that hitting was useless, and that the key had to be taken hold of when met. Thus arose one of his most important teachings; that one must adjust oneself for every note to the resistance experienced after reaching the key. Thus, the law of ATTENTION TO KEY RESISTANCE.[76]

Matthay's enthusiasm for Rubinstein had been honed barely a month before his arrival, when he heard the artist generally considered to be the greatest performer of the nineteenth century—and another of his "great initiates"—Franz Liszt. Long retired from the concert stage, the Abbé Liszt arrived in England in April 1886, not to play, but to be present for a number of concerts in his honor, including a 6 April performance of his oratorio *Saint Elizabeth* at St. James's Hall under Alexander Mackenzie—according to *The Times*, its first

London performance since Henry Wylde had conducted it 16 years earlier.[77] Forty-five years had elapsed since Liszt had toured England as a pianist, but his sixth visit proved to be his last since he died just four months later. Although London had once embraced his virtuosity, in 1841 his generosity had moved him to reimburse his concert agents when his recitals lost money in the outlying towns—at the time because many provincials found him "too dazzling and too unaccustomed a phenomenon."[78] It was said that bitterness over this incident had always precluded his return to the British Isles, but the ensuing decades had brought about a change in English tastes. Liszt was thrilled that London was now receptive to Wagner, Berlioz, and his own compositions, and no doubt this new acceptance served as a type of vindication for earlier rejections.[79]

On Saturday, 3 April, Liszt arrived at Dover from Calais and boarded a direct train to Victoria Station, but his eminence was so pronounced that officials arranged to have the train stop at Penge, so that he could proceed directly to Sydenham, where he was staying at the home of Novello's head, Henry Littleton. Soon after he arrived he was fêted at a soirée whose honored guests included Mackenzie, Hallé, Dannreuther, Manns, Sullivan, Sir George Grove, and his longtime pupil and friend, pianist and RAM professor Walter Bache.[80] Throughout Europe, many had sought ways to celebrate the composer's seventy-fifth birthday, and Bache, who over the past decade had given annual Liszt programs in London with little success, had extended the invitation to his former mentor—with assistance from a chain of supporters that extended up to the Royal Family. He had hoped Liszt would perform, but the Abbé declined on the grounds that "my seventy-five-year-old fingers are no longer suited to it."[81]

Nonetheless, he did play informally a number of times over the next 17 days, and on the afternoon of 6 April he was escorted to the Academy, where he presented Macfarren with a check for £1100, a sum raised largely by Bache to inaugurate the RAM Liszt Scholarship. Then, in response to the cheering students, Liszt gave a brief, impromptu recital, which included his *Cantique d'amour*. The next day, he performed for Queen Victoria at Windsor Castle, and the following evening, Bache gave an enormous party for him at the Grosvenor Gallery, where Joachim was among the 400 guests. Liszt performed again on that evening, and George Grove remarked on how his playing was remarkably "unlike" that of the so-called "Liszt School."[82] Matthay heard him at both the Academy and the Gallery, and Jessie summarized his reaction in a single sentence: "At this time he was within a few months of his death, but even then the piano was sublimated at his touch."[83] Matthay was so moved that he even had a virtuosic etude he had completed four months earlier copied and presented "with hommage [sic] to the master Dr. Franz Liszt in commemoration of his visit to the Royal Academy of Music[,] April 6th, 1886." Liszt responded across the title page: "*Accepté avec plaisir la dédicace/F. Liszt.*"[84] At the Grosvenor Galleries, Matthay also noted the difference in sound quality between Bache and his teacher, and a few years later, he attributed their tonal differences to the condition of their upper arms, noting that Bache played with far more stiffness:

> Though the wrong way makes possibly more noise close by . . . this will not "carry" at all compared to the correct, elastic method. This is easily heard in a larger room, and it was forcibly brought under my notice when I heard Liszt play at a reception at the Grosvenor Gallery where our genial and talented host, Mr. Walter Bache, himself also played. Liszt, though an old, weak man, produced far more resonant and "filling" tone, without any effort whatever, than did our late friend [Bache suddenly died two years later] (energetic and splendid teacher indeed that he was) [;] poor Bache.[85]

Toward the end of his life, Matthay even testified that this brief encounter left such an impression that he believed Liszt had a "slight edge" over Rubinstein as a performer.[86] At this final stage in Liszt's career, he was no longer storming through pieces with virtuosic thunder, but Matthay was astonished at the orchestral-like colors he drew from the instrument—an experience reinforced by his exposure to Rubinstein a month later—and a new world had opened for him.

One of Liszt's greatest pupils, and Matthay's third "great initiate," returned to London two years later for a cycle of four recitals dedicated to Beethoven's works—his last appearance in the English capital. Hans von Bülow (1830-94) had been a regular fixture on the London concert scene since 1873, so it is unclear why Matthay had not previously experienced his artistry. Born in Dresden, Bülow studied briefly with Friedrich Wieck as a youngster, and he later branched out to conducting, becoming close to both Liszt and Wagner, whose advice he frequently sought. In 1851 he began to study piano with Liszt at Weimar, and in Christopher Fifield's words, he soon "completely rethought his piano technique, embarking on a regimen of hard work."[87] Liszt thought he was one of the greatest talents he had ever taught and believed him destined to join the first rank of pianists, but—Bülow's well-documented lack of tact notwithstanding—he continued to conduct, even to the point of defining many practices used today for opera preparation. He gave the Munich premieres of both *Tristan* and *Meistersinger,* and throughout his life he remained steadfastly loyal to Wagner, even after his wife—Liszt's daughter Cosima—left him to live with the composer. In 1880 he began to mould the forty-eight-piece orchestra at Meiningen into one of the marvels of Europe, requiring the musicians to play always from memory while standing, and in 1885 he astounded his audience when he conducted Brahms's D minor Concerto from the keyboard.

But although he was highly esteemed, Bülow was also one of the most controversial figures of his day, as evidenced by this report from the 6 December 1884 issue of the *Musical World*:

> A musical scandal, the like of which has never been witnessed before, was enacted on Monday evening December 1st, at a concert given in the large hall of the [Vienna] Conservatoire by Dr Hans von Bülow.... The concert hall was crowded, and amongst the audience were the Archduchess Valérie, Archduke Karl Ludwig, Duke Karl Theodor of Bavaria, and many leading members of the aristocracy. The programme included Beethoven's overture to *Egmont*. After the previous numbers

had been played, Herr von Bülow stepped forward to the front of the platform, and, taking from his pocket Tuesday morning's issue of the *Fremdenblatt*, addressed the audience in a tone of mingled ill-temper and irony. He said that the journal in question had found fault with his previous rendering of Beethoven's *Egmont*, and that, as he would like not to wrong the great composer again, his orchestra would play instead the "Academical Overture" of the Austrian Brahms. The public indignantly protested, and called for Beethoven's overture, which, after some hesitation on the part of Herr von Bülow, was produced. Brahms' "Academical Overture" was then expected, but Herr von Bülow, after putting on his overcoat, once more addressed the audience. "I cannot render it upon the pianoforte," he said, "and my musicians are too tired to play it themselves." It would be difficult to describe the angry feeling roused amongst the public by Herr von Bülow's behaviour. It is questionable whether he will ever be asked to play in Vienna again. Neither the presence of Royalty, nor the fact that he was performing to the most musical and appreciative audience in Europe, prevented him from giving vent to his wounded vanity by an unseemly and unjustifiable manifestation.[88]

At times, Bülow's piano concerts aroused comparable indignation. Liszt's pupil Amy Fay greatly admired him, but she noted that he always kept two pianos on stage facing opposite directions, observing that "he plays alternately on both. His face seems to say to his audience, 'You're all cats and dogs, and I don't care what you think of my playing.'"[89] Many thought him too cerebral, and as Fifield points out, Dannreuther's complimentary label of "passionate intellectuality" was often reworded derisively by those who suggested the word "passionate" be omitted.[90] But there was no questioning his stamina, and it was characteristic of him to perform the last five Sonatas of Beethoven—from Op. 101 to Op. 111—in a single evening, often without pausing between movements.[91] In 1888, Bülow's London recitals were scheduled on weekday afternoons at St. James Hall between 4 and 26 June, all beginning precisely at three o'clock.[92] After he played the first program, *The Times* was ecstatic:

> That Dr. von Bülow is one of the leading pianists of our time, that his intellectual grasp is as large as his technical skill is phenomenal—these are facts generally acknowledged. But he is more than a mere virtuoso. We talk in literature of novels "with a purpose;" Dr. von Bülow might be called a pianist "with a purpose," or, if the word should be preferred, with a mission, that mission being the active advocacy of all that is highest and purest in art, to the exclusion of the vulgar, the artificial, the showy. . . . It has been declared that Dr. von Bülow thinks rather than feels music, that his expression comes from the head, not from the heart. The truly "pathetic" manner in which the *adagio cantabile* of the C minor sonata [Op. 13] was given should go far to shake such a prejudice.[93]

Matthay was also enchanted, and Jessie notes Bülow's "commanding authority of interpretation, his magnificence of line, his lifting of keyboard music up to the plane of the Universal."[94] In December of 1885 he had purchased Bülow's edition of the "Appassionata" from the Lucas shop, and immediately he even began to pencil in aspects he remembered of the artist's interpretation which were not indicated on the score.[95] Although he occasionally marked tempo fluctuations, Matthay often seemed more interested in questions of voicing. For example, in bars 38 and 39 of the Sonata's Finale, he circled the quarter notes in the right hand and wrote above them: "Bülow brought these out:"

Example 3.7 Beethoven: Sonata in F minor, Op. 57, third movement, mm. 36-39. (Matthay's notations are indicated with square brackets.)

Chapter 3

 A more subtle effect was captured at bar 158, where Matthay circled the C which occurs on beat two in the right hand, and the C an octave lower which occurs on beat one of bar 159. Above this section he wrote "Bülow brought these well out," indicating that the pianist made much of the imitative effect which occurs through the entire sequence, even underscoring the effect of extended chromatic movement:

Example 3.8 Beethoven: Sonata in F minor, Op. 57, third movement, mm. 158-62. (Matthay's notations are indicated with square brackets.)

 He was obviously captivated by Bülow's performances, and at this point it was as though a catalyst had taken effect, for the thirty-year-old Matthay had found his life's work. It was to be a crusade, and he often confessed that whenever he felt weary or defeated, it was enough simply to recall the wondrous sounds that these three pianists had created. But it was more than clarity of line or technical execution that attracted him, because those features had been amply provided by Hallé, Dannreuther, and the others who were such viable London fixtures. Rather, these three artists had brought exquisite sounds—orchestral tone colors—and Matthay struggled to unlock the secrets enabling him to reproduce what he had heard. He wondered what role the choice of instrument had played in the effects that thrilled him, and soon he turned his attention to the Bechstein, which had been Bülow's choice since 1855, when he performed the Liszt Sonata on the Berlin-based company's first grand. He helped the firm garner much acclaim, and its production figures increased substantially after 1860 when—in response to a serious fire—it successfully mechanized its plant without compromising artisanship.

Matthay as well soon made a permanent switch to Bechstein, the instrument which Jessie indicates "captured his interest and attention and completely satisfied his ear with its wealth of tonal colour."[96]

But therein lay a paradox, for if in fact the instrument possessed a "wealth" of tonal color, it was incumbent on the performer to unlock those possibilities, and Matthay eventually grew to dislike pianos capable of only one basic sound—even if that sound was attractive. But he also reasoned that unlocking the inherent possibilities demanded skill, and that skill—at least for him—could only be obtained by understanding how the instrument worked. Fortunately, his experience and inclinations led him to feel at ease with the mechanics of machinery, and it felt entirely natural for him to remove a piano's action from its case, which he soon did almost daily. He began to question one of the maxims so often presented to him over the years by his teachers Dorrell and Macfarren: that to produce singing tone, "one should squeeze the key(bed) like ripe fruit," and his examination of the instrument's mechanisms soon led him to the conclusion that he had been told a half-truth. As Jessie put it:

> [It was] a direction not quite bad if properly applied, since the sensation of that necessary "acceleration at increasing ratio" during key-descent certainly seems like squeezing a resistance that gradually gives way.
>
> The sensation of "singing tone" might mislead one into thinking that the tone was produced on the key beds, but the fact that the hammer rebounds from the string in the act of tone-making proved this theory to be impossible.
>
> To make sure of the point he one day removed the pads under the keys so that the hammers would "block" or be jammed against the string if the keys were taken down too far. He then found that his singing tone was as good as ever, and that the "squeeze" experienced was due to the intense acceleration up to tone-emission accurately delivered. (He does not recommend this experiment to the careless student: as inaccuracy of tone-production under such circumstances would certainly wreck the piano action!)[97]

Matthay was about to embark on a sixty-year war against key striking, or "hitting," for he had discovered that the key was essentially a lever for moving a hammer to its strings, and that the secret to all tonal effects required control of its leverage. He discovered very quickly that volume was not related to force per se, but to the speed at which the key was moving when it reached the point of escapement, that is, the point at which the hammer broke free of its supporting mechanism and traveled unimpeded to the string. He noted that on most pianos this was a spot about three-quarters of the way down in key descent which could be felt by the player, and after that point no further control of the hammer was possible. This led him to develop the term "sound spot" or "tone spot," which he began to share with his students, explaining that it was impossible to obtain the desired volume or quality unless the key's acceleration were timed or "aimed" for that spot—in essence the target or goal to which the key's energy must be directed. This immediately brought him into sharp conflict with conventional teaching, because many simply taught that the key was an object to be struck like the head of a drum, while others taught that its energy should be aimed for the pad which lay underneath it. Matthay was able to refute these long-established maxims simply by removing and examining an action, but other aspects of tone production were far subtler, and Jessie reports that he later viewed a lot of his early investigations merely as misguided, blind experimentation:

> In fact he experimented with every known technical method and mechanical device. In the early eighties, when "strengthening the fingers" was the prevailing obsession, he himself devised and manufactured an arrangement of strong springs for his old upright piano [probably his family's instrument in Clapham] which he could adjust to any desired pressure; and then with these springs well screwed down upon the opposite end of the key lever, he practiced rapid brilliant finger passages, such as those in Mendelssohn's E flat Rondo for Piano and Orchestra! He now looks back with amazement on the fact that his fingers and arms came unscathed through such diabolical experiments.[98]

Evidently he was also beginning to develop the nocturnal work habits which characterized him for the rest of his life: "He also at that time fitted to the same old piano an arrangement of felt-strip which could be inserted between hammer and strings, to enable him to work late at night without disturbing the slumbers of his family."[99]

Even before he had heard Bülow, Matthay had become well acquainted with the popular fascination for "strengthening the fingers," for six months earlier he had attended a lecture on the subject sponsored by the Musical Association. Founded in 1874 under the leadership of John Stainer, the Association met monthly at the Beethoven Rooms at 27 Harley Street to pursue "the investigation and discussion of subjects connected with the art, science, and history of music." Their programs ranged from conventional fare such as George Macfarren's lecture on "The Lyrical Drama," to high-tech topics such as the "music electrograph," a device invented by J. Föhr of Stuttgart and designed to notate "on a band of paper unwound from a cylinder by clockwork any music played extemporaneously on a pianoforte to which it may be attached."[100] The meeting which Matthay attended on 2 January 1888 was convened to discuss apparatus intended for strengthening a pianist's muscles designed by W. MacDonald Smith. Smith, an American living in London, was in Portugal at the time, but he sent samples of his equipment—guaranteed to achieve in 20 minutes what pianists normally spent hours honing through keyboard exercises—along with a lecture read in absentia by Thomas Southgate, then the guiding force behind both the *Musical Standard* and the *Musical News.* Although mechanical implements promising enhanced keyboard dexterity had been popular for decades, Smith's devices included the added novelty of a bell sound when the exercises were completed successfully. His philosophy represented a curious blend of the old and the new, for while he accepted earlier views that successful playing required brute strength, he sought "scientifically" to avoid injury by taking pianists away from their instrument to perform carefully structured exercises aimed at the attainment of speed and power.[101]

After Southgate's presentation, Matthay took an active part in the brief discussion, and his remarks demonstrate that he had not yet

Chapter 3

fully shaken the widely held view that technique could be enhanced without reference to a musical effect. However, he did recognize the folly of trying to base a serviceable technique on strength alone, and his strongest objection was reserved for Smith's device for strengthening the vertical muscles of the finger:

> Mr. MATTHAY.— . . . There is a very general objection to anything of this kind, because the touch is hard on account of having to move springs or weights. The result of this is that instead of having great rapidity of the movement of the finger, which is the object of this apparatus, you have great force used, which is not at all desirable. The use of great force produces bad touch and bad tone, not because the shank of the hammer bends, but because the hammer is driven up in such a way against the string that it does not recoil immediately, and by not recoiling immediately the tone is damped and deadened.[102]

Although he later revised his position, labeling the "slower recoil" theory as merely a likely hypothesis, his thinking was clearly influenced by scientific considerations. Walker, who nearly chose piano as a first-study at the RAM before switching to violin, later recalled that Matthay was virtually a lone pioneer in this regard when contrasted with England's most prominent teachers:

> When I started piano playing at the age of fifteen I came under the influence of a friend who was a disciple of Arabella Godard. I learned to run a scale with a coin on the back of my hand. Even with this awful inhibition I gained quite some execution. Sir G. Macfarren and my piano teacher (Walter Fitton) each complimented me. They said, I had "some fingers."[103]

But Matthay was not the only Royal Academy professor bent on reforming the field of piano teaching at the time. Although fourteen years his senior, Oscar Beringer should have had much in common with his younger colleague, since both of their fathers had been *Achtundvierziger*, Beringer's father arriving in England exactly in 1848. But though largely reared in London, Beringer capitalized far more extensively on his German lineage than Matthay, to the point that as late as the 1890s he was still labeled by some in the press as a "foreign professor."[104] He described himself as an "infant prodigy," performing at the Crystal Palace as early as 1857,[105] and he spent much of the next decade in Germany, where his teachers included Moscheles, Reinecke, and Tausig. In 1869 he began teaching in Berlin at Tausig's Schule der höheren Clavierspiels, an institute on which he modeled his own school four years later in Portland Place: the "National Academy for the Higher Development of Pianoforte Playing." Well respected both in Germany and England, Beringer moved in prestigious circles, and in March 1884 he even played host to, and interpreted for, Dvořák during his appearances with the Philharmonic. He also frequently turned pages for Clara Schumann, and in 1888 he performed Brahms's *Variations on a Theme by Haydn*, Op. 56b, with Bülow.[106]

Beginning in 1877, Beringer gave annual recitals in London, and his programs were often enormous. For example, his concert at St. James Hall on 2 February 1881 included four massive sonatas: Beethoven's "Hammerklavier," Weber's Sonata in A-flat, Brahms's Sonata in F minor, and Liszt's Sonata in B minor.[107] But despite such Herculean efforts, the only mention he received that year in *The Times* came on 1 November, after he performed the Liszt E-flat Concerto "admirably" for one of Corder's concerts at the Brighton Aquarium.[108] For many years, he sought to earn a living from concertising and from his school, which was designed "for amateur and professional students," and was divided into "two sections, the one for ladies and the other for gentlemen."[109] But although his staff included Bache and Prout, he still encountered stiff competition from Wylde's Academy, which was boasting 350 students by the fall of 1878,[110] and Beringer no doubt welcomed the appointment he received to the RAM in 1885. Although his compensation for his first term was only £27, 6s—compared with Matthay's £57, 2s, 6d—his prominence immediately brought him the stature of a senior professor, and he was soon having "first studies" routinely assigned to him.[111]

Beringer was apparently an intelligent teacher who saw himself as representative of the best pedagogical methods from the

German tradition, and later he heartily endorsed the latest German scientific theories. But since Matthay was soon to renounce many of those teachings, there may have been some friction between them. Beringer's short book *Fifty Years' Experience of Pianoforte Teaching and Playing* was published four years after Matthay's *Act of Touch* appeared, but he grants Matthay no credit at all as an innovator, categorizing him only as one of many who have "recently seen the light."[112] Clearly, he believes that the most impressive books in the field are Breithaupt's *Die Natürliche Klaviertechnik* (1904) and Steinhausen's *Die physiolgischen Fehler und die Umgestaltung der Klavier-technik* (1905). He is particularly impressed by Steinhausen's background as a physician, citing his book as "by far the most important work upon technique, from the physiological point of view, that has appeared up to the present date."[113] One of his pupils recalled that Beringer taught that singing tone should be produced by "pressure" from the "fleshy part of the finger" which influences the "harmonics" of the sound—an observation with which Matthay strongly disagreed.[114] But some of Beringer's students enjoyed a pronounced success, and whatever their relationship, Matthay was generally too gracious to initiate rivalry.

However, when the Committee of Management convened on 1 December 1888 to discuss what it termed "The Case of Miss Meadows," Matthay must have been prompted even further to question traditional teaching methods. Jessie Meadows of Regent's Park had entered the Academy in the Easter Term of 1886 as a student of Walter Bache. When he died in March of 1888 she went to his good friend Fritz Hartvigson, with whom she was undoubtedly studying when her request came before the Committee.[115] The recorded minutes of that day's meeting speak with poignancy, and they strike an uncomfortable parallel with many such cases today:

> The Principal informed the Committee that from great & continued practice one of Miss Meadows['s] hands had given way and that in consequence she had been compelled to leave the Academy during the present Half Term.

> According to last year[']s arrangements Miss Meadows would be precluded from the examinations in July but the Committee decided that as Miss Meadows had studied in the Academy for more than 3 consecutive Terms and that her retirement was wholly due to accident, she should be allowed to enter for the Annual Examinations in July 1889.[116]

Whether or not Matthay had experienced injuries among his own students, he was no doubt eager to share his recent "findings" with them. Jessie reports that about this time no fewer than four RAM pupils defected to his studio from the class of another professor "which they found stagnant," and they were soon thrilled when Matthay "was making things hum."[117] She provides neither the name of the students nor the professor. The other teacher could have been Hartvigson, but could just as easily have been Macfarren, who records in his autobiography that George Aitken (1868-1942) joined his class in 1885.[118] Twenty years later, Aitken, a skilled pianist and organist, wrote a pamphlet comprehensively explaining and extolling Matthay's teaching.[119] Macfarren also indicates that Claude Pollard began working with him in 1893,[120] but in little over a decade, Pollard was teaching at Matthay's school. The studio migrations were also noted by other RAM students, such as Jessie's older sister Margaret, who was then studying voice at the Academy and remarked that Matthay's students seemed "unusually happy and enthusiastic."[121] Jessie also indicates that Matthay had begun to assign a substantial amount of four-hand and two-piano work to his students, which proved very popular, although such repertoire had not been appreciably pursued at the Academy before then. To some extent, his interest in ensemble work may have been inspired by the fact that his class as yet contained few outstanding soloists, although Dora's progress must have been substantial, since on 5 June 1889 she performed Rubinstein's D minor Concerto with Manns at the Crystal Palace.[122]

In the fall of 1886, thirteen-year-old Maude Rihill, who had been sent to Matthay by his old friend William McNaught, entered the Academy, and she was followed in the Lent term by fourteen-year-old Myra Kate (sometimes "Katie") Goodson, who was immediately

Chapter 3

assigned to Beringer. Nearly ten years Matthay's senior, McNaught began his professional life as a businessman and entered the Academy at 23 to study choral conducting. By the mid-1880s, he was assisting Stainer at the Education Department, overseeing music in schools and training colleges, and establishing a reputation as one of the finest music educators in Britain. He authored numerous publications, and from 1910 until his death in 1918, he served as editor of the *Musical Times*. Rihill and Goodson became fast friends and evidently Beringer and Matthay were cordial enough to allow them to appear together as duo-pianists in November 1890 at the Bow and Bromley Institute in East London, where McNaught served as choral director. Their program, which included works by Saint-Saëns and Raff, featured several solo pieces as well, with Rihill offering the Chopin C-sharp minor Scherzo and Goodson performing the Liszt twelfth Hungarian Rhapsody. Corder, who was in attendance, presented a glowing report:

> Besides commending the pluck and good example thus shown, it is our pleasing duty to record how both performers equally received a most warm and enthusiastic reception from a crowded house. This from so critical an audience as the "Bow and Bromley" ought to prove a great encouragement and stimulus to them . . . for the audience certainly did say "Bravo, first rate!" with right good will, a recall being insisted upon after every item. Without doubt, if they go working as their talents demand, they will indeed become artists of whom not only the Royal Academy, but England may yet be proud.[123]

Walter Mackway soon engaged Rihill to appear in a chamber music program at the Clapham Philharmonic Concerts for the coming season, and in the spring of 1891, she won the Academy's Thalberg Scholarship, which had been inaugurated in 1877 for female pianists. On 25 June 1891, Matthay featured his own pupils in an "Invitation Pianoforte Recital" at the Clapham Assembly Rooms, where she performed some of his compositions.[124] At the same concert she also teamed with Dora to play "Grieg's new Variations for two pianos" (undoubtedly the Romance and Variations in F, Op. 51), a work they repeated for the Clapham Philharmonic Concerts on 30 March 1892, where they also performed two-piano works by Schumann and Saint-Saëns. On 12 March, Rihill performed on one of the Academy's Fortnightly Concerts playing Liszt's twelfth Hungarian Rhapsody, the same work which had brought Goodson such high praise at the concert they shared a year and a half earlier. Whatever the relationship was between Matthay and Beringer, the two students were obviously highly compatible, since in December 1892 the Academy magazine *The Overture* reported that "Miss Kate Goodson and Miss Maude Rihill are having some additional training and experience under Leschetizki at Vienna."[125]

The women remained in Vienna for about three years, and in November 1895 Rihill presented her London debut at St. James's Hall, the first of Matthay's students to appear in such a major venue. The concert was prominently advertised in *The Times* on 31 October: "MISS MAUDE RIHILL, ex-Thalberg Scholar (pupil of Mr. Tobias A. Matthay, A.R.A.M., and of Leschetizky), will give a PIANOFORTE RECITAL on Tuesday Afternoon, November 12, at 3, St. James's Hall."[126] She had almost certainly returned to Matthay's studio in preparation for the event, and she probably continued to work with him for the next several years, since his compositions frequently appear on her programs. But unfortunately, her *Times* criticisms were highly mixed:

> The first part of her programme was well chosen, and Schumann's "Papillons," with the exception of the last [no. 12 in the suite] were capitally played. A very neat rendering of a set of variations by Paderweski followed, but the pianist's performance of Chopin's F minor fantasia was rather lacking in smoothness, and the middle part of the B minor scherzo was dull. The nocturne in B, however, was given with excellent taste. A new piece, "La Piccola," by Leschetitzky, and several pieces, bearing the curious title "Monotheme," [Matthay's *Monothemes,* published in March 1893] were well played, but are not interesting as music; and the recital closed with one of Liszt's rhapsodies. Miss Rihill has a clear and

sympathetic touch, but is deficient both in power and in sense of rhythm, but despite these faults, her playing is not without some charm.[127]

Nonetheless, she returned to the same venue for another program on 7 December 1897, featuring Chopin's G minor Ballade, an unidentified Beethoven Sonata from Opus 31, and numerous shorter works, including Matthay's demanding impromptu, "Die Elfen" (Elves). By now, Rihill's success as an Academy prize winner had been followed by other Matthay students, such as Lilias Pringle, a gifted pupil from Edinburgh, who won the Sterndale Bennett Prize, and the accolades continued when Ida Betts won the Liszt-Bache Scholarship—as the award was renamed in 1888 to commemorate Bache's untimely passing. Throughout his career, Matthay stressed public performance as the main goal of piano study, and he consistently devised trial venues to prepare his pupils for more major appearances. In 1888, he initiated informal programs called "Practice Concerts," where his students were encouraged to try out repertoire. Since the Academy facilities were generally considered off limits, he first presented these gatherings in Clapham, but the distance was inconvenient for most of the students and he soon moved to the Bechstein showrooms on Wigmore Street. Since the firm as yet had built no suitable concert hall, the participants had to contend with "pianos shrouded in overalls, the audience seated upon steps and odd piano stools, and even on the floor." Nonetheless, according to Jessie, the students found all of these occasions "important and enormously happy affairs." A few years later, Matthay removed his private teaching to a Chelsea studio which he shared with portrait painter C. Kay Robertson, and the Practice Concerts were soon transplanted to more comfortable surroundings.[128]

Maude Rihill and others were beginning to enhance Matthay's reputation, but by all accounts his first bona fide prodigy was Gertrude Peppercorn, a gifted thirteen-year-old who entered the Academy on 4 May 1892. The Academy Register records her address as West Horsley in Surrey, and cites the Reverend H. D. Cerjan as her sponsor. She was the daughter of A. D. (Arthur Douglas) Peppercorn (1847-1924), a successful landscape painter, and according to Jessie, "she inherited a magnificent physique and equipment for piano playing."[129] When she first entered Matthay's studio, Jessie observed that "she was little more than a child," but she found it difficult to resist "large-canvas music," and dispatched many of the grander works with great authority. At the Academy she won a number of prizes and her work was considered so distinguished that on 25 November 1897, at the age of 16, she appeared under management at St. James Hall, which—remarkably—she filled. In the advance publicity for her debut—which occurred one week before Maude Rihill's return engagement to the same hall—Matthay was prominently mentioned as her teacher, and *The Times*'s reaction to her appearance was highly positive:

> That an English girl should be able to fill St. James's-hall for a pianoforte recital at which no extraneous attraction was offered is as good a sign of the sanity of English musical taste as Miss Gertrude Peppercorn's artistic and refined playing is of the soundness of English educational methods. Even those who have watched her career as a student most carefully will hardly have been prepared for such an amount of finish and real artistic insight as the young lady displayed yesterday afternoon. The slight uncertainty of finger occasionally perceived in the earlier part of her recital wore off as time went on, and is clearly to be ascribed to nervousness. Her touch is nearly always sympathetic, her tone nicely graduated, and her phrasing that of a sound musician. If the slow movement of the "Appassionata" sonata seemed a little too much for her powers of interpretation, and a little lacking in poetry, there was plenty of sentiment in her playing of Chopin's [B]arcarolle and of Schumann's "Des Abends," while a couple of brilliant studies by Zarembsky and Moszkowski, as well as some pieces by Mr. Matthay, were played with a great deal of effect. Liszt's studies on a theme of Paganini's, given with admirable virtuosity, and Balakireff's "Islamey" brought this very successful recital to a close.[130]

A year later, barely 17, she performed Liszt's E-flat Concerto with Manns at the Crystal Palace,[131] and after that time she began appearing with increasing frequency as a soloist and chamber musician. She was so warmly embraced by London concertgoers that on 11 February 1905 she was one of a small number of artists chosen to participate in one of the final concerts at the venerable St. James's Hall before it was razed. She shared the program with nine singers and pianists, performing Liszt's sixth Hungarian Rhapsody and *Liebestraum* No. 3. With Gertrude Peppercorn, the "Matthay trademarks" were beginning to achieve public recognition. As Jessie observed, "although she was finely equipped for larger sound effects, it was the finer shadings and gradations of tone that made the most memorable artistic impression."[132]

But from the day that his first talented pupils began to appear, Matthay knew that his mission could not be fulfilled through teaching alone. If he had anything truly original to offer, his ideas had to see print, and he was determined to use his pen to shape the revolution he soon hoped to forge.

Notes

1. JHM, 21.
2. From Davison's review of Wagner's first Philharmonic Concert, *TT,* 14 March 1855, 11, col. A.
3. See Sterndale Bennett, 243.
4. The first concert of the Musical Arts Union, conducted by Klindworth at the Hanover Square Rooms on 31 May 1861, was reviewed by *The Times* on 3 June (9, col. F). The reviewer (probably Davison) attacked Rubinstein's Symphony as "empty and inexpressive as it is loud, incoherent, and pretentious."
5. Dannreuther's career in England had been assisted by Chorley, the editor of *The Atheneum*, who intended to make him his heir until the pianist's Wagner loyalties became "increasingly conspicuous." See Jeremy Dibble, "Dannreuther, Edward," in *RNG*. Dibble's outstanding biography of Parry also has an illuminating discussion of Dannreuther and his relationship to Parry.

6. JHM, 21.
7. Parker, *Several of My Lives*, 129. Hereafter cited as Parker.
8. Parker, 129.
9. Parker, 129.
10. The autographs indicating times and dates are in the RAMMC.
11. In March 1880, she participated in a program at her husband's home on Devonshire Place, where one of her songs was sung. The concert was held in honor of W. H. Holmes, who performed some of his own music and was still teaching piano at the Academy at the time. Also featured was Florence Baglehole, the first winner of the Sterndale-Bennett Prize and an early classmate of Matthay, who discussed and performed some of Bennett's music. See *TT*, 13 March 1880, 1, col. D.
12. The autographs to both cadenzas (MS2026 and MS2026a) are in the RAMRBC. A slightly revised version of the "Wagner" cadenza was published in 1929 by Augener.
13. JHM, 18.
14. RAMRBC MS1934.
15. RAMRBC MS1950. On the same page, he also wrote "Look at this again," suggesting that he considered revising it nearly 60 years later.
16. RAMRBC MS1951.
17. RAMRBC MS1931.
18. RAMRBC MS1932. He completed the orchestral score on 3 January 1883.
19. JHM, 18.
20. The winner was chosen on 12 April 1883 by Julius Benedict and Otto Goldschmidt, "Acting at the request of the Directors in the unavoidable absence of MICHAEL COSTA, who was attacked by illness after he had nearly completed his examination." See *Philharmonic Society Analytical and Historical Programme of the Fourth Concert*, Wednesday, April 25, 1883, 11-12. Oliver King, described as "about 25 years of age," was an English pianist then living in Ottawa, but he soon returned to London, where, like Matthay, he served as a piano professor at the RAM.
21. BL, RPS MS 355, vol. 23, f. 52. Matthay to Philharmonic Society, 21 Apr. 1883.
22. BL, RPS MS 355, vol. 23, f. 53. Matthay to Philharmonic Society, 16 Jun. 1883.

Chapter 3

23. RAMRBC MS 1946.
24. Matthay's comments are written across the title page of the score. Two months later he conceded that despite some "splendid moments," it was "not worthy to spend time over" since it "would need totally re-writing."
25. RAMRBC MS 1947.
26. RAMRBC MS 1954 and RAMRBC MS 1956 (parts).
27. BL, RPS MS 355, vol. 23, f. 55. Matthay to Berger, 10 Nov. 1885.
28. Quoted in JHM, 19.
29. BL, RPS MS 355, vol. 23, f. 57-58. Matthay to Philharmonic Directors, 19 Sept. 1890.
30. Cf. Michael Musgrave, *The Musical Life of the Crystal Palace* (Cambridge, 1995), 77 ff.
31. JHM, 22. Jessie indicates that the Society's "real" founders were "Amy Horrocks, a composer, and Winifred Robinson and Edith Parker, two enthusiastic string players," while Matthay, Corder, and Bantock were its "sponsors." In later years, Matthay and his pupils frequently collaborated with Robinson, a violinist, in chamber performances.
32. JHM, 19.
33. See "Births" in *TT*, 9 May 1864, 1, col. A.
34. The piece bore no opus number when it was published by the London Music Publishing and General Agency Co. in the 1880s, but when Matthay's Anglo-French Music Company reissued it sometime after 1915, it was published as his Opus 8.
35. See *The Childhood of the World* (London, 1872), and *The Story of Creation* (London, 1894).
36. Matthay later said that he first encountered Spencer when he heard a lecture at the age of 16 in which Spencer argued that "every effect must have a cause," and that "this prompted me to seek for 'Causes' in Piano playing." MA. Matthay to Bruce Simonds, 13 Dec. 1941.
37. See Walker, "Student-Days with Matthay," *AMAJ*, 1932, 14.
38. See J. D. Y. Peel, *Herbert Spencer: the evolution of a sociologist* (New York, 1971), 22.
39. Spencer first used the term in an 1852 essay titled "A Theory of Population, deduced from the General Law of Animal Fertility." See Peel, 137-38.
40. See Peel, 234-37.

41. See Charles Darwin, *The Origin of Species*, ed. Philip Appleman (New York, 1975), 122. Appleman's edition is taken from the sixth edition of *Origin*, first published in 1872.
42. See Ch. 4. Matthay quotes from this work in the one of the pieces he wrote for *The Overture*.
43. Herbert Spencer, *Education: Intellectual, Moral and Physical* (New York, 1861), 79-80.
44. See Spencer's *Literary Style and Music* (New York, 1951), for a complete exposition of all his revisions to this piece.
45. For example, on 20 Dec. 1882 (4, col. E), *The Times* reported that "Receipt was acknowledged at the under-mentioned police-courts of the following sums for the poor-box:—Mansion-house—Mr. William Teetgen, £10."
46. See "The Bishopsgate Institute," *TT*, 26 Nov. 1894, 10, col. B.
47. JHM, 20.
48. "Sir M. Montagu-Pollock," *TT*, 18 Aug. 1938, 13, col. F.
49. JHM, 20.
50. JHM, 19.
51. For example, the years 1880-81, while they exist at the BLN, are considered "unfit for use." (*Clapham Observer* volume requested on 12 July 2004.)
52. For example, see the ad which ran in the *Observer* on 30 July 1887, 2, col. 1.
53. *Observer*, 15 Oct. 1887, 5, col. 1.
54. The Prince of Wales announced the honors on 7 May 1883 for Macfarren, Sullivan, and George Grove, who were all summoned to Windsor Castle on the same day. See Janet Ritterman, "Grove as First director of the RCM," in Michael McClelland, ed., *George Grove, Music and Victorian Culture*, (London, 2003), 249.
55. *Observer*, 28 Nov. 1885, 4, col. A.
56. *Observer*, col. B.
57. JHM, 22.
58. Program reprinted in JHM, 23. Ernest Ford was a long-time friend of Matthay, and had also been a member of Prout's class several years earlier. They were evidently so close that Matthay even wrote a song for him, "To Ernest" (with a text beginning "Ich liebe dich") in 1883. RAMRBC MS1925. Matthay seems to have been fascinated with Byron's poem. He even orchestrated "There be none of beauty's daughters." See RAMRBC MS1909 through MS1910C.

Chapter 3

59. *The Musical World*, 18 Dec. 1884, 786.
60. *MT*, 1 April 1887, 219.
61. *MT*, 17 Nov. 1888, 4, col. 6.
62. COMM, 3 Nov. 1892.
63. COMM, 10 May 1894.
64. See *TT* ads, 25 Nov. 1885, 1, col. D, and 9 Mar. 1887, 1, col. B.
65. *TT*, 16 Sept. 1885, 1, col. F.
66. JHM, 16.
67. *TT*, 6 May 1876, 7, col. E.
68. *TT*, 21 Nov. 1885, 5, col. E.
69. *TT*, 8 Apr. 1886, 5, col. C.
70. *TT*, 20 Apr. 1886, 5, col. C.
71. *TT*, 14 June 1886, 12, col. B.
72. *TT*, *The Times* published Rubinstein's entire program and the only works which he composed which were programmed that day were his Sonata in F and excerpts from his Sonatas in C minor and A minor.
73. For example, both companies ran brief classified ads in *The Times* on 31 May 1886 (13, col. B) citing Rubinstein's endorsement. Becker went so far as to say, "ANTON RUBINSTEIN plays only the BECKER PIANO."
74. JHM, 17.
75. The Frederick Collection in Ashburnham, Massachusetts, maintained by E. Michael and Patricia Frederick, contains two beautifully—and faithfully—restored instruments: an 1871 Broadwood and an 1877-78 Erard that I played in June 2004. The responsiveness of the Erard was remarkable.
76. JHM, 17.
77. *TT*, 5 April 1886, 9, col. B. Alan Walker, in *Franz Liszt: The Final Years* (485), indicates that Bache also conducted the work on 24 February 1876, which I have been unable to confirm, but he may have learned this from examining the complete run of Bache's annual Liszt programs at the Bodleian. He also indicates that neither Wylde nor Bache gave the work a complete performance. Hereafter cited as Walker, *Liszt*.
78. *TT*, 5 April 1886, 9, col. B.
79. Ironically, one of Liszt's scheduled events, an afternoon Crystal Palace concert on 10 April at which Manns conducted his pupil Bernhard Stavenhagen in the E-flat Concerto, was juxtaposed directly opposite an appearance by

Clara Schumann at St. James's Hall—so Matthay and other London pianists may have faced a difficult decision. Among other works, Clara performed the *Carnaval*, and her audience was "filled to overflowing." See *TT*, 12 April 1886, 5, col. F.

80. *TT*. The guest list was a veritable *Who's Who*. The gathering also included several foreign ambassadors, as well as Lady Walter Scott and Sir John Stainer.
81. Letter from Liszt to Bache dated 11 February 1886, taken from *Franz Liszts Briefe*, vol. 2 (Leipzig 1893-1905), reproduced in Walker, *Liszt*, 478.
82. Walker, *Liszt*, 488.
83. JHM, 16.
84. RAMRBC MS1986. Matthay called his study "Frivolity." It was the first of three "Vagaries," etudes which he dedicated to Liszt.
85. Matthay, "On Technique," 8-9. RAMRBC (uncatalogued at this writing).
86. In the 1930s, Matthay expressed this view to his pupil Guy Jonson. Interview with Jonson at his home in Hampstead, 8 July 2004.
87. See Christopher Fifield, "Bülow, Hans (Guido) Freiherr von," *NRG*. Hereafter cited as "Bülow."
88. *Musical World*, 62 (6 December 1884):49.
89. Fay, *Music-Study in Germany*, 176.
90. Fifield, "Bülow."
91. For example, he accomplished this feat in London ten years earlier. See *TT*, 21 Nov. 1878, 10, col. C.
92. See *TT*, 15 May 1888, 1, col. D.
93. *TT*, 5 June 1888, 12, col. A.
94. JHM, 16. Alan Walker provides the most outstanding, definitive study of Bülow the pianist, conductor, and musical intellect in his recently published *Hans von Bülow[:] A Life and Times* (New York, 2010). His discussion of Bülow's intentions concerning the Beethoven cycle is especially illuminating, since unlike Rubinstein, Bülow was consciously attempting to reveal Beethoven's intellectual development as a composer. See *Hans von Bülow*, 354-58 and 396-97.
95. Matthay owned Sonate Op. 57, from the series *Sonaten und andere Werke für das Pianoforte von Ludwig van Beethoven in kritischer und instructiver Ausgabe*, edited by Dr. Hans von Bülow (Stuttgart, 1882).

96. JHM, 17.
97. JHM, 17-18.
98. JHM, 18.
99. JHM, 18.
100. Now known as the Royal Musical Association, much useful information about the society may be obtained at its web site: http://www.rma.ac.uk. For details about Macfarren's talk and the "electrograph," see *TT*, 8 June 1880, 10, col. E, and 7 June 1882, 9, col. G.
101. Smith also thought his devices would be helpful to violinists ("making the right wrist supple for bowing") and typists ("an increase of rapidity in ordinary writing, and also with the type-writer, is very marked when these finger exercises are made use of."). See W. MacDonald Smith, "The Physiology of Pianoforte Playing, with a Practical Application of a New Theory," *Proceedings of the Musical Association*, 14th Sess. (1887-1888), Oxford University Press, 60.
102. Smith, 63. Discussion following the lecture.
103. Walker, "Student-Days with Matthay," *AMAJ*, 14-15. Arabella Goddard (1836-1922), a student of Kalbrenner and Thalberg, was considered by many to be the ranking female pianist in late nineteenth-century Britain. A good friend of Bennett, she premiered several of his works, and she was married to *Times* critic J. W. Davison. She taught at the RCM from its opening in 1883.
104. On 31 July 1896, *The Times* (13, col. D) carried partial transcripts of a complicated civil trial in which Alexander Mackenzie, then Principal of the RAM, sued the *Saturday Review* for libel. One of the issues revolved around the Academy allowing Beringer's student Vera Margolies, the daughter of naturalized Russians, to compete for a prize restricted to British students. The magazine wrote that Mackenzie "permitted a foreign professor to 'manipulate' in favor of a foreign student a scholarship given for the express purpose of assisting British students." The jury found that this and other statements made by the magazine were libelous, and awarded Mackenzie £400.
105. Beringer, 1-2.
106. Beringer, 41.
107. Program reproduced in Beringer's book, 66.

108. See *TT*, 1 Nov. 1881, 5, col. F.
109. See *TT*, 1 Oct. 1878, 9, col. C.
110. *TT*, 1 Oct. 1878, 9, col. C.
111. COMM, 19 Dec. 1885.
112. Beringer, 48.
113. Beringer, 48.
114. See William H. Cummings, "The Art of Clavier Playing, Past and Present," a lecture given before the Musical Association on 12 Dec. 1893. After Cummings spoke, the discussion was joined by Walter Wesché (1857-1910), an Italian-born pianist and composer who taught at Beringer's school.
115. See RAMR for 1887, 242 and 250-51.
116. COMM, 1 Dec. 1888.
117. JHM, 25.
118. Macfarren, 323.
119. See his "Tobias Matthay and his Teachings" (London, 1907).
120. Macfarren, *Memories: An Autobiography,* 325.
121. Macfarren, 26.
122. *TT*, 5 June 1889, 1, col. D.
123. *TO*, Dec., 1890. 128.
124. *TO*. The program also included Matthay pupils Lily West, performing Chopin's F minor Fantasy, and Zola Cohen, performing the Beethoven C minor Variations.
125. *TO*, Dec. 1892, 132.
126. *TT*, 31 Oct. 1895, 1, col. C.
127. *TT*, 13 Nov. 1895, 10, col. B.
128. JHM, 34. C. [Charles] Kay Robertson also painted Matthay's portrait in 1899 (Photo 8), and did a charcoal drawing of Jessie (Photo 9) about the same time. Both are now housed at the RAM.
129. JHM, 30.
130. "Miss Peppercorn's Recital," *TT*, 26 November 1897, 6, col. A.
131. On 6 October 1898. See *TT* for that date, 1, col. C.
132. JHM, 30.

Sir Alexander Mackenzie about 1912

CHAPTER 4

THE OVERTURE . . .

On 31 October 1887, Sir George Macfarren died suddenly, "almost literally at his work."[1] Since he left no clear-cut successor, for a time the Academy was governed by a committee led by his brother Walter. Then on 22 February 1888, Alexander Campbell Mackenzie—whom Corder later termed a "dark horse"—was appointed Principal. Mackenzie, then aged 40, was one of the youngest men to have held that post,[2] and though his musical accomplishments had been substantial, he was still an unlikely choice. Born in Edinburgh, by the age of 10 he had entered the Realschule in Sondershausen, Germany, where he studied violin with the orchestra's concertmaster, K. W. Uhlrich. He also studied harmony with *Kapellmeister* Eduard Stein, whose adventurous programming enabled him to participate in the local premieres of numerous works by Berlioz, Liszt, and Wagner.[3] In 1862 Mackenzie entered the RAM to study violin with Prosper Sainton and he gained much experience performing with London theater orchestras, even as he completed a number of original compositions which were performed at the Academy. In 1865 he returned to Edinburgh, where he remained for the next 14 years, teaching, performing, and composing—often for the string quartet which he formed in 1873. In 1879 he relocated to Italy, where he remained until he returned to London in 1885 to assume the conductorship of the newly reorganized Novello Choir. The following year, his reputation was enhanced when he conducted Liszt's *Saint Elizabeth* before the composer, and after Macfarren died, Academy officials decided to take a chance on a younger man from outside the London establishment. Mackenzie, an intimate of Joachim, Rubinstein, and Bülow, was well connected, but his candidacy still provoked a nasty fight among RAM personnel who favored Joseph Barnby, the conductor of the Royal Albert Hall Choral Society. An unprecedented election was held in which Mackenzie narrowly triumphed, but it prodded him "to prevent the possibility of so undignified an election ever occurring again."[4] No doubt his supporters hoped he would have the energy and vision to rescue the institution from a new series of difficulties which had been brewing for several years.

Although he had weathered many storms in the five years following Bennett's death, it was clear by 1880 that Macfarren's astute powers of management were again to be tested. In September of that year the City of London founded the Guildhall School of Music, designed to nurture an appreciation for the "higher forms of music among all classes of society."[5] Under the directorship of Weist Hill—who had formerly conducted the RAM orchestra—the School fostered an openly populist orientation, and the night classes it offered for working people caused its enrollment to grow at a staggering rate. Opening with a mere 62 pupils, within a few months that number had expanded to 216, and five years later, it reached an astounding 2400. Municipal funding was sought to rescue the students and staff from the house it had outgrown in Aldermanbury, and the Court of Common Council soon appropriated £20,000 so that the City's architect, Horace Jones, could design a new building on the Embankment, whose appointments overshadowed anything the RAM had known. With 42 classrooms, "well secured from extraneous noises by double doors and double sashes," and a multi-purpose room, 70' x 28', for concerts and lectures, its exterior was adorned with "incised ornaments representing various musical emblems, and forming as a whole an 'Academic Italian' design."[6] The cornerstone was laid on 21 July 1885, and despite the press's assurances that the Guildhall in no way competed with the Academy (which was not exactly true), Macfarren—who could remember blood feuds once waged over the RAM's annual £500 stipend—must have surveyed the City's ample largesse with regret, if not bitterness. In fact, *The Times* even rubbed salt in the wound by declaring the Guildhall facility "a new departure in the history of English music," and condemning the same deficiencies in its briefly occupied townhouse that the RAM had endured for decades:

> The rooms are too small and too few; some of them are divided only by thin wooden partitions, incapable of isolating the sound. The evil involved in this state of things is obvious. How can a singer be expected to keep in tune with the accompanying piano while not many yards off another pupil practices on the French horn in a different key, and the organ placed at the top of the house swells the confused noise arising from below with its mighty voice? Strange to say, human nature, aided by habit, overcomes the difficulty to some degree. Mind and ear concentrate themselves on the task immediately before them, and cease to perceive what is extraneous to it. But this can be done only by means of a corresponding waste of mental energy and what philosophers call unconscious cerebration.[7]

But even if the Academy did not regard the Guildhall School as a threat, there was no way it could ignore the challenge it was facing from South Kensington. Although the National Training School had folded in 1882 and was no longer an issue, it had been succeeded in April of 1883 by the Royal College of Music. Under the directorship of Sir George Grove, the College began its operations in the Training School's former facilities next to the Albert Hall, and it opened with 50 students on full scholarship, complemented by 42 who paid tuition. There was little question that highly influential partisans were pressing to make the RCM the nation's premier conservatory, since the Royal Family was directly involved in its governance and the Prince of Wales even served as its President. Grove and the Royals had spent nearly a year scouring the country for contributions, and by its inauguration ceremony on 7 May 1883, the RCM had amassed an endowment of £110,000, a sum which exceeded anything the RAM had ever seen—but which Grove still dismissed as "niggardly."[8] In addition, Sir Charles Freake, who had built the Training School's building at his own expense, now made a gift of it to the Royal College, insuring the institution's immunity from the perennial landlord-tenant problems that still confronted the Academy. Grove had also recruited an impressive performance faculty—Jenny Lind was even one of his voice professors—and his *Dictionary of Music and Musicians*, which had first seen print four years earlier, assured that the RCM was also to be a citadel of scholarship. And less than a month before Mackenzie's appointment, Grove announced that Samson Fox—who had made a fortune as the inventor of the corrugated iron flue for steam boilers—had given the Prince of Wales £30,000 for a new RCM building to stand on Prince Consort Road, to "relieve the College from a serious amount of inconvenience."[9]

It was probably no coincidence that Mackenzie and Grove were friends— Mackenzie addressed him familiarly as "G" and they soon became neighbors in Sydenham—and this connection may have helped sway Mackenzie's supporters.[10] Corder entered as an RAM professor some seven months after Mackenzie arrived, and despite his lack of seniority and the controversy that ensued, he was soon made Curator, the Principal's second-in-command, "taking charge of such details of management as needed not the Principal's personal supervision."[11] Years later, he wrote that he believed Mackenzie's appointment to be "the most important event in the history of the Academy:"

> He assumed the reins of government with a firm hand that never relaxed, no matter what other calls there might be on his energies. One can hardly, even at this distance of time, disclose the troubles and obstacles which he had to encounter; I personally . . . was an edified spectator of many a conflict and of his invariable triumph, and my admiration of his masterfulness and unswerving integrity grew and grew.[12]

Changes were effected almost immediately. By taking over both the choir and the orchestra, Mackenzie immediately put a stop to the custom of professors second-guessing the conductor in public when their students performed, and he abolished the archaic regulation confining male and female students to separate sides of rooms and corridors.[13] He also allowed Corder and Matthay to sponsor the

Excelsior Society, an organization openly devoted to Wagner, which would have been unthinkable during Macfarren's reign. Out of its weekly meetings soon grew the R.A.M. Club, which although at first limited to men, undertook a broader focus and became a kind of cheerleader for all aspects of Academy life, even as the Society continued on for a time. No doubt with an eye toward the increasing importance of scholarship—even from composers and performers—in March 1890 the Club launched *The Overture*, a monthly journal which eventually filled four volumes, ceasing publication in February 1894.[14] Jessie described it as "a jolly little magazine" and lamented that it eventually disappeared for lack of funding. The new publication had adopted one of the Excelsior Society's stated purposes: to "interest the more alert students," and to "inspire if possible the duller ones with the desire for more alertness."[15] Its target audience also included the R.A.M. Club members—professors and alums—and it combined timely reports on their activities with reviews of books and music, interspersed with faculty commentary covering a wide range of musical subjects. Corder served as editor through its entire run, and although some of Matthay's contributions may be explained by their close friendship, the fact that *The Overture* featured no other professor's views so abundantly suggests that his insights were, in the main, well received. In addition to Matthay and Corder, Jessie identified Orsmond Anderton, Granville Bantock, Henry Davey, and Ebenezer Prout as part of the editorial board, all of whom occasionally contributed articles.[16]

Many considered the journal's commentaries so insightful that even 30 years later, Robin Legge of the *Daily Telegraph* was urging serious musicians "to beg, borrow, or steal" a compilation of its contents, adding that such a collection "to me is beyond price:"

> The other day, while dipping yet again into these fascinating little volumes—you may open them at any page and find something you did not know about the then state of contemporary and earlier music in England—I was amused to find how many topics were then discussed and threshed out seemingly for ever that have cropped up as hardy annuals ever since.[17]

When the first issue appeared, Matthay had just turned 32, and although he had already honed his pen on some *Clapham Observer* reviews, he had as yet published no technical articles aimed at professionals. He was in the eleventh year of his RAM professorship, but he still had little contact with serious piano talent, since understandably, he was forced to defer to Walter Macfarren's seniority. But the *Overture* articles already document the development of his pedagogical thinking and confirm that although he believed his theories explained the practices of finished artists, he found them equally applicable to those of more modest talent—at least enough that he could prescribe them with confidence to the entire RAM readership. The roughly 20,000 words he penned through the magazine's run also dramatically illustrate the detailed argumentation he was already making in defense of his theories. Clearly, he believed the pianist's art could be explained by reference to scientific principles, and he was ready to give those principles such intellectual defense as required—even if it meant stretching his audience's mental capacities. Matthay was still several years away from arriving at revolutionary formulations, but *The Overture* provides a telling documentation of the embryonic steps he traveled.

He was a frequent contributor to two series which ran through the life of the journal, "Chats on Technical Subjects," in which he dealt specifically with piano playing, and the far broader "Thoughts and Reflections," in which he covered topics ranging from vocal instruction to acoustic wave theory. In the first issue in March 1890 he inaugurated the "Chats" series with a thousand-word essay titled "On Technique." This first entry demonstrates that Matthay was already echoing Adolph Marx, and grappling with what was to become the most fundamental of his teaching principles—that technique and musical expression cannot be separated:

> The practice of technical exercises has, as it appears at first sight, two ends in view, the attainment of facility in "execution in general," and facility in the "execution in particular" of some passage form often occurring in music, such as the scale, arpeggio, &c. These, only

apparently, separable aims, however, ultimately merge into one, and this aim is the acquirement of "technique."[18]

He then reasserts a principle for which Marx and Kullak had laid the groundwork—that technical finesse springs not from innately endowed reflexes, but from an intellect which has been consciously programmed. He adds that "real practice is that which tends towards increasing the power of the brain over the fingers," or "tends to strengthen the memory of those mental impressions which accompany each separate muscular motion."[19] As a predictable corollary, he also dismisses the view that genuine technique is likely to be acquired through blind repetition, or even trial and error, since although such activity may awaken one's musical taste and perhaps invoke a greater desire to release the composer's message, "not at all necessarily will *muscle-command* follow," or as he succinctly states it, technical mastery requires "*remembering the sensations* accompanying each particular movement."[20] But obviously, since some gifted pianists do not seem to require extensive muscular analysis, he closes his first piece with a reference to those students for whom verbal explanations often seem superfluous: "A word remains to be said on the phenomenon of so-called 'natural execution.' Endowment of this sort is unfortunately not at all invariably found to be concomitant with a *natural determination towards music*." He adds that prodigiously gifted artists "are able to give the requisite 'concentration' without much *conscious* effort, and as every application of 'will power' means so much expenditure of vital energy, these favoured ones manifestly here begin with a great advantage on their side."

In the coming years, Matthay maintained that all technical command originated from proper mental functioning, allowing for the fact that a musical genius—like a savant or prodigy in any field—may not be aware of all the intervening thought processes. But those who lack such a gift may compensate for their lack of "natural" execution by striving to "induce it artificially,"[21] which he saw as a thoroughly realistic goal for the intelligent aspirant. He also stressed a corollary of this view, since he believed that while a natural aptitude for technical proficiency assured a "great advantage," it did not assure artistry. Therefore, if only one aptitude should be present in a given individual, the "natural determination towards music" was by far the more valuable, and throughout his career he proved remarkably consistent in this view. In fact, over the next six decades, stories were legion concerning the patience he showed toward students who felt the emotional message of a score, even if their technical attainments were at first unimpressive.

In the April issue—introduced by Victorian language bordering on the opaque—he begins to lay out his theory of tone production. He seems fully conscious of the anti-scientific bias which had previously clouded such discussions, but confident that the path is now clear for systematic, rational analysis:

> Until within comparatively recent years, the broaching of a subject such as [tone production] would decidedly have been a piece of temerity which would summarily have been punished by opprobrious epithets. . . . Indeed, it would have been thrown in the face of any rash one who should have dared to venture on such a path that good performers, as well as good musicians, "are born, not made." . . .
>
> Happily those days are quite past now. The student, instead of being merely directed to work as hard as possible—which, indeed, is even more necessary in these days than before—is now at all events more or less made acquainted with the elements of the problem he has before him.[22]

Matthay seems assured that a new era of aesthetic enlightenment has arrived, in which artists are willing to be guided by the dictates of science. And he pays homage to the man he regarded as its principal architect—Herbert Spencer—by quoting a paragraph, reproduced here in part, from his *Education: Intellectual, Moral and Physical*: "That science necessarily underlies the fine arts becomes manifest, *à priori,* when we remember that art products are all more or less representative of objective or subjective phenomena; that they can be good only in proportion as they conform to the laws of these phenomena, and that before they can thus conform, the artist must know what these laws are."[23] With Spencer's scientific and philosophic foundations thus laid, Matthay continues: "The first element of the problem may perhaps be defined in these terms: *that the greatest possible effect may be obtained from the least necessary expenditure of force.* [Emphasis original]"[24] In the interests of space, he foregoes an extensive discussion of the piano's mechanisms, but he explores the known physics of tone production in some detail:

> The tone being the result of a blow [of the hammer to the string], we are here face to face with another of those chief facts which ought to govern our behaviour at the keyboard. A steel string is struck—*i.e., a swift motion* is delivered to it by means of the hammer. . . .
>
> A vibrating string has, too, a strong family likeness to an oscillating pendulum. Now, within certain limits of arc, a pendulum fulfils practically *the same number of beats* (complete oscillations) *in a given lapse of time, whether the impulse first given be strong or weak*; and in the case of the string the *rhythm* is even more invariable than in the case of a freely suspended weight. Here arises then the question, what becomes of the extra motion given if it does not increase the *number* of vibrations? The answer to this is, that it simply increases—within certain limits— the *actual space traversed* by the pendulum during that natural rhythm which its particular length determines. The same holds good with the string, the space-extent of each complete to-and-fro motion is increased, "the amplitude of its vibration is increased."[25]

His observation leads him to the conclusion that just as force or mass per se cannot alter a vibrating string's frequency (what we hear as pitch), so it cannot alter its amplitude (what we hear as volume). In other words, the amount of tone heard is entirely dependent on the speed with which the hammer travels, and therefore on the speed with which the key travels: "What is required from our fingers, or hand (wrist-action), or arm (elbow-action), is not force taking the form of *pressure*, but force taking the form of speed—quickness of movement; *swiftness* of finger, hand, or arm, *descent*."[26] In subsequent years, this focus on key speed rather than "pressure" became

Chapter 4

a cardinal element of his teaching, and as will be shown, he later refined his precepts to include physiologic subtleties enabling the performer to summon the desired differences more easily.

In the next series of "Chats," which ran from May through July, he began in earnest to explain what he later termed the "physiological details" of piano technique. Beginning where he left off with a discussion of key speed, he enters into an examination of the pianist's muscular functioning and, at the outset, argues against the simultaneous invocation of *opposing* sets of muscles (that is, those which raise, as against those which lower a limb). In addition to inhibiting freedom of movement, he believed that the inadvertent, concurrent use of these opposite sets was the root cause of muscular tension— and of most faulty technique. It was a tenet he maintained throughout his career: "Quantity of the sound entirely depending on the quantity of the motion delivered . . . clearly, if this motion has to take place *against the resistance of the player's own muscles*, then this must detract from the speed—must create a distinct obstacle tending to annihilate the desired effect; and effort taking the place of freedom of movement, the result can, at best, be but clumsy and inartistic."[27] Then for the first time, he resolves a controversy resurrected by Otto Ortmann some 35 years later (See Chapter 10). It was a debate he was often forced to revisit, for Ortmann and others later devoted considerable attention to what Matthay termed "useless" anatomy teaching, or as he put it, teaching the "names and addresses" of individual muscles:

> However, we are not able directly, consciously, to set in motion a single muscle, for we are unable deliberately to concentrate thought on a single bundle of muscular fibre. Certainly, we do realise the possession of muscle on a contact from outside taking place, and by perceiving its motion, but the reverse nervous action we are unable immediately to determine. But what we can do is to organise the *sensations resulting* from muscular movements and the consciousness of the nerve-impulses required to bring them about. We can experiment with our fingers, &c., until we succeed in obtaining the correct impulse—correct movement—in

The Overture . . .

one muscle without the slightest opposition on the part of the particular muscle endowed with the reverse function.[28]

His language is still cumbersome, but he later simplified this concept to the maxim that, since our muscles are all interconnected, we cannot mentally isolate the action of a *single* muscle. He concluded that the acquisition of effective piano technique is therefore dependent on *limb* training, rather than individual *muscle* training. But the precepts he offers in *The Overture* are not always consistent with the principles later outlined in *The Act of Touch*. For instance, at times he insists that the finger be raised high above the key, making no mention of his later precept that the key mechanism must always be accelerated, rather than struck: "A blow having to be given by the finger, the preliminary condition must therefore be, that the finger tip be well raised from the key. And this cannot be done unless the hand itself, to begin with, be held well away from the surface of the keyboard."[29] Indeed, his later view that the hand should lie loosely on the surface of the keys, and that "position" was the result of doing, rather than the fixation of a limb in a given location, seems nowhere in evidence. In June, he continued his discussion of technique, but the language is rather dense—even when contrasted with his later writings—and his stated theories concerning the use of the finger stand in contradistinction to what were eventually accepted as "Matthay Principles." He advises that after the finger is "well raised from the key-surface; the third phalange (from the knuckle-joint) moving most; not, *though the whole finger is to unbend* in preparing for the blow—not, however, to such an extent as to interfere with the full raising of the *second* joint, nor so as to place the finger in a line pointing away from the keyboard."[30]

Nowhere does he suggest the later distinctions he formulated between "thrusting" and "clinging" finger touch (see Chapter 6), nor does he even hint that the fingers may remain in contact with the keys, which he promoted extensively 12 years later in *The Act of Touch*. He also advocates exercises from Book I of the *Tausig-Erlich Daily Studies* ("of which an English translation is obtainable") that demand an element of fixation, a muscular condition he later disavowed: "The elbow is held fixed against the performer's body, as an exercise, this having a most salutary effect on the wrist joint, particularly tending to render horizontal movements from it free and unimpeded."[31] It is difficult to reconcile Matthay's later insistence that the elbow be continuously free and floating, with the claim that a held, fixed elbow breeds "a most salutary effect on the wrist joint." Though he may have seen such an exercise purely as preliminary to sensing a freed wrist, he nowhere mentions the "balanced" arm, which he later insisted was the essential basis for all successful playing. Through this period he may have been grappling for a middle ground between tension and relaxation, and it appears that many issues still remain to be settled. However, again harkening back to Marx, Kullak, and Deppe, he seems to harbor no illusions about the damage which can be caused by excessive tension: "Arm-pressure, with its corollary, a stiffly held wrist joint, is absolutely fatal to good quality of tone and a 'liquid' touch. Any tendency therefore in this direction should be most carefully eliminated."[32]

In the July 1890 issue, another of Matthay's important principles makes its first appearance: that the piano cannot be played by the fingers alone. In this he was also preceded by the Germans, but he seems to grapple for a level of detail beyond what Deppe had discussed:

> Manifestly, it is difficult, if indeed not impracticable, to strike chords by means of finger-action alone. Hence wrist and arm actions are here employed. These are of three very distinct kinds.
>
> I. Arm-action—movement from the elbow. II. Wrist-action—movement of the hand from the wrist-joint. III. A certain combination of these two, in which the hand is thrown into motion by a jerk given by the fore-arm; this might be described as "wrist-elbow" action.[33]

In this context, the word "strike" eventually disappeared from his vocabulary, and over the next decade, the three distinctions identified here became far more precise, particularly with respect to the arm's interaction with the finger. Matthay eventually formulated three "species" of touch involving the finger, the hand, and the arm respectively, accompanied by six possible modes of arm functioning, all of which as he reasoned, could and should merge effortlessly at the artist's will depending on the desired musical effect (see Chapter 6). And it should be noted that although muscular ease and convenience always factor into his thinking, the *quality* of tone also governs his precepts: "Bad tone does, however, often result even when the correct arm-movement is employed. Yes! even with first-rate artists—simply from the striking limb being held in a state of absolute *rigidity instead of in a naturally elastic condition*." But admittedly, his grasp of the underlying scientific causes of harsh tone is still somewhat empiric:

> The correct theory *may* be, that although the pianoforte mechanism does provide for the hammer's falling away from the string immediately after impact, yet, when the blow given is of the rigid nature above alluded to, then, after all, the hammer does not immediately leave the string, and so the vibration is stopped in its very birth. We have the familiar instance when a bell or other vibrating body is struck with an un-recoiling action. Direct experiment at the pianoforte will, however, demonstrate quickly and conclusively enough how the bad tone arises and how it can be avoided. Let two chords be struck forcibly, holding every tendon in a state of tension in one case, and in the other throwing the hand down freely and in a state of relaxation, and the thing is done![34]

The passage above demonstrates that Matthay was almost certainly familiar with Helmholtz's *The Sensations of Tone*, which had first appeared in English translation in 1875, and which contrasts the effects of vibrating piano strings with "rigid" versus "elastic" mediums.[35] The issue of qualitative differences in sound would soon become one of the most heated controversies in twentieth-century pedagogy, but Matthay never wavered in his insistence that the artist can—and must—influence the instrument's tone quality, an argument which he always sought to support on scientific grounds.

Beginning in March 1891, he became a regular contributor to the *Overture's* "Thoughts and Reflections" column, and his preoccupation with these pieces delayed his final "Chat" until November 1892. When that installment finally appeared, he addressed the topic of effective practicing, and his piece often assumes a surprisingly sardonic tone. In fact, several passages are devoted to what is arguably a superfluous moralizing, even bordering on the cynical: "A day arrives in many a student's life when he discovers he has not yet learnt what real, fully effective practice should be. . . . He has for awhile enjoyed the music, and then got heartily sick and tired of his pieces and studies (techniques he has of course not adopted, for they are 'so uninteresting and unmusical, don't you know') . . . Now it is doubtful whether it is possible to show such a student, whether arrived at this point or not, *what* real practice is; but a hint or two may happen to prove of avail."[36]

This excerpt strikes a sharp contrast to the tone of Matthay's later writings, and it may shed some light on his professional attitudes in this time period. There can be little doubt that his students still failed to inspire him consistently, and it appears that the benevolence for which he was later so noted had its limits. That his anger could be aroused when he sensed students (or professionals) were turning away from thoughtful analysis has been well documented elsewhere, but in his earlier days it appears that such behavior may at times have driven him to sarcasm—and even bitterness—a reaction that may have only been mollified when he saw his ideas taking hold with the musical public. And the content of his article offers few, if any, fresh insights. Predictably, he advocates a vigilant analysis of all passages, but—short of the expected caveat to pay attention—he offers little concrete advice to guide the process, so perhaps he felt that he had already sufficiently explained the particulars in previous installments. As always, the goals are lofty, and the executant's mental faculties are meant to direct the entire process of music making: "And the true practiser does not rest satisfied until he feels he is able to give absolute and conscious attention to each and every detail."[37]

His final "Chat" did not mark the end of his *Overture* articles on piano playing, for a mock Socratic dialogue called "Piano and

The Overture . . .

Forte" appeared in the December 1893 issue and, though unsigned, its authorship is unmistakable. Matthay has chosen once again to address the subject of tonal volume, and one can only presume that the fictional conversation he created reflects, at least to an extent, the model to which he aspired when he gave lessons:

> *Professor.* What is it that you do when you intend to play a note louder?
> *Student.* I strike it harder.
> *Professor.* Can you put that in other words? What constitutes the hardness where the finger is the same?
> *Student.* I put more force into the blow.
> *Professor.* And how do you do that? You must *do* something different, you know.
> *Student.* I suppose so, but I can't imagine what. I can't describe putting force into a blow in any other way.
> *Professor.* You haven't described it all: you have merely asserted that you perform the act. Can you tell me at least what happens to the piano? I will first inform you that when a string sounds softly the middle of it vibrates in a small loop; when it sounds strongly it vibrates in a wide loop. You may see that for yourself with a violin string.
> *Student.* Well, the hammer strikes a more or less hard blow, and that makes the difference.
> *Professor.* Does the hammer always weigh the same?
> *Student.* I suppose so—yes, of course it must.
> *Professor.* And it is lifeless and unchangeable in substance?
> *Student.* Yes.
> *Professor.* The same hammer traveling the same distance and hitting the same string must surely produce the same effect always unless some other element enter [sic] into the matter?
> *Student.* Yes, the force of the blow.
> *Professor.* There you go again with your word *"force"!* Have you any notion what you mean by the term?
> *Student.* Of course I know very well, but it is as difficult to define force as to define light, or sound, or electricity.

Professor. Just about. And yet, you know, people measure sound and light and electricity (which you may be surprised to hear, are one and the same thing) so they must be able to translate their expressions into other terms.

Student. I am beyond my depth. I give it up.[38]

Now that the student has been brought face to face with his own ignorance, the teacher explains the laws of tone production by bringing forth the applicable scientific principles. And again, Matthay makes no concession to those who might be resistant to such analysis:

Professor. My good child . . . the term *force* is a generic one for all kinds of movement taken in combination with all kinds of matter. Thus if a grain of shot moves at a certain velocity another of ten times the weight moving at the same speed, or one of the same weight moving at ten times the speed would be said to have ten times the *force* of the first. When you strike a pianoforte wire with increased *force* the wire vibrates in larger loops, as we said. There is a natural law called the "law of isochronous vibration" which compels those loops large or small to be executed in the same space of time, and I hope you will perceive that to perform wide loops in the same time as it made narrow ones the wire will have to move more quickly. This gives us the first link in our chain of reasoning. *The louder the note the quicker the wire moves.* With this hint can you not see what [must] happen to the hammer and the key of the piano?[39]

Matthay's final contribution to *The Overture*—also neither a "Chat" nor a "Reflection"—appeared in the journal's last issue in February 1894. Entitled "Pianoforte Teaching: A Retrospect and Prospect," it offers a brief summary of what he has presented thus far. But more importantly, it serves as a paean to science:

The great advance in the pianoforte teaching of to-day lies in the fact that it has followed the tendency, manifested everywhere else, of discarding antiquated "empiric" methods in favour of scientific and more direct ones. Instead of first trying this way and then that, and thus only perhaps *finally* hitting on the easiest (and maybe only possible) way to success, the tendency now-a-days is to look into "first principles"; to enquire first what is to be done before attempting the doing; to enquire at the outset on what principles the easy doing depends; and, knowing so much, then proceeding to apply in practice what then is a "known quantity."[40]

Interestingly, he gives no hint that he sees himself as a lone pioneer, but rather, he asserts his membership in a growing community of enlightened professionals. One cannot help but draw a parallel between his beliefs and the rhetoric of the Darwinists. For Matthay, piano teaching was "evolving" and, as he calls it, "the higher development of pianoforte teaching"[41]—undoubtedly a veiled, perhaps satirical, reference to Beringer's academy—was an inevitability: "All that is now much changed for the better, anyway with those teachers who aspire to be 'with the times.' Not merely technique, but the means of it, are never lost sight of for a moment. Technique is shown to the student at every point. . . . Indeed, it is the 'higher development of pianoforte playing' that we have here, or, rather, the higher development of pianoforte teaching!" However, he seems quite aware that the renaissance has not yet penetrated to all corners of the profession and that the most progressive teachers are still in the minority: "But in mitigation of this roseate view, it has to be admitted that the great majority of teachers are not as yet, by any means, 'up to date.'. . . For though the best teachers are now fully alive to the necessity of more science, yet the vast majority, both of students and teachers, still utterly fail in this respect."[42]

Matthay began his contributions to the *Overture*'s "Thoughts and Reflections" series by taking over its fifth entry in March 1891. Although he occasionally referenced piano issues in this column, the scope was generally broader—and the tone more evangelical. Here are some excerpts from the March installment:

HABIT! How vast the changes wrought by it, and yet how slight the attention vouchsafed by most of us to this, the most powerful lever in Education! . . .

Truly, education at bottom is nothing but this continuous and unavoidable process either artificially or naturally guided into *useful* channels. Indeed, has not the most evident fact we are aware of—our own *being*—and also the very existence of animal and vegetable life, been probably brought about by this very same, so all powerfully insinuating means? . . .

"The higher the adaptability, the higher the life," is virtually what Herbert Spencer teaches in his "Biology." Like all far-reaching generalisations, this one, also, may be made instructive in small matters.[43]

But, not surprisingly, he still relates his "reflection" to piano study: "Do we not even find it exemplified in Pianism? For the greater the player is, the greater are his powers of adapting himself to any pianoforte he may happen to sit down to. To be more precise, the greater his executive facility, the greater the ease with which the artist can modify his technique."[44] He made similar, seemingly moralistic, pronouncements throughout the series, exemplifying the Victorian trait of conjoining science and virtue. In his third "Reflection" in May, he tackled yet another character trait common to many students: "OBSTINACY! What an ever-present cause of misery to the possessor and his surroundings! What waste of energy, and how pitiful it seems! . . . This quality, which, when *guided by reason* can produce such marvellous results, what is it but 'will' to carry through a thing? . . . Obstinacy, no doubt, is 'will' exerted just unreasonably—the desire to have one's way, not because reason and conscience say it is right so to persist, but merely from a false-pride; a taking *pride* in forcing the fulfilment of one's wishes."[45]

Matthay also occasionally contributed letters to right injustices he felt had been inflicted on his fellow professionals. The plight of the British composer had always been dear to his heart and already in the magazine's second issue in April 1890, he quarreled with an unsigned review that had appeared the previous month. Although the review had been somewhat complimentary, it spoke derisively of composers who specialized in miniature works. H. A. J. Campbell, an Academy graduate, had recently published *Six Songs with German and English Words,* his Opus 5, but with titles such as *Frühlingslied* and *Gute Nacht,* some regarded his efforts as derivative and redundant. Matthay's letter, presented here in part, provides insight into his thinking at the time, as he attempted to reconcile various philosophic, aesthetic, and commercial aspects of the composer's profession:

TO THE EDITOR OF "THE OVERTURE."
SECOND-RATE MUSIC.

SIR,—A set of songs by Mr. H. A. J. Campbell, one of our "old students", was reviewed in the March number of this journal. From the reviewer's words it would appear that the songs are on a level with those of, say, Lassen or Robert Franz—no mean compliment, as a matter of fact; on the other hand, the reviewer seems to assert that it is of no use writing any more vocal music of this calibre.

Now on this point I should venture to disagree with him. Possibly, nay, probably it is true that the German *Lied* of the present day is not a thing that may have a long individual life predicted for it; doubtless only that which is really new abides with us for long—for some centuries or so. There are, however, but few Griegs, Dvořàks, and Brahms [sic]—if your reviewer will permit me to put the latter master's name with the others!—living amongst us at one time. Few are they indeed that possess sufficient power of initiative to strike out a new path for themselves! But, nevertheless, is it then altogether quite useless to write pretty, pleasing, and musicianly little trifles, such as some of the better songs of Lassen are—and as Mr. Campbell's seem to be—even though they perhaps evince but little of that subtle element—"the spirit of originality"?

Surely a thing that gives no particular offence to even the most fastidious ear, and which is about 500 times higher art than the ordinary shop-ballad, must have some intrinsic value, must be not quite "useless"?[46]

Continuing his compositional advocacy, a year later in the April 1891 issue, he offered a series of observations on the training of

Chapter 4

young composers, and Bennett's pedagogical imprint is unmistakable. Matthay speaks with an eloquence that may resonate even today with teachers who struggle with similar problems:

> Amusing it is what a sense of martyrdom many young student-composers labour under, when their professors attempt to restrict them to the rules of harmony as laid down in the various theory-books. Appearing to resent this restraint as a sort of injury and attempt on their personal liberty! . . .
>
> Obviously enough, this whole tendency of mind is, however, an utter mistake. It simply shows non-comprehension of the object of harmony lessons and of harmony "rules." That the spirited student could only be brought to see that rules have NOT been framed for his particular restraint and annoyance, but, on the contrary, just for his particular assistance! That harmony rules are but the RULES OF GOOD TASTE, as discovered by the GREAT MASTERS thus far, and formulated into the musical etiquette of the day, but to save future incipient "masters" the laborious process of re-discovering them![47]

Occasionally, he left the realms of piano and composition, as when in the April 1891 issue he mused over the state of contemporary singing. No doubt his views were shared by at least some of his RAM colleagues, but his tone is surprisingly caustic, and one wonders at the circumstances which provoked him to attack an entire category of students and—by extension—their teachers:

> We have been asked why we do not give any "thoughts and reflections" for VOCALISTS. Surely the reason is obvious enough. Vocalists, as a rule, require none, for they manifestly never do think or reflect! Else, how could they sing the twaddle they do with such zest, and then vocalize through beautiful music without the slightest sign of comprehension; and allow the only reflections they appear to indulge in, to relate but to the beauty of their voices, the perfection of their own particular system of voice-production, and the utter wrongness of every other "method" in the world! . . .

> Certainly, there are some vocalists and vocal students who are, and who strive to be, ARTISTS. And the number of these increases daily, owing to better training, and to a tendency being abroad for the public to select rather artistic performances than mere "voice"—a hopeful sign indeed!
>
> But perhaps, after all, the typical vocalist is but the type of humanity at large! Deplorably limited indeed is the number of those who humbly—and maybe uselessly, unably, and inexpertly enough—do yet try, though groping in the dark, to do more than merely VEGETATE![48]

With similar candor, the following November he contributed a letter published under the title "Charity Concerts *versus* The Profession." It serves as evidence of his strongly profit-oriented stance in professional endeavors, but it offers arguments on the grounds of principle, rather than immediate, pecuniary concerns. By the late nineteenth century, the British "charity" concert, which had long been associated with children's church choirs, had expanded to more secular realms. It is clear that nothing could arouse Matthay's indignation more quickly than proposals or movements which threatened the commercial stability of his colleagues, and by the century's final decade the line between professional and amateur was often being blurred in the name of philanthropy. For example, on 30 June 1890, *The Times* advertised a "Grand Welsh Charity Concert" to benefit the families of the 87 men who had died on 10 March in the Morfa colliery explosion in Glamorgan, Wales. Overseen by Clara Novello Davies, the program combined the talents of noted organist Edmund Turpin with several amateurs and a one-hundred-voice "Welsh Ladies Choir."[49] A year later, the "South Kensington Ladies' Choir" gave a "Charity Concert" in Prince's Hall, headlined by soprano Liza Lehmann and violinist Joseph Ludwig.[50] Matthay felt he could no longer remain silent:

> The universal cry is that Concerts are "paying" less and less, and that singers' and instrumentalists' fees are dwindling slowly, but only too surely. . . .

Artists fancy they are doing "good work" by *giving* their services in these cases; apparently they do not yet perceive what an evil thing they are doing to their profession, to their brethren, to themselves, and even in the end to Art itself!

Let every artist therefore make it an inflexible rule never to "give" his services, excepting really for the benefit of a brother artist. There are plenty of sufficiently capable amateurs who can supply the Charity Concert platforms. Then, if the Public desires to hear the professionally educated, it will be compelled to patronise the *bona fide* Concert, instead of, as at present, paying for very mixed fare at what may aptly be described as a Charity *dis*-organisation *fête*; which latter contrivance, put into plain words, just means: that the poor struggling musical artist has his slender purse mulcted for only too often quite an unworthy object; that the public are enabled to hear performances at far lower than fair prices; and that two or three nonentities have their names for a time brought forward as shining benefactors of mankind!

Shall this state of things continue, or will musicians for once use their heads as well as their voices, fingers, and hearts?

TOBIAS A. MATTHAY[51]

In December's issue, he addressed the criticisms stemming from the increasingly acerbic London press which, as will be shown, frequently plagued his appearances as well as those of his students in the coming years. Although it could be argued that he was exaggerating the evils caused by their negativity, his words might strike a chord today with those also in quest of more humane conduct from musical "authorities:"

Even amongst REAL LISTENERS, how great is the difference in their attitude towards the Artist!

There are two very distinct tendencies amongst such, the two extremes being very marked; and what an extreme difference it makes to the performer too! And to the effect of a new work!

The one may be said to *subtract* continually, the other to *add*.

Both listen acutely; but with the first, it is felt he is all the time counting and laying up against the artist every point where failure can be perceived; whereas with the other, it is obvious that he is grateful for each little successful point, and though he, as well as the artist himself, need not be blind to the latter's shortcomings, yet, as he does not store these up, but, on the contrary, it is felt forgives them, and waits for and accepts the *good* things that happen to be done: this one certainly forms the ideal listener. To play to such an one is an unmitigated delight, and the artist is led to play his very best, out of sheer wish to please him. Whereas the other "criticising" species of listener makes "playing" next door to an impossibility. To be aware of one such amongst even a large audience, is quite enough to kill a whole afternoon's performance.[52]

His final contribution to the "Thoughts and Reflections" series, which occurred in July 1892, offered a caveat concerning inferior pianos. One wonders how often the scene he describes—which again parallels many contemporary situations—was played out in the homes of wealthier patrons:

It is astounding what people will put up with in the shape of bad Pianofortes! They spend huge sums on a fine house, and on "keeping up style," and cheerfully pay hundreds for a bit of table or chair—and then grudge the small sum required for the purchase of a really efficient Piano; and instead, have a wooden, leathery, voiceless thing in their drawing-room or boudoir—and then feel a bit surprised and aggrieved, when, on asking a musician to "play" on such a fraud, he refuses to disgrace himself and his Art, and speaks a bit of his mind on the indignity offered him![53]

Some of his *Overture* commentaries are far more theoretical, and a year earlier, the July 1891 installment featured his most technical excursion into science thus far. The topic, which consumes the entire article, is wave motion, and the thorough-going analysis he employs is impressive. In all probability, he was responding to the "substantial" theory of sound offered by an American, A. Wilford

Hall (1819-1902), who had for several years been engaged in a feud with Sedley Taylor (1834-1920), an accomplished musician and a lecturer in acoustics at Cambridge. Taylor, a member of the Musical Association, was acquainted with Matthay since he had also participated in the MacDonald Smith piano apparatus seminar early in 1888. Fifteen years earlier he had written *Sound and music: a nonmathematical treatise on the physical constitution of musical sounds and harmony,* in which he advocated the modern theory of sound wave propagation.[54] Hall proposed instead what he termed a "substantial" theory of sound, or in his words,

> The volume or intensity of sound produced by any sounding body, depends entirely upon the sonorous property of such vibrating body itself, or in other words, upon its inherent quality of liberating this form of force from the fountain of natural energy, and in no sense does it depend upon the air-waves or atmospheric disturbance such vibrating body may send off.[55]

Hall's "theory" offered no explanation at all for the physics of sound, and his attacks on Taylor were supported largely by misconstruing the mathematical formulas offered by scientists, and "proving" them to be absurd. But rather than taking Hall to task, Matthay used the attacks as a point of departure to clarify what was currently understood about the subject—although his preamble leaves little question as to how he viewed Hall's efforts:

> Scientific knowledge means progress towards a less confused apprehension of the things around us. So, when people "REJOICE" that some scientific theory or other seems likely to be overturned, this either means that they rejoice in the victory of ignorance over knowledge, or else, that they know not the real sphere of Science, which certainly is not the sustaining of any particular theory, but the following [of] Truth wheresoever it may lead.
>
> It seems, then, that the "WAVE-THEORY" of sound has lately been called in question. Perhaps it is only one other of those fanatical attacks

The Overture . . .

against accepted facts, such as that one from time to time raised against belief in the rotundity of our globe, by certain half-demented individuals.[56]

Later in the article he begins to write more like a science professor than a music master—so much so that one wonders how eagerly his words were received by their intended audience:

> Perhaps the best way to gain a notion of the manner sound-waves travel, is, first to apprehend the idea that all matter (whether gaseous, liquid, jelly-like, or solid) does consist of ultimate particles, molecules, or atoms (ultimate unsolvables!), which never, so far as we can judge, are in absolute contact, but are, according to their place in the range between gas and "solid," held more or less apart, thus rendering even the hardest solid elastic, and enabling its constituent particles to oscillate, each one on its own account. So that when some of these arc dislodged for a moment through a knock (or other disturbance of equilibrium), these, before resuming their position of comparative repose, do for an instant infringe on the domain of their next-door neighbours, and so these again do then elbow the adjacent ones, and so on, until the motion, having reached those nerve ends in the ear capable of receiving it, and thence transmitted to the animal sensorium, is there changed into that psychological effect we term "sound."[39]
>
> The cause of the difference to the ear between a musical sound and mere noise, lies in the first representing regular vibrations, and the other, irregular waves; and the difference may be likened to the effect produced on the eye by the familiar phenomenon of "retention," *though it is not the corresponding one. . . .* A similar effect is produced on the ear. A regular series of knocks presented to it, at a slow rate, are heard as separate percussions, but when they exceed sixteen per second or thereabouts, and up to about 40,000, they also merge into a continuous sensation, the ear mechanism being so arranged as to allow us to appreciate the difference in vibration number between sixteen and about 88,000 as a difference in pitch.[57]

In "Reflections" XI, which appeared in November's issue, he offers an inkling of the view he later championed: that musical

Chapter 4

interpretation was also a science. Writing for the first time on the subject of rubato, he (sardonically) suggests that contemporary musicians not only fail to understand its components, but he offers evidence that there was then a widespread resistance to its mere presence:

> People are, after all, not so much more advanced now than a couple of centuries ago, when they were so astounded by MOZART'S daring to give the "RUBATO."
>
> We hear the schoolmasters and *soi-disant* critics cry out, howl, and affect to be shocked by a true, real, living performance, such as only can be given by an artist of such pre-eminent genius as a PADEREWSKI. "Talk of *Rubato!* Goodness!" is the ejaculation of such a sanctimoniously-minded "STIGGINS"—in—music! Being possessed of neither any natural nor delicate sense of rhythm, he requires everything to be chopped into mechanically unflinching beats, like the music of a metronome! Yes, undoubtedly it is difficult to "play in time"—but then it is more difficult still to keep in view the bar pulsations with unfailing accuracy of *feeling*, and yet to CURVE around these; to caress the rhythm. Now lagging behind, and anon dancing in advance, and yet ever again infallibly recurring to the persistent under-current of bar rhythm. And that is the higher acquirement or sense.[58]

The Overture also provides a useful record of Matthay's less prominent performances through this period. The March 1890 issue reports that the Excelsior Society gave an extended concert at 12 Granville Place (Bantock's home) on Monday evening, 24 February—a program which was unfortunately "somewhat too long, for there were evident signs of weariness among the listeners." The Society had unwisely chosen to perform on the same day as an afternoon RAM student concert at St. James Hall, and the journal argues that it would be "wiser in future to restrict the music on these evenings to one important work only, with a few instrumental songs and solos in addition." That evening Matthay performed two of Schumann's three Romances, and he appeared with Dora in Grieg's four-hand work *Walzer-Capricen*, Op. 37. Academy student Gerald

Walenn closed the concert performing Matthay's violin miniature "A Pamphlet," to Dora's accompaniment.[59]

Not surprisingly, Dora and Tobias had also remained active in Clapham's musical life, and the March issue reports the activities of the "Clapham Philharmonic Concerts," which were in fact confined to solo, choral, and chamber renderings. The dates are not provided, but the journal indicates that a "Pianoforte and Violoncello Recital" by Matthay and W. E. Whitehouse, an RAM cello professor, had recently occurred at the Clapham Assembly Rooms. They repeated their program on 15 February at the Bow and Bromley Institute, where they performed the Grieg cello Sonata in A minor, Rubinstein's D major Sonata, and Matthay's as yet unpublished Ballade for cello and Piano.[60] On 5 March, Matthay returned to the Clapham Assembly Rooms for a solo program shared by some of his students, who "acquitted themselves in a most creditable manner."[61] On 13 May, he again appeared before the Excelsior Society, this time at 24 St. John's Wood Park, performing an unidentified Liszt Rhapsody—perhaps the second.[62]

The Saturday evening Fortnightly Concerts were a staple of Academy life through this period, and *The Overture* records that Matthay's students were frequent participants. On 30 May 1891, Maude Rihill performed four miniatures by Matthay's pupil Cuthbert Nunn. On 24 October, Lily West again performed the Chopin F minor Fantasy which she had played for Matthay's class the previous June, while Macfarren's (or perhaps Matthay's) pupil George Aitken performed a Chopin Prelude and a Heller Etude. Aitken was also a skilled organist, and on 4 June 1892, he performed a movement from Widor's Fifth Symphony. On the 13 February program, Dora sang a Haydn canzonette, supported at the piano by Lily West, and on the 21 October program, Matthay's pupil Edith Purvis played an Alkan Etude.[63] These concerts were often supplemented by other gatherings that occurred less frequently, such as The Royal Academy Students' Orchestral Concert on 15 June 1891, which—despite its name—seems to have been limited to solo and chamber works. On that program Rihill performed the Chopin G minor Ballade, while

Dora shared the stage with pianist and composer Stanley Hawley to perform the Grieg Romance and Variations, which she also performed the following season with Rihill.[64]

Matthay's pupils were frequently sought by the Bow and Bromley and by the Clapham Philharmonic. In January 1892, Lily West played for the Bow and Bromley, and on 11 February she accompanied Walter Mackway at the Clapham series in songs by Beethoven, Mozart, Handel, and Matthay. On 22 April she appeared again at the Bow and Bromley in a concert devoted to Matthay's pupils, where she was joined by Dora, Ida Betts, and Edith Purvis. The repertoire included the Brahms G minor Rhapsody, the Beethoven "Moonlight" Sonata, the Chopin fourth Scherzo, and some Liszt "Paganini" Etudes. On 21 June, Matthay presented his own studio class at Bechstein Hall "by kind permission of Messrs. Bechstein's [sic],"[65] and on 24 July, his students gave him a "testimonial in the shape of a beautiful dressing case."[66] Such as it was, Bechstein offered its "hall" for another "Practice Concert" on 11 November, and his class again made a pilgrimage to Wigmore Street on 16 March 1893.[67] On the same day, the Academy Directors voted to award the A.R.A.M. (Associate of the Royal Academy of Music—the Academy's mark of special distinction sometimes awarded well after graduation) to Dora, Stanley Hawley, and Cuthbert Nunn.[68] Nunn also gave a concert devoted to his own compositions at the Elliot Rooms in Leytonstone on 29 November 1892, and again the following season on 6 October 1893.[69]

Matthay also remained active as a solo performer, and on 8 January 1892, he appeared at the Lecture Hall in Hawkhurst, Kent, in a program which included Brahms's B minor Rhapsody, Liszt's second Hungarian Rhapsody, works by Schumann, Chopin, Henselt, Beethoven, Raff, Grieg, and Nicodé, and his own recently published *Love Phases*, Op. 12, which he subtitled "Minne-Lieder." Composed two years earlier, these three miniatures (somewhat unusually for Matthay) bear no dedication, and their titles—"Doubt," "Avowal," and "Response!"—suggest the inspiration of a genuine romance. By the time they appeared, he had become enamored with his future wife, and this may have served as a motivation to have them published. His harmonic language is still heavily chromatic, but not exclusively Wagnerian. Bars five and six from "Doubts" are especially striking, echoing—respectively—Mussorgsky and Franck:

Example 4.1 Matthay: "Doubts" from Love Phases, Op. 12, mm. 4-7.

He repeated the program on 12 January at the Town Hall in Kelso, Scotland, with several vocal works. He was assisted by Jessie's older sister, Margaret (Maggie), a soprano, who then served as an Academy sub-professor in harmony.[70] He also repeated the solo portion of the program for the Clapham Philharmonic series on 11 February, and again on 5 March for the Bow and Bromley, where he added Nunn's "Bourée in D." He performed *Love Phases* for the Excelsior Society on 19 July.[71]

Beginning in late 1892, he gave several concerts devoted exclusively to his own compositions. He appeared at the Bow and Bromley on 10 December, Clapham on 15 December, Leytonstone on 19 January, and the RAM on 23 January (See Chapter 5).[72] At these performances he was also assisted by several singers and by his pupil Emily ("May") Christie, who served as accompanist. On 12 June he appeared at Prince's Hall at the invitation of violinist Winifred Robinson, who assembled a string trio to premiere his Quartett in F for Piano and Strings. On the same program Matthay accompanied Robinson in Grieg's third Violin Sonata.[73] His catalogue of published compositions continued to expand through this period, and in March 1893 *The Overture* announced the publication of *Monothemes*, six miniature works for piano, which both the composer and Maude Rihill soon performed in various public settings.

Chapter 4

In November it announced the publication of two additional suites, *Lyrics* and *Scottish Dances*, both discussed in Chapter 5.[74]

The June 1892 issue reports that at the Bow and Bromley concert on 26 March, a Miss Jessie Kennedy "pleased greatly by her sympathetic interpretation of Gounod's 'When all was young.'" The same issue reviews the 4 May concert given by the Farnham Choral Society, and bestows special praise on several of Arthur Thompson's voice pupils: "Miss E. Bradshaw, Miss Jessie Kennedy, and Mr. James Brand—all three having a most unmistakably cordial reception." Actively sought as a soloist, Jessie was soon assisting Tobias in several of his concerts. In a sense, Janet (Jessie) Henderson Kennedy was born to sing. She was the eleventh, and youngest, child of the late David Kennedy—perhaps the most famous of all Scottish folksingers—and her entire family had preceded her in the pursuit of intensive musical studies. She first met Matthay in September 1891—a meeting which soon changed both of their lives.

Notes

1. "Death of Sir George Macfarren," *TT*, 1.Nov. 1887, 9, col. E.
2. Cipriani Potter, born in October 1792, was appointed Principal in 1832 on the dismissal of the Academy's first Principal, William Crotch. He was less than a month away from his fortieth birthday when he assumed office.
3. Sir Alexander Campbell Mackenzie, K.C.V.O., *A Musician's Narrative* (London, 1927), 30-31.
4. Ibid., 158.
5. See "A new departure in the history of English music," editorial in *TT*, 21 July 1885, 9, col. D.
6. Ibid.
7. Ibid.
8. Percy H. Young, *George Grove* (Washington, D. C., 1980), 167. Grove's target had been between £250,000 and £300,000. See Janet Ritterman, "Grove as

First director of the RCM," in Michael McClelland, ed., *George Grove, Music and Victorian Culture*, (London, 2003), 250. Hereafter cited as Ritterman.

9. Letter from Grove to *The Times*, 30 Jan. 1888, 8, col. C. Fox eventually donated £45,000 to underwrite the RCM building, over twice the sum the City had appropriated for the Guildhall building a few years earlier. See Ritterman, 261-63.
10. See Meirion Hughes and Robert Stradling, *The English Musical Renaissance: 1840-1940*, 2nd ed. (Manchester, 2001), 39.
11. FC, 82.
12. Ibid. Of course, it should be mentioned that Mackenzie was still Principal when Corder wrote these words.
13. See Mackenzie, 164.
14. The full title was: *The Overture:. A Monthly Musical Journal for Students and Friends of the Royal Academy of Music*. To coincide with the Academy's calendar, it was published monthly, with the exception of January, August, and September.
15. JHM, 23.
16. Ibid.
17. Robin H. Legge, "The Overture and R.A.M.," The *Daily Telegraph*, 8 July 1922.
18. Tobias A. Matthay, "Chats on Technical Subjects. I.—On Technique," *TO* 1(March 1890):8.
19. Ibid., 9.
20. Ibid. All italics in quoted material are Matthay's.
21. Ibid.
22. Tobias A. Matthay, "Chats on Technical Subjects. II.—Pianoforte Tone Production," *TO* 1(April 1890):26.
23. Ibid.
24. Ibid.
25. Ibid. 26-27.
26. Ibid. 27.
27. Tobias A. Matthay, "Chats on Technical Subjects. III.—Pianoforte Tone Production," *TO* 1(May 1890):44.
28. Ibid. See also Tobias Matthay, "Additional Note No. XI: Useful *Versus* Useless Anatomy Teaching," in *VIPT*, 156 ff.

29. Ibid. See Tobias Matthay, *The Act of Touch in all its Diversity: An Analysis and Synthesis of Pianoforte Tone-Production* (London: Longmans, Green, and Co., 1903). Hereafter cited as *AOT*. In a section dealing with Key-Contact (128), he goes out of his way to stress that the fingers need not be lifted above the keys: "On the other hand, contact with the key *need not be deferred until the last moment*. On the contrary, it may be accomplished sometime before the key is due to be provoked into movement. In quick, light passages, several fingers may indeed be thus ready beforehand. In fact it is in this way that that 'general judgment' of the key-board (rather than of its distinctive units) is brought about which forms the distinctive mode of applying the Resistance-sense in rapid passages, as already indicated in the last chapter."
30. Tobias A. Matthay, "Chats on Technical Subjects. IV.—Pianoforte Tone Production," *TO* 1(June 1890):58.
31. Ibid., 59.
32. Ibid.
33. Tobias A. Matthay, "Chats on Technical Subjects. V.—Pianoforte Tone Production," *TO* 1(July 1890):74.
34. Ibid., 74-75.
35. See Hermann L. F. Helmholtz, M. D., *The Sensations of Tone*, 3rd ed., trans. Alexander J. Ellis (London: Longmans, Green, 1895), 74 ff.
36. Ibid.
37. Ibid., 107.
38. "Piano and Forte," *TO* 4(December 1893):128-29. Over twenty years later, Matthay employed a similar, Socratic style of prose in his "On Method in Teaching," (London: 1921), which was actually the final installment in his *Six Lectures on Psychology*. See Ch. 8.
39. Ibid.
40. Tobias A. Matthay, "Pianoforte Teaching: A Retrospect and Prospect," *TO* 4(February 1894):141.
41. Ibid.
42. Ibid., 141-42.
43. T[obias] A. M[atthay], "Thoughts and Reflections by T. A. M.: V.," *TO* 2(March 1891):5.
44. Ibid.

The Overture . . .

45. T[obias] A. M[atthay], "Thoughts and Reflections by T. A. M.: VII.," *TO* 2(May 1891):42.
46. Tobias A. Matthay, "Correspondence [to the Editor]," *TO* 1(April 1890):31.
47. T[obias] A. M[atthay], "Thoughts and Reflections by T. A. M.: VI.," *TO* 2(April 1891):23.
48. Ibid., 24.
49. *TT*, 30 June 1890, 1, col. C.
50. *TT*, 11.May 1891, 1, col. D.
51. Tobias A. Matthay, "Charity Concerts *versus* The Profession," *TO* 1(November 1890):110.
52. T[obias] A. M[atthay], "Thoughts and Reflections by T. A. M.: XII.," *TO* 2(December1891):122.
53. T[obias] A. M[atthay], "Thoughts and Reflections by T. A. M.: XVI.," *TO* 3(July 1892):77.
54. Sedley Taylor, *Sound and music: a non-mathematical treatise on the physical constitution of musical sounds and harmony, including the chief acoustical discoveries of Professor Helmholtz* (London: Macmillan, 1873).
55. A. Wilford Hall and Sedley Taylor, *The "Substantial" and "Wave" Theories of Sound: Two Letters* (London: Macmillan, 1891), 12.
56. T[obias] A. M[atthay], "Thoughts and Reflections by T. A. M.: X.," *TO* 2(October1891):85.
57. Ibid.
58. Ibid.,123.
59. "The Excelsior Society," *TO* 1(March 1890):12.
60. Ibid.
61. Ibid., 13.
62. "The Excelsior Society," *TO* 1(June 1890):63. Matthay performed the second Liszt Rhapsody frequently during this period, including a performance in Kent on 8 January 1892.
63. "Fortnightly Concerts," *TO* 4(March 1893):15, and "Fortnightly Concerts," *TO* 4(November 1893):117.
64. "What our Old Students are doing," *TO* 2(July1891):78-79. Stanley Hawley appears to have specialized in accompaniment through this period. For example, at the Fortnightly Concerts of April 26, 1890, he was partnered

with six different singers and instrumentalists. See "Fortnightly Concerts," *TO* 1(May 1890):45-46.

65. "What our Old Students are doing," *TO* 2(July1892):80.
66. "What our Old Students are doing," *TO* 2(October 1892):99.
67. "What our Old Students are doing," *TO* 2(December 1892):132, and "What our Old Students are doing," *TO* 3(April 1893):31.
68. Ibid.
69. "What our Old Students are doing," *TO* 3(December 1892):132, and "What our Old Students are doing," *TO* 4(March 1893):116.
70. "What our Old Students are doing," *TO* 2(February 1892):148.
71. "What our Old Students are doing," *TO* 3(December 1892):132, and "What our Old Students are doing," *TO* 4(March 1893):116.
72. "What our Old Students are doing," *TO* 3(February 1893):146.
73. "What our Old Students are doing," *TO* 4(July1893):79.
74. "What our Old Students are doing," *TO* 4(March 1893):15, and "What our Old Students are doing," *TO* 4(November 1893):116.

CHAPTER 5

. . . SCOTTISH INTERLUDE . . .

The Register of the Royal Academy of Music records that Jessie Henderson Kennedy, of 5 Mayfield Road, Edinburgh, matriculated in the winter of 1891, her fees guaranteed by her mother, Mrs. E[lizabeth] Kennedy. Her London address is given as 28 St. Marks Crescent in Regent's Park, but she remained enrolled only through the Michaelmas term of 1892. After nearly a four-year hiatus, she returned to complete her studies in the fall of 1896, earning her RAM Certificate on 11 January 1898 and receiving her A.R.A.M. on 22 March 1899.[1] Her absence was not unplanned, since by then she was married, and the Register records her married name as Jessie Henderson Kennedy Matthay. Matthay later wrote that she was "my inspiration, my helper and advisor in everything . . . and I ascribe to her all the success I have achieved."[2] But whatever debt he may have owed to Jessie, his life was also enriched by contact with her many siblings, who helped script a family saga like none other in British musical history.

Jessie's father, David, was born in Perth, Scotland, on 15 April 1825, the only son of a weaver. His father also gave singing lessons, served as precentor to thousands of parishioners, and took his theoretical studies so seriously that the townspeople nicknamed him "Auld Supertonic."[3] He taught his son so well that by the time David was 20 he had assumed the role of precentor at South Street Church.[4] He was also developing a yearning to follow in the footsteps of John Wilson (1800-49), by singing the "songs of Scotland to the exiled Scots scattered throughout the world."[5] Born in Edinburgh, Wilson, an accomplished tenor trained in the *bel canto* tradition, had enjoyed spectacular success in America in both opera and Scottish folksong, and in 1842 he even published a collection of tunes which no doubt served as inspiration to young Kennedy. But David married young

Chapter 5

and while he was still in his twenties, his wife, Helen Henderson Kennedy, succumbed to a fatal illness, leaving him a widower with three children. By the time he was 32, he was remarried to Elizabeth Fraser, with whom he soon had two children, and the seven of them eventually relocated to Edinburgh.[6] He was so determined to realize his dream that he burned all of his bridges, leaving a "prosperous" business in Perth to establish himself as a singing teacher, while frequently traveling to London to pursue intensive training with Michael Costa. Since by then, Costa's eminence left him little need of teaching unpromising pupils, one can infer that he regarded Kennedy's talents as exceptional. Predictably, when Kennedy confided his dream to his teacher, Costa told him that if he really intended to devote his vocal gifts to Scottish folksong, he was "a fool."[7]

His first important appearance was in 1859 at the Liverpool centenary celebration for Robert Burns. His rich tenor voice was so warmly received that he was soon encouraged to present a series of recitals in Edinburgh, touring Scotland extensively in the summer of 1860, and the Orkney Islands in 1861. On 23 September 1862, he performed his first London recital at the newly renovated Queen's Concert Rooms in Hanover Square, inaugurating a long-standing collaboration with pianist Edward Land, who had frequently served as Wilson's pianist-conductor. The concert proved so successful that they had to repeat it three times in London and again on 10 October at the Brighton Pavilion. Their *Times* advertisements listed some of their selections:

> SONGS of SCOTLAND.—Mr. KENNEDY will, at the Hanover-Square-Rooms, THIS EVENING, and at the Pavilion, Brighton, on Friday, SING the new song, Gentle Bessie; composed expressly for him by Mr. Land, and which was so favorably received on Thursday last.
>
> SONGS of SCOTLAND.—Hanover-Square-Rooms.—TO-NIGHT (Thursday). Oct. 9th. Fourth and Last Night. Mr. KENNEDY will SING "Highland Mary," "Scots wha hae," "Waes me for Prince Charlie," "Hame cam our guid man," &c.; and give Selections from the "Gentle Shepherd." Commence at 8. Pianoforte, Mr. Land.[8]

. . . Scottish Interlude . . .

By now he had moved his family to London and on 22 December, while undertaking further study with Costa, he and Land began a short series of appearances seven times a week at the Dudley Gallery in Egyptian Hall, an elegant facility overseen by the Lord Mayor and frequently used for more popular forms of entertainment. The press was overwhelmingly positive, and although it denied that Kennedy's voice was equal to Wilson's, in a review of nearly a thousand words, *The Times* proclaimed him as "Scotch to the backbone:"

> Since John Wilson, indeed, no entertainer of the monologue class, more eminently, more exclusively "Scotch," has appeared before a London audience. Without the voice and without the vocal proficiency of his renowned prototype (who, it must not be forgotten, had the advantage of more than a quarter of a century's experience of public life, on the stage and elsewhere . . .), Mr. Kennedy so nearly approaches him as a characteristic delineator of Scottish poetry and Scottish song, that he may be fairly styled John (or "Jock") Wilson's legitimate successor.[9]

Acknowledging him as a raconteur as well as a singer, the *Daily Telegraph* observed that Kennedy could "cause tears to trickle down those cheeks that a few minutes before were bulged out in boisterous glee," while *The Times* was especially taken with his *Noctes Ambosianae*, in which he acted out the parts of various characters.[10] On 31 December, the paper praised him as "one of the most recent novelties of the year,"[11] and the following season he gave over 100 recitals throughout the city and neighboring countryside.[12] By 1866, the War Between the States was over, and he decided it was time to try his luck in America. Since Land wanted no part of an extended overseas journey, Kennedy was forced to replace him with his eldest daughter, Helen. Though she was still in her teens when the tour began, she acquitted herself admirably, her father showing the same patience and enlightened guidance that he displayed toward all his children. There were now nine Kennedy offspring, and Elizabeth left the four youngest girls with her mother in Perth while the rest of the family embarked on a North American adventure which proved

Chapter 5

so successful that they remained abroad for four years.[13] David also endeared himself to audiences in more traditional repertoire, both in Canada and in the States. On numerous occasions he was asked to sing "The Star-Spangled Banner" for appreciative Americans— once before several thousand at the opening of the Union Pacific Railroad in San Francisco—and twice he performed *Messiah* tenor arias for the Toronto Choral Society.[14] The extended journey also saw the addition of two more Kennedys, when John (Jack) was born in 1867, and Janet (Jessie), the youngest, began life in Detroit on 30 December 1868.[15]

When their American tour had been in progress for about a year, Elizabeth returned briefly to Perth and removed her four daughters to Edinburgh, where Marjory, the eldest of the group, began her musical studies with a local piano teacher. Inasmuch as he occasionally "read his *Scotsman* while I careened through my sonata," she remarked years later that her learning owed more to luck than to "gude guidance." But he did expose her to worthwhile music, and he provided a strong enough theoretical background that "I got over the measles of dominant sevenths, &c., before I was ten." After her father returned home, he actively groomed her to assist Helen with the accompaniment duties, working with her for at least an hour daily. On 14 February 1870, at the age of twelve, she made her concert debut with him at Lanark, and by summer he thought she was ready for an extended tour of the northern coast. He could be understanding, but he was a demanding taskmaster. As Marjory later remarked: "He chaffingly told me then that he was prepared to accompany *me* for the first month, but that after that he would expect me to accompany *him*."[16]

A year later, when Kennedy discovered that his eldest son, twenty-two-year-old David, had a fine tenor voice, he began vocalizing with him regularly, and he soon followed suit with several of his younger children. He observed that Helen, 17, was a lyric soprano, James, 16, was becoming an arresting baritone, and Marjory, a mere 13, was holding her own as contralto. The quartet made its first appearance at Edinburgh's Music Hall in the fall of 1871, and continued

. . . Scottish Interlude . . .

concertising as a group for the next eight years. As time passed, they gradually assumed more of their father's repertoire, thereby lessening the performance demands on him.

By 1872, David Kennedy was arguably the most famous folksinger in Britain, and the time now seemed ripe for the family's first world tour. On 6 March, with Elizabeth and the newly formed quartet, he boarded a clipper in Glasgow, and they spent three months at sea before finally docking at Melbourne on 18 June. There for another three months, they sang six nights a week and before they left the city they were fêted with a farewell ceremony rivaling those reserved for heads of state. Then they began an eighteen-month trek through the bush country—complete with dust storms and highwaymen—riding horses and ponies at daily stretches of 50 miles or more. They survived locusts, hailstorms, and poisonous snakes. They sang in barns, huts, and aborigine villages, and spent six weeks traversing the 500 miles between Melbourne and Sydney, where Robert joined them from Canada to make a party of seven. They traveled to Tasmania and then to New Zealand, where they lived among the Maori. They crossed the 750-foot chasm of the Manawatu Gorge before any bridge had been built, "launched out over the abyss and perilously jerked across" by a crude pulley mechanism some 200 feet above the river.[17] When they finally sailed from Sydney toward California, they were nearly lost at sea, tossed about by a week-long storm which "washed the boats adrift—broke into the captain's cabin," and "tore the door off its hinges," before it "plunged with a great smash through the skylight of the saloon."[18] Through the summer of 1875 they toured the States, and by autumn they had reached Canada, "once again under our own flag."[19] During a wintry Ontario "white night," at temperatures of minus 20 degrees Fahrenheit, they traveled the 22 miles from Listowel to Wingham in two open sleighs, before finally sailing home from Halifax in June of 1876.

The Kennedys had toured with a two-hour program titled "Twa Hours at Hame," featuring "standard Scottish songs, humorous stories, five-part harmonized Scottish airs, English glees, madrigals, &c." The following March they offered the same presentation in

Edinburgh "before a large and sympathetic audience," and beginning on 24 September they gave 12 additional concerts—four per week with a "change of programme each evening"—at St. James's Hall in London. In the advertisements they placed in *The Times*, David saw to it that his children were always billed and, for example, on 20 September their extensive notice indicated that he was to be joined by: "Miss Helen Kennedy, soprano; Miss Marjory Kennedy, contralto; Mr. David Kennedy, tenor; Mr. Robert Kennedy, tenor," and "Mr. James Kennedy, baritone."[20] Concerts were at 8 pm on Mondays, Wednesdays, Fridays, and Saturdays for three shillings, two shillings, and one shilling, and for an extra 2s, 6d they offered a travelogue recounting their adventures abroad:

> TWA HOURS at HAME.—Under this distinctive and appropriate title Mr. KENNEDY and FAMILY have given their entertainments on the SONGS of SCOTLAND, in Australia, Tasmania, New Zealand, California, Utah, Canada, and Newfoundland; and the Narrative of the Four Years' Tour Round the World may be had (price 2s. 6d.) at the Great St. James-hall, every Monday, Wednesday, Friday, and Saturday.[21]

For the next several years the family confined their tours mostly to Scotland, but there was nothing provincial about the youngsters' outlook, whether in the sphere of music or politics. Jessie reported many fond memories of the entire clan seated around the dinner table passionately debating the merits of Irish home rule or Gladstone's latest speech. They discussed the "revelation" wrought by Richter's conducting, and later—as David was also a fervent Wagnerite—the "miracle" of the performances he heard at Covent Garden.[17] Their library was filled with musical classics and, despite their growing fame, David insisted they all undertake further training. By February of 1879 Robert and James were in Milan studying with Francesco Lamperti, one of the acknowledged masters of *bel canto*, and their thorough-going musicianship stood them in good stead since they were soon chosen over several native Italians to appear as Edgardo and Enrico in a Brescia performance of *Lucia di Lammermoor*.

. . . Scottish Interlude . . .

Some of the Kennedy children were now old enough to pursue separate professional activities, so that spring only three of the siblings journeyed with their parents to South Africa, where the Dutch Boers greatly enjoyed their concerts, "in spite of the foreign language."[22] In the same summer Marjory joined Robert and James in Milan to study with a pupil of Rossini—one Signora Gambardella—who gave her daily instruction lasting for an hour and a half, and Helen soon arrived to follow suit. In October, only ten days after the family had returned from South Africa, Helen sailed for India with her parents, Lizzie, and young David, where they toured until March. After a 713-mile train journey from Lahore to Allahabad lasting 37 hours, they gave their final concert in Calcutta, after which they met Marjory, Robert, and James in Milan. Their father remained in Italy for several months, attending his children's lessons at Lamperti's summer home on Lake Como, and learning "much that proved useful to him during the next six years."[23]

By March of 1881, Kate and Lizzie had also journeyed to Milan to work with Lamperti, but as he was still wintering in Nice, they joined with James to follow him to the French resort, while Robert remained in Milan to pursue more operatic roles.[18] Within a week, Kate, Lizzie, and James had begun a regimen of daily lessons with the Italian master, and were sending home frequent reports on their progress. Kate wrote of her first lesson: "We'll have to keep our wits about us, for old 'Lamp' mumbles. . . . Madame [Lamperti] bangs the piano and you don't know whether your head or your heels are uppermost."[19] But although they all encountered some rough sledding, the general pattern was encouraging, and in a few weeks Lizzie wrote: "At Kate's last lesson Lamperti was mightily pleased. Said she had made quite a *salto* (leap) and called her in Milanese a *brava tosa*."[20] James was also optimistic: "We study with all our mind and soul and each day the road seems clearer."[19] Within several weeks the three Kennedys were blissfully happy in Nice, and Lizzie wrote to Marjory, "I wish you could all be here, Madge. The sky is deep blue, the sun bright, the sea glorious."[21] James echoed the sentiment on Sunday, 20 March: "Weather here divine! Health never better—we

Chapter 5

all feel well and strong and hearty and fresh as paint. Early to rise, &c." They were excited by the musical climate as well, and Lizzie wrote that they went *"au paridis"* when they heard Bianca Donadio in Rossini's *Barbiere* at the Théâtre des Italiens. They resolved to hear her again in *Lucia* on Wednesday, 23 March, and were grateful when they were able to take their seats early. But on that evening, the theater caught fire, and within the next few moments—tragically—they were asphyxiated, trapped by an hysterical audience stampeding for the exits.

Robert was the first Kennedy to hear of the disaster, and he repeatedly wired Nice from Milan in a vain attempt to obtain precise information. Finally, when his sisters' landlady answered that they had never returned from the theater, he cancelled an important Naples engagement and hurried to Nice. By the time news of the fire reached Scotland, the death toll had mounted to 46, and the family waited in agony. Finally, their worst fears were confirmed when Robert cabled: "It must be told—they are all dead." He described the tragic scene with a poignant eloquence:

> Under the budding branches of the trees, encased in rude and cleanly coffins, I found them. . . . Lizzie seems but to sleep and none of them have suffered bodily. There would simply be time for an acute mental pang and then all would be over.[24]

Robert made a decision to have them buried in the English cemetery several miles outside of Nice. The services were held the following Monday and he wrote to his family: "At four o'clock today, I kissed them all for you, Mother, and nailed them down." Then he returned to Edinburgh, forever abandoning an Italian opera career, and in time, rejoining his family on their tours. Marjory later wrote that the sudden loss was "a staggering blow from which our father never recovered," but nonetheless he soon undertook another twelve-month concert tour of North America.

By the summer of 1882 the family had returned home, and Marjory and Helen found themselves in Paris studying with Mathilde

Marchesi, acclaimed by many as the greatest vocal teacher of her generation. Their lessons were often attended by their older brother Charles, now a doctor working in Paris, who held a special interest in the physiology of tone production and found Marchesi's pseudo-scientific approach to be of interest. But she was a difficult woman, and the sisters found her biting sarcasm disparaging. Marjory later noted that "We all believed that she enjoyed her own cruelty," and that her teaching was not "sufficiently analytical to be of lasting value." In fact, "Compared with the . . . teaching of a Matthay, alike in tone-production and in interpretation, it could hardly be called teaching at all."[25] However, Marchesi did awaken in her the latent possibilities of various forms of diction, and when she returned to Scotland she resolved to investigate her maternal grandfather's native tongue: Gaelic. But in the 1880s there were few songs published in Gaelic, and the bias against the language was so pronounced that even those who grew up speaking it often disavowed it. Marjory finally located a woman in Inverness who published a few works, and after much effort, she discovered an elderly man in Grantown-on-Spey who could read the language. She then arranged several songs for a trio consisting of herself, Helen, and Maggie, and to her delight, her father "fell in love with them."[26] With his support, they soon began working regularly with Mary MacKellar, a Gaelic poet who had recently settled in Edinburgh, and late in 1882 a new family tradition was born, as they began adding a few of these songs to their programs.

The following year they were off to Australia, where their first stop was once again Melbourne, and their first order of business was to attend Robert's wedding. Robert, who had become engaged to an Australian woman, proclaimed this to be his last tour with the family, and by prior arrangement, he remained with them only through the New Zealand segment. He then settled permanently in Melbourne, where he later forged a successful career as a singer and teacher. On this tour, given their lighter schedule of only three Melbourne concerts a week, the family was able to attend outside musical events, and they were quite taken one afternoon with the daughter of a wealthy Scottish immigrant, a Mrs. Armstrong, who was introduced to them as an "amateur singer." She sang only a few selections, but on leaving the hall, Marjory remarked to Helen, "If that is an amateur, then all the professionals may hide their heads."[27] A few years later, after she too had studied with Marchesi in Paris, Mrs. Armstrong was reincarnated on the world's opera stages as Nellie Melba.

The Kennedys found Australia much modernized since their previous visit ten years earlier, but such was not the case with New Zealand. Although they were no longer required to ride horses, their coach imprisoned them on twelve-hour journeys over nearly impassable roads, as they limped their way through primeval forests. They finally emerged in the Hot-Lake District, where the Maori again tended to their needs, but where the ground was heating up intolerably. Marjory later wrote: "It seemed the pathway to Hades—the whole but a section of the infernal regions broken loose. Sulphur fumes, terrific intermittent geysers, rumbled in the bowels of the earth, as if to give warning of their upward thrust." After awaiting the passage of some earthquake tremors, they crossed the torrid lakes by canoe, while the girls sang Gaelic trios to the Maori boatmen. Wherever they appeared, whether primitive village or industrialized city, they were venerated, and this tour proved every bit as successful as their first. But when they returned home, Robert's absence created a practical problem, since he had been serving as the group's business manager for the last several years, and none of the older boys were any longer singing with the group. David Kennedy finally had little choice but to allow Marjory to assume those duties—reluctantly— since as she later wrote, "girls had not then invaded business premises." She remembered, "There was some slight flutter in newspaper and printing offices and occasionally a look of dazed surprise when M. Kennedy, Esq. (a young girl) appeared to settle the accounts."[28]

In March 1886, the Kennedys appeared in London at St. James's Hall, and David used the occasion to introduce his youngest daughter, Jessie, then 17. Their appearances were designed to precede their farewell American tour, and they performed three times within a two-week span. Their first program on 9 March, devoted exclusively to Scottish folksong, was promoted extensively in *The Times*, which listed the titles of their selections. Jessie, Helen, and Marjory even played piano duets:

> KENNEDY'S SONGS OF SCOTLAND, St. James's-hall (last appearance prior to farewell tour in America). Mr. Kennedy will be assisted by his daughters, Miss Helen Kennedy, Miss Marjory Kennedy, Miss Maggie Kennedy, Miss Jessie Kennedy, To-morrow, March 9, Twa hours at hame; Thursday next, March 11; The Jacobites; Tuesday, March 16, Burns; commencing at 8. Tickets, 5s., 3s., 2s., 1s., at Austin's office, St James's-hall.
>
> KENNEDY'S SONGS OF SCOTLAND, St James's-hall.— PROGRAMME for To-morrow, March 9—Twa hours at hame, O sing to me the old Scotch Sangs, The Banks of Loch Lommond, There's nae luck about the house, Gaelic trios, Fear a Bhata (the boatman), Mo Nigbean donn Bholdheach (the nut-brown maiden), Caller Herrin, The land o' the leal, The auld man's mare's dead, Willie's gane to Melville Castle, Scots, wha hae wi Wallace bled, Pianoforte duet, Scottish airs, Roy's wife o' Alldivaloeb, Jenny Nettles, Bonnie Laddie, Bonnie Dundee, the Misses Helen and Marjory Kennedy; Mr. Kennedy will recite Burns' [sic] address to the mouse; Burns' address to the haggis. Quartet, the broom o' the Cowdenknowes, the Misses Kennedy; This is no' my plaid, Get up and bar the door o', Annie's Tryste. Pianoforte duet, Scottish airs, The haughs of Cromdale, Ye spires o' Banff, The bonnie hoose of Airlie, The barren rocks of Aden, the Misses Jessie and Marjory Kennedy.; Song, with chorus, The Scottish blue bells; The laird o' Cockpen. Gaelic trio, Mo run geal dileas (My faithful dear one), the Misses Kennedy. Finale, Auld lang syne.[29]

Marjory later wrote that when David proclaimed Jessie as "not only the latest but the last of the Kennedys," the enormous audience received her so enthusiastically that "she might well have been embarrassed by the unceasing roll of applause."[30] Her debut was so auspicious that he decided at once to include her on his farewell tour, scheduled to begin in the early summer. But since the Nice tragedy, the family had noticed a downward pattern in David's health and wellbeing, and they expressed reservations about his undertaking another strenuous overseas tour. However, they relented when he insisted that the work was therapeutic, and plans were finally laid for the new quartet—Helen, Marjory, Maggie, and Jessie—to accompany their parents on the voyage to Halifax. After they arrived, they continued on to Quebec, Montreal, and Toronto, plotting a steady course to British Columbia. But David soon developed Canadian cholera, making him progressively weaker, and his refusal to miss any of his scheduled appearances only exacerbated his condition. By autumn he was seriously ill, and on the evening of 5 October in Stratford, Ontario, he was unable to leave his bed for a performance—forcing the family to carry on without him. A week later, he was dead.

Marjory recounted the moving story of his final hours, as her mother and sisters gathered round his bedside and sang two verses of his favorite hymn:

The sands of time are sinking;
The dawn of heaven breaks;
The summer morn I've sighed for;
The air, sweet morn awakes.[31]

He was too ill to sing with them but he understood perfectly and he mouthed the words silently. He did not achieve his dream of dying in Scotland, and ironically, like John Wilson—who had sailed the ocean to sing the songs of Scotland—he also passed in Canada. But as Marjory later confirmed, the family was gratified by the warmth and sincerity of David's Canadian admirers: "He did not die a stranger in a strange land. He was a man who loved much and was loved in return. There were men there who had known him in boyhood and others who were friends of his manhood, and all proved most true friends."[32] He was embalmed in Stratford and transported to the station by a funeral wagon "followed by hundreds of the citizens."[33] The family carried his remains back to Edinburgh and buried him "where he had wished to rest, by a quiet wall in the Grange

... Scottish Interlude ...

Cemetery."[34] But although his passing was peaceful, neither Marjory nor her siblings could ever quite rid themselves of the notion that the real cause of death had been the unspeakable catastrophe which occurred in Nice five years earlier.

At the time of Kennedy's passing, all of his children had reached adulthood, and there was little chance of continuing the public concerts. Helen was engaged to a Scotsman who was settling in Nova Scotia, and Marjory was planning marriage as well, so the two most experienced members of the group were soon to be separated by an ocean and by discrete family responsibilities. Their last performance took place that autumn in the Edinburgh Music Hall to commemorate a stone memorial to be erected in their father's honor, and after that, the singing Kennedys fell silent. Marjory devoted the winter to penning her father's biography under the title *David Kennedy, the Scots Singer*, and in the spring of 1887, she married her mother's cousin, Alexander (Alec) Fraser, a brilliant mathematician. They soon had two children: a son, David, and a daughter, Patuffa (a name Marjory always insisted had Milanese, rather than Gaelic, roots). After a few years, Alec was appointed headmaster of Alan Glen's Technical School in Glasgow, but he soon developed respiratory ailments and was advised to relocate briefly to South Africa in search of drier air. The hiatus seemed helpful, but after they returned to Glasgow, his health problems recurred, and in November 1890, while preparing to return south, he died of pneumonia in the Kennedy home at the age of 33.[35]

Now at 32, Marjory was a widow with two children to support. Using the name Marjory Kennedy-Fraser, she turned to piano and voice teaching in her mother's home, where she became even closer to her two younger sisters, Margaret (Maggie) and Jessie. Both girls were no less serious about their musical careers, and Maggie was soon to complete her vocal studies at the RAM. The Nice tragedy had still loomed too ominously for Elizabeth to sanction more Continental study for her daughters, so she insisted that Maggie and Jessie pursue their training in London. At the time, the Academy seemed a propitious haven for Scottish students,

Chapter 5

since Alexander Mackenzie, now its Principal, was making special overtures to his countrymen, wooing young Scots with accolades such as "they have brains."[36] The Academy proved a good fit for Maggie, and she spent over three years there, eventually serving as a sub-professor of harmony, and even receiving the A.R.A.M. However, her highest praise was reserved not for her vocal training, but for a piano teacher with whom she had never studied: Tobias Matthay.[37]

Through 1890, Jessie could hardly contain her excitement as she contemplated journeying to London to follow her professional dreams. At 21, she was older than most of the entering students, but the family's financial circumstances required her to wait until Maggie's studies were complete so that her mother could comfortably underwrite her expenses. In the meantime, Jessie pumped her older sister relentlessly to obtain the lay of the land on Tenterden Street. As a Kennedy, she was being strongly encouraged to pursue voice as her primary study, but she seemed to vacillate daily: at times she thought she might study composition (she was determined to work with Corder), and she also had not ruled out piano as her primary focus—although she was resolved to have a teacher far more prominent than this "Matthay" her sister kept promoting. Maggie's persistence only intensified Jessie's antagonism, and at one point she even quipped that "Tobias" was "too Biblical" a name to engender modern, effective instruction.[38]

When she finally arrived in London in January of 1891, she had just turned 22, but she still had not yet narrowed her professional focus. With the recklessness of youth, she resolved to pursue voice, piano, and composition with equal commitment. She played for Beringer and was thrilled when he accepted her. The intoxication of discovering that Kate Goodson was his star pupil almost muted the realization that Maude Rihill, considered by most to be Kate's equal, came from Matthay's studio. She was delighted when Corder took her as a composition student and, as Curator, also served as her mentor/advisor. She also managed a spot in the class of Arthur Thompson, one of the finest vocal professors at the Academy, but they were all demanding taskmasters, and her multiple obligations soon made untenable demands on her time and energy. Her first six months at the RAM were a humbling, dizzying experience which took its toll on her mental and physical health. When she returned to Edinburgh in July, she was so ill that she hoarsely confessed that she "had no voice left to sing with," and a family conclave was convened to assess the damages. She finally gave in to their suggestion that she concentrate on voice, because she began to realize how much it meant to her, and as she later wrote, "the eleven Kennedys just had to be singers!"[39] But if piano were to become only her "second study," she would have to leave Beringer, and Maggie again stressed that Matthay was a better choice. But Jessie now resisted for an entirely different reason, for at close range she had observed that Matthay was far from the marginal presence she had imagined him to be. In fact, as a teacher, he was clearly Beringer's equal, and singers rarely, if ever, were assigned to his studio. Six months earlier, Matthay's name had evoked condescension; now it provoked intimidation.

Knowing that Corder and Matthay were close, Maggie urged Jessie to capitalize on their friendship by arriving a few days early in the fall to convince her mentor to intercede on her behalf. To Jessie's relief, Corder agreed, but Matthay had become increasingly ambitious, and by then his career path was clearly rising. Corder later reported that when he finally broached the subject, he had to endure Matthay's "thunderous refusal" to accept another "second study." He only relented when his friend stressed the young woman's talent and unique family background, and he finally agreed to an audition, but nothing more. That afternoon, Jessie was grateful when Corder provided moral support by leading her through the hallways, because her nerves had begun to fray: "Matthay's room was in a remote part of the old R.A.M. building in Tenterden Street, and many were the ups and downs in the long and narrow passages before it could be reached. There was plenty of time for all courage to ooze out from finger tips and toes before the ordeal had to be faced." But as soon as she entered his studio, all apprehension

Chapter 5

vanished. She described a "kindly though tired pair of eyes" looking at her through gold-rimmed spectacles. He drew the Schumann G minor Sonata from a pile of music and, after some discussion, she sauntered through the first movement. Years later, she recalled the dialogue that followed:

"Now what was there to be alarmed about? You're very musical."
"Yes, but I am *so* slow."
"But what does it matter if you feel the music? Lots of quick people never feel the music at all. That's all right."[40]

He accepted her as a pupil and their relationship soon broadened to more personal dimensions. Jessie provides few details concerning their courtship, but it reached a decisive plateau by May, when Tobias completed a song for her entitled "There's nae Lark." His "Sketch Book 14" contains a piano sketch which he dated "May 16th/92[;] Monday night[.] After that thankful Sunday,"[41] suggesting that Jessie accepted his marriage proposal on Sunday, 15 May. The first "Lark" sketch was created the following weekend and appears on the next page with the caption: "This phrase written at 26 St. Marks Crescent May 21st/92"—Jessie's address. Not surprisingly, the song's text is filled with Scottish dialect, but Matthay disregarded the authentic poetry of his fiancée's heritage to set two brief stanzas from Algernon Swinburne's *The Sisters*, a short tragedy in blank verse which had just been published. The poem, copied in Jessie's hand, is taped to page 57 of the Sketch Book, so it seems likely that she suggested it. It is also irresistibly romantic to speculate that she was drawn to Swinburne's verses because they embraced the sincerity of her own sentiments. Those sentiments are scarcely deep, but no doubt she rendered the poetic brogue with a *panache* that few English singers could have matched:

There's nae lark loves the lift, my dear,
There's nae ship loves the sea,
There's nae bee loves the heather-bell

. . . Scottish Interlude . . .

That loves as I love thee, my dear,
That loves as I love thee.

The whin shines fair upon the fell,
The blithe broom on the lea,
The muir-side wind is merry at heart,
It's a' for love of thee, my dear,
It's a' for love of thee.[42]

Marjory gives no suggestion of Jessie's vocal range, and although the B-flat version of "Lark" published in 1908 is best suited to a *mezzo*, it seems likely that 16 years earlier she was still searching for an appropriate vocal classification. Matthay's earliest sketches for the song are in C, and on page 57 of his Sketch Book he wrote "in A[;] best key for contralto." Her comfort with lower pitches seems confirmed by his comment two pages later: "probably a 4th lower (in G) for Jessie." Undoubtedly they discussed range, but for whatever reason, he returned to the key of C when he completed the song in Clapham on 25 May 1892,[43] so perhaps this is the key in which she first sang it. Although an autograph in A also exists, it was probably a later transposition, and Matthay's caption of "May 1892" may merely record the month of composition.[44] Perhaps he considered offering the A major version to Ricordi in 1908, since at some point he scribbled "in a bad key" in red pencil above his C major draft, but precisely why he settled on B-flat is unknown. Although it is also tempting to speculate that Matthay may have issued "Lark" to commemorate his fifteenth wedding anniversary, a surviving memo in his hand indicates that he first planned to include it in a suite of five songs, four of which remain unpublished and have no demonstrable connection to Jessie.[45]

Perhaps Matthay's simple, strophic setting of Swinburne's poem was meant to capture the folk-like atmosphere so associated with the singing Kennedys, and certainly Scottish evocations can be found in the Lombardic rhythms which permeate the vocal and piano lines:

Example 5.1 Matthay: "There's nae Lark," mm. 38-39 (original key C)

However, the song also presents several curiosities, such as his "Agitato" tempo marking, which intrudes a tempestuousness not necessarily suggested by Swinburne's poetry. He evidently wrote the first four bars (the piano introduction is the first sketch to appear in his Sketch Book) before he began to set the text, and one wonders if Jessie had yet submitted the poem to him:

Example 5.2 Matthay: "There's nae Lark," mm 1-4 (original key C)

Exactly where Jessie sang "There's nae Lark" is unknown, but throughout 1892 she occasionally assisted Tobias in some of his performances. She sang with him at the Clapham Philharmonic on 15 December, and again at a concert at the RAM (at which Dora also sang) featuring his own works on 23 January 1893, so perhaps the song was heard by London audiences on those occasions. If so, *The Times* gave it only a lukewarm reception:

> A programme consisting entirely of the compositions of one musician is naturally likely to be to some extent monotonous, and, as

. . . Scottish Interlude . . .

such, Mr. T. A. Matthay's concert on Monday evening must be described. Pianoforte and vocal music were judiciously mixed, and in nearly every instance the former surpassed the latter in musical value. Spontaneity and coherence are lacking in both classes, but in the instrumental numbers a certain brilliancy of execution occasionally atoned in part for other defects. The most important work produced was a set of 17 variations on an original theme in C; other numbers included such fancifully-named compositions as "Mono-themes," "Love phases," and so forth. A set of arrangements of Scottish airs [see below] merely shows a lamentable want of taste, as a good deal was done to rob them of their national characteristics. The concert-giver played his works effectively, and was well received; and Miss Jessie Kennedy, Miss Dora Matthay, and Mr. Walter Mackway sang songs acceptably.[46]

Although the full program is not indicated, Matthay may have withheld his most recent set of piano pieces—also dedicated to Jessie and simply called *Lyrics*—because they were not "brilliant" and he probably intended them for her personal use.[47] The whimsical titles he has given to these seven charming miniatures—"A Presentiment," "Des Mädchens Klage [after Schiller]," "Secret à deux," "Bei gutem humor," "Sing-Song," "Pleading," and "Peace"—suggest a man who has recently fallen in love. For the most part the pianistic demands are modest, and Jessie could have easily managed any difficulties they presented. However, they are often harmonically sophisticated, as suggested for example, by the progressions in his hypnotic ode to Schiller's "Mädchen:"

Example 5.3 Matthay, from Lyrics, Op. 14, "Des Mädchens Klage," mm. 16-19

Chapter 5

On 10 August 1893, Jessie and Tobias were married in Edinburgh. Their Banns were entered in Book 39 of the Clapham Parish Church on 2 July, 9 July, and 16 July respectively, and attested to on 21 July by the Reverend Noel P. Tower.[48] Several days later on 25 July they also entered Banns at the Mayfield Parish Church in Edinburgh, and the marriage was performed there by the Reverend John S. Burton. No doubt their timing enabled Tobias's family to travel more easily to Edinburgh since the summer holidays had temporarily freed his father and Dora from teaching commitments, and the wedding was almost certainly attended by Jessie's mother and her nearby siblings. Jessie reports that almost immediately Tobias and the Kennedy family were drawn to one another, since "he admired their spirit of adventure, and they responded to his grit."[49]

Matthay also loved the Scottish countryside and soon after the wedding, Jessie took him hiking in the Pentland Hills southwest of Edinburgh—along with Dora and Maggie—an excursion which found them unprepared for the difficulties masked by the Pentlands' benign appearance. Their plan was to scale a two-thousand-foot peak, and then descend to the village on the opposite side to board the last train for Edinburgh. But the party was so taken with the beauty of the region that they delayed their climb too long and they lost the sun, forcing the four of them to grope awkwardly down the hill without benefit of road or illumination, in quest of a train "that would wait for no man."[50] Jessie recounts the narrative's finale: "The rest of the tale can be guessed, seeking tracks with lighted matches, stumbling over sleeping sheep, scaling unfriendly walls, and eventually arriving home long after midnight to an anxious family, by means of a leisurely horse and trap. Needless to say, Tobias's respect for Scottish hills became profound."[51]

Matthay was also fascinated with the intellectual climate that Edinburgh University enjoyed each summer through the 1890s, and Jessie cites the presence of Marjory's friends and acquaintances, such as Darwin disciple Sir Patrick Geddes (1854-1932) and literary critic William Sharp (1855-1905), who began to publish a highly successful series of novels in 1892 under the pseudonym Fiona

McCleod. Marjory was first embraced by this community of scholars in 1888 when she and her husband began attending their "Summer Meetings," conclaves devoted primarily to the study of biology and sociology, but which included evening *ceilidhs*, "as the Gaels would have called them—social and musical gatherings that followed each day's work."[52] Soon after Alec's death, the group began to engage Marjory professionally, and for the next decade her annual lecture-recitals became an integral part of their programs. She enhanced the cultural atmosphere by introducing them to the songs of Grieg, Tchaikovsky, and Hugo Wolf, as well as a wide variety of European folk music. For the next several years, the Matthays spent their Augusts in Edinburgh, and one summer Marjory and Jessie even collaborated on a series featuring the Celtic music of Brittany.[53]

Matthay also played for the group, at some point performing the four *Scottish Dances and Melodies* he had completed in January of 1893 with "true Lisztian skill and fervour."[54] But although Jessie speaks of them positively, Matthay reports that their first performance was received with near hostility by the Scots for whom they were intended. Some 35 years later, he recalled that their inspiration occurred to him while he was still engaged, after he had given two recitals on the Scottish border:

> I had to wait three hours [for the train] at Berwick in the snow and moonlight and as I had the 'flu, I walked the rampart, for all that time and got very hot and got rid of the 'flu, <u>and</u> got the idea of what I <u>thought</u> should be Scottish Dance music, looking across the Border in the moonlight and hearing the bagpipes in the distance! I played them at Edinburgh after, and I believe the audience <u>nearly killed</u> me for meddling with the sacred tunes! However, these things are all common-place now so they may be played un-scathed.[55]

The set, which Matthay dedicated to Marjory, was soon published by the Glasgow firm of Paterson and Sons and assigned Opus 15, close on the heels of his *Lyrics*, which became his Opus 14. Terming the collection a "Concert Arrangement for Pianoforte," Matthay

Chapter 5

offered transcriptions of familiar dances which, despite the negative reactions of both *The Times* and Marjory's Edinburgh associates, are often surprisingly true to the traditional character of Scottish folk music. The first of his two strathspeys, "The Braes o' Tullymet," is a raucous essay in Lombardic rhythms and open fifths, in which the tonic and dominant are only rarely relieved by richer harmonies, such as the episode which begins at bar 10:

Example 5.4: Matthay: Scottish Dances and Melodies, Op. 15, "The Braes o' Tullymet" mm. 10-11

The first of his two reels, which he titles "The Drummer," is based on the familiar "The Piper o' Dundee," and at bar 17 he begins to iterate the tune in the bass, suddenly shifting from G major to A minor to preserve the characteristic "double tonic" found in so many Scottish tunes:

Example 5.5 Matthay: Scottish Dances and Melodies, Op. 15, "The Drummer" mm. 17-20

But to be sure, he does end the piece with a Lisztian flourish, shocking the ear with the sudden intrusion of a prominent Neapolitan chord:

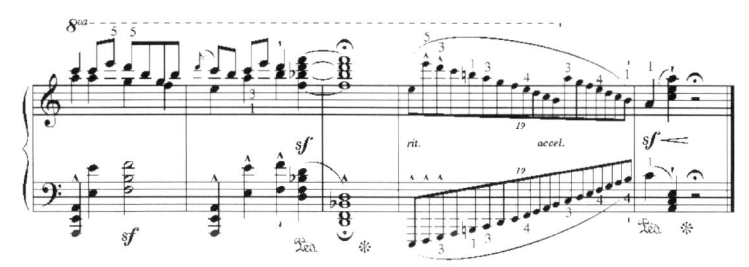

Example 5.6 Matthay, Scottish Dances and Melodies, Op. 15, "The Drummer" mm. 35-39

His finale, another reel, and the longest piece in the set, is a blazing transcription of "The de'il amang the tailors." The last several measures freely transform the original tune into a concert paraphrase:

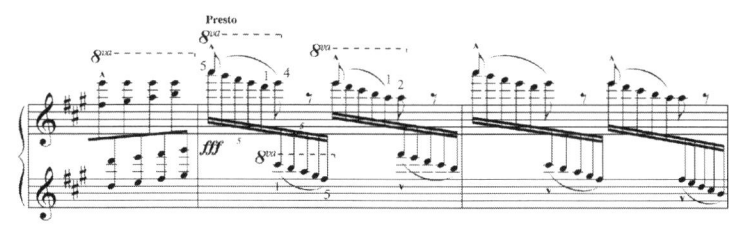

Example 5.7 Matthay: Scottish Dances and Melodies, op. 15, "The de'il amang the tailors" mm. 100-103

Through Marjory, Matthay also met the man who was arguably Edinburgh's most schooled and influential musician: Friedrich Niecks (1845-1924). Inasmuch as Niecks, born in Düsseldorf and naturalized in 1880, shared a common heritage with Matthay's father, the German-Anglo bond that drew the two musicians together can readily be appreciated. They were both close to Alexander Mackenzie as well, since Mackenzie had sought Niecks's skill as a violinist (he had studied with Leopold Auer), and induced him to leave Germany in 1868 to accept the viola position in Mackenzie's Edinburgh Quartet. In Mackenzie's words, he had been "warmly recommended to me as one highly deserving of such consideration."[56] In Britain Niecks quickly established himself as a scholar as well as a performer, and he was soon a regular contributor to the *Musical Times*. After further studies at the University of Leipzig, he returned to Scotland in the late 1870s, where he demonstrated an astonishing breadth in disciplines ranging from philosophy, to psychology, to history. In 1888 his biography of Chopin was published in London, and it was soon recognized as the most authoritative study in the field.[57]

His erudition so impressed the trustees of Edinburgh University that in 1891 he was appointed Reid Professor of Music, a position he held for 23 years.[58] At the time he accepted the post, his duties were simply to provide musical performances for the academic community, but he soon inaugurated the University's first musical instruction classes, which he eventually expanded to a full-scale, co-educational degree program. By the mid-1890s, Niecks was giving over 100 lectures each term, and for at least a decade, Marjory was one of his most faithful attendees. She readily absorbed his views on history, form, program music, and other subjects, stressing that he "did not carelessly repeat himself," but opted instead to present "ever fresh results of thorough study and research."[59] They soon became close friends, and with several of his other students, she became a frequent visitor to his study in Dick Place, which was near the Kennedy home:

> I could not find an unoccupied chair, they were all plied with books he was consulting for his lectures. Thus his students—we were but few—without the eye-strain and fatigue of personal "bookworming" got the sense of proportion in history only possible by dint of long traveling down the road of history in successive centuries, even should much of the detail of the road be forgotten in the end.[60]

After their marriage, Tobias and Jessie needed a home, and they soon acquired "Barlemere," a house on Brighton Road quite near the Surrey Downs in Purley, then barely a suburban village adjacent to Croydon.[61] Although Jessie insists that Matthay was so taken with the Scottish landscape that he was moved to scour the English countryside in search of a suitable residence, there is little evidence that his finances allowed him much choice, and undoubtedly Purley was far less expensive than central London. Though he was now over forty minutes away from the Academy by train, Jessie also reports that he was "overjoyed to find a music-room large enough to take two grand pianos, and opening on to a real garden; and this in a house not large enough to be exacting."[62] This was their home until 1901, and for at least some of those years Dora resided there as well, along with Sarah Osborne, their live-in cook and housekeeper.[63] Tobias senior and Dorothea remained in Clapham, but they were frequent visitors to Purley, and Jessie often entertained them in her garden.[64] Eventually Matthay (and possibly Dora) taught there as well, and visitors were often taken aback by the large complement of "technicons" and dumb keyboards which Jessie claims lurked "in almost every corner."[65] Matthay was still an incessant experimenter, and for the next several years he played with different key weights and resistances, until he felt he had learned all he could from these devices. He eventually retained only one small, two-octave keyboard which he used to take back and forth on the train, where he could often be seen "getting his fingers in"—an activity which, according to Jessie, amused onlookers:

> It used to intrigue his fellow-travellers to see this be-spectacled student sitting in the corner of the carriage, lost in thought, drumming away industriously with his fingers and executing gymnastics on this little set of keys. One day, when he left the carriage to change to another train, someone asked "Who in the world is that?" A Purley neighbour answered: "Oh, that's Professor Mathias Mathey;" and, tapping his brow, nodded significantly![66]

Jessie reports that Matthay's first student at his Purley studio was Maud Samuel's sister, Ida Scharrer, who had sought him out on Maud's recommendation after living for several years with her husband in Australia. Maud and Ida were the granddaughters of Moses Samuel (1795-1860), a Liverpool watchmaker whose determination to protect his Jewish heritage from Christian evangelizing had led him to translate and circulate the writings of Moses Mendelssohn (the composer's grandfather), whom he once praised for his "inimitable mellifluence."[67] Although Samuel left his family an estate valued at less than £100, his descendants expanded his modest jewelry shop into an empire, and by the time Ida, an accomplished pianist, began studying with Matthay, the firm of H. Samuel was becoming the largest jewelry chain in Britain. She was eager one afternoon for Matthay to meet her six-year-old daughter, Irene, an energetic, enthusiastic child who was determined to greet the master with a formal bow. Unfortunately, once Irene entered the Matthays' music room, a rug mercilessly slid across the polished floor and she landed feet first, momentarily losing a dignity which she quickly recovered.[68] But the child proved remarkably gifted, and soon Matthay was teaching both mother and daughter. From this small nucleus grew a private "country" class, and even though it appears he had given up some of his London private teaching by this time, his outside work was expanding. But his RAM class was also growing in size and stature, and during this period Matthay began to guide a number of aspiring musicians who were soon to leave a mark on British music.

The Academy Register records that John Blackwood McEwen entered the RAM on 25 September 1893. His home address is given as 19 Onslow Drive in Glasgow and his fees were guaranteed by his father, the Reverend James W. McEwen.[69] At the time of his matriculation, he was 25, and he had already had an active career in Scotland. Born in Hawick in 1868, from the age of 17 he worked steadily as a church organist, and in 1888 he earned an M.A. from the University of Glasgow.[70] His decision to enter the Academy was motivated by a growing interest in composition, and on his entrance, the Register records his first study as counterpoint, overseen by his principal professors, Prout and Corder. He also studied harmony and organ with Charles Steggall, but since for him piano was merely a second study, in his first year he worked only with Oliver King, then still a sub-professor.[71] But in the following year, his decision to accept a piano scholarship necessitated elevating piano to a first study, and although King had just been made an assistant professor, McEwen may have elected to join Matthay's studio.[72] Soon the two men grew close, for not only was McEwen older than most RAM students—he was exactly Jessie's age—but like Cuthbert Nunn before him, he exemplified Matthay's personal ideal in music: an accomplished pianist with an equal or greater love for composing.

Unquestionably, Matthay viewed such talents as cast in his own image, and throughout his career, he opened as many doors to have their works published as he did to assist their performing careers. After a three-year stint teaching at The Athenaeum School in Glasgow—during which time he also served as parish organist at nearby Greenock—McEwen was appointed Professor of Harmony at the RAM in 1898, and Matthay may have provided a helping hand in the Academy's decision, since he supported him in similar ways throughout his career. Several years after his appointment, McEwen married Matthay's pupil Hedwig Cole, who in Jessie's words, was "delightful, affectionate, and musical to her fingertips."[73] Soon McEwen began to establish himself in England as a musician of vision and intelligence, and Tobias and Jessie—who always called him "Mac"—regarded him as one of their closest friends and confidantes.

Another close friendship soon developed with Ernest Read. Born in the village of Shere, near Guildford, he was younger than McEwen, and he entered the Academy in 1896 when he was 17. Though a proficient pianist, he was eventually drawn more to conducting, and during his time with Matthay he also studied with Henry Wood, a relationship that continued for nearly ten years.[74] He entered the RAM a full two years before he began studies with Matthay, and decades later, he provided some valuable insights into the perceptions then shared by some of his fellow students:

> In the first place, a certain group of us amongst the students always looked forward to a performance by a Matthay pupil, for we soon discovered that not only would it be a well finished and highly polished performance, with no untidy ends, but also that the rhythm would be clear and absolutely under control, the tone varied, the climaxes perfectly timed, the melodic passages—whether in the bass, treble, or middle part—would sing, and the difficult passages would be played with great

ease and complete muscular freedom. The pupils, more-over, seemed to have that power of concentrated listening such as we had noticed in the great artists—Paderweski and others. . . . Small wonder, then, that those who had ears to hear clamoured to become pupils of Matthay in order to find out his secrets of teaching.[75]

Understandably, since he had not sought a piano concentration—his "first studies" included organ and harmony[76]—Read considered himself fortunate when he was finally admitted to Matthay's class:

> I was one of those admiring crowd but it took me a long time to pluck up courage and ask him to take me as a pupil, for I had no ambition to become a concert pianist, being much more interested in music as a whole, especially choral and orchestral music. Eventually the day came when Matthay invited me to play to him and the thrill I got when he said he would teach me is something I shall never forget. To my great surprise at my interview, he said he was more interested in teach[ing] the young musicians who were prepared to think rather than the pianist who wanted to play and not think.[77]

Read also offered a highly detailed portrait of his experiences with Matthay in the studio:

> What were my first six lessons like? I did not play a note! He went over the whole gamut of piano playing and musical interpretation and it was a revelation to me as I had been ploughing my lonely way through every book I could find that dealt with piano playing, only to realize that what I read in one was contradicted in another. Matthay's "talks" made me see what was true or false in all I had read, the good and bad in the Schumann method, the Stuttgart method, the dawning of the light in Leschetizky's principles and method, etc. Then came my first piece, *Mozart's Rondo in A minor*—what an easy piece, thought I to myself; but for the moment I had forgotten those polished and beautifully moulded performances by his pupils, and did not realize how difficult that degree of perfection was to achieve. But I soon discovered!

. . . Scottish Interlude . . .

I had to get some real singing tone—how? Just refer to the notes I had made during his talks. The passages were not fluent or even—why? Refer to my notes. There was no life in this phrase—what had I learnt about the laws of interpretation? Apply them! "You had better do a little technical drill to enable you to play this or that passage—Czerny, Op. 740, (*Fingerfertikeit*)—but play each study in a dozen different ways!" "What about Beringer's Daily Studies?" "Yes, they are all right." "Tausig?" "Yes, they are excellent, but here a few technics (now found in his *Relaxation Studies*) that will help you to play these studies and exercises correctly."

By that time you knew that if you had the time and will to practice, you could be certain of performing any passage, for you were able immediately to diagnose the fault and would have a method of tackling it. So the lessons proceeded, every one a voyage of discovery that sent you away in a seventh heaven of delight.[78]

Matthay respected Read's intelligence, and they grew closer as the lessons progressed. Read later confided to his wife, Helen, that he even availed himself of every opportunity to sit in Matthay's studio to watch him teach.[79] On a number of occasions they caught the same train, with Matthay departing at Purley and Read remaining on to Guildford,[80] and Jessie recalled that they often lost themselves in conversation:

One remembers certain Saturday nights after the R.A.M. "Fortnightlies" when Matthay and Ernest Read ran a neck-and-neck race to catch the 9:50 at Charing Cross. After subsiding into their respective corners and regaining their breath, they would enter into prodigious discussions on the psychology of teaching until, braving the danger of a casualty, Matthay had to precipitate himself out of an almost moving train. As the years went on this discipleship developed into a comradeship which brought them many happy years of co-operation.[81]

But Matthay was still being largely denied the recognition he sought as a composer-pianist. On 17 May 1895, he premiered a sonata which was never published, in what was evidently his first recital in the newly opened Queen's Hall. Unfortunately, *The Times* offered him no better reception than it had given him two years previously for his RAM recital. And although he received positive comments about his performance, the critic's approval was still somewhat qualified:

> MR. MATTHAY'S RECITAL.—At his piano recital on Friday night in the small room of Queen's-hall, Mr. Tobias Matthay introduced a new sonata of his own in B minor, playing it with much skill. In plan it conforms to an extremely modern type, a "motto" theme preceding, and more or less supplanting in prominence of treatment, the technical first subject of the opening movement, and returning in the finale; that the work as a whole produces an effect of incoherence cannot be denied, and not the less so because the form of its passages is often almost old-fashioned, assorting, therefore, rather oddly with the structural type chosen. A graceful intermezzo suggests the idea of an improvisation, and this is confirmed in the finale, in which certain rhythmical experiments have been tried which, justifiable as they undoubtedly are, do not tend to clearness of outline. Among the most successful of the miscellaneous pieces played were Brahms's E flat minor scherzo [Op. 4], two of the "Kreisleriana" of Schumann, a couple of musicianly pieces by Christian Sinding, and Rachmaninoff's effective prelude in C sharp minor. Chopin's ballade in A flat was also played, with a good deal of exaggeration in the matter of *tempo*, and some pieces by Zarzycki, Goetz, Chaminade, and Liszt completed the programme.[82]

The criticisms offered by the *Musical News* were far more positive, but still somewhat mixed:

> Mr. Matthay's style of writing is pianistic and highly effective; entirely his own, too, though nearer the manner of Liszt than of any other. The sonata is in three movements, the usual allegro, an intermezzo, which

. . . Scottish Interlude . . .

is unfortunately akin to the Rhine-daughters' "Rheingold, reines Gold" trio, and a remarkably brilliant finale, in which the melody struggles to the front in a tangle of persistent rhythm in a clever and interesting manner. Mr. Matthay's programme was unconventional, and included a prelude in C sharp [sic] by Rachmaninoff of very original character, with a species of "ground" of three notes (A, G sharp, C sharp) that seems to have some sort of dramatic significance.[83] . . . Brahms' [sic] scherzo, Op. 4, was finely interpreted; the rendering of two of Schumann's "Kreisleriana," and Chopin's ballade in A flat, we found rather fussy, noisy, and too *rubato*. Liszt's twelfth Hungarian rhapsody brought to a close a very interesting concert, which was attended by a large and enthusiastic audience.[84]

But if his critical reception did not always fulfill his desires, he no doubt found consolation toward the end of the decade when three talented composer-pianists entered the Academy in close succession. Unquestionably, the most gifted performer from the group was fourteen-year-old York Bowen, who began his work with Matthay "in knickerbockers" in the fall of 1898 as the recipient of the Erard Scholarship.[85] Born Edwin Yorke Bowen in 1884, the Crouch Hill native, who also became a pupil of Corder, soon distinguished himself by winning virtually every major prize the Academy could offer, both in piano and composition. In July 1902 he won the Charles Lucas Prize, and a year later Mackenzie awarded him the Academy's Dove Prize, which was given annually to the student who had demonstrated the most "general excellence, assiduity, and industry" over the past year. *The Times* noted that great achievements were expected from the young scholar not only as a pianist and composer, but also as an instrumentalist, since by then Bowen had also mastered the horn, with the viola soon to follow.[86] A year later his compositions had achieved national prominence when one of his orchestral overtures was chosen from a field of 42 to be included in a special concert for the Royal College of Music Patron's Fund, placing his work alongside that of Bridge, Holst, and Vaughan Williams.[87]

In the same year—he was 20—his London recital debut was greeted with extraordinary praise by the *Daily Telegraph*, and two years later in 1906 he performed his first piano concerto with the Philharmonic in Queen's Hall under Frederick Cowen, a concert that paired his work with Holst's setting of Whitman's *Mystic Trumpeter* for soprano and orchestra. *The Times* was euphoric:

> Times are indeed changed for the better when a Philharmonic Concert can attract an exceptionally large audience to two new English works, at a concert where all the soloists are of English origin. . . . The first of the English pieces was a pianoforte concerto in D minor, by Mr. York Bowen, who played the solo part in a masterly manner. He not only scores with great skill and real feeling for orchestral "values," but his themes are happily invented and treated with a spontaneous ingenuity that is most attractive. The three short movements follow without a break, and are bound together, as it were, with a strikingly individual phrase. The concerto won immediate success, the composer being repeatedly called at its close, and at last being compelled to play an encore; he gave the "Shadow Dance" of Macdowell.[88]

Though his gifts were prodigious, Bowen always gave full credit to Matthay for his pianistic attainments. As a young man he conferred the "highest praise" on his teacher's "remarkable method,"[89] and in later years he freely admitted that Matthay had "transformed" his approach to the instrument.[90] His repertoire was enormous, and as he dashed off works such as Liapunov's demanding Transcendental Etudes with ease, his playing was admired not only for its astonishing technical command, but for his cultivated phrasing and tonal subtleties—the *Telegraph* even called him a pianist "of culture."[91] As his compositional catalogue (which eventually embraced over 160 entries) continued to grow, the elderly Saint-Saëns remarked that he regarded Bowen as Britain's "most remarkable" young composer.[92]

But even though his compositional efforts were initially overshadowed by Bowen's achievements, Arnold Bax eventually overtook and surpassed his eminence. Born in Streatham in 1883, Bax was 17 when he arrived at the RAM in September 1900, where he immediately began working with Matthay and Corder. After winning several awards for composition, in 1905 he tied for the Walter Macfarren Prize in piano. Bax was a facile, gifted pianist, unexcelled at score reading, who according to Jessie, "cared not a straw for public performance," but through his ability to devour difficult music at sight, became "a centre around which lesser lights revolved."[93] Once in Liverpool at a concert for the Musical League, he virtually sight-read the difficult piano part to Joseph Holbrooke's Sextet for Strings and Piano, after which *The Times* wrote, "A very fair performance was given," spoiled only by "the roughness of the strings" in places.[94] Bowen was so astonished at his classmate's talent that he once considered withdrawing from a sight-reading competition when he learned that Bax planned to enter:

> While still a student, he showed a most remarkable gift and avidity for reading at sight, and after a time there was no one who could touch him in this way. . . . It was almost magical to hear Bax trying over something like a piano quintet from a small score and being able to read all the staves at once and giving a remarkably good idea of it at sight, even if it were a modern and complicated work. The other unmistakable sign of his growing creative gift was his power of extemporization, altogether beyond anything I have ever heard since at the piano keyboard. He took little interest in developing his piano technique and gradually dropped it.[95]

At the London Music Club, Bax played for both Debussy and Schoenberg, and Matthay was instrumental in getting Boosey and Company to publish his "Concert Valse" in E-flat, an early piano piece which, in Jessie's words, "all his fellow students had to have a shot at."[96] But if Matthay appreciated his pupil's compositional gifts, he could not abide his lack of discipline in the practice room, and Bax evidently felt so constrained that in later years he characterized Matthay as "a benevolent Svengali."[97] Although he conceded that

Chapter 5

Matthay "achieved magical successes with quite stolid and musically unimaginative students," he regarded his "highly scientific" approach as "dry," adding that his methods were "something of a trial to the highly strung:"

> I, for one, could never play anything approaching my best at my lessons with him. It nearly always happened that just as I would begin to forget my self-consciousness and to play something like freely, "Tobs" would bump my forearm from underneath and cry excitedly, "What's this? Key-bedding? To the sound and no further, remember! Again now! Don't think of yourself! Think of the music! Beethoven!!" (and he would assume an expression and attitude of sublimity). "Beethoven's messenger!!!" (in a thrilling voice). "That's *you!*" and he would poke a long forefinger hard into one's midriff. Another trick he had was to charge one off the piano-stool like a heavy-weight footballer, and play the passage quite unintelligibly himself.[98]

By his own admission, Bax seems to have been rather an unresponsive student. But given that his view of Matthay scarcely constitutes an unqualified endorsement, one wonders why he remained for five years with a teacher who evidently invoked such discomfort, and even resentment. Jessie insists that Bax was "much beloved and appreciated" by Matthay, so perhaps he benefited—at least to some extent—from the instruction. However, it must also be noted that Matthay's eminence in London was growing, and that before the first War—as will be seen later—Bax profited immeasurably from his teacher's expanding sphere of influence. His biographer, Lewis Foreman, points out that a great many of Bax's friends and associates during this period were Matthay pupils, and he was careful to retain ties with many of them after he left the Academy.[99]

Concurrent with Bax's entry to the RAM in 1900 was the appearance of Benjamin Dale, then 15. Another Londoner, when he first entered he began studying with Corder and he later worked with Matthay.[100] At 17 he began composing his massive Piano Sonata

...Scottish Interlude...

in D minor, a project which occupied him for the next three years, and which Foreman praised for its "remarkable command of 19th-century Romantic pianism, looking not only to Liszt and Schumann as models but also to Balakirev and other Russian composers."[101] Inasmuch as Dale's primary instrument was organ and he was not a piano virtuoso, the Sonata's difficulty made it an attractive vehicle for Bowen (to whom it is dedicated) and Myra Hess, both of whom frequently performed it and did much to popularize it (see Chapter 7). Corder championed his pupil's work and was even instrumental in publishing it, although he believed its difficulty had kept it from receiving the recognition it deserved.[102] Nonetheless, over the next two decades it enjoyed considerable popularity in England, and in her book on the British piano sonata, Lisa Hardy notes that it was performed by many pianists both inside and outside of Matthay's circle, including Irene Scharrer, Moura Lympany, Benno Moiseiwitsch, and Frank Merrick.[103]

Bowen premiered the work—then still in manuscript—to a packed house at Bechstein Hall on 14 November 1905, and although the *Musical News* praised him for his "brilliant technique and accurate phrasing," the journal was somewhat less kind to Dale:

> [Bowen] began his programme with a Sonata in E minor, by Mr. J. B. McEwen, a work which is dignified and impressive, and moreover clearly devoid of the kind of cleverness that imitates—in a word, musicianly. Mr. B. J. Dale's Sonata in D minor, made up of four movements, does not merit such praise, for in certain passages he adheres too slavishly to his models, Chopin and Grieg, especially the former. Still, for so young a composer, he shows great promise, and, even in this early composition, Mr. Dale, who received a double call, asserts his individuality.[104]

But *The Times*, which lauded Bowen as "a clever pianist," praised Dale's work with far less qualification:

> The pianist did [McEwen's sonata] full justice, as he did to the other, a work by Mr. B. J. Dale, in D minor, in which a very old experiment is

tried once again—that namely, of making the successive movements into a set of variations, and so combining two of the recognized forms into one. Some suites of the 18th century, by Pergolesi and others, show the same system, of course in a far simpler form than in this sonata, where the fine opening allegro is quite distinct from the variations—and extremely interesting, too—and where the theme is given out at the beginning of the slow movement, which contains the first four variations, leaving three for the scherzo and an introduction and finale for the last section. All are genuinely expressive, admirably written, and very original in invention. Exactly where the scherzo group of variations passes into the finale it was a little hard to discover by the ear alone; but the whole conception is most interesting and the experiment quite successful.[105]

Matthay was also taken with the Sonata, and for several years he assigned its second movement, a set of four imaginative variations, to many of his students. For example, on 19 July 1906, the ink was barely dry on the published copy when Dorothy Grinstead, one of his RAM pupils, gave a "good account" of the variations at Steinway Hall.[106] Although modern listeners might regard Dale's virtuosic Sonata—with a harmonic vocabulary ranging from Liszt to MacDowell—as a wildly overblown expression of romantic temperament, his contemporaries rarely saw it as excessive or sentimental. Years later, Bax's brother, Clifford, tried to encapsulate the spirit and ethos of the age, although time has perhaps belied his prophetic abilities:

> Years have outmoded [the Sonata's] manner, but, in my lay judgement, it is so vibrant with the Arcadian romanticism of early youth that it well may last as long as *Endymion*. Indeed, if any one who is now eighteen were to ask me how we at the same age felt toward life, I should willingly let that Sonata stand for my answer.[107]

. . . Scottish Interlude . . .

Example 5.8 Benjamin Dale: Sonata in D minor, first mvmt, mm. 1-15

Chapter 5

 In 1901 the Matthays left Purley to move to Hampstead. Jessie provides little insight into their motivation, but Tobias's recent salary raise at the RAM to 10s, 6d per hour may have factored into their decision. She does mention that as the Victorian era drew to a close and a new century approached, their "quiet little Surrey village . . . was to wake up and think about suburban tram lines,"[108] so perhaps the rural peace they had enjoyed was rapidly disappearing. Hampstead was scarcely open country at the time, but it was one of the last boroughs in greater London to be served by horse-drawn buses, and the Matthays' new home, a handsome residence at 21 Arkwright Road, was situated in a quiet neighborhood.[109] The area had also become a haven for London's artists and intellectuals, and Jessie recalled that poets, painters, and novelists could often be found "grouped under the friendly spire of the old parish church."[110] In March 1895, Bax's father had purchased a large house on Rosslyn Hill at the end of the Hampstead High Street, and Jessie noted that the family "kept open house to all clever people."[111] Other neighbors included Annie Curwen and her husband, John, whose determination to carry on his father's solfegge work had made him one of Britain's most prominent music educators and publishers. Annie, born in Dublin and trained at the Royal Irish Academy, had taught piano for her entire life and in 1886 she published *The Child Pianist*, a popular approach that was later known as *Mrs. Curwen's Pianoforte Method*. Though nearly 13 years Matthay's senior, she soon became one of his most ardent disciples, and their mutual admiration for Spencer's psychological concepts sparked many lively discussions. Jessie indicates that "she straightaway grafted herself on to the Matthay circle as Godmother," and Matthay thought so highly of her that he later hired her to teach at his school.[112]

 The Matthays' garden was smaller and the house less spacious than what they had enjoyed at Purley, but Tobias was still able to crowd two grand pianos into the sitting room and seat enough people so that small recitals could be staged on the premises. These events were becoming increasingly important, because his private class continued to grow, and no doubt a Hampstead address proved far more convenient for most of his pupils—perhaps such considerations had even prompted the Matthays' decision to relocate. After his family had settled in London's Westbourne Grove, New Zealand-born Arthur Alexander recalled his first lesson on Arkwright Road, where the ringing of the bell was muffled by an "unearthly clanking" of empty cocoa tins attached to a wire on the wall next to Matthay's piano. He was told that this was his teacher's invention, a doorbell "enhancement" designed to spare the elderly servant the necessity of leaving her basement kitchen every time a student appeared.[113] Even after it was explained that Matthay found it simpler to dispatch one of the auditing students to admit callers, young Arthur returned home that afternoon and confided to his mother that not only was his teacher "mad," but that he was "shaky and frail," and that "it was unlikely that he would last more than a month or two."[114] Though he was only in his mid-forties, Matthay's towering frame had begun to stoop, but Arthur—at least at first—was more taken aback by his "strange, husky voice:"

> From a long series of buzzing sounds (*legatissimo*), accented words stood out here and there. At first . . . I could understand almost nothing, however, once accustomed to those strange mumblings, I found them both expressive and helpful. Uncle Tobs was capable of the amazing feat of giving a whole lesson without the use of a single intelligible word.[115]

Like most of Matthay's pupils, Alexander was soon swept away by his teacher's warmth and benevolence, but he was often put off by his unrestrained expressions of affection: "His greeting and farewell took the form of a brushing glissando kiss. I well recall my embarrassment at being kissed in Oxford Street at a busy time of day, and worse, the terrible occasion when he rushed on to the platform at Queen's Hall and embraced me as I left after playing *The Emperor*." But most welcomed Matthay's demonstrative expressions and found them to be natural extensions of an endearing nature, merely complementing Alexander's observation that his "patience and kindness were inexhaustible." After he entered the Academy a few years later, Alexander provided brief but colorful portraits of both Matthay and Corder:

Chapter 5

Matthay was tall and very stooping—his arms were long and he had enormous hands. His bald and quite flat head was fringed at the back with long—and for many years—light-coloured hair. His complexion was youthful and healthy, and it seemed that only his chin ever required shaving. He wore a moustache and glasses (he was very short-sighted). His brown velvet coat, oatmeal tweed trousers and Harris tweed overcoat were particularly noticeable in the days when professors wore frock coats and silk hats. (My composition professor Frederick Corder relaxed a little in the summer—*he* wore a dingy straw boater with *his* frock coat.) Matthay's expression was that of a kindly German professor of the old school. His movements were quick and shuffling—his entry into a room blowing kisses, was *allegro agitato murmurando.* In cold weather [indoors] he wore an overcoat as a rug when the rug was not handy, and on his hands, mittens.[116]

Matthay was also incapable of practicing elitism, and inasmuch as he believed that public performance should transcend status and class, he was soon intermingling his private pupils with his Academy students at Sunday afternoon Hampstead "Practice Concerts." Typically, the Arkwright Road sitting room so quickly overflowed with students and invited guests that the performers were often asked to wait upstairs. G. M. B. Wigton, who was seated in the audience one afternoon in 1903, recalled Matthay's kindness in offering to turn pages for a student experiencing some memory problems. But the next performer, who needed no such assistance, left an indelible impression which he remembered for the rest of his days. Gazing up the staircase, Matthay simply said, "Your turn now, Myra," and with that, a young girl, barely 13, came sailing down the banister—her waist-length hair flowing behind her—before she landed "in the hall with a bump!"[117]

At the time, Julia Myra Hess, born to Orthodox Jews and reared in and around Hampstead, had studied with Matthay for about a year. She began piano lessons at five, but within two years her instructor, a Miss Reason, informed her mother that she had nothing left to teach her, advising that she be given a musical exam at Trinity College. At the age of seven, Myra emerged as the youngest child ever to receive the coveted Trinity College Certificate, and the occasion was captured by a Baker Street photographer.[118] The accolades continued as she entered the Guildhall School, where she remained until she was 12, studying under various teachers. In March 1901 she performed a Liszt Rhapsody for a London women's gathering, and was praised in the press for "a clever piece of work."[119] In 1902 she won the school's Steinway Prize and shortly thereafter her picture appeared in *The Sketch*, a London weekly which dubbed her "a particularly promising young pianist."[120] At the age of eleven, Myra entered St. Leonard's School for Girls, an institution recommended to her mother perhaps by Ida Scharrer, since it was already her daughter's school and the two women were friends. Irene was two years older than Myra, but despite the age difference, they soon became inseparable.[121] At the time, Irene was the dominant force in their relationship, and it seems probable that she frequently praised "Uncle Tobs" in Myra's presence. After she had won a scholarship to the Academy, she urged Myra to audition as well. "Little Hess," as the Matthays called her, was thrilled when, at 12, she earned one of the first Ada Lewis Scholarships, guaranteeing her tuition to the RAM for three years—and two lessons per week with Irene's hallowed "Uncle Tobs."[122]

Irene was present for Myra's first lesson with Matthay, a practice he encouraged with all of his students, and which he thought might prove especially beneficial to Myra since Irene was then the more advanced player. Years later, she recalled that she was "shocked" when Myra offered her teacher only a "silly little piece by Edward Schütt," but Matthay's newest pupil was soon studying more suitable literature.[123] Sometimes the girls took their lessons at the Academy, and sometimes they appeared at Arkwright Road, where Jessie remembered their music-room antics while they awaited their teacher's arrival: "While waiting for their lessons, they would often indulge in high-jinks on the studio-pianos, extemporizing simultaneously in a wildly exciting manner, making rhapsodies out of everything."[124]

Though none could have known it at the time, Matthay had captured lightning in a bottle, for these two young women—whom Bax remembered as "very small and eternally giggling girls," and whom Corder was once forced to physically remove from his classroom

Chapter 5

for their disruptive behavior—were one day to change the face of British pianism.[125] But within months of the day that "Little Hess" had bolted down the Arkwright Road banister, Matthay's work was to have a far more immediate and controversial impact—an impact which would soon be felt the world over.

Notes

1. RAMR, 1891, 86, and COMM 22 March 1899.
2. Tobias Matthay, "Mrs. Tobias Matthay," *AMAJ* (1937): 3. Matthay offered a four-paragraph tribute to his wife when she died in May 1937, first published that month in *The Musical Opinion*.
3. Marjory Kennedy-Fraser, *A Life of Song* (London: Oxford University Press, 1929), 4. Hereafter cited as MKF.
4. Jean Mary Allen and Ruzena Wood, "Kennedy, David," *RNG*. Hereafter cited as Allen, "Kennedy."
5. Ibid., and MKF, 4.
6. MKF, 4-5.
7. Ibid., 5.
8. *TT*, 9 Oct. 1862, 1, col. C.
9. "Songs of Scotland," *TT*, 22 Dec. 1862, 3, col. F.
10. Ibid. and Marjory Kennedy, David Kennedy[,] *The Scottish Singer: Reminiscences of his Life and Work* (Paisley, 1887), 38. Hereafter cited as David Kennedy.
11. *TT*, 31 Dec. 1862, 10, col. C.
12. Allen, "Kennedy."
13. MKF, 6-8.
14. David Kennedy, 46.
15. MKF, 12. The 1901 Census for England and Wales, now available on line at http://www.1901censusonline.com/ records Jessie's place of birth as Detroit, Michigan, and her age (in March 1901) as 32. See RG Number 13, Series 637, Piece 66, Folio 10, Page 214. Hereafter cited as Census 1901. Last accessed on 23 Feb. 2011.

16. MKF, 8-9.
17. Ibid., 12-36.
18. David Kennedy Jr., *Kennedy's Colonial Travel: A Narrative of a Four Years' Tour through Australia, New Zealand, Canada,* &c. (Edinburgh: Edinburgh Publishing Company, 1876), 315-16. David, the eldest Kennedy son, kept a journal of their adventures, installments of which were regularly sent to Scottish newspapers. With some revisions, these were later published in book form.
19. MKF, 39.
20. *TT*, 20 Sept. 1877, 1, col. D.
21. Ibid.
22. David Kennedy, 67-68.
23. Ibid., 72.
24. Cited in MKF, 73.
25. MKF, 75-77.
26. MKF, 78.
27. MKF, 81.
28. MKF, 80-86.
29. *TT*, 8 Mar. 1886, 1, col. C.
30. MKF, 86.
31. MKF, 87.
32. MKF, 87-88.
33. MKF, 88.
34. Ibid.
35. MKF, 91-94.
36. MKF, 95.
37. Maggie studied piano with Septimus Webbe.
38. JHM, 26-27.
39. JHM, 27.
40. JHM, 27.
41. Tobias Matthay, "Sketch Book 14," 54. RAMRBC. Matthay left a total of 14 compositional Sketch Books, numbered 2 through 15. All are uncatalogued at this writing.
42. See Tobias Matthay, "There's Nae Lark" (London: Ricordi, 1908).
43. The C major autograph is in the Matthay Archives.

44. RAMRBC MS 1919.
45. The memo was found inserted between the pages of the A major autograph.
46. TT, 26 Jan. 1893, 13, col. A.
47. Almost certainly Matthay wrote these pieces before he married Jessie, since they are inscribed "To J. H. K."
48. The Matthays' Banns and Marriage Certificate are in the RAM Archives.
49. JHM, 29.
50. JHM, 28.
51. JHM, 29.
52. MKF, 100.
53. MKF, 100.
54. JHM, 29.
55. MA. Matthay to Bruce Simonds, 1 Dec. 1927.
56. Mackenzie, *A Musician's Narrative*, 73. Niecks was also a skilled organist and he was immediately sought to fill the post at Dumfries.
57. *RNG*, s.v. "Niecks, Friedrich [Frederick]" by Robin H. Legge and Duncan J. Barker.
58. Niecks was succeeded in this position by Donald Francis Tovey.
59. MKF, 98.
60. MKF, 98.
61. See the "Matthay, Tobias Augustus," entry on 42 of John Warriner, ed., *National Portrait Gallery of British Musicians* (London: Sampson, Low, Marston and Company, c.1893) The name of the house is misspelled as "Barliniere" in the 1901 British Census. Jessie (JHM, 29) discusses the move to Purley, but provides no address. Although the Matthays were still resident in their home when the census was taken in March, it may be inferred that 1901 was also the year they left Purley for Hampstead. A photo of Matthay's parents faces p. 38 in Jessie's book with the caption, "Father and Mother, 1901, at Arkwright Road."
62. JHM, 29.
63. Sarah H. Osborne's name is provided by the Census. Her age is given as 40 in March 1901.
64. A photo of Jessie pouring tea for her in-laws at Purley faces p. 30 in her book.
65. JHM, 29-30.
66. JHM, 29-30.

67. Bernard Wasserstein, *Transactions of the Jewish Historical Society of England*, vol. XXXV, 2. http://www.manfamily.org/PDFs/MosesSamuel.pdf. Last accessed on 22 Jan. 2011.
68. JHM, 30-31.
69. RAMR, 1893, 25.
70. Bernard Benoliel, "McEwen, John (Blackwood)," *RNG*.
71. The RAM Prospectus for August 1894 indicates that King had by then been made a assistant professor.
72. RAM Register, 1893, 25.
73. JHM, 31.
74. Lynda MacGregor, "Read, Ernest," *RNG*.
75. Ernest Read, "Tobias Matthay: An Appreciation," *The R. A. M. Magazine* (January 1946) No. 133:2-3. Hereafter cited as Read.
76. Conducting was not then taught at the RAM. Read also chose "sight singing" as a "first study," which was then a concentration designed for choir specialists. See Frances Zagni, *'Uncle Ernie'—a biography of Ernest Read* (New Malden, Surrey, 1989), 20-21.
77. Read, 3.
78. Read, 3-4.
79. Zagni, 22.
80. Read was fortunate to have a network of support in his village to help underwrite some of his Academy expenses. During his first year, Zagni (p. 15) reports that one Mr. Beaumont, a "wealthy bachelor," provided "the first term's fees and the rail season ticket."
81. JHM, 31.
82. *TT*, 21 May 1895, 3, col. G.
83. Rachmaninoff's famous Prelude had been written only three years earlier, but by 1895 it was easily obtained in the West, partially because the Gutheil firm had not bothered to secure a copyright—much to Rachmaninoff's regret in later years.
84. *Musical News*, 25 May 1895, 487.
85. *MT*, 1 March 1906, 175.
86. *TT*, 25 July 1903, 14, col. E. Bowen was also a highly accomplished violist.
87. See "The Royal College of Music Patron's Fund," *TT*, 9 May 1904, 12, col. E.
88. *TT*, 1 June 1906, 11, col. C.

89. *MT*, 1 March 1906, 175.
90. Interview with Bowen's student Monica Watson Chard at her home in Woodside Park, London, 12 July 2004.
91. JHM, 40.
92. Francis Pott, liner notes for *York Bowen: Piano Music*, Stephen Hough, piano. Hyperion CDA86838, (Recorded September, 1995), 4.
93. JHM, 40.
94. *TT*, 27 Sept. 1909, 7, col. E.
95. Quoted in Lewis Foreman, *Bax: A Composer and his Times*, 3rd ed. (Woodbridge, Suffolk: Boydell Press, 2007), 37-38. Hereafter cited as Foreman, *Bax*.
96. JHM, 40.
97. Arnold Bax, *Farewell, My Youth*, Edited by Lewis Foreman (Aldershot: Scolar, 1992), 14. Hereafter cited as Bax, *Farewell*.
98. Ibid., 14.
99. Ibid., 171. Foreman makes this comment in an endnote.
100. See Lisa Hardy, *The British Piano Sonata: 1870-1945* (Woodbridge, Suffolk: Boydell Press, 2001). Hardy observes that Dale studied piano at the Academy with Frederick Lake and Evelyn Howard-Jones, neither of whom studied with Matthay. However, a few years later Howard-Jones began teaching at Matthay's school so one can presume there was some affinity between the two teachers. Guy Jonson, who knew Dale personally and also played his Sonata, maintains that Dale did indeed study with Matthay, and Dale's closeness to the Matthay circle seems to confirm this. Matthay even hired Dale to teach music history at his school. Interview with Jonson at his home in Hampstead, 16 Jun. 2006.
101. Lewis Foreman, "Dale, Benjamin (James)," *RNG* Hereafter cited as Foreman, "Dale." The first movement of Dale's Sonata is 310 measures and the finale is 376 measures. The Charles Avison edition, published early in 1906, extends to 62 pages. Dale indicates that the work was completed in July 1905, and since he was born 17 July 1885 he could have completed it before his twentieth birthday.
102. See Corder's extensive essay "Benjamin Dale's Pianoforte Sonata in D" in *MT*, 1 April 1918, 164-67.
103. Hardy, 48.

104. "London Concerts," *Musical News*, 25 November 1905. Hardy (p. 47) mentions that Bowen had already performed the first movement of Dale's Sonata at Queen's Hall the previous February. As testimony to Bowen's endurance, he concluded his Bechstein Hall program with a performance of the Glazounov Sonata in B-flat minor, which the *News* described as "capital." The review ends by suggesting that Dale's Sonata did not receive the optimum venue for its premiere: "Messrs. Bechstein would do well to improve the ventilation of the Hall. As it was, the atmosphere was suffocating."
105. *TT*, 16 Nov. 1905, 10, col. E.
106. *TT*, 21 July 1906, 9, col. D.
107. Clifford Bax, *Inland Far: A Book of Thoughts and Impressions* (London: L. Dickson, 1933), 35.
108. JHM, 38.
109. In *Bax*, Foreman reproduces portions of an unpublished memoir by Matthay pupil Arthur Alexander, who indicates that he used to catch a horse-drawn bus from Westbourne Grove to Finchley Road to reach Matthay's Arkwright Road residence. See Foreman, *Bax*, 17-18. In the early 1970s, the Greater London Council placed a plaque on the house's exterior, which reads, "Tobias Matthay[,] 1858-1945[,] Teacher and Pianist[,] lived here."
110. JHM, 39.
111. Ibid.
112. JHM, 41.
113. Alexander memoir, quoted in Foreman, *Bax*, 17.
114. Foreman, *Bax*, 18.
115. Ibid.
116. Ibid.
117. G. M. B. Wigton, "Your Turn Now, Myra!," letter to *Radio Times* 69 (15 November 1940):10.
118. Marian C. McKenna, *Myra Hess: A Portrait* (London: Hamish Hamilton, 1976). The photo is reproduced in McKenna's book, opposite 19.
119. McKenna, 11.
120. Ibid.
121. Ibid., 12. The claim is so often made that Myra and Irene were *cousins* that it seems to have assumed the status of folklore. It has been reiterated by two

Chapter 5

recent contributions to the *RNG*: see Bryce Morrison, "Hess, Dame Myra," and Frank Dawes, "Scharrer, Irene." However the rumor began, McKenna (p. 12) insists that the two women were not related, a fact which was confirmed to me by Denise Lassimonne, who knew both of them intimately. Perhaps the claim was perpetuated by the fact that Irene and Harriet Cohen, both descendants of Moses Samuel (see Ch. 7), were in fact second cousins.

122. McKenna, 16. See also Irene Scharrer, "A Unique Friendship," in Denise Lassimonne and Howard Ferguson, eds., *Myra Hess By Her Friends* (New York, 1966), 2. Hereafter cited as Scharrer. Dublin-born Ada Davis Lewis (1844-1906) was the widow of Samuel Lewis (1838-1901), England's colorful, best-known moneylender, who rose from the slums of Birmingham to leave an estate of £2.6 million. During his lifetime he generously endowed hospitals, schools, and housing for the poor. Three years after her husband's death, Ada married an army officer 30 years her junior, but she continued to disburse her wealth with extreme generosity for another two years until her death. Samuel's will stipulated that about £1,000,000 be given immediately to charity and in 1901 Ada granted £18,000 to the RAM—in Mackenzie's words—to "establish the fifteen scholarships bearing her name." Subsequently, they were awarded annually to entering students in a variety of concentrations. Out of the blue, while taking tea with Mackenzie one day, she offered him £1,000 to produce his opera *The Cricket on the Hearth*, but he passed on it, because as he said, "the spirit moved me to decline the generous offer." It was an inclination he later regretted. See Mackenzie, 207.

123. Scharrer, 2. After Myra died, Irene recalled her performing the Schütt at her first lesson, but 25 years earlier, both women seemed to agree that Myra had first played Beethoven's "Moonlight" Sonata for Matthay—although this "memory" may have been contrived for the benefit of a radio audience (see Ch. 12).

124. JHM, 40.

125. Scharrer, 3.

John McEwen in 1924 as he became principal of the RAM

Portrait of Tobias Matthay painted in 1899 by C. Kay Robertson

*Charcoal sketch of Jessie Matthay done by Robertson in 1899
as she began her elocution career*

Frederick Corder about 1910

CHAPTER 6

... AND THE FIRST "ACT"

Jessie withdrew from the Royal Academy of Music over eight months before her 1893 wedding, but her book offers no explanation as to why she remained absent for nearly four years. During her hiatus, it seems unlikely that she pursued a teaching career, since the competitive London climate would have made an RAM Certificate a virtual necessity, and she had every incentive to complete her studies first—Tobias could even have negotiated a reduction in her Academy fees. Although she may have sought some temporary employment to assist with the household finances, no such activity can be documented, and if she was professionally less active through this period, it is even possible that the couple tried to start a family. The Matthays never had children, perhaps in part because for much of her life, Jessie suffered from a particularly debilitating form of rheumatoid arthritis. But in the years immediately following their wedding, the disease was not yet apparent, so if they did desire children, one can presume that at some point they either reconsidered, or they encountered some additional impediments.

But the fact that she left the Academy a full two terms before her wedding suggests that she suspended her studies for other reasons, and her prolonged absence may even have been due to vocal problems. By the summer of 1891, after working for two terms with Arthur Thompson, she was exhausted, admitting that she "had no voice left to sing with," and her last documented student performance occurred about eighteen months later in January of 1893. Matthay's song "There's nae Lark," completed the previous May, was obviously written with her vocal capabilities in mind, but it encompasses a surprisingly narrow range. When Jessie finally did return to the RAM in September of 1896, she left Thompson to work with Manuel Garcia (1805-1906), who years earlier had invented the laryngoscope. The teacher of Marchesi, Jenny Lind, and countless others, Garcia—then in his nineties—had brought an unprecedented degree of scientific acumen to vocal study, and he was undoubtedly the most logical choice for RAM students encountering physical difficulties. Thompson then was far from retirement, and almost certainly Jessie could have remained with him had she chose, but Garcia may have presented alternatives that even Matthay endorsed.

But whatever help she received, she soon abandoned a career of singing for that of dramatic elocution, an area which was clearly expanding at the Academy. In 1891 the RAM prospectus listed only one professor of elocution, but within ten years there were six.[1] There is no known record that Jessie studied with any of them, but monologue had always been an integral part of the Kennedy family performances, so it was probably a natural transition for her to realign her focus. She received her R.A.M. Certificate early in 1898, and soon thereafter, she began appearing with increasing frequency in various London venues, occasionally interspersing a few songs into her presentations. Since her recitations often required piano music, she frequently featured Tobias's most favored pupils, often allowing them to contribute their own solos. Her first appearance was at the Erard showrooms on Great Marlborough Street on 4 May 1898, and her second—consisting of entirely different repertoire—took place a week later at the same location. The brief ad that ran in *The Times* indicates that her first program was assisted by Gertrude Peppercorn, arguably Matthay's most outstanding student at the time, who six months earlier had given a successful debut at St. James Hall:

SALLE ERARD
MRS. TOBIAS MATTHAY
Will give her First
DRAMATIC RECITAL TO-NIGHT, at 8.
Grieg's "Bergliot," "Graih My Chree," "Bianca Among the Nightingales,"
and Pianoforte Solos by Miss Gertrude Peppercorn.
Tickets—reserved, 5s; unreserved, 2s.; Concert Direction Adlington,
224, Regent-street, and at Salle Erard, Great Marlborough-st., W.[2]

... and the First "Act"

From her earliest appearances, Jessie received support from her Scottish countrymen Alexander Mackenzie and John McEwen, and her first performance featured a recitation of Hall Caine's "Graih my Chree," enhanced by McEwen's accompaniment for piano, strings, and drums, "in a manner that increases the eerie character of the story."[3] And two years later, with both Dora and Cuthbert Nunn assisting at the piano, the two composers offered music which was cited in her first *Times* review:

> MRS. TOBIAS MATTHAY'S RECITAL.—Mrs. Tobias Matthay gave a recital at the Steinway-hall on Wednesday evening, at which she appeared in the double capacity of reciter and singer. Among the recitations on the programme was Tennyson's "Romney's Remorse," to which incidental music has been written by Mr. J. B. McEwen. In this Mrs. Matthay displayed very considerable dramatic power; in fact, the performance was in some ways the most satisfactory that she gave. Mr. McEwen's music is unpretentious in character and is sparingly used; it includes a graceful setting of "Beat, little heart." The programme also included Hood's "Queen Mab" and "Faithful Nelly Gray," with music by Sir Alexander Mackenzie; Hans Anderson's charming fable "The Butterfly," and other pieces. As a vocalist Mrs. Matthay was heard to advantage in two Scots ballads, "Barbara Allen" and "Last May a braw wooer." Mr. Cuthbert Nunn produced a graceful set of four "Miniatures" and two valses of his own composition, and Miss Dora Matthay played Chopin's "Polonaise" in A flat.[4]

Jessie promoted the music of Matthay's friends and colleagues as readily as she supported his pupils, and on 25 May 1903, in the newly opened Bechstein Hall on Wigmore Street, she premiered Corder's setting of his own translation of Ernst von Wildenbruch's *Das Hexenlied*—a work composed especially for her:

> At her dramatic recital at Bechstein-hall on Monday evening—an excellent entertainment of its kind—Mrs. Tobias Matthay brought forward for the first time in public a new piece entitled "The Witch's Song,"

Chapter 6

words and music by Mr. Frederick Corder. A hidden orchestra is used—consisting mainly of a couple of "strings," a harmonium, and a harp; and the music evolved from this combination certainly does much to create the "atmosphere" sought for. Here and in a large number of other pieces by Tennyson, Hood, Poe, Austin Dobson and others Mrs. Matthay was quite successful in her performance; for she has a very natural delivery, happily free from the melodramatic vices so common to the reciter, and an excellent command of vocal changes and of gesture.[5]

There can be little question that she was developing a following, and soon she was being featured at larger events. On 5 December 1902, she enhanced a performance by Samuel Coleridge-Taylor, as he led the Croydon Conservatoire string orchestra in the premieres of several of his own works, and on 11 February 1904, she appeared in Bristol with the Clifton Quartet, narrating Strauss's *Enoch Arden*.[6] By 1906, she was filling smaller halls three to four times annually and tickets were at a premium. On 27 October she shared the stage at Steinway Hall with Matthay's pupil Felix Swinstead, and the *Times* reviewer complained that the ladies' headgear obstructed his view, so that he "had to be content with listening to her voice." But he added that it was "well worth" listening to, except "when, as in Rossetti's 'Sister Helen,' she raises it to a squeak in an injudicious attempt to imitate the probable tones of the 'little brother.'" However, he seemed more impressed with the quality of Jessie's voice than with her acting:

It is rich and full and in almost perfect control; if its high (speaking) notes are hard, its low notes are organ-like, and its middle notes superb. That she is singer as well as reciter a charming little "Sing-song cycle" of poems for children by Christina Rossetti, set to music by Mr. Felix Swinstead, was there to prove; and here the high notes were above reproach. Whatever might be the attitude towards recitation of individual members of her audience, all must have joined in enjoying her songs. The reciter has a harder task than the actor; and so has his audience than the actor's audience. When we see Mrs. Tobias Matthay gazing at the roof of Steinway-hall it is really hard to persuade ourselves that it is not the roof of Steinway-hall she is looking at but Mr. William Watson's "First Skylark of Spring"; and when Sister Helen throws herself into a chair instead of on to the ground, we realize, for all our efforts, that it is not really Sister Helen but Mrs. Tobias Matthay. Still, taking the art with all its difficulties, Mrs. Matthay is a very clever exponent of it, good alike (if a little heavy) at tragedy and (if a little arch) at comedy; and a programme which includes one of the "Just-so" stories [of Kipling], love poems by Browning and Henley, and "The Courtship of Saunders McGlaushan," besides the pieces we have mentioned, shows no intention of keeping in a groove. Mr. Swinstead at the piano played a polonaise and four preludes of his own composition.[7]

Exactly six weeks later on 8 December, she appeared again at Steinway Hall, this time with Myra Hess, who performed the variations from Dale's recently published Sonata. Once again, *The Times* critic, if not effusive, was overwhelmingly positive:

In spite of the rain only a few seats were empty at Mrs. Tobias Matthay's third recitation [of the season] Saturday. There are many good reciters, and many recitals; but it is clear that good reciters, like Mrs. Tobias Matthay, can and do acquire a large and faithful following. Her program on Saturday was as varied as ever; we had Tennyson and Whitcombe Riley, Margaret Deland and Mr. Gilbert. We had "Peter Pan" and we had the dullest of sham fancy in a passage on Little Rivers by Van Dyck. But there were none of the things which ought never to be recited, and the programme as a whole was of a light and pleasant character. Mrs. Matthay is especially good in passages of gentle humour which require a light touch and a neat technique. To hear Tennyson's ballad of "The Revenge" recited is to compare the reciter's tones with Dr. Stanford's music,[8] and perhaps to find the latter the more dramatic; but those who like Hans Andersen would find nothing of his delicacy destroyed by Mrs. Matthay's manner of telling the story, and those who like Margaret Deland's poems would probably find their beauty enhanced by the musical accompaniment and the little snatch of song, which showed the reciter's voice at its best.[9]

Matthay doted on his wife, virtually obsessing over her performances for weeks in advance, to the point it was said that he could think of little else.[10] Although the custom of the day dictated that Jessie use his name rather than her own in public, it is unlikely that this elevated her reception with the London press since she was soon outdistancing the notices her husband had received. In fact, it had taken Matthay years to be recognized by the major critics, and when he finally got their attention, his own reviews were far more mixed. In 1888 the praise he received in the *Musical Times* had been undercut by adjectives such as "eccentric" and "slipshod," and five years later *The Times* dismissed some of his compositions for their "lamentable want of taste." In May of 1895 the paper chided his unpublished Sonata for its "incoherence," while the *Musical News* criticized his Chopin as "fussy" and "noisy." Whether or not such assessments were objectively justified, they could not have seemed trivial to a man whose entire professional life had been shaped around the dual arts of composition and piano, and for whom many had once predicted extraordinary accomplishments. By now Matthay was certainly convinced that the art of piano playing required words as well as deeds, but if he needed further encouragement for writing a book, the cool reception the London press often afforded his efforts may have provided an additional incentive.

In the summer of 1897, as Jessie completed her first full year after returning to the Academy, the Matthays went on holiday to Germany. They stopped first at Bayreuth, so that Matthay could hear "his beloved *Parsifal*," but he found the performance—overseen by Wagner's widow, Cosima, and conducted by his son, Siegfried—"a bitter disappointment," and "totally lacking subtlety." They then went to Munich, where they found Strauss's rendering of *Tristan und Isölde* far more satisfying, but they were even more impressed with his "*perfect Mozart*."[11] How much of Matthay's proposed book had already been written is unknown, but Jessie reports that he chose an unlikely spot to augment it:

> The hills of the Tyrol called him, irresistibly as always. He pitched his camp at Sölden, a remote village in the heart of the mountains, and for

four weeks devoted himself entirely to the writing of his book. Every now and then there were expeditions to the snow peaks, guided each time by a stalwart young Tyrolean to prevent mischance or miscalculation. An urgent telegram from Scotland hastened our steps homeward, for my mother had suddenly passed away.[12]

The Matthays' unexpected return to Edinburgh no doubt brought them closer to Marjory, who for a number of years had been supporting herself as a piano teacher. She had already visited them several times at Purley, where she first learned of Matthay's work, and she keenly tracked its progress. Although Jessie makes no mention of it, Marjory indicates that she read and corrected many of the proofs for the forthcoming book, and Matthay acknowledges her contribution in his Preface. She also claims that he labored over the work for ten years, and this is substantiated by several bound volumes filled with handwritten notes now housed at the RAM. The first of these, titled "On Technique," was begun sometime in 1894 as *The Overture* was finishing its run, and its earliest entry illustrates that Matthay had now reached two of the main principles he was to stress throughout his career:

> Whether teaching oneself . . . or "teaching" others (in helping others to practice correctly)
> a. <u>Never allow a note "to play itself"</u> but always determine the <u>movement</u> continually.
> b. <u>Never allow the opposing contrary muscle to be used at the same time as the one intended.</u>
> These two are the chiefest [sic] rules with regard to all practice and playing whatever. If attended to, practice will be beneficial, if not, most probably pernicious.[13]

His "thinking on paper" is rarely confined to lists or summaries, and most often he authored full-scale essays, as evidenced by an entry which occurs two pages later. This brief excerpt from a larger piece illustrates that his views on relaxation were not only informed

Chapter 6

by a careful study of earlier theorists, but that he was determined to explain the facts as clearly as possible:

> When Deppe for instance speaks of playing with the mere "weight" of the fingers he wishes for exactly the same thing [the avoidance of stiffness]. He says "let" the fingers sink down to the bottom of the key, i. e. he desires the impression of no resistance during descent. Whether he himself really believed in the absurdity that the "weight of the fingers" could be increased by practice, or whether he merely made such statements as "suggestion" for his pupils so that they might receive the impression which would lead to a correct movement, does not really matter. But it is quite conceivable that a person not even knowing the merest elements of scientific thought (and most artists are at a disadvantage) might be led to believe when the finger is successfully brought the more downward with a larger tone result that it is the finger that has "learnt to be heavy"!![14]

His notes were often conceived during the summer meetings—the *celidhs*—which he and Jessie attended at Edinburgh University. In the later summer when the gatherings were over, they generally remained in Scotland, and at some point Matthay began writing drafts of the book. Years later, Marjory remembered summer holidays "I spent lying among the heather on the Scots hill-sides, helping with the revision of his proofs, or suggesting difficulties of comprehension that might be likely to arise on the part of the reader."[15]

As the work neared completion, Matthay was fortunate to have it accepted by one of the most venerable publishing firms in Britain: Longmans, Green, and Company. In continuous operation since 1725, the House of Longman had branches the world over and its catalogue included Gray's *Anatomy*, as well as works by Wordsworth, Coleridge, and (no doubt to Matthay's delight) Herbert Spencer. The Education Act of 1870 had prompted the company to bring forth a fresh spate of instructional titles, and by the century's end, educational books were one of its mainstays. At the time, Longmans had few musical titles, but the fact that they offered some selected works by former RAM professors—notably George Macfarren's *Lectures on Harmony* and John Hullah's *The History of Modern Music*—may have influenced their decision. The firm also had a reputation for treating its authors with extreme generosity, and in 1880 they even paid Benjamin Disraeli £10,000 for the rights to *Endymion*—"believed to be the largest sum ever paid for a work of fiction."[16]

The completed work, titled *The Act of Touch in All its Diversity: An Analysis and Synthesis of Pianoforte Tone-Production*, first appeared in December of 1903. No record remains of what Matthay earned from its sales, but as Annabel Jones reports in a study of Longmans' history, the royalty system was in common use by the late nineteenth century, and a 15 per cent royalty on the list price for each copy sold was not an unreasonable expectation.[17] Initially, *The Act of Touch* retailed for 7s, 6d, and since it was reprinted 13 times during Matthay's lifetime, his profits could have been substantial. A modern reader might well view the book's thirty-nine-page table of contents as formidable, and its 328 pages of highly detailed text as encyclopedic to the point of distraction. It was also deliberately repetitious, since the author admitted that he sought "a *useful*, rather than an ornamental work," and that he did "not hesitate to sacrifice all literary exigencies . . . for the sake of the student."[18] He was also insistent that he was not offering a mere set of rules—a pedagogical "method" as the term is generally used—since ease of execution, while necessary, was not synonymous with artistry:

> Much of that conflict of opinion, and apparent contradiction, we find between the upholders of rival "methods" and "systems" of pianoforte playing (and of singing!) arises from non-perception of the fact, that a really great Master-artist, be he Pianist, Violinist, or Vocalist, never restricts himself to one single form of "touch" or tone-production. On the contrary, we find, that he constantly changes from one tone-kind to another. It is mostly by such means, indeed, that he is able to express those subtly-varying moods he perceives in the music he undertakes to interpret.

The "method" maker, on the contrary, having discovered one or other way of effectively using the Pianoforte-key, or human-voice, allows himself to be misled into fancying, that that particular way is the only "right method." Consequently he then decries everything that does not happen to fit in with his narrow views; and forces his pupils to perform whole works with but one tone-colour throughout, varied merely in its intensity.[19]

The above maxim is premised on a recurring theme which runs through Matthay's entire career: that artistry requires the pianist to effect qualitative changes in the piano's tone. Although he may have insisted on this point more strongly than many of his contemporaries, few challenged what was then often regarded as a self-evident observation, and his book no doubt benefited from the fact that most believed that altering the piano's "color" was an obtainable ideal. To Matthay it certainly seemed apparent that Liszt, Rubinstein, and Bülow could imbue a given instrument with a kaleidoscopic palette, and to that end he sought merely to elucidate the scientific explanation by which those effects had been achieved. At the outset of *The Act of Touch*, he freely enters the realm of aesthetics, distinguishing the "intellectual" from the "emotional" aspects of music, and asserting that while high artistry requires the cultivation of both, the expression of "emotion" is largely dependent on tone color:

The *Intellectual* interest of Music is made evident in performance, by clearly *showing* the musical "shapes"—the musical architecture.

The *Emotional* effect of Music, on the other hand, mostly depends upon the use of Tone-*Colouring*. . . .

By "colouring" is here meant not only contrasts of tone-*Amount* but contrasts in that far more important department, that of *Quality*.

Evidently it is range of "colouring"—range of contrast in tone-*kind*, that constitutes the most important item in one's technical equipment.

The proof of this is: that this very item is the point that most distinguishes the *Technique* . . . of a really great performer-artist from that of the less great; for his range of tone-shadings is far greater; his distinction between shadings far more subtle.[20]

If the logic establishing his "proof" seems circular, it should be remembered that a century ago Matthay was faced with the same conundrum challenging today's scholars, since many will argue that aesthetic beauty in music is impossible to verify scientifically. For example, that Rubinstein was once highly popular cannot be disputed, but popularity alone does not "prove" a performer's artistic worth, and even the pianist's most fervent admirers might have disagreed about the precise effects they claimed to hear when he performed. No doubt Matthay took solace in the fact that many, if not most, concertgoers agreed that the greatest artists of the day produced qualitative tonal differences, but he was fully aware that not all listeners recognized such properties. And since he saw no means of further arguing the proposition, he simply reduced it back to the level of observation—although not always kindly:

> There are some who even deny the very existence of the fact, that variety in Tone-QUALITY can be produced from the Pianoforte! The explanation is obvious enough. Either, they suffer from a physical disability which prevents their discerning such contrasts; or they have never happened to discover the *Doing*. Possibly, they may never have experimented on an instrument sufficiently good![21]

Just as Matthay took qualitative tonal differences for granted, so he accepted scientific proof as the final arbiter, and in keeping with the spirit of his age, he accepted the tenet that science could at least explain, if not substantiate, the underlying principles of beauty. In fact, the most fundamental, Aristotelian law of science—"There can be no effect without a cause"—although filtered through Spencer, serves as the motto inscription to *The Act of Touch*, and it provides the philosophic underpinning of the book's substance. However, he also saw the limits of science, and although he believed in the sanctity of reason, he did not believe that scientific explanations alone could create artistry. Throughout his career, although he insisted that rationally deduced principles could nurture a pupil's imagination and reveal the laws of technique, he also maintained that no one could "teach" a student to acquire artistic vision. He took it for granted that most of his readers would be serious aspirants who already had a message within them, but perhaps had not fully discovered the means by which to release it. And as a corollary, as he had first indicated in an *Overture* piece some 13 years earlier, he recognized that a great many gifted artists would find such explanations superfluous:

> To many Artists, self-analysis seems totally denied. Hence, such fail to recognize the *processes* of their own acts, both mental or physical. Indeed, once having learnt to act properly, knowledge of the process appears useless to such, and may be so, in some measure. This is the reason why artists, as a rule, actually resent the mere idea of "attention" or "execution"; since the very fact of their giving such good attention prevents their personally becoming aware of the act. This is also the reason why most artists prove themselves such indifferent teachers, although they often do stimulate (as Liszt did) by their exhibition of unbounded enthusiasm. Obviously, as we cannot show that which we have not perceived, it follows, that without conscious or unconscious analysis we cannot hope to become cognizant of what there is to teach.
>
> And as the self-analysis required must be that of an actual artist, we here see why really "great teachers" are even rarer than great artists.[22]

He divides his work into four large sections meant to cover the substance of his theoretical investigations, while a fifth section devoted to keyboard exercises was planned for a later date. With deliberate consistency, each section has a similar structure, all beginning with a Preamble, followed by individual chapters covering the topic in detail, each of which generally concludes with a "Recapitulatory" in boldface. A "Recapitulatory and Summary," also in boldface, appears near the end of each larger section, followed by an extensive Appendix of endnotes in reduced type to augment the ample footnotes peppered throughout the main body of the text. The book is also generously adorned with charts and diagrams. In his Preface, Matthay explains the necessity for such a seemingly cumbersome arrangement:

> In endeavouring to place the many unfamiliar facts and new ideas before the reader, there was however this dilemma to face: that innumerable prejudices and fallacies would have to be combated, and that to do this would render the treatise too elaborate for the Schoolroom; whereas to limit it to direct information in its conciscest [sic] form (as required for the Schoolroom) might render its teachings liable to misconception, and unacceptable to the prejudiced.
>
> To overcome this difficulty, the work has been laid out in four Parts, as follows:—Part I, is purely introductory, and purposes [sic] to show the relation the study of Touch bears to the general problems of Pianoforte-education. This is followed by the practical Parts, II to IV.[23]

Part I is foundational to an understanding of Matthay's entire output, for it lays the philosophical basis that guided his pedagogical career. After the Preamble, his second chapter addresses "The Problem of Pianoforte Training," in which he is careful to defend the necessity for explaining the laws of touch, leading him logically to his third chapter, "The Problem of Education in the Art of Tone-Production." The "problem," he is quick to observe, is one of science:

> Tone-production is hence a question of Mechanics, Physics, Physiology, and of Psychology too. It is an art that does not rest on mere "rules," mostly at the mercy of taste—like those of language, or of harmonic-etiquette; for it rests on physical LAWS, inexorable as those of mathematics.[24]

But he rarely misses an opportunity to conjoin theory to practical situations, as he illustrates later on the same page:

> The idea that there are "stiff" hands and fingers which have to be ground down to suppleness by interminable exercises, is also mostly based on fallacy; except in those rare cases of incapacity through rheumatism, etc.

"Stiff" wrists, "stiff" fingers, are as a rule, merely the outcome of incorrect muscular action—*impeded* action, *i.e.*: Action impeded by the unnecessary, and harmful associated action of *opposite* muscles.[25]

A few paragraphs later, he discusses the pianist's "physical endowment"—a quality he carefully distinguishes from "musical endowment"—and the concept of "arm-weight" (a term which he did not invent, but which followed and occasionally tormented him for the rest of his career) makes its first appearance:

It is evident then, that physical endowment for the Pianoforte is as divergent as that for vocal performance, and that at the Pianoforte we may evince a naturally large "voice." This depends on the actual size of the Arm-muscles, etc.,—that is, provided these are... easily *fully relaxable*. For it is the amount of Arm-weight we can set free, that forms the possible extent of our real voice, *in "singing" tone-quality*, at the Pianoforte.[26]

This passage is joined to a footnote which offers a lucid and uncompromising stance on "muscular relaxation," another concept by which Matthay's teaching would be characterized—and occasionally parodied—in the coming years. But even here, he was careful to associate the term only with "muscles that should be passive," implying that more detailed discriminations were to follow:

Really complete relaxation may possibly be physically unobtainable, perhaps even undesirable, pathologically considered; but the term thoroughly conveys, what has *practically* to be striven for. For it is the completest possible *Relaxation* of all muscles that should be passive, that forms the real "secret" of all good tone-production (including Agility) at the Pianoforte.[27]

Chapter IV, "The Problem of Muscular Education," offers a fuller explication of those discriminations, as the author summarizes the central problem in teaching all physical skills at the piano: "We must learn mentally to distinguish the muscular conditions that *are necessary*, from those that *impede* the desired result in Tone."[28] This leads him naturally to one of his most important pedagogical precepts: that the *cessation* of muscular activity is as vital as its commencement:

> We must learn to *time* [the muscular exertions] to CEASE the very instant they have completed their duties against the key—so that the energy set free by the muscles shall fulfill its purpose in making *Sound* only, and shall not instead be wasted (and worse than wasted) against the pads under the key.... We must learn similarly to *gauge* and *time* the beforementioned horizontal movements of Finger, Hand, and Arm, so that we may with *certainty* always find the required notes,—having already learnt to make the requisite movements themselves with perfect ease.[29]

Part II is devoted to the workings of the piano and it culminates in an extensive two-page diagram of the instrument's inner mechanisms provided by Bechstein. In Chapter XI, his considerably detailed discussion further underscores the necessity for muscular cessation:

> The key therefore *ceases* to induce string-speed the moment the beginning of Sound is heard; for the key-lever as it were *falls in twain* at that moment; *i.e.*: the hammer at that moment slips off the hopper, rendering it impossible for us further to influence the string through its agency, unless we first allow the key slightly to rise, and thus regain control over the hammer....
>
> This very potent fact in tone-production must always be kept in view.[30]

He also expresses his antipathy to key hitting, relying on Helmholtz for an explanation of the underlying science:

> It is found that a too sudden application of energy tends to cause the string to move off rather into segmental vibration, than into those complete vibrations—of its whole length—that enforce the fundamental sound.

The more these segmental vibrations (or harmonics) preponderate, especially the higher and harsher ones, the worse is the sound in every respect; it is less beautiful, and less full, and is less able to travel and "carry."[31]

Part III, "Key-Treatment from its Muscular Aspect," forms the core of Matthay's physical principles. He separates the "muscular components" into three separate categories: the "down-activity (or exertion) of the Finger," the "activity (or exertion) of the Hand," and "Arm-weight." However, while these modes of functioning may be mentally separated for pedagogical purposes, in practice they are typically conjoined "in an infinite variety of ways," depending on the musical effect desired.[32] His exposition also includes an identification—brilliant in its simplicity—that scientific law demands that downward exertions against the key result in upward reactions against the wrist, and at times the shoulder. Therefore, the desired sensation accompanying effective touch must always be experienced as an *upward*, rather than a downward feeling, lest the energy be wasted or misapplied. As a corollary, in Chapter XII he cautions that this reaction cannot be easily felt if the performer contravenes the downward energy of a limb by simultaneously invoking the contrary, "upward" muscles. Matthay returned to this maxim throughout his career, repeatedly insisting that muscular tension was not created simply by the use of muscles, but by the concurrent use of opposing sets of muscles:

> However strongly we may wish to urge any particular set of muscles into activity, we must under no circumstances permit this exertion sympathetically to prompt the *opposite* set of muscles into action. If we do, it will infallibly prevent our attaining any accuracy, either in tone-amount, kind or quality; and it will consequently destroy all accuracy and subtlety in Expression; it will besides prevent our attaining any true Agility.[33]

Later in the book—expanding on ideas first presented in his *Overture* articles—Matthay presents a more comprehensive codification of these physical conditions. In Chapter XIX he identifies the three "species" of touch formation, which allow for the full range of tonal effects possible from the instrument, and serve as one of his most important teaching principles:

1. Finger-activity alone, with loose-lying Hand, and self-supported Arm.
2. Finger-activity with Hand-activity behind it, and self-supported Arm.
3. Finger-and-hand activities, with relaxed Arm-weight (and its coöperatives) behind them—*i.e.*, with Lapse in the self-support of the Arm momentarily added.[34]

Because the fingers alone are not strong enough to draw much power from the instrument, "first-species" is a choice best employed in passages demanding lighter, more filigreed-type effects, although it has the advantage of allowing extreme speed when desired. Matthay adds that this technique "has often been aptly described as the 'pearling' touch."[35] "Second-species"—far more frequently used in piano repertoire—is characterized by a discrete hand exertion, however slight, to assist each finger, with the degree of hand assistance governed by the amount of sound desired. This is the touch most often required for louder scale passages, rapid chords, and double notes, since the key's resistance is multiplied proportionately to the number of notes being depressed, as well as the speed with which it must be moved, and the hand's assistance is therefore desirable. The "third species" of touch conjoins hand and finger exertion to released arm weight, and is necessary for resonant, *fortissimo* chords, but Matthay is quick to point out that the released weight can also impede speed and agility—hence the necessity for re-poising the arm at the moment sound is reached, or even for "merging" one touch form into another at will depending on the desired musical effect.

Although "third-species" allows the greatest power possible from the instrument, it is often also helpful—paradoxically—for obtaining extraordinarily soft effects. Throughout his career, Matthay stressed the value of employing "muscular" versus "weight-initiated" touch

Chapter 6

for various colors, and it was only the third species that allowed for either. If the keys were accelerated quickly into motion by the hand and fingers and backed by released weight, the sound would be large and powerful, whereas if the hand and fingers were far more passive and the keys depressed more slowly, the sound would be quieter and less brilliant:

> We must recall that this combination includes Arm-release and Muscular-exertion of Hand and Finger, and that we may therefore start (or "initiate") the whole of this combination into operation against the key in either of two ways. . . . That is: we may directly prompt either of the two implicated elements into use—either the element of Weight, or the element of Exertion, when the remaining element will automatically respond to the other's initiative. In the first case—Weight-initiative—we have the conditions that make for "sympathetic" tone-colour; whereas in the second case we have those that tend towards brilliancy.[36]

Artists customarily combine the three "species" of touch into myriad "hybrid" forms to obtain their desired effects, and understanding the usages of a fully, versus a partially, supported arm was paramount to apprehending the laws of technique. By contrast to Breithaupt, Matthay never suggested that the arm be continually released, but rather that it exist in a state of "balance" preceding most tonal acts, thereby enabling the performer to choose the amount of weight—if any—necessary for the appropriate musical result:

> Variety in QUALITY of tone, mainly depends on the fact, that when we do employ the element of WEIGHT . . . we then have the option of prompting the complete combination of Weight (arm-release, etc.) and Muscular-exertion (Hand and Finger activity) into operation against the key, by "willing" the employment of *either* of these two Elements. . . .
>
> Touch, thus initiated by muscular-*exertion* (with its more or less *sudden* key-descent) tends to make the tone-quality more or less aggressive or harsh; whereas Touch, initiated by a partial or complete *lapse* of the whole arm . . . furthers a more gradual increase of speed during

key-descent, and therefore tends to make the tone-quality more carrying, round, full, sweet, and singing.[37]

Matthay thought these qualities important enough that throughout his career he insisted on distinguishing between "muscular" and "weight"-initiated touch—each requiring a different mode of finger functioning:

> These ... contrasts in muscular-attitude have been recognized by many, as "Hammer-touch" and "Clinging-touch" respectively, or as the French have it: "*Avec attaque*" and "*Sans attaque.*"
>
> In the *first*, or "hammer-touch" variety, which we will term the BENT-FINGER attitude, or "Thrusting attitude," a greatly curved or bent position (like the hammer of an old-fashioned percussion-gun) is assumed by the finger when it is raised as a preliminary to the act of tone-production. . . .
>
> In the second, or "clinging" variety of touch, which we will term the FLAT-FINGER attitude (or "Clinging attitude") a far less curved position is assumed by the finger as a preliminary, and it may indeed be almost unbent or "flat." Exertion in this case is almost entirely restricted to the *under*-tendons of the whole finger. . . .
>
> The first kind of finger-attitude (with its correlated upper-arm conditions) is exceedingly less *elastic* than the second.
>
> When the most sympathetic quality of tone is required, we must therefore choose this second (flatter) attitude—with its elastic Knuckle and Wrist, and consequent furthering of *gradual* key-descent, and must employ this in conjunction with Weight-touch,—touch initiated by lapse in arm-support.[38]

Matthay's students later became especially noted for the "singing tone" he attributed to the "clinging" type of touch, which he recommended for warmer sounds. But he also maintained that "thrusting" touch was necessary for brilliance and a great many other effects, and that the two touch forms could—and often should—be invoked at will, even in rapid alternation. To clarify these concepts, some

Chapter 6

pages later, he offered illustrations which may have been taken from photographs. Although no credit is given, it is even possible that Matthay drew them himself, since his skills as artist and draftsman have been well documented:

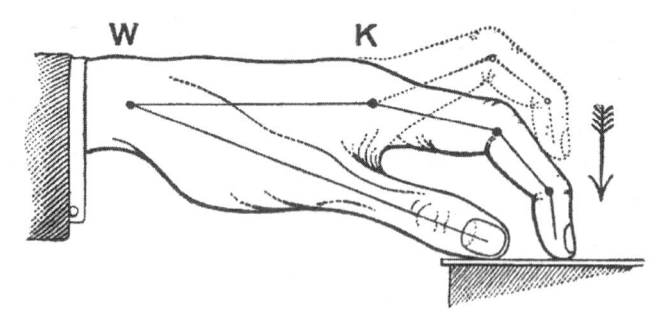

Fig. 6.1 "Thrusting" Finger illustration from The Act of Touch, p. 151. The caption reads: "The position is with depressed key; the dotted lines exhibit the index-finger fully raised. W is the Wrist, K the Knuckle."

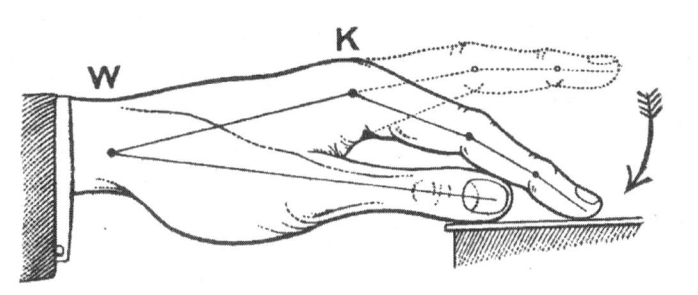

Fig. 6.2 "Clinging" Finger illustration from The Act of Touch, p. 151. The caption is identical to the one above.

But it should be noted (and Matthay later confirmed) that the drawings above were somewhat misleading to many, since it is difficult to illustrate motion in a still frame. Many believed Matthay thought the finger should always come from some distance above the key, which was never his intention. In addition to begging the question of how such extraneous movement can be reconciled with passages demanding speed and agility, such a procedure would make it impossible to measure the key's resistance during descent, and it would be difficult to reconcile such an approach with his insistence that the key never be struck or hit. It is not until he reaches Chapter XXIII, well past his first presentation of this subject, that he clarifies the matter in a brief passage:

> Ample preliminary movement of the finger is healthy, provided it is not excessive, and does not lead to "hitting," and provided there is time for it. Provided also, that such ample raising—or "playing from a distance"—is undertaken solely for the purpose of attaining *freedom* during the subsequent stepping-upon the key, or key-attack. We must be particularly on our guard, lest we fall into the common error of allowing such raising, itself, to be looked upon as the object to be attained, instead of its being regarded merely as the accompaniment of free action.[39]

His clarification is also followed by an extensive footnote, from which this passage is particularly instructive:

> It may be well here to point out, that as regards the finger-action of that greatest of Pianoforte-wizards, FRANZ LISZT, it often seemed (as observed by myself and others) *"as if his fingers hardly moved at all,"* his marvelously soft, rapid passages appearing merely to glide along, absolutely without effort,—so *"close to the key-surfaces"* was his technique at such times.[40]

It could be argued that Matthay's initial explanation of "forearm rotation," one of the most widely discussed—and misunderstood—aspects of his teaching, lacked completeness, and in fact it was introduced merely as a peripheral issue near the middle of the book. Although various kinds of forearm rotary movements had been advocated by others before Matthay, his specific identifications in this regard are one of his most revolutionary formulations. In essence, he maintained that slight adjustments felt at the elbow were necessary to create the effect of five equally strong fingers, since by their nature the fingers cannot be equally strong without such assistance. He also suggested that even though such sensations should be invisible during actual performance, making visible movements was

Chapter 6

helpful as an aid to initially grasp the condition—a suggestion that caused no little confusion to later commentators. But even though he admits that "many players never discover its necessity," his first presentation of the subject is surprisingly brief:

> Besides these main facts of muscular condition, there are several subsidiary ones that must be understood. Chief among these, is, the principle of FORE-ARM ROTATION:
>
> The rotary exertions and especially the rotary *lapses* of the fore-arm, play a very important part in Technique. Unfortunately such necessary changes in the state of the fore-arm remain practically invisible, unless deliberately made visible by exaggerating them.[41]

Four years later he enhanced his explanation with exercises in the muscular *Relaxation Studies*—discussed below. By his own admission, the subsequent attention he paid to rotation was due precisely to the unanticipated misconceptions he later encountered from so many students and professionals.[42]

As one example of how the various components of touch can merge at the performer's will to create the desired musical effect, Matthay cites the first movement of Beethoven's *Appassionata*, in which a great many passages demand the "bent-finger" type of touch. The passages beginning at bar 51 clearly demand rotational freedom, and while the inner voice moves at a rapidity calling for the "second-species," the accented tones in the upper voice (A-flat, A-flat, C-flat, B-flat, A-flat, etc.) demand some "third-species" assistance with the arm, used only instantaneously and then re-balanced.

Example 6.1 Beethoven: Sonata, op. 57
"Appassionata," first movement, mm. 52-53

> Many of the more rapid passages of BEETHOVEN have thus to be played "bent-finger." For instance, the passage commencing bar 52 of the first movement of the "Appassionata," must have all the non-accented played "bent" finger and second Species of touch, while for the accented notes we must add the arm-element.[43]

Matthay spent much of his career stressing that most of the important sensations and muscular conditions in touch were in fact *invisible*, that is that their discriminations could not be sensed visually, and he often took issue with conventional teaching which stressed only such familiar canons as "hand position." But he did not entirely discount the visual element in teaching, and Part IV of his book is titled "On Position"—although at 48 pages, it is clearly the shortest of the book's four main sections. Not surprisingly, he begins his discussion with a forceful caveat:

> Bad Position and incorrect Movement no doubt form valuable *warnings*, since they form visible signs that totally inefficient muscular conditions are being employed not at their easiest. Correct position, on the other hand, unfortunately does not form any guarantee whatsoever that the very fundamentals of Technique are correct. . . .
>
> It is necessary to insist on this point, since a degree of importance has been attached to Position that is absurdly out of all proportion to its real significance.[44]

He further counsels that since no two players are built exactly alike, no one should expect their respective positions at the keyboard to be identical. However, he does provide some general maxims which allow relatively little deviation. The most important of these is that the player sit far enough away from the keyboard so that the arm can be free to bend or unbend as required, allowing an easy lateral traversal of the instrument, as well as the full benefit of arm weight if required. He also favors centering the piano bench, and positioning it "of such height as to allow the lower part of the fore-arm to be on a level with the keys; since a lower position will render brilliancy more difficult, although it rather tends to further clinging touches."[45]

A few weeks after *The Act of Touch* rolled off the presses—in the very week the Academy began its Lenten term—Matthay presented a copy of it to the RAM Library with the following inscription:

> For the Library of the Royal Academy of Music—my
> Music mother—from Tobias Matthay/ Jan. 13th 1904[46]

Initial press reaction to the book was highly positive. Four months later, on 1 April 1904, the *Musical Times* praised the "long-expected" work as "welcome" and proclaimed that "Mr. Matthay has recently staggered humanity, or at least that considerable portion of it interested in pianoforte playing."[47] The reviewer, who seemed to have thoroughly digested the book's arguments, appeared to bring a degree of sophistication to the issues:

> The motto chosen for the book is that "there can be no effect without a cause." If the first impressions on poring over the volume are bewildering and astonishing because of the extraordinary fullness with which minute points are argued, one soon after gets deeply interested if not fully convinced. Every page has its deep, pregnant idea expressed in carefully chosen language. In Mr. Matthay's explanations and arguments there is always an undercurrent of appeal to the first principles of the relations of mind and matter and natural law generally. Physiology, anatomy, psychology and evolution are applied with Spencerian insistence. The book is no mere meandering round and toying with obscure transcendentalism; the tread of its logic is firm and the clearness of its diction bears witness to the amplitude of Mr. Matthay's vocabulary and the width and depth of his reading. The arrangement of the material of the book is masterly, even though it involves much repetition—a repetition which no good student will regret, inasmuch as it serves to drive the important points well home.[48]

Over a column is then devoted to a detailed summary of the book, and the reviewer concludes with an accolade (couched in excessive alliteration) granted to few teachers, then or now:

> What will be the influence of this extraordinary book? It should be deep and widespread even if its doctrines are not all accepted. But we have to reckon with the imperviousness of teachers and performers who have already found salvation or think they have, which in this connection amounts to the same thing. . . . But when all is said it must be acknowledged that Mr. Matthay has earned a place on a pedestal in a prominent position in the pantheon of pianoforte pedagogues.

Though unsigned, the piece may have been written by Matthay's friend William McNaught, an experienced pianist and teacher. McNaught had not yet taken over as the *Musical Times* editor, but he contributed articles to the journal on a regular basis, and a year earlier he had even been the subject of an extensive biographical feature within its pages.[49] But even if McNaught did write the review, Matthay's interest—some argued obsession—with the accurate reporting of his ideas immediately prompted him to contribute a correction, which appeared in the next issue:

> Mr. Tobias Matthay writes: "May I point out a little slip of the pen occurring in that very kind review you gave of my work "The Act of Touch," as it might lead to a misconception of my teachings? Your reviewer quotes me as saying, that "The more rapid the key-depression the harsher is the quality" of the sound. Instead of "rapid," this should read "sudden." For my teaching is, that the difference in key-attack between sympathetic and harsh quality consists in the key-depression being more gradual or more sudden respectively; whereas it is the degree of loudness that is determined by the *rapidity* of the descent."[50]

By July, the magazine's "advice" column was counseling a reader that "Mr. Matthay's book . . . will give you unlimited food for thought."[51] And by August, Longmans was offering a "Prospectus"

Chapter 6

to be "sent on application," and adorning its advertisements with an excerpt from the *Musical News*: "Surely never was any subject gone into more thoroughly and methodically by anyone than this of Pianoforte-Playing by Mr. Matthay."[52] By September, one "Presto," who claimed to hold the L.R.A.M., had written the *News* wondering how Matthay could claim it was possible to obtain brilliant touch without striking the key from a distance.[53] The letter also suggested that Matthay favored only one type of touch, which the writer charged would make a "lengthy composition" become "more or less monotonous." Matthay of course answered, and the *Musical News* ran his lengthy reply on 15 October, which read in part:

> Such misconceptions of my teachings it is not right to pass without protest, seeing how widely read your paper is; although these misconstructions arise from carelessness on the part of a writer who has obviously merely read (or heard?) at random one or two sentences of my work. Even a casual perusal of this would prove, that so far from teaching that a "lengthy composition" should be performed with one single kind of touch(!) I point out that it is possible to enumerate at least 42 well-defined modes of key-treatment, not to speak of their inflections! . . . I certainly do insist that if one desires *accuracy in musical-result*, one must no more *really* hit a key (however much it may seem so), than one would, for instance, hit any object, which one wishes to snatch up rapidly from a table.[54]

And a week earlier, even Corder had jumped into the fray, challenging the magazine's reviewer for proclaiming Moscheles to be one of the greatest teachers: "The man who could see no merit in either Chopin's or Liszt's writing for the piano and who could talk of 'squeezing tone' from the instrument stands proclaimed as an ignoramus."[55]

Nine months later, *The Act of Touch* was already in its second printing, and it was now available in America. Interestingly, as early as October of 1902 the New York office of Longmans had announced the book as available—over a year before it was published—under the title *Pianoforte Tone Production in all its Diversity. An Analysis and Synthesis of "Touch" Considered as the Means of Expression*, and perhaps this was the title Matthay had originally intended. It was advertised under that title in the *New York Times Book Review* on 11 October 1902, but it does not seem to have materialized in the States until shortly after its British publication over a year later. On 2 January 1904, the *Book Review* announced a forthcoming book titled "The Art [sic] of Touch" with a brief synopsis, but the reviewer seemed to enjoy his own witticisms more than the subject matter:

> *Longmans, Green & Co.* are about to publish a highly scientific work on pianoforte playing. The book store habitué, who carelessly may pick it up and glance through its pages, may possibly imagine that it deals with an entirely different subject, for its title reads, "The Art of Touch in All Its Diversity," and some of the chapters are entitled "Key-Treatment from Its Instrumental Aspect," "The String," "The Concepts of Touch," "The Three Chief Muscular Tests," and "Details of Position." It is not, however, a "bunco-steerer's" vade-mecum.[56]

Four months later, the book was reviewed more seriously by Richard Aldrich, who had recently succeeded W. J. Henderson as chief music critic for the *New York Times*. Educated at Harvard, Aldrich, like Matthay, was an ardent Wagnerian, and as a former student of John Knowles Paine, he was thoroughly immersed in Germanic traditions.[57] Matthay was no doubt fortunate that his work seemed to resonate so positively with one of New York's leading critics, but Aldrich was far from impressed with the author's means of expression:

> Mr. Matthay's book is a prodigiously thorough, logical, and learned application of scientific principles to one important and fundamental matter in pianoforte playing. It is the art of tone production with which the book deals in a way that has never been attempted before. . . . There is a vast amount of verbiage in the book, which is written in a crabbed

and unidiomatic English style. But its idea and the general method of carrying it out are admirable. . . .

[Matthay] insists on a thorough learning of the treatment required for "each and every sound—kind [sic][58] and shading," (to quote a specimen of the curious Teutonic English that he uses,) and secondly, on acquiring and forming into habit all those different sets of muscular conditions of activity and relaxation that are necessary to give that treatment. The balance of the muscles brought into play is a subject into which the author goes deeply: he distinguishes a large number of different varieties of touch and of "key attack"—no fewer than forty-two, in fact. . . . It may be feared that the formidable detail, minuteness of classification, and attempt at the highest refinements of scientific analysis may deter many from going far in this book. Yet it is clear that Mr. Matthay has expressed some important facts in it—facts that would repay consideration. It is rather unfortunate that they are not presented in a manner, if not more alluring, at least more accessible.[59]

Americans appeared to have far less tolerance for what many regarded as an unwieldy German syntax, and Aldrich's reservations were in fact mild compared to those of New York's most noted critic, the *Tribune's* Henry Kriehbel, who offered his review five months later. Despite his reverence for German culture (both of his parents were German and he later translated Thayer's mammoth *Life of Beethoven* for English-speaking audiences), Kriehbel seemed so offended by Matthay's approach that he virtually dismissed the entire work:

Of economy, either in time, words, paper or printing ink, Mr. Matthay has no conception. He writes a book to tell what he is going to say in a book which follows; supplements that with a book promulgating what he has written; amplifies all this in another volume of appendices. The result is so bewildering that the reader is not likely to carry away much more than this: that to play upon the pianoforte one must press upon a lever called a key sufficiently hard to cause the hammer to hit the string. Of course there is much more in the book, and many things that have pedagogical value; but it is laborious to dig them out of Professor Matthay's verbal tumulus.[60]

Matthay was keenly—and at times painfully—aware of these criticisms. Jessie reports that they were both touched by the "warmth" of the *Musical Times* review, but that he was quite concerned about his perceived "verbal tumulus."[61] She indicates that his determination to clarify awkward wordings led him to produce his next work, a briefer distillation of the maxims contained in *The Act of Touch*, called *First Principles of Pianoforte Playing*. The book was issued by Longmans in 1905, and at 129 pages it was far shorter than its predecessor. Notwithstanding Jessie's claim that Matthay was seeking to simplify his language, *First Principles* consists mostly of verbatim extracts from the larger work—even the same plates have been used—deliberately pared down "for the School-room and Class-room, and as a Text-book for Examinations."[62] But Matthay did add a twenty-six-page chapter called "Directions and Definitions for Learners," along with seven pages of "Advice to Teachers and Self-Teachers." As might be expected, he opens his advice to "learners" with a brief discussion of the piano and its mechanisms, albeit somewhat simplified for younger audiences: "When you move the key down, its other (hammer) end tilts up like a see-saw, and in rising it gives up to the String any motion which you may have succeeded in imparting to the key while you were moving your end of it down."[63]

His essay for teachers begins with suggestions for teaching adult students, and his advice seems reminiscent of the studio experiences once recounted by his pupil Ernest Read: "In dealing with adults, it is best to devote the first two, three (or more) lessons to a general consideration of the main principles and laws which must be obeyed during Practice and Performance if one would succeed technically and musically."[64] He modifies this approach only slightly when teaching children:

> With an intelligent child one need not hesitate to start with a recital of the facts to be learned, even as advocated for adults. Of course

this must be reduced to the simplest and barest outline; the teacher being careful to draw attention rather to *what has to be done*, than to the explanation of *why* it has to be done; for a child cares not to know the Wherefore so much, as the *How*-fore! Every intelligent child will indeed be found quite interested to know "the rules of the game" before starting to play; much therefore depends on the way these matters are presented;—one can only expect the child to be interested, provided the teacher makes plain the *immediate* and *practical* application of these rules.[65]

However, for neither adults nor children should lessons be allowed to remain purely abstract, and he adds that, "Experiment at the instrument itself, both by teacher and pupil, should constantly accompany this description and outline of these main facts."[66]

For students of all ages, Matthay suggests "Exercises, Studies, and Pieces best suited to the pupil's stage of advancement," and he even recommends several "well-planned" sets of finger exercises, including Oscar Beringer's *Daily Practice*, which he calls "very sensible."[67] It was a compliment Beringer scarcely repaid in kind, since two years later the highest accolade he offered his colleague was that Matthay had "recently seen the light." Beringer may have sensed an even greater competition afoot, because within the year Matthay had completed his long-promised set of technical exercises designed to form in effect, a fifth section to *The Act of Touch*. His one-hundred-fifty-page *Relaxation Studies in the Muscular Discriminations Required for Touch, Agility and Expression in Pianoforte Playing* was issued by Bosworth (also Beringer's publisher) in the first week of February of 1909, at the price of six shillings. Since the work was unlike any technical studies that had yet appeared, the author opens it with an extensive foreword echoing his leading pedagogical principle—that technique cannot be separated from music:

My "Method"—of teaching—does *not* consist in the use of any special exercises, nor even of mere explanation of and attention to "rules." It consists in giving properly selected pieces of actual music, to the student, and while making clear to him the interpretative requirements of such actual music, it consists in showing him at the same time how to conquer the difficulties of its performance—the technical and interpretative difficulties therein met with. Studies and Exercises are then given to serve as concentrated material for the study of the difficulties found to be barring the way, the nature of which difficulties having been previously fully explained to the student.

I do not approve of any "method" which separates the study of Execution from the study of Music. The two things, although quite distinct, should nevertheless be always studied conjointly as far as possible. Since we must acquire such habits that our musical sense will in the end serve to prompt the requisite technique, it is necessary that we should all along endeavour to weld these two—our musical faculty and our technical faculty—into a most intimate relationship; and we must never therefore, even during the early stages of learning, lose sight of that which should always form our ultimate aim—the achievement of the Beautiful in Music.[68]

In fact, the *Relaxation Studies* contains comparatively few technical exercises. Instead, it is a book largely of printed instructions for acquiring muscular conditions, conditions which are tested by exercises often done away from the keyboard. It is also peppered with photos of Matthay's highly accomplished class of RAM scholars—including a teenaged Irene Scharrer and Myra Hess—engaged in demonstrations of these exercises. Matthay clearly intended it as a book to be read as well as played, and he carefully follows the plan he presented in *The Act of Touch* concerning the hierarchical nature of the physical skills which require mastery. And though he remains a steadfast Darwinist, he eschews dogmatism with respect to the order in which the material is presented to a student:

Regarding the ORDER in which these exercises should be undertaken, the answer must be the same as to all such enquiries, and that is, that there should be no fixed "course of study," since the result of such "method" must always be to mis-fit the vast majority of cases. Therefore, also here, the actual order in which the exercises are begun, must be determined by the requirements of each individual case. Certain laws do, however, somewhat control our choice. For the laws of Evolution do indeed apply as strongly during the process of learning to play the Piano as during every other form of growth in Nature; and we cannot transgress those laws, and yet hope to obtain the best results from our study. Thus, in learning, we must always try to master the more simple facts before proceeding to the more complex ones.[69]

The book is divided into three main sections. Part I is titled "The Chief Muscular Tests and Other Permanent Daily Studies," and it consists of four sets of studies: 1) the Freeing or "Balancing" Exercises, 2) the "Aiming" Exercises, 3) the "Throw-Off" Exercises, and 4) the Rotation Exercises. The "freeing" exercises are designed to eliminate the "contrary exertions in finger and hand actions" which Matthay believed to be the root cause of tension, and they involve allowing the hand to lie loosely on the surface of the keyboard. The player is asked to undulate the wrist slightly to test for hand freedom, and to move the hand slightly forward to test for finger freedom. The "aiming" exercises can be done both at and away from the keyboard, but they all amount to testing whether the player has ceased applying energy before the key-bed has been reached, as opposed to misapplying exertion by continuing to press against the key-beds. In its most advanced form, Matthay suggests practicing it in double-note groups in each hand at dynamic levels ranging from *ppp* to *fff*. The passage below is tricky—in fact practically impossible—to play smoothly unless the player has ceased exertion at the point of sound. Matthay also provides multiple fingering suggestions and groupings indicated by the two sets of brackets in the right hand, "to prevent one's becoming accustomed to commencing the fingering groups at the same moment in both hands."[70]

Quadruple Arpeggio

Example 6.2 Advanced "Aiming" Exercise from Relaxation Studies, p. 14

The "Throw-Off" exercises are designed "for the elimination of arm-force" and "the isolation of finger and hand down-exertions from those of the arm."[71] This exercise also comes in various forms, but generally the trick is to perform an arpeggio or scale while kicking against the key-bed on the last note only, thereby sending the free-floating arm into space:

Example 6.3 "Throw-Off" Exercise from Relaxation Studies, p. 26.

Once again, the player will fail this test if the arm is in the least bit stiff, for it will not rebound easily, that is, it will not "float." Obviously, this test requires a highly visible component, and although Matthay did not invent it, many of his most famous artist-pupils were known for the grace with which they performed this gesture in public—occasionally leading some (wrongly) to believe that Matthay advocated distance, rather than proximity, to the keys in performance.

The "Rotation Exercises" can also be done away from the keyboard, and Matthay chose to feature photos of twelve-year-old Vivian Langrish (in a period sailor suit) to demonstrate some of the "preparatory gymnastic exercises" designed to facilitate their employment. Born in Bristol, Langrish (1894-1980) won an Ada Lewis Scholarship in 1906, which brought him immediately into Matthay's studio at the RAM. The photos simply show him holding a stick with his right hand and twisting his right forearm so that the stick's end is made to touch his left hand.[72] At the keyboard, Matthay advocated a wide variety of exercises to insure rotational freedom which he recommended practicing in all keys. In more preliminary forms, he advocated practicing them in octaves, and for more advanced players he recommended playing them in tenths, as illustrated by this exercise in E-flat:

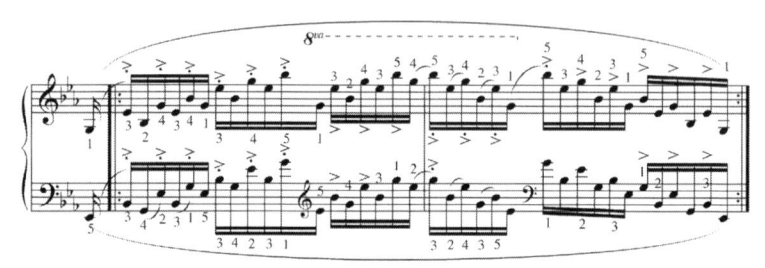

Example 6.4 Advanced Rotational Exercise from Relaxation Studies, p. 49.

Matthay wrote much about rotation in subsequent years, and he grew even more to respect the fundamental role it played in technique. The only exercises he provides in the *Relaxation Studies* are in parallel motion, or in other words, the passages in each hand move in the same direction. Later, he came to believe that contrary-motion passages were more fundamental and should be mastered first, and he reflected this in his teaching materials.[73]

Part II of the *Relaxation Studies* consists of "Preparatory Exercises," all of which are to be done away from the piano. He provides exercises in turn for relaxing the hand, the forearm, the upper arm, and the shoulder, as well as for exerting the forearm while the upper arm is lax. Again, photos of Matthay's students serve to illustrate these procedures, and young Langrish (this time looking more mature in coat and tie) is joined by Irene Scharrer, nearly twenty, and a very young Harriet Cohen, barely into her teens. Part III is devoted to "Special Exercises" earmarked for the advanced player. These include a modified version of the "throw-off" exercise designed to be done so quickly that the arm must be "kicked off" at each end of it, and performed in thirds so that "the slightest *prolongation* of any of the notes sounded by the *preceding hand*, will under these circumstances instantly mar (or even entirely prevent) the sounding of notes by the *succeeding hand*, and will thus warn the student of his misdoing."[74]

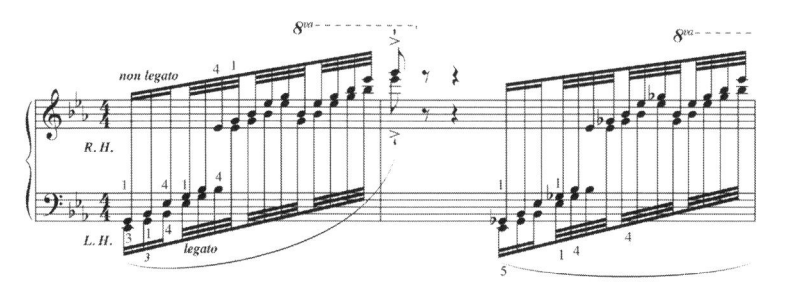

Example 6.5 Advanced "Throw-Off" Exercise from Relaxation Studies, p. 81

A similar skill is demanded by the playing of rapid scales where the hands are separated only by a tone:

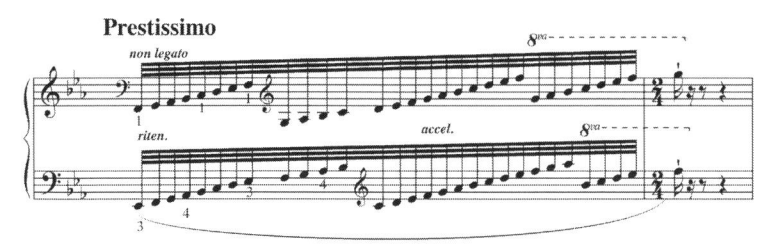

Example 6.6 Advanced "Throw-Off" Exercise from Relaxation Studies, p. 84

After offering studies for octaves and hand touch, Matthay provides what he terms "easy" and "advanced" forms of "technic for lateral freedom." In one of the "advanced" forms illustrated below, the little finger is required to sustain the G through the entire exercise while the thumb is required to move successively toward and away from it. Not only does this study test lateral freedom, but it virtually mandates that the performer hold notes freely without "key-bedding."

Example 6.7 Advanced Form of Lateral Freedom Study from Relaxation Studies, p. 115.

The last sentence in Matthay's Preface to the *Relaxation Studies* is: "At a future period I hope to issue a book of additional exercises and technics under the title of 'Occasional Technics,' giving further material on the same lines."[75] He wrote this about 40 miles southwest of London at Haslemere, Surrey. Jessie indicates that Matthay had once again been longing for a country home, at least as a weekend retreat, but as yet he had found nothing to his liking:

> In the summer of 1906, while working at "RELAXATION STUDIES," he spent a very delightful holiday at Moses Hill Farm on a spur of the Surrey Hills running south from Hindhead and parallel with Blackdown, where Tennyson, some thirty years earlier, had found the ideal spot for his home.
>
> Here it was that Matthay discovered the hilltop of his dreams. Here from the extreme point of MARLEY HEIGHTS one could have a thirty-mile view, east, west, south, and north, over country as yet unexploited. A poet friend, Wilfred Wilson Gibson, described it as being "on the prow of a great ship surging forward and cresting green billows of tumbling grandeur stretching far away into the distance." Walking and cycling had taken Matthay the length and breadth of the beautiful southern counties, but nowhere had he met with such buoyant freedom, such widespread beauty and quietude. There would be difficulties, of course;

ordinary comforts would have to be sought and fought for, but this was an adventure entirely after his own heart.[76]

Matthay believed he had found paradise. Now, all he needed was a castle worthy of it.

Notes

1. The July 1890 RAM catalogue lists two professors of elocution: Walter Lacy and John Millard. By August of 1891, only Millard was listed. The fall 1900 catalogue, now calling the area "Diction & Elocution," lists a Miss Bateman (Mrs. Crowe), plus Annie M. Child, William Farren, Henry Lesingham, Ian Robertson, and Katie Thomas.
2. *TT,* 4 May 1898, 1, col. E.
3. *MT,* 1 January 1905, 41. Jessie appeared at Aeolian Hall on 6 December 1904, under the auspices of the Royal College of Music Patron's Fund. Bowen and Bax appeared on the same program.
4. *TT,* 18 May 1900, 15, col. B.
5. *TT,* 27 May 1903, 14, col. D.
6. *MT,* 1 January 1903, 52, and 1 March 1904, 186.
7. *TT,* 29 Oct. 1906, 12, col. B.
8. Charles Villiers Stanford (1852-1924), then the reigning composer at the Royal College of Music, composed a large choral setting of Tennyson's poem entitled *The Revenge: A Ballad of the Fleet,* which had first been performed at the Leeds Festival ten years earlier.
9. *TT,* 11 December 1906, 17, col. C.
10. LI.
11. JHM, 32. Strauss had been appointed *Kapellmeister* in Munich in 1894 and had yet to establish a following for his own operas, but had garnered much acclaim for his productions of both Wagner and Mozart, staples of the Munich summer festival since 1875.
12. Ibid.
13. Matthay, "On Technique," 3. RAMRBC (uncatalogued at this writing).

14. Ibid., 5-6.
15. MKF, 85.
16. Annabel Jones, "Disraeli's *Endymion*: A Case Study," in Asa Briggs, ed., *Essays in the history of publishing in celebration of the 250th anniversary of the House of Longman*, (London: Longman, 1974), 153. Jones quotes from Robert Blake's 1966 biography *Disraeli*.
17. See Jones's discussion, 147.
18. *AOT*, 10.
19. *AOT*, 6
20. *AOT*, 16.
21. Ibid.
22. *AOT*, 11-12.
23. *AOT*, x.
24. *AOT*, 20-21.
25. *AOT*, 21.
26. *AOT*, 22.
27. Ibid.
28. *AOT*, 25.
29. *AOT*, 26.
30. *AOT*, 80.
31. *AOT*, 74-75. See also Helmholtz, *The Sensations of Tone*, 74 ff.
32. *AOT*, 102-103.
33. *AOT*, 103.
34. *AOT*, 215.
35. *AOT*, 224.
36. *AOT*, 220.
37. *AOT*, 107-108.
38. *AOT*, 109-110.
39. *AOT*, 281-82.
40. *AOT*, 282.
41. *AOT*, 117.
42. As late as 1932 he wrote, "In spite of all that I have written and lectured on this very point, I am still persistently and stupidly misrepresented." (*VIPT*, 30).
43. *AOT*, 224. This comment is contained in a footnote.
44. *AOT*, 273-74.

45. *AOT*, 276-77.
46. Inscribed on the title page of *The Act of Touch*. As last as 2004, this was still the copy in circulation in the RAM Library.
47. *MT*, 1 April 1904, 245.
48. Ibid.
49. See "W. G. McNaught," *MT*, 1 Mar. 1903, 153-59.
50. *MT*, 1 May 1904, 326.
51. *MT*, 1 July 1904, 471.
52. See, for example, the ad in *MT*, 1 Aug. 1904, 547.
53. "The Act of Touch," letter to the *Musical News* 17 Sept. 1904, 247.
54. "'The Act of Touch.' to the Editor of 'Musical News,'" *Musical News* 15 Oct. 1904, 288.
55. "The Act of Touch," letter to the *Musical News* 8 Oct. 1904, 277.
56. *New York Times Book Review*, 2 Jan. 1904, BR14.
57. In the year this review appeared, Aldrich's *Guide to Parsifal* also appeared and the following year he published a *Guide to the Ring of the Nibelung*.
58. Aldrich may have intended a hyphen here rather than an em dash.
59. *NYT Book Review*, 9 Apr. 1904, BR241.
60. *New York Tribune*, 28 Sept. 1904, cited in JHM, 38.
61. JHM, 37-38.
62. Tobias Matthay, *First Principles of Pianoforte Playing*, (London, 1905), v.
63. *FP*, 1.
64. *FP*, 121.
65. *FP*, 125.
66. *FP*, 121.
67. *FP*, 122-23.
68. *MRS*, i.
69. *MRS*, iv-v.
70. *MRS*, 14.
71. *MRS*, 24.
72. See *MRS*, 45.
73. See *The Nine Steps to Finger Individualization* (App. III) and Ch. 8.
74. *MRS*, 80.
75. *MRS*, ii.
76. JHM, 49-50.

CHAPTER 7

BUILDING AN EMPIRE

On 1 February 1907, Tobias Matthay paid Sir Jonathan Hutchinson £575 for slightly over two acres of land. Hutchinson (1828-1913), a Fellow of the Royal College of Surgeons, was then an Emeritus Professor of Surgery at the London Hospital and Medical College and one of the most noted physicians in Britain. He was also highly acclaimed for his research into leprosy, which he pursued with trips throughout Europe, Africa, and Asia well into his eighties. After he died at his home in Haslemere—which he called "The Library"—*The Times* noted that over the years he had become

> a considerable proprietor at Haslemere, and built houses there for his own habitation and also for members of his family, among whom at last he came to hold a sort of patriarchal position, and where he was at once beloved for his amiability and benevolence and honoured for his scientific eminence. He built and endowed a museum at Haslemere, and devoted much time and thought to rendering it useful for the instruction of the children and the young people of the vicinity.[1]

The conveyance to Matthay's property designated a plot situated "at Moses Hill in the Parish of Fernhurst in the County of Sussex," but his purchase was so close to the Surrey county line that his mailing address was always identified as Haslemere. The document further describes his land as "bounded on the East and South sides thereof by the road leading from Kingsley Green to Marley Common and all other sides thereof by land belonging to the said Jonathan Hutchinson."[2] At that time Marley Common was a vast expanse of forest and hiking trails generally thought "common" to public use, but this was often contested by the third Lord Leconfield, who lived at nearby Petworth House and occasionally

Chapter 7

erected barriers around its perimeters.³ Nor was Hutchinson's property free from liens, for Matthay's tract was but a small part of some 40 acres he had purchased several years earlier, an area overlooking the Sussex Downs known as Marley Heights, and he was still carrying a £9,000 mortgage. But after three years of payments, Sir Jonathan's mortgagors agreed that a two-acre sale still left him with sufficient collateral to secure the loan, so Matthay was able to acquire the crown of his beloved Moses Hill freehold and absent any encumbrance.

That crown was more than 700 feet above sea-level, and on a clear day an observer's southward gaze could span over 40 miles—as far as the English Channel. The hill jutted outward to the south to form a sharp angle, suggesting—in Gibson's words—"the prow of a great ship," but the property was also landlocked, so Hutchinson was required to provide Matthay with an easement so that he could travel the only access road. Matthay also agreed to share in the maintenance of the road, to which both parties pledged £5 a year, and there were several more significant conditions: Matthay was required 1) to erect and maintain in perpetuity a "good and [substantial] wood or iron fence" adjacent to Hutchinson's land on the west and northwest portions of his property; 2) to abstain from carrying on "any [trade] or business whatsoever" on the premises without Hutchinson's approval (if he considered piano teaching a "business" he probably waived his objection); 3) to build no more than one dwelling house on the property at a minimum value of £500—or a value of £750 if "a lodge or bungalow and stabling" be included; and 4) to produce documents on demand either to Hutchinson or his heirs proving that the house met the stipulated value when confined purely to construction costs, or "labour and materials."⁴

Jessie recounts that Tobias threw himself into his adventure with unbounded enthusiasm, although it was over two years before the new house began to take shape. Soon they had erected a temporary shelter on the hilltop, and their weekends were spent eagerly transforming a wilderness:

> Nothing gave him greater pleasure than surmounting difficulties, for in spirit he was an excellent colonist. Clearings had to be made, and a little wooden house erected for the first settlers until the home should eventually be built. It recalled the little house among the treetops in Peter Pan. The shape and position of the big house were to be a snare to catch the sun—for Matthay was always a sun-worshipper—and to coax the thirty-mile view in at the windows.[5]

Finally in the spring of 1909, Jessie notes that "the bursting of buds and the song of thrushes were intermingled with the cheery ringing of hammers,"[6] and the construction of "High Marley" was under way. Architecturally, it bears some resemblance to the forward-looking Arts and Crafts styles wrought by Charles Voysey and others—particularly with respect to lighting—but the overall style is profoundly eclectic. Matthay either closely collaborated with an architect or designed the house himself, for many of its ingenious innovations were cast entirely in his own image, even to lighting the music room from the southwest since he rarely taught before noon. The floor plan unfolds to an extreme oblique angle, with the northern, less sunny side lit mostly by smaller openings, and the southern side consisting largely of rooms with expansive windows. On the first floor, Matthay's 15'6" x 14' bedroom faced the southeast corner with an unbroken semi-circular pattern of casement windows. Directly below on the ground floor was a slightly larger (16' x 14'6") dining room sporting similar fenestration, except that the casements were taller. Not surprisingly, the largest room in the house was the music room which ran from the southwest to the northwest corner on the ground floor, expanding to an area of 29'3" x 24'8". It was reached from the entrance way through large double doors, so that Matthay's pianos could be easily moved in or out. A stone fireplace dominated the west wall, complete with Baxi grate and stone mantel, both below an elegant carved panel showing a galleon "in full sail."[7] An enormous three-sided bay window—made taller by the addition of clerestory casements above the long, narrow panes—extended

Chapter 7

out toward the southwest, with a cushioned window seat wrapped around its interior.

 A small extension projected from the northwest wall looking like nothing so much as a tiny, gabled house flanked by high, narrow casements. By day, it flooded the interior staircase with light, facilitating guidance to a large bedroom, 18'6" x 13'6", directly above the music room. Framed by three exterior walls, this room opened onto a balcony directly over the music room's extended bay windows. A smaller room, 11'6" x 7'9", was adjacent with a connecting door, suggesting that Matthay may have originally planned both rooms as a suite, perhaps for his parents, since both were still living when he purchased the land. A connecting door also joined Tobias's bedroom to Jessie's, a substantial room of 17'9" x 15'9", opening onto extended bay windows facing the south, east, and west, a design which formed a protective roof over the house's southern entrance. Directly above Jessie's room was Tobias's study, which crowned the house with a towering gable, and at 25'6" x 13'6" traversed its entire width, looking out over both the north and the south. Matthay also attached a two-story servants' cottage at the northeast corner of the house, complete with sitting room, bedroom, and kitchen, and this was adjacent to an 18'6" x 12'6" garage.

 The exact date the house was ready for occupancy is unknown, but Jessie implies that the two of them had moved in by September of 1909.[8] At some point they also brought Sarah Osborne down from London to reside in Marley's attached cottage as permanent cook and housekeeper, and Jessie reports that she was soon happily "installed in her brand new kitchen."[9] They also hired a Scottish gardener named Middleton, whose "strong Aberdeenshire accent, fiery hair, and temper to match" offset his determination to landscape their grounds "in the spirit of the first chapter of Genesis."[10] As a housewarming present, the Bechstein firm graced Tobias's study—his "turret sanctum" in Jessie's words—with the gift of an upright "composer's piano." The piano's upper case converted to a drafting board so that music could easily be notated directly above its keyboard, and Jessie maintains it was designed especially for her husband. The underside of the fallboard is adorned with a silver plate directly above the familiar "C. BECHSTEIN" logo, bearing the inscription:

To Tobias Matthay
a token of esteem and friendship
from
C. Bechstein—April 1909

For over 35 years, Matthay kept the piano in his upstairs study, and for decades many locals could recall the men hired to carry its bulky mass up the two flights of narrow steps, who were prone to commemorating their journey with a series of unrestrained expletives.[11]

About two and a half years passed from the purchase of the land till the house's completion, and although no exact record remains of Matthay's expenditures over this time, they undoubtedly approached £2,000. With the £575 he paid for the land, and a £750 house enhanced by brick construction and a clay-tiled roof, he was already crowding or exceeding £1,500. He also had to clear the site, erect the required fence, construct and raze a temporary dwelling, purchase new furnishings, move two grand pianos and other belongings down from London, and hire additional staff. Since a decade earlier, so many cash outlays would have been prohibitive for the Matthays, questions concerning the source of their income are understandably raised. The couple undoubtedly had saved some money in their fifteen years of marriage, and their various professional pursuits, including the publication of *The Act of Touch*, and Jessie's success as an elocutionist, were no doubt having a positive impact on their financial status. But Matthay also came into some money when his parents died unexpectedly within about six weeks of each other, and although he had already purchased the land, his small inheritance may have enabled him to begin building sooner than he originally planned.

Tobias senior passed on 28 October 1908, leaving his widow a net estate of £693, 13s, 10d, which included their freehold house at 40 Clapham Manor Street. But before his will could even be probated, Dorothea died on 15 December, leaving her son an estate valued at

£472, 17s, 11d. Matthay never sold the Clapham home (Dora lived there till nearly the end of her life), but whatever cash he received probably helped offset Marley's expenses, which may even explain why construction began in April, immediately after Dorothea's estate had been settled.[12] The question of Matthay's financial stability in 1909 is important, since earlier in that year—before ground had even been broken at Marley—he made another major investment.

For years he had been developing a private class, and by the early 1900s it had grown to the point that he was prompted to hire assistants. For generations, nearly all Academy professors had pursued outside teaching—often through economic necessity—but it might well be asked why Matthay did not simply refer his overflow to favored colleagues or former students, as others did. Jessie's explanation is somewhat over simplified: "Matthay's responsibilities became still heavier after the appearance of his books. There came a steady stream of pilgrims, both from the provinces and the colonies and America, to seek advice and instruction—as well as many advanced students already in London, who had been arrested by the appeal of his penetrative mind."[13] But in fact, relatively few "pilgrims" appeared before World War I, and with very few exceptions his earliest private pupils were Londoners—often of modest talent. Why then did he elect to run the risk of founding a new institution?

Although he may have been inspired by the earlier models of Henry Wylde and Oscar Beringer, both of those schools were now closed, and their demise in large part could be attributed to the fact that London's musical climate had changed radically in the past 25 years. When Matthay first began his studies at the RAM, it had no significant competitors, but now two major conservatories—and a host of smaller institutions—aggressively pursued much of the same talent. If Matthay really believed his new school could be commercially viable in such a market, he must have regarded it as distinctive from anything then being offered. To be sure, his lower overhead gave him a competitive advantage with respect to fees, and he also saw his school as a valuable training ground for future RAM students— merely expanding the preparatory instruction he had offered on an individual basis for decades. No doubt economic ambition played a role as well, because he had reached the maximum pay rate—ten shillings and sixpence an hour—then offered to RAM professors, and to an admirer of Spencer's unfettered capitalism, this was not an acceptable ceiling. But even more importantly, only an academy could fully vindicate what he had written in *The Act of Touch*. Unlike his predecessors, he believed he had something to prove, and only the dissemination of his theories in a controlled, institutional environment could validate them scientifically.

Nonetheless, the Tobias Matthay Pianoforte School was as much the product of evolution as of deliberate conception. In subsequent years Matthay identified 17 February 1905 as its birth date, but he always admitted that determining a precise date was difficult since his decision to create an institution merely consolidated what had already existed "in fact although not in name."[14] When he finally formalized his enterprise, he was still teaching in his home on Arkwright Road, but in January 1906 he rented a suite of rooms at 309 Oxford Street, which he soon identified as the School's "central address." The location, directly north of and conveniently in the same block as the Academy buildings on Tenterden Street, could be reached on foot within a few minutes. Jessie indicates that Matthay's first faculty members were Dora and two of his former RAM pupils, Cuthbert Whitemore and Lily West. But *The Act of Touch* must have made a substantial impression on at least some of his RAM colleagues, for he also hired Evlyn Howard-Jones and Claude Pollard, who Jessie avows "submitted themselves to intensive training in his ideas."[15] Howard-Jones (1877-1951) was an especially impressive pianist, having studied with Eugen d'Albert in Germany, where he befriended Brahms, whose music he later performed to much acclaim. He was also Benjamin Dale's teacher, and no doubt this connection strengthened Dale's relationship with Matthay's own pupils. Pollard entered the Academy in 1893 as a student of Macfarren, who probably did not live long enough to see his former student switch allegiances.

Jessie reports that the first TMPS Invitation Pianoforte Recital was held in July 1908 in Bechstein Hall on Wigmore Street, and the

Chapter 7

program confirms that by then Matthay had added Hedwig McEwen, Felix Swinstead, York Bowen, and Percy Waller to his staff, all former students who stayed with him at least through the early 1920s.[16] The program featured a total of 18 performers and included such substantial offerings as the Chopin Barcarolle, the first Bach Partita, the first movement of Beethoven's "Waldstein" Sonata, and a few newer works, such as a Prelude in F-sharp by Corder's son, Paul.[7] The repertoire appears to be somewhat graduated in difficulty, suggesting that the most advanced students appeared toward the end, but some of the earlier selections are also challenging. For example, twelve-year-old Harriet Cohen (then studying with Dora) was third, rendering a Chopin Waltz in A-flat, while the sixth performer, a Mrs. Enid Stoker, played Matthay's demanding impromptu, "Elves." No doubt twenty-three-year-old Harold Craxton (then studying with Whitemore) was one of the School's more senior scholars, appearing twice: first in two movements of an unidentified Mozart Concerto (probably with Whitemore at the second piano), and closing the concert with an unspecified Chopin waltz. Claude Pollard is identified as the teacher of Marjory's teenaged daughter, Patuffa, who was fifth on the program, performing Tchaikovsky's *Doumka*, Op. 59.

The same program also reveals Matthay's penchant for identifying himself as "The Founder," a title he used continuously throughout the School's existence. He uses this term exclusively in a formalized, typewritten agreement he offered his teachers sometime before 1908, which set the terms of their employment.[8] It exemplifies the high degree of fiscal acumen—perhaps even shrewdness—that characterized the School's business operations, and one can appreciate the precise wording Matthay employed to protect himself from the possibility of exploitation. For example, he reserved the right to set the fees charged by his faculty, but kept his own fees off the books, so that the school's advertised rates would not affect those paid by his private pupils, who "have the right to consider themselves Members of the School, although no account of them will be rendered."[17] The contract also makes reference to the School's substantial start-up costs, which leave him no alternative but to demand 50 per cent of each teacher's fee. He does not elaborate, but one can imagine the expenses connected with renting pianos and space on Oxford Street, as well as hiring a secretary to monitor scheduling, accounts, and other matters. Jessie indicates that from the beginning, Matthay was assisted by the genial and competent Edward Cole, who in 1911 married his RAM pupil Marion White. Notwithstanding such significant financial outlays, he also opens the door, however tentatively, to the possibility of profit-sharing: "If, at any subsequent period, owing to any extreme success the School may achieve, it is found that the Founder's profits become unreasonably great, he may at his discretion, reduce this 50% to a more favourable percentage."[18]

Potential largesse aside, his document leaves little to chance, and Matthay gives himself sole discretion in all financial matters—even if it means setting aside his stated policies. For example, although the School's cut is always capped at fifty per cent, he recognizes that it may be advisable to increase the percentages of the lower-paid teachers who provide ancillary instruction, and it is clear that even from the beginning, he saw the necessity of offering such services:

> Harmony Teachers, may at the Founder's discretion, receive a higher percentage in fees than received by the Piano-Teachers.
>
> Preparers' fees, if lower than two guineas [per 12-week term], may also receive the same favour: it being to the advantage of the School to have such Preparers.[19]

He also recognizes that where talent is concerned, one size rarely fits all, and he allows himself leverage to attract the staff of his choosing: "The Founder also reserves the right to make special arrangements with any Teacher, if he considers that best in the interests of the School." However, he has also wisely installed a deterrent to gossip and elitism: "Such special arrangements will be recorded in the School books: they will therefore be known by the staff."[20] Personal initiative is also to be rewarded, but again—with legalistic precision—he insists on written confirmation to minimize the possibility of in-house fighting:

Chapter 7

> The fees of pupils introduced to the school by a Professor, will provisionally have only 30% deducted, instead of half. It will not be considered an "Introduction" unless the student brings a letter or card of introduction from the Professor concerned. Nor will the rule apply when a student exchanges professors in the School.[21]

Predictably, he also includes a "non-competitor" clause to protect the School's interests: "No Professor can be allowed to accept lower fees outside the School for private lessons within the Metropolitan District, than at the scale published by the School unless notice and permission is given in each particular case." However, seeing the wisdom of retaining prominent artist-teachers, he allows enough flexibility so as not to inhibit their pursuits: "Such permission, will however, not be with-held without strong grounds."[22] Matthay promises his teachers an annual financial report—implying that they are to be treated more like stockholders than employees—but he also reserves the right to dismiss any teacher at will. So far as can be determined, the TMPS Agreement served as the School's principal employment contract until at least 1925, and it was probably revised only in 1927 when the School was incorporated.[23]

To assess precise enrollment figures for the School's earliest years is difficult, but Jessie insists that "during the first twelve months it grew like a young beanstalk,"[24] so most likely Matthay found his new enterprise lucrative. His personal lesson fees were not advertised—perhaps deliberately—but it may be presumed that he charged more per hour than the 10s, 6d the Academy was then paying him. And even after withholding the stipulated 50 percent, he probably compensated his staff more generously than the RAM did. It is not always easy to infer Academy wages after 1900, because payment records were generally entered with less precision than in previous years. On more than one occasion Mackenzie instructed the Committee of Management to study the issue of Professors' fees via subcommittee, and although raises still required a vote of the full Committee, quite often only the amount of the increase was indicated in the Minutes. A notable exception occurred on 26 February

1911, when York Bowen delivered an ultimatum threatening resignation if his five-shilling fee were not raised to seven shillings and sixpence, a request which Matthay strongly supported. What he was being paid at the time through the TMPS is unknown, but less than two weeks later—in an uncharacteristic gesture of benevolence—the Committee granted his increase.[25]

By the end of 1908 the TMPS had outgrown its Oxford Street facilities, and although many of his professors continued to give lessons in their homes and personal studios, Matthay felt that a central location was still essential. He decided that his best means of expansion was to lease an entire house, and his gaze naturally fell northward to the largest tract of housing in the vicinity, a region known historically as the Portland Estate. The area, which dated back to the late eighteenth century, extended from Oxford Street up to Marylebone Road (including Cavendish Square), and it had always been predominantly upscale. Many of its homes were designed by the Adam brothers—once London's most fashionable architects—whose masterpiece according to many was the general plan of Portland Place. The neighborhood included Harley Street, which by 1914 housed nearly 200 doctors, and one block west was Wimpole Street, where Elizabeth Barrett Browning's family had once lived. Almost all of the property in the region was owned freehold by the Howard de Walden Estate, one of the most venerable firms in London, which sold long-term leases to affluent brokers. Matthay knew that if he wanted a house in this area he would have to rent, and at first he may have found this arrangement preferable, for he could not have remained had the property proven unsuitable for his school.

In late 1908 or early 1909 Matthay and Jessie were shown a residence at the bottom—the "busy end" in Jessie's words—of Wimpole Street.[26] The house, No. 96, was somewhat north of the School's previous location, but still convenient to both the Oxford Circus and Bond Street tube stations, and even closer to Bechstein Hall, which was just around the corner on Wigmore Street. The house was built in 1726, but it had been extensively remodeled in 1859, and almost totally rebuilt about 1896, so its appointments were extremely modern.[27] For

Chapter 7

years, it had been owned leasehold by George J. Elgood, whose firm renegotiated a 999-year lease on the property with the Howard de Walden Estate in 1913.[28] Like most London townhouses, it was tall and narrow—its front spanned only 17'11"—but exceedingly deep, extending back from the street for nearly 47 feet.[29] The Matthays planned to dedicate four of its five floors to teaching studios, and to use the remainder of the house as their London residence. Jessie remembered the "estate agent"—most likely Frederick J. Stevenson, the Surveyor for the Howard de Walden enterprise—offering resistance to Matthay's commercial plans, and insisting that it would be "no use" to open a school in such a predominantly residential neighborhood.[30] She indicates that the agent also forbade them to display a brass plate, but when Matthay determined that such opposition was dictated only by "custom," he softened his antagonism. In actuality, Elgood would have needed to renegotiate his sublease with the Estate, and the Matthays were fortunate that Stevenson permitted them to carry on, since his permission was essential and establishments such as dance studios, for example, were strictly forbidden. Whatever understandings were struck, Matthay was soon allowed to install two 2'6" by 6" plates, one on the door and another on the balcony railing, and his new location was soon open for business.[31] However, the neighborhood was far from exclusively residential, since the merchandising giant Debenhams was then using the three houses immediately to the north—Nos. 93 through 95—as dormitories for female employees working in their Debenham & Freebody shops. They also used part of No. 97 for the same purpose. No. 98 was occupied by Elgood and Company, listed in the city directory as "auctioneers," and the house also contained the offices of Frank Minshull Elgood, a practicing architect who had probably overseen the rebuilding of No. 96 twelve years earlier.[32]

The rent Matthay paid is difficult to establish definitively, but it may be approximated by studying some related figures. The 1909 Rate Book for St. Marylebone Parish assesses No. 96 at £180 for tax purposes, although its market value was probably far higher. In January of 1909 Elgood advertised a four-bedroom flat located in a

"Wigmore-Mansion" near Cavendish Square for £210 per annum. Although Matthay's property had many additional rooms, it was less elegantly appointed (the building in Elgood's ad even featured a "passenger lift"), so it may be safe to assume that he paid no more than £400 per annum—and perhaps far less.[33] He was also responsible for the annual tax bill, which was then figured at 3s, 5d per £1 of value. For the tax period from 1 April 1908 to 31 March 1909, the taxes came to £30, 12s, 6d, and they remained fairly constant for well over a decade.[34] Although such an outlay clearly involved a substantial commitment, Matthay may have reasoned that a net yield of even £40 a month from the School would comfortably underwrite his rent and taxes, and the fact that he was then employing over a dozen teachers made such a figure seem realistic. But the only way the plan could work was for him to leave his Hampstead home, which he probably owned leasehold, so he most likely waited until its sale was imminent before signing a lease with Elgood. The likeliest scenario is that his inheritance enabled him to complete Marley a few months later, so that Tobias and Jessie were soon able to become weekend commuters, a status they enjoyed for nearly thirty years.

Since No. 96 was merely a *pied à terre* for the Matthays, their needs were simple and they probably took their time about acquiring furniture. But pianos could not wait. From early on, Matthay's studio contained two Bechstein grands, and most likely the company—whose showroom was a two-minute walk from his new residence—provided their instruments at reduced rates, perhaps even as a form of advertising for one of their most cherished clients. Other firms may have followed suit, but most of the instruments were more modest and may have been acquired over a period of time. At some point Matthay obtained another Bechstein grand, and eventually a Bösendorfer, but Broadwoods, Chappells, and Challens predominated. The house's cellar was devoted to the kitchen and servants' rooms, while the ground floor consisted of a dining room along the south wall where Tobias and Jessie took meals, and a sitting room at the front (east wall) of the building which they used as a general living area—in later years its simple furnishings included

Chapter 7

a Bechstein upright. The first floor was dominated by Matthay's studio, also facing east, which overlooked Wimpole Street and was large enough to accommodate the constant flock of students who were encouraged to observe one another's lessons—long a customary practice at the RAM. At the rear was a smaller room which Cole used as his office, and the next two levels had similar floor-plans, each with a larger and smaller room used for teaching. In all, counting the concert room, the TMPS soon enjoyed a total of six teaching spaces.[35]

Since most of the studios were shared by multiple teachers, Matthay had numeral plates installed on the doors as a means of identifying the rooms. His studio was often referred to as "No. 3" and the corresponding studios on the upper floors were known as Nos. 5 and 7 respectively, with the smaller room on each floor carrying the appropriate even numbers.[36] The top floor, a characteristic mixture of split levels common to such dwellings, housed the bath and bedrooms. Although the surroundings were generally comfortable, the house's exterior walls—following the pattern of many such London dwellings—were built entirely of stone and brick and tended to be chilly year-round. The electric fires scattered throughout the building were the principal source of heat, but most visitors conceded that they helped little. Matthay had a coal-fire in his studio, but many a student remembered suffering through lessons with chattering teeth.

One of the earliest known advertisements for the new address appeared in the *Musical Times* on 1 March 1909. By then, Howard-Jones was evidently out of the picture, but the "Chief Professors" who remained—with the exception of Pollard—were all Matthay's former RAM pupils:

96, WIMPOLE STREET, W.
TOBIAS MATTHAY PIANOFORTE SCHOOL
FOR INSTRUCTION UNDER HIS TEACHERS ON THE LINES
LAID DOWN IN "THE ACT OF TOUCH," ETC.
OPEN TO PROFESSIONALS AND AMATEURS.

<u>Chief Professors:</u>

York Bowen	Dora Matthay	Percy Waller
Claude Gascoigne	Frederick Moore	Lily West
Dorothy Grinstead	Claude Pollard	Cuthbert Whitmore
Hedwig McEwen	Felix Swinstead	

Branches at Bournemouth, Bristol, Croydon,
Eastbourne, Ipswich, and Manchester
SPECIAL SHORT COURSES FOR TEACHERS
DURING TERM & VACATION TIME.
Owing to the rapid expansion of the School, more
extensive premises have been opened as above
KINDLY NOTE CHANGE OF ADDRESS
For further particulars, write EDWARD H. COLE, Secretary[37]

The "branches" generally designated studios maintained by former pupils who were now resident in outlying cities, but some of Matthay's London-based professors commuted to these areas weekly, or more often, if interest warranted. For example, Dora taught for a number of years—and eventually built a sizeable following—in Bristol. And curiously enough, directly above a TMPS ad which ran two months later in the same journal was a notice for the "Huddersfield College of Music and Northern Centre of the Tobias Matthay School of Music," which offered "HIGHER MUSICAL EDUCATION, with or without Residence."[38] Its piano studies were overseen by a Miss L. W. Ingham, undoubtedly another former student. In 1908, one of Matthay's former pupils was billing himself as Matthay's Manchester "representative," and when he enlisted in HM Forces in 1914, his pupils were taken by another longtime Manchester resident, Hilda Hester Collens (1883-1956). Collens first began lessons on Wimpole Street in 1909, and on 22 September 1920, she formally reopened the Manchester Branch of the Tobias Matthay Pianoforte School with Matthay's blessing. During her time in London she had become well acquainted with Ernest Read, who maintained a long relationship with her School, and was deemed responsible for much of its success.[39] Exactly how each of these branches were handled financially is unknown, but in many cases the proprietors simply paid Matthay a commission for the use of his name. Undoubtedly they also agreed to purchase the ever expanding array of books and teaching materials that he was producing.

And those materials were soon being marketed aggressively. Matthay immediately had letterheads printed to reflect his new address, and soon nearly all of his business and personal correspondence bore the Wimpole Street logo, suggesting that he sought to publicize his enterprise wherever possible. He even had postcards printed, and on 25 October 1910, he sent one in his own hand to the Arthur Schmidt firm in Boston, offering them the American rights for an instructional practice card with recommended fingerings for scales in thirds—which no doubt the various branches were expected to buy. This was the first entry in a catalogue of correspondence with Schmidt that spanned nearly 30 years, and it exemplifies his characteristic brevity in business matters. It also indicates that, although as yet he had no "branch" operations in America, he was striving to develop a market across the Atlantic:

Dear Sirs.

May I add your name to the Double Third Scale Practice Card which Gilson Co are printing for me, as the American Agents? or publishers[?]

Yours truly
Tobias Matthay
Messrs Schmidt & Co.[40]

In effect, Matthay was offering Schmidt the complete inventory of cards then being struck by the Boston firm of F. H. Gilson, the parent company of Stanhope Press. Evidently Gilson had no interest in distributing the title, because they were retained only to engrave and print it. When the plates were ready on 2 March 1911, they were shipped to Wimpole Street and one can presume that Matthay found Gilson's fees attractive, or he would have avoided the shipping costs by using a London firm. Evidently the agreement also called for Gilson to print 200 copies for the American market, for this was the number eventually shipped to Schmidt's, who agreed to sell the title. Gilson also struck a few additional copies for Matthay's examination, and the plates were then transferred to London publisher Joseph Williams, Limited, who had already printed some of Matthay's music and was granted the British and European distribution rights.[41] Through many years of entrepreneurial activity, Matthay produced a large volume of correspondence on TMPS stationery, but he seems never to have engaged Cole or any of his other secretaries to assist him with publishers or merchants. On 4 October 1911, a year after the first Schmidt communication, he sent them a letter which he probably typed himself, since it contains numerous handwritten insertions, and a great deal of his surviving business correspondence is entirely handwritten. Although the omnipresent letterheads scarcely suggest that he sought to segregate the School from his other commercial interests, he evidently allowed little or no intervention by subordinates in his business dealings.

By now Matthay's professional focus and stature were moving well beyond his position at the Royal Academy of Music, but this can be little documented by examining surviving Academy records. The seeming indifference he encountered is all the more surprising, since given his nearly 30 years of service—and a burgeoning international reputation—he should have been well positioned to become the institution's most esteemed piano professor. A decade earlier, he had even been given an unexpected, and perhaps undesired, advantage when Macfarren fell from grace early in 1899. On 1 February, the Committee of Management (of which Macfarren was a member) met to discuss a letter from a Miss E. J. Bentley of Leek, who complained that he had twice failed one of her students in an exam. She declared Macfarren to be "incompetent," with an "irritating, sneering nature," and alleged that his "cruel" manner had made her student suicidal.

Undoubtedly, many negative allegations were made about Academy professors from time to time, and although the Committee promised Bentley a full investigation, nothing much came from this. Still, Mackenzie's decision to affix her acerbic, three-page typewritten letter to the Minutes ledger was unusual, and could only have meant that in his eyes Macfarren's eminence was fading.[42]

For a number of years, Macfarren held a privileged position as the only Academy piano professor permitted to give weekly supplementary lectures, for which he was compensated at the rate of £2, 2s. Generally held on Wednesday afternoons, these evidently meant so much to him that even when the RAM closed to honor Queen Victoria's passing on Wednesday, 23 January 1901, he insisted his lecture be moved to Saturday.[43] After Macfarren died in 1905, Matthay dared to fill the void when on 21 June he offered to give two lectures on "The Foundations of Pianoforte Playing," which he had distilled from his recently published *First Principles*. But no sooner had the Committee of Management agreed to schedule him (at Macfarren's rate) when Beringer, then a Committee member, chimed in with a similar offer which his colleagues agreed to take under consideration.[44] However, there was no stopping the accomplishments of Matthay's pupils. In March of 1906, Marjorie Middleton Wigley, a native of Simla, India, won the Sterndale Bennett Prize (by then reduced to ten guineas and awarded for the best performance of a Bennett composition), while Myra Hess received honorable mention. Four months later, Myra was awarded the Frederick Westlake Memorial Prize,[45] and the next year, Dorothy Grinstead received the Sterndale Bennett Prize, as Myra tied for the Macfarren Gold Medal, which Bax had tied for two years previously.[46]

Such awards were routinely announced in the press, and by now, even before their studies were completed, many of Matthay's pupils were accustomed to a high degree of media exposure. Thus in December 1905, before Myra had reached her sixteenth birthday, *The Times* praised her as "a very richly-gifted pianist," for having performed the Grieg Concerto "quite superbly."[47] Still, the aggressive competitiveness of London's musical climate made chance factors occasionally welcome, and Myra was soon able to make the most of a minor scandal surrounding Benjamin Dale's Sonata, which Bowen had just premiered a month earlier. For several years the Russian-born pianist Mark Hambourg had sponsored an annual competition at the RAM to reward the best "virtuoso" piece by a student, and in 1906 an impartial committee chose Dale's Sonata over some 60 entries. On 16 June, the pianist was scheduled to play the work at Queen's Hall and personally award Dale his prize of £20 at the interval. But since Hambourg's program also included many additional pieces, he felt it necessary to trim the Sonata by omitting the first and last movements, thereby inaugurating a practice that soon became common among performers. He played the four variations of the second movement, following them with the three additional variations comprising the scherzo, thereby making a continuous fabric of seven variations. But he also made substantial cuts and took liberties so extreme that even the *Times*'s critic was taken aback:

> How far Mr. Hambourg, having virtually acquired the piece by awarding it a prize, has an artistic right to present it in a version varying at so many points from the written indications of the composer is not for us to decide; but as before presented [referring to Bowen's premiere the previous November] the piece had an artistic unity which it lost in Mr. Hambourg's version, in which many alterations of shades of force were made, apparently for the mere sake of display.[48]

Dale was so indignant that he refused to appear on stage with Hambourg and even returned the prize, which—perhaps as a consequence—was never awarded again.[49] Undoubtedly, Matthay's pupils rendered the work with greater textual fidelity, and his students soon became the Sonata's principal advocates, receiving—as Lewis Foreman notes—unusually generous press coverage for their efforts.[50] On 19 November 1906, Myra, then 16, performed the Variations at Queen's Hall at an RAM chamber concert, and the *Musical Times*—praising a "remarkable performance for so youthful a player"—went out of its way to contrast her presentation with that which had occurred in the same hall some five months earlier:

> It was an open secret that the virtuoso had so altered many passages that Mr. Dale would not appear on the platform at the close of Mr. Hambourg's rendering. Miss Hess proved that the variations as left by the composer are quite satisfactory from a constructive point of view, and are sufficiently brilliant, not to say exacting, to satisfy the majority of professional pianists.[51]

On 8 December at Steinway Hall Myra also complemented one of Jessie's poetry recitals with the Variations,[52] just four days after the eighteen-year-old Irene Scharrer had opened her recital with them at Aeolian Hall. Irene's performance prompted the *Musical Times* to label her a "clever young pianist," who performed them "most brilliantly" and with "apparent ease."[53] The following November, Myra shared the platform with Johann Kruse's string quartet at Bechstein Hall, sandwiching the Variations between Stanford's recently completed Fourth Quartet and the Beethoven "Razumowsky." Although *The Times* lamented that the work's "diffuseness and apparently fortuitous structure are qualities which contrasted unfavorably with the clear and logical form of the two quartets," the critic also observed that she performed them with "remarkable skill."[54] And less than three years later at Bechstein Hall, at a program dedicated to Matthay's RAM scholarship students, fourteen-year-old "Master Vivian Langrish" was deemed "precocious" by *The Times* after his performance of the Variations demonstrated that he was "already something of a virtuoso."[55]

It was not entirely coincidental that Matthay's pupils were associated with Dale's massive work, because he so admired it that he even had a hand in publishing it. In 1905 he joined with Corder and McEwen to form the Society of British Composers, an organization very much taken with the spirit of the "English Musical Renaissance," and designed to give a greater voice to young composers who were by then shedding Teutonic inspiration in favor of their own national heritage. Dale's sixty-three-page Sonata was the first work they published under the imprint of Charles Avison, Ltd., a press name chosen to honor an unsung eighteenth-century musician—a figure the *Musical Times* noted had "gained fresh notoriety by having been discovered by Robert Browning."[56] Although it could be argued that Matthay's strategies were occasionally self serving, his crusades to promote British music were emphatic and uncompromising. In January of 1906, he cancelled one of his subscriptions to the Philharmonic Society's series, resuming it only when the orchestra agreed to perform Bowen's first Piano Concerto at its May concert. But he was equally concerned about opportunities for British performers, and early in 1907 he wrote Francesco Berger to announce that he was cancelling both of his subscriptions and resigning from the Society's roster of Associates. Berger immediately asked him to reconsider, and on 27 January, Matthay sent the Board a letter, which read in part:

> As I have also been appealed to by one of the Directors, privately, I feel compelled to state my reasons to you, although these must have been self-evident.
>
> The Society has consistently ignored its DUTIES towards British Art all through its career. Lately this has been so accentuated that to every out-sider it must appear as a deliberate boycott of the British Instrumentalist.
>
> This year's prospectus, instead of showing any improvement in this respect, is worse than ever, seeing the number of British Pianists and String Artists now so prominently before the public of this country, Germany and America, and whose great "drawing" powers cannot be questioned.
>
> For this reason I felt it my duty, as a Patriot, to take the step I did. Since, however, I now learn from my personal friends on the Directorate that there is an intention to repair the slights thus inflicted upon native talent, I will suspend my intention to resign for another month, and will await the publication of the Society's amended prospectus.[57]

Whatever intention the Society may have had to "amend" its prospectus, its 1907 roster of soloists was framed by Teresa Carreño at its first concert (6 February), and Mischa Elman at its sixth (16 May), both of whom were already receiving frequent exposure in London. And the Directors evidently had no interest in appeasing Matthay, since Berger immediately accused him of spewing "so many inaccuracies as regards the Phil. Soc. that they do not feel called upon to reply in detail."[58] On 11 February, Matthay responded that, "I assure you I shall only be too delighted to find that things are not quite so bad as they look." But he continued:

> In the meantime I fear the letter, describing as "inaccurate" my statement that the present prospectus of the Philharmonic Society forms a "boycott of the British Instrumental Artist", is only a further proof of that obliquity of vision on the part of some of the Directors, which has brought the Society to its present financial straits, and has prevented it from seeing the trend of the times and from following sound advice.[59]

Berger may have felt especially justified in his remarks, since a week earlier he had promised McEwen a performance of his *Coronach* Symphonic Elegy on 17 April. The same program featured Clara Butt singing an aria from *Samson and Delilah*, but such interspersions were common at Philharmonic concerts, and Matthay's "instrumental boycott" assertion was supported by the fact that the only instrumentalist featured that evening was Hungarian violinist Tivadar Nachez, premiering his own concerto.

Matthay continued to promote British music wherever he could, and a year later, Myra gave "a very able and interesting performance" of Dale's Variations at a benefit concert he sponsored with Jessie at Steinway Hall. Devoted entirely to the works of British composers, the program included Jessie's recitation of Thomas Hood's "The Song of the Shirt" (to Stanley Hawley's music), and Tennyson's "The Mermaid" (to Swinstead's music). The songs of Matthay, Vaughan Williams, Charles Wood, and Arthur Somervell were also heard, sung by Jessie's youngest brother, John (Jack).[60] Jack Kennedy had practiced law in Edinburgh for a number of years, and now as he was entering his forties, he sought to return to his family's roots by teaching voice. A widower with two children, he began to grow closer to Dora, and within a year they were married and dividing their time between Clapham and Bristol, where they both taught.

Undoubtedly, Myra had a prodigious ability to learn and retain repertoire, because her Steinway Hall appearance came exactly one week after a recital in Aeolian Hall which did not even include Dale's Sonata. Her two grandest works for the afternoon were Schubert's "Wanderer" Fantasy and Franck's Prelude, Chorale, and Fugue, but she also offered d'Albert's transcription of Bach's D major Prelude and Fugue for organ, Chopin's third Ballade, and several shorter works by Brahms and Matthay. Her reviews were extremely favorable, but *The Times* chided her for a "hard edge" in her *forte* playing, despite her "great command of piano tone." If such criticisms were less common for Matthay pupils, she was at least praised by the same critic for her "untiring energy and very little appearance of effort."[61] Just one month later on 22 February, the seventeen-year-old returned to Aeolian Hall for an all-Beethoven recital, with offerings which included the "Moonlight," the Op. 2, no. 3, and the Op. 110 Sonatas. Perhaps understandably, Myra had not yet acquired all the poise and refinement for which she was later noted (Jessie claims she even "bolted" through works, much to Matthay's disdain), and on at least one occasion she was publicly taken to task for shallow "glamour"— although she may have been the victim of a blatant Liszt animus. On 2 September she played the composer's E-flat Concerto at Queen's Hall under Henry Wood, and *The Times* critic, after praising works by Mendelssohn and Dvořàk, made no effort to conceal his bias:

> After that, however, came the dreary wastes of Liszt's pianoforte concerto in E flat, which gave Miss Myra Hess ample opportunities of exhibiting her very considerable technique; any genuine musical feeling was precluded by the nature of the music. The rapturous applause with which the performance was greeted showed once again that the glamour of virtuoso playing is not yet a thing of the past.[62]

Myra also had a penchant for absorbing newer, more esoteric works, as when she performed Vincent d'Indy's difficult Sonata about six months later in the composer's presence. D'Indy was the guest of honor at Novello's for a gathering co-hosted by the Society for British Composers, an affair to which Bax later confessed he escorted Myra merely as an excuse to meet the composer:

> Amusedly I noted d'Indy's expression of enhanced suspicion as she sat down at the piano, an apprehension made evident by the restless twitchings of his nervous face and hands. But after a few moments, his anxiety allayed, he relaxed and listened in calm appreciation, and at the end of the sonata expressed himself as delighted—albeit not a little astonished—that so young an artist [Myra had just turned 19] could triumphantly overcome the complexities of such a work.[63]

Irene, two years Myra's senior, also devoured difficult works with apparent ease, and she executed them with a virtuosity that soon evoked comparisons to Liszt. During their Academy days, Myra and Irene were both regulars at RAM concerts, appearing as Jessie notes, "in the regulation white concert dress of the Academy student, with a red sash across the shoulder."[64] Matthay no doubt relaxed the dress code when he presented his students each July in Bechstein Hall, and Jessie reports that at one such gathering the pianist Vladimir de Pachmann was "enraptured" when Irene played a group of Chopin Etudes—repertoire which soon became her specialty: "Rushing into the artists' room with much Pachmannesque gesticulation, he exclaimed: 'I could not play them better myself,' and then with a sly look added, 'certainly I could not play them faster.'"[65] Irene not only brought a spectacular command to her performances, but a seemingly effortless facility. For a number of years the Academy had organized year-end picnics at Hedsor in Buckinghamshire, reached via a small steamer which sailed up the Thames to mingle professors with "some lucky students who could spare the money."[66] As impromptu concerts were the custom on the return journey, the boat always included a piano, and on one such occasion Mackenzie asked

Irene to play some Etudes. After she rendered the "Black Key," he asked her, "with his merry twinkling eyes,"

> "You couldn't play that on the white keys, could you now?" "I don't know," said Irene; "I've never tried, but I will." And she did; and made it sound just about as well as though the keys had been black.[67]

Shortly thereafter in October 1904—perhaps even more prodigiously than Myra—the sixteen-year-old Irene made her debut in Bechstein Hall while still a student. Although she played the entire B-flat minor Sonata of Chopin, she offered only the first movement of Schumann's G minor Sonata, which *The Times* dismissed as "a habit which is no doubt fostered in the students' concerts in the school from which she comes."[68] The critic was also hopeful that in time, she would "find out that music means a good deal more than she now seems to imagine." But he did praise her technique and "clearness of articulation," and conceded that she had "but little to learn."[69] And fifteen months later, at 17, she was sounding like a finished pianist. Henry Wood invited her to appear as soloist in both the Liszt E-flat and Saint-Saëns G minor Concertos, and—somewhat boldly—Irene insisted that Matthay's *In May* be included on the same program under his own baton. The *Musical Times* observed that "her touch was delightfully sympathetic and delicate, and florid passages were rippled off with fascinating clearness and lightness."[70] Four months later, she returned to Aeolian Hall to re-perform the Chopin B-flat minor, and this time *The Times* acknowledged that she even made the "weird last movement sound wonderfully poetical."[71] Her program also included the Chopin Barcarolle, a number of smaller Chopin pieces, and Matthay's "Elves," and she seemed to have arrived as an artist. The reviewer continued, "Not only is her technique as neat as can be wished, but she possesses in a rare degree the art of tone-gradation, and her touch is of unusual beauty."[72]

Myra and Irene were inseparable through this period, and once at an RAM chamber concert they even performed Corder's two-piano transcription of Weber's *Invitation to the Dance*.[73] Seventeen-year-old

Rebecca Clarke, then studying violin at the Academy, captured their likenesses in charcoal caricatures, and she later recalled that "Myra was always giggling."[74] But although they could be reduced to school-girl antics in each others' presence, their temperaments were radically different. Fundamentally, Myra was quiet, even shy, while Irene could be dramatically extroverted. Harriet Cohen's mother was her second cousin, and Harriet later recalled that when she performed at her first TMPS recital, Irene came "sweeping" into Bechstein Hall to cheer her on "in an enormous hat and feather boa."[75] After Harriet entered the Academy, she so admired both Myra and Irene that she even volunteered to be their messenger girl: "I fell off my bicycle countless times going on their errands. They gave me odd lessons and overwhelmed me with teas, luncheons, suppers, and even breakfasts. Irene spoiled me very much, but I was rather more in awe of Myra, who could be severe."[76]

In a sense, Harriet was born to the world of Tobias Matthay. Her mother, Florence, had also been his pupil for a time, although she was evidently less responsive than many.[77] Harriet reports that Florence had "a phenomenal musical ear and memory," supporting herself for some years as a cinema pianist, but she approached the piano intuitively with little patience for Matthay's explanations, which "she could never understand."[78] Harriet also insists that Matthay was biased against her mother because she had once been a student of Hambourg's father—a Leschetizky pupil—and was therefore "not quite in the fold."[79] Since Matthay's entire career was spent training, or retraining, the pupils of far less esteemed teachers—some of whom he even sent to Leschetizky[80]—her remark seems curious, but not nearly so curious as her claim that Matthay gratuitously wounded her. Dora had been Harriet's teacher at the TMPS, but when she was twelve (following in Myra's footsteps), she won an Ada Lewis Scholarship, and she had her first lesson with Matthay in the fall of 1908. On that occasion, she maintains that—in front of several other students—he chided her with, "I suppose you are like your mother. She had cotton wool in her head."[81] The story begs for corroboration, because it seems wildly out of character with Matthay's personality, but Harriet is probably correct that she studied with Matthay very little that year, having approximately three times as many lessons with Swinstead.[82]

Her account is especially important because it confirms that Matthay was permitted to assign his RAM class to assistants who held Academy appointments, which explains how he was able to manage the increasing demands on his time. Since the Academy paid all teachers by the hour, it was actually cheaper for them to pay Swinstead, given their respective rates, so there was probably little objection. Harriet mentions that Matthay began to give her more time after she had risen to the head of the class, and this was a pattern he also employed at his own school. But when she refers to Matthay—perhaps sardonically—as "the great man," she offers a view that is little confirmed by the Committee of Management Minutes, where deference is rarely shown to his suggestions or convictions. On 4 May 1910—at the age of 52—Matthay was finally asked to join the Committee, but his arguments still seemed to hold little sway with the other members.[83]

For example, by 1911 the entire Academy was excited by the impending move to a new facility—its present building on Marylebone Road—and Matthay thought it an opportune moment to propose a better instrument for the new concert hall. The school had had a long relationship with Broadwood, and on 1 August 1911, the firm sent the Committee a letter advising that they would repair five of their own grands at the rate of £12 per instrument. Corder was told to authorize repairs for four of them, but there was some discussion of what Broadwood would allow for a trade-in on the fifth instrument if a concert piano were purchased for the new concert room. No doubt Matthay thought it fortunate that no firm decision was then reached, for the following March he sent a formal letter to the Committee, suggesting they instead purchase a Bechstein. However, "Sir A. C. Mackenzie gave reasons for considering this action inadvisable and it was resolved that no change be made at present."[84]

But as it turned out, the choice of instrument mattered little, because even after 32 years of continuous service, Matthay was still not permitted to schedule the new hall—or any other space in the

Chapter 7

building—for programs by his own students. Two months later on 12 May, the Committee read

> a letter from Mr Matthay suggesting that he should be permitted to give a Concert by his students in the new Room on some convenient date in July on special terms. . . . Sir A. C. Mackenzie made a brief statement of the reasons which led him to consider the giving of such Concerts in the Academy Concert Room as undesirable. Mr Matthay gave his reasons for considering the giving of such Concerts highly desirable. Eventually after consideration it was agreed that the Subcommittee should take this matter into consideration and advise there-upon.[85]

Two weeks later, Matthay reiterated his suggestion to the Subcommittee overseeing opening ceremonies for the new building. But not only did they vote him down, they even rubbed salt in the wound by opening the new hall to any group in London *except* Academy students and faculty:

> The Secretary reported that the Sub-Committee for dealing with the Official Opening and the question of letting the Concert Room had considered Mr Matthay's letter of the 28th inst and made the following recommendations:
>
> 1. That the Concert Room be not let to any professor for a Concert the executants at which are Academy students.
> 2. That in the case of Concerts given to Professors at other Concert Rooms at which any of the Academy Students shall be among executants the consent of the Principal shall be first obtained in accordance with Regulation XI.
> 3. That the fee of ten guineas for afternoon Concerts and twelve guineas for evening Concerts be charged for the use and an additional guinea for orchestral concerts on either occasions, & that no reduction be made to anyone except the RAM Club & the RA Musical Union, these two bodies to have the use of the Concert Room as heretofore for the cost of lighting and cleaning.[86]

Regulation XI was a long-standing section of the Committee of Management General Regulations which gave the Principal the right to approve outside concert appearances by RAM students, but it was almost never invoked against professors of Matthay's stature. The Subcommittee's curious decision to reiterate it as part of its resolution can only be read as a message, for no other professor at the Academy organized as many concerts as Matthay, and many of these routinely received press coverage. Now that he had opened his own school, he was being further warned that the mingling of RAM with TMPS students would be carefully monitored. Two weeks later, Matthay sent a letter of protest to F. W. Renaut, the Academy Secretary, for inclusion in the Committee Minutes. He was particularly upset that professors were forbidden from using "the Concert Hall for Concerts by their pupils at cost or one of the large rooms for the same purpose."[87] And even in smaller arenas he was granted few concessions, for two weeks later, he sent a personal letter to Mackenzie urging that the Saturday night "Fortnightly" concerts be resumed now that the hall was open. Because of construction delays the concerts had "been omitted for nearly the whole of the year," and Matthay thought that if they were rapidly resumed, the students would have sufficient repertoire to produce two per week before the term's end in late July. The Committee was far less enthused: "It was agreed that it would be extremely inconvenient to carry out Mr Matthay's suggestion but as it appeared that it would be possible to give one Fortnightly Concert during the remainder of the Term that course was agreed to and the Secretary was instructed to carry it out."[88]

A few months later the concert situation had gone from bad to worse. By October it seemed that the new Concert Hall had produced little of the hoped-for revenue, and the proposed cure—at least to Matthay—seemed worse than the ailment:

> The Secretary stated that in consequence of various delays, County Council and others, he had not yet been able to make any public announcement with regard to the letting of the Concert Room but he had already let it once for a concert given by the Theosophical Society of which a rent of thirteen guineas was received, and he had also secured

Chapter 7

an engagement of a large room for twenty-eight rehearsals by the Stock Exchange Operatic Society for a fee of £31.10.0. He further stated that in order to be prepared to deal effectively with the Concert Room he had appointed Mr Harry Ross [a local concert promoter] on probation, and subject to be approved by the Committee at a salary of thirty shillings per week. Mr Matthay objected to the appointment on the ground that it was unnecessary and that such work as there was might be done by the present staff. The saving having been discussed and it being pointed out that every member of the present staff had as much as he could possibly do, the secretary's action was approved.[89]

Ironically, just as Matthay fought his Academy colleagues over the right to present his—and their—students in concert settings, he was having almost a reverse problem with the teachers in his own School, many of whom were performing so frequently that they were becoming stars in their own right. In May 1913, he sent the following memo to his entire staff, which now numbered over 20:

> To the Professors of the Tobias Matthay Pianoforte School:
> All private schools and some public ones insist upon the Regulation that no professor on the staff is allowed to take private pupils within a radius of four miles. Otherwise these schools could not grow as they do, or exist, since it is only the good work done by the Professors which draws pupils to them.
> This regulation I have not insisted upon at the School, but in common fairness I feel that all pupils drawn to a Professor through pupils of the School must be considered as School pupils and should as such be notified to the Secretary.
> Please note, however, that pupils not drawn to the School by its reputation for music, but for the express purpose of studying under one of the Professors will not have the same percentage deducted from their fees but only 15% of them will be retained;—which barely covers studio hire.[90]

The exact percentages then being deducted from various teachers' lesson fees are unknown, but it may be presumed that many

Building an Empire

ing more than the 50 percent net that Matthay
ral years earlier. At first sight, it might appear an
e to reduce the School's percentage even further,
teachers to have studios "at cost," but it virtually
at even the most celebrated members of his staff
would continue to teach under TMPS auspices and—by discouraging under-the-table tactics—it saved him the unpleasant drudgery of having to police their ethics throughout the city. In addition, the more successful a teacher became, the more likely he or she would breed overflow, and the School would most assuredly be the beneficiary—for indeed it was Matthay's own overflow that had provoked the necessity for a school in the first place. Finally, as with many institutions, some prominent names may have served primarily to decorate the marquee, but this was to the benefit of all and served as valuable advertising. For example, by 1913 York Bowen, Myra Hess, and Irene Scharrer had all become "names," and Matthay's generous arrangements virtually assured that whatever amount of time and attention they devoted to teaching, they would continue to remain on his staff, lending their support to the School in the coming years.

But it is also possible that Matthay's compassion for Myra may have inspired the new policy—at least partially—since her biographer recounts that these were very difficult years for the aspiring pianist. The annual London recitals she had given since 1907 generally met with positive notices, but she lost money on all of them and was forced to support herself through teaching. Her family's assistance had always been minimal, and after her father declared bankruptcy in 1910 she was even pressured to give them financial aid. They were soon obliged to leave their opulent residence on Belsize Road for a smaller home on Boundary Road, where Myra was forced to cram all of her possessions into an attic room and—until repeated frictions forced her out of the household in 1914—it was here that she did most of her teaching. Rebecca Clarke later recalled that Matthay treated Myra "like a daughter, almost,"[91] and when she made her orchestral debut under a little-known Thomas Beecham in November 1907, he prepared her assiduously. Since Myra's biographer also reports that she had to lay out £87 for the hire of Queen's Hall and the New Symphony Orchestra—and that the source of her funding is unknown—it is tempting to speculate that Matthay may even have provided some financial assistance. Beecham had scheduled an enormous program, demanding that Myra sandwich the Saint-Saëns Fourth and the Beethoven Fourth Concertos between a number of orchestral works, and Matthay was suspicious of the brash newcomer, advising Myra that "if he doesn't accompany you properly, I shall come and do it myself."[92] On 25 February 1909—her nineteenth birthday—he probably also paid her for the inaugural recital she gave in the small concert room on Wimpole Street, for he was no doubt well aware of her financial circumstances.[93] He soon added Myra's name to his roster and he probably sent her as many pupils as he could, but even when she recruited her own students she averaged less than 16 shillings per lesson.[94] Undoubtedly, whether she taught at home or on Wimpole Street, Myra benefited from Matthay's new policy, and since he had vowed that such arrangements be public, he may have felt obliged to extend the same benefit to all.

By now, Matthay had expanded the offerings at his School beyond a purely pianistic focus, which may be verified by observing that on 2 November 1910, he invited Stewart Macpherson to inaugurate a series of lectures on "musical appreciation."[95] Macpherson (1865-1941) had entered the RAM in 1880 as a recipient of the Sterndale-Bennett Scholarship, where he studied piano with Macfarren, and he now served as a composition professor at the Academy. He was also collaborating with his—and Matthay's—former pupil Ernest Read to break ground in a field then little explored by music educators. For many years, Matthay and Macpherson had both been active in the R. A. M. Club, an organization dating from 1889 which grew out of the Excelsior Society. Its stated purpose was to maintain "a friendly intercourse amongst gentlemen who are past Students of the Royal Academy of Music,"[96] and it changed presidents on an annual basis. Matthay was honored to be elected President of the Club (by then expanded to include women) in January 1910, and the June *R. A. M. Club Magazine* carried the obligatory Presidential biography, accompanied by a full-page photo. Not surprisingly, the text seems to bear the imprint of its subject's influence:

> His first *great* pupils indeed came to him through his painstaking work with sheer dullards musically—thus was his "luck" brought about, and he never spared himself whatever the opportunity. His motto has throughout been, whatever the achievement or the lack of it, "try to do better," and that motto he hopes to retain to the end of his days.
>
> He also insists that much of his success must be attributed to the fact that he married "the right woman"—for in 1893 he found a worthy mate in Jessie Kennedy, who has since made so great a position for herself as a dramatic reciter and teacher of singing and recitation. He has lately built himself a house on a hill-top near Haslemere, and there he spends all his week-ends and holidays, and there he hopes to accomplish much work of a permanent nature, and even to return to composition once again.[97]

Matthay relished the ceremonial duties required of him during the year, and with Jessie at his side, he presided over the annual Club dinner at the Criterion Restaurant on 20 July 1910. Before 87 assembled members and visitors, he toasted the King, the Royal Family, and the Club. Corder then led the gathering in a toast to Matthay, which he respectfully acknowledged. On 25 January 1911, he relinquished the gavel to Macpherson, and in compliance with custom, he made his final speech. No one who knew him could have been surprised by any of the sentiments he expressed, for he was now clearly in the vanguard of a movement to venerate British—and especially RAM—composers:

> In acknowledging your vote of thanks, I must say it has given me much pleasure to serve the Club this year.
>
> Several things, particularly, have much gratified me during my year's tenure of office as President. . . .
>
> What gratified me perhaps more than anything else, was, that the evening we devoted to the younger School of Royal Academy composers

and executants drew such a large audience; an attendance almost as large as that for the [Elena] Gerhardt-Nikisch evening [250], and this in spite of the inclement weather which the Royal Academicians had [on] their evening.

I was all the more gratified, since my suggestion was at first received very pessimistically. I was told that Royal Academy Clubites would refuse to turn out to hear merely their own kith and kin. But I refused to believe in this libel, and my trust in our members, as the event proved, was more than justified. Indeed, how can we expect the foreign nations to listen to our music if we, ourselves, refuse to take our home-products seriously? As a matter of fact, the foreigner now grows enthusiastic over these products, so we no longer need feel any false modesty on the subject.

I heartily agree that a visit from really great artists, such as we had this session, is an undoubted benefit to all of us, but I do venture to maintain that as a rule, our Club-meetings should be devoted to Royal Academy products only. Thus again will be furthered the purpose for which the Club exists. I assure you that although I am no longer your President, my interest in the Club will continue to be of the keenest.[98]

The *R. A. M. Club Magazine* also provides a useful record of many of Matthay's activities during his "Presidential" period. On 10 February 1910 in Bournemouth, he conducted his concert overture *In May*, as well as his *Concert-Piece* in A minor for Pianoforte and Orchestra (Concerto in One Movement), which he had begun over 25 years earlier. Although the magazine does not indicate the soloist, it was probably Bowen, who had premiered the work the previous August at a Queen's Hall Promenade Concert under Henry Wood. For that occasion, at Wood's request, Matthay provided some program notes, which read in part:

> While this is a continuous movement in the usual sonata (or duplex) form, it nevertheless also presents the contrasts found in a short concerto of three movements; for the exposition may stand as first movement, the working-out as slow movement, and the *Coda* as *Finale*. Also it forms a

true example of what has been termed "unary" form, since the whole of the subject-matter employed is logically evolved either directly or indirectly from its initial Motto phrase.[99]

The Times reviewed the premiere, and while the critic's approval was somewhat qualified, the audience was ecstatic:

A remarkably clever "concert piece" in A minor for piano and orchestra by Mr. Tobias Matthay, the piano part of which was played by Mr. York Bowen, took the central place in the programme of Saturday night. The ingenuity of its structure is the most striking feature, since it is written in the form of the first movement of a sonata, while all the material is derived from a single short theme metamorphosed into a variety of shapes according to the principles Liszt propounded.

The theme itself has the merit of simplicity, so that when once it has been clearly stated there is no difficulty recognizing it through all its disguises; but it carries with it the disadvantage that it has not really sufficient distinction to warrant such elaborate treatment. The transition from its first terse statement into an expressive second subject is charming, but before the end of the development section the ear begins to tire of its insistent character, and the full recapitulation and coda seem redundant. The piano part is adorned with a number of brilliant passages, and their instrumental effectiveness probably accounts for the unusually enthusiastic reception which the work received. Mr. York Bowen was recalled over and over again, and the composer had to bow his acknowledgements from his seat in the grand circle.[100]

The crowd's euphoria may have been somewhat understandable, for Matthay's tempestuous work is filled with Lisztian bravura. Jessie indicates that he actually began the piece shortly after he completed *In May* in 1883, but he labored over it for years, revising and re-revising it extensively.[101] Like most of his orchestral works, it lay dormant for decades, but the amount of revisions he made suggests that he was hopeful about having it performed. He sketched a two-piano arrangement dedicated "to his Sister on her twenty-first birthday," which occurred in April of 1890, so perhaps Dora was fond of the work, although there is no evidence she performed it with orchestra.[102] The completion date of the orchestrated version is more difficult to pin down. The fair copy from which Matthay—and probably Wood—conducted is filled with handwritten annotations, and he indicates in ink that he used his summer holiday to complete a "Revised sketch" at Hunstanton on 25 August 1889, while the "New Score" was completed at Bexhill the following year on 13 August 1890. The next indication appears in blue pencil: "Latest revised copy/TAM Oct 1903/for York Bowen's rehearsal!" If Bowen performed it then, it must have been outside London, because the Proms program clearly indicates that the 1909 concert was the work's "First performance in London." Matthay's last annotation on the score is in pencil: "Final revise [sic] for publication/January 1908," so this was undoubtedly the version which Bowen performed at the Proms, and it matches note for note the piano-orchestral reduction published by Ricordi a year later, which Matthay inscribed to Dora.[103] However, it seems unlikely that Ricordi ever printed a full score or orchestral parts, since surviving correspondence suggests that as late as the 1930s, Matthay was still supplying parts to conductors such as Adrian Boult and Sir Dan Godfrey.[104]

Example 7.1 Matthay: Piano solo section from Concert Piece in A minor, Op. 23; mm. 304-305.

But his most important professional activity through this period was not chronicled by the *R. A. M. Club Magazine.* In fact, the Academy's records make but one solitary reference to the work that had been occupying him for the last several years. On 20 July 1910 he was required to miss a Committee of Management meeting because of the annual TMPS recital occurring at the same time in Bechstein Hall. But in his absence, the Committee read a request he had presented to give two lectures on "The Principles of Interpretation," a proposal they "considered and agreed to."[105] Matthay was now 52, but many close to him were starting to believe that his greatest work still lay ahead of him.

Notes

1. "Death of Sir Jonathan Hutchinson[,] A Great Scientific Observer," *TT*, 24 June 1913, 9, col. G.
2. The conveyance title is on file at the Land Registry, Chancery Lane, London. Hereafter cited as LR.
3. Several months after he moved into his new home in 1909, Matthay sent a letter to the Haslemere Parish Council, which they read at their 21 December meeting, complaining that Lord Leconfield had erected signs around the Common with the words "Trespassers on this property will be prosecuted." Allen Chandler, the president of the Council, advised him that the Commons' Preservation Society was "ready to take proceedings, but none of the commoners were willing to act as plaintiff." See "Marley Common," *TT,* 23 Dec. 1909, 9, col. E.
4. Conveyance title.
5. JHM, 50.
6. Ibid.
7. Taken from the Cubitt & West "sales Particulars," a promotional brochure offered when the house was put on the market in the early 1980s. All dimensions given are taken from the same source.
8. JHM, 50-51. Jessie does not provide every date, but the sequence of the dates she does provide suggests that they had moved in by late summer.

Chapter 7

9. JHM, 50-51.
10. Ibid.
11. Interview with Gwen Paul, who owned the house for over 30 years. August 1980. The Bechstein today is housed in the Matthay Room at the RAM.
12. Tobias senior's will was probated on 19 Feb. 1909 (Matthay's birthday), and Dorothea's was probated on 2 April 1909. Both wills are on file at the Family Records Office (FRO), Holborn.
13. JHM, 43.
14. Jessie (JHM, 46) indicates that 17 February 1906, marked the School's first anniversary, and Matthay's staff chose to commemorate it by staging a dinner that also honored his forty-eighth birthday which occurred on 19 February. The quote "in fact although not in name" appears in the School's Prospectus of November 1921 (p. 3). The Prospectuses were generally published annually until 1939.
15. Ibid., 41.
16. The program is reproduced in JHM, 47-48.
17. The RAM Archives have an uncatalogued folder of materials on the Matthay School compiled in 1925 by John McEwen, then Principal of the RAM. By then, McEwen was embroiled in a bitter feud with Matthay and compiling information to initiate legal action against the TMPS. It is believed that he obtained the "in-house" Matthay documents from his wife, Hedwig, who by then had taught at the School for nearly twenty years. See Ch. 9.
18. Ibid.
19. Ibid.
20. Ibid.
21. Ibid.
22. Ibid.
23. McEwen would have had no access to TMPS documents after 1925, but it is likely the original document still governed the School's policies, or he would have made no reference to it in building his case.
24. JHM, 44.
25. See COMM, 8 Mar. 1911.
26. JHM, 12.
27. HDWEA.

28. In 1928, a large number of properties, including Nos. 91 to 98 Wimpole Street, were sold to Debenhams Ltd., whose central offices were then at No. 91. The conveyance on file at the LRO includes a schedule of previous transactions for all the included properties.
29. HDWEA. Its exact depth was 46"11".
30. Stevenson's name was provided by HDWEA.
31. JHM, 12.
32. See *Kelly's Marylebone and St. John's Wood Directory for 1910*.
33. See *TT*, 25 Jan. 1909, 20, col. C.
34. Marylebone Rate books are available at the City of Westminster Archives.
35. LI.
36. Matthay refers to possessions he bequeaths to family and friends by their position in various rooms on Wimpole Street, all of which he refers to by number. Last Will of Tobias Augustus Matthay, dated 13 January 1944, FRO.
37. *MT*, 1 Mar. 1909, 146.
38. *MT*, 1 May 1909, 290.
39. Many Northern College archival entries are on line at http://www.rncm-archive.rncm.ac.uk (last accessed on 16 Jan. 2011). During World War II, the Manchester branch of the TMPS faced sharp enrollment declines and in September 1943, after 23 years of continuous service, "the Matthay School, Manchester branch, formally became a public institution under the name The Northern School of Music." Eventually, Collens saw that other instruments were represented as well, including the clarinet, which the Manchester branch later taught to a young Harrison Birtwhistle.
40. A. P. Schmidt Company Archives, Music Division, Library of Congress, Washington, D.C.
41. Ibid.
42. See COMM, 1 Feb. 1899. Bentley sent her letter, dated 7 Jan. 1899, to J. J. F. Ainsley, Principal of the Widnes Academy of Music in Widnes, Lancs., where the exams took place. Ainsley then forwarded her letter to the RAM.
43. See COMM, 23 Jan. 1901. The Committee agreed to Macfarren's request. In his autobiography Macfarren wrote (p. 269) that "the death of this august lady affected me greatly," but evidently he was undeterred from approaching the Committee on the very date that the RAM had cancelled its classes.

44. COMM, 21 June 1905.
45. See *TT*, 21 Mar. 1906, 9, col. F, and 19 July 1906, 10, col. F.
46. See *TT*, 20 July 1907, 12, col. C.
47. *TT*, 16 Dec. 1905, 12, col. B.
48. *TT*, 18 June 1906, 14, col. F.
49. Hardy, 47-48. See also Lewis Foreman, "Benjamin J. Dale," from *Benjamin Dale[:] Piano music*, Peter Jacobs, piano, Continuum, CCD 1044.
50. Foreman, 6.
51. "Royal Academy of Music," *MT*, 1 Dec. 1906, 832.
52. *TT*, 11 December 1906, 17, col. C.
53. *MT*, 1 Jan. 1907, 43.
54. *TT*, 28 Oct. 1907, 14, col. F.
55. Ibid., 15 Jul. 1910, 13, col. C.
56. *MT*, 1 Sept. 1909, 582. The Society's works were, at least initially, printed and distributed by Breitkopf und Härtel, before their catalogue was absorbed by Novello in 1909. See the excellent discussion in Foreman, *Bax*, 41 ff.
57. Matthay to the Board of the Philharmonic Society, 28 Jan. 1907, BLPS, fol. 65-66.
58. Draft of Berger's letter to Matthay, 1 Feb. 1907, BLPS, fol. 68.
59. Matthay to the Board of the Philharmonic Society, 11 Feb. 1907, BLPS, fol. 68.
60. *TT*, 4 Feb. 1908, 14, col. F.
61. *TT*, 27 Jan. 1908, 8, col. C.
62. *TT*, 5 Sept. 1908, 11, col. C.
63. Arnold Bax, *Farewell, My Youth*, Edited by Lewis Foreman (Aldershot, Hants.: Scolar, 1992), 52. Bax seems to have incorrectly remembered the occasion as occurring two years later at the London Musical Club, but Myra first performed d'Indy's Sonata for the composer on 27 March 1909, and that is the only occasion where he was likely to have been "astonished" by her performance. See *TT*, 29 March 1909, 5, col. B.
64. JHM, 44.
65. JHM, 43.
66. Ibid.
67. JHM, 43-44.
68. *TT,* 28 Oct. 1904, 4, col. C.
69. Ibid.

70. *MT*, 1 Mar. 1906, 190.
71. *TT*, 22 May 1906, 8, col. A.
72. Ibid.
73. *TT*, 23 July 1904, 9, col. D.
74. For the sketches, see Plate 4 in Foreman, *Bax*. Clarke remembered Myra in an interview for New York radio station WQXR on 25 Feb. 1976, reprinted in "Rebecca Clarke Remembers Myra Hess (Interview with Robert Sherman)," in Curtis, 162-69.
75. Harriet Cohen, *A Bundle of Time: The Memoires of Harriet Cohen*. (London: Faber and Faber, 1969), 33. Hereafter cited as Cohen.
76. Ibid., 31.
77. The claim is occasionally made that Matthay's pupil Toni Cohen was related to Harriet, but I can document no family connection, and Toni, who began teaching at the TMPS in 1911, is nowhere mentioned in Harriet's autobiography. Toni may have been the wife of Joseph Cohen, a surgeon who passed at the Royal Surrey County Hospital in Guildford on 4 Feb. 1946, at the age of 79. Harriet's father was also named Joseph, but he was not a physician. Toni was evidently widely literate, since in 1914 she completed a German translation of Matthay's *First Principles*, a project doubtless undertaken with Matthay's help and guidance, but which may have been ill timed, since it appeared on the eve of the first War. The full title was: *Die ersten Grundsätze des Klavierspiels, Auszug aus dem Werke des Verfassers "The act of touch" [Der Vorgang des Anschlags] nebst zwei neuen Abschnitten: Anleitungen und Erklärungen für Schüler, Ratschläge für Lehrer und Selbstlernende; für den Schulgebrauch und Selbstunterricht* (Leipzig: C. F. Kahnt, 1914).
78. Cohen, 21.
79. Ibid.
80. In addition to Maude Rihill, who spent three years with Leschetizky, Matthay recommended that his pupil Ida Betts be allowed to complete the last two years of her Liszt-Bache Scholarship "under the care of Mr. Leschetizky in Vienna." See COMM, 15 Nov. 1894.
81. Cohen, 21.
82. Ibid., 23.
83. COMM, 4 May 1910. Matthay's membership was proposed by Mackenzie and seconded by Beringer.

Chapter 7

84. COMM, 6 March 1912.
85. COMM, 12 May 1912.
86. COMM, 29 May 1912.
87. Letter from Matthay to Renaut on TMPS stationery, dated 11 June 1912. COMM, 12 June 1912.
88. COMM, 26 June 1912.
89. COMM, 2 Oct. 1912.
90. RAMA.
91. Curtis, 164.
92. Marian C. McKenna, *Myra Hess: A Portrait* (London: Hamish Hamilton 1976), 30. Hereafter cited as McKenna.
93. Ibid., 29. Jessie (p. 46) gives the date of Myra's recital as 25 February 1905, but this is probably incorrect, since it was several years before Matthay had moved to Wimpole Street.
94. See McKenna, 52-57. McKenna indicates that in 1914 Myra taught at times in her home at the rate of nine guineas per twelve lessons.
95. See *MT*, 1 Nov. 1910, 732.
96. RAMCM, 11 (Jan. 1904):16.
97. RAMCM, 30 (June 1910):10.
98. RAMCM, 32 (Feb. 1911):10.
99. The Matthay Archives contain Matthay's fair copy of the *Concert Piece*, from which he conducted. Among the many notes it contains is the date of Bowen's Proms performance with Henry Wood. He also pasted the printed program notes to the inside front cover. Hereafter cited as *Concert Piece*, fair copy.
100. *TT,* 30 August 1909, 9, col. E.
101. JHM, 18.
102. RAMRBC MS 1949. At the end of the sketch, he wrote that the "solo copy" was completed at Purley, which dates it after September 1893.
103. MA. *Concert Piece*, fair copy.
104. It should be noted that the list of Matthay's published works contained in Jessie's biography (published in 1945) indicated that the parts could be rented from Ricordi. But Matthay supplied the parts to Boult, who broadcast it on the BBC with Vivian Langrish in May 1931, and to Godfrey, who performed it with Langrish at Bournemouth in June 1932. See Chap. 11.
105. COMM, 20 July 1910.

Arnold Bax about 1922

York Bowen about 1905

Benjamin Dale about 1914

Irene Scharrer about 1925

The Royal Academy of Music building on Marylebone Road at the time of its opening in 1911

CHAPTER 8

LIFE AT THE SUMMIT

On 23 September 1911 the Royal Academy of Music began its Michaelmas term in what Mackenzie dubbed a "Spanish castle"[1]—a virtual palace beyond anything its students and staff had experienced in its eighty-nine-year history. The concert facility alone—shortly to be known as "The Duke's Hall" in honor of the Duke of Connaught—was a separate wing, 122' x 45', "estimated to accommodate an audience of about a thousand persons."[2] It soon housed an elegant concert organ built by Norman and Beard, the gift of Mrs. Thomas Threlfall, whose late husband had chaired the Committee of Management for over a decade. According to the *Musical Times,* the main building was even more opulent, containing

> about fifty class-rooms [including teaching studios], in the construction of which the latest devices for deadening sound outside the rooms have been adopted. There are double doors to all the teaching rooms. The west wing is devoted to offices, libraries, &c., and there is ample dining room accommodation in the basement, and two practice organs on the top floors are placed well out of hearing. The entrance leads to a marble hall where, in the centre of a tessellated pavement, and surrounded by a wreath, is inscribed the motto of the Academy . . . "SING UNTO GOD."[3]

Corder indicates that the new building cost nearly £60,000, and although its construction had not been achieved without a struggle, the Academy's decision to leave Tenterden Street was not totally unexpected. The lease George Macfarren had helped renegotiate in 1876 was due to expire in the summer of 1912, and the Academy desperately needed to expand its floor space. On 7 December 1908 they were presented with an enlargement scheme by their landlords, the coach makers Laurie and Marner, which involved the cooperation of

Lord Carnarvon, the freeholder of much of the property surrounding Hanover Square. Laurie and Marner were already extracting a rent of £820 a year for Nos. 4 and 5 Tenterden Street, but after the Academy's proposed expansion had been approved by all concerned parties, the new rent was to be £2,254 per annum, a figure Mackenzie dismissed as "impossible."[4] Nonetheless, the negotiations continued for a while, until one of the Academy Directors found, in Corder's words, "a far more eligible situation in the Marylebone Road." The RAM broke off discussions "at the eleventh hour," and soon plans were laid to lease a plot of ground on Marylebone Road near York Gate, the main entrance to Regent's Park. The setting was quieter than the area they were then occupying, a neighborhood which Mackenzie complained had frequently "tormented" them with the "hideous din" of "fearsome and raucous" auto horns.[5] The new site was bounded by Madame Tussaud's Wax Museum, which stood two blocks to the west and offered far less distraction, and the Baker Street Underground station in the next block assured that the new location could be easily reached from anywhere within the metropolitan area.

The "eligible situation" Corder had described was actually somewhat complicated from a legal standpoint. Not surprisingly, the Howard de Walden Estate owned the property freehold, but in 1837 it had granted a lease to the St. Marylebone Charity School, an orphanage and educational facility for girls. The School moved to Ealing in 1907 but it continued to lease the Marylebone property from the Estate, so the Academy became in effect a sub-lessee of the Charity School. After the deal was finalized, the RAM also paid £176 to raze the School's old building, so that the cornerstone of the new building could be laid on 14 July 1910. Corder reports that they were wise to take the highest demolition bid, since the firm chosen managed to salvage all the older building's ornaments and "the marble mantle pieces alone fetched £200."[6] But most of the expenses were met by the Academy's Building Fund, which had been escrowing substantial sums for decades. Corder also indicates that, pursuant to an archaic law, the RAM was assessed a fee of £2,500 for "dilapidations" to their

Tenterden Street facilities (even though the houses were immediately condemned) and another £500 in legal fees,[7] but that nothing could quell the excitement of the "realisation of a long cherished dream!"

> To pore over architects' plans, to watch foundations being dug, to follow the marvelous procedure of modern building operations, to clamber about on steel girders at giddy heights, and watch the silent growth of concrete walls—all this was a new and delightful experience.[8]

When he first settled at Wimpole Street, it is unlikely that Matthay knew where the new building would be located, so he was fortunate that No. 96 was situated almost equidistant from the old and the new sites. After the Marylebone Road facility opened, a brisk ten-minute walk up Wimpole Street brought him within sight of the new Academy, which soon loomed like a regal presence over the surrounding terrain. Far from the confusing tapestry of Tenterden Street corridors which Bax remembered as "tortuous tunnellings,"[9] the new building had been designed by the firm of Ernest George and Yeates, who worked in close consort with Academy staff. The plans were completed in March 1910, and each drawing was stamped with the Howard de Walden insignia, since the Estate's approval was required for all construction on the property. The building even contained a lift adjacent to the basement dining room, housed in a shaft spanning the whole of its five stories so that music stands and other equipment could be easily transported to various levels. The teaching studios were spacious, and Matthay's room—designated as "Classroom 20" on the second-floor plan—was situated directly opposite the central staircase, affording an expansive view of Marylebone Road.[10] The studio was an auspicious location befitting one of the Academy's most senior professors, and any conflicts Matthay had endured with the Committee of Management were most likely imperceptible to the many who passed his door on a daily basis. Other factors also testified to his eminence, since his books, his highly publicized school, and his growing legion of prominent students continued to attract attention and admiration.

Chapter 8

And he was now also lecturing publicly far beyond the Academy's boundaries. He was invited to speak before the Edinburgh Musical Education Society on 28 March 1910—possibly by his friend Friedrich Niecks, who chaired the event.[11] His topic, "Principles and Teaching of Interpretation," was a subject which had begun to occupy more and more of his time, and his views were evidently finding a wide acceptance. He gave the same talk in Manchester on 3 March,[12] in Southampton on 7 May, and he journeyed to Scotland again in December to speak before the Aberdeen chapter of the British Music Teacher's Association.[13] On 18 February 1911, he spoke before the London chapter of the MTA at Broadwood's Rooms, a talk which *The Times* found "very interesting." It even offered a brief summary, which read in part:

> The lecturer, whose name is chiefly known to the world in general in connexion with a carefully-elaborated system of pianoforte technique, kept a large audience interested in his subject for some two hours, and the special needs of teachers and pupils were fully discussed, of course exclusively in connexion with the pianoforte. That the teacher must be always on the alert, the pupil always concentrated and imaginative, that musical analysis is of inestimable value at every stage of training, that the mere imitation of favourite performers is unlikely to lead to great results—all these rather general principles were dwelt upon very earnestly and persuasively.[14]

The May 1911 issue of the *R. A. M. Club Magazine* printed a far more extensive synopsis, which revealed that Matthay continued to insist that the student's *mind* be trained:

> Mr. Matthay directed attention to the difference between practice and mere strumming on the piano, between teaching and mere cramming; he considered how the pupil's mind could be brought upon his work, his ideas of time, the elements of rapidity and duration, and pedal. Good teaching made the pupil think; work really became play. It was fatal to delude ourselves that we were listening to music, when we were not really

listening. Ear-training which concentrated upon pitch or time was worse than useless; it must be mind-training with a musical purpose; we must feel the musical content and shape of every bar; we must know what to do better physically and what to avoid doing physically at the keyboard. To concentration we must add vividness of imagination. The power of pre-hearing could be cultivated to a greater extent than people supposed.

Analysis in teaching implied analysis in four distinct ways (1) we must analyse what the pupil was actually doing, (2) we must analyse the faults thereby perceived, (3) why the pupil was making those faults, and (4) we must analyse the pupil's attitude of mind, so that we might know how to treat him. Before we could form any judgment, we must know the music and must analyse that. To rely upon example led to disappointment, if not disaster.[58]

And the often controversial topic of rubato was quickly making its way to the forefront of his interpretative theories:

Rubato might take two distinct forms: (1) where we emphasised a note and gave more than the expected time value, and made up by accelerating the remaining notes of that phrase; (2) where we began by pushing on or hurrying the time and then retarded the phrase so as to bring back the correct time at the end of the phrase. A rubato curve should vary with the mood of the performer. We might also use rubato to emphasise a single note only, or to give a graceful curve to a whole sentence. Rubato would, in fact, enable us to make clear the climax of a phrase, even in the case of a *decres.* [sic] The coming back from a rubato might give more importance to the phrase than anything else. When we are required to express vitality, aggressiveness, etc., we must make the music as clear as day, and avoid rubato.[15]

Matthay was then pioneering a form of presentation that some later said he invented: the lecture-recital, or highly scripted discussions of technique and interpretation punctuated by his own illustrations at the piano. To be sure, Macfarren and Beringer were also experienced speakers, and once Macfarren had even lectured on all 32 Beethoven Sonatas, but their talks were invariably illustrated by performances from their students. By contrast, Matthay was always ready to demonstrate his own points at the piano, and he regularly worked far into the night to assure that he would be sufficiently prepared. These late-night practice sessions were frequently preceded by several hours of writing, and surviving manuscripts of his lectures confirm that he generally read from a prepared text—often typewritten. The presentations were sufficiently polished that they transferred easily to print, and late in 1913 Joseph Williams issued several of his talks as an octavo-sized, 163-page volume titled *Musical Interpretation[:] Its Laws and Principles and their Application in Teaching and Performing*. Perhaps because Matthay's lectures had already been so favorably received by the press, the book itself evoked little comment. It was published almost simultaneously in America by the Boston Music Company, and even the "review" which appeared in the *New York Times* on 8 February 1914 was little more than a summary.[16]

In his Preface, Matthay conceded his work might have seen print somewhat prematurely, but since several who had attended his lectures were already acknowledging his concepts in their own writings, he decided the time was ripe for an initial presentation—with the promise of later elaborations. He once again thanked Marjory for her encouragement and assistance with his proofs, and elsewhere in the book he cites her—and Jessie's—brother Jack, whose thirty-eight-page pamphlet *Common Sense and Singing* (published by Williams in 1911) made use of some of the same principles applied to singing. Like *Musical Interpretation*, Jack's work was also a printed version of a lecture given in various locations, including the TMPS, where he wrote his Foreword on 29 March 1911.[17] His bibliography cites works by Darwin (*Expression of the Emotions*), Tyndall (*On Sound*), and Helmholtz (*The Sensations of Tone*), as well as Huxley's *Elements of Psychology*, so Matthay's endorsement was understandable. Jack's commitment to science seemed as pronounced as his own:

> The everyday man or woman "shies" at Science, and nothing makes a fact more indigestible than labeling it with a technical name. But we

often forget that the common sense of this generation was the science of the past. While we smile, with a touch of pity, as we think of the primitive lives of our grandfathers, yet in Musical Art, and especially Singing, we reverence the very words our forefathers used, to describe effects, of which they did not, and we do, know the causes.[18]

Matthay also praises McEwen's newly issued *The Thought in Music*, a copy of which he received as he readied *Musical Interpretation* for press in October 1912. He lauds the author's "masterly" transformation of his own concepts into "a work full of original thought and research."[19] McEwen's book traverses far more ground than piano playing, and Matthay is quick to observe that *Musical Interpretation* also espouses principles designed to enhance musical execution in any realm:

> Many of the same laws of Interpretation which apply to Piano-forte playing also hold good whether we are players of stringed instruments or wind instruments, or are vocalists, organ-players, or conductors. We cannot play even on a penny whistle without coming under the sway of such laws![20]

He also uses his Preface to reiterate his oft-expressed claim that no teaching can "create" artistry, thereby clarifying some of the most essential goals of his profession:

> To prevent misunderstanding, I must at once state that I do not claim that artists are "made" by the mere enunciation and teaching of such laws and principles as here given, or by those of instrumental technique—although no success can be attained without obedience to these same laws and principles. No, the really great artist always has been, is now, and ever will be, a most rare phenomenon. His advent depends on so many things uniting in one single individual—the highest gifts of imagination and invention, therefore high, mental powers (yes, the really great artist must also have high reasoning power), physical and mental endurance, extreme enthusiasm for his chosen art, good health, and the

opportunities to acquire the requisite skill *to work in strict obedience to the laws of his art.*

Hence, it is not claimed that the truthful Analysis and Synthesis of art or its technique can transform dullards into poets and seers, but what has been amply proven is, that such teachings do inevitably help the ordinary student to succeed in attaining to far higher ideals that he could have reached without such help, and that the "heaven-born" Genius (when he does appear) has many years of useful life added to his career, years otherwise wasted in futile experiments, while his path toward still higher perfections is thus rendered possible and easy—and his appreciation of truth in art made more sound.[21]

In one sense, the ideas contained in *Musical Interpretation* are simply an extension of the logic employed in *The Act of Touch*, a work undertaken to explain the physiological components of artistry in a scientific manner. But they added a new dimension to Matthay's thought, because now—with Spencerian consistency—he was maintaining that even intelligent artistic *choices* rested upon scientific principles. The book also marks Matthay's first published foray into the realm of psychology, a burgeoning field which he revisited many times in subsequent writings, and it could be argued that it was his first work undertaken to address the *mental* components of artistry. And perhaps more significantly, it centers on the successful teaching of those principles, or in other words, it is designed to make pupils more musical. The book is organized into six sections, the first of which presents "Some General Principles of Teaching and Learning." Although today not all of these ideas may seem revolutionary, they no doubt resonated strongly with many teachers in his own time—as they might with many today:

> The first general conclusion we are thus driven to accept is the need for purposeful brain-use, on the part of both teacher and pupil. With regard to the pupil, not only is brain-use (i.e. reasoning) imperative during

lesson-time, it is even more imperative during the practice-hour when there is no help available from the outside. How often indeed do we find the pupil's work brought back worse than at a preceding lesson, in spite of what would seem to have been the most judiciously thought-out and carefully worded advice! And why is this so? Simply, because the pupil in the interval, instead of really practicing, has tried with might and main to make himself (or herself) into an automatic *strumming-machine*. Yes, often it is the pupil's fault, he either will not, or cannot use his brains.

But believe me, far more often still, it is the teacher's fault, owing to his not having correctly *shown* the student *how* to use his brains during practice, or not having diplomatically enough insisted on real practice, in place of such mere gymnastic strumming.[22]

Section II is devoted to "The Nature of Musical Attention and of Musical Shape," and it contains some of Matthay's most distinctive concepts about the phenomena underlying the experiencing of music. For example, he believed that rhythm was the most important constituent of musical structure, even with respect to the nature of pitch discrimination, since differences in pitch were in essence nothing more than differences in rhythmic oscillations. But he also believed that the mere exertion of musical attention implied a rhythmic act, and he devoted considerable space to explaining this concept:

> We cannot, therefore, definitely think a note in playing unless we *think* the time-place of its *beginning*—the beginning of the sound. Moreover, we must try to realize, that the law has a far deeper significance even than this. The fact is, we cannot experience any act of consciousness, we cannot direct our minds and think about or realize anything definitely, without just such an act of *timing*—a timing of our consciousness. The act of bringing or directing our thought or attention upon anything is therefore a *rhythmical* process; Thought and Rhythm are inseparable. Again, we see the reason why in the absence of Rhythm there can only be Nothingness—emptiness, non-being!![23]

Since music exists in time rather than space, a pupil's rhythmic sense must be directed toward an expanse of individual elements, or in other words, a *progression*. Matthay certainly did not invent the concept of musical progression, but he uses it far more precisely than most commentators, and he believes it lies at the core of all musicality:

> In Music we choose some particular sequence of beats or pulses, and upon this particular form of *extension in space*, or Time-spacings, upon this thoroughly tangible *time-canvas* of Pulse we lay out the *progression* of our musical picture, whether as composers or players—just as the painter must lay out *his* work on his canvas.
>
> It may strike you at first that this is "a very waste of words" but I assure you we are here face to face with one of the most fundamental laws of our art, and the teaching of it.[24]

But since the concept of "progression" cannot be experienced by consciousness without some sense of purposeful movement, Matthay insists that the student must feel all music as movement *toward* some specific point:

> This doctrine of Progression or Movement, which I insist upon as the basis of all Shape in performance, is indeed a most important teaching principle—one might say perhaps *the* most important of all. The old way of teaching Form, Form-analysis, Structure, and Interpretation with its false ideas of dead, disconnected segments of music (blocks or chunks) was perfectly useless, musically, to the student. It not only failed to give him any real insight into what constitutes Music in the act of performance, but it failed to draw his attention to Movement as the basis of all Music, and it was therefore positively deadening from a performing point of view.[25]

Quite naturally, this leads him to the view that musical phrases must often be sensed without respect to the bar lines which appear on the page. In fact, he observes that some composers, such as Schumann, are notorious for mis-barring their works, and as an example he provides the opening measures of his Novelette in F as written:

Example 8.1 Schumann: Novelette in F, Op. 21, no. 1, mm 1-4

Because the piece opens firmly in F, Matthay believes the V-I cadences to be paramount to understanding its musical sense, and he thus re-bars it so that the three tonic chords in the above example all appear on the strongest beat of each measure. In the example below, the lower case *a* represents the positions of Schumann's bar lines, while the lower case *b* represents Matthay's suggested re-barring:

Example 8.2 Schumann: Novelette in F, Op. 21, no. 1, mm 1-4, as re-barred by Matthay from Musical Interpretation, 38

But he is careful to acknowledge that not all phrases are as predictable as the Schumann example above, and he cites a passage from

Beethoven's Sonata, Op. 22, to illustrate the principle of progression in a different context:

Example 8.3 Beethoven: Sonata in B-flat, Op. 22, mm 30-33, with "progression" markings by Matthay from Musical Interpretation, 48

At first sight this Beethoven excerpt, from Op. 22, almost looks like a case of mis-placed bar-lines; but it is quite correctly barred, for the *sfs* are here true syncopations, which are felt to go against the true rhythmical pulse, and which last must persist in spite of these *sfs*. The bar-line (or true pulse) may be shown by making the notes *on* it slightly staccato.[26]

If progression is essential to intelligent musicianship, then the performer's *memory* must also be activated to maintain a sense of shape across the entire expanse of a composition:

> Whether we are laying out a large movement, or a small one, it is absolutely essential that we should vividly *remember* the exact proportion of *musical importance* attaching to each of its component sections and climaxes, to its variously contrasting subjects, sentences, phrases, ideas, down to the actual importance of *each note* employed.
>
> Only by such perfect *memory* of all its constituents can we hope to produce a musical picture perfect in its perspective, perfect in its outlines—perfect as a WHOLE.
>
> This kind of memory is, indeed, the hardest task of the player—and I think it really is harder in our art than in any other.[27]

But if the artist finds the task of memory to be a challenge, what does this imply about the (largely unskilled) members of a given audience, who will probably know the work far less well? Matthay's consistency in this regard leads him to ideas that are innovative, perhaps even visionary, since such suggestions are commonplace in many venues today:

> Here we clearly see why it is that a new musical work, even of the highest merit—or because of that—takes so long before it is accepted. In the case of lengthy works, there is no remedy available; it is not practicable to repeat a "Götterdämmerung" several times in one evening, even were a hearer capable of enjoying the process, and so we must trust to the audience taking the trouble to study such huge works before trying to appreciate an actual "first performance."
>
> But in the case of *short* instrumental or vocal works of serious content, given for the first time in public, I do seriously put forward and plead for the adoption of the custom of an immediate repetition of them; such works should be performed at least twice in immediate succession. This would give worthy new music a far better chance of being accepted forthwith.
>
> The old masters unconsciously felt this, when, in their Sonata movements, they insisted on repeating all the subject-matter, before proceeding to its amplification.[28]

Memory was also critical to an understanding of "The Element of Rubato," which forms Section III of *Musical Interpretation*, and later became one of the most controversial tenets of Matthay's teaching. He begins with unusually pointed criticisms of professionals who either forbid their students to use rubato or—at the other extreme—offer up directives such as "You must not play Chopin in time!" Although he pardons such sins when committed by the inexperienced, he insists that such teaching "amounts to crass stupidity in the case of men who have worked at their profession for years."[29] He is quick to embrace Chopin's dictum of rubato as "borrowed," rather than "stolen" time, and insists that time must be artfully bent—rather than broken—to preserve a sense of rhythmic continuity. This

Chapter 8

bending can begin either with a push forward or a pull back in time, and in that sense it can take two "quite distinct forms:"

> The most usual is that in which we emphasize a note (or a number of notes) by giving *more* than the expected Time-value, and then subsequently make-up the time thus lost by *accelerating* the remaining notes of that phrase or idea so as to enable us accurately to return to the pulse. This return to the pulse must always occur at the most important part of the phrase—that is, near its end. Remember, this law is inexorable, we must always look ahead, and *come back* to the pulse at the chief syllable of the phrase, however much we may have swerved from it beforehand. Indeed, the very fact of our returning to the main pulse after having swerved from it forms the strongest means of emphasis we can give to any note.[30]

He illustrates with the opening bars of Chopin's F-sharp Nocturne, where the curved line above the time-line represents the holding or pulling back, while the curve below the line represents the push forward. He also offers another more detailed way of representing the motion visually which is closer to the way the ear actually senses the phrase, that is, a coiled line indicating the degree of "hold," balanced by a straighter, more direct line to illustrate the pushing forward:

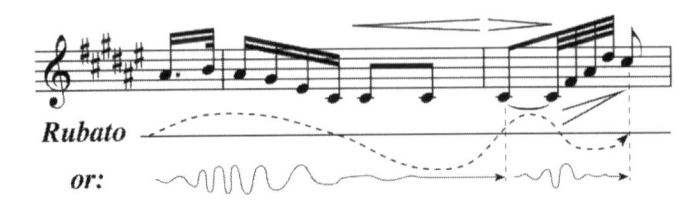

Example 8.4 Chopin: soprano line from Nocturne in F-sharp, Op. 15, no. 2, mm. 1-2, with Matthay's rubato indications from Musical Interpretation, 70

Here we have a double Rubato: the main Rubato is caused by wavering over the first notes of the phrase, and the delay thus caused must be made up by hurrying over the first two quaver C sharps, so as to bring us back to the pulse accurately at the bar-line—the chief syllable of the phrase, with its resolution of the dominant harmony of the previous bar; and a smaller, subsidiary Rubato then prevents the subsequent demisemiquavers (32nd notes) from appearing square—this subsidiary rubato being in the form of a slight lingering over the first C sharp of that bar, while the time is again made up by a corresponding acceleration of these demisemiquavers towards the final note of the phrase, which thus forms an unaccented (or "feminine") phrase-ending. Played any other way, the phrase would prove totally unmusical. Both time-swerves (even the first one) are here most delicate and minute.[31]

He is also careful to acknowledge the differences germane to different style periods:

Now, please do not misunderstand me to maintain that Beethoven and Bach are to be treated in the manner of Schumann, Brahms, Chopin, and Debussy! It is true, indeed, that the more shapely, the more architectural the music, the less ornately may it be treated. To smudge over the majestic arches, columns and domes of a really fine cathedral with tinselly colors and gew-gaws, is of course nothing short of a crime. But do not let us pretend that we can see the cathedral without *light*—without the strong shadows and colors, and mysteries—and rhythm—which light brings with it! As I have already said, in playing great works, works continuous and large in their construction, such as Beethoven's, we must often restrain the impulse to color each detail too strongly, lest we lose sight of the larger shapes of the piece, its general feeling and the majestic shape of its great proportions. We must play Beethoven not sentimentally, but we must play him with sentiment—with strong feeling, and dramatically.[32]

Chopin, arguably, requires the most assiduous, unrelenting attention to the application of rubato, and in addition to the F-sharp Nocturne,

Chapter 8

Matthay offers numerous examples of suggested approaches. One of his most interesting observations concerns the opening of the A-flat Ballade, which he maintains is actually mis-notated as 6/8 time:

Example 8.5 Chopin: Third Ballade in A-flat, Op. 38, mm. 1-4, with Matthay's rubato indications from Musical Interpretation, 80.

The Time-signature 6/8 is misleading, it should really have been notated as 12/8; and the piece, therefore, begins with a *half*-bar of this 12/8 time. The structure of the phrase is a swing towards the tonic chord; the opening E flat is therefore not a down-beat (as it looks in the original) but is an *up-beat*—a *syncopation* in fact; and as such it requires considerable tone and time-emphasis. This time-leaning on the opening E flat is the *cause* of the Rubato, and we are compelled to hasten the remaining quavers (eighth-notes) of that bar, so that we may swing back to the pulse at the crisis of the phrase—the A-flat chord at the true bar-line. In this way we are able to draw attention to it without undue tonal emphasis, while yet rendering clear the true rhythmical swing. This chief point of the phrase is followed by a "feminine" ending, and here again a very slight Rubato assists its rhythmical swing; and thus you see, we really have a *double* Rubato in this simple little phrase.[33]

Matthay's chapter on rubato contains over 40 musical examples from various style periods, including an excerpt from Dale's "wonderful" Sonata and another from a Nocturne by Bowen. But regardless of style, he always insists that tempo fluctuations be dictated by loyalty to the score rather than whim or caprice, and he is careful to observe that Romantic melodic lines are often broader than those from other periods. In Chopin especially, a rubato can often only be meaningfully experienced across an eight-bar span, as in the Mazurka in F-sharp minor from Opus 59:

Example 8.6 Chopin: Mazurka in F-sharp minor, Op. 59, no. 3, mm 65-74, with Matthay's rubato markings from Musical Interpretation, 96-97

The vertical arrows here denote the *only* places where the written rhythm really coincides with the *played* "Time-spot"—all the remaining bars and beats are off the *straight-on* line of beats.[34]

Similarly, the chapter which follows on "tone-inflection" indicates that *quantitative* variations of tone must follow phrase patterns dictated by the composer's intentions. Most notably, he here insists on awareness of a physical limitation built into the piano's nature, that is, that the tone begins to die immediately once evoked, and the artist must be cognizant of this quality if a sense of line is to be maintained. In other words, when notes within a given phrase follow longer notes, the amount of sound must be "matched" to the amount still lingering. He illustrates the effect with several compositions, including the lyrical section of the "Funeral March" from Chopin's B-flat minor Sonata, the inflection of which he felt might be more easily sensed with a mental re-barring to an 8/4 time-signature, beginning at the half-measure:

Example 8.7 Chopin: Sonata in B-flat minor, Op. 35, third mvmt, mm 31-34, with Matthay's inflection markings from Musical Interpretation, 111

To Matthay, "interpretation" involved the artful manipulation of sounds on the page, all of which could be grouped under the general category of "coloring." Rubato represented coloring with respect to time, and inflection represented coloring with respect to tonal quantity. But since the piano also allowed strings to be damped at the artist's discretion, *duration* formed another significant category of color, and hence Matthay devotes a brief chapter to pedaling. His concerns may provide insight into the customary performance practices of his day, because he feels that pianists tend to over-use, rather than under-use, the damper pedal. He provides numerous examples of how a more rhythmic damping of chords can add buoyancy and life to passages such as the opening of the "Davidsbündler" March from Schumann's *Carnaval*:

Example 8.8 Schumann: Marche des "Davidsbündler" contre les Philistins, from Carnaval, Op. 9, mm 1-4, etc., with Matthay's pedal markings from Musical Interpretation, 127

With the publication of *Musical Interpretation*, the essence of Matthay's pedagogical approach had reached print, and his future writings consisted almost exclusively of elaborations, reformulations, and polemics, since in the years to come he was to devote an increasing number of pages to answering his critics. Even before the book appeared, he had become further entwined with the Kennedys in matters both musical and personal, since Dora had married Jack on 15 April 1909, and within a few weeks they joined Marjory, Jessie, and Margaret at Steinway Hall for a program of Marjory's recently published arrangements of Hebridean folk songs. Marjory was enjoying considerable success with a series of programs she simply titled "Songs of the Hebrides," and after she sang at Bechstein Hall on 20 March 1912, she eagerly anticipated another appearance with Jack in the spring. But on 15 April 1912, Jack and Dora's third wedding anniversary—and the very day the *Titanic* sank—the Matthays were engulfed in a far more personal tragedy. When Jack offered to help a woman with her baggage on a Bristol-bound train, he was suddenly seized with excruciating pain, and when he arrived he underwent an emergency hernia operation. But he suffered a heart attack while on the table, and he died the next day at the age of 45. Marjory mentions that he was cremated in Golders Green on the day their concert was to have occurred, and that his friend Ernest Read organized a choir to sing a few selections from Brahms's *Requiem*. Then Marjory, Jessie, and (presumably) Dora carried the urn back to Edinburgh where his ashes were placed alongside "those of his father and mother in the Grange Cemetery."[35] In its brief obituary, the *Musical Times* hoped (in vain, so it seems) that his unpublished writings might one day see print:

> Here he directed his keen legal, analytical mind on the problems of voice-production, and his only recently published booklet, 'Common-sense and singing,'[36] proved how he had been working on these problems in a far more rational way than had so far been done; and many a young artist had found his teaching indeed practical and to the point. It is to be hoped that his many recent lectures and MSS. will be rendered available,

Chapter 8

so that the valuable work he had accomplished may not be lost to the public.[37]

On 8 May 1912, barely three weeks later and perhaps in response to Dora's tragic circumstances, the Committee of Management voted to appoint her to the Academy staff. She was also granted the unusually high starting wage of seven shillings per hour, in view of the fact that she "had attained a certain position in the musical world."[38] But surviving documents from the period give little hint of any underlying grief the family may have been feeling. Three months later Jessie gave recitations at both of the student recitals Matthay scheduled in Bechstein Hall, the first on 10 July for his RAM pupils, and the second eight days later for the TMPS. Perhaps he was playing with fire, but he printed both programs in a single booklet, with his own name virtually dwarfing the tiny font chosen for "Royal Academy of Music" on the cover. He also elected to place "Tobias Matthay Pianoforte School" in boldface, an honor he did not bestow on the RAM. The program of Academy students included Arthur Alexander performing a Prelude and Fugue by Taneyev and Dale's "Night Fancies," while Harriet Cohen played Chopin's Fourth Scherzo in E. The printed program also confirms that Harriet was then having at least some lessons with Swinstead, and Matthay indicates that Bowen and Percy Waller, who both held Academy appointments, were also assisting him with his RAM class.[39]

Harriet ended the evening with a two-piano Scherzo by Saint-Saëns, for which she was joined by Vivian Langrish. Langrish, who also performed Franck's Prelude, Chorale, and Fugue, was then 17 and had been at the RAM for six years. Matthay was now regarding him as one of his most impressive prodigies, and as the years passed they grew increasingly close. The program also featured one "Master Jim Ching" in Bach's Chromatic Fantasy and Fugue,[40] and several other students performing major works such as the Mendelssohn *Variations sérieuses*, the Chopin Fourth Ballade, and substantial portions from the composer's B minor Sonata and Beethoven's Op. 110. Since the Academy had refused to assist Matthay with his recital efforts, he had no compunction about mingling TMPS students with the RAM group, and on the same evening Mary Lediard, listed as a "Private Pupil," performed the complete Schumann *Kinderscenen*.

The TMPS program, which occurred on 18 July, seems almost lackluster by comparison. Ten students performed in the "Junior" division before the interval, followed by nine "Seniors" in the second half. Curiously, except for Evelyn Dawkin, a Senior listed as an "Ex-Student of the R.A.M.," none of the performers studied with Matthay, although many of them later worked with him at the RAM. The "Junior" list included Moiseiwitsch's niece, Lily Kennard, whose name had been anglicized from "Kanewskaya," and who studied with Dorothy Grinstead. She was then in her third year, and the program confirms that the TMPS was then awarding annual prizes, since she is listed as the "Junior Silver Medalist" for 1910. Evangeline Livens, the Junior Silver Medalist for 1911, studied with Hedwig McEwen and had already been praised by the *Musical Times* for her ability to play "cleverly" given her "extreme youth."[41] Like her younger brother Leo, she was a gifted composer—then studying privately with John McEwen—and at the concert she performed her own "Impromptu and Gossamer." In addition, the first half included Hilda Dederich, also with Hedwig, and Egerton "Bob" Tidmarsh, then with Dora, both of whom later became RAM prize winners. They also performed the most difficult repertoire from this group, with Dederich rendering the complete Schubert Impromptu in B-flat, and Tidmarsh offering another performance of the Mendelssohn Variations.

But for the most part, the "Seniors" offered far less virtuosic works than those heard from the RAM scholars eight days earlier in the same hall. The second half included both Brahms Rhapsodies from Opus 79, the Allegro from Bach's *Italian* Concerto, Debussy's *Cathédrale engloutie*, the Schumann *Papillons*, and two Chopin Waltzes. One of the most difficult offerings was given by Ivan Phillipowski, then studying with Bowen, who ended the evening with Dohnányi's Rhapsody in C. Matthay was now listing only 17 teachers on his staff, and he seems to have given the lion's share of the "Seniors" to Myra, who taught four of the advanced group. As far as can be determined, Matthay and Jessie did not overly intrude themselves into the personal lives of students, but they spared no compassion when they felt that deserving members of their extended family were in need, and for some time they had regarded Myra as a surrogate daughter. In August of the following year as they celebrated their twentieth wedding anniversary, they took her with them to Scotland, where they met Marjory and her friend Kenneth MacLeod, the Scottish folklorist and lay minister who had collaborated on her published collections of folk songs. MacLeod led a group of "friends"—15 in all, according to Jessie—on a scenic journey across his native isle of Eigg, and Marjory could not help but note that Tobias had long since learned from his ill-fated adventure in the Pentlands 20 years earlier. In fact, he was approaching such obsessive overcompensation that MacLeod soon dubbed him "The Wizard," a reference to his seeming ability to produce "every device of civilization" from a large bag he always carried. But that summer, Marjory also expressed her gratitude that Matthay was the only member of the party who remembered to bring a camera.[42]

But despite instances of occasional compassion, the Committee of Management remained at loggerheads with Matthay on many substantial issues. By 1910, a nationwide movement emphasizing the training of music teachers was taking hold in Britain, but Mackenzie stubbornly resisted such measures at the RAM, advising Matthay that it was "impossible to teach anyone to teach."[43] Nonetheless, by 1911 he had begrudgingly authorized the formation of a subcommittee, and on 1 March, Matthay and Macpherson presented the Committee with a recommendation that the RAM adopt a "special course designed for students who desire to be specially prepared for the teaching of music."[44] Predictably, the matter dragged along slowly for the next several years, but in the interim Matthay was also moved to advocate changes in current Academy competition rules. On 25 May 1914, he wrote the Committee suggesting a host of reforms, including measures to insure anonymity, such as screens hiding the contestant from the examiners, and identification by number rather than name. But when the vote was taken, the tally was 5 to 1 against all of his suggestions, except the minor one that predictable faults be printed in advance so that the judges need only insert check-marks in certain categories.[45]

Less than two months later, Matthay was again indiscriminately mingling RAM and TMPS students at Bechstein Hall, but by this time his class had grown to the point that he needed to divide his Junior and Senior groups into separate recitals. These were preceded by another Academy recital on 2 July 1914, and the program reveals that a number of the performers had already made their formal London debuts. Langrish, who had appeared at Bechstein Hall the previous February, opened the evening with Matthay's brief "Romanesque" ("by request"), and ended the first half with the first movement of Beethoven's "Emperor" Concerto—assisted by Bernard Symons at the second piano. Symons, who had given his debut at Blackheath in 1911, was one of several pupils studying with Matthay toward the L.R.A.M., and he also joined Langrish to close the evening with several of Corder's demanding two-piano transcriptions of Czerny studies from the *School of Velocity*. Mary Lediard, again listed only as a "private pupil," performed the entire Schumann *Carnaval*, while Tidmarsh offered the Franck Prelude, Chorale, and Fugue. Harriet performed Bax's recently composed *Two Russian Tone Pictures*, the second of which—"Gopak"—the composer had "affectionately" dedicated to Matthay before offering its premiere to Myra a year earlier. The printed program denoted former TMPS students with asterisks, and seven of the eleven performers could claim this distinction. Jessie also recited Maeterlinck's "On the Death of My Little Dog" at the interval.

The "Junior" recital occurred two weeks later on 15 July, and Matthay co-mingled his 20 performers with two former TMPS students, both now at the RAM. Evangeline Livens performed two Chopin Etudes, and Tidmarsh played Paderweski's Variations and Fugue in A minor, while the two of them combined to end the program with Corder's *Fantasia on Mendelssohn Lieder* for two pianos. The "Juniors" offered more ambitious repertoire than in previous years. Eleven-year-old Frieda Swain (then studying with Dora) performed Chopin's Introduction and Variations from Hérold's *Ludovic*, Lily Kennard played Liszt's tenth Hungarian Rhapsody, and Hilda Dederich rendered Weber's *Konzertstücke* with Hannah Smith at the second piano. The "Senior" concert which followed on 23 July contained a mixture of 17 present and former TMPS students, although only two—Mary Lediard and Margaret Bennett—actually studied with Matthay. Lediard opened the program with five of Matthay's six *Monothemes*, and returned later with Chopin's Scherzo in B-flat minor, while Bennett gave the first movement of Beethoven's "Waldstein" Sonata. One of Dora's students played the Chopin G minor Ballade, while another ended the evening with Liszt's twelfth Hungarian Rhapsody. Myra remained loyal to her RAM friends, with one of her students playing sections of Bowen's Second Suite, another playing the Variations from Dale's Sonata, and a third offering Bax's early "Concert Valse." She also took the stage with violinist Winifred Smith to perform the first movement of Bax's Violin Sonata No. 1 in E, which the two of them had premiered in the same hall four years earlier.

But this was the last concert Matthay organized in a climate of normalcy—at least for several years. By then, the Matthays were hosting annual year-end picnics at Marley, and a photo taken on Saturday, 18 July 1914, shows 24 RAM and TMPS scholars—along with Matthay, Jessie, Corder, and Myra—posing on the south edge of Moses Hill. The weather was cloudy that morning, and although the sun later broke through, Jessie reports that it was no ordinary July afternoon:

> In the midst of their jousts and tournaments they stopped to gaze at a fleet of aeroplanes (a rare sight in those days) circling in the sunshine like a flight of silver birds over the Solent where it lies hidden behind the Sussex Downs.
>
> It seemed just the right climax for a memorable day, but had the young folks known its portent they would have been dumb-struck.
>
> These manoeuvres were not being carried out in play. The fourth of August was only three weeks distant.[46]

But in fact there was every reason to know the "portent" of the display, because on that day several thousand people had descended on nearby Portsmouth to watch the most highly publicized naval spectacle in decades. The Royal Navy was preparing some 22 miles of warships—the largest fleet in British history—for the King's inspection on 20 July, and the planes and airships seen from Marley—38 in all—were circling as part of an elaborate staged salute.[47] Exactly two weeks after *The Times* lauded "the glory of England's naval might" in its 21 July edition,[48] war had broken out, and Matthay may soon have felt a sense of relief that his parents had been spared the indignities he now saw inflicted on Germans living in his father's adopted country. England's determination to deny aid to its enemies was necessary and understandable, but the draconian measures soon invoked against the Bechstein firm were arguably fueled by home-grown interests who sought merely to feather their nests. Less than two weeks after Matthay's friends Edwin and Carl Bechstein were forced to return to Germany, the Westminster Bank, their principal creditor, sued to award custody of the London office to Bechstein's assistant manager, Winchester Berridge, which was granted on condition that he not "remit any monies or goods" to the owners.[49] For well over a decade, the Bechsteins had shown untold kindnesses to scores of British musicians, and even welcomed Matthay to Marley with a housewarming present, but now they were being pilloried in absentia, and within a year the firm was enjoined from selling any instruments in Britain. The brothers who ran the London division were said (not surprisingly, by several British piano manufacturers) to be subversives, and on 14 April 1915 *The Times* even labeled the company "An Enemy Alien Firm." It reported that after long deliberations, Bechstein's Royal Appointments had been cancelled, adding that "the Home Secretary does not intend to renew Messrs. Bechstein's licence empowering the firm to trade."[50]

A few weeks later, the sinking of the *Lusitania* intensified anti-German sentiment in many parts of Britain, and Matthay should have seen the handwriting on the wall. But he was oblivious to the paranoia of his colleagues who were concerned that their past actions

Chapter 8

might soon provoke attacks on their patriotism. On the Committee of Management alone, Beringer, Corder, and Mackenzie—all closely connected with German musical life and fluent in the language—had good reason to fear the volatile climate at home, but no more so than Matthay, who was every bit as vulnerable and, arguably, naïve not to have taken greater precautions. He blithely scheduled another concert by his RAM students—by invitation only—at Bechstein Hall on 16 June 1915, which forced him to be "unavoidably absent" during a Committee of Management meeting:

> The chairman [E. E. Cooper] drew attention to the programme of a recital which was to be given by some of Mr Matthay's students at Bechstein Hall on the 16th inst., in which the name of the Royal Academy of Music appeared prominently in conjunction with a Bechstein Concert grand pianoforte. After considerable discussion it was resolved unanimously:
> "That the Committee registers its protest against the name of the RAM being associated with that of the Bechstein pianoforte, and calls upon Mr Matthay for an explanation."[51]

The "conjunction" that caused so much concern was the small (and customary) caption at the bottom of the page which read "Bechstein Concert Grand Pianoforte," acknowledging merely that Bechstein provided the piano used in its hall. To add insult to injury, the Matthays were even designating this particular concert as a benefit for "Relief of Belgians in Belgium"—a cause profoundly sympathetic to British interests. The *Musical Times* reported that the event, which was attended by 600 people, brought in £21, 15s, 6d, but the Committee was undeterred.[52] On 23 June, they read Matthay's letter of "explanation," and immediately drafted a response but—oddly—the contents of neither document are contained in their Minutes. No doubt Matthay was infuriated at their demands because, somewhat unusually, several weeks later he lashed out at his colleague (and former employee) Evlyn Howard-Jones, who had also scheduled a concert for 12 of his RAM pupils at Bechstein Hall for 21 July—another War-time benefit which *The Times* reported collected £42 for the "Officers' Families' Fund."[53] But in flagrant violation of Academy rules, a large poster advertising Howard-Jones's event had been placed on its "notice board" some days in advance, to which the Committee turned a blind eye. By then Matthay had completed 35 years of teaching at the RAM, and he was understandably indignant at the double standard. The Committee ignored two of his letters of protest, which prompted him to write a third, evidently worded so strongly that they censured him at their 21 July meeting:

> Considerable discussion followed in the course of which the writing of such letters was strongly deprecated, and Mr Matthay agreeing to consider the incident closed, it was not considered necessary to take any further action.[54]

On 4 November, conditions for Bechstein went from bad to worse when an alliance of local piano manufacturers pressed the London County Council to deny renewal of Bechstein Hall's concert license. They argued that the Wigmore Street venue was used only "for the purpose of advertising and furthering the sale of German goods"[55]— a contention supported solely by the observation that Bechsteins were the only pianos allowed on its stage. Three weeks later, solicitors for the Westminster Bank eloquently appealed the decision, observing that about 70 British workers would be left jobless, and that there was not the "slightest danger that a single farthing would be sent to Germany," but their arguments fell on deaf ears.[56] For over a year the hall remained vacant until the Board of Trade, ostensibly prodded by the Trading With the Enemy Act of 1914, ordered the entire Bechstein enterprise sold at public auction. On 7 November 1916, at a sale which *The Times* characterized as "one of the most remarkable ever held in London," the gavel fell in just under four minutes as Debenhams, Limited, was granted ownership of all Bechstein's British operations for the meager sum of £56,500.[57] Included in the sale was the leasehold conveyance of the Hall itself, for which the Howard de Walden Estate was then charging £925 a year (but which contained studios, offices, and flats that Bechstein had been letting for £1,480 a year), an inventory of 104 Bechstein grands, 30 uprights, motor delivery vans, and the tuning contracts on over 3,000 instruments grossing between £6,000 and £7,000 a year.[58] A new license was rushed through, and the concert venue re-opened on 16 January 1917 as "Wigmore Hall," with a recital of three Beethoven Sonatas by violinist Albert Sammons.[59] Matthay next utilized the building for concerts the following July, but the printed programs have not been located.[60] He returned on 11 July, 16 July, and 18 July 1918, with programs for his RAM and TMPS students given in aid respectively of "Concerts at the Front," the Royal National Lifeboat Institution, and the "Musicians' Y.M.C.A. Gift to the Troops." Now beneath each printed program was the terse caption, "The Weber (British) Concert Grand Pianoforte Will Be Used."

A mere glance at Matthay's printed programs helps dramatize the stress the war had inflicted on the country as a whole. Of the eleven performers in his RAM recital, the only male—"Master Harry Isaacs"—was present merely because he was too young to serve. In the three concerts combined, only one additional performer was male, and Matthay appeared to be doing more of the teaching himself. Jessie later wrote that "One after another, the members of the teaching staff were called away, until it seemed as though a darker moment could not be."[61] A similar fate afflicted the RAM, as reflected in a surviving Students' Chamber Concert program from 4 March 1916, in which the oldest male performer was cellist "Giovanni" Barbirolli, then 17, who performed Beethoven's Sonata in A. He was joined by Matthay's pupil Ethel Bartlett, then 19, who accompanied nearly the entire program, and who was soon assisting young Barbirolli in major London venues. But Matthay's older male students—and younger teachers—were clearly thinning as they were called to the front. Bowen was out of commission for months after he joined the Scots Guards Regimental Band and caught pneumonia in France.[62] Langrish enlisted as well, and Arthur Alexander returned to New Zealand. Some absences inflicted consequences more emotional than practical, and Matthay and Jessie were undoubtedly saddened by Benjamin Dale's internment in a civilian camp at Ruhleben for the war's duration.⁶³ But the most serious blow came in August 1915 when Edward Cole, the "enthusiastic and energetic" secretary of the TMPS as well as the RAM's "second clerk," lost his life at Suvla Bay—one of 18,000 British casualties.⁶⁴ His widow, Marion, soon stepped in to assume his duties at the Matthay School on a permanent basis.

When the War first started, Jessie reports that Marley had almost immediately become a magnet for homesick Scottish soldiers:

> In less than four months [by December 1914] the whole Sussex weald was one vast camp—"Kitchener's army." The soldier lads, most of them from Lanarkshire, became our neighbours. Every Saturday night some thirty of them climbed the hill to High Marley and made merry, dancing reels in their stocking-soles and singing all their favourite songs. These parties continued till the day came for them to sail to France.⁶⁵

But in spite of their wartime benevolence, the Matthays were subjected to another indignity when two MI-5 agents paid a visit to Marley one evening to investigate Matthay's "German loyalties."⁶⁶ By May 1916 German Zeppelin raids had killed nearly 600 British civilians, and 13 months later the first raid by a Gotha G-V bomber had been staged over Kent. As the war moved increasingly into aerial arenas, Marley's extreme height—coupled with Matthay's bi-linguality, his Germanic roots, and his friendship with German citizens—provoked apprehensive officials to seek assurance that he was not operating a signaling tower. Their suspicions were quickly allayed, but perhaps as a consequence, in July 1918 he offered a short pamphlet to the War Department called *The Problems of Agility: A Summary of the Laws governing Speed in Reiteration and Succession for Wireless Operators, Telegraphists, and Typists, and for Pianoforte and Organ Students*. He begins with a Preamble clearly designed to contravene any suggestions of disloyalty:

> It having been brought to my ears that certain "Wireless officers of a squadron of H.M. Navy" (the location of which must not be divulged

Chapter 8

for fear of D.O.R.A. [a reference to the 1914 Defence of the Realm Act, which gave the Government broad powers to censor civilian publications that compromised the War effort]) had found the "Act of Touch" of immediate help in their work. I felt it might be doing a service to such, and others, if I summarized in concentrated form the laws governing agility in utterance—laws which were formulated for the first time in that rather ponderous work.[67]

Students of Matthay's earlier works would have found nothing radically new in his eight-page pamphlet, although his principles had now been expanded to some unexpected applications. For example, he had always insisted that the arm be balanced or poised as a basis for all touch at the piano, and noted that the resistance of five un-depressed piano keys was generally sufficient so that the weight of the hand could lie loosely on the keyboard. But since this was less likely to be the case with telegraph and typewriter keys, he noted that it might be necessary that "the hand itself must also be kept more or less completely self-supported, and poised like the arm:"

> For instance, with a *shuttle*-typewriter, such as I myself use, the springs keeping the keys at surface level are so slight that they will not successfully support the *fully*-released weight of my (rather large) hand; therefore the hand must here be kept in its more or less fully-supported state, in between the successive typing impulses. Nevertheless, I find that in very rapid typing, that I may allow greater latitude to the hand, since the greater number of keys covered in a short time will bear more weight.[68]

He distills his suggestions into three "injunctions," which came as no surprise to those already familiar with his teachings: 1) "Insist on accurately *timing* and *ceasing* the impulse-providing exertion," 2) "Eliminate *Down-arm Force*. Depend instead upon the assertion of the finger and hand alone," and 3) "Insist on limiting the muscular exertions to those required, eliminating *all contrary exertions*."[69] It is widely believed that in the last few months of the War,

Matthay's booklet was well received by the Navy and other departments, though its presence in government offices is difficult to document. No doubt Matthay was able to surmount wartime exigencies by releasing it through his own publishing house, the Anglo-French Music Company, which he founded with McEwen in 1916 to produce, in Jeremy Dibble's words, "educational music in lieu of German publications stemmed by the war."[70] Although this was partly true, Jessie observes that Matthay also viewed the AFMC as a useful and natural extension of his School: "There was a rising generation of composers, both men and women, to be encouraged; and by bringing their work before the public, both by publication and performance, something quite definite could be achieved."[71] Matthay had long been critical of the pedagogical materials aimed at children, and now the TMPS gave him a vested commercial interest in improving the available literature. While he sought to provide carefully graduated levels of difficulty, he also strove to present works of substantial musical value, and—perhaps not so coincidentally—few, if any, of the compositions he published seemed "Germanic."

For example, in February 1919, a few months after the War ended, the AFMC issued McEwen's charming three-movement Sonatina in G minor, whose abrupt modal shifts from minor to major were highly suggestive of English folksong:

Example 8.9 John B. McEwen: Andante semplice
from Sonatina in G minor, mm. 17-24

Chapter 8

Matthay also contributed a few selections, and two months later he completed a suite of four miniatures at Marley titled—fittingly enough—*On Surrey Hills*, which he issued later that summer. Possibly, the youngest contributor to his catalogue was seventeen-year-old Denise Lassimonne, whose brief homage to Debussy, "Les longs cheveux de Mélisande," was completed in the summer of 1920, and published four years later. The month of its release is unknown, but when Langrish performed it at Wigmore Hall on 31 October, *The Times* noted that it won such "deserved applause" that he was required to repeat it.[72] Replete with ninth, eleventh, and thirteenth chords, her colorful essay shows an impressive harmonic sophistication:

Example 8.10 Denise Lassimonne: "Les longs cheveux de Mélisande," mm. 1-4

Nor was this her first offering, for though it also remained unpublished for several years, she completed a charming lullaby, "Petite Berceuse," in March of 1919, two months before her sixteenth birthday, which she dedicated to "Uncle Tobs." By then she had been studying composition with McEwen and piano with Matthay for over two years, having won an RAM Associated Board Scholarship in 1916.[73] She performed in July 1917 at Matthay's Wigmore Hall RAM recital, barely a week after she had "distinguished herself" on 9 July by performing the difficult piano part to Taneyev's Quintet at an RAM Chamber Concert.[74] On 11 July 1918, she appeared on Matthay's RAM recital performing some of his own pieces as well as the Finale to Beethoven's Third Concerto (with Hilda Dederich at the second piano), and again on 18 July as an alumna guest artist for the "Junior" TMPS program, where she played the Chopin Nocturne in E, Op. 62, no. 2.

Denise's family background bore a striking resemblance to Matthay's in at least one respect: both of their fathers had fled their native lands to become language tutors in England, and both households were bicultural and bilingual. She was the daughter of (Eugène) Lucien Lassimonne (1861-1921), who by the age of 30 was living in Camberley, where he taught French at the Royal Staff College and occasionally advertised for private students.[75] Several years later he was well established as a member of the Société Nationale des Professeurs de Français en Angleterre, and on 17 July 1897 he even spoke on "La Lecture en Famille" at the Westminster Town Hall.[76] Five years later his first daughter, Lulu, was born, and shortly thereafter he and his wife were evidently lodging (or willing to lodge) well-to-do boys in their home, as evidenced by an advertisement carried by *The Times* on 13 August 1902:

> A LIMITED NUMBER of SONS of GENTLEMEN, under 15, can receive special TUITION in French and German, besides usual subjects, in the family of the French Instructor at the Royal Military College, Sandhurst. Apply to L. Lassimonne. Montjoie, Camberley.[77]

Denise always maintained that her father had taught Churchill—who entered Sandhurst in 1893—and if so, he had been teaching there for a decade or more by the time this ad appeared. He was generally well liked and seemed to exude an irrepressible *joie de vivre*, and very soon he was also serving as French tutor to the Royal Family. His principal duties were to instruct the children of the Prince of Wales (later George V) at Osborne House, Queen Victoria's summer home on the Isle of Wight, and Denise was born in Cowes in May 1903 during one of her family's visits to the Isle. Despite a reputation for aloofness, particularly where youngsters were concerned, Princess May (later Queen Mary) regarded it as propitious that she shared a birthday with Denise—26 May—and every year until her death she sent her a birthday card. In 1905 Lucien Lassimonne left Sandhurst to assume the post of Senior French Master at the newly opened Royal Naval College at Osborne, where most cadets remembered him as an "excellent teacher." As Matthay's father had done before him, he also issued grammar books and readers, and by 1910 he was even collaborating on a French series with W. Mansfield Poole, the Head of the Modern Language Department at Osborne.[78] However, his short, rotund figure often made him the object of ridicule, and some even labeled him as a "caricature of a Frenchman." As one cadet remembered, "His top hat tapered outwards to start the ample eclipse of his figure which came in at his ankles and small feet."[79]

Denise and Lulu were also quite short, but Denise never showed a propensity to gain weight, and in fact for most of her life she suffered from the opposite problem. Her musical abilities were pronounced from an early age, so much so that when Lulu became ill and the family returned briefly to Paris in 1912 in search of treatment, Lucien was persuaded to take his nine-year-old daughter to Isidore Philipp (1863-1958), the noted teacher of many distinguished pianists. But despite an audition consisting of Beethoven's "Waldstein" and other demanding works, Philipp made no comment about Denise's playing, merely pointing to her unusually long arms and remarking to her father: "Votre enfant est déformé."[80] On their return to England, Lulu and Denise were enrolled at a convent school in Farnborough, Surrey, where she continued her piano studies with a Mr. Sewell, "who came down from London each week to teach the best talent."[81] When she was eleven, Sewell was helping her prepare Matthay's recently revised "May Morning," which was then on the list for the Associated Board Examinations, but as she recalled years later, "neither of us could make head or tail of it!"[82] Sewell, who was acquainted with Matthay, asked him for some help, and Matthay soon agreed to hear Denise at Marley, which was nearby:

> So the day came, and I found myself in the room I was to get to know and love so well, especially the benevolent figure sitting in an armchair, wrapped in rugs and mittened hands, by the big Bechstein piano giving a lesson. When it finished he welcomed me and sat me comfortably on the stool making me feel at ease and off I started on "May Morning"—after

I had ended he patted me on the head saying "You're a very good little girl" and pushed me from the stool to play it himself.

I shall never forget that performance—I had never heard that kind of controlled but *very* free playing before—It was my introduction to RUBATO! . . . It seemed as though the left hand was in one world and the right hand in another yet bound by a mystical cord which swept the music in a flow of inevitableness.[83]

Example 8.11 Tobias Matthay: "May Morning," from From my Sketch Book, Op. 24, Book 1, mm. 1-3, with Matthay's handwritten rubato suggestions

Matthay also listened to her other pieces, and he was so impressed that he asked her father if he could work with her fortnightly over the next two years while she remained with Sewell. She entered the RAM on full scholarship at 13, but her award expired at the end of three years and she sought to extend her funding by trying for the Sterndale-Bennett Prize in 1920 and again in 1921—only to receive "high commendation" both times.[84] No doubt Matthay understood the realities of educating children on a language master's salary, and in an unprecedented move he placed Denise on the staff of the TMPS when she was merely 16. He was impressed with her insightful intelligence, and as her students were primarily children, the pieces she then composed were largely an extension of her professional focus.

Like a great many of Matthay's pupils, she also longed for a concert career, but for whatever reason, success on the stage seemed just out of reach. Without question she was a gifted performer, and decades later her friend Clifford Curzon remembered her "wonderful" performances of the Beethoven "Appassionata" and the Chopin E major Scherzo.[85] The few recordings she left also testify to the refinement characteristic of many Matthay pupils, but her press approval often

Chapter 8

seemed so hard won that one wonders if she might occasionally have been the victim of unjustifiable criticism. For example, in November 1922 RAM violinist Rowsby Woof collaborated with Bowen to premiere Dale's Violin Sonata at Wigmore Hall, and *The Times* was almost totally negative, complaining that the Finale should have been "compressed." But the review was even harsher on the selections which Denise performed with Woof, calling their rendition of the Bach E major Sonata "very unfinished," their Franck Sonata "rough and ill-balanced," and their interpretation of McEwen's recently composed Little Sonata "flippant."[86] On 15 February 1924 she gave her solo debut at the age of 20, and despite some lukewarm praise, the paper's brief comments were again largely unflattering:

> This was a first performance at Wigmore Hall on Friday, and nerves must be held responsible for some things which a sober judgment will condemn later on—inadequate finger work in Bach's English Suite in G minor and doubtful phrasing and a hectic pedal in Franck's Prelude, Choral, and Fugue. Chopin's rarely heard Prelude in C sharp minor, Op. 45, was nicely played.[87]

The Times's critic may have assessed the evening accurately in one respect, since Denise could be highly strung, and throughout her life she suffered from a nervous condition which often manifested itself as stage fright. Three years earlier, on 8 May 1921, her future had been substantially altered when Lucien Lassimonne died of kidney disease at his home in East Cowes.[88] He left his widow, Georgette, with a modest estate of slightly over £3,300, and she soon chose to return to France with Lulu.[89] The Admiralty's much publicized decision to close the highly troubled Osborne Naval College two weeks after Lucien died (it had long been criticized for unsanitary conditions which left the cadets overly susceptible to communicable diseases) may have contributed to Georgette's decision, because even had her husband lived, he would probably have been dismissed, rather than reassigned.[90] Although Denise was nearly 18 and old enough to be somewhat self sufficient, the Matthays offered her their home and she soon became—even more than Myra—the daughter they never had. Matthay's largesse was not unprecedented, since Myra had virtually been forced from her dysfunctional family's household by the summer of 1914, and very soon she too was using 96 Wimpole Street as her address. Her biographer also reports that when the War began, she accompanied the Matthays to Marley most weekends, and even after she found more permanent lodgings at Carlton Hill late in 1915, she returned whenever possible to Matthay's "magical" expanse to "re-set her compass."[91]

But the Matthays' generosity still begs for some explanation, since although a great many of Matthay's students might have benefited from similar gestures, Myra and Denise were the only ones so favored. Harriet, for example, also spent many weekends at Marley during the War, and in the summer of 1915 Jessie even took her to the Glastonbury Festival to accompany her on stage as she recited some Celtic poetry. At the War's end, Matthay gladly added Harriet to the TMPS staff, but when her incessant practicing forced her out of her family's tiny West Hampstead flat to an unfurnished room in Swiss Cottage, not even her inability to purchase a mattress moved Tobias and Jessie to offer her lodgings.[92] Denise rarely spoke of the details surrounding her entry into the Matthay household—referencing only "difficulties occurring at my Father's death" as a causal factor[93]—but it seems likely that she had engaged their affections more emphatically than most of Matthay's other pupils. Julian DeGray, one of her closest friends (see Chapter 11), maintained that Matthay had actually hastened Lucien's death by involving him in a motor accident, which might further explain their behavior, but even though Denise often spoke of Matthay's reckless driving, the evidence for this story is too fragmentary to be conclusive.[94] What is certain is that when Lucien died, Matthay was 63 and Jessie was 52, and if they had ever desired to expand their family, this was likely to be their final opportunity.

It is also worth noting that six months earlier, on 8 December 1920, Jessie had undergone surgery to remove an ovarian growth, a procedure Matthay deemed "a somewhat serious operation."[95] She recuperated within walking distance of Wimpole Street at a nursing

Chapter 8

facility in Dorset Square, and she returned to Marley several days before Christmas.[96] But despite Matthay's assurances that she was "quite normal and well,"[97] three months later she was packed off—somewhat against her will—to a spa in Bath, prompting her to joke that the city was "lovely beyond compare, but every other person walks with a stick!!"[98] She spent much of May in Scotland adjudicating elocution competitions, which probably tired her out since by late August Matthay had taken her to a German spa—Kurhaus zur Helenenquelle near Bad Pyrmont—and on 14 September he wrote Corder that "I hope my wife will feel the benefit of it next term."[99] But the following March, Jessie feared that she might not be well enough even by July to deliver a recitation for the RAM Centennial Celebration, advising Corder by letter that "I am doing all I possibly can to recover my health by then."[100] Perhaps Denise appeared precisely at the moment that an impending sense of mortality prodded Matthay and Jessie to consider leaving more to the world than just a musical legacy. And very soon, Denise considered herself virtually adopted, referring to Matthay as "Panunck"—a combination of "Papa" and "Uncle"—and Jessie as "Mummy II."[101] Jessie's arthritis now largely confined her to a wheelchair, and Denise remembered her being in severe pain much of the time, though she could never remember her complaining.[102]

Jessie also continued to work, and she was now propagating her own artistic legacy through teaching. As early as 13 October 1909, the Committee of Management had considered her suggestion that Elocution be added to the L.R.A.M. syllabus, and after the War, it allowed her to accept a few Academy students at Wimpole Street.[103] One of her pupils, Dulcie Bowie, recited a Fiona McLeod poem at a TMPS program at Morley Hall on 23 October 1923, and another, Phyllis Keeves, presented Walter de la Mare's *Four Queer Poems* in the same location on 19 December. Shortly after Denise arrived at No. 96, she also remembered visits from several fledgling actors not connected with the RAM, including a young Alastair Sim and an even younger John Gielgud. Most likely Sim was in London to audition for the Old Vic, but he was unsuccessful, and before returning to Edinburgh (where he later opened his own school of speech and drama), he may have sought Jessie out to assist him with Shakespearean diction.[104] Denise, then about 20, soon developed a severe crush on young Gielgud (which came to nothing), and she recalled once even absent-mindedly following him out of the TMPS and aboard an Oxford Street bus "as if in a trance."[105] Jessie was also writing, and in 1922, the Glasgow firm of Paterson published her *The Art of the Spoken Word*, a brief pamphlet issued as part of its "Festival Series," an undertaking spurred by Britain's growing Festival movement, which had been gathering momentum since the War's end. The Glasgow Festival of 1921 lasted for eleven days—from 4 to 14 May—and the *Musical Times* noted that it had become "one of the largest in the kingdom," with "about eleven thousand competitors in ninety-two classes."[106] Elocution had recently been added to the plethora of solo singing and choral events, and Jessie spent the first two weeks of May judging the Festival's many contestants, along with her friend, poet and playwright John Drinkwater. The magazine also spoke approvingly of the new category:

> The Elocution Classes, successfully inaugurated last year, were again a very popular feature of the Festival. The inclusion of Ecclesiastes xii, and I Corinthians xiii, was a brilliant idea, and so impressive was the delivery of these fine passages of Scripture that had the audience been composed mainly of clergymen—comparatively few of whom seem to be alive to the religious, moral, and social value of the Festival movement—much improvement would result in their reading of the 'lessons.'[107]

Frequently the various provinces spared no expense procuring Britain's finest talent to adjudicate these events, and a week later Jessie was in Edinburgh to judge its second Festival—which boasted 78 categories—where her name was prominently displayed alongside those of Holst and Ernest Newman.[108] She probably began her *Spoken Word* pamphlet sometime later, and perhaps not surprisingly, her advice is remarkably consistent with the counsel Matthay had long been offering teachers and pupils. Predictably, she is quick to note that the current emphasis on competitions and "winning" might not always be compatible with the deep reflection and thought necessary for moving interpretations of a poet's sentiments: "Without doubt, it is a fine thing to see one's name, or the name of a pupil, at the head of the list, but it is only a fine thing when it is clear that the general standard of endeavour is mounting ever higher and higher."[109]

Jessie's views on poetic expression are remarkably similar to Matthay's views on musical interpretation:

> Each branch must be grown to fulfill the poet's requirements; articulation, vocalization, to give the requisite character to his words; sense of pulsation, accentuation, to provide the necessary rhythm; inflection, together with a sense of continuity of thought, to show forth the shape and duration of his phrase.[110]

She even mirrors Matthay's physiological principles:

> The essentials to be remembered are that the throat must be kept perfectly free, most carefully watched, so that none of the functions belonging to the articulatory organs are shared by it (except on very rare occasions when a rough tone is desired), that the tongue is exercised into great nimbleness, so that it achieves its vowel shapes with absolute certainty and purity and its articulations with precision and elasticity, that the lips are not lazy, but are made muscularly fit to do any work demanded of them, with whatever degree of energy required.[111]

A year before Jessie's pamphlet appeared, the AFMC published Matthay's "On Method in Teaching," a thirty-two-page booklet (which later appeared as the sixth in a series of lectures on "psychology for music teachers") prepared in the summer of 1919 for his "Special One Year Complete Training Course for Teachers." His interest in the science of psychology had been growing, and although he was convinced that some rudimentary understanding of the subject was essential for effective teaching, he cautioned that his presentation was far from exhaustive:

> These lectures are intended purely as an *Introduction* to this vast subject, to stimulate the teacher towards a real study of the practical aspect of Psychology, to persuade him to realize how much study has immediate bearing upon his work during every moment of his teaching duties, and with special reference to the teaching of Music, and Pianoforte playing and teaching in particular.[112]

He is careful to note that a method of *teaching* should not be confused with a method of *playing*, which "usually implies a set of mere fads consisting of quite false ideas as to the causes of things and effects."[113] Rather, a method of teaching refers to a hierarchical exposition of facts to be presented to the student, in which "the steps enumerated are in purely logical order, each one psychologically leading to the next," on those occasions when "their succession cannot beneficially be altered."[114] As an example, he then presents eight of his "Nine Steps toward Finger Individualization," a systematic approach to the acquisition of rotational freedom which he issued in pamphlet form the following year. (See Appendix III) He is careful to contrast "method" with "teaching devices," necessary approaches "which must be changed, modified and adjusted, to suit the requirements of each individual student, and his particular mental stage at the moment."[115] In other words, as with all his teaching, the mental and physical context of the student must always be taken into account, but the facts of reality which underlie the acquisition of the necessary mental and physical skills must be apprehended as needed—and they must be grasped logically if they are to be meaningfully understood.

The War's end also signaled a heightened level of talent at the TMPS, which is verifiable by even a cursory examination of its concert programs. By 1921 Matthay had added a fourth recital to conclude the customary three he gave each July at Wigmore Hall, this one featuring his *crème de la crème* at the much larger Queen's Hall, and offering a mixture of RAM and TMPS students. On 21 July that program began with Denise and Désirée MacEwan performing Bax's two-piano work *Moy Mell*, which he had written several years earlier for Myra and Irene. Three of the four Chopin Scherzos were also heard by various artists, as well as the Schumann Toccata and Ravel's *Ondine* performed by an American, Bruce Simonds. Matthay's RAM program, which occurred a week earlier, featured several students who were soon to leave a mark on British music, including thirteen-year-old Betty Humby and twenty-year-old Alan Bush (who played only his own compositions). The two remaining TMPS programs offered no less than 40 separate performers.

The following year's events were overshadowed by the Academy's Centenary Celebrations, and on 10 July 1922 Matthay opened a week of RAM chamber concerts with a special program at Aeolian Hall, which he presented in lieu of his customary RAM recital. Supported by nine of his present and former students, he gave an afternoon lecture under RAM auspices entitled "Some Royal Academy Pianoforte Composers," which he acknowledged gave him "a lot of happiness."[116] The program featured two RAM scholars—Betty Humby performing a piece by Bennett, and Désirée MacEwan playing works by Matthay and Mackenzie—and seven graduates. Hilda Dederich played two short pieces by McEwen plus two short works of her own, Arthur Alexander played Dale's "Night Fancies" and two of Bax's pieces, Bowen played his own Second Suite, and Dorothy Howell—who had studied with Matthay during the War and was already making a name for herself as a composer—played one of her own Studies. Her contemporary, South-African-born Adolph Hallis, who was already developing a reputation as a champion of modern music, performed one of Sydney Rosenbloom's difficult Concert Studies. Langrish and Tidmarsh ended the program with two of Langrish's duo-piano transcriptions of Bach Chorales. *The Times* praised Matthay's commentary as "clearly put and given," illustrating how the composers' "painstaking efforts had built up a society of which we could be proud." The critic added, "The performances we listened to were quite worthy of the occasion: they were capable, musical, and modest."[117]

By 1923 Matthay was no longer devoting an entire evening to his RAM students, for his TMPS concerts had mushroomed to the point that five were now required to comprise what he termed his "Summer

Festival," and the repertoire had become increasingly ambitious. On 24 July, his series ender at Queen's Hall featured Désirée MacEwan performing a Ravel set—including the *Alborado del gracioso*—Nan Dove in Scriabin's Fifth Sonata, and an American, Jeffry Reynolds, rendering one of d'Albert's Scherzos. The following year, even before the interval, the selections included offerings from another American, sixteen-year-old Eunice Norton, who opened with Rachmaninoff's Prelude in B minor from Opus 32, as well as his demanding Prelude in B-flat from Opus 23. She was followed by Virginia MacLean, who performed the first movement of Beethoven's "Hammerklavier" Sonata, Betty Humby, who played two demanding Chopin Etudes—including the "Winter Wind"—Anthea Skimming, who performed Schumann's Toccata, and Denise, who offered the Bach Chromatic Fantasia and Fugue. But it should be noted that of the eleven performers presented, only three were then receiving lessons exclusively from Matthay, since his attentions had become increasingly difficult to obtain. On average, his former pupils were now appearing in major London venues three to four times a week, and most were still playing their programs to him before they ventured on stage. Myra, Irene, Harriet, and Langrish performed every new work for him, and many others played for him at least intermittently. Denise also recalled that it was an optimum time to be in Matthay's good graces, since "all Uncle Tobs had to do was pick up the telephone and you had a concert engagement."[118] Arguably, no other professor then wielded as much influence in the London concert arena, and if some were already regarding him as royalty, the summer of 1922 soon witnessed a more formal coronation.

As the Academy's Centennial year approached, it fell to Corder—pending Mackenzie's approval—to oversee the vast array of festivities scheduled for July of 1922. For many months, he had been hard at work lining up participants, and on 14 September 1921, Matthay wrote to him from Bad Pyrmont. His unusually candid remarks reveal that he harbored no false modesty:

> My reason for writing just now, particularly, is the Centenary Celebration. No doubt Mackenzie will wish to acknowledge my services to the

Academy during this Century, and what I have done for the Academy, and incidentally what I have done for the world? He would cut his own nose off if he did not express what all the world knows! Well, what I should like to request, and I beg <u>you</u> to suggest it to him, is, that this acknowledgement, partly, anyway, takes the form of a performance of my <u>Concert-Piece in A minor.</u> I really think, after consideration, that it <u>would best represent me</u> although it is an earlier work—and everyone seems to think it is one of the best things I've done! And—I would suggest that <u>Vivian Langrish</u> be asked to play it! He played it as a student under A. C. M. [Mackenzie] himself—and even then had a great success with it! He has played it a number of times since—I think <u>three</u> times at the <u>Proms</u>! . . . I feel its performance could not be in better hands. Also this would give an opportunity of putting him in the programmes; and he deserves it, as he has gained quite a following by his many Recitals, etc. and is really a very fine player—and besides—(at least <u>I</u> think so) one of our most painstaking, careful, enthusiastic, and self-sacrificing professors—he certainly is at my School, anyway!

I shall be quite pleased to <u>conduct</u> the work myself, if so desired; and I do hope my wish will be acceded to.[119]

After the War, Langrish had married and soon had a son who developed substantial health problems, so he was denied the career of a touring pianist—at least for the time being. Matthay thought highly of his playing and his character, and strove to assist him wherever possible. But Mackenzie—while allowing Matthay to conduct his concerto—insisted that Myra be the soloist, since she had just returned from her first American tour with extremely positive notices, and he was leaving no stone unturned in his efforts to make the celebration an unprecedented publicity coup. Since the RAM held a Royal charter, a visit from the King and Queen had been arranged, and on the evening of 18 July 1922 their presence, accompanied by the King's uncle, Prince Arthur—the Duke of Connaught—created virtual pandemonium outside the three-thousand-seat Queen's Hall. *The Times* noted that "by 8 o'clock it was quite impossible to get near the doors [the hall had 17 separate entrances], and the possession of tickets was of no avail."[120] Even *The Times*'s critic was unable to procure a seat, conceding that "we can only record what the program promised."[121] However, the report he provided the next day was inaccurate, for although Henry Wood did present scheduled works by Bennett, Bantock, Coates, Dale, and Stanley Hawley, composer Edward German was unable to fight his way through the throngs, and Wood was forced to delete the two pieces he had agreed to let him conduct.[122] But he did grant the podium to Matthay for his own work, which formed the centerpiece of the program. Matthay was so self-possessed that he was unwilling to make wardrobe concessions even in the presence of royalty, where formal attire was mandatory. He owned only two velvet jackets, a brown one for everyday wear and a black one for slightly more formal occasions, and he petitioned Buckingham Palace for an exemption which allowed him to conduct in his black coat, a waiver granted with surprisingly little hesitation.[123] A few months later, he wrote to an American student that 18 July 1922 was "the red-letter day of my life:"

> Myra . . . played my best work, my Concert Piece, most wonderfully and I had a wonderful orchestra to conduct—all artist players and the King and Queen there compelled to listen to it!! And such a nice ovation afterward![124]

But the honors were not yet complete, for 1922 also marked the end of Matthay's fifty-first year of continuous association with the RAM, or as he belatedly referred to it to interact with the Academy's celebrations, "my Jubilee." Several days earlier, he and Jessie had been honored by a dinner "at which the Principal—said far more nice things about [me] than I would possibly have expected—as we are rather at loggerheads!"[125] And after the Queen's Hall concert, Matthay was further taken by surprise when he was escorted back to Wimpole Street for another ceremony, the unveiling of an exquisite triptych, hand-crafted by Stanley Kennedy North, the husband of Jack's daughter, Elizabeth. North, who was a cousin to the Kennedy clan, was Keeper of the King's Paintings, and a gifted illustrator. His elegant memorial, which stands 21¾ inches high and expands to a width of 34 inches, contains a total of 82 signatures on its centerpiece and two interior wings. Some were provided by close friends, such as Marjory and Frederick Montagu-Pollock, but most were Matthay's former students—many dating from his earliest days as an Academy professor. Some, such as May Christie, Maude Rihill, and Gertrude Peppercorn, had left the Academy well before 1900, while others, such as Read, Bowen, and Bax, had flourished slightly later. In addition to Read and Bowen, a great many others were current RAM professors, such as Langrish, Tidmarsh, McEwen, and Harold Craxton. Irene (and her mother, Ida), Myra, Harriet, and Denise also signed, as well as scores of other present and former students who strove to pay homage to their musical mentor. The triptych, now housed at the RAM, is best described by its catalogue entry:

> Illuminated testimonial in the form of an encased triptych on parchment, with signatures in ink of former pupils and colleagues on the side panels, gilt framed in the style of a mediaeval manuscript. The central panel contains the following text: 'Amicitia et Reverentia, Tobias Matthay, Student and Professor of the Royal Academy of Music, Founder of the Matthay Pianoforte School, Author, Composer and Teacher, having won the admiration of his students and incalculably advanced the Art of Music by his zeal, his research and his intellectual brilliance, we in homage and friendship, desire by this record to commemorate his Jubilee. AD MDCCCLXXII (bottom left), AD MCMXXII (bottom right). The marginalia includes tiny musicians in a mediaeval style—to the left a bagpiper, in the top right, a figure trumpeting Fame, whilst a further figure below plays the harp, with seven strings as thought to have been used by Apollo. The corners are tied with a Celtic knot design, as is the central lower border, above which is a wreath of laurel. The borders are decorated with gilding, plants and flowers. The main image, formed by a historiated 'T' & 'M', shows a tiny mediaeval-style lutenist in a [nocturnal] landscape, seated beside a muse who is composing music. The Gothic columns to each side and the central column of the 'T' form the 'M'. Each is topped with a trumpet-playing figure, tracery and two

figures sharing a banderole. It is snowing. The outer wings are painted with a pattern of peacock-feathers in blues, greens, black and some gilding, with the name 'Tobias Matthay' in a banderole.[126]

In the same year, as part of the Centenary celebration, the AFMC published Corder's illustrated history of the RAM, a somewhat worshipful, but largely candid, chronicle of his alma mater's first century. But the final copy was subject to Mackenzie's approval, and Corder was not always at liberty to express his own views. The RAM Archives contain the complete manuscript, including numerous pieces he was forced to remove, such as this glowing tribute to his long-time friend and colleague:

> It would be invidious to mention the names of any present professors as being more distinguished than others, save in one single case. The incontestable supremacy of our Institution in the important branch of piano playing, it is but bare justice to own, is due to the labours of one man, Tobias Matthay, who though of alien family, is of London birth and breeding. He it was who among teachers devoted many years to the scientific investigation of the dynamics of tone-production and successfully solved them. Like most pioneers he was at first regarded as a crank and a faddist, then when his results were undeniable they were credited to the work of others; still he continued to turn out one marvellously [sic] equipped pianist after another, in scholarship and prize competitions his candidates nearly always swept the board, and what was more to the purpose, his pupils proved to be nearly as successful teachers as their master. At the present time his influence upon English pianoforte playing and teaching is almost paramount, and the old "methods" involving fixed positions of the hands, or mechanical drill of any sort are becoming a thing of the past. How many of the overseas "artists" owe their fame to the once despised English teacher may not be told, but it is one of the Royal Academy's chief glories that the man who has not only revolutionised pianoforte teaching but really expounded its principles for the first time accomplished his training and triumphs within our walls. To say this is not to disparage for one moment the efforts of other brilliant

teachers: it is to give simple acknowledgement to a fact hitherto ignored by our writers on musical matters. This year Mr. Matthay completes fifty-one years of unremitting labour in this Institution—as student, sub-professor, and teacher: it is hard to say whether he or we should be most proud of this record.[127]

Beneath his copy, Corder has written, "This article had to be cancelled, 'for fear of exciting jealousy,' according to the excuse given; the real cause I leave the reader to guess."[128] He was no doubt referring to the rift that had developed between Matthay and Mackenzie which, despite the Principal's public accolades, had long colored their more private interactions. But Mackenzie was now in his late seventies, and eighteen months after the Centenary Celebration, his retirement was announced in conjunction with the appointment of his successor, John Blackwood McEwen, one of Matthay's oldest and most trusted friends.

Matthay had fought a long, and at times painful, battle to reach the pinnacle from which he now surveyed the musical world. And to most observers, it seemed as though his life could only get better.

Notes

1. "The New Royal Academy of Music," *TT,* 24 July 1911, 10, col. C.
2. "The Royal Academy of Music, Pt. II," *MT,* 1 Sept. 1911, 576.
3. Ibid.
4. FC, 94, and COMM, 9 December 1908. The mimeographed, typewritten letter from the RAM solicitors, Treherne, Higgins, & Co., is pasted to the Minutes.
5. "The New Royal Academy of Music," *TT,* 24 July 1911, 10, col. C.
6. FC, 95.
7. FC, 94.
8. FC, 95.
9. Bax, *Farewell, My Youth,* 13.

10. Ironically, the Academy today designates this as the Arnold Bax Room.
11. *RAMCM*, No. 30 (June 1910): 11.
12. Ibid., 10
13. *RAMCM*, No. 32 (February 1911): 9.
14. "The Principles of Interpretation," *TT*, 20 February 1911, 12, col. A.
15. RAMCM, No. 33 (May 1911): 11.
16. See "New Books on Musical Subjects," *NYT*, 8 Feb. 1914, X5.
17. The exact wording in Kennedy's Foreword is, "The following pages hold the substance of a lecture I gave recently to private audiences in London." See John H. Kennedy, *Common Sense and Singing* (London, 1911), 3.
18. Ibid. 6.
19. *MI*, 34.
20. *MI*, vi.
21. *MI*, vii.
22. *MI*, 3-4.
23. *MI*, 31.
24. *MI*, 33.
25. *MI*, 35.
26. *MI*, 48.
27. *MI*, 6-57.
28. *MI*, 58.
29. *MI*, 62.
30. *MI*, 70.
31. Ibid.
32. *MI*, 66.
33. *MI*, 81.
34. *MI*, 97.
35. MKF, 151.
36. Marjory (MKF, 137) indicates that Jack's book was published by Ricordi, but if so, surviving copies appear to be even more rare than the Williams version.
37. Obituary of "Mr. John Henderson Kennedy," *MT*, 1 May 1912, 314. See also Marjory's account in *A Life of Song*, 151.
38. COMM, 1 May 1912.
39. MA. The program for this recital and all others cited in this chapter are in the Archives.

40. When he reached adulthood, Ching opened his own piano school in London, and wrote several books disavowing Matthay's teachings.
41. *MT*, 1 July 1911, 471. On 26 May 1911, she was soloist in Ole Olsen's Suite for Pianoforte and Strings with the Woltmann Orchestra at Bechstein Hall.
42. MKF, 152.
43. Tobias Matthay, *An Introduction to Psychology for Music Teachers* (London, 1939), v.
44. COMM, 1 March 1911.
45. COMM, 27 May 1914.
46. JHM, 55.
47. See "Naval Spectacle at Spithead," *TT*, 20 July 1914, 9, col. G.
48. See "The Naval Might of Britain," *TT*, 21 July 1914, 10, col. C.
49. See "Messrs. Bechstein's Business," *TT*, 19 Aug. 1914, 10, col. C.
50. *TT*, 14 April 1915, 5, col. B.
51. COMM, 16 June 1915.
52. *MT*, 1 July 1915, 430.
53. *TT*, 9 Aug., 1915, 11, col. C.
54. COMM, 21 July 1915.
55. See "The Bechstein Hall Licence," *TT*, 5 Nov. 1915, 5, col. F.
56. "Bechstein Hall Licence Refused," *TT*, 27 Nov. 1915, 5, col. B.
57. See "Bechsteins' Sold," *TT*, 8 Nov. 1916, 5, col. A.
58. Ibid.
59. See "Beethoven's Violin Sonatas," *TT*, 17 Jan. 1917, 11, col. E.
60. Marjory's daughter, Patuffa, sang "Hebridean airs" at two of the programs. See *MT*, 1 Aug. 1917, 374.
61. JHM, 55.
62. Watson, 23.
63. Lewis Foreman, "Dale, Benjamin (James)," *RNG*.
64. JHM, 55.
65. Ibid.
66. LI.
67. *POA*, 1.
68. *POA*, 7.
69. *POA*, 7-8.

70. See Jeremy Dibble, "McEwen, Sir John Blackwood," *Oxford Dictionary of Biography*.
71. JHM, 55.
72. "Mr. Vivian Langrish," *TT*, 3 Nov. 1924, 21, col. D.
73. *MT*, 1 Jan. 1917, 33.
74. *MT*, 1 Aug. 1917, 374.
75. He gave his address as "Montjoie," on Cranfield Road S.E. See *TT*, 29 Sept. 1891, 12, col. A.
76. See *TT*, 17 Jul., 1897, 15, col. A.
77. *TT*, 13 Aug., 1902, 2, col. C.
78. Their "Lectures Scolaires Intermédiaires" series included works by Dumas (père) and George Sand.
79. Michael Partridge, *The Royal Naval College Osborne[:] A History 1903-21* (Phoenix Mill, U.K.: Sutton Publishing, 1999), 89.
80. LI.
81. MA. Denise Lassimonne, "My Introduction to Tobias Matthay," a brief, unpublished memoir. Hereafter cited as DL "Introduction."
82. "May Morning" was the second of five brief pieces entitled *From my Sketch Book*, Op. 24, Book 1, originally composed in 1887-88, and revised in May 1914. Matthay dedicated the revised set to Mary Lediard.
83. DL "Introduction."
84. See *MT*, 1 Apr. 1920, 267, and 1 April 1921, 281.
85. Author's conversations with Curzon in Hampshire and London, August 1975.
86. "Mr. Rowsby Woof," *TT*, 10 Nov. 1922, 8, col. B.
87. "Miss Denise Lassimonne," *TT*, 18 Feb. 1924, 17, col. D.
88. Lassimonne's death certificate is on file at the General Register Office for the Isle of Wight. Since it lists "chronic nephritis" and "arteriosclerosis" as the causes of death, it seems likely that he had been in poor health for some time.
89. The exact value of his effects was £3,328, 16s, 4d. Lassimonne's will is on file at the FRO.
90. See Partridge, 140 ff. A memo (see p. 148) from the Admiralty to the Naval Commander-in-Chief at Portsmouth on 22 December 1920 read, "It has been assumed . . . that it will not be necessary to transfer more than one-half of those now employed at Osborne [to the Royal Naval College at Dartmouth].

Chapter 8

Every effort, however, should be made to reduce the number as much as possible below that figure."

91. McKenna, 63-64.
92. Harriet, 31-32.
93. DL "Introduction."
94. Conversation with DeGray at his studio in New York City on 7 Nov. 1982. Denise also once confided to her friend Oscar Yerburgh that Matthay had been involved in a serious auto accident in the early 1920s, which moved him to revise his Prelude in E, which he later published. Interview with Yerburgh at his London home on 6 July 2005.
95. MA. Letter from Matthay to Bruce Simonds, 12 Dec. 1920.
96. MA. Ibid. and letter from Jessie to Bruce Simonds, 1 Jan. 1921.
97. MA. Letter from Matthay to Simonds, 12 Dec. 1920.
98. MA. Letter from Jessie to Simonds, 8 Apr. 1921.
99. Letter from Matthay to Corder, 14 Sept. 1921, "Large Corder," RAMA. "Large Corder" is the term used informally by RAM archivists to designate the expurgated sections of Corder's history discussed at the end of this chapter.
100. Letter from Jessie to Corder, 16 Mar. 1922, "Large Corder," RAMA.
101. For her nineteenth birthday, Jessie presented Denise with a copy of the *Lyrics* piano pieces Matthay had written for her years earlier, inscribing it, "Denise/from "Mummy II,"/May/22 [sic]." MA. Denise often claimed that she later shortened "Panunck" to "Punky," but many close to Matthay, including Myra, Harriet, and Bax, were using this nickname many years before she entered the household.
102. LI.
103. See COMM, 13 Oct. 1909.
104. LI. Sim knew a number of Matthay pupils. See Naomi Sim, *Dance and Skylark* (London, 1987), 74.
105. LI.
106. *MT* Supplement, "The School Music Review," 1 June 1921, 4.
107. Ibid.
108. See, for example, *MT*, 1 Mar. 1921, 148.
109. Mrs. Tobias Matthay, *The Art the Spoken Word* (Glasgow, 1922), 2. Hereafter cited as *Spoken Word*.

110. *Spoken Word*, 5.
111. *Spoken Word*, 8.
112. Tobias Matthay, "On Method in Teaching," (London: AFMC, 1921), Preface. Hereafter cited as "On Method."
113. "On Method," 4.
114. "On Method," 6.
115. Ibid.
116. MA. Matthay to Bruce Simonds, 30 Sept. 1922.
117. *TT*, 11 July 1922, 12, col. E.
118. LI.
119. Letter from Matthay to Corder, 14 Sept. 1921, "Large Corder," RAMA.
120. *TT*, 19 July 1922, 12, col. D.
121. Ibid.
122. See "The Royal Academy of Music[:] The Centenary Celebrations," *MT*, 1 Aug. 1922, 580.
123. LI.
124. MA. Letter from Matthay to Bruce Simonds, 30 Sept. 1922.
125. Ibid.
126. RAMA, item 2003.1774.
127. "Large Corder," RAMA.
128. Ibid.

*High Marley seen from the south as it appeared in the mid-1920s
Denise's bedroom is at left with balcony directly above the music room;
Jessie's bedroom is directly above the entrance, while Matthay's bedroom with the
circular wall is at right directly above the dining room. The southern windows to
Matthay's study are directly below the center gable.*

*The Matthay School at 96 Wimpole Street
as it appeared in the mid-1920s. The townhouse
that originally stood at No. 97 has been replaced by an oculist's shop.*

*Tobias Matthay in his studio on Wimpole Street about 1920.
The piano is a Bechstein.*

*Matthay at High Marley with Myra Hess
shortly before she left for her American debut in 1922.*

CHAPTER 9

STORM CLOUDS

On 21 July 1925, Professor Tobias Matthay sent the following letter to each member of the RAM Committee of Management, "to reach them all at [the] same time:"[1]

Dear Sirs,

After the most searching reconsideration of the whole situation I feel the best thing is definitely to resign with the end of this term.

Quite apart from the episode now closed, (re Patron's Fund) obviously the Principal desires my name no longer to be a power in the Academy. There are other outstanding differences between us.

For instance, I feel proud to have helped to bring the Licentiate Diploma into its present proud position amongst professional diplomas. That position, however, in my opinion, is now being jeopardized. Again, the Teachers' Training Courses are being weakened all round, by an attempt to docket into separate compartments things, which educationally, should never be separated.

No man can be, or should be coerced to take another's advice; but I feel that when it comes to questions of education in special subjects, that the views of those who have spent their lives (successfully) in coping with them should at least receive careful or polite attention. It is of no use having world-specialists on the Committee of an Institution, and then insist on their being mere ciphers, and not allowed to open their mouths—even at Specialists' Meetings[!] . .. [sic]

There are also other matters, unnecessary to allude to here, which render it impossible for me to continue as a teacher under Mr. McEwen.

It is with the greatest sorrow and pain that I find this old friendship shattered, and my withdrawal from the R.A.M., a necessity. I assure you, however, that the love I have borne my old Alma Mater (these fifty years and more) still remains.

Perhaps my drastic action now may yet prove to be my greatest service to the old place—perhaps even to one who was my oldest and dearest friend!

Yours always,
Tobias Matthay[2]

The next day the Committee read Matthay's letter at its weekly meeting, but its Minutes record no discussion. And the following week its members approved a perfunctory response from their Chairman, Philip Agnew—which could have applied equally well to a retiring custodian. It read in part:

> I am requested to convey to you on behalf of my colleagues an expression of their regret that, for the reasons stated in your letter, you have decided to sever your connection with the Royal Academy of Music, also to assure you of their sincere appreciation of the great services you have rendered to it during a long period.[3]

Matthay wrote his letter on the same day that his annual Queen's Hall program was scheduled, but by now only two of the performers—Hilda Bor and Betty Humby—were at the RAM. As was customary, at the interval he gave his annual report on the progress of his School, and on that evening he felt obliged to reference the action he had taken earlier that day. But his public remarks in no way reflected the tone of the letter he had mailed a few hours earlier. In fact, he confined himself purely to tactful half-truths:

> It is gratifying to be able to say that the School forges ahead every year. We now have some 400 students, and the quality is higher every year. Literally, they come from all quarters of the globe. This year, indeed, we have a record number here of our American cousins—and the reason

Storm Clouds

is not far to seek! Indeed, I feel very proud of our students and of our Professors, and I wish again to thank all for their wonderful work.

Here I must take the opportunity to make an important announcement, both unhappy and happy.

After much anxious consideration, I have decided that the moment has arrived when I must <u>cease to divide my time between my own School and the Royal Academy of Music!</u>

I have been in intimate connection with the Royal Academy of Music for over fifty years. Indeed, I was (as it were) bred and born there, musically. Also, I used to place all my most talented pupils in the Academy and therefore I earnt my first laurels there. Hence my decision now to sever my connection with the old place was come to with much regret. But I feel it was unavoidable. In the meantime my own School has been making more and more urgent demands upon my time; and I shall now be free to devote myself exclusively to its welfare. Its fine professors and wonderful students deserve nothing less from me.[4]

By 31 July, Matthay had issued two formal press releases, but his remarks to Langrish the next day were far more candid:

The paper's got hold of it—and I've been quite a <u>notorious</u> person last week—interviewers poured in upon me—and I did all I could to keep my mouth shut, and in desperation I had a few lines typed to minimize the evil—nevertheless some of them got hold of the wrong end of the stick—so I've had [the] enclosed typed out and I am now sending that to them all—perhaps they'll do a little correcting after that.[5]

Although Matthay's second press release contained an element of truth, he again took the high road, somewhat soft-pedaling his conflicts with McEwen and disavowing any conflict with the Academy:

As there seems to be some considerable misunderstanding with regard to my withdrawal from the Royal Academy of Music, may I be allowed to correct this?

Chapter 9

> When Mr. J. B. McEwen became Principal a year ago, he begged me, as a personal favour, to give much more time to the Academy than had been possible for me of late years. Regretfully, I could not accede to this. The reason is that so many of those claiming my time outside the Academy are too advanced in the profession for the benefits of an Academy curriculum—in fact artists and head-teachers from all over the world.
>
> Mr. McEwen has persistently refused to accept this explanation. That has been the beginning of the breach between us. Further differences have gradually aggravated this. Hence my drastic action of the 21st, inst. was the only possible solution. I have no quarrel with the Royal Academy of Music.[6]

But no informed observer could have taken Matthay's denial seriously, because his "quarrel" with the RAM had been building for decades. Nearly forty years earlier, on 2 July 1887, he had given his first RAM student recital at the Belmont Lecture Hall in Clapham,[7] and at no time subsequently had the Academy allowed him to present such a program on its premises—even when he offered to advance rental fees. And in recent years his limited—yet hallowed—presence had aggravated the political climate, so that McEwen, who was formally installed in September of 1924, had inherited a difficult situation. Despite the fact that Matthay lived within walking distance of the Academy, Denise remembered that by the early 1920s he was appearing only twice a week—once for the Committee of Management meetings which occurred Wednesday afternoons at 5:30, and again on Friday afternoons to teach no more than two or three students. Nonetheless, his influence was endemic throughout the building. For example, on 5 November 1924, about six weeks after McEwen took office, 15 piano professors—including Matthay—were appointed to L.R.A.M. examining committees.[8] Of the remaining 14, six had studied with him—Whitemore, Pollard, Moore, Swinstead, Craxton, and Langrish—and two others, Carlo Albanesi and Ambrose Coviello, were ardent admirers. In addition, Tidmarsh was held in reserve as an alternate, so that nearly two-thirds of the examiners were "Matthayites." Moreover, Dora, Bowen,

Dale, Read, Lily West, and even McEwen's wife—Hedwig—were also then sharing professorships between the RAM and the TMPS. In the few years before he retired, Mackenzie had taken measures to head off mounting resentments from non-Matthayites, so that Matthay was no longer farming out his RAM students to assistants, but many of these had become so established that they now had their own followings—and most granted a worshipful deference to their former master.

In addition, Matthay's press release neither exaggerated the demands his School was making on his time nor overstated the eminence of his pupils, because a growing number were performing in major settings, and it could be argued that he was now spending more time coaching than teaching. For example, in the spring of 1927, the TMPS blitzed Wigmore Hall with a torrent of recitals from both aspiring and established artists—many from far beyond the British Isles. And as Matthay confided to an American student that March, he planned to mentor each program in turn:

> We are having a terribly busy time here in May and June—recitals by so many of my present pupils! Eunice Norton [Minneapolis] (two) Lyell Barbour [Illinois] (He has just done very well in Holland a week or two ago and has an orchestral [engagement] there fixed up) Frank Mannheimer [Ohio] (end of May), Dora Kircher [Germany] (early May), M[argaret] Harvey Samuel [Denmark] (early June), Betty Humby [London] (May), Clifford Curzon [London] (early May)—a fine player—Lilian Smith (early May) Denise early June—and our annual Festival Concerts starting July 5 this year.[9]

In a very real sense, Matthay had "outgrown" the Royal Academy of Music, because its students were no longer competitive with the artists he encountered daily at his own school, and arguably, no conservatory in the world was then nurturing so many finished pianists. In all probability, McEwen had prevailed on their friendship by asking him to accept more RAM pupils, but the considerations that might have been extended are far from clear. Even decades

Chapter 9

earlier, long before the TMPS had become a force in the concert world, Matthay often merely oversaw the training of Academy pianists he assigned to his assistants, many of whom were now well established teachers, and there was no way he could have—or would have—turned back the clock. Moreover, it is not known what financial inducements McEwen offered, nor what the political consequences might have been had he granted Matthay his TMPS fee, which by 1922 had risen to nearly £3 an hour—over five times the Academy's highest rate of compensation.[10] McEwen may also have been placed in the middle of an impossible conundrum fueled by competitive RAM colleagues who demanded a greater Matthay presence while insisting on less Matthay influence. No doubt the situation was even more complicated by the fact that Matthay still had a few RAM students who needed to complete their studies—hence the necessity for tact on his part—but this merely raises questions concerning the timing of his decision. And nothing in any of his reasons explains why, as he informed the Committee of Management, he now regarded his thirty-year friendship with McEwen as "shattered." In fact, to understand the gravity of the situation, the "other matters, unnecessary to allude to here" must be identified. Eleven days after he resigned, he still gave Langrish only a partial accounting, though he did confide essential details which had been withheld from the press:

> As Mac called a Meeting of the Piano Staff on Prize Day morning [Friday, 24 July, the date set aside for the Academy's year-end ceremonies] and told them a very inadequate version of the Patron's Fund Episode and also told them that the question of Schools like mine doing [the] same ground as RAM v. the RAM would have seriously to be gone into—and in fact making out that that was my cause of leaving—!!—I am countering that false impression by sending to the whole of the Piano staff a copy of my letter and also the one I am sending the newspapers. I don't believe for a moment that Mac will succeed in carrying through Committee his proposed boycott of my School. The Committee will have something to say first! And I should think also a great many of the professors![11]

Obviously, McEwen had begun to see the TMPS as a threat to the Academy's viability but—even disregarding the personal dimensions of their long friendship—he had to know that engaging Matthay in a full-scale war was like playing with dynamite, since a critical mass of RAM faculty were still unswervingly loyal to him. Nonetheless, as will be shown, the Principal of the Royal Academy was about to embark on a ten-year campaign to destroy the Matthay School. And although many of his actions were carried on behind closed doors, so much of the animosity was public that by July of 1925 numerous observers already regarded Matthay's resignation as inevitable. But ironically, even after their dispute became a matter of record, Matthay was always reluctant to name the real cause of their estrangement, which centered around McEwen's public attacks on his teaching—something Mackenzie had never dreamed of doing, no matter how severe their differences. Understandably, Matthay loyalists quickly branded McEwen as an audacious turncoat (especially since Tobias and Jessie had actively campaigned for his appointment as Principal), but even years later, Matthay was more charitable, as confirmed by the account he offered Langrish early in 1937:

> It might be well to put the facts <u>on record</u>—There has never been any quarrel between myself and the Academy—I was a student there for nearly ten years and I taught within its walls for near on 60 years!!! Hence there never has been anything but a feeling of friendship for the old place.
>
> McEwen and I quarreled, but this only on <u>One Point</u>. He discovered one day that his <u>Duo-Art</u> records showed that certain well-known artists did not always adhere to my doctrine, that in playing <u>Rubato</u> one <u>must</u> "come back to the beat"—if it was to be true Rubato. He however jumped to the conclusion that these rolls showed my teaching to be untenable!—Just as silly as it might be that a student must <u>not</u> have an ideal of pitch intonation held before him, because most great Violinists do at times fail to "keep to the rule"! The cases are absolutely parallel!
>
> Unfortunately, Mac related his "discovery" at a <u>luncheon table</u>, and then—his pride forbade his backing out. I was quite unable to shake him

in his mis-belief, and as I refused to give way (and knowing I was right) he said he would make the matter public, and would ask the public "to decide between us." I warned him that if he did so, I should refuse to continue at the RAM. Nevertheless, he wrote articles in the M.T. [*The Music Teacher*] attacking my views, so there was no alternative (for my own self-respect) but to leave—as one could not serve under a Principal who publicly denounced ones [sic] most important teaching! Agnew and the Committee most kindly tried to shake me in my decision [not surprisingly, no record of such activity appears in their Minutes], but it could not be changed.[12]

The underlying causes behind Matthay's conflict with his "oldest and dearest friend" were complex. When McEwen was installed as the Academy's Principal, he was 56—16 years older than Mackenzie had been when he assumed the same post. And although by then he had earned a reputation for high intelligence and integrity, scarcely anyone regarded him as one of Britain's major composers. His output had been substantial and at times of excellent quality, and in 1893 he even began the first of what eventually culminated in a cycle of 19 String Quartets.[13] But for over a decade his work had been largely unsung and even overshadowed by Corder's younger students, such as Bax, Bowen, Dale, and Bantock, to say nothing of the impressive roster of RCM-trained composers, including Holst and Vaughan Williams. During the Academy's Centenary Celebration in 1922, he was finally given a belated spotlight when—at Corder's urging—an entire evening devoted to his own works (mostly quartets) was scheduled on the same day as Matthay's afternoon composers' lecture. The *Musical Times* was in attendance and highly taken with what it regarded as McEwen's personal and artistic humility:

> Here was a stack of music of which—except perhaps the *Biscay* String Quartet—the public knows next to nothing. One could see why. His music does not shout from the hill-tops; nor could it have been written by a self-advertiser. It shows a man who loves the Art of composition with a big A, and for those who are ready to forego excitement and take

measured delight in fine quality and the expression of a kindly nature and wise intellect—for all this is spelt out in Mr. McEwen's music—the evening was one of prolonged satisfaction.[14]

Two months later, the journal published a letter from McEwen, who—now in his twenty-fifth year of service to the Academy—seemed bemused that he had recently been "discovered:"

> Musical opinion in this country groups the native composer into two categories: 'The Promising Young Composer' and the 'Old Fogey'—the 'May-be' and the 'Has-been.' There does not seem to be any intermediate stage, and one never knows exactly when he makes transition from the one to the other.
>
> Twenty-five years ago I was told that I belonged to the first of these; and I had believed that I had long since been promoted—or reduced—to the other. However, I am glad to see that in [your] opinion . . . I am still to be regarded as vociferating a promise which the expiry of a quarter of a century has not stifled, even if it has not succeeded in bringing it to fruition.[15]

Jeremy Dibble observes that McEwen was "seemingly unconcerned about the dissemination of his own works,"[16] but since few composers are totally indifferent to the issue of public acceptance, one wonders if limited recognition (or failed promise) was, at least on some level, an ongoing issue in his life. Today, McEwen's underlying motivations are difficult to determine with accuracy because he was extraordinarily private, even to the point of resisting photographs after he was installed as Principal, so that surprisingly few images of him survive in the RAM Archives. But he was a dynamo of energy from behind the scenes, enthusiastically assisting Corder with the formation of the Society of British Composers and the Avison Press, and later assuming the lion's share of administrative duties for the Anglo-French Music Company. By the early 1920s, he had donned yet another administrative hat by agreeing to serve as artistic advisor to the British wing of the American-based Aeolian Company, which was then producing the Duo-Art Reproducing Piano, generally acknowledged as the industry leader in a growing field. After World War I, electrical reproducing pianos had become a rage in Europe and the United States, and most well-known pianists were approached to cut rolls on mechanisms which often captured their nuances with surprising sophistication. Instruments fitted with these devices were even featured in concert settings, and on 27 October 1922, Harold Bauer was heard—"*in absentia*," according to the *Musical Times*—in a Duo-Art performance of Saint-Saëns's Second Concerto at Queen's Hall under Henry Wood, who was praised for timing the orchestral *tuttis* with exact precision: "We reflected that to direct an orchestra in these conditions must require a new kind of technique on the part of the conductor."[17] On 4 November 1924, Wood again "conducted" Bauer's Saint-Saëns in Edinburgh with the Queen's Hall Orchestra, along with Duo-Art rolls by Myra and Percy Grainger, who "performed" the Grieg Concerto and the Tchaikovsky First, respectively.[18]

By 1921 Aeolian was boasting 12 factories throughout the world,[19] but pianos fitted with their mechanisms were not inexpensive, and even second-hand Duo-Art instruments were advertised for as much as £500.[20] Nonetheless their popularity was such that by the mid-1920s the *Musical Times* was devoting a monthly column—"Player-Piano Notes"—to the latest releases. Since many pianists did not yet feel comfortable in the recording studio, most found the technology of the reproducing piano—which allowed for editing—less nerve-wracking, although the possibility of editorial tampering has prompted some modern scholars to raise questions about the "authenticity" of the finished product.[21] But most concede that the rolls manufactured by Duo-Art and others provide an accurate record of a pianist's tempo and rhythmic fluctuations, especially in the realm of rubato. On 1 September 1925, the *Musical Times*'s William Delasaire reviewed a new set of Duo-Art Chopin performances by pianist Vladimir de Pachmann:

> Every subtlety of *rubato* is infallibly caught and reproduced—sometimes to the extent of an inch of [roll] paper between the hands in one chord!

Mr. McEwen, principal of the Royal Academy of Music, has recently been discussing the question of *Tempo Rubato* in the *Music Teacher* [the journal of the British Music Teachers' Assoiciation], his analysis being based largely on an examination of these rolls. Those who wish to inquire into the subject further could hardly do better than obtain them—indeed no complete study of the matter could be made without these rolls.[22]

Seven months earlier, on 3 February 1925, McEwen's interest in the new medium had prompted some of Britain's most esteemed music educators to gather at the Academy to form the "Honorary Advisory Committee on the Educational Use of Player-Piano Rolls," an organization chaired by Mackenzie, who happily emerged from retirement to oversee its mission. In addition to McEwen, he was joined by the heads of the other major conservatories, Sir Hugh Allen of the Royal College, and Sir Landon Ronald of the Guildhall School. Also present were four additional members: Sir Henry Wood, Robin Legge of the *Daily Telegraph*, and Percy Scholes of the *Observer*—then a prominent commentator for the BBC—who agreed to serve as "honorary secretary." Curiously, the eight-member Committee, organized for the purpose of guiding "the knowledge and appreciation of music by means of the player-piano, including recently recorded rolls by great artists,"[23] contained no prominent pianists, and in fact the only active performer in the group was Charles Kitson, an organ professor at the Royal College. Though the principals all had extensive keyboard training, all had long since moved into other areas, and perhaps this was the meeting Matthay referenced a few months later in his resignation letter, in which he claimed that "world-specialists" had been required to act as "mere ciphers."[24] Within a month of the meeting, the Duo-Art rolls were being touted as a watershed in the history of music education, and beginning on 14 March, the company even hired Scholes to give a series of Saturday morning lecture-demonstrations for children at Aeolian Hall, which were broadcast simultaneously on the BBC.[25]

Chapter 9

Precisely what led McEwen (or Delasaire) to believe that Duo-Art rolls provided indispensable *scientific* data concerning rubato may never be known, particularly when many precautionary injunctions—to say nothing of common sense—might easily have steered him in another direction. Scholes even issued an important caveat in one of his lectures after he played Arthur Rubinstein's Duo-Art release of Chopin's Nocturne in F-sharp, Op. 15, no. 2:

> Between you and me I did not quite approve of everything that the player did in playing that piece. I did not think the *rubato* was always quite purposeful. It was sometimes just a little erratic, but of course the very virtue of a Duo-Art Roll is that it gives you a performer's actual performance, absolutely true in all the nuances of speed and rhythm. The instrument cannot err in those matters, and so you may try a roll and compare the great pianist's reading with your own and perhaps learn something from it, either something to do or something to avoid.[26]

But by then the first installment of McEwen's "Tempo Rubato" had already appeared in *The Music Teacher*, and two months later Matthay resigned from the RAM. Although McEwen's first article does not mention Matthay by name, he is quick to observe that at one time he had subscribed to the "regular-pulse" theory of rubato (that an artist must return to the pulse) as expressed thirteen years earlier in his book *The Thought in Music*. Although he proposed no alternative theory, he now stressed the impossibility of artists conforming to a regular pulse, leaving open the question of how a performer (or a listener) could discriminate between a true rubato and mere rhythmic fluctuation:

> That belief in the convincing power of his intuition, which is usually an unanswerable reason for the practice of the artist, is quite a sufficient and adequate explanation for [the practice of rubato]. No one, except the most hide-bound pedant, will expect the artist to regulate his practice by reference to a set of rules and regulations, formulated by intellectual process and operating independently of his intuition. In the heat of

artistic performance things are done and peculiarities of treatment can be justified, which are too personal and individual ever to be crystallised into a guide or reason for universal practice, or to be compressed into the defining limits of a general "rule" or "law."[27]

The second installment offered the results of an "experiment," for which McEwen selected two versions of Chopin's "Raindrop" Prelude, one by Pachmann and another by the recently deceased Busoni. His objective was to compare the rubato time-swings of the two artists, and to this end he created two fairly complicated graphs. In the top curve of each, he represented the Prelude as though it had been performed in metronomic time, and this he compared, with the assistance of linking vertical lines, to curves of the Busoni and the Pachmann performances. Inasmuch as all artists will naturally take their own tempos, he identified an average pulse for each reproduction, and drew his graphs according to the *relative* time each pianist spent on the notes of the composition. The first graph (Figure 9.1) relied on measures 1-4 of the Prelude as a means of determining the eighth-note pulse, and showed that Busoni and Pachmann "met" at the end of the first phrase on the fourth beat of the fourth measure. But since McEwen was determined to prove that such a return did not validate a performance "law," he added a fourth curve which charted, in his words, "an absurdly out-of-time performance." This was put forth as a *reductio ad absurdum* (his term) to show that even profoundly distorted performances could meet at the same juncture. Inasmuch as he was now left without any meaningful "baseline," he created a second graph (Figure 9.2), which used the first bar only as the standard of pulse. This graph was presented as the more meaningful of the two, showing that although both Pachmann and Busoni returned to the beat by the end of measure 1, by the middle of the fourth bar they were hopelessly out of synch. McEwen now reasoned that since neither pianist returned to the pulse that had first been established, he had proven that no "law" of rubato governed either performance.

Chapter 9

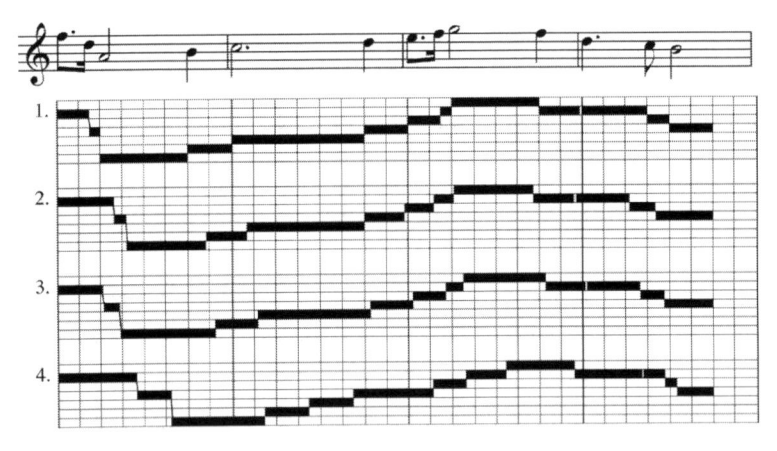

Fig. 9.1 McEwen's first graph from The Music Teacher, *July 1925 (p. 427) showing rubato curves for Chopin's Prelude in D-flat, Op. 28. Using the first four bars as the standard of pulse, the first curve (1) shows the Prelude performed in "strict" time, the second (2) shows Busoni's rubato, and the third (3) shows Pachmann's rubato. The fourth (4) shows a "reductio ad absurdum" performance, or a rendition ridiculously out of time offered to show that all the performances could still meet by the fourth beat of the fourth bar.*

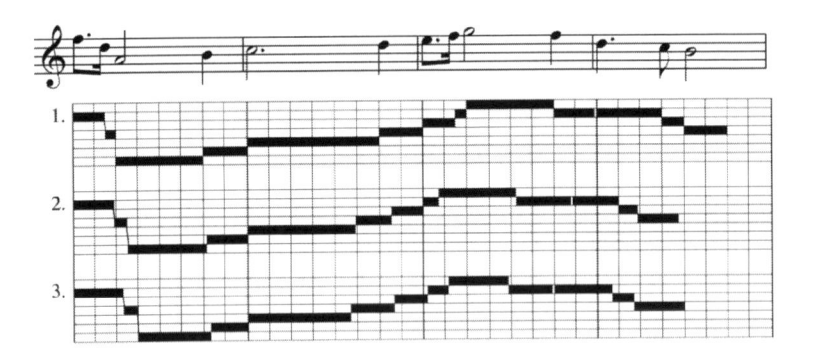

Fig. 9.2 McEwen's second graph (p. 428) showing 1) "strict" time, 2) Busoni's rubato, and 3) Pachmann's rubato, this time using the first bar only as the standard of pulse.

After three installments of McEwen's series had appeared, Matthay could no longer contain himself. On 16 August 1925, he drafted a brief letter which *The Music Teacher* agreed to publish, in their words, "in pursuance of our policy of conducting this journal as a platform, not a pulpit." But it prefaced his letter, which ran under the title "The Vexed Question of Rubato," with an editorial admonition:

> It has happened before, and we feel sure will happen again, that some point of musical aesthetics has aroused keenly differing views among men of standing. In such cases the bystander ought, we suggest, to consider all sides, to add his own experience, and to remember (what we think is often insufficiently taken into account) that there are a great many things in the world which can neither be proved nor disproved. The ancient tag "A thing either is or is not" has done more harm to human thought than all the lies that were ever uttered. Concerning very many things it is simply impossible to form a finite judgment.[28]

Matthay confined himself to a single objection regarding McEwen's methodology—his manner of determining the average pulse in each performance:

> [McEwen] admits that it is "impossible" to determine by such measurements whether a player has or has not obeyed the laws in question unless a mean or straight time Tempo can first be determined upon. Nevertheless, in taking the first four bars of Chopin's Prelude in Db as an example, he quite arbitrarily chooses the *first* bar of that strain as offering a standard by which to determine the mean or straight time of the remainder!
>
> Everyone, however, who in the least understands the nature of the problem, pedagogically, must realise that one bar of a four-bar Rubato-*curve* cannot possibly give such a standard of measurement! As this particular first bar will naturally be played by most artists with a considerable lingering over it, it follows that the extra time thus spent must be made up subsequently in the same strain—as a matter of fact, one of eight bars, not four. As Mr. McEwen has taken this first false bar by which to make his experiments, the natural consequence is that both of the artists in question *seem* to fail to "come back to the beat." But the fault is not Pachmann's nor Busoni's, but of the wrong standard of measurement employed by Mr. McEwen in his experiments.[29]

McEwen was offered the opportunity to respond to Matthay's letter in the same issue, but he declined. In his absence, the editors again urged agnosticism on their readers:

> In commending again the wise Paulist injunction, "Prove all things; hold fast to that which is good," we would emphasise again the point that it is worth while trying to find out first if a thing *can* be proved. Frankly, our own opinion is that not only this, but other points raised in Mr. McEwen's articles, cannot at present be proved or disproved to such a degree that a completely satisfactory aesthetic system can be founded upon one's conclusions—a system, that is completely satisfactory to all.[30]

In 1926 Oxford University enhanced McEwen's eminence by presenting him with an honorary Musical Doctorate, just as his Duo-Art work was placing him increasingly in the vanguard of modern music educators. Matthay objected to the veneer of scientific objectivity ascribed to the Duo-Art reproductions, noting that the same data could have been obtained from conventional gramophone records. But McEwen persevered, insisting that science had now refuted the "regular-pulse" theory of rubato—a fundamental tenet of Matthay's teaching. For the next two years—through the spring of 1928—*The Music Teacher* served as a forum for the Matthay-McEwen debate, which continued to build in intensity. In the January 1928 issue, Matthay published a complete article, "The Truth about Rubato," which was to date, his most extensive refutation of Mc-Ewen's assertions. By now, their public debate was assuming an acrimonious tone:

> Dr. McEwen has no right to say that my first law of rubato [that time borrowed from one portion of a phrase must eventually be replaced in another portion] is grounded on the "fallacy" that the development of musical expression "must be regulated by reference to mechanical time-measurers." He has intimately known the results of my teaching and its manner for the last thirty years or more, and he knows it is precisely the opposite of a worship of mechanism. The laws of rubato are founded on the necessity of *Continuity in Performance*—which again is founded

on Universal Law. It is he who has now tried to use the micrometer-callipers and stop-watches, and I have had to answer him by reference to the Metronome.[31]

McEwen had posed a challenge to Matthay in the form of a simple question: If the first bar of a composition could not be taken as a reliable unit of pulse, how would the performer or the listener be able to distinguish a satisfactory rubato from simple distortion? Matthay soon responded:

> You cannot decide whether a couple of chords reiterated at the beginning of a piece are "in time" or not, so long as you have no knowledge what tempo is going to be taken up! Subsequent events only will prove it. An artist, therefore, having in view a rubato-curve, must *project* his mind "in front of his performance" in sympathy with his mood of the moment so that he may arrange the time fluctuations within the limits of the pulse-scheme he has decided upon. . . . This projection of the mind seems to appear a difficult proposition to Dr. McEwen—he speaks of the "jugglery" possible to great artists, but I assure him it is successfully done every day where performances are convincing and "inevitable." This is no more "difficult" or "impossible". . . than it is for the experienced reader to read some four bars or more ahead of what he is actually playing at the moment.
>
> As to the audience, the impression of a piece of music is *not* formed by the impression produced by its *first complete span* of pulsation (whether it be of one quarter of that first bar, or a span of four bars by eight) but by the impression produced by the series of contexts afterwards. We must also not overlook the fact that musical *memory* plays an important part in our appreciation of a musical work, even on its first hearing. For if we are unable to connect what we are hearing with what we have already heard of a piece, how can we gain any idea of the shape of its performance as a whole? Of what use is it trying to be a very BEETHOVEN in shapefullness if one's audience can only feel each successive bar as an entity by itself, without memory of what has gone before?[32]

But in the next issue, it was McEwen's turn, and the rhetoric was now erupting into near-hostility:

> A reckless disregard of accuracy both in statement and in quotation, a voluble irrelevance which evades and confuses the real issue, and a positive genius for misrepresentation, are more likely to obscure than to illuminate this so-admirable and so-much-to-be-desired Truth.[33]

McEwen claimed that Matthay had deliberately misrepresented his two graphs of the "Raindrop" Prelude. He maintained that his first graph, which used the first four bars to determine the average pulse, exonerated him from Matthay's charge that he used the first measure only as a standard. But in point of fact, McEwen had created the second graph precisely *because* he claimed that the first was unreliable, since any random distortion of tempo could be made to come out evenly at the end of the phrase. Predictably, Matthay was not taken in by the inconsistency, and in March, the forum was again his:

> [McEwen] founded this allegation of "fallacy" solely on the result of his measurements of certain Duo-Art rolls. Yet he admits, that for the crucial Diagram, No. II., [Fig. 9.2] he chose the *first* bar of a *four*-bar Rubato-phrase as the standard of measurement for the complete phrase. . . .
>
> He now, however, insists . . . that this crucial Diagram (No. II.) was put forward as a *Reductio ad absurdum*! It is impossible to reconcile this cryptic utterance (whatever it may mean) with his statements in 1925. Possibly one may hope that the futility of those measurements has at last dawned upon him?[34]

McEwen had made a serious blunder, and his editors, who (despite their protestations of impartiality) favored his side, knew it. Underneath Matthay's rejoinder, they announced they were shutting down the debate:

> This discussion tends to range over too wide a field, and it is impossible to allow it to proceed further. It will be understood that this application

Storm Clouds

of guillotine does not imply that the arguments set forth on this page by Mr. Matthay are accepted by Dr. McEwen. They have not been submitted to him. It would be interesting if the [British Music Teachers' Association] could induce the parties to finish the argument in public, where arguments could be illustrated more effectively.[35]

But no such meeting ever occurred, for Matthay and McEwen never spoke again.[36] Not surprisingly, in the ensuing years their paths did occasionally cross, and Denise recalled that they and their wives, who held season tickets for the London Symphony, once came face to face in the lobby of Queens Hall. She remembered Matthay extending his arms in a gesture of embrace with a heartfelt "Mac!" but McEwen only scowled defiantly and turned away. The rift was also painful to those around them, for Denise, who had once entertained thoughts of becoming a serious composer, had adored McEwen and grown extremely close to him during her years of composition study. She held an equal affection for his wife, Heddie, who was forced to resign from the Matthay School in 1925 at her husband's insistence—a break which some said caused her unspeakable pain. Even before Matthay submitted his resignation, McEwen had begun assembling data to support his campaign against the TMPS, and the documents he collected—some confidential—were almost certainly provided by Heddie, who had been a member of the School's teaching staff from its earliest days. McEwen was very much in earnest about carrying through a "boycott" of the Matthay School, and further evidence of Matthay's impending break with the RAM is provided by a letter which TMPS Secretary Marion Cole sent the Academy on 23 June 1925, a full month before he resigned. McEwen was obviously threatening to forbid dual appointments between the two institutions, and it fell to the Matthay School to document those members of its faculty who might be exempt by virtue of their longevity. Matthay also insisted that his school was not an Academy competitor, but rather a vital training ground for its future prospects:

> Enclosed we are sending as required 4 prospectuses[.] Mr. Matthay wishes me to say that we are collecting statistics <u>as to students who have</u>

Chapter 9

migrated to the R.A.M. from here. He also wishes me to point out that all the pianoforte professors on this staff taught here before doing so at the RAM, in most cases for many years before being appointed there. Possibly Mr. Frederick Moore is the only exception: He was teaching here in 1906 and even sooner.[37]

In fact, even the question of Moore's longevity was a moot point, since he had not been appointed to the RAM until 2 October 1907, and then on Mackenzie's personal recommendation.[38] The Academy received Cole's letter on 24 June 1925, and beneath her signature McEwen wrote, "Please place this letter before the Chairman of the Sub-Committee,"[39] indicating that he had already mobilized a group to address the "threat" posed by Matthay's School. On a separate page, he added his own handwritten notes to guide their deliberations:

The Matthay Pfte. School
   Founded in 1905 for the special purpose of teaching Pianoforte.
   In March 1925 there are (vide prospectus) 400 students
   The subjects now taught include all branches of Music Theory, Aural Training etc. Stringed Instruments, Singing & Elocu[tion]
   On its staff are 17 professors of the R. A. M.
   It runs a Teachers' Training Course on the same lines as the R. A. M. at a fee of £5.5 per session. (This is complicated by the fact that on paper the Course includes lessons in pianoforte playing, but as there are charges for extras to the course & as they can be dispensed with (vide 3 of special prospectus) the actual Course fee is as above £5.5 i.e. lower than the R. A. M.)
   One serious objection is the explicit & open advertisement of classes to prepare for the L. R. A. M. Examinations & as most of the Academy [are] certified Examiners for the L. R. A. M.[,] the objection is obvious.
   The whole curriculum is obviously modelled on that of the Academy—even to the Student's Aid Fund!—& the growth & development of this School is now such that it is a serious competitor with the R. A. M.[40]

By singling out the School's L.R.A.M. preparatory curriculum, it could be argued that McEwen was merely flaunting the appearance of impropriety, because over the past two decades, Matthay had gone out of his way to minimize potential conflicts between the two institutions, only to meet with resistance from Academy officials. For example, in 1914 when he attempted to inject greater anonymity into RAM scholarship auditions, his several proposals were resoundingly defeated by the Committee of Management. Moreover, if McEwen really feared an inappropriate favoritism, he had a sufficient number of L.R.A.M. adjudicators to remove Matthay faculty from panels where TMPS pupils were heard, a far simpler solution than the divisive measures he now proposed. He was correct that by 1922 the TMPS had expanded its offerings well beyond piano playing, but his language, while technically accurate, was highly misleading. Most of the "general" classes were there to support the School's year-long "Special Training Course for Pianoforte Teachers," which certified music teachers for the government schools and required specific subjects to maintain accreditation from the Teachers' Registration Council. As part of the course, Frederick Moore alternated Wednesday evening demonstration lessons with Matthay, who was then lecturing on "Psychology and its Application in Teaching Music." The curriculum also included Read's lectures on "Training in Teaching Aural Culture," Annie Curwen's "The Teaching of Elements to Children," and organist and choir master Stanley Marchant's "Training for the School Singing-Class." By 1925, Dale's ten-lecture series, "History and Evolution of Music," was also being offered as an optional component at a reduced rate for those already enrolled. No doubt McEwen had long been aware of Jessie's elocution lessons, but these were never advertised, and Denise maintained that they were offered only as separate concessions, as were Herbert Walenn's cello classes for youngsters (see Chapter 11).

Even though Matthay probably never intended becoming "a serious competitor with the R.A.M.," he nearly doubled his floor space in the spring of 1922 when he acquired the house next door at No. 95 Wimpole Street—which may have seemed like *déja vu* to McEwen, who no doubt recalled the days when most RAM activities had been confined to two houses on Tenterden Street. For several years Debenhams had been acquiring substantial parcels of land, and since they no longer required No. 95 as a women's dormitory, they sub-let it to Matthay, who in turn let the ground floor to the AFMC. There is no known record of the rent Matthay paid Debenhams, but it was probably comparable to what he was then paying Elgood for No. 96. By October 1927 each house had a ratable value of £205 and the annual tax on each was £52, 19s, 2d, so Matthay was no doubt careful to insure that the income from No. 95 exceeded its expenses.[41] The rear of the property contained a far larger room than its counterpart at No. 96, and this immediately became the School's concert hall—and also the location where several months later Matthay was presented with his Triptych.

In 1925, as a casualty of their schism, the Matthay-McEwen business relationship was dissolved, and the Anglo-French catalogue was absorbed by Oxford University Press. It is likely that very little money changed hands in this transaction, since by 1924 the AFMC was advertising fewer than 60 short piano teaching pieces, and most of these were by little-known composers.[42] In 1925 Debenhams purchased some 40 acres freehold on the southern edge of the Portland Estate from Howard de Walden, including No. 95,[43] and they were far more receptive to commercialization than the former freeholder had been. By a fortuitous coincidence, by then the OUP music division had outgrown its facilities on Paternoster Row, and it now agreed to take over the ground floor of No. 95 as a combination business office and retail shop. Matthay may even have sub-let his space to the firm at a reduced rate in exchange for a promise that Oxford would continue to distribute AFMC titles for a specified period of time. Perhaps the Committee of Management saw these developments as supporting evidence of TMPS "competition," for in July 1926 they granted McEwen's request by banning dual appointments between the RAM and "competing institutions," although the regulation allowed for a "grandfather" clause to protect pre-existing situations. But McEwen continued to press for a total segregation of Academy faculty and the TMPS, and within a short time he was demanding such extreme sanctions that Matthay felt obliged to write the Committee in June of 1928:

Dear Sirs,

I am told that pupils of mine are forbidden to continue their lessons with me on the ground that they are on the staff of the R.A.M. May I ask whether this is a fact or a misunderstanding?

Your not wishing them to appear as students or to appear at the concerts of another school (even though it be not a "competing institution") is a conceivable standpoint. But to prevent anyone from having lessons with me PRIVATELY is surely an inconceivable attitude?—considering that professors from truly "competing institutions" do come to me, and are actually encouraged to do so by the authorities; and that the great American conservatories send their head teachers to my School? To say the least it would seem anomalous, if true, coming from the R.A.M. to which institution I gave my life's blood for some 50 years!

Anyway, my school cannot be considered to be a "competing institution" by the wildest fancy, in the meaning of your regulation passed in July 1926. It is NOT a "general" music school, but is a highly specialist one, since it is only for Piano students, and moreover, only for one particular method of teaching it. And Specialist schools, so far from being "competitive" with the R.A.M. are indeed its most valuable "feeders", as mine has been all along and still is; and the late Principal's [Mackenzie's] description of it as "The R.A.M. Nursery" was indeed fully merited.

I must beg you to answer my question as soon as possible, as some twenty of my old pupils are on your staff, and as some of these still think that I know my job better than they do, they naturally appeal to me for help when under the stress of Recitals, etc., and I must know, as I have no wish to be a party to the contravening of R.A.M. regulations.

Yours as ever,
Tobias Matthay[44]

Chapter 9

Matthay was responding to a letter the RAM had sent him on 24 May, but he evidently received no response, because he wrote again on 1 October. Two days later, the Committee read his letter and directed A. Alger Bell, the Academy's Secretary, to draft a response assuring him that its May letter expressed no such prohibition—although precisely what it did permit was less than clear:

> The Committee instructed me to refer you to their letter of the 24th May 1928, in which it is said that there is no rule forbidding professors at the Academy taking private lessons from you or any other teacher—They wish me to draw your particular attention to the word "private"; the place where the lesson is given is immaterial.[45]

Over the next decade, Matthay received numerous "clarifications" of Academy policies, but as will be shown, the wording was often deliberately ambiguous and subject to McEwen's interpretation. However, there is no evidence that penalties were ever invoked against RAM professors who sought his instruction. Even Dora continued teaching at the Academy well past McEwen's tenure, as did many others who remained loyal to Matthay. McEwen's actions may have been provoked by an additional threat he sensed in 1927 when a TMPS Trust Deed was executed to make the School a "permanent institution."[46] It is tempting to speculate that Matthay undertook this action as a result of his break with the RAM, but undoubtedly it was more related to his advancing age (he was then 69) and his desire to leave a viable legacy for Jessie, Denise, and his teachers, who now numbered 45, without even counting those—like Dale, and Corder's son Paul—who taught harmony and other supporting subjects.[47] In accordance with Article 59 of the Articles of Association governing English companies, the TMPS was now a corporation with provisions for continuity and governance following Matthay's death. A new set of by-laws was created, although in most respects they were remarkably similar to the older set Matthay had drawn up in 1913. The chief difference was the installation of corporate officers and three governing committees, all of whom were required to answer to

Matthay ("The Principal") during his lifetime. Myra was installed as the School's President, while Irene served as Vice-President. Myra also served as an ex-officio member of a General Committee of 18 (including Matthay, Dora, and Irene), an Executive Council of eight, and a four-person "Programme Advisory Committee," consisting of Jessie, Denise, Langrish, and Hilda Dederich.[48]

Honors and financial awards, though meager at first, had been offered by the TMPS as early as 1909, and by 1920 the School had instituted the Students' Aid Fund, an endowment to assist financially needy scholars. Matthay and Jessie served as its Treasurers and each year's donors were always listed in the School's Prospectuses, and guaranteed free admission to all TMPS events. This was undoubtedly one reason Matthay and McEwen had come to blows, because the TMPS regularly reached out to the same pool of prospective donors as the RAM Patron's Fund. The scholarships rendered by the School evidently came exclusively from the interest, since the cumulative amounts are given for each successive year and it appears that the principal (deposited at Barclay's Bank) was never tapped. In the Fund's first year, most of the donors gave extremely modest sums, and a benefit concert at Queen's Hall pushed the total to just over £40. In 1921, the donors gave only a little over £15, but Matthay was now charging admission for his Wigmore Hall programs, and the gate receipts that July sent the total to £154, 12s, 1d. Most years the average donation per person remained well under £5, although in 1925 Myra—on hearing of Matthay's break with the Academy—gave £50, while the proceeds from the School's five concerts for that year tallied to over £150. After the TMPS was incorporated in 1927, the endowment was recognized as a Charity Fund by Inland Revenue, and by the end of 1929 the principal had risen to £1,836, 19s, 4d.[49]

By now, Matthay was peppering his annual Queen's Hall speech with appeals for donations, and he was even more concerned with "quality control," so that performances sponsored by the School might elicit the maximum interest from prospective patrons. In effect, he was "auditioning" his pupils throughout the year with regular "practice concerts" held in less prominent (and less expensive) settings—events that were generally open only by invitation, and for which weekly screenings usually occurred at No. 96. Most of these "practice" venues were within walking distance of the School, such as Morley Hall at 93 Mortimer Street (where Chappell pianos were used) and Grotrian Hall (known as Steinway Hall until 1925) at 115-117 Wigmore Street (where Grotrian-Steinwegs were used). In December 1930, Jessie wrote:

> The practice Concerts this year are being given at Conway Hall, Red Lion Square, Bloomsbury; not in the accustomed Concert hall area, but in a more romantic spot, [far] less than a stone's throw from its threshold is the house where William Morris and Burne Jones did their pioneering work in the sixties of the last century. The hall has only recently been built, and it carries an air of youth and vitality that infects both artists and audiences and makes the evenings doubly enjoyable.[50]

For nearly a decade, the majority of these concerts remained at Conway Hall, just over a mile away from the TMPS, where Bechstein—now re-established in new showrooms on Brook Street—provided the pianos. For all of the recitals—or "concert meetings" as they were sometimes labeled—Denise simply typed the programs on Foolscap E (8" x 13") sheets, and by 1928, she was using paper monogrammed with the TMPS logo and the hall's name at the top. The atmosphere was a bit less formal at these events than at the Summer Festivals, and not infrequently the same program offered performances by students and their teachers. Thus, the Morley Hall program of 20 November 1923 featured Denise performing six Chopin Mazurkas on the same evening that her students Peggy LeLiévre, Henry Elman, and Oroya Sewell offered works by Schubert, Beethoven, and McEwen respectively. It is clear that Matthay's teachers often used these gatherings to try out fresh repertoire, for Denise also performed on 23 October (a Mozart Sonata), 4 December (a Chopin Nocturne and two additional Mazurkas), and on 19 December she accompanied Désirée Mac-Ewan in the slow movement of the Rachmaninoff Second Concerto, and Dorothy Hess in the Scherzo and Finale from the Saint-Saëns Second.

Three of the four "practice" concerts that fall featured Argentinean-born Carlos Buhler, then studying with Matthay, who made his first TMPS appearance on 23 October with the Schumann Toccata. He followed up on 4 December with Liszt's transcription of Bach's Organ Prelude and Fugue in G minor, and on 19 December he offered a Polonaise by Emile-Robert Blanchet and "El Albaicín" from Book 3 of Albeniz's *Iberia*.[51] Buhler (1897-1976) had been born in Buenos Aires while his father was serving as Chilean Ambassador to Argentina, and for most of his life his diplomatic passport supported his aspirations to live as a citizen of the world. A brilliant intellect, he held degrees from the University of Geneva and the Sorbonne, and he had studied extensively with Busoni before coming to Matthay. Within a year of his first Morley Hall appearance, Matthay added him to his staff, although Buhler preferred to teach lessons at his Chelsea flat, where he delighted in playing roles. As one of Matthay's pupils remembered, "Often he greeted a student at the door of his studio in a Spanish costume or some unexpected garb which, unfortunately, threw the person off balance for his entire lesson."[52] Buhler's notoriously caustic tongue could also be intimidating, but all agreed that he was a remarkably analytic musician, and by 1924 Matthay had placed him in charge of the growing number of Americans who were flocking to the TMPS each summer. Matthay would have given the task to one of his senior teachers or undertaken it himself, but the American summer holidays generally began in June, and the calendars of both the RAM and the TMPS—which ran until later July—interfered.

Although their numbers increased substantially after 1920, only a few Americans sought Matthay out before the War. Jessie reports that several who had read *The Act of Touch* came as early as 1904,[53] but his first documented American pupil was Fannie Judson Farrar, a professor at Ohio's Denison College, who studied in Dresden and Vienna before arriving in London in 1906, where she worked with Matthay and Pollard.[54] The following year Hamilton MacDougall, a professor at Massachusetts's Wellesley College, appeared at Arkwright Road to interview Matthay for an American music journal, remaining with Percy Waller until 1908.[55] Then came Wesley Weyman (1877-1931), whom Matthay once described—perhaps inaccurately—as "my very first American pupil."[56] Descended from Myles Standish, Weyman was born in Boston and graduated from Harvard in 1899, where he studied composition with John Knowles Paine. He soon went to New York, where he began piano studies with William Mason while appearing frequently as a soloist and chamber musician. He joined the faculty of the Institute of Musical Arts (now Juilliard) in 1905, but as reported by the *New York Times*, he "left in 1908 to study under various famous teachers in Europe."[57] On 22 March 1911, he gave an all-Liszt program in London's Aeolian Hall which was generally well received, *The Times* noting that "he treats Liszt in the only right way, that is to say, as a musician who is speaking very earnestly and not as a virtuoso who is trying to show off."[58] From the late nineteenth century onward, many American instrumentalists regarded study in Berlin or Leipzig as a necessary rite of passage, but the War had shattered America's fascination with Germany just as surely as the Teutonic bonds had been broken in Britain. Still, by the early 1920s, London was not the first choice for most aspiring Americans, and far more seemed to gravitate toward other European capitals—especially Paris.

Bruce Simonds (1895-1989), born in Bridgeport, Connecticut, had received two degrees from Yale before arriving in Paris in 1919 to seek a diploma in Gregorian Chant from the Schola Cantorum—studies that were largely underwritten by a two-year fellowship from his alma mater. His musical training was extensive, as he had studied composition at Yale with Horatio Parker, and worked briefly in New York with Harold Bauer. But despite serious intentions, his piano studies had been largely unproductive, and for a time he even considered refocusing on music history or composition. He later remembered that Yale's Stanley Knight had been able only to "tell me what not to do," and Bauer's rubato advice had been limited to "You must practice with the metronome."[59] During his first year in Paris he studied composition with d'Indy, but he had no piano teacher at all, recalling only that he used the piano in his flat to "read a good deal of music."[60] By chance, that spring he met a young English woman at a tea who suggested that Matthay had "a lot of new ideas," and in August, during the Schola's summer vacation, he played to Matthay at Marley, surprising even himself by remaining in England till November.[61]

Simonds was not only a stunning intellect but a gifted performer, and after just four months of study, he seemed convinced that even a Proms appearance was not out of the question. By now he had endeared himself to Matthay and Jessie, who were thrilled at the prospect of his extending his scholarship for another year and transferring the venue from Paris to London. Matthay was eager to offer advice and wrote to him that December:

> Most certainly, if you can get another years' [sic] study, take it. It is fully justified by your talents and prospects. You have "<u>platform</u>" talent too, which is a great asset! I see no reason why you should not give a Recital in a years' [sic] time, and get press notices to take home—if you can afford Recital-expenses. As to getting with the Promenade Concerts (Queen's Hall) that one cannot <u>promise</u>, as it depends a good deal on the mere caprices of certain men—But as an American—a foreigner—you would have [a] better chance of getting in than a native, in a measure. Also, I think your merits—especially with another years' [sic] progress behind you, should give you a good chance, as your playing sounds like that of someone <u>who has something to say</u>. Work away and you will succeed in expressing yourself. I am sure you will work through all right—and get "a place in the sun" eventually.[62]

Simonds appealed to his scholarship committee and succeeded in extending his stay, but because money was tight, by early March he was installed well outside of London at Burley, Hampshire, on the outskirts of the New Forest. He remained in England through August, receiving lessons both at Marley and on Wimpole Street as Matthay's schedule permitted. On 19 July 1921 he made his debut at Wigmore Hall, and though the program has not been located, he undoubtedly performed the Schumann Toccata, Ravel's *Ondine*, and

Chapter 9

Szymanowski's third Etude from Opus 4, "In modo d'una canzona," since he offered this repertoire two nights later at the first TMPS Queen's Hall concert. Unfortunately, the press seems to have largely ignored his recital, but Matthay was so moved that he drafted a brief and touching note on the same evening:

My Dear Bruce,

This has indeed been one of <u>the</u> happiest evenings of my life, to hear you come out right on top of your work! Indeed, you will come out <u>At the top</u>, in the bigger sense; & by sheer real musical perception—like Myra has done. I am proud I have had the privilege of helping you a bit—you are a real [and] good Human-being—and it is that which shines through your playing and illuminates it and makes it the real thing as it should be, a prophet speaking. Go on and win the victory <u>most</u> worth having—victory over people's hearts through art.

All my love to you
Uncle Tobs[63]

Whatever desires Simonds may have had to remain abroad, personal circumstances intervened, for Yale offered him a teaching position that September. He was then engaged to Rosalind Brown of New Haven, who had graduated from the Yale School of Music in 1916. At the War's end she also went to the Schola Cantorum, remaining there till the spring of 1920, shortly before Bruce went to Matthay. They were married on 30 June 1922, and by then Bruce had been teaching at Yale for a year. The following year, their daughter, Elisabeth, was born, but Bruce soon confessed to Matthay that he still had a "hankering" to return to England. The letter Matthay sent him on 31 December 1923 reveals not only that he wanted him to join his staff, but that he even regarded him as a possible successor:

What <u>I</u> should <u>like</u> would be to have you on the staff of my School here! I have thought that ever since I realized what you were. I wonder whether it could ever become a fact? Unfortunately I don't see how I could manage—at present anyway—to get a sufficiently large class together for you—right off—to enable it to become a possibility and worth your while, financially—it always comes to that in the end—<u>to join us</u>!! I can't go on (at the rate I am tearing along) for ever—and it would need someone like yourself to take over <u>my</u> lecturing-work <u>when I cave in</u>—which is something I <u>don't mean to do</u>, however, for a long while yet!

I expect you get a good big stipend at Yale—and it would be necessary to better yourself if you gave that up![64]

But Simonds was intrigued at the possibility of teaching at the Matthay School and their discussions continued. As the summer of 1925 approached, he began making plans to house himself and his family just south of London at Richmond Hill in Surrey, and Matthay found the timing ideal to provide Buhler with some assistance. He typed a letter to Simonds on 21 March which reveals a good deal about the School's financial arrangements and practices:

My dear Bruce,

We are all very delighted to hear that you are going to be here again this summer, and shall much look forward to seeing you.

Indeed, I should like to put work in your hands. I do not know of any rule preventing you from taking any pupils here. [In fact, there was no rule forbidding Americans from working in England, but the legal formalities proved so complex that Simonds was almost forced to abandon the project.[65]] It would be well to make an enquiry. Mr. Carlos Buhler was taking most of my American visitors of last year, as Langrish and Tidmarsh were unavailable. Also both of these will be away examining this year. I have discussed the matter with Mr. Buhler (who has promised to stay on) but he also thinks there will be too much work for one man to deal with, so in that case we should be glad of your help. You would have to take the same fees as Mr. Buhler. For <u>holiday</u> lessons we charge somewhat more than for ordinary lessons. These holiday course fees are:—6 half hour lessons for £4. 4. 0 <u>of which the professor gets</u>

£2. 16. 0. 6 hour lessons are charged £6. 6. 0. <u>of which the professor gets £4. 4. 0</u>. On enclosed prospectus—the "ordinary fees"—the professor receives <u>half fee</u>. [No doubt Matthay included the most recent fee list as an additional inducement, since the summer fees were higher than those charged during the year. Though the "ordinary fees" varied greatly according to the teacher (and the 50 percent cut was by no means universal), very few would have been clearing £4, 4s, during the year for six hour-long lessons.] So far as I can see there will be a far greater influx of Americans this summer than before, and in that case I shall be delighted to have your services, but of course Mr. Buhler's time will have somewhat [Matthay inserted the word "somewhat" by hand] to be filled up first as he has already promised to stay on. Also there may be a difficulty with Americans not wanting to go to one who already is teaching in America? Or New Yorkers? [By this time Simonds was also keeping a studio in New York City.] But perhaps there is nothing in that? Anyway, we will certainly do our very best for you, and all your friends will welcome you back. I only wish we could keep you here.

Love from all of us,
Ever affectionately from
Uncle Tobs[66]

Simonds kept highly detailed records of his summer's work, noting that he gave his first lesson at Wimpole Street on 30 June and taught till the second week of September. He gave a total of 78 lessons to 13 students, all at the rate of one guinea (£1, 1s), and Matthay allowed him exactly two-thirds of the £81, 18s gross. On 8 September Simonds submitted a final accounting to Marion Cole, and four days later she sent him a check for £40, 12s, which, when added to the £14 advance he received when he first arrived, made his total income for the summer £54, 12s.[67] Over half of his pupils were American, including Arthur Hice, who taught privately in Philadelphia, and Marie Sloss, who taught at Carleton College in Minnesota. But not surprisingly, none of his students performed on the July TMPS recitals—since they had not appeared in the earlier

Storm Clouds

"practice" concerts. Nor did Bruce or Rosalind play, even though both of them studied extensively with Matthay that summer. Nonetheless, a number of Americans did perform, since some had been resident in London for many months. Raymond Havens, who had taught at Dartmouth before moving to Boston University, appeared at Queen's Hall on 21 July with four Chopin Etudes. Havens had been concertizing for nearly 20 years before arriving in London in 1924 for studies with Buhler and Matthay, and in 1920 the *New York Times* had praised his "capital Chopin."[68] He was joined that evening by his BU colleague Frederick Tillotson, who performed Medtner's "Tragedy Fragment," and Wellesley College professor Jean Wilder, then also with Swinstead, who completed her year and a half in London by performing his Impromptu in C.

No doubt many of the Americans were surprised—if not shocked—by the speech Matthay gave that evening announcing his resignation from the RAM, but he did his best to keep the mood light by hosting a party for the entire School the next afternoon at Marley, which lasted far into the evening. Since Langrish was away examining, Matthay filled him in by letter on 1 August:

> We had a most wonderful Party day after Queen's Hall—enormous enthusiasm—Americans in strong force—Myra and Irene played Duos—[Lyell] Barbour represented America [by performing]—and [Harold] Craxton and Jessie did some things together to finish with—It was an unforgettable [evening].[69]

There was also a dinner, preceded by considerable toasting. Bruce and Rosalind were in attendance, as Bruce had been taken by surprise several weeks earlier when Jessie made his life "miserable" by asking him to "respond" for the Americans:

> I am sure that she had no idea of how appalled I was at this perfectly reasonable request. I had never made an after-dinner speech; I never attended dinners at which this was done. So I agonized over this for several weeks until the fatal evening arrived and I found myself seated at

413

Chapter 9

a little round table with the Matthays, Myra Hess, and Irene Scharrer, I don't remember the others. I can't recall what I said, beyond mentioning the successes of Myra and Irene, but at the close, in some desperation to find something constructive to say, I remarked that it would be appropriate if we Americans could get together and form an Association. To my surprise the suggestion was taken up and shortly after that a few of us went out one afternoon to a place near Chenies [in Buckinghamshire] for tea.[70]

Another New Englander, Albion Metcalf (1902-76), who had also come to Matthay after enduring frustration in Paris, reported that the tea was taken about two miles from Chenies—on the 3 August Bank Holiday—in Flaunden, (now) in Hertfordshire. He wrote his parents that same week:

> Monday was a holiday here, and about twenty of us Americans went on a hike in the afternoon. We rode about twenty miles out of London by train, then walked into the most beautiful country, through fields of sheep, along lanes bordered with new-mown hay, over a hill and into the tiny hamlet of Flaunden, where we had tea at "The Green Dragon."
>
> There the American Matthay Association was formed, and a Provisional Board chosen to act till the first annual session in New York next December, where the full organization will take place in a three-day program filled with social activity, business, recitals, conferences, and lectures.
>
> The Board plans to have a two-day meeting in Boston at Thanksgiving time to perfect plans. The Chairman is Richard McClanahan of New York, other members are Bruce Simonds of Yale, Miss [Gertrude] Leonard of New York and Tillotson. For the present at least, I have the job of Secretary-Treas., so the next few months will be "full up."
>
> Then another four-mile hike through forests and the village of the Duke of Bedford [Chenies], a gorgeous sunset, and two rainbows overhead.[71]

Richard McClanahan (1893-1981), then engaged to Gertrude Leonard, chaired the Provisional Board by virtue of his having journeyed to Richmond several days after the Marley party to exchange thoughts with Simonds concerning the proposed organization. McClanahan, a native of Rushville, Indiana, had graduated from the Northwestern University School of Music in 1917 and was immediately called to service in a band attached to the 22nd Infantry in France, where he served alongside Percy Grainger. When he returned to Evanston for a brief visit in 1919, he encountered Northwestern's Dean, Peter Lutkin, who showed him a copy of *Musical Interpretation*. His interest in Matthay increased strongly after he attended a summer course at the Cincinnati Conservatory stressing "firm finger-tips, high, arched knuckles, and a heavy arm," which he said brought him such pain that "whenever I played I had to go to an osteopath for relief."[72] By the time he arrived in London in 1924 he was teaching at New York University, and three years earlier he had founded the Riverdale School of Music, a division of the Riverdale Country School in The Bronx. McClanahan was only too happy to devote its facilities to the first AMA conference meeting, scheduled for 28-30 December 1925. By then, the Board had set the organization's annual dues at $5, and on 2 December, Metcalf—until 1927 he was spelling his name "Metcalfe"—drafted a form letter at his home in Reading, Massachusetts, promising a number of specially selected Americans (Matthay had provided the names earlier that summer) the status of "Charter Member" if they paid up before the conference began. They were also advised that food and lodgings could be obtained for three nights at the Riverdale School dormitories for $12.

The program consisted of a reception, dinner, and a dance on Monday, 28 December, with day-long deliberations concerning elections, a proposed constitution, and future plans on Tuesday, followed by a recital that evening by Simonds, who was billed as "the first American assistant of Matthay, summer of 1925." The final day was devoted to "studio discussions," a display of new teaching materials by G. Schirmer, and a talk by McClanahan called "Some comments on Matthay, the teacher." An afternoon recital by Tillotson and transportation to midtown evening concerts were also promised,[73] but it appears that neither of these occurred. Instead, McClanahan's talk was preceded by a discussion of "various developments in the art of pianoforte playing," given by LeRoy Campbell, the Director of the Warren Conservatory in Warren, Pennsylvania, who at 52, was undoubtedly one of the senior statesmen of the group.[74] A total of 35 "charter" members had paid dues by the stipulated deadline, but only ten of these attended the Tuesday meeting to draft the organization's constitution.[75] Those assembled also voted Simonds in as President, while retaining Metcalf as Secretary-Treasurer, at least for the first year. Several weeks before the meeting, Matthay had prepared a touching greeting to be read in his absence at the opening dinner, but it was delayed in the mail and appeared only in the conference Minutes:

> My dear friends all!
>
> It gratifies me immensely to see what you proposed last summer has become actuality. It makes me feel as though my home now embraced America! The new Association will indeed bind us all together more than we could feel as individuals only.
> Indeed I shall be with you in spirit at all your meetings,—perhaps some day even in person—who knows the possibilities of the future?
> In the meantime, All Luck to the A. M. A.! They are initials of good omen—they suggest "amare"!—may the Association indeed foster the growth of love between us all—affection, the only thing worth striving for in the end.
> My blessing on you all at the Association.[76]

Indeed, the possibility of bringing Matthay to America for a 1927 AMA summer school was much discussed at the first meeting, but the project was soon abandoned for financial reasons. However, the tiny group was so determined to raise scholarship funds to send Americans abroad that Simonds immediately appointed a Ways and Means Committee with sub-chairs throughout the United States. Over the next decade, many Association members gave benefit concerts to advance this cause, and they continued sending students to London even at the height of the Depression. By the following summer, Matthay was eagerly promoting new prospects to enhance the Association's modest beginnings, and the Board asked him to group his suggested candidates into the classes of "Active," that is, those he deemed fully qualified to teach his principles, and "Associate," or those who as yet still had only a partial understanding. Simonds took the typewritten names and addresses of 15 proposed "Actives" and 13 proposed "Associates" with him to the next Riverdale meeting on 29 December 1926, and by then 18 had been contacted. He placed checkmarks next to those from both groups who had accepted (a total of 11) and penciled an "N" next to those who had refused membership—a total of nine.

One of the "Actives" who refused was Frank Mannheimer (1895-1972), an accomplished performer then studying with Buhler and Matthay, whose address was given merely as "TMPS." Mannheimer, a native of Dayton, Ohio, had arrived in London that spring by way of Paris after two years of study in Berlin with Leonard Kreutzer. On 6 July 1926, he made his first appearance at a TMPS Wigmore Hall program performing Beethoven's Sonata, Op. 110, and Matthay was so impressed that he presented him two weeks later at Queen's Hall, playing Busoni's transcription of Bach's Toccata and Fugue in C. The 22 July Queen's Hall program may have represented a turning point for the TMPS, because of the 11 students heard that evening, six were non-British. Allanah Delias, who performed the first Bach Partita, and Raie Da Costa, who performed three Chopin Etudes, were both from Cape Town, and Erzi Breiner, who performed the first movement of the Schumann F-sharp minor Sonata, was from Budapest. Besides Mannheimer, there were three additional Americans: Metcalf, who performed the Chopin B minor Scherzo, Barbour, who played the Mozart Sonata, K. 310—before ending the program with Denise and Rae Robertson in the Bach Triple Concerto—and Eunice Norton, then 18, who performed the Chopin E major Scherzo.

Despite her youth, the Minneapolis-born teenager was already in her third year of study with Matthay and Langrish, and six months earlier Simonds had made her the London sub-chair of the AMA

Scholarship Committee. She had been viewed as a child prodigy by William Lindsay, her teacher at the University of Minnesota, who arranged an audition with Myra when she passed through the Twin Cities in 1922. Although Myra strongly encouraged Eunice's mother to take her to Matthay one day, no one expected Mrs. Norton—described by many as a somewhat overbearing stage-door parent—to establish residence in London a year later with her fifteen-year-old daughter in tow. Eunice made her first TMPS appearance at a Morley Hall practice concert on 20 November 1923 with a portion of Schumann's *Faschingschwank*, and she appeared again on 19 December with the first movement of Beethoven's Sonata, Op. 2, no. 3. Recognizing her gifts, Matthay immediately took her under his wing, and she became a fixture at the TMPS for the next seven years. But he also sought a peer group for her, and a year after her arrival, he allied her with three teenaged RAM students—Hilda Bor, Virginia MacLean, and Anthea Bowring[77] (a pupil of Irene)—to perform Bach's rarely heard four-keyboard transcription of Vivaldi's concerto for four violins, which they performed under Wood's baton in October 1924. Despite the fact that *The Times* found the work "a good deal less interesting" than Bach's triple concerto, the young women were acclaimed for their "delicately balanced *ensemble*."[78]

Eunice made her Wigmore Hall debut on 26 May 1927, but the press reactions were mixed. *The Times* praised her Bach G Major Toccata, which was performed with "admirable clearness" and "complete understanding of the proportions," but it found the theme of her Brahms Handel Variations "much too fast" and the dynamic gradations in the rest of the work "too violent."[79] She gave another program in the same hall five weeks later, and although the notice was briefer, it was generally more positive. The same critic noted that "she has an excellent technique and her playing is usually rhythmical," but he also observed that "at times, the tone became unpleasantly hard."[80] Matthay worried about Eunice's musical development, and she even recalled that he and Jessie once scowled at her after she admittedly turned the first movement of the Tchaikovsky No. 1 into shallow virtuosity.[81] By the fall of 1927, after repeating the Bach Concerto with her three colleagues at the Proms in September, she returned to Minneapolis to solo with the Orchestra in Chopin's F minor Concerto, and she sent the reviews back to Matthay. On 21 November, Jessie confided to Simonds:

> Eunice Norton seems to have excited the Minneapolis folks with her Chopin Concerto. She makes it really fascinating. I hope they won't spoil her. She needs a year or two of living without thought of réclame [publicity], and I'm afraid that is the predominating thought just now. She is a dear child—and is growing in personality tremendously—her technique is quite astounding—but there is not much spirituality as yet. She will be back again in London in January.[82]

On 9 November 1928, Eunice gave another Wigmore Hall program, but the reviews were again somewhat lackluster. The reviewer found her three early Stravinsky Etudes the most satisfying, commenting that they "displayed fine virtuosity in their presentation." But she was criticized for her tempos in the Beethoven Sonata, Op. 27, no. 1 ("the allegro movements were taken too fast, and the adagio movement too slowly"), and she evidently suffered a memory lapse in Schumann's *Symphonic Etudes*, creating "an atmosphere of uncertainty, which rather pervaded the rest of the performance."[83]

However, by now Matthay also had American pupils who compared favorably to his finest British artists. Lyell Barbour (1897-1967), born in Champaign-Urbana, Illinois, gave his Wigmore Hall debut on 9 February 1926, and *The Times*, although noting that he sometimes forced his tone, was generally positive.[84] But a year later, the paper offered not a single negative word:

> The piano playing of Mr. Lyell Barbour is distinctively attractive. He gives you the music, does not obtrude himself, yet makes whatever he plays alive and interesting; best of all he plays *to* you, not *at* you. The paradox of giving musical pleasure, like the paradox of hedonism, is that you must not seek to do it. Mr. Barbour does not strive to please, but ends by pleasing you because he is a conscientious and extremely capable artist. His programme at Wigmore Hall on Tuesday night began with Mozart and Beethoven,

proceeded through Brahms to Albeniz and Debussy and several more miscellaneous pieces demanded as encores by an enthusiastic audience.[85]

When Simonds returned to Wigmore Hall on 4 July 1928, he made an even more dramatic impact on the London concert scene. Although his *Times* review was mixed (he was "very accomplished," though "immature," and his Ravel was "brilliantly played," but lacking in "definition of outline"[86]), the *Musical Times* regarded him as a near-deity:

> Bruce Simonds is a pianist of whom any nation might be proud. Not only are his executive attainments of the highest order, but his power of communicating the thought of music to his audience is commanding, and, in not a few respects, unique. Beginning with Bach's Caprice 'on the departure of his beloved brother,' the Fugue was played with remarkable insight and with deft touches of humour. Beethoven's Sonata, Op. 101, followed, and at once revealed the mental stature of the player. . . . Perhaps Ravel's 'Gaspard de la Nuit' gave Mr. Simonds the best opportunity to display his great powers of thought and invention. In tone, style, and intellectual grip the interpretation of these pieces will always remain a fragrant memory to those who heard them.
>
> In brief, Bruce Simonds is a benefactor to his race. He has reminded us of the kinship between ourselves and our brethren across the Atlantic, and the reminder is as opportune as it is delightful. For years untold, great artists have come to us from the Old World. If Mr. Simonds may be regarded as a sample, we shall presently have to welcome equally great exponents of music from the New. Yet we would warn our American friends of the obvious dangers attending the prodigiously high standard they have set in the person of Bruce Simonds.[87]

Matthay was ecstatic. He had coached Simonds extensively, particularly on the Bach and the Beethoven, and he wrote to him on the same evening with the terse accolade: "You are A Very Great Man!"

> I don't think I've ever had a happier evening. It really was great, masterly, playing Music all through. No one can touch your Gaspard—it was

an immense achievement—so were many of the other things. Most of us were just rendered speechless!

You must go all over the world doing that and teaching people—by your fingers-and-mind—behind what Music really means[.]

Bravissimo!!![88]

Simonds's success came about three months after Matthay's final installment had appeared in the March issue of *The Music Teacher*. But as distasteful as his battle with McEwen had been, he may not have grasped the full significance of an unsigned essay which appeared thirteen pages later in the same issue. Indeed, the magazine's pledge of impartiality in the Matthay-McEwen debate was belied by a series of unsigned pieces it had been carrying which indicted not just his teachings on rubato, but *all* of his principles. Authored by an anonymous contributor who signed himself as "One of the Crowd," the first installment appeared in January:

> A teacher must be ready to face the fact that what was new and revolutionary fifteen years ago is a commonplace these days, and is encountering the criticism that usually overtakes the commonplace. Many teachers, for example, are still teaching the Matthay system, as something entirely novel and startling, whereas there is now a great mass of well-founded criticism of the system, almost as formidable as that which the Matthay system levelled against the old German technique.[89]

Predictably, Matthay countered with an angry letter which appeared in the February issue:

> The remarks of your correspondent . . . transcend all limits of journalistic licence. I am sorry I must ask for an unquallified apology from you and the anonymous writer of what I consider to be a serious libel.[90]

In March, as *The Music Teacher*'s editors were terminating the Matthay-McEwen dialogue, the same writer offered "In Reply to Mr. Matthay:"

> I might say that I have, in my time, been as ardent a missionary for Matthay methods as anyone could wish. . . .
>
> Mr. Matthay's own mind is one of the most keenly analytical in the teaching world of the present day, and for students of an analytical turn of mind, his works are of incalculable value. . . .
>
> I myself feel strongly that Mr. Matthay's laws and directions will someday have to be re-stated in more simple language for the benefit of those to whom his books, with their wealth of detail and abundance of (quite necessary) digression, are sometimes baffling. . . .
>
> The Matthay system, beyond question, contains the truth, and nothing but the truth on questions of piano technique, but I doubt if anyone would be so bold as to claim that it contains the *whole* truth. It is unthinkable that one—or even one school of minds—should evolve the whole truth about one of the most subtle and delicate of the arts. I am amazed to find Mr. Matthay protesting, as though his reputation and very honour were at stake, at the criticisms referred to in my remark. Surely he does not consider himself infallible, and his system impeccable![91]

A few sentences later, the author suggests that his views are also shared by a growing community of British musicians from whom Matthay has merely insulated himself:

> I assure Mr. Matthay that the criticism I spoke of is a sincere and understanding criticism; it is not to be found in quantity among the written and spoken words of the eminent in the musical profession—although occasionally some of it comes from them [no doubt a reference to McEwen]—but among the rank and file of the profession, whom I have the honour to represent.[92]

Though his anonymity precludes verifying his "rank and file" status, he seems convinced that while Matthay principles are indispensable, they are also inadequate:

> If Mr. Matthay will carefully re-read the whole of the paragraph to which he objects he will see that I was making a vigorous plea for the

thoughtful teaching of this system, in place of the one-sided, over-enthusiastic teaching which I assure him is very common in many parts of the country, and that I was emphasising the fact that we must expect to meet criticism of the system, and know how to meet it.

I hope that as a result of this discussion readers will look up for themselves their Matthay books and study them, not just in detail, but as a whole; at the same time realising that the whole of the system may not be the same thing as the whole art of piano-playing.[93]

Although no specific principle or idea had been attacked, an anonymous voice now aroused a generalized skepticism toward Matthay's ideas. Similarly, although McEwen's charts and measurements were too complex to be refuted by many who followed the controversy, a widely respected journal now assured the musical public that *neither* viewpoint was rationally defensible. For decades, Matthay had proudly invoked the banner of science, but now a new "science" was arising— a science which, curiously, bred doubt rather than understanding.

And very soon, his critics would no longer require the cloak of anonymity.

Notes

1. MA. Matthay to Vivian Langrish, 1 Aug. 1925.
2. MA. Matthay sent a carbon copy of his resignation letter to Langrish.
3. COMM, 29 July 1925. Agnew wrote his letter on 23 July.
4. MA. Matthay gave Langrish a carbon copy of his typewritten "Speech[:] Queen's Hall, 1925, July 21st."
5. MA. Matthay to Langrish, 1 Aug. 1925.
6. MA. Matthay sent a copy of his 31 July press release to Langrish with his 1 Aug. letter.
7. JHM (p. 36) reproduces the entire program.
8. COMM, 12 Nov. 1924.
9. MA. Matthay to Simonds, 18 April 1927.

10. His advertised rate was then £2, 2s for a forty-five-minute lesson. See Revised Fee List, September 1922, McEwen RAM.
11. MA. Matthay to Langrish, 1 Aug. 1925.
12. MA. Matthay to Langrish, 22 Jan. 1937.
13. Fortunately, at this writing the RCM's Chilingirian Quartet has recorded three volumes in its McEwen Cycle and Geoffrey Tozer has recorded his complete piano music on the Chandos label.
14. *MT*, 1 Aug. 1922, 579. The concert took place at Queen's Hall on the evening of 10 July 1922.
15. *MT*, 1 Oct. 1922, 726. The letter was dated 12 Sept. 1922.
16. Jeremy Dibble, "McEwen, Sir John Blackwood," *Oxford Dictionary of Biography*.
17. *MT*, 1 Dec. 1922, 873.
18. *MT*, 1 Dec. 1924, 1127.
19. See their full-column ad in *TT*, 30 Aug. 1921, 7, col. E.
20. *MT*, 1 May 1923, 366.
21. See Frank W. Holland and Arthur W. J. G. Ord-Hume, "Reproducing Piano," in *RNG*.
22. *MT*, 1 Sept. 1925, 826.
23. "The Educational Use of the Player-Piano," *MT*, 1 Mar. 1925, 253.
24. Allen was also an accomplished organist, and earlier in his career Ronald had been acclaimed as a collaborative pianist.
25. See "Broadcasting. Week-End Programmes," *TT*, 14 Mar. 1925, 17, col. E. Scholes's highly entertaining lectures were soon issued in book form by the Oxford University Press. See Percy A. Scholes, *The Appreciation of Music by Means of the Duo-Art[:] A Course of Lectures Delivered at Aeolian Hall, London* (New York, 1926). By 1926 there was an American equivalent to Mackenzie's Committee, which sponsored Oxford's New York publication of Scholes's lectures. Its 18 members included Clarence Hamilton of Wellesley College in Massachusetts, one of the first Americans to study with Matthay.
26. Scholes, 114.
27. John B. McEwen, "Tempo Rubato," Article I, *The Music Teacher* 4 (June 1925): 370.
28. *The Music Teacher*, Sept. 1925, 624.
29. Ibid.

30. Ibid.
31. Tobias Matthay, "The Truth about Rubato," *The Music Teacher*, 7 (January 1928): 13.
32. Ibid.
33. "The Rubato Problem: Dr. McEwen's Rejoinder to Mr. Matthay," *The Music Teacher*, 7 (February 1928): 89.
34. "The Truth about Rubato: Mr. Matthay's Answer to Dr. McEwen's Question on 'The Point at Issue,'" *The Music Teacher*, 7 (March 1928): 150.
35. Ibid.
36. On at least one occasion in the mid-1930s, Matthay sent a letter to McEwen, but it was answered through intermediaries. See Ch. 11.
37. McEwen RAM.
38. COMM, 2 Oct. 1907. Moore was appointed at a salary of six shillings an hour.
39. Ibid.
40. Ibid.
41. Westminster Archives.
42. For example, see the catalogue page listed on the back of Matthay's *Playthings for Little Players*, published by the AFMC in 1924.
43. LRO.
44. MA.
45. Bell's draft reproduced in COMM, 3 Oct. 1928.
46. TMPS Prospectus, July 1928, 2.
47. Ibid., 3-4.
48. Ibid., 1.
49. All amounts taken from TMPS Prospectus, July 1930.
50. *AMAJ*, 1931, 4.
51. MA. The Archives have a number of these "practice concert" programs.
52. Eunice Norton, "In Memoriam: Carlos Buhler," *MN*, Fall 1976, 19. Hereafter cited as Norton.
53. Jessie, 60.
54. See *AMAJ*, 1931, 17.
55. Jessie, 38-39. Oddly, in his year of study MacDougall seems only to have worked with Percy Waller, though he attended many of Matthay's lectures. See *AMAJ*, 1931, 19.

Chapter 9

56. Matthay, "Outline Lecture on Technique," from June of 1934. RAMRBC (uncatalogued at this writing).
57. "Wesley Weyman Dead," *NYT*, 31 Oct. 1931, 17.
58. "Mr. Wesley Weyman's Recital," *TT*, 23 Mar. 1911, 10. col. E.
59. Virginia Gaburo, *Who Is Bruce Simonds?* (La, Jolla, California: 1978).
60. Ibid.
61. Ibid.
62. MA. Matthay to Simonds, 12 Dec. 1920.
63. MA. Matthay to Simonds, 19 July 1921.
64. MA. Matthay to Simonds, 31 Dec. 1923.
65. MA. No fewer than seven letters have survived between Simonds, Yale, and the British Passport Office. The matter was not straightened out till early June, a week before he sailed.
66. MA. Matthay to Simonds, 21 Mar. 1925.
67. MA. Simonds to Cole, 8 Sept. 1925, and Cole to Simonds, 12 Sept. 1925.
68. *NYT*, 16 March 1920, 18, col. C.
69. MA. Matthay to Langrish, 1 Aug. 1925.
70. MA. Simonds evidently typed his reminiscences for publication in *Enjoy the Music[,] 1925—1975*, the Golden Anniversary Booklet of the AMA (1975), but they were not used.
71. Metcalf's letter was reproduced in part in *Enjoy the Music*, 4. The booklet gives the date as July 1925, but Bank Holiday did not occur until 3 August.
72. Ibid., 10.
73. MA.
74. MA, Minutes of Dec. 1925 meeting.
75. Ibid.
76. Ibid.
77. Anthea Audrey Bowring Skimming, then 14, had begun to perform under the name "Anthea Bowring," which she used for the rest of her career.
78. *TT*, 20 Oct. 1924, 12, col. C.
79. *TT*, 28 May 1927, 10, col. D.
80. *TT*, 4 July 1927, 12, col. B.
81. Eunice Norton, "A Turning Point," *Enjoy the Music*, 11.
82. MA. Jessie to Simonds, 21 Nov. 1927.
83. *TT*, 12 Nov. 1928, 21, col. C.

84. *TT*, 12 Feb. 1926, 10, col. C.
85. *TT*, 13 May 1927, 14, col. B.
86. *TT*, 6 July 1928, 14, col. C.
87. "Bruce Simonds," *MT*, 1 Aug. 1928, 747.
88. MA. Matthay to Simonds, 4 July 1928.
89. The article appeared as an installment in an ongoing series entitled "The Ups and Downs of Professional Life," by "One of the Crowd." See *The Music Teacher*, 7 (January 1928).
90. *The Music Teacher*, 7 (February 1928): 88.
91. *The Music Teacher*, 7 (March 1928): 163.
92. Ibid.
93. Ibid.

Some Americans on the steps of the TMPS in 1924.
Richard McClanahan sits at far left next to Eunice Norton and her mother.
Jessie sits directly behind Eunice, and Carlos Buhler stands to Matthay's left.

Matthay and Denise Lassimonne on the southwest hill of High Marley about 1930.

Tea at Marley in the summer of 1928. Gertrude McClanahan stands between Matthay and Bruce Simonds. Denise is kneeling to Jessie's right, while Rosalind Simonds and her daughter, Elisabeth, are seated on the grass.

Three Americans at Marley in the summer of 1928; from left, Bruce Simonds, Julian DeGray, and Albion Metcalf

The concert room at the TMPS, which was completed in 1929. By day it served as the administrative offices for the music division of Oxford University Press.

CHAPTER 10

THE AFTERMATH

On 9 May 1926, in a long, typewritten letter to Bruce Simonds, Matthay discussed a recent book in some detail:

> With regard to Ortmann, I have read his book with great interest. As you say some of his experiments do corroborate my teachings. Where his experiments fail is that I suppose he has experimented with pianists who force their tone <u>whenever they go beyond</u> a [sic] mf or forte. I do not remember having one American artist over who has not done so until put in better ways. This quite easily accounts for his belief that quality of tone always becomes harsher as you play louder. Our aural experience seems entirely to be the contrary. Certainly with a push forward of the upper arm, and down force of forearm one makes more noise than by playing a properly produced forte, and it is this forcing of the arm which I find in most artists I meet with. Of course, in the end it makes no difference whatever to ones [sic] teaching whether we <u>call</u> it "differences of quality," or not, so long as the treatment of the key is put on the lines I have indicated if the performance is to be beautiful and effective.[1]

The first in a series of ongoing studies from the "Psychological Laboratory" of the Peabody Institute in Baltimore, Otto Ortmann's *The Physical Basis of Piano Touch and Tone* had been published in London the previous year. The title is arguably misleading, since Ortmann's book is centered almost exclusively on the physical properties of the piano rather than on the "bodily movements" employed by pianists: "The nature of these bodily movements, their variability and usefulness . . . do not concern us here. We have to investigate only their effect upon the action, and through this, upon the sound-complex of the piano."[2]

If he seems determined to reach a certain conclusion, it should be noted that even his preface announces his conviction that performers cannot effect purely qualitative distinctions in piano tone, an observation he suggests is already self evident to scientists. In fact, it could be argued that his book is not so much a "study," as a recitation of scientific data designed to enlighten musicians who have been misled by their senses:

> The present investigation is addressed primarily to the musician; the physicist will necessarily find in it much that is repeated and apparently superfluous. He, however, who knows the reluctance with which musicians, both professional and amateur, accept the limitation of all tone-colour on the piano to key-speed and duration, will readily understand the necessity for both repetition and detail. If this book contributes a little to the acceptance of this limitation, its object will have been attained. This it proposes to do by using as a starting point proved laws.[3]

But even though the book is filled with discussions and illustrations of scientific principles, the "proved laws" he mentions primarily concern aspects of mechanics and acoustics and often have little relevance to practical issues of performance or musical effects. Even his insistence that his study is aimed at musicians rather than scientists seems somewhat disingenuous, since as early as page 6, the reader is asked to grapple with sentences such as the following:

> If l be a length of vibrating string, r the radius of the string, d its density, P the stretching weight or tension, and n the number of vibrations per second, it is known that $n = \dfrac{l}{2\,rl} \sqrt{\dfrac{P}{\pi_4 d^l}}$ in which π is the ratio (3.14159) of the circumference of the diameter.[4]

Nonetheless, he reports a number of meticulous experiments which, as Simonds observed, offer corroboration for many findings expressed in *The Act of Touch*. For example, he vibrated a tuning fork of known frequency in proximity to a smoked microscope slide and traced the outline of its wave pattern. Then he attached the same slide to the side of the corresponding piano key and moved it at various speeds to produce tone, creating a series of sine curves, each of which he traced for purposes of comparison. By comparing wave amplitudes he then established that volume was entirely a function of key speed, or as he states it: "The faster the key is depressed, the louder is the resulting tone."[5] He also established that tone could be initiated by weight, rather than muscular action, by placing metal cups on the keys and filling them with various amounts of "small shot."[6] To be sure, he was not the first to conduct such experiments, for decades earlier Matthay had undertaken similar investigations as a prelude to his first published work, but Ortmann's data still provide much useful information. He compared two grand pianos which he believed to be "good representatives of the normal conservatory or student's piano,"[7] and demonstrated that different weights were required to depress keys depending on the tonal range represented, or in other words, on the size of the hammers. And he established that a minimal weight was required to create a *ppp* tone—usually at least three ounces. But he remains steadfast in his conviction that tone "quality" as such can only be imbued by the instrument's manufacturer.

Up to this point, the leading attacks on Matthay's teachings had been confined to Britain, but in their immediate aftermath, Ortmann now fired a shot heard round the world. Even so, his first book was not so much an attack on Matthay's means as on his ends, since it merely challenged some widely held beliefs about the instrument's tonal capabilities. But in 1929, his next book, *The Physiological Mechanics of Piano Technique*, completed the assault, for now Matthay's methods were also to be "disproved" by science—or at least by Ortmann's version of it. Peppered with plates from Gray's *Anatomy*, charts, graphs, and time-lapse photos, his book stresses the names, locations, and functions of individual muscles to the point that it often reads like a physiology primer, and muscular fixation is taken as a given. For example, in an effort to demonstrate that a relaxed arm can produce no better *fortissimo* quality than a stiff arm, he simply instructed (unidentified) pianists to conjure up both states. And since his participants were unsuccessful at achieving maximum sound with a relaxed condition, he concluded that stiffness was essential to reach greater volumes of tone:

> In all loud chordal work, therefore, the arm is fixed as, or immediately before the tone is produced. This rigidity is essential from a mechanical standpoint in order to obtain the desired tonal intensity. . . . Any "give" in any part of the arm between this and the keyboard, will cause the force to bend the arm at such a point as soon as resistance is encountered. . . .
>
> Two types of records were made to prove this. In the first type nothing was said to the player about arm condition and the instructions were merely to produce a tone of a given degree of intensity. . . .
>
> In the second type the player was told of the effect of stiffness upon intensity and was then asked to produce *fortissimo* tones with a relaxed wrist and arm. Although quite loud effects were thus obtained, they were uniformly below the intensity levels obtained with rigidity and as soon as the player felt that he had produced a true *fortissimo* the recording lever showed stiffness of the wrist, although the immediate subsequent relaxation frequently deceived the player.[8]

Although the English press did not immediately applaud Ortmann's book as revolutionary, it was received with considerable respect. A reviewer writing in the *Musical Times* on 1 December 1929 was impressed with its modern methodology, noting that "the same methods used originally with 'Motion Study' in connection with the efficiency of workers in factories are here used to study the motions of pianoforte playing."[9] Though a deferential nod is given both to Matthay and Breithaupt, the writer regards Ortmann's advice as equally valuable—even while acknowledging that his science is questionable: "The research technique is not such as would satisfy the scientist, and the pianist would do well on the whole to ignore the semi-scientific parts of the book, attending only to those parts where, as a result of physiological arguments, practical advice can be given."[10] But not only did Ortmann's "practical advice" contradict much of what Matthay had written, it was not even clear *how* it could be implemented:

> The records have shown, beyond any doubt, that a muscular coördination changes with each change of tempo, intensity, or pitch of the tones. In order, therefore, to exercise the muscles used in the actual movement, we should, from the beginning, have to practise each passage at the tempo, intensity, and pitch of what it is finally to be played. The practical impossibility of doing this does not invalidate the statement.[11]

Nonetheless, there was little significant opposition to Ortmann's work on either side of the Atlantic, and the appearance of his two books almost certainly hastened Matthay's decision to complete his long-promised condensation of the principles he had first expressed in *The Act of Touch*. But even before Ortmann's first book appeared, he had completed "On Memorizing," arguably the most popular of his six psychology lectures, judging from the fact that it remained in print long after his death.[12] Although much of what he says about memorization might be viewed as little more than common sense, he offers several insights which are not easily or readily inferred from his earlier writings. For example, he distinguishes three main forms of memory, all of which can be further subdivided:

1. *The Musical Memory*: this divides into Melodic, Harmonic, Rhythmical, and Moodal memory, and this last includes the required inflexual memory of the Tone, Time, and Duration inflexons. All these four are forms of *Musical* Memory.
2. *The Visual Memory*: includes (a) Eye-memory of the page, and (b) Eye-memory of the keyboard progressions and combinations.
3. *The Muscular Memory*: comprises (a) The sense of *Place* and movement from note to note—the spaces traversed—*on the keyboard*, and (b) the sense of Key-motion (key-resistance)—the going down, and also the coming up, of the key—the duration-sensation.[13]

Paraphrasing psychologist A. A. Lindsay, he begins by affirming that a memory "simply implies a *continuity* of something. In other words, an impression once made . . . remains alive, although, maybe, the mind becomes sleepy with regard to its presence."[14] Hence, the act of learning should always be undertaken carefully with an eye toward retention. But he distinguishes "care" from "routine," since the exact steps taken to memorize must necessarily vary with the individual, allowing for the fact that overtaxing one's mental faculties can only result in fatigue. Instead, he recommends "frequent and short exercises," stressing that nothing will really stick unless it is analyzed. His understanding of the subject also seems to embrace the cutting edge of what was then understood about the physiology of memory:

> Memorizing, from its *physical* aspect, is obviously a change of state in the grey matter of the brain. It may be pictured as the forming of the physical fibrous connexions or channels between one brain corpuscle and another—so that when one corpuscle is excited this excitation is transmitted to any other corpuscles that may have been thus connected-up by such physical fibrous channels.[15]

He then revisits several passages from *Musical Interpretation* which emphasize the "connections" which must be consciously made in the learning process, such as, "In short, remembrance of any piece means that the suggestion-channels are all in good working order."[16] He continues:

> The point to realize is, that in memorizing it is useless to try to "memorize" the thing we wish to note, as such—as an isolated thing, as an entity in itself. That is [a] waste of time. We can only successfully note a thing by our fixing up for it an association with other things, other thoughts, and experiences already present in our brain. The secret of Mneumonics is that we must note, must realize the *whence* for each musical thing; we must make a relation for it in our minds, so that when its relative, the preceding note, etc., is sounded, this relative will then automatically call

up a consecution to the next note, etc., and thus we find it to be fixed in our mind—in fact, *memorized*.[17]

Conversely, he stresses that the act of playing from memory demands the unrestricted flow of these connections surfacing at the desired moment, but he adds that this can only be prompted by focusing on the intended musical effect in the present:

The moment you begin to doubt your memory's capacity to "follow on", that moment you will hinder, if not completely stop, its continuity of action. Thus, if you commit the fatal blunder of *trying to recall the next note*, this will at once paralyse the natural and safe action of the previously-made sequential memory-ways or channels. . . . Here is not a case of your memory being incomplete or unreliable, but simply that you are *preventing* its natural action.[18]

Even as he prepared his memorization pamphlet for press, Matthay was at work on his next major book. On 16 June 1931 he wrote Simonds from Wimpole Street that he had "finished the last page of my new book a fortnight ago—so that is off my mind—but the Proofs—wont [sic] be for some time to come!"[19] And a year later, Oxford published *The Visible and Invisible in Pianoforte Technique*, graced with Tobias's heartfelt inscription to Jessie, "without whose constant encouragement no book of mine probably would ever have seen the light." Its Preface conveyed Matthay's motivation for presenting a new, 120-page "Digest" of his views:

It is now over a quarter of a century since my "Act of Touch" appeared—in 1903—my first essay on Pianoforte Technique.

Necessarily it was cumbrous, since there was little, if any, common-sense knowledge of the subject; and as the great majority of the ideas I had put forward were new, these were of necessity protected and fenced round with defensive arguments. But now all this has changed, the basic principles of my teachings are generally accepted, and indeed have become axiomatic as pianistic knowledge.[20]

Chapter 10

Notwithstanding the fact that Ortmann and others no longer found his teachings "axiomatic," Matthay cited an unpleasant byproduct of his success, which also explained his choice of title:

> There have been issued lately a number of *piratical works and writings* founded on my ideas, sometimes avowedly so, which, while showing much felicity in expression, are nevertheless inadequate, and most inaccurate upon very important matters, thereby forming actual *perversions* of my teachings. To mention only one instance, these writers have almost entirely overlooked the important changes of state of exertion and relaxation of the playing limb which form THE REAL BASIS OF GOOD TECHNIQUE, but which, *being invisible*, have escaped their attention.[21]

In the last decade, Matthay had begun to accentuate the importance of certain "invisible" conditions of the arm as the "basis" for all effective technique, so much so that in 1923 the AFMC issued his *Nine Steps towards Finger Individualization through Forearm Rotation* (See Appendix III), a four-page pamphlet which he regarded as the most concise articulation of his principles' foundation. In the twenty years since *The Act of Touch* had appeared, he had made no substantial revisions to his theory of rotation, but he had gained a greater appreciation for its fundamental importance. And he confessed to being surprised at how often his views were misrepresented on this subject—so much so that he now devoted an entire chapter to its use, while stressing the importance of "invisibility:"

> Success or failure technically (and therefore musically) depends on a clear understanding and due mastery of these Forearm Rotatory-adjustments. Just here, however, we find perhaps more vagueness and misunderstanding than anywhere else. In spite of all that I have written and lectured on this very point, I am still persistently and stupidly misrepresented as dealing solely with rotatory MOVEMENTS—movements which had already been recognized and approved "for occasional use" in tremolos, etc., half a century ago! Whereas, throughout, I am

referring to rotatory actions or stresses, inactions, and reactions, mostly *unaccompanied by any movements whatsoever.*[22]

The Digest portion of *The Visible and Invisible* is followed by 19 "Additional Notes"—over 50 pages in all—and in the wake of Ortmann's work, Matthay was careful to title one of these "Useful versus Useless Anatomy Teaching." He begins by acknowledging that while some basic understanding of anatomy may be helpful to the student, immersion in the subject can actually hamper serious work, since the physiological connectivity and interdependence of the muscles precludes the possibility of knowing precisely which ones are involved at any given moment in performance:

> True, by dissection we can discover which are the main muscles attached to the various portions of our playing-limb, but dissection cannot tell us exactly how and where we must use them in playing. Experiments, on the other hand, made on the living body, are not only unreliable and misleading, but are often even impossible to attempt. Mechanical tests of the tension or laxity of muscles and tendons during the actual performance of a sufficiently competent artist suffer from the grave disadvantage and uncertainty that the player is quite unlikely to "be himself" under such ordeal, and is instead likely to become more self-conscious and tense, and to do quite unusual things muscularly at the critical moment. Moreover, it is manifestly impossible to test the more deep-seated muscles in the living subject by calipers or other machines. . . .
>
> Finally, even were such analysis not impossible, it would yet be useless and quite futile for the simple (but quite final) reason that it is physiologically and psychologically *impossible* for us *directly* to prompt, influence, or stimulate any muscle into action by *any exertion of our will*, however concentrated our attention.
>
> Muscles will only consent to spring into action in response to our desire *for a particular limb-exertion or limb-movement*. All we can do is earnestly to *will* and time the exertion or movement of the *limb*, or portion of it, by recalling the accompanying *sensations*, and the suitable

muscles may then spring into responsive activity. To think of a particular muscle is futile! . . .

To be "scientific" signifies to be in accord with attainable Truth. Whereas, to try to bring the student's mind upon the names and addresses of muscles is a totally wrong road by which to achieve Limb-control—and therefore *un*-scientific![23]

At the end of his Note, he reveals some personal history, suggesting that he speaks from experience:

During the years I was engaged upon my "Act of Touch," being of German descent, I was therefore naturally bent on being "recht gründlich" [quite thorough] as to my facts; I, also, for a time was misled into the anatomical field. Consequently I misspent (?) [sic] a good deal of time trying to master, anyway, *our* part of Anatomy; and was well abetted therein by my late brother-in-law, Dr. CHARLES KENNEDY, of Edinburgh, an excellent anatomist. When, however, it dawned upon me that it was impossible to obtain any muscular response by directing one's attention upon the concerned muscle, I had the common sense to throw all this overboard. . . . I therefore restricted myself on this point to about one single page (p. 148 of "The Act of Touch") devoted to rudimentary facts, and that single page is ample for the aspiring Pianist![24]

For the first time in over 30 years, Marjory, who had passed in November of 1930, was unavailable to read Matthay's proofs, and his Preface acknowledges that he turned instead to his "devoted disciple," Alvin Goodman.[25] Though he never joined the American Matthay Association, Goodman was a young New Yorker who had distinguished himself by earning the TMPS Chapell Gold Medal in the summer of 1930. He had also developed an interest in Denise, and for a time the Matthays were seriously expecting him to join their family. But the relationship soon ended, and though the Matthay household remained generally happy, there were occasional undercurrents of tension. For example, by the early 1930s Jessie was at work on a full-scale biography of her husband, and although she includes many personal anecdotes about Matthay and his family, she never mentions Dora's three-year marriage to her brother Jack. Nor is Dora so much as referenced in Marjory's 1929 autobiography, *A Life of Song*, even though her book provides a detailed account of Jack's death.[26] After Denise entered the Matthay household, she recalled that Dora had adopted the manner of an eccentric spinster, always sporting a large valise and acting giddy and childish whenever she visited Marley, where she preoccupied herself with posy arrangements. The fact that she and Matthay spoke only in German—which Jessie did not understand—merely exacerbated the household frictions, and Denise could recall a few occasions when Matthay even lost his temper, virtually screaming at Dora (in both English and German) to "stop being silly!"[27]

Perhaps not surprisingly, Jessie's last will, dated 9 October 1927, made no specific bequests to Dora, despite the fact that—in warmly adoring language—she bequeathed numerous items to over 20 close friends and relatives. With legalistic formality—and undoubtedly with her husband's guidance—she stipulated only that in the event Matthay predeceased her, Dora and Denise were each to receive an amount not to exceed £500 per annum.[28] And nowhere in her lengthy document does she refer to Denise as an "adopted daughter" (a status perhaps legally precluded by the fact that Denise's mother was still alive),[29] describing her only as "my Husband's dear protégée," and bequeathing to her two oil paintings and an assortment of furnishings from Marley and Wimpole Street. But surprisingly, Jessie makes no bequest at all to Marjory, who was then very much alive—even though she allocated £2,000 to her other surviving sister, Margaret (Maggie). Since she left £250 each to Marjory's two children (plus numerous items of furniture to Patuffa)—and even £250 to Jack's daughter, Elizabeth—one might speculate that some type of rift had developed between the two sisters. But if so, it must have been short lived, since four months after the will was drawn, Jessie wrote Simonds and his wife that Marjory was staying at Marley, reading them passages from her forthcoming book every afternoon over tea.[30] And in December 1930, about two weeks after Marjory died,

Chapter 10

Jessie wrote to Simonds, "I have come through dark days lately, my sister Marjory of the songs has passed away, and I cannot but feel desolate. But I know time brings its compensations."[31] Still, the fact that Marjory is not even mentioned in Jessie's will is curious.

On the afternoon of Thursday, 27 November, five days after her passing, a memorial service was given at the Church of St. Martin-in-the-Fields in Trafalgar Square, and Marjory, who had received the C.B.E. six years earlier, drew an impressive crowd. Her son-in-law, Patuffa's husband, the Reverend J. C. F. Hood, officiated along with the church's Vicar, and in addition to Jessie, Tobias, and other immediate family, the attendees included well over 100 people, many of whom had journeyed from Scotland. C. Patrick Duff, then Private Secretary to No. 10 Downing Street, represented the Prime Minister, and the titled guests included the playwright Lady Alix Egerton, whose brief poem to Marjory—"My Friend"—was included in the six-page printed program. Mourners from the musical world included Maud Karpeles, a close associate of the late Cecil Sharp, with whom *The Times* had favorably compared Marjory several days earlier.[32] Irene also attended, along with Toni Cohen, Marion Cole, Paul Corder and his sister, Dolly, and representatives from Boosey and Company, Marjory's publishers. Myra, then on tour in America, sent her close friend Anita Gunn.[33]

Also in attendance was Arthur Broadhurst, who with his wife, Annie, had resided below stairs at No. 96 for over a decade. Annie was the Matthays' cook at their London residence, and Broadhurst ("Broady," if he knew you well)—with a face and physique resembling the mature Churchill—was always impeccably attired in coat and tie. Generally beloved by staff and students alike for what many described as an endearing, gentle nature, he functioned as the School's general factotum, receiving daily visitors and requiring everyone to sign the guest book. In addition, he monitored the schedule assignments of the teaching studios and practice rooms, and addressed all the invitations to the many concerts sponsored by the TMPS. His unswerving loyalty to the Matthays made him indispensable in myriad personal ways as well. He regularly hoisted

Jessie's wheelchair onto the stairway track designed for the mechanical conveyance which pulled it up the several flights to her room, and he guided her to Queen's Hall and other locations whenever she needed assistance. No doubt his presence at Marjory's memorial service was as much to assist Jessie as to pay his respects to her sister, for Jessie's arthritic problems had now progressed to the point where she required constant care. But her spirits remained high, even when the medical science of her day imparted more promise than substance.

By 1926, she was largely confined to a wheelchair, but she was so determined to walk again that she repeatedly endured intense physical pain. In February, she was performing grueling exercises at a spa in Hereford, and a year later, after appearing at Yale, Irene Scharrer advised Bruce and Rosalind Simonds that Jessie was undergoing a "new treatment." In March, Simonds asked Tobias, "Is this new treatment, which Irene tells me is very painful, proving to be beneficial?"[34] and a month later, Matthay responded, "Jessie has been ordered off to Wales for the time being, and I am hoping it will help her. She has had her legs straightened and hopes to be able to walk again later on.[35] At present in <u>splints</u> [braces]!" One of many such trips, her visit focused on painful, at times bone-crunching, leg "straightenings," and walking by small degrees. By June, Tobias was highly optimistic: "I went to see Jessie in Wales last week-end and found her really much better—with health restored, and walking much better—with slight help from sticks still—but immensely freer and bolt upright!"[36]

In September, she was permitted to spend "some family time at Marley—in the rain and fog. But she is gradually getting better—but it is a slow process; but she can walk along [the] <u>creek</u> now again, with sticks."[37] And two months later, with unfazed optimism, Jessie informed Bruce and Rosalind that "my own story is quite a good one:"

> I'm pegging away, under the supervision of a nurse, doing exercises that take the best part of the day; but I am getting quite straight, and there

only remains now to get my knees to bend far enough to get my feet under a chair. They wont [sic] go as far as that yet, so next Monday I'm going to have another anaesthetic—my last, I hope, and then there ought to be a fairly straight road to the happy ending.[38]

Eighteen months later she was still optimistic, despite occasional setbacks: "I am pegging away, I think always walking better, but I am obliged to face yet another operation."[39] She was home for most of the summer of 1929, but by late August she had returned to the Hotel Bellevue—a spa in Trefin, North Wales—seemingly convinced that a cure was just around the corner. Tobias had accompanied her, waiting expectantly to see the braces removed, but when this proved impossible after a few days, she sent him home to finish his book. She wrote Bruce and Rosalind on 28 August, "I am still in bed after nearly five days, having much massage and then I am to be put on my feet by very easy stages; and then after about a fortnight I may—or may not—be pronounced 'A1 at Lloyd's.'"[40] But her problems continued. The proximity of the TMPS to Harley Street may have been a mixed blessing, for whenever Jessie disliked a given prognosis, she was able to shop for doctors with greater ease. On 1 February 1932, she quipped to Simonds,

> I'm just trying out another doctor, who will probably have all my remaining teeth out and dig my tonsils out, and perhaps "if my right hand offends me," he will cut it off. I hope he'll leave my eyes to see you with when you come again. That sounds as if he were an ogre, no such thing—he is the most delightful chap & recommended by Myra.[41]

The doctor may have been C. Yarrow Eccles, whose father had been the Hess's family physician, and to whom Myra was deeply devoted.[42] Myra's biographer describes him as a "homeopath," and by then Jessie's proclivities were clearly leaning more toward "natural" remedies. Denise reported that she was soon obsessed with an all-pudding diet suggested by a physician, but it did little good. In March, as she was preparing for another visit to Hereford, Matthay revealed to Simonds the full extent of her condition. He also added a poignant afterthought:

> Jessie is returning to Hereford next week for a 3 month's treatment, and we are hoping it may bring her back again to some degree of normality and freedom from pain.
> If you have a touch of arthritis <u>do</u> take steps at once—<u>kicking</u> it—don't let it grow on you! Fight it early![43]

A few days later, Jessie spoke of herself in the third person as she expressed her determination to Simonds: "Aunt Jessie is static, rather like a Surrey Hill, but she has got herself on wheels, and hopes to conquer the garden to its very last pathway."[44] Exactly how she emerged from the three months of treatment is unclear, but by October, Matthay reported to Simonds that "Jessie's health fluctuates from time to time—was getting on splendidly, but has had a set-back again this week."[45] But nothing in Jessie or Tobias's letters gives any hint that the prolonged absences placed a strain on their household or on their devotion to one another, even though they were now forced to take separate holidays. In September of 1927, during Jessie's first stint in Wales, Matthay wrote Simonds: "Denise and Dora and I fled to Italy for a fortnight after the U. S. army of visitation left us, and we had some sunshine there (even [though] it was not the real blue sky all the time[)]—and here it rained all the time we were away, and has rained ever since!"[46]

Jessie also made every effort to live as normally as possible and—allowing for her absences—the family's routines were highly predictable. When Denise entered the household, they were dividing their week evenly between London and the country, generally arriving at Wimpole Street on Tuesday afternoons and returning to Marley late Friday evenings. Despite the ease of train connections between Haslemere and Waterloo Station, Matthay always insisted on driving, a decision no doubt influenced by his wife's disability. Over the years he indulged his fascination with machinery through a series of motor cars such as

Chapter 10

the Morris Standard, and at Marley he worked on them as often as once a week. He generally kept his vehicles for some time, and he was fastidious about their mechanical condition, always lubricating them and changing the oil himself. But oddly, his mechanical skill never seemed to extend to the operation of the machine. Denise remembered that he nearly frightened his passengers to death when he took the wheel, driving with utter recklessness, and often paying more attention to the surrounding scenery than to the road ahead. She recalled a holiday in the Scottish Highlands where he became so fascinated with the beauty of the view that she and the other passengers were terrified that at any moment he might take them over a cliff.

In London his car was always housed in its own garage at nearby Wigmore Mews, and on Friday evenings he had it brought to Wimpole Street. Normally, the trip to Marley took slightly over an hour, and in winter, the normal routine was to leave after the evening meal, while in warmer weather they generally packed a cold supper, stopping on the way for an evening picnic at the southwestern edge of London in Richmond Park. Since Jessie did not drive, Matthay had little need for more than one auto, but for a time in the 1920s he owned two simultaneously, and after Denise obtained her license and purchased a car, there were three available in the household. At some point, she wrested the wheel away from him (perhaps in self-defense), and began to handle the driving on their weekly commutes. But as she got older, her schedule became less predictable and she was delighted when, by the mid-1920s, a Mr. and Mrs. Coates had joined the Marley staff as gardener and cook. Coates also served as chauffeur for Matthay and Jessie, appearing like clockwork at Wimpole Street every Friday evening in full-dress uniform to return them to Marley.[47] His precise dates of service are unknown, but it should be noted that on 21 November 1927, Jessie informed Bruce and Rosalind of the family's "latest acquisition," a Scottish chauffeur named Macmilen, "so like the Prince of Wales, that he says it is 'berry embarrassing!'"[48]

The Aftermath

Denise's lack of self confidence also concerned the Matthays, and in retrospect it might even be argued that her virtual fixation on Myra—whom she idolized as an older sibling—was not altogether healthy. In November of 1927, soon after Myra had left for another American tour, Jessie digressed from her discussion of Marley's gardening chores to share some observations with Bruce and Rosalind: "I wish you could have seen Denise this morning holding a spade bigger than herself. I begged her to take pity on her Schumann Concerto, which she is working at to console herself for Myra's absence."[49] Simonds's interest in Denise was understandable, since he thought so much of her that he wanted her to teach all the Americans he sent to the TMPS, and he confessed to Matthay in 1929: "I am getting a little shamefaced about wanting everybody to go to Denise."[50] Inevitably, since the Matthays regarded Myra and Denise virtually as daughters, they fostered a sense of sisterhood between them, but since Jessie's letters often devote more space to Myra's activities, one wonders if Denise was not inadvertently being measured against an impossibly high standard.

To be sure, she was not without ambition, and in the spring of 1932 she even scheduled a pair of Wigmore Hall recitals within two weeks of each other. She concluded her 20 May program with Bach's Concerto in D minor (accompanied by a small string orchestra led by violinist Marjorie Gunn, the sister of Myra's friend Anita), and two weeks later her program included the Brahms Handel Variations. Her reviews on both occasions were mixed, but filled with compliments. *The Times* praised her Bach Concerto for its "forceful rhythm and vitality,"[51] and noted that her Brahms Variations "went behind the notes to the music," featuring "charm of tone," and "a delightfully intimate style."[52] Matthay was thrilled with her efforts, "which have greatly enhanced her reputation as a real 'maker of music,'"[53] and Jessie's report to Simonds five days later was optimistic: "Denise's two recitals would have gladdened your heart. I think now she will believe in herself just a little more."[54]

But on 20 November, as Denise prepared to play the Beethoven Third—as well as an upcoming Wigmore Hall program with cellist Antonia Butler—Jessie's remarks still bore traces of concern:

Chapter 10

> Denise is almost this very moment rehearsing the Beethoven C minor at Eastbourne, that is if the fog allows her to get through. She has her hands full just now with her London recital looming. We are always so glad when she really gets going. I think her fortnight in Holland with Myra spurred her on to realize the joy and forget the nervous misery.[55]

Ironically, though Myra was then enjoying substantial success both in America and Europe, her life was far from stress free. Within a few months, she was diagnosed with fibrocystic breast disease, a condition which troubled her for over a year, prodding her to have both breasts removed at Boston's New England Hospital for Women in the spring of 1934—operations that may have been unnecessary.[56] By June she was home and headed for an extensive recuperative holiday in Devonshire, and not surprisingly, Denise accompanied her.[57] When Myra was in England, the two often seemed inseparable, and as late as November 1935, Jessie was still expressing concerns to Simonds and his wife about Denise's career and—perhaps—her self image:

> Denise is spending the week-end with Myra. She went to Bradford with her on Friday when she played a Mozart Concerto, and now on Wednesday, she will play the [Beethoven] G major at the B.B.C. Orchestral [broadcast]—this is Myra—not Denise. I wish *she* were playing.[58]

The concern Tobias and Jessie showed for Denise was no doubt well intentioned, and in all probability well received. But at times Matthay was drawn into personal matters he would have preferred to avoid. On 12 September 1932, he sent Simonds a somewhat agitated letter from Marley:

> My Dear Bruce,
>
> Harriet Cohen has written one of her periodical lamentations, saying that I am not "proud" of her—etc—also she says that her agent in the States says that the A.M.A. don't do anything for her, and apparently that *you* don't worship her as you should etc etc!!! and asks me to write

The Aftermath

you and tell you her New York Recital is on <u>Nov 18</u>, and that she plays at Boston with Kousevitzki on the 11th and 12th.

Of course I tell her that this is all rubbish and that if she plays as people like it, they will. But if you can do anything to further her—if you think she deserves it—I am sure you will. Perhaps you can tell me <u>how really she has got on in the States</u>? Certainly, she has got to the front rank here and composers choose her to play their works. She played twice at the Proms this week, last night the De Falla (a <u>splendid piece</u>) "in a Spanish Garden" [*Noches en los jardines de España*] and she certainly played <u>remarkably well</u>, and she has a personality quite her own. She has also done well on the Continent and played at the Geneva Conference [Harriet played a recital on 19 June 1932 at the International Disarmament Conference in Geneva] at the invitation of [British Foreign Minister Sir John] Simon etc, so this is to be reckoned with! Her "pushing" proclivities of course go much against the grain with many of us, but still there she is![59]

Ironically, Simonds may have inadvertently roused Harriet's ire, because in February of 1927—some three and a half years before her American debut—he expressed pessimism to Matthay about Irene Scharrer's chances for success in New York:

I'm afraid that she is running up against the same thing which confronts us all here, namely the slight disadvantage of having Paderweski, Hofmann, Rosenthal, Bauer, Godowsky, Cortot, Samuel, Brailowsky, Gieseking, Novaes, Schnelling, Lamond, Rachmaninoff, Gabrilowitsch, Dohnanyi, Prokofieff, to say nothing of hordes of mediocre pianists you never heard of, but followed by a train of admirers, all playing in New York in the same week. If Harriet Cohen or anyone else wants to come to New York, do head her off!! The competition is appalling, and next year we are losing our most important concert hall, Aeolian, which is being turned in[to] a cigar shop or something equally exciting. So piano recitals will doubtless be given in the streets.[60]

When Simonds replied to Matthay about Harriet's "lamentations," he brought forth matters confided only to him—matters that

Chapter 10

Myra had not even shared with Matthay, though he strongly suspected as much. A few weeks later, Matthay's next letter referenced the real roots of Harriet's antagonism:

> My Dearest Bruce,
>
> So many thanks for your candid letter re H. C.—<u>it is exactly as I thought myself</u>! For her to say that Myra has been spoiling her success by ["]running her down" that really is lunacy! I knew she was frantically jealous of Myra, but had no idea it went so far as that! Glad my reading of the matter was no <u>mistake</u> on my part![61]

And less than a week later, after baiting a trap for Harriet, Matthay again wrote to Simonds:

> My dearest Bruce,
>
> I thought it might do some good—as I have been having arguments with Harriet—to tell her that it was reported from America that one had been saying that her success had been spoiled by <u>Myra running her down</u>. Of course I gave no hint where I had heard this. But she was furious, and I have promised to let "my correspondent" know that she categorically and indignantly denies <u>ever having said such a thing</u> of Myra! So I have done my duty by transmitting this denial to you. Sorry to worry you over such matters. They are sordid and have nothing to do with Music-making. Yet one gets drawn into them!!![62]

Whatever the truth of Harriet's assertions, her conflicts with Myra had been building for over 15 years, triggered by the relationship each of them had once had with the composer Arnold Bax. For nearly a decade Myra was Bax's favored interpreter for his piano works, a status that—for whatever reason—she seemed to covet, but which probably worked more to his advantage before the War, since Myra was quickly becoming established, while many still saw Bax merely as a promising newcomer. On 16 February 1910, Bax dedicated his first published piano piece to Myra—his Concert Valse in E-flat—and by May she had performed it three times.[63] Whatever their personal relationship, Bax was not above a bit of manipulation—particularly with women—when it suited his purposes, and it should be noted that beginning in 1910, Myra turned down three marriage proposals in rapid succession: from Aldo Antonietti, Mischa Elman, and Benno Moiseiwitsch.[64] Bax married early in 1911, and whatever feelings Myra may have had for him, she continued to perform his music. But their relationship changed dramatically after she discovered he was having an affair with the nineteen-year-old Harriet.

For years Myra had felt a warm affinity for Irene's cousin, treating Harriet much as a younger sister, and even augmenting her lessons with Matthay with weekly coaching sessions. The precise beginning of the Cohen-Bax liaison is somewhat difficult to determine, because much of their affair was conducted through undated, often melodramatic, correspondence, and—since he was still married—for nearly two years they were each committed to a policy of secrecy. For some time after they first met, Harriet regarded Bax as something of a kindly uncle, but the lengthy letter he wrote her on Christmas Eve 1913, shortly after her eighteenth birthday, suggests that he longed to be more than a mere mentor: "Ah what a wonderful world this would be if we were all perfectly natural, but I suppose it would be a little uncomfortable. But I do want to see you again sometime soon if it can be managed."[65] And exactly one year later, Harriet, who was then spending Christmas at Marley, wrote him with unrestrained passion from her "tiny bed" in Matthay's study: "Dearest in the world—O I am so weary for you. And would give my soul to have your arms about me."[66] Although they were still discrete about their public meetings, two months later she implored him to attend a party Corder and his wife were giving at their Swiss Cottage home: "Do come to the Corders on Sunday—tomorrow—<u>early</u> and I <u>will</u> sit next to you and talk to you!!!"[67]

The gathering proved to be a turning point in their musical relationship. Stunningly beautiful, she wore a dress adorned with a single daffodil, and almost immediately Bax wrote a short piano piece,

Chapter 10

"To a Maiden with a Daffodil," in her honor, subsequently showering her with periodic daffodil bouquets. When the piece was published several months later by Joseph Williams, it bore the inscription "To Tania"—Bax's nickname for Harriet—and Myra may have been unaware of the dedicatee's identity when she premiered it at Aeolian Hall on 24 March. Undoubtedly, Bax finessed some ticklish situations, since he immediately wrote several short pieces for Harriet—all of which he wanted Myra to premiere, as Harriet had yet to make her London debut. The autograph of his rousing "In a Vodka Shop" identifies "Tania" as the dedicatee, but the inscription on Augener's published copy reads "To Miss Myra Hess." Myra premiered the piece on 29 April, sometime after she had introduced Bax to Augener's chief executive, Willy Strecker, and it was largely through her efforts that Bax got the firm to publish it, as well as several additional works. But Bax neglected to mention Myra's involvement when he wrote to Harriet the following week: "I thought it best not to dedicate "The Vodka Shop" to you in print as the "Daffodil" is just coming out, so I have written Myra's name on it. This is better, isn't it, don't you think? Anything makes people talk."[68]

Period photos show that Myra was also beginning to struggle with the weight problems that plagued her for the rest of her life, and even though Bax continued to treat her as one of his closest friends, he could be brutally duplicitous. A week later, after praising Harriet for her performance of several of his pieces, he added a gratuitous, cruel comment: "It is rather pleasing aesthetically to be interpreted by some-one who (to put it vaguely) does _not_ disgrace the human race in her appearance."[69] But Myra gave no hint of any waning admiration for him, and by the fall Harriet felt the need to confide in her. She reported their candid meeting to Bax on 24 October:

> My darling—Myra knows. She said she has known for ages about _you_— but wasn't quite sure about me. O the relief of telling a woman about it!! Myra was perfectly wonderful—and I had a hard fight not to cry—She didn't seem _too_ happy about it . . . . [sic] she was thinking of the "world" I suppose and our suffering. . . .

She said—<u>She</u> would love you whatever you did—but that you were very naughty! She said—"You are only 19 or 20 and have all your life to live yet"—And I told her how I could never love anyone but you in the wide world.[70]

But soon thereafter Harriet was stunned when Myra approached Bax directly "to try to part us," even though she insisted that "my darling friend meant well."[71] And although she may have been overdramatizing for effect, her letters were soon laced with dark, even morbid, thoughts, as when she wrote Bax the following summer while on holiday with friends in Cornwall:

> Tonight the Bechstein Grand for Myra came—Oh!!!!! Think of working here—in this lovely place on such an instrument. I nearly died of envy. Mother Mab [Mabel Galsworthy Reynolds—John Galsworthy's sister—owned the cottage where Harriet was staying] won't let me ever touch it—for fear of sending it out of tune!!! My fingers <u>ache</u> to play. O dear— dear!
>
> I can swim—sometimes I think drowning wouldn't be a bad idea—I thought so this morning again—I wonder why.[72]

And soon she felt that Myra had turned against her, trying to get their mutual friends to take sides: "It's no use—I----yes <u>I am</u> jealous!!! I do believe Myra wants you to fall in love with her and all her friends instead of me!!"[73] But Harriet continued to tempt fate by taking daring risks, and on 11 July she even wrote Bax a love letter on TMPS stationery as she sat at Matthay's desk waiting for a lesson: "O you wonderful lover. I am so happy I have you. Was there ever such completeness in love in this world before?"[74] Within a year, the affair had become common knowledge, and the Matthays—especially Jessie—were pressuring Harriet to break it off:

> I told Uncle Tobs that you were the most generous and unselfish man alive and that you had been Father and Brother to me as well as Lover. . . . It hurt me when Auntie Jessie talked of your "affairs"—but I have been nearly as bad, and <u>in our own case quite</u> as bad.[75] . . .

Chapter 10

But Heavens could Auntie Jessie doubt that whatever you were like—whatever your fault[s] I should stop loving you ever because of them! And I thought her a nice woman. Why I believe the baby of 21 as she called me knows more about Love than she does. And yet everything she says has gone deeply into me. And everything he said too.[76]

Two months later, matters came to a head when Harriet was dealt a severe blow. She wrote to Bax with unusual poignancy:

Darling—You have no doubt seen by now in the papers about the hideous tragedy that was enacted at 8 Carlton Hill—Topsy and Baby (the Burnett girls) never went away at all----I can't write about it—I enclose a paper cutting. From what I know of them I don't think it's an overdose[—]I think it's suicide. It wouldn't be so terrible if they hadn't lain there dead a fortnight—Vera & Judy might get into serious trouble about that I'm thinking—and to think that I was there on Monday night! Poor <u>poor</u> girls . . .

I hope I don't have to go to an inquest or something—I was the only one . . . whom they knew & liked etc. etc. etc. And to think that I—such a little time ago—when the Matthays worried me—nearly did the same thing. You nearly lost me Arnold—sometimes the Russian in me will out.[77]

Stephanie Primrose Compton-Burnett ("Baby"), 18 at the time of her death, and Katharine ("Topsy"), 22, had been living with their two older sisters, Vera and Judy, in a large house at 8 Carlton Hill in St. John's Wood for over two years. Vera and Judy had studied with Matthay at the RAM, and after he referred them to Myra for additional lessons, they all became so close that Myra was soon keeping her studio and lodgings in their basement, to which Harriet was a frequent visitor. According to the partial transcript of the inquest which appeared in *The Times*, Baby and Topsy were last seen alive on Monday evening, 10 December, at about 10:30, when they informed their housekeeper, Ellen Smith, that they were leaving early the next morning for a three-day holiday in the country. When they failed to return home, Smith even went to the West Wickham farm where they had previously stayed, only to discover that they had never arrived.

The Aftermath

When their half-sister, Iris, forced the young women's locked door open on 27 December, she found a gruesome scene in which both "were lying on their right sides. The left hand of the second body was holding the dressing gown of the other."[78] Though the cause of both deaths was unquestionably an overdose of veronal—which both sisters had frequently used to help them sleep—the jury was unable to determine whether the excessive amounts had been inflicted deliberately or accidentally. But their deaths proved to be a watershed in Harriet's relationship to both Myra and the Matthays, as evidenced by the bitter account she offered to Bax the next day:

> Arnold dear—It is very distressing here about the Burnetts. They are at Tor Gardens [the London home of Mabel Reynolds] with Winnie [violinist Winifred Smith, one of Myra's closest friends] and Myra—I've tried & tried but can't get hold of Vera to come and sleep here—I was her best friend you know—I say was because—O well I've hidden a lot from you since last summer[.]
>
> Winnie is taking them to Marley for a fortnight! 3 month[s] ago that would have been me—Since the summer they have been as thick as thieves with Winnie—I have only seen them thrice! They are dear *dear* girls but Winnie has an insidious tongue—is that woman going to leave me a single friend? I ought to have told you this before—but somehow I was too proud to. See how they pay me out for loving you! . . .
>
> And I read of the affair in the paper as I stood on the platform at Swiss Cottage [underground] station—and my first impulse was to throw myself under the oncoming train—it was probably mechanical---sort of "suggestion" I suppose. Myra, Winnie, Ruth [Ruth Howard, a close friend of Myra], Clare [Clare Mackail, a close friend and traveling companion of Myra], Vera, Judy, Mrs. Reynolds, the Matthays, all gone—all loved me so much once[79]

By this point, the Hess-Cohen feud, which continued for the rest of their lives, was well under way, but the Matthays still tried to be amenable. Although only one letter each from Jessie and Matthay have been discovered among Harriet's voluminous British Library

Chapter 10

correspondence, both are filled with glowing compliments. On 5 February 1926, as she was preparing a Bach recital for Academy students, Jessie wrote to her from Hereford: "How I wish I could be there, but I send—blessings—& blessings."[80] And several years later, Matthay praised the "delicacy" of Harriet's rendering of a Haydn Sonata, as he lauded a broadcast performance which "came through splendidly—it was most excellent and really musical throughout. Brava!"[81] But there was never a reconciliation with Myra. Their mutual friends often felt caught in the middle, and Denise tried repeatedly (and unsuccessfully) to counsel Myra out of carrying a grudge—though she knew that such advice would be to no avail with Harriet.[82]

Although Harriet had a knack for connecting with influential people, her American debut in October of 1930 was confined to two chamber works, and probably made less of an impact than she might have wished. Now 35, over the past decade she had specialized in two opposite poles of the repertoire which often connoted intellectuality: the works of Bach (and at times, pre-Bach), and contemporary works—especially those of British composers. The recognition she had received for the latter category gained her an invitation to participate in a four-day festival of largely contemporary chamber works sponsored by Elizabeth Sprague Coolidge at Chicago's Field Museum, and on 13 October Harriet performed Frank Bridge's Piano Trio with members of London's Brosa String Quartet, as well as Bax's *Legende* for Viola and Piano. But though the *New York Times*'s Henry Prunieres found Bridge's work "the great surprise of the festival," full of "ingenuity and the spirit of invention," he said nothing at all about Harriet.[83]

Mrs. Coolidge, who sat in the front row, had also arranged for Harriet to play at the Library of Congress, as well as at Harvard, Princeton, and Yale during her two-month stay, and no doubt Simonds heard her recital when she reached New Haven. Perhaps he also attended her New York debut in Town Hall on 12 November, but the *New York Times* found her program merely "interesting." She brought along some of the chamber players who had worked with her in Chicago, and flutist Georges Barrère assumed the conducting chores in her opening piece, Bach's D minor Concerto. But the *Times* complained that despite "reasonable accuracy" there was "little of the majestic soul of the composer."[84] She also played William Byrd's "A Fancie." which she informed the audience she had personally transcribed from *My Lady Neville's Booke*, and Bax's one-movement Sonata No. 2 in G. The reviewer found both works of interest, but he felt that her Falla group suffered from too much introspection, which he blamed for the pieces' "lack of subtlety, climax, and contrast."[85]

The following year, her next Town Hall appearance, on 30 December 1931, coincided almost exactly with the annual meeting of the American Matthay Association. But she gained nothing from this, since that year—for the first time ever—the meeting was held in Boston rather than New York. Two nights earlier, on Monday, 28 December, Raymond Havens played a recital at Boston University's Jacob Sleeper Hall (for which "formal dress" was required), and the next day the AMA business meeting was held at the Hotel Kenmore on Commonwealth Avenue. It did not escape Harriet's attention that not only had the meeting been moved over 200 miles to the north, but that Myra, who had agreed to judge the annual AMA Scholarship Auditions, was the Association's honored guest, having specially arrived in the States a few weeks before her first American concert in January.[86] She even gave a brief address at the business meeting, where she lamented the "ingratitude" some showed to Matthay:

> There are two remarks often made to me, which sooner or later, will make me lose my temper. The first . . . [all ellipses original] "Do you still have to practice, Miss Hess?" . . . The second . . . "Of course you would have played just as well without a teacher."
>
> We all know the absurdity of these idiotic remarks, but it is the insinuation of ingratitude which hurts me, when people want me to say that I owe nothing to Uncle Tobs. It is for all of us, who have had the advantage of studying with him and coming close to his rare spirit, to uphold the traditions with which he has inspired us, and with all our ability to try and help others, as he has helped us.[87]

Chapter 10

The conference ended that afternoon with a tea in Havens's studio on Copley Square, so McClanahan (then the AMA President) and others who lived in the New York area could have easily attended Harriet's program the next evening. But (perhaps confirming her complaints to Matthay) no mention was made of her concert in any of the AMA publicity materials. Her program opened with two transcriptions of Bach Choral Preludes—one by her, and another by Walter Rummel—followed by Bach's Prelude and Fugue in A minor, probably from Book I of the *Well-Tempered Clavier*. Although she was mildly praised, the review she received in the *New York Times* did little to solidify her reputation as a Bach specialist:

> Miss Cohen's interpretation of Bach was forceful, energetic and faithful to the letter if not to the spirit of the composer. Her tone was dry, sometimes harsh, and her playing did not always achieve the depth and breadth of Bach's conception. This was particularly apparent in the fugue.[88]

But any success Harriet may have sought in America was virtually eclipsed by Myra's popularity, which had already surged to nearly unmatchable heights. Ever since her debut at New York's Aeolian Hall on 17 January 1922, it seemed as though she could do no wrong before American audiences. Even Harriet's Bach expertise had been trumped early on after *New York Times* critic Olin Downes expressed astonishment at Myra's April 1925 recital:

> An incident probably without a precedent in the concert annals of this city occurred at the end of the piano recital given by Myra Hess last night in Aeolian Hall. Miss Hess had completed her program as announced, and had played as an encore a composition of Scarlatti when some one in the hall called out "Bach." The name was taken up by many others in different parts of the auditorium until "Bach" could be heard from every part of the house.
>
> The compositions of Bach do not customarily serve as encores at piano recitals, nor has Bach ever enjoyed the reputation of being food and

The Aftermath

sustenance for the encore fiend. But it was Bach last night who figured as the most popular composer of Miss Hess's program. She responded to her audience with a prelude and fugue from the "Well-Tempered Clavichord." This was not enough. The cry came again, "More Bach," and was taken up as before. Miss Hess played another one of the preludes and fugues of the "Forty-eight" before the audience was satisfied. She then played two more compositions of Scarlatti and finally two etudes of Chopin, thus adding half again to the length of her program—a program which had opened with four of the Chorales of Bach in arrangements for piano by Busoni, and, in the instance of the chorale "Herz und Mund und That und Leben," arranged by Miss Hess herself [published by Oxford the following year as "Jesu, Joy of Man's Desiring"]. . . .

It is precisely in Bach . . . that Miss Hess excels and appears with special distinction among her colleagues. All of the performances of last night were technically brilliant, musicianly and sincere, but probably the wishes of the audience led it aright to the music of Bach, which seems part of the birth-right of a singularly accomplished pianist.[89]

And within ten years, many believed that Myra belonged in a select pantheon of pianistic gods. In June 1935 the American music magazine *The Etude* ran an article called "Lessons from Hearing Great Pianists" by Walter Spry, then the "Musical Director" of South Carolina's Converse College. The article placed Myra's portrait in the middle of an elite dozen, the others being: Anton Rubinstein, Bülow, Paderweski, Rachmaninoff, Hambourg, Hofmann, Godowsky, Gieseking, Iturbi, Horowitz, and Novaes (the only other woman)— all of whom the aging Spry had heard. Although English readers might have felt somewhat patronized by his comments, he no doubt spoke with sincerity:

Last winter I heard Miss Hess play the "Concerto in F major" of Mozart and the *Variations Symphonique* of César Franck. It is seldom that I use the word *perfection*, but to me both performances lacked nothing. Miss Hess is an example of fine talent and training, and we can gather from her how important it is to preserve the spirit of the composer. Her manner is pleasant but confident; and it is interesting to note that the English people have made such advancement that they may now take their place among the most musical nations.[90]

Years later, Simonds observed that any popularity Matthay had enjoyed in the United States was directly related to Myra's American success: "Certainly his books, excellent as they are, would not have made the impact on the public that was made by her playing."[91] But although Myra's eminence with American audiences can scarcely be overstated, she was not the first Matthay-trained artist to enjoy success in the New World. Matthay's first pupil to appear in New York was probably Gertrude Peppercorn, who performed Beethoven's "Emperor" Concerto in Carnegie Hall on 21 February 1904 under Hermann Hans Wetzler, then leading his own recently formed orchestra.[92] She followed this with two recitals at New York's Mendelssohn Hall—on 3 March and again on 24 March, where her program included the Schumann G minor Sonata and the Liszt Sixth Hungarian Rhapsody. She was so well received that three years later she agreed to another extensive tour of American and Canadian cities, beginning on 16 January 1907 with a recital in Washington, D. C. She might have been on the verge of a major career, but on the day she was to have sailed, she sent a cable claiming illness—an excuse her managers immediately questioned. A few weeks later, the *New York Times* reported that she had feigned sickness as a ruse to cover her wedding to painter (later, writer) Stacy Aumonier, who actually sent the cable.[93] Somewhat begrudgingly, the newlyweds arrived on the *Amerika* on 8 February, and the *Times* strongly implied that it was only because she had been threatened with legal action that she now agreed—over the next twelve weeks—to punctuate her honeymoon with performance engagements.

Though she may have been eight years his senior, Peppercorn was smitten with Aumonier, and her amorous lapse may have seriously sabotaged her future prospects with American managers.[94] She began her tour in Boston on 12 February, and she played again in Mendelssohn Hall three days later. Her reception in New York was at least somewhat positive and the *Times* gave generous coverage to her "refreshing unconventionality"—a reference to her opening her program with the Allemande and Gavotte from d'Albert's Suite in D minor, which she followed with a single Brahms Intermezzo and seven of his Waltzes. But the reviewer did not think she was fully effective in Liszt's Sonata:

> Miss Peppercorn is a player of attractive and musicianly qualities and of intelligence, and though she is at present by no means a great artist, her performance was interesting, and gave pleasure in many ways. She was at her best in the lesser pieces, such as those of d'Albert and Brahms, which she played with a clean and incisive technique, crispness and fluency. Liszt's sonata is a matter of a very different sort. It takes a pianist of powerful and imposing personality, who can fill the bombastic measures with a certain sweep and swelling flamboyance. It is pretentious music, but it never rises to the pitch of great art. Miss Peppercorn did some interesting things in her analysis of its musical structure; but she has not the temperament nor the command of sensuous color effects to present the music in the Lisztian spirit. She showed a surprising command over certain of its technical difficulties, and the fugato passage she delivered with clearness and at a rapid pace.[95]

She was heard again in America in 1910, but she did not return until 1924. Although her career was far from over, this was evidently her last appearance in New York, where she played twice in Aeolian Hall. Her second program, on 19 February (exactly one week after Whiteman and Gershwin premiered *Rhapsody in Blue* on the same stage), included Beethoven's "Moonlight" Sonata and Chopin's Sonata in B-flat minor, as well as shorter works by Liszt, Brahms, and Dohnányi. She also played the "Bloomsbury Waltz" of Poldowski, the pseudonym of Polish-born Lady Irène Paul, the youngest daughter of Wieniawski, who had years earlier become a British subject. But the *Times* was merely cordial, noting only that Peppercorn's fans still remembered her: "It was noteworthy that a numerous audience turned out for the English artist in the finest [first?] storm of New York's belated winter."[96]

Chapter 10

Perhaps understandably, when Irene Scharrer finally appeared in the States, she made a far stronger impression. She arrived in February of 1926 on an odd sort of double bill overseen by Otto Klemperer—then serving as guest conductor for the New York Symphony—which placed her in exalted pianistic company. For his program the week of 25 February, he offered the American premiere of Krenek's Concerto Grosso No. 2, followed by Strauss's *Till Eulenspiegel*, and the Prelude and Finale to Wagner's *Tristan*. But on Thursday afternoon and Friday evening he included Josef Hofmann playing the Schumann Concerto, while on Saturday and Sunday afternoon—using the same orchestral repertoire—he accompanied Irene in the Beethoven Fourth. According to the *New York Times*, she acquitted herself admirably with "poetic feeling and refinement of style." The reviewer added, "She was well received and repeatedly called back to the platform."[97] Four days later, she gave her first recital in Aeolian Hall, and although Olin Downes was present only for the first half, he was charmed by her Scarlatti, which he praised for its "fleetness and transparency of tone quality." He also loved her C-sharp minor Prelude and Fugue from Book I of the *Well-Tempered Clavier*, which had "a lyrical grace that became it well," to create the character "of an improvisation of unusual loveliness." He was somewhat less impressed with her Schumann Fantasy, for even though he admired the "imagination, tenderness and also dramatic impulse" in her first movement, he felt that the March was "a little beyond her technical grip." And he added: "The prevailing impression of these performances was of a musician of unquestionable gifts and attainments, but one who has yet to gain her full stature as a virtuoso and her complete individuality as an interpreter."[98]

But within a month, she was back with an all-Chopin program, including the C-sharp minor Scherzo and the B-flat minor Sonata, and on this occasion the *Times* offered not a negative word:

> Miss Scharrer was intimate and suggestive in the short pieces, where her musical tone and her admirable pedaling served well, but she also compressed the bigger and more heroic expressions of Chopin, and understood his more fantastic pages, which often escape the imagination of pianists.[99]

And less than a year later, Downes was so captivated that he drafted an entire essay of tribute. After observing that she played "with a beautiful feeling for the capacities and limitations of the piano, which were always respected, and with unfailing taste," he wrote:

> Miss Scharrer reminded us that the [Chopin] B flat minor prelude is a mildly dramatic utterance in a small compass. The frame is restricted; the mood is headlong, gigantic. No wilder was the ride of Mazeppa on his steed! By contrast was the lyricism and the improvisational character of the A flat impromptu, and its conclusion, so simple, so elusive in its slowly vanishing fragrance. . . At the end of the A minor étude ["Winter Wind"] Miss Scharrer achieved a superb climax.[100]

By November, she was filling Town Hall, where one month later she gave a two-piano program with Myra. Their selections included Mozart's D major Sonata, Schumann's Andante and Variations, the Saint-Saëns Variations on a Theme of Beethoven, and Bax's *Moy Mell*, which he had written for them 11 years earlier. The *New York Times* was overwhelming in its approval, remarking that "it is to be hoped that this will be the first of more performances by them, of the same nature, in the future."[101]

But although neither Myra nor Irene achieved their greatest impact as duo-pianists, another Matthay-trained couple thrived on the medium. In September of 1921, Matthay's RAM pupil Ethel Bartlett (1896-78) married another of his Academy scholars, the Scottish-born Rae Robertson (1893-1956)—who hailed from the village of Ardersier near Inverness—and they soon began working together. For the first three years, they continued to work in England both as soloists and collaborative artists—Ethel most notably with cellist John Barbirolli before he began to focus more on conducting. Rae's appearances were more varied: for example, on 15 August 1923 he performed Strauss's seldom heard *Burleske* at the Proms; on 13 October 1925 he appeared with (then) violinist William Primrose at Wigmore Hall; and on 12 July 1928 he participated in a revival of Stravinsky's *Les Noces* at His Majesty's Theatre—in which

Matthay allied him with Lyell Barbour, Clifford Curzon, and Frank Mannheimer. As duo-pianists, Bartlett and Robertson made their London debut at Wigmore Hall on 17 June 1924 to lukewarm praise, *The Times* reviewer noting that "they have not fully understood yet that the point of playing on two pianos is not to get more sound but to work out intricate detail more clearly."[102] But by 1927, the negativism had been largely replaced by accolades, as when they performed the Mozart E-flat Concerto at the Proms "with exactly the right kind of tone, crisp but not dry, and in exactly the right style, light and also warm."[103] By the end of the decade they were the ranking two-piano team in Britain, if not Europe, and they undertook world tours virtually every season until the War.

But it could be argued that their greatest success came in America, which perhaps influenced their decision to settle in California at the War's end. They made their New York debut at the Guild Theater on 4 November 1928, traversing over three centuries of unconventional repertoire, from Giles Farnaby to Daniel Gregory Mason to Bax, who had recently composed three short works for them: *Hardanger* (1927), *The Poisoned Fountain* (1928), and *The Devil that Tempted St. Anthony* (1928). A year later, he again added to their repertoire with a substantial three-movement Sonata (which the *New York Times* praised as an "impressionistic musical picture of Celtic lore" filled with "delicate and poetic charm"),[104] and in 1931 he presented them with *Red Autumn*. Bartlett and Robertson distinguished themselves by performing virtually all the standard two-piano and four-hand repertoire, but they commissioned new works almost annually. In 1933 Germaine Tailleferre wrote a two-piano concerto for them that they soon performed in Britain and America. In Washington on 31 January 1934, they premiered Lennox Berkeley's transcription of his own Polka—which paraphrased an excerpt from Disney's "Who's Afraid of the Big Bad Wolf?"—for Eleanor Roosevelt. The *New York Times* noted that it "was received with a ripple of amusement quickly followed by an outburst of applause."[105] In New York's Town Hall in 1937, they gave the first performance of *Concerto quasi una fantasia* by Mischa Portnoff, a thirty-six-year-old Brooklyn composer.[106]

The Aftermath

they presented the first New York performance
...ar *Scaramouche* suite—although the *Times* dis-
...vements as "artificial trifles of small moment."[107]
In the spring of 1936, John Barbirolli was given a ten-week contract as interim Conductor of the New York Philharmonic—which soon led to his appointment as its Musical Director—and a reunion with the Robertsons was inevitable. On 10 January 1937, at the final concert in his interim series, the *Times* noted that "he was obviously moved" as he expressed his gratitude to the audience and to the orchestra for being named its permanent conductor.[108] The story added that he also had the cooperation of his "two compatriots" in the Mozart Concerto in E-flat:

> Miss Bartlett and Mr. Robertson form one of the best two-piano teams that are heard here currently. They play Mozart with special felicity. Their performance yesterday had grace and charm and refinement. Their tone rose seldom above forte, but within their scale of dynamics they achieved a wide gamut of expression. This was more than a display of rapport between pianists; it was a recreative performance. Mr. Barbirolli and his orchestra collaborated in the same spirit.[109]

After spending the summer in Britain, Barbirolli returned to New York via the *Britannic* on 10 October. He was met at the pier by Bartlett and Robertson,[110] who also joined him about six weeks later for the Poulenc Concerto for Two Pianos, a composition completed five years earlier which as yet had been little heard in America. Olin Downes spent no less than four paragraphs berating the work, which he found "precious thin stuff," overburdened with musical events "just as inconsequential as what went before, or what comes after. Then the composer suddenly stops. He could have stopped just as well five minutes later, or, better, ten minutes earlier."[111] But he was far kinder to the soloists:

> The interest of the music lay in its performance, which was admirable, scintillating, vigorous, explorative of everything there was in the piece

Chapter 10

to explore. Miss Bartlett and Mr. Robinson, [sic] as they are professionally known, were right worthily applauded for the precision, authority, and vivacity of their playing.[112]

But even as Matthay's pupils were solidifying his reputation at home and abroad, other more immediate, practical problems were confronting the recently incorporated TMPS. On 14 September 1928, about six weeks before Bartlett and Robertson made their New York debut, Matthay took the unusual step of writing British Prime Minister Stanley Baldwin to request government funding for his neediest students. Although his appeal was no doubt wildly misplaced, it was treated with respectful, if bureaucratic, deference as it was shuttled from office to office. His plea rested upon several contentions, but his strongest arguments were 1) that other schools—such as the RAM and the RCM—received annual government grants; 2) that his school was no longer a "proprietary," but now a "permanent" institution; and 3) "that no one else can do this work so well as ourselves."[113] Within two months, Matthay had been steered to the Board of Education, and the letter he sent them on 20 November revealed that his Student's Aid Fund was then yielding only about £100 a year in interest, while he was also careful to stress that the TMPS had achieved greater international stature than any other British musical institution: "Last Summer some 52 artists and head teachers came to our 2 months 'Summer School' <u>for America alone</u>."[114]

On 5 December, W. R. Davies, the principal assistant secretary for "technical and continuation schools," sent an internal memo to S. H. Wood, Private Secretary to Lord Burnham, the Minister of Education, in which he virtually dictated Wood's reply to Matthay:

> With reference to your letter of the 20th ultimo, I am directed to state that the Board of Education have no power under their Regulations to pay direct grants for the assistance of promising pianists.
>
> Local Educational Authorities are enabled to incur expenditure on Maintenance Allowances to students or places of Higher Education, and certain Authorities have made arrangements whereby students have

The Aftermath

been assisted to pursue their studies at Schools of Music. The Board can only suggest that a student who desires to obtain such an allowance should make application to the Local Education Authority of the area in which he resides and give such evidence as maybe available of his need for assistance and of his capacity to profit by the instruction which he desires to obtain.[115]

Wood was also instructed to advise Matthay that the yearly £500 grant made to the RAM (which had begun under Gladstone) was conferred directly by the Treasury. And in a private postscript, Davies informed Wood that he had shown all the Matthay correspondence to the Duchess of Atholl, the Parliamentary Secretary to Education, who "does not feel that the Tobias Matthay School is in any case a national institution of the type that might deserve special consideration."[116]

Perhaps not surprisingly, when Matthay applied to the London County Council, it refused to accede to his requests. As late as August of 1932, he was still unable to obtain assistance for any needy students from the Metropolitan area, and the LCC advised him that such funding was prohibited by law unless the TMPS had first been "recognized" by the Board of Education. But when Wood's successor, G. G. Williams, investigated the matter, he found that Matthay had originally been told by P. G. Fawcett, an LCC education officer, that his school had been denied funding because she regarded it as a "proprietary institution." Only when Matthay corrected her did she bring up the issue of "recognition," an arguably inappropriate response, since the Board of Education had no authority over universities or institutions like the RAM or the RCM, where LCC funds regularly offset the fees of needy Londoners. In a letter dated 17 September, Williams took Fawcett to task for her inconsistency and requested the "real reason" for her refusal, even suggesting that "your advisers do not think much of Matthay's School."[117] Three days later she answered him—albeit in bureaucratic doubletalk:

> Thank you for your letter about the Matthay School. I do not think we have exactly shifted our ground because if the school were still as it once

was a proprietary institution, that reason would be sufficient in itself. As, however, it is said not to be a proprietary institution we have to consider its suitability for the attendance of Council scholars. I am afraid that the phrase "recognized by the Board of Education" was perhaps not quite happily chosen. It is a stock phrase which we use in regard to secondary schools and training colleges, but it is perhaps not quite applicable to a place like the Matthay School, though of course the school would have to be "recognized" by the Board in the sense that the Board would have to regard our expenditure on paying the fees of scholars there as qualifying for 50 per cent. grant. [sic] But the real condition is that the institution would have to be inspected by the Council's inspectors. . . . As I said on the telephone, our scholarship system is intended for the benefit of the scholars and not for the benefit of the schools, so that if we have sufficient suitable places recognized we do not feel under any obligation to recognise another place, even though it might be very nearly as suitable.

I suggest, therefore, that you should reply . . . that the question of the place of tenure of awards is one for the L. E. A. [Local Education Authority—or in this case the LCC, which was evidently asserting the right to withhold funds simply because it chose to do so.][118]

With an enrollment nearing 400 by 1925, Matthay had easily lived up to the additional floor space provided by his next-door annex at 95 Wimpole Street, but in 1927 Debenhams decided to demolish the house, and the TMPS was soon forced to vacate its premises. For a time, the merchandising giant considered razing most of the block (which it now owned freehold), but since No. 96 had been rebuilt some 30 years previously, the School was finally permitted to remain. Eventually, Debenhams even allowed the airshaft and smaller rooms at the back of the house to be expanded into a one-hundred-seat auditorium. The project was well under way by March of 1929, when Jessie informed Simonds and his wife that "the new lecture-concert room is already almost as high as the roof."[119] While this was a welcome, even superior, replacement to the old TMPS concert room at No. 95, one wonders at Jessie's comment in her book that the building's "Owners" volunteered "to build a little Concert-Hall at the rear of '96,'" since she makes it appear that Debenhams presented it to the School as a gift, and this is extremely unlikely.[120] In all probability, the TMPS was required to advance all or most of the funds, which may explain some of Matthay's financial concerns through this period. On 28 August 1929, Jessie wrote Bruce and Rosalind that the summer had been "very happy," in spite of "terrible dust and noise at Wimpole Street," and that Tobias had "thoroughly enjoyed most of the work."[121] Oxford's music division had agreed to use the new hall for its offices during the day and the TMPS arranged to rent additional teaching spaces from the Wigmore Galleries—housed in the Hall of the same name—around the corner.

But though Matthay was spared the anxiety of a complete relocation, his renovation expenditures were augmented by the increased tax bill he faced after improving the Wimpole Street property. When he first moved to No. 96, he paid rates of around £30 a year, and by 1927 they had risen to £52, 19s, 2d. However, by April of 1932 the ratable value of No. 96 had jumped to £288 (an increase of more than £100 from its 1909 value), and he was now paying £132 annually in taxes.[122] The timing of these additional outlays was unfortunate, because the TMPS was now also experiencing substantial enrollment decreases. Matthay's own figures, provided on a form he completed for the Board of Education on 14 March 1933, indicate that the School's enrollment dropped from 285 in 1930, to 249 in 1931, to 235 in 1932. These totals did not include the Americans who appeared in the summer, but those numbers showed an even more dramatic decline—from 60 in 1931 to about 30 just a year later.[123] The economic woes wrought by America's Depression were now surging through Europe as well, but the speech Matthay gave at Queen's Hall on 21 July 1931 showed that—despite his pleas for public assistance—he still held fast to the virtues of Spencerian self reliance:

> The financial conditions in this country, as in every other country, are indeed grave. We cannot look for any betterment here—so long as those

Chapter 10

of us who have sufficient Self-Respect to wish to work, and wish to work their best, are penalized for the upkeep of the many who refuse to work!...

While the roll-call of this School, like that of every other Music-school in the world, continues to give anxiety, yet we can record with much satisfaction the fact that the actual standard of talent and achievement is ever higher. This year is, in fact, a record in this respect.[124]

Matthay then made reference to a number of students whose work had been especially distinguished in the previous year:

> Mrs. [Annie] Woodward-Smith, an ex-pupil of the School [she actually first studied with Matthay when he served as an RAM sub-professor of harmony in the 1870s[125]], has munificently presented us with £600 for the endowment of a scholarship in memory of her late husband. The first competition for this scholarship was held last April [the competition was actually held in late March and adjudicated by Bartlett and Robertson], and was awarded to a worthy recipient indeed in Miss Eileen Joyce from Australia.[126]

The Woodward-Smith fund was then yielding £27 per annum in interest, and at the request of the donor, the Scholarship was renewable once by open audition, so that a recipient could hold it for two consecutive years. Eileen Joyce, then 23, had been born to a miner in Zeehan, Tasmania, and her childhood was spent in abject poverty. The fourth of six surviving children, she was forced to wear whatever garments her mother could devise when she began attending a convent school in nearby Boulder, and she received sharp taunts from classmates for "wearing pants made from flour sacks with the brand still visible on the fabric."[127] Her father finally permitted her to study piano with a nun for sixpence a lesson, and she was soon rising at four so that she could practice for several hours before her classes began. After disgruntled neighbors threw a rock through the window, she developed the habit of playing just to "the point of sound" (a term she later learned from Matthay), which enabled her to perform her pieces with precision at a *pianissimo* level.[128] She was forced by financial circumstances to leave school at 13, but three years later, through the generosity of several priests and townspeople, she was sent to Osborne, a boarding school near Perth run by the Loreto Order. There she was taught by Sister John More, an accomplished musician who successfully prepared her for the L.R.A.M. exam, and soon her musical abilities were beguiling a chain of admirers extending up to the Prime Minister of Western Australia. When the town's "Eileen Joyce Fund" fell short of the £1,000 it sought to send her abroad, Sister John intercepted the Melbourne-born Percy Grainger during a concert tour, who wrote an impassioned letter to a Perth newspaper, dubbing her "the most transcendentally gifted young piano student I have heard in the last twenty-five years."[129]

Grainger was adamant that she not be "needlessly 'Europeanised' or 'Continentalised,'" but sent instead to "an Australian master in his prime," or more specifically, to New York's Juilliard School, where she could study with another Melbourne native, Ernest Hutcheson, "whom I consider to be the greatest living piano teacher anywhere."[130] The fund raising continued, with Eileen frequently performing at parties and at a local cinema, but when Wilhelm Backhaus passed through Perth, the committee eventually agreed with his suggestion to send her to the Leipzig Conservatory, where Hutcheson had trained years earlier with Reinecke. She was accepted by Max Pauer, the Conservatory's Director, and on Boxing Day, 1926, sporting several "freshly washed, starched and pressed" school uniforms packed in a battered trunk on which an Osborne art student had painted her initials, she set sail on the *Mooltan*.

But when she reached Leipzig, Pauer decided she was not prepared for his class and sent her to his colleague Robert Teichmüller, who insisted that she "practice scales and exercises (rather than pieces) for weeks on end, often using a hard tabletop instead of a keyboard."[131] For a variety of reasons—not the least being that the money raised by her committee was nearly gone—Eileen felt compelled to leave Leipzig after graduating from the Conservatory, and with the assistance of a New Zealand couple, she relocated to London. But she aroused little interest with concert agents, who told her that she lacked "the imprimatur of London's leading piano academy."[132] After Myra arranged for her to play for Matthay, she was well settled into the School's regimen by

Chapter 10

the fall of 1930. In February, Matthay referred to her as "an Australian artist of 19"[133] (by then she had shaved four years off her age), and a year later he told Simonds that she was "an Australian genius."[134]

Though she stood less than 5'2", she was often capable of aggressive self promotion. Shortly after she began at the TMPS, her first break came when she took the score of Prokofiev's Third Concerto to conductor Albert Coates, who had been a classmate of Teichmüller years earlier in Leipzig. Coates was so flabbergasted by her command of its difficult passages that he brought her to the attention of Henry Wood, who asked her to perform the work at a Proms concert on 7 September 1930. Although *The Times* deigned to review the fledgling newcomer, Wood was so impressed that he promised her another engagement if she agreed to learn Franck's *Symphonic Variations*.[135] Her first TMPS Practice Concert appearance was on 6 February 1931 at Conway Hall, where she performed the Glazunov Theme and Variations, a great favorite of Bowen, who may have first brought the work to Matthay's attention. Understandably, after she won the Woodward-Smith prize, she was also prominently featured in the TMPS Summer Festivals, performing the Scherzo and Finale from Saint-Saëns's Second Concerto at Wigmore Hall on 7 July (with Denise at the second piano), and repeating the Glazunov two weeks later at Queen's Hall. On 7 December she returned to Conway Hall with Chopin's Scherzo in C-sharp minor, and the following summer she performed three Scriabin Preludes for the Festival in Aeolian Hall on 30 June, before offering Haydn's Sonata in A-flat, Hob. XVI/43, at the final Queen's Hall concert on 12 July.

At Conway Hall on 28 October she performed a Brahms Capriccio plus two Bach Chorale transcriptions, including Myra's "Jesu, Joy of Man's Desiring." On 16 February 1933, she played Grainger's "Handel in the Strand" and Liszt's "La Leggierezza," pairing the latter with his "Waldesrauschen" for the Queen Hall's closer later that season on 11 July. Ten days earlier at Wigmore Hall she performed Hummel's Rondo in E-flat with the demanding Etude in A-flat by Paul de Schlözer (1841-98), and three weeks before that, on 8 June, she had paired the Schlözer with "Leggierezza" for her first Parlophone record, a "vanity" recording to which one of her male admirers had committed £20. The disc was meant purely to enhance her marketability to concert agents, but when Parlophone executives listened to it, they were so overwhelmed with her virtuosity that they had it placed in record shops by August.[136] Wood had made good on his promise to feature her in Franck's *Variations*—on which Myra coached her—and they performed together at Hull in April 1931. This led to a Queen's Hall performance in December of 1934 with the LPO under Beecham, who paired the work with Franck's Symphony. *The Times* was impressed, noting that:

> A new pianist, Miss Eileen Joyce, made a good impression of judgment and sensibility. She played her opening phrase without the pedal and was very sparing throughout of mere sonority for sonority's sake. This clean definition and the consistent finesse of her playing fitted in well with Sir Thomas Beecham's general approach to Franck, which is to divert attention from colour to line.[137]

But notwithstanding the success of yet another of his graduates, Matthay was still unsuccessful in obtaining government assistance for any TMPS scholars, regardless of nationality. And despite Fawcett's assertions, he knew all too well that the LCC's policies were clearly designed to favor specific schools, rather than individual students. But he tenaciously continued his fight to effect changes in the government's practices, and although naïveté may have offset an increasing sense of desperation wrought by a bleak economy, he doubtless believed that such changes would be to the good of all. On 16 March 1933, he informed the Board of Education that yet another paradox of government policies was embodied by the fact that the TMPS had long been approved by the Teacher's Registration Council as a training ground for teachers who taught in the schools served by the LCC:

> One would think that the greater includes the less, and as we <u>are</u> accepted as "efficient" enough to teach the teacher we ought to be sufficiently

efficient to teach the student. But unfortunately, the London County Council regulations are blind in this respect, and insist on the recognition by <u>your Board</u>. Hence we shall be compelled to continue worrying you.[138]

But by this point the wagons had been firmly circled, and no government agency was willing to grant largesse to the TMPS—even when highly influential voices were raised in its advocacy. On 1 June 1933 Lord Irwin, the recently appointed Minister of Education, received a letter from Lady Ethel Snowden, the wife of Viscount Snowden, former Chancellor of the Exchequer:

Dear Lord Irwin,

I am enclosing a letter from a cousin of my husband (Viscount Snowden), Miss Marion Keighley Snowden, which speaks for itself. [Marion Snowden was a long-time student of Matthay, and had taught at the TMPS for a number of years.]

I do not know anybody on the Board of Education, but I feel sure you will do what is necessary to enable Dr. Tobias Matthay [sic] to have his very excellent school treated as it deserves to be.

Amongst his pupils are numbered such famous Artistes [sic] as Miss Myra Hess and Miss Harriet Cohen, and a host of others too many to be named.

Not only is Dr. Matthay a great teacher, but he is a man of the very highest ideals. I have heard him lecture, and have been very much moved by his wise and inspired words.

The name "Uncle Tobs" used in Miss Snowden's letter is the affectionate designation of some hundreds of admiring pupils in every part of the world.[139]

As a result of Irwin's intervention, Matthay received a highly deferential letter from his secretary, G. G. Williams, several weeks later. Once again, Williams assured him that no "recognition" from the Board was necessary, and that he should simply re-apply to the

The Aftermath

LCC.[140] He even offered to grant him a personal interview to discuss the matter further, but in Matthay's response of 23 June, he declined. He assured Williams that he would re-apply to the LCC, thanked him for his time and attention, and sent him five complimentary tickets to the Summer Festival.[141] But after five years of struggling, the fight was over, and Matthay had finally conceded defeat.

Several months before he engaged in his final correspondence with the Board of Education, Tobias Matthay had turned 75. He had spent his entire life sowing seeds which he might have expected to blossom in his maturity, and unquestionably many of them had. But much to his amazement, after devoting his life to science, he now found his work attacked as "unscientific." The School he had spent much of his life building was now also experiencing financial difficulties, largely due to a worldwide economic depression which he could not have foreseen. And any personal discretionary income he may have had was being rapidly eroded by Jessie's escalating medical expenses. Years earlier, Matthay might have envisioned a calm, perhaps serene retirement in his later years. But now the rules had changed so substantially that it was as though the world he had once known no longer existed.

Many close to him now saw the road ahead—or what remained of it—laden with disturbing uncertainties.

Notes

1. MA. Letter from Matthay to Simonds, 9 May 1926.
2. Otto Ortmann, *The Physical Basis of Piano Touch and Tone* (London, 1925), 14. Hereafter cited as Ortmann, *Basis*.
3. Ortmann, *Basis*, viii.
4. Ortmann, *Basis*, 6.
5. Ortmann, *Basis*, 18.
6. Ortmann, *Basis*, 36.
7. Ortmann, *Basis*, 38.

8. Otto Ortmann, *The Physiological Mechanics of Piano Technique* (New York, rep., 1962), 157-58.
9. *MT*, 1 December 1929, 1084.
10. Ibid.
11. Ortmann, *Physiological Mechanics*, 376.
12. See Tobias Matthay, "On Memorizing" (London: Oxford University Press, 1926).
13. "On Memorizing," 8.
14. Ibid.
15. "On Memorizing," 4.
16. "On Memorizing," 5. The quote is taken from *MI*, 42.
17. Ibid.
18. "On Memorizing," 6.
19. MA. Matthay to Simonds, 16 June 1931.
20. Tobias Matthay, *VIPT* (London, rep. 1964), ix.
21. *VIPT*, x.
22. *VIPT*, 50.
23. *VIPT*, 157-59.
24. *VIPT*, 160-61.
25. *VIPT*, xii.
26. See MKF, 151.
27. LI.
28. This was to be raised to £600 per annum in the event one of them died, and this amount could be met from TMPS income if necessary. The Will of Jessie Henderson Matthay, probated on 14 April 1937, is on file at the FRO.
29. In Matthay's letter to Simonds dated 16 June 1931—four years after Jessie drew her will—he mentions a desire to go to Paris in September, "to see Denise's mother's new flat." MA.
30. MA. Jessie to Bruce and Rosalind Simonds, 21 Nov. 1927.
31. MA. Jessie to Simonds, 7 Dec. 1930.
32. "Mrs. Kennedy-Fraser[:] The Songs of the Hebrides," *TT*, 24 Nov. 1930, 14, col. D.
33. *TT*, 28 Nov., 1930, 19, col. C.
34. MA. Simonds to Matthay, 8 Mar. 1927.
35. MA. Matthay to Simonds, 18 Apr. 1927.

36. MA. Matthay to Simonds, 9 Jun. 1927.
37. MA. Matthay to Simonds, 19 Sept. 1927.
38. MA. Jessie to Bruce and Rosalind Simonds, 21 Nov. 1927.
39. MA. Jessie to Bruce and Rosalind Simonds, 17 Mar. 1929.
40. MA. Jessie to Bruce and Rosalind Simonds, 28 Aug. 1929.
41. MA. Jessie to Simonds, 1 Feb. 1932.
42. Eccles had attended Myra's mother in the final stages of her cancer in 1929-30, and he counseled Myra after her two radical mastectomies (performed in Boston in April 1934), both of which he thought were unnecessary. That summer she took Eccles and his entire family with her to Devonshire to recuperate. See McKenna, *Myra Hess*, 94-102.
43. MA. Matthay to Simonds, Easter Sunday [27 Mar., 1932].
44. MA. Jessie to Simonds, [Apr. 1932].
45. MA. Matthay to Simonds, 7 Oct. 1932.
46. MA. Matthay to Simonds, 19 Sept. 1932.
47. LI.
48. MA. Jessie to Bruce and Rosalind Simonds, 21 Nov. 1927.
49. Ibid.
50. MA. Simonds to Matthay, 24 June, 1929.
51. "Miss Denise Lassimonne," *TT*, 23 May 1932, 12, col. D.
52. "Miss Denise Lassimonne's Recital," *TT*, 6 June 1932, 10, col. D.
53. MA. Matthay's speech to the TMPS at Queen's Hall, 12 July 1932.
54. MA. Jessie to Simonds, 8 June 1932.
55. MA. Jessie to Bruce and Rosalind Simonds, 20 Nov. 1932.
56. See McKenna, 101-02. Less than half a dozen people knew the nature of Myra's surgery. Years later, Denise implied that Myra had never even confided it to her. LI.
57. MA. Jessie to Simonds, 17 June 1934.
58. MA. Jessie to Bruce and Rosalind Simonds, 25 Nov. 1935.
59. MA. Matthay to Simonds, 12 Sept. 1932.
60. MA. Simonds to Matthay, 2 Feb. 1927.
61. MA. Matthay to Simonds, 7 Oct. 1932.
62. MA. Matthay to Simonds, 12 Oct. 1932.
63. Foreman, *Bax*, 75.
64. McKenna, 45.

Chapter 10

65. Bax to Cohen, 24 Dec. 1913, BL.
66. Cohen to Bax, 24 Dec. 1914, BL.
67. Cohen to Bax, 27 Feb. 1915, BL.
68. Bax to Cohen, 5 May 1915, BL.
69. Bax to Cohen, 14 May 1915, BL.
70. Cohen to Bax, [24 Oct.] 1915, BL. The date is established by a letter Bax wrote to Cohen on the same day.
71. Cohen to Bax, dated only "Saturday morning," boxed in sequence with letters from late 1915, BL.
72. Cohen to Bax, 10 Aug. 1916, BL.
73. Cohen to Bax, undated from 1916. In the text Harriet says "it is spring now." BL.
74. Cohen to Bax, 11 July 1916, BL. Harriet even mailed the letter in a TMPS envelope.
75. Cohen to Bax, 22 Oct. 1917, BL.
76. Cohen to Bax, written between 24 and 28 July 1917, BL.
77. Cohen to Bax, 29 Dec. 1917, BL.
78. "St. John's Wood Veronal Poisoning Case[:] The Death of Two Sisters, *The Times*, 31 Dec, 1917, 10, col. G. The inquest was held two days after the bodies were discovered, on Saturday, 29 December.
79. Cohen to Bax, 30 Dec. 1917, BL.
80. Jessie to Harriet, 5 Feb. 1926, BL.
81. Matthay to Harriet, 31 July 1933, BL.
82. LI.
83. Henry Prunieres, "The Coolidge Festival in Chicago," *NYT*, 19 Oct. 1930, 120.
84. "Harriet Cohen's Recital," *NYT*, 13 Nov. 1930, 36.
85. Ibid.
86. McKenna, 98.
87. *The American Matthay Association Summer Journal*, 19. The date of Myra's address is incorrectly given as "December 28th, 1931," but the Association's Minutes confirm that the business meeting was held the following day. MA.
88. "Harriet Cohen in Recital," *NYT*, 31 Dec. 1931, 22.
89. Olin Downes, "Myra Hess's Recital," *NYT*, 2 Apr. 1925, 18.
90. Walter Spry, "Lessons from Hearing Great Pianists," *The Etude* (June 1935): 378.

91. Bruce Simonds, "Myra in America," in Denise Lassimonne and Howard Ferguson, eds., *Myra Hess by her Friends* (London 1966), 55.
92. *NYT*, 21 Feb. 1904, 8. At the time Wetzler was such an imposing figure that the following week he turned his baton over to his friend Richard Strauss, who conducted a program of his own works, including *Ein Heldenleben*. See "Richard Strauss Appears," *NYT*, 28 Feb. 1904. 7.
93. See "Gertrude Peppercorn Ill," *NYT*, 16 Jan. 1907, 7, and "Will Sing on Honeymoon," *NYT*, 8 Feb., 1907, 9.
94. Some sources give Aumonier's year of birth as 1877, insisting that the 1887 date often given is incorrect. However, his 1928 *Times* obituary gives his age as 41, which seems to verify the 1887 date. See *TT*, 27 Dec. 1928, 17, col. D.
95. "Miss Peppercorn's Recital," *NYT*, 16 Feb. 1907, 9.
96. "Gertrude Peppercorn Plays," *NYT*, 20 Feb. 1924, 23.
97. "Irene Scharrer Soloist," *NYT*, 1 Mar. 1926, 16. Ironically, her Carnegie Hall performance on 27 February was directly opposite a solo recital by Simonds in Town Hall.
98. Olin Downes, "The Scharrer Recital," *NYT*, 5 Mar., 1926, 25.
99. "Irene Scharrer's Recital," *NYT*, 10 Apr. 1926, 15.
100. Olin Downes, "Irene Scharrer's Recital," *NYT*, 13 Feb. 1927, 28.
101. "Myra Hess in Recital with Irene Scharrer," *NYT*, 8 Dec. 1927, 33.
102. "Two Pianos, *TT*, 20 June 1924, 12, col. B.
103. "Promenade Concert," *TT*, 14 Sept. 1927, 8, col. D.
104. "Recital for two Pianos," *NYT*, 24 Jan. 1930, 30.
105. "President's Wife A Hostess to Five," *NYT*, 1 Feb. 1934, 16.
106. "Duo-Pianists Give Town Hall Recital," *NYT*, 1 Nov. 1937, 25.
107. "English Duo-Pianists," *NYT*, 6 Nov. 1938, 48.
108. "Barbirolli Ends his Season Here," *NYT*, 11 Jan. 1937, 16.
109. Ibid.
110. "Barbirolli Here after Trip Abroad," *NYT*, 11 Oct. 1937, 19.
111. Olin Downes, "Poulenc Offered at Carnegie Hall," *NYT*, 26 Nov. 1937, 27.
112. Ibid.
113. Matthay to Board of Education, 20 Nov. 1928, PRO ED7416/102740.
114. Ibid.
115. Memo from Davies to Wood, 5 Dec. 1928, PRO ED7416/102740.
116. Ibid.

117. G. G. Williams to G. Fawcett, 17 Sept. 1932, PRO ED7416/102740.
118. Fawcett to Williams, 20 Sept. 1932, PRO ED7416/102740.
119. MA. Jessie to Bruce and Rosalind Simonds, 17 Mar. 1929.
120. Jessie, 83. Jessie also implies that the concert room was built in 1927, but this is contradicted by the letters she wrote Simonds.
121. MA. Jessie to Bruce and Rosalind Simonds, 28 Aug. 1929.
122. Cavendish Ward Rate-Books at the Westminster Archives. In 1927, No. 96 was moved to Ward 9 in the City of Westminister.
123. Matthay to the Board of Education, 14 Mar. 1933. PRO ED7416/102740.
124. Matthay's Queen's Hall Speech to the TMPS, 21 Jul. 1931. MA. Hereafter cited as QHS.
125. JHM, 24.
126. QHS.
127. Richard Davis, *Eileen Joyce[:] A Portrait* (Fremantle, Australia, 2001), 22. Hereafter cited as Davis.
128. Davis, 25-26.
129. Davis, 37.
130. Davis, 38.
131. Davis, 50-51.
132. Davis, 57.
133. MA. Matthay to Simonds, 16 Feb. 1931.
134. MA. Matthay to Simonds, Easter Sunday [27 Mar. 1932], Davis (p. 14) indicates that Eileen frequently changed or embellished biographical details. For a number of years, she told Londoners that she had been born in a tent in Tasmania and that no record existed of the year, though she believed it to have been 1912.
135. Davis, 62.
136. Davis, 70-72.
137. "London Philharmonic Orchestra," *TT*, 22 Dec. 1934, 8, col. C.
138. Matthay to the Board of Education, 16 Mar. 1933. PRO ED7416/102740.
139. Ethel Snowden to Lord Irwin, received 1 Jun. 1933. PRO ED7416/102740.
140. Williams to Matthay, 19 Jun. 1933. PRO ED7416/102740.
141. Matthay to Williams, 23 Jun. 1933. PRO ED7416/102740.

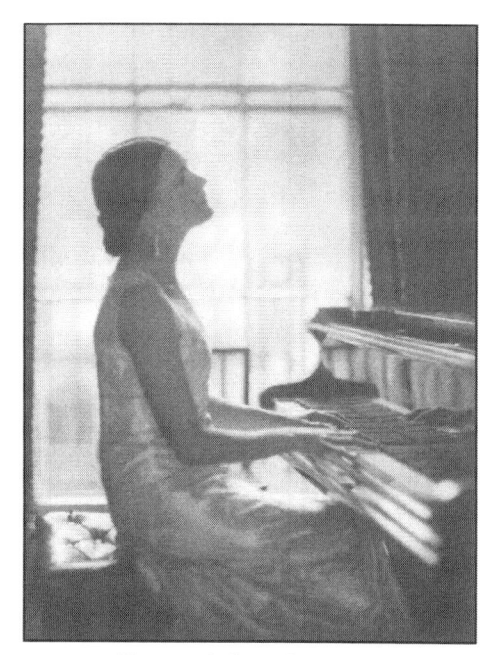

Harriet Cohen about 1930

Photo of Matthay taken about 1935 by his American pupil Paul Snyder

CHAPTER 11

"WHETHER HE IS WRITING REAL MUSIC"

On 22 March 1933, Jessie penciled a long letter to Bruce and Rosalind Simonds, which read in part:

> We took part in the 4th of March Inauguration [of Franklin Roosevelt], and Miss [Pearl] Waugh [a student of Matthay who lived in Washington, D.C.] sent us an enormous number of the Sunday papers, and America doesn't feel far away at all. We are beginning to feel very Eastery, just another week of the School term so that the concerts and other fixtures are beginning to head on each other's heels. Edwin and Ina Gerschefski took leave of us last week for where—I don't quite know. He was eagerly expecting news of gaining the Guggenheim Scholarship [annual fellowships awarded in America by the Guggenheim Foundation to further graduate studies in the arts] but as he has not written it looks as if it were not coming his way. He has developed greatly in many ways, but in respect of his musical idiom [as a composer] he is perplexing. It is difficult to believe that one can so completely outgrow the understanding of those to whom music has been the language of a lifetime. And yet, there is no doubt about his sincerity.[1]

Simonds had sent Gerschefski to Matthay soon after his graduation from Yale, and he arrived no later than July of 1931 at the age of 22, already married (his wife studied with Denise) and determined to make his mark as both composer and pianist.[2] On 11 November he made his TMPS debut with the Schumann Toccata, and after he won the School's Silver Medal six months later, Jessie wrote Simonds approvingly that "his playing surprised one at every fresh hearing."[3]

Chapter 11

But the Matthays could neither understand nor endorse his compositional idiom, which troubled Jessie so much that she complained about it whenever she wrote to Simonds. The following November, Gerschefski convinced Gertrude Peppercorn to perform some of his unpublished Preludes at Aeolian Hall, and Jessie was scarcely surprised at the press reaction:

> Gershefski [sic] is forging ahead. Gertrude Peppercorn played some of his things at her recital last Tuesday. The Daily Telegraph, I fear, did not like them, rather underlining Uncle Tobs' fears as to whether he is writing real music. Gershefski is, of course, sure about it. It may be that after all he is sharpening his tools for something better.[4]

If anything, Jessie understated the *Telegraph*'s negative reaction. Peppercorn surrounded Gerschefski's pieces with the Schumann *Symphonic Etudes*, the Beethoven "Waldstein" Sonata, and several shorter works by Debussy and Chopin, and the fact that she was praised for her efforts merely underscored the paper's devastating assessment of the young composer:

> Since it is good to hear new things, one may be grateful to Miss Peppercorn for having played them. Assuredly few pianists will trouble to wrestle with their technical difficulties which emphasise the composer's crudity of expression and do not conceal his emptiness of thought.
>
> Miss Peppercorn afterwards, in some Debussy pieces showed how a master writes for the piano, and offers incidentally plenty of opportunity for legitimate virtuosity.[5]

But it was not merely Gerschefski's complexity that caused Jessie to lament that his music "might come from another planet,"[6] because his harmonic palette also tended toward uncompromising, even savage dissonance. For example, his *Three Dances*, composed about the same time, contain several pounding excursions into bitonality:

Ex. 11.1 Edwin Gerschefski: Dance, Op. 11, no. 2, from Three Dances, mm. 29-31

The 1930s wrought a cruel irony to Matthay, who had spent a lifetime championing the efforts of younger composers. The new wave which Gerschefski represented sought at times to inflict the aural equivalent of Edvard Münch's *The Scream* on its audiences, and many older listeners, including the *Telegraph*'s critic, found such an idiom repugnant. But if the *avant garde* often seemed unintelligible to Matthay's generation, the irony was compounded by the fact that so many Matthay artists—including Peppercorn—were regarded as pace setters in the cause of contemporary music. By 1930, they had introduced dozens of British works to the public, and in addition, they were often seen as leading promoters of the newest European styles. Bartlett and Robertson performed all of Stravinsky's four-hand and two-piano works, and Bartók even dedicated his *Six Dances in Bulgarian Rhythm* to Harriet Cohen.[7] But no Matthay student ever did more for contemporary music than his South African pupil Adolph Hallis (1896-1987), who left his native Port Elizabeth in 1912 for the RAM, where he studied with Beringer. The War forced him home in 1915, but by the early 1920s he had returned to London for study with Matthay, who included him in his 1922 RAM concert that paid tribute to Academy composers. Through this period Hallis also toured extensively in Europe, though largely with traditional repertoire. In 1926, Matthay added him to the staff of the TMPS, and by the end of the decade his performances of solo and chamber works had become virtual staples of early BBC programming. His interests were wide, and soon he had even composed symphonic soundtracks for two early Hitchcock films: the visually opulent *Rich and Strange* (1931), and the taut, suspenseful *Number Seventeen* (1932).[8]

In April 1936, he performed the recently composed Shostakovitch Concerto for Piano, Strings, and Trumpet in Birmingham,[9] and in the same year he founded The Adolph Hallis Chamber Music Concerts which, as Caroline Mears observes, were "notable for their enterprising programmes."[10] Three years later, the second War forced him to return to South Africa, but through this brief period he was one of the most visible figures on London's contemporary music scene—even though his stated purpose was to promote "forgotten works of the past" as well as "new works of the immediate present."[11] For example, on 15 February 1937, he oversaw a Wigmore Hall performance of Couperin's *Concert instrumental sous le titre d'Apothéose*, 14 pieces for two violins, cello, and harpsichord, composed in memory of Lully. This was conjoined to songs by Monteverdi and Debussy, as well as Alan Rawsthorne's Chamber Cantata for voice, string quartet, and harpsichord. A month later, he presented Palestrina and Mozart alongside Berg's String Quartet and Stravinsky's *Duo Concertant*, and his April concert opened with Beethoven's Trio in C minor for Strings, Op. 9, no. 3—after which he performed the second book of Debussy Etudes with "remarkable virtuosity and a nice sense of tone colour."[12]

The following season brought string quartets by Haydn and Schoenberg on the same program with two solo piano works of Busoni, "which served to show once more what an odd mind that very great musician had."[13] A month later, Hallis joined violist Frederick Riddle to perform three sonatas, opening with Brahms's Op. 120, no. 1, in F minor, premiering a new work by Elizabeth Maconchy (criticized by *The Times* for her insistence on "harsh harmonies" which failed to "expand into beauty"[14]), and concluding with Hindemith's early Sonata, Op. 11, no. 4. By November, his series had relocated to Aeolian Hall and *The Times* announced that the programs would occur "on the 14th of every month till March."[15] The December concert opened with Webern's Trio for Strings, before Hallis turned his considerable virtuosity to Balakirev's *Islamey* and Bartók's *Three Burlesques*. In March, the final concert in the series sandwiched his "purposeful and vigorous" premiere of Rawsthorne's Concerto for

Pianoforte, Strings, and Percussion between works of Schoenberg and Kodály.

Matthay's American students were no less enthusiastic in their support of the newer styles. Frank Mannheimer, a close friend of American composers Roger Sessions and Leo Sowerby, did much to promote their music to European audiences, and in July of 1931 he even participated in a festival featuring their works at the German resort of Bad Homburg.[16] And the following November, Stravinsky's intellectually demanding Sonata was performed at Grotrian Hall by Matthay's pupil Julian DeGray, prompting *The Times* to remark that the composer's "displaced accents and irregular rhythm" were treated "as to make the whole flow forward in a smooth, logical, and completely convincing manner."[17] DeGray, whose tastes soon extended to the music of his friend Carl Ruggles, as well as to the works of Messiaen, was a native of Harrisburg, Pennsylvania, and in June 1922 he graduated from Harrisburg Technical High School, which he attended with his close friend Jacques Barzun. They both soon entered Columbia, where DeGray took fifth entrance prize in Greek, thanks to a stunning intellect, and an extraordinarily rigorous high school curriculum that immediately prepared him for graduate courses. He also studied French—having profited from the tutoring he received from Barzun's mother—and, after graduating Phi Beta Kappa, within a decade he was fluent in no less than eight European languages, including Russian, Norwegian, and Swedish. Like Simonds and Metcalf, he elected Paris for further musical studies, which he funded with Columbia's prestigious Cutting Fellowship.[18] He had sought piano instruction from Cortot, but finding him virtually inaccessible, went instead to Lazare Lévy at the Conservatoire, who had also once taught Metcalf. In the spring of 1926, some visiting Columbia friends observed that his playing was sounding strained and tense, and by the fall he found himself in London, where Matthay suggested he work with Carlos Buhler at Chatou, while he completed his Paris composition studies with Jean Huré.[19]

DeGray soon became thoroughly committed to Matthay principles, and even though Buhler never returned to Wimpole Street, over

Chapter 11

the next year they grew close. Just as Simonds had done, DeGray soon beseeched his alma mater to transfer his remaining fellowship funds to London, and by the spring of 1927 he was working regularly with Matthay, who happily added him to the staff of the TMPS. Because money was tight, DeGray was also introduced to Eunice Norton and her mother—then in search of a lodger—and he was thrilled to use the studio grand that Mrs. Norton had rented for their sitting room at 8 Greville Road. But frictions soon developed when she tried to supervise his practice sessions, and even stronger issues ensued over repertoire, especially when Eunice and her mother suggested that the Scriabin Sonatas he had studied with Buhler were inferior to the works of the German masters.[20] Whatever its genesis, this became a recurring theme in her thinking, and by 1931, she was convinced that her nearly seven-year relationship with Matthay should end. And if Gerschefski regarded Tobias and Jessie as insufficiently tolerant of newer styles, Eunice was prepared to lodge exactly the opposite criticism:

> I am afraid that I am compelled to say that, if there was any weakness in the Matthay School, it was "tolerance" concerning qualities of music. This led to confusion in the minds of students about musical values and left them with an undeveloped capacity to distinguish between music that is consequential and that which is trivial. During my long study in London I learned most of the keyboard works of Bach, Mozart, Beethoven, Schumann, Chopin, and Brahms. Many hours were also spent on pieces I no longer like[:] pieces by Rachmaninoff, Medtner, Franck, Albeñiz, Saint-Säens, Palmgren, and Poulenc.[21]

Liszt and Debussy also soon disappeared from her "consequential" list, and she rarely, if ever, performed their works after 1930. She conceded that leaving Matthay was a "dreadfully difficult decision," and "if I had not been urged by friends whom I knew had my interest at heart I would never have left him."[22] But by 1932 she was in Berlin working with Artur Schnabel, and repertoire was clearly a pivotal issue:

Schnabel, in drawing an uncompromising boundary between qualities of music, challenged one to take a stand. Your integrity as a performer or teacher was measured by your own uncompromising adherence to the music you preferred. By including lesser pieces in programs because of their appeal to the public, your integrity was damaged. If you were incapable of appreciating the best, you left Schnabel and went home; and there were those who fell by the wayside either immediately or later when on their own.[23]

Matthay, who had once been on the cutting edge of *Kunstwerk der Zukunft*—at least in England—had devoted much of his life to the new and the modern, but now he was often caught between two opposite poles. The *avant garde* of his youth had still been Romantic, but now if Romanticism were tolerated at all, many sought to resurrect it only through a highly selective lens—one where the virtuosity of Liszt, for example, was far less acceptable. But a more severe censorship could exist at the other pole, since those focused exclusively on the present were often avowedly anti-Romantic. This newer aesthetic was slow to invade the nation's concert halls, but between the Wars, the BBC was a major proponent of the "ultra-modern"—to use the contemporary term identified by Jennifer Doctor—due in large part to its influential music programmer Edward Clark, a former pupil of Schoenberg.[24] Ironically, this was the very period Matthay sought to pursue broadcasts for some of his earlier compositions, and to his delight, he eventually succeeded with many of them—but often only after considerable perseverance. One of his earliest surviving letters to the Corporation is dated 4 January 1928, when he offered the score of his youthful overture *In May* to its Booking Manager, Terrence Tillett, adding that "I should be prepared to conduct it myself if thought desirable."[25] Several weeks later, for Matthay's seventieth birthday, the professors of the TMPS sought to encourage his fascination with the latest technology by giving him "a five-valve wireless set" (a present his students augmented with a "Kodak-cinema" camera),[26] but while it may have piqued his enthusiasm for the new medium, the BBC was still unresponsive.

Although he never received a firm rejection, neither *In May* nor any of his other works were broadcast over the next two years, and on

Chapter 11

24 September 1930, he wrote to Adrian Boult, its recently appointed Music Director. It was Boult's job to oversee the BBC Symphony Concerts, and since he was also an occasional visitor to Wimpole Street, Matthay discretely prevailed upon their friendship:

My dear Boult,

Perhaps it is too late already, & it is with the greatest diffidence indeed I make the suggestion, knowing your very kindly feeling towards me upon which I should be most loth [sic] to impose. But I do wish room could be made in the forthcoming Symphony Concerts for <u>Vivian Langrish</u> with my own Concerto in one movement (Concert-Piece).

Vivian Langrish has played it magnificently several times at the Proms, and elsewhere of course, and so has York Bowen, and each time they have "brought the house down" so that must be my excuse for venturing proposing my own work! But he really does deserve an appearance, he is a really fine—really serious artist & has been before the public for long years past, & his playing grows in maturity every day—& he deserves to come into his own. He has had to support himself and his family by teaching and that has hampered his public work—& incidentally as professor he is <u>one of the main stays both at the R. A. M. & my School</u> & has a big reputation behind him.[27]

Not surprisingly, Boult was unfamiliar with Matthay's Concert-Piece, and his Chief Assistant, Kenneth Wright, soon received a terse "Do you know it?" from senior programmer Victor Hely-Hutchinson. Wright's response, while not totally negative, suggests a changing aesthetic tide: "No; & we must see it before committing ourselves. Matthay's compositions are usually on the frozen edge!" Although he added, "I quite agree about Langrish. He is a fine pianist."[28] Matthay promptly sent the score, and Hely-Hutchinson sent Boult a lengthy memo on 31 October, which read in part:

I have read through this score and, although I do not think it is a bad work, neither do I think it is a good one. Its best points are the effectiveness of the piano writing and the good straightforward scoring for the orchestra. Apart from this, it seems to have no virtues or vices at all. The musical invention strikes me as simply negligible. I would suggest that somebody else should see it and give an opinion as, with a man of Matthay's standing, one wants to as sure of one's ground as possible. Perhaps Mr. Buesst and Mr. Clark might both see it.[29]

Aylmer Buesst, an opera conductor who had once worked with Boult at the RCM, does not seem to have had any official post at the BBC before 1933,[30] so it is unclear whether he or Clark actually examined the score. Curiously, Boult's answer to Hely-Hutchinson six days later suggested the matter be decided entirely by "Langrish's wish. If he would genuinely like to play it then we should do it; otherwise not."[31] But the question was also referred to the BBC's Music Executive, Owen Mase, whose 31 October memo to Boult confirms a climate bordering on condescension:

> I have chased this matter as far as possible and the situation is:—
> 1. It's a rather dull work
> 2. Langrish would like to play it.
> 3. Lewis has done it at Birmingham and is not enamoured.
> Now—will you put it down for a Studio Concert or do you wish Lewis to?[32]

Joseph Lewis, recently transferred from the Birmingham Station, was now assistant conductor of the newly formed BBC Orchestra, but at the bottom of Mase's typed memo, Boult scrawled, "I think TM would appreciate my doing it."[33] On 11 November he informed Matthay that the Concert-Piece would be scheduled for a January broadcast,[34] and Matthay followed up with a letter of thanks on 14 November, in which he offered to conduct the work if Boult were unavailable. Although this proved unnecessary, the event was delayed five months, and Boult did not perform it until 19 May 1931, on a program beginning at 7:47 pm in the BBC's Savoy Hill Studios,

Chapter 11

just weeks after he had appointed himself Chief Conductor of the Orchestra.[35] Matthay received studio passes for himself, Jessie, and Denise, and the next day he sent a congratulatory note to his friend, thanking him for a "splendid performance" and "all the trouble you took to get it:"

> It was indeed a great joy to me. The Orchestra is indeed delightful—and Vivian Langrish played it indeed most sympathetically. He deserves to be heard again in it! Indeed it was a red letter day for me—I can't thank you enough for it.
>
> Affectionately yours,
> "Uncle Tobs"[36]

Langrish again performed the work—this time under Matthay's baton—at the Eastbourne Festival on 24 November, and Matthay had the opportunity to conduct *In May* on the same program. The following day he pressed Boult for a broadcast of the overture, revisiting the desire he had expressed nearly four years earlier:

> I must say after this experience that I <u>envy all conductors</u>—it is a delightful sensation having a body of men expressing one's feelings! But why I am worrying you with this, is, that I found I was quite right in my hankering after this old score—<u>of nearly 50 years ago;</u> and its mood of <u>Youth</u> quite <u>moved</u> me myself!—I suppose memories of when I was <u>young</u>!! But I am sure it is the best piece . . . Ive [sic] ever written—much better musically than the Concerto; and I do hope the BBC will give it a chance next year[.] I would like to hear it once with a really fine orchestra like yours! Too bad to write all this when you are madly busy![37]

Exactly three months later on 24 February, *In May* was given a "remote" broadcast from Bournemouth under Sir Dan Godfrey, and Boult agreed to look over the score. But the BBC returned it several months later "saying that they had no room for it," and on 30 June, Matthay, who suspected Boult had never seen it, informed him that he found the rejection "a bitter disappointment."[38] But Boult in fact had seen it, and he drafted a sensitive reply on 29 July, which perhaps captured the frustrations felt by many whose ideals had been nurtured in an earlier age:

> Works like your "In May" give me anxiety because they represent an idiom, in fact an artistic ideal, that I find myself more in sympathy with than are many colleagues, not necessarily in the B.B.C., both of my own age, and younger. The present pursuit of colour and of immediate effect appeals to me far less than the ideal of design coupled of course with beauty, which I take to be the basis of the work of the whole group headed by Parry and Stanford, in which I would also put composers like [Sir Arthur] Somervell, Walford Davies (his early work anyhow) and many others (even [Sir George] Henschel, whose 'Requiem' has so much beauty) and the work we are discussing, and your Pianoforte Concerto.
>
> I am <u>convinced</u>—and I told Somervell so the other day—that there will be a renewal of interest in these ideals, and I think it will come soon; and I look forward to it. But I cannot feel that it is up to us here to try and push it prematurely. There will be sure signs when the time is ripe, and then we shall be able to help it along, and then (incidentally) one of the B.B.C. conductors will enjoy himself! In the meantime he must deny himself in patience.[39]

Although Matthay might have argued convincingly that the BBC was already "prematurely" pushing currents such as the Second Viennese School, he put the matter aside. But much to his surprise, several of his smaller works were heard on the air far sooner than he might have expected, as he informed Simonds about two months later:

> It will amuse you to know I am <u>broadcasting</u> for the first time in my life on Oct. 25 Tuesday at <u>10.10</u> pm! During the holiday with long vistas of supposed free time ahead, in an optimistic moment I thought why not give a little Recital of my compositions for the B.B.C? So I wrote off to them and to my astonishment found myself nailed down to give one!! So, instead of letting my playing slack away during this term—as I generally

Chapter 11

do, as I have only <u>Psychology</u> lectures needing no playing—and doing some more writing, I've had <u>to set to, and practice hard</u> to get into playing form!!!—although it is only a ½ hour Recital—Here is what I have chosen:

1. Studies[:] Prelude in E[;] Intermezzo in E[;] Bravura in E[;]
2. No[.] 1 and 4 [from On] Surrey Hills
3. Romanesque
4. No[.] 5-6 Monothemes

Try and pick up "National" that night (lw [long wave]) and hear me play across the Atlantic![40]

Matthay's broadcast went off as scheduled at the recently opened Broadcasting House in Langham Place, which was adjacent to Queen's Hall, within convenient walking distance of the TMPS. Although—with the exception of the playing he used to illustrate his lectures—it was his first documented recital appearance in nearly 40 years, those close to him maintained (despite his comments to Simonds) that he rarely allowed his playing to "slack away." His general pattern was to rise late in the morning and, after a full day of teaching and perhaps an evening concert, begin his correspondence and writings around 10 or 11. Then as late as 2 in the morning, he regularly practiced, often till 3 or 4. Although no recording of the broadcast is known to survive, it was undoubtedly well received, because almost immediately, he recorded four of the selections—including the two miniatures from his 1919 Suite *On Surrey Hills*—for Columbia.[41] In a charming gesture, the company released them on a twelve-inch disc on 19 February 1933—Matthay's seventy-fifth birthday—and on the same day *The Gramophone* dubbed him the "G.O.M. [Grand Old Man] of the piano world."[42] Although most of the London press ignored the record, Columbia amassed no less than 24 positive notices from various journals throughout Britain and the Commonwealth, including the *Johannesburg Sunday Times*: "The facile fingers of the old man might easily arouse the envy of younger players. His technique is brilliant, while his sense of temperament is pleasantly marked, particularly in the Prelude and Bravura."[43]

The Prelude and "Bravura" were from eight *Studies in the Form of a Suite*, Op. 16, which Matthay had completed by the spring of 1887—but only Numbers 1, 7, and 8 (all in the key of E) were published. He originally labeled five of the pieces "Etudes" and the remaining three "Intermezzi," but by the time they reached press, only No. 7, an Intermezzo, kept its original title. At some point (no later than 1897) he revised the E major Prelude, No. 1 from the set, and "affectionately dedicated" it to Gertrude Peppercorn and Lily West. In September of 1909 he also revised the "Intermezzo" (No. 7), which he dedicated to Fanny Robertson, and "Bravura" (No. 8), which he dedicated "affectionately" to Bowen—both also in the key of E.[44] Curiously, although Myra occasionally performed the Intermezzo, neither the Prelude nor "Bravura" appear with any regularity on programs by Matthay's students, and their inclusion probably stemmed more from his fondness for lecturing on them—in fact his own copies are so covered with pedagogical comments that the printed music is at times virtually unintelligible.[45]

The two Opus 16 pieces he recorded are only somewhat harmonically adventurous, but both are profoundly Lisztian in spirit, and the Prelude is clearly a study in cantabile playing. Though the published score does not include a metronome marking, Matthay's penciled notation reads: "72-76 ♩ is quick enough—it is a slow movement!"[46] But whatever tempo he chose for the broadcast, his recording is closer to ♩ = 84, and since its length is only 2:09, he was not speeding up merely to accommodate the limited disc space characteristic of 1930s technology. In all probability, he played the piece as he felt it, and however many takes may have been involved, this performance, which occasionally features a few prominent wrong notes, has the spontaneous character of a "live" improvisation. As written, the Prelude requires legato, sustained lines, almost all in the tenor, which must sing out against highly decorative, arpeggiated soprano textures. *The Gramophone* observed that Columbia's "admirable" engineering was "clear as a bell,"[47] and it should be noted that the pianist's kaleidoscopic tonal palette was well captured:

Chapter 11

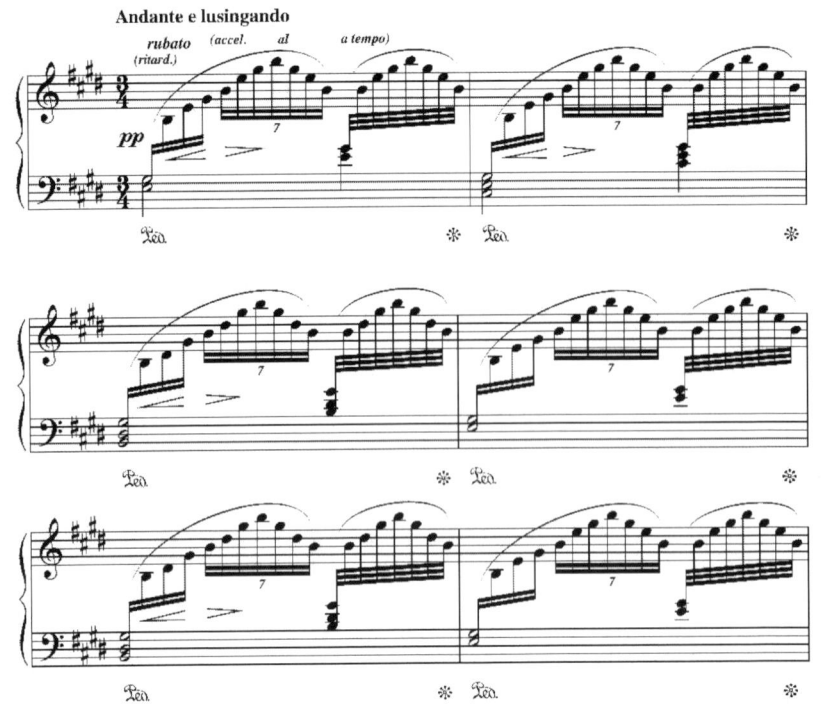

Ex. 11.2 Matthay: Prelude from Studies in the Form of a Suite, Op. 16, mm. 1-4

"Bravura," which Matthay has marked "Vivacissimo," is a virtuosic frolic in parallel scales. His pencil notations suggest a tempo of ♩ = 120-126, but his whirlwind recording is often closer to ♩ = 180. Many of the reviews noted that his technical wizardry was impressive for an artist of any age, and the *British Musician* even observed that "in every respect of flexibility, ease, speed and strength, one would fancy that some youthful prodigy of the piano were the performer."[48] The number of takes required to capture the finished product is unknown, but Matthay's handwritten comments leave ample documentation that he conferred extensively with Myra before and during the sessions. To guide his own practicing, he wrote on the page facing the opening bars: "Not too heavy an accent for 1st note for record[,] says Myra,"[49] indicating she had learned from experience that microphones can sometimes distort louder tones unless the performer exercises caution. Given the nature of Matthay's opening passage, it was probably advice well taken:

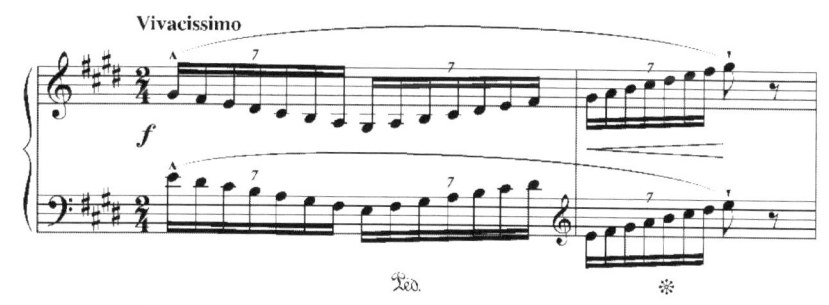

Ex. 11.3 Matthay: "Bravura" from Studies in the Form of a Suite, Op. 16, mm. 1-2

Myra acted as a virtual session producer, providing important feedback on balance issues. At Bar 9, perhaps after hearing a test cut, she asked him to bring out the right hand more in a passage, even though the left hand carried the tune: "Myra says accompaniment too light!"[50] And at Bar 18, she gave the opposite advice: "Myra says R. H. not heard enough!," prodding Matthay to scratch out the printed "*mf*" dynamic mark in favor of a penciled "*f*."[51]

Ex. 11.4 Matthay: "Bravura" from Studies in the Form of a Suite, Op. 16, mm. 18-20. (Matthay's penciled dynamic notation in brackets)

Ironically, of all Matthay's artist-students, Myra was arguably the least comfortable in a recording studio, although her biographer suggests that her aversion developed over a period of several years.[52] Her first contract had been signed only five years previously in the American offices of Columbia, and her earliest discs—a collection of Debussy pieces—were released in the States in 1928, nearly two decades after Irene had cut her first wax cylinders (in 1909) for the Gramophone Company.[53] But in the interim, many of Matthay's students had been quick to embrace the new medium. For example, Bowen made a number of acoustic recordings for Vocalion in the mid-1920s, including collaboration with Stanley Chapple in what seems to have been the first commercial release of Beethoven's Fourth Concerto—which appeared on four 12" discs in the fall of 1925. The *Musical Times* praised it as "one of the very best concerto records," noting that the pianist's "fluent, happy style is well suited here."[54] Several months earlier, Harriet Cohen had recorded Bach's D minor Concerto with Henry Wood for Columbia, and by December of 1930, her recording of the first nine Preludes and Fugues from Book I of the *Well-Tempered Clavier* secured her photo above the fold on the "Newly Recorded Music" page of the *New York Times*. For some reason, Columbia had chosen Evelyn Howard-Jones to record the second volume in the series—which ran from numbers 10 to 17—and the *Times* lamented the company's decision:

> For choice, we would take the first, and are left wondering why Harriet Cohen was not selected to continue the series she commenced. Her touch is essentially sympathetic, and where Mr. Howard-Jones's manner is at all times too scholarly, in places almost mechanical, Miss Cohen brings out the melodious, romantic nature of her material without in any way sacrificing what may be considered in some quarters as the essential features of the contract. A product of Tobias Matthay, which she shows very definitely in spots, Miss Cohen . . . is justly regarded as one of England's foremost Bach players.[55]

While Myra, for the most part, confined her studio sessions to conventional repertoire, many of Matthay's artists used recordings to popularize unfamiliar works—at times with marked success. Late in 1933, Columbia released Irene's rendering of Litolff's sparkling Scherzo from his *Concerto Symphonique No. 4*, Op. 102, which she recorded with Wood and the LSO. Supposedly, Paderweski was the first to extrapolate this single movement from the four which comprise the work, but precisely how Irene discovered it is unclear. Despite the faint praise afforded by the *Musical Times*—which dubbed it "a sprightly piece" that makes "pleasant hearing so long as you don't mind music that goes round and round in a small space"[56]—its Lisztian flourishes suited Irene (who had already issued a stunning twelfth Hungarian Rhapsody), and the disc sold well.[57] It soon became—at least informally—the virtual "property" of artists with Matthay connections, and in subsequent years both Curzon and Moura Lympany recorded it.

Following the success of her first disc, Parlophone signed Eileen Joyce to a three-year contract late in 1933 which was enthusiastically renewed, and by the end of the decade she had recorded more than 70 sides for them. Most were popular staples of the repertoire, but in 1938 she made what was evidently the first recording of two Rachmaninoff Preludes from his Opus 23: No. 6 in E-flat and No. 7 in C minor. She also left a stunning Scherzo in F-sharp minor by d'Albert—which the American pianist Earl Wild praised as "a recording to die for"[58]—and in February 1936 she even recorded the recently discovered Mozart Concert Rondo in A, K. 386, with the BBC's Clarence Raybould. Joyce had a long, intimate relationship with the BBC, and it was she, rather than Hallis, who gave Britain its first performance of Shostakovich's recently composed Concerto, which aired from Broadcasting House under Henry Wood on 4 January 1936. Five years later, she recorded it with Leslie Heward and trumpeter Arthur Lockwood for Columbia. However, Hallis is credited with the first complete recording of Debussy's Etudes (for Decca in 1938), predating Gieseking's EMI offering by more than 15 years. Predictably, Bartlett and Robertson also committed unfamiliar repertoire to disc, and in 1930 they recorded Bax's Sonata for the National Gramophonic Society which, according to the *Musical Times*, "could hardly be better done."[59] In the same issue, the journal reviewed Ethel's recording of the Bach F minor Concerto—also for the NGS—noting that "her tone records unusually well,"[60] while the *New York Times* added that "the piano recording is equal to anything that has come this way."[61]

Chapter 11

    If Schnabel and his disciples sought to narrow the range of acceptable musical styles, Matthay's pupils often seemed on the verge of unbridled aesthetic expansion. Raie Da Costa arrived at the TMPS from her native Cape Town in 1924 at the age of 19, and soon established herself as a major talent. In the summers of both 1925 and 1926 she performed Chopin on Matthay's Queen's Hall programs, and almost immediately thereafter she was being heard regularly on the BBC as both soloist and chamber musician. But by early 1928 her career had taken an unconventional twist, as evidenced by the program log published in *The Times* on 14 February, which places the word "syncopations" after her name.[62] As a girl in South Africa, she had longed for the career of a dancer, and her slender, graceful frame assured many that her goal was realistic. But as *The Times* reported years later, a fall, "by which her hip was injured, and which resulted in a long illness, caused her to abandon dancing and to take up the piano."[63] She may have relinquished her dream of dancing professionally, but she always retained a feel for complex, exotic rhythms, and in 1926 she even wrote a song, "When I Say Goodbye to You," for the popular American singing team of Layton and Johnstone. What in America was soon being hailed as "The Jazz Age" had a somewhat less specific identity in Britain, where the term "syncopation" covered a multitude of novelty styles, embracing everything from rag to Broadway. At the time, its leading exponent was pianist Billy Mayerl (1902-59), a prodigy who had studied at Trinity College, before abandoning the classics to perform in hotels and West End cinemas, eventually signing with Columbia in the early 1920s to issue a series of "syncopated" recordings.

    When Parlophone executives discovered Raie Da Costa, they found a photographer's dream, as well as Mayerl's technical equal, and they soon plastered her picture in record shops all over London, with the caption: "The Parlophone Girl—Dance Pianiste Supreme." She issued her first recording in April of 1928, and by August she was headlining at the Alhambra in Leicester Square, where she played Chopin, Debussy, and Liszt. Accompanying dancers choreographed by June Radbourne of the Margaret Morris Theatre, she enhanced what *The Times* described as a "novelty of movement and costumes:"

> *Ballet* would be too pretentious a name for a simple entertainment, but the "Clair de Lune" of Debussy, creating a thought of moonlight and fountains, an opening episode, "Modes Nouvelles," and a dance in the Russian style, full of vigour and colour, are *ballet* in miniature. Miss Raie da Costa, "the Parlophone Girl," uses the technique of a concerto soloist, supported by a rainbow range of lighting effects, to play the dance melodies of the moment at the piano.[64]

Her jewelry, her auburn bobbed hair, and her "flapper"-style dresses complemented a tall, curvaceous figure to create an air of cool seduction, and when, for example, she performed Gershwin's *Rhapsody in Blue* at the Palladium (a Mayerl specialty), audiences were enchanted. But it was her effortless, improvised "syncopations"—characterized by flawless rhythm and virtuosic flamboyance—that garnered the most attention. Of the over 100 stylizations she placed on disc, some are whimsical novelties couched in pseudo-Romantic gestures, some are pop hits recorded with ensembles such as Ray Noble's Orchestra, and some include uninhibited mezzo vocals—her 1932 recording of Harold Arlen's "I've Got the World on a String" even employs "scat." But her most remarkable work is shown by her solo, purely instrumental renditions of popular standards, including the songs of Gershwin, Walter Donaldson, and Vincent Youmans. In May of 1929, *The Times* praised three of her latest Parlophone "foxtrot piano solos," which were "almost entirely made by her playing," and which demonstrated "mental as well as technical agility."[65] In 1930, she left Parlophone for HMV, and three years later the company staged a publicity coup when Cole Porter's *Gay Divorce* opened at the Palace on 2 November 1933. A mere two weeks earlier, Da Costa had recorded the show's hit song, "Night and Day," and on the morning it opened, HMV was already advertising it, along with three additional versions:

> Brilliant records of "Night and Day," the tune from "Gay Divorce" that everyone is singing, humming, and whistling. Fred Astaire, the star of the show, sings the vocal refrain in Leo Reisman's record. Paul Whiteman plays it, Raie de Costa gives her interpretation of it, and the

Chapter 11

Comedy Harmonists give their unique male-voice version of it. All on "His Master's Voice." They are on sale to-day at your dealers; call and hear them now![66]

Now that she was ranked with Astaire, Whiteman, and the Harmonists (a classically trained, six-man, German *a cappella* group that had developed a cult following), Raie Da Costa's career had peaked. But she never abandoned her earlier ideals, and in June of 1930 HMV even released her rendering of Liszt's Paraphrase on Themes from *Rigoletto* (which Irene had recorded a year earlier for Columbia). With a blazing technique that was routinely compared to Liszt's own, she negotiates its torturous passages with staggering ease, but the *Musical Times* may have tainted her by this point, since it accused her of "wasting twenty-four valuable inches" of disc space. However, it should be mentioned that the reviewer, one "Discus," refers to Liszt in the same article as the "arch-transcriber," and demonstrates his bias against the composer by dismissing one of his Rossini transcriptions as "a vulgarity."[67] But whatever her commercial reception, her support and loyalty for the TMPS never wavered, and on 16 July 1926 she even performed the orchestral part of the first movement of Beethoven's Third at Wigmore Hall, "flawlessly," for twelve-year-old Guy Jonson, stepping in at the last minute for his teacher, Betty Humby, who was ailing.[68] Before long she had little time for such largesse, and by January of 1933, she was appearing in Monte Carlo in a massive revue called *La Navire l'aventure* (The adventure ship), conceived by painter Jean-Gabriel Domergue, and advertised as "A plethora of virtuosos under the baton of Maitre Paul Paray."[69] She now had royalty at her feet, and her Riveria appearances soon captivated the Kings of both Sweden and Denmark.[70] But she worked incessantly, and by the summer of 1934, while appearing at a seaside hotel in Hove, she was suffering from exhaustion. She was further weakened by a sudden attack of appendicitis, and a brilliant career was extinguished on 26 August 1934, when she died following complications after surgery. She was only 29.

Nor was Raie Da Costa the only Matthay School graduate to forge a career in more popular mediums. At Wigmore Hall on the evening of 9 July 1919, fourteen-year-old "Master Dick Addinsell"—then studying with Dora—performed a movement from Ravel's *Sonatine* at a TMPS concert given on behalf of the Royal National Lifeboat Institution.[71] Several years later, he briefly attended the RCM, and by the late 'twenties—now as Richard Addinsell—he was contributing songs and other music to West End stage shows. In 1928, he began a lifelong collaboration with writer Clemence Dane (of whose plays Jessie was especially fond), creating operettas and other pieces to her libretti.[72] In 1932, he composed the score for *His Lordship*, a musical film directed by Michael Powell (*The Thief of Baghdad*), and for the next 35 years, cinema was always a second love, with *Goodbye, Mr. Chips*, the 1939 film starring Robert Donat, being one of his most remembered scores. During the War, he also began writing songs for Myra's close friend, Joyce Grenfell, but his score for the 1941 British propaganda film *Dangerous Moonlight*—in the words of David Ades—"eclipsed all others as far as the public was concerned."[73] His *Warsaw Concerto*, composed in a mock-Lisztian style, was eventually recorded in over 100 different versions, with total sales exceeding five million.[74] During the War, Eileen Joyce performed a concert version of it throughout England with the LPO,[75] and Addinsell's music soon set the tone for a plethora of "piano concerto"-type film scores in the late 'forties and early 'fifties. And although no TMPS appearances can be documented for him, the highly successful light arranger and orchestral leader Stanley Black (1913-2002), composer of the theme for the BBC's popular *Goon Show*, told Raie Da Costa's biographer that he had "fond memories" of his studies at the Matthay School.[76]

Understandably, Matthay took pride in the radio and gramophone successes of his students, and on 17 January 1934, just as the TMPS winter term was beginning, Jessie shared some of his exhilaration with Bruce and Rosalind Simonds:

> Everybody is back at work again (except me)[.] Uncle Tobs has gone off with a light in his eye, hoping very much that it may mean plenty of

Chapter 11

staying power. He would just adore to play himself, he says he understands better than ever he did how to get himself ready for the big tournaments. It is quite possible that he will have a broadcast in February. Yesterday was quite a field day for him. Five of his disciples on the programme[.] Denise—Handel & Debussy Sonatas with [cellist] Antonia Butler [the broadcast was actually on Monday, 15 January, at 4 pm on the National Service], Eileen Joyce on Foundations of Music [a daily fifteen-minute educational series]—Mozart Sonatas for pf & violin [with violinist] (David Wise)[,] Vivian Langrish—recital including [Schumann's] 'Carnival! [sic] [Langrish's broadcast was actually on 15 January, at 9:15 pm, on the London Regional Service. He shared an hour with contralto Enid Szantho] Ernest Lush [one of the BBC's staff pianists and a long-time Matthay pupil] accompanying Lieder recitals & Irene Scharrer in a ½ hour group of new gramophone records. A busy day?[77]

But Matthay's second BBC broadcast, scheduled for 11 March 1934, did not occur. Two nights earlier, writing from Marley, Jessie confided the explanation to Simonds and his wife:

My Dear Bruce & Rosalind

I feel I must tell you about Uncle Tobs. It will soon be a month since he had to lay up with a capricious temperature that kept on alarming us, and after about 5 days hoping that it would steady itself, steps were taken to track the trouble to it's [sic] source. First X ray photos of intestines—all right—Water examination [urinalysis]—also encouraging, but showing some foreign matter, & a little blood[.]

Blood test—Quite all right

I dare say he has told you for the last two years or so he has had some trouble with the prostate gland. He was examined before he went to Italy [on holiday, the previous August], but was passed O.K. So now here it is again in an agravated [sic] form, and two operations must be performed. The first took place last Sunday morning, and the other probably in the middle of next week. He has a lovely room at the Haslemere hospital, built only a few years ago, and equipped with the very latest.

His surgeon from the 'London' [The Royal London Hospital in Whitechapel] and the young doctor here has [sic] worked and still works with him, and two nurses trained to all their requirements are carrying out their instructions. We all have every confidence in the work of such a team. The nurses live up here when not on duty, one on day and one on night, and we can get down to the hospital in ten minutes should he want us. We have all been through a hectic time. But now that things have been straightened out both here and at the School, he is already better nervously, and jubilantly playing the game to win back his health. . . . Denise is taking Uncle Tobs' place at BBC tomorrow, when he was to play another group of his own pieces. [Jessie probably finished her letter on 10 March. Denise filled in for Matthay with a half-hour program on Sunday, 11 March, at 12:30 pm on the National Service. She also had to cancel an appearance in Madeira, which was taken "at a moment's notice" by Matthay's pupil Dorothy Hesse.] I will write you again in about ten days when he has pulled round from the major operation.

Dearest love to you both,
Aunt Jessie[78]

By 1934, operations had become a way of life for Jessie, but now Tobias, whose health had always been excellent, was undergoing two major surgeries at the age of 76. But the second could not be performed until mid-April—some seven weeks after his first one on 4 March—because the doctors were unable to stabilize his temperature. Fortunately, by the end of April he was through the worst of it, and he felt well enough to dictate a letter from his hospital room to his American students who were planning to travel abroad for summer study. He revealed that before the crisis hit, he had been practicing exceptionally hard, not only for his BBC appearance, but because "I also decided to make some more gramophone records," all of which had to be cancelled.[79] But by mid-May he was home at Marley, and Jessie's major concern was simply restraining him from over-exertion. A

Chapter 11

few weeks later, she informed Bruce and Rosalind that everyone's spirits were high:

> It hasn't been all dark & desolating. We have had lots of fun in one way and another. The little nurse that he has had for the last three months has been worthy of a play or a book all to herself. She has tackled him to a way that only one in a million could (if that)[.] He is going to be allowed to give his first lesson next Sunday. It was scrumptious having Myra home again. She has returned more sweetly human & strongly modest than ever. [Recovering from mastectomies which had been performed in Boston in April, Myra stayed at Marley briefly after she returned to England.[80]] The [TMPS] Concerts are all going on as usual, and I shall be greatly surprised if T. M. won't be at Queen's Hall [in July]. He has started to play, and is finding that his fingers are not duds. So it is all a very happy time[.][81]

Jessie's letter was written on a Tuesday, and whether or not Tobias waited until Sunday to give his first lesson, he scrawled a note to Simonds at the top of her page before she posted it: "Gave a <u>lesson</u> today (special one) first in 3 months!!!"[82] He taught a few others through the month of June, but most of his students who performed at the Summer Festival were assigned to other teachers. And he was still not fully back to normal by the time the opening concert occurred on 2 July, since Jessie got him a room at the Dysart Hotel on Henrietta Street, "with no stairs to climb," just around the corner from the TMPS, where "he could be out of the mêlée at the School."[83] The first Wigmore Hall concert on Monday evening proved a poignant experience, as Jessie informed Simonds from Marley the following Saturday:

> Here we are in Mid-Summer—three of the Concerts over & two more to come. Uncle Tobs had a most moving reception at the first one[.] The whole audience stood up. It was a great return. Everyone thought it best, after he had managed the first two, to have "an interval for refreshment," so he came home & I donned my party frock, and made a speech for

him. So it was a resurrection for me too.... Myra is giving a lecture this morning [for the TMPS Summer School] at Carlton Hill in her own studio. She will have an audience of almost 40—I think. [Irene also agreed to do a master class on Chopin Etudes for the Summer School.] ... Uncle Tobs and I are having a Darby & Joan lunch under the old apple tree, with the <u>two</u> dogs sprawling in the sun, and the bank of Surrey poppies that have always been there in former days to welcome you, are looking very fairy like.[84]

Two days later, Matthay's appearance at the final Festival concert in Queen's Hall was even more moving, as recounted by Philadelphia pianist Arthur Hice:

At the Queen's Hall concert on July 10, the audience accorded Mr. Matthay a heart-warming welcome such as I have rarely, if ever, seen given anyone. When he appeared on the stage, the audience rose *en masse* to its feet, applauding and cheering as if for a returning hero! There was also a very warm greeting for Myra Hess, who again presented the annual awards. [As TMPS President, this was one of Myra's duties.] Mr. Matthay called on the audience to cheer the "Empress of Pianists," but Myra, in a manner so characteristic of her, bade the audience to "hail the master once more."[85]

Hice indicated that Matthay's doctor had cleared him to give his first lecture at Marley nine days later on Thursday, 19 July, and that over 50 enthusiastic students and friends—including some 25 pupils brought from Pennsylvania by LeRoy Campbell—traveled down from London to socialize on the south lawn in the afternoon sun:

After a very jolly tea-time and much picture-taking by the group, we settled down to hear what was perhaps the most comprehensive single lecture I have heard Uncle Tobs give. Starting off with most amusing parodies of the many so-called "methods" of playing in vogue, and including a killingly funny one of what some claim to be the "Matthay Method," with exaggerated pumpings of the arm and ludicrous finger-slidings,

Chapter 11

> Mr. Matthay then gave a most clear and concise exposition of the vital points of piano technic and interpretation, punctuated throughout by his pungent wit and apt illustrations of the "Act of Touch" in its different manifestations. There were memorable performances of several Chopin Etudes, notably those in C major (Op. 12) [sic—this was probably Op. 10, no. 1] and F minor and A flat (Op. 25) [probably Op. 25, no. 2 and no. 1], all done with the verve and abandon of a youthful artist. . . .
>
> At this point the lecture had gone on for almost two hours, and members of Uncle Tob's [sic] household appeared anxious to call it a day, as several tip-toed in and whispered to him—all to no avail—until Nurse appeared, who gently but firmly led Uncle Tobs away from the piano, as he exclaimed with his typical droll mock-pathos, "But I have practiced a lot of other pieces also, and now you are not going to let me play them."[86]

By the fall, Matthay was beginning to resume his normal schedule, but the TMPS was still reeling from the impact of a worldwide economic depression. Two years earlier on 20 September 1932, the School's secretary, Marion Cole, had died suddenly, and Denise later remembered that her unfortunate passing may have actually resolved a difficult situation, since her organizational skills had been deteriorating to the point that the Matthays planned to dismiss her. Matthay's former pupil and Denise's close friend Hilda Dederich briefly stepped in to fill the void, but her sister Elsie soon became the permanent secretary, bringing a much needed financial acumen to the post. Since both Hilda and Elsie could remember the stigma attached to Germanic-sounding names during the War—and the problems such associations had once visited upon Matthay—Elsie immediately changed her professional name to the more Anglo-sounding "Elsie Neville."[87] Whenever Matthay stayed at Wimpole Street, Denise recalled that the two of them met each morning for nearly an hour, so that "he could account for every penny."[88] Since the British government had refused to offer scholarship assistance, the School was becoming increasingly dependent on other sources of funding, and Matthay was especially grateful when, for example, as early as 1923, the Dutch government had funded the studies of Maria

Erdtsieck. In 1930, the Chilean government conferred a far more substantial scholarship on Arnaldo Tapia-Caballero, a brilliant pianist who remained at the TMPS for several years, performing extensively in London to critical acclaim. In 1927, the American Matthay Association sent its first scholarship winner, Simonds's pupil Eleanor Goddard, and she was followed in 1928 by Irene Greenleaf Drake. But the most impressive AMA Scholar, Ray (Rachel) Lev, appeared in 1930, and her scholarship was extended for two additional years by the New York Philharmonic. By the end of the decade, she had garnered a wide following on both sides of the Atlantic.

But despite Matthay's public assurances that the School was financially sound,[89] much evidence suggests that by the mid-1930s its earlier troubles had not yet abated, and his increased medical expenses could only have exacerbated his personal difficulties. Of the 50 or so students who had assembled to hear his lecture at Marley in July of 1934, most were visiting only briefly, with fewer than 25 paying the full Summer School tuition. Throughout 1935, he considered a number of measures to produce extra income, and by the year's end he had even resolved to seek an endorsement from the Royal Academy of Music. On 30 January 1936, he wrote a formal letter to McEwen (who five years previously had been knighted):

My dear Sir John,

I am sorry to have to trouble you in this matter but I have no alternative. Mr. Herbert Walenn I hear has explained to you the nature of a Vienna Children's Music Course which it is hoped may be introduced here, and I understand you kindly told him his taking it up would not affect his position at the R.A.M. As he decided after all not to pursue the matter I have been appealed to, and am much inclined to adopt it here. As you did not object to Walenn's doing so I presume also that there will be no objection to my carrying on, although we have a number of professors in common; and I shall conclude that this is correct unless I hear from you to the contrary. It seems to me to be a project that is worth while trying. It must help to increase general interest in music, and also it will help to increase the numbers of music students later on, both here and at the R.A.M. and elsewhere, since after the specified age limit of ten, many from these classes will feel inclined to continue their studies more seriously. The scheme consists of two class lessons per week of 1½ hours, and <u>includes</u>

    20 minutes Aural Training,

    20 " Rhythmical gymnastics,

    20 " vocal study of a foreign language,

    ½ hour of class instruction in either Pianoforte, Violin or Violincello [sic].

The age limits are 6 to 10 years of age. In fact it is a musical form of advanced Kindergarten.

Yours always,
Tobias Matthay[90]

In deference to his rift with McEwen, Matthay did not risk posting his letter, but instead gave it to Walenn to hand deliver. Herbert Walenn had long been a cello professor at the RAM (Barbirolli had been one of his students), and in the 1920s, he had even briefly run a series of cello classes for youngsters at the TMPS, in addition to his own highly successful London Violoncello School, which enjoyed the patronage of Casals. In 1935, he went to Vienna to observe the classes of Joseph Reitler at the Vienna Children's Academy, and he returned to London with a plan for creating a "branch" enterprise with the support of the Austrian government. Soon he invoked the assistance of Baron Georg Frankenstein, Austria's Minister to Britain, who eventually sought to organize a committee of London's most eminent musical educators. But when Walenn was unable to commit his facility at 10 Nottingham Place, they both turned to Matthay to provide a home for their proposed activity. Since before the first War, the RAM had also run a Junior Academy, but as Walenn had already secured McEwen's approval for the new undertaking, Matthay probably sought further sanction merely as a precaution, since by then he was in an unfavorable position to risk confrontation. Predictably, McEwen dealt with Matthay only through intermediaries, and the

Committee of Management discussed his letter on 5 February. The next day, a response was drafted by L. Gurney Parrott, the RAM Secretary:

> I was asked to reply to you that while . . . the Committee have no intention of interfering with any engagement entered into by any Professor of the Academy prior to July 1926, no R.A.M. professor can be permitted to undertake an engagement at any competing Institution without first obtaining the Principal's sanction.
>
> The word "competing" means any School or Institution which professes the same aim as the Royal Academy of Music, viz. the training of professional musicians in any branch of the Art.[91]

Although it could be argued that McEwen and the Committee were being deliberately opaque, it should also be said that Matthay was certainly in a position to have known better, for he immediately assumed that Parrott's ambiguous response constituted an endorsement of his proposal. On 7 February, Elsie Neville informed him that "Mr. Matthay . . . is much relieved that there will be no trouble," while Matthay added a handwritten P. S. at the bottom of her letter: "Glad to hear the definition re 'Competing' institutions[.] I was not quite clear on this point. Anyway, we shall continue to be an 'RAM Nursery.'"[92] But whatever the Academy's true "position"—which no doubt fluctuated according to McEwen's whim—Matthay was arguably imprudent to represent it as he did several weeks later to his friend Sir Hugh Allen, the Principal of the Royal College of Music:

> My dear Sir Hugh,
>
> We are negotiating with Dr. Mosco Carner representing the Neue Wiener Konservatorium with a view to introducing at my School the special Children's classes there held and which have proved such a great success in Vienna. Now as I was not quite sure whether this fact might not alter the standing of this School in the eyes of the R.A.M. and as we have many

Chapter 11

professors in common I placed the matter before the R.A.M. authorities. In their reply however they see no such objection. But before signing the Agreement I feel I ought also to ask you, as one of my most esteemed teachers, Arthur Alexander, also teaches at the R.C.M. [Matthay then includes a description of the proposed classes, taken verbatim from the description he had provided McEwen.]

In my view, the inclusion of these two class lessons per week in stringed instruments cannot affect our standing as a specialist school for Piano, and I have no intention of its so doing, in fact our trust deed precludes its ever being anything else but a Piano School.[93]

Matthay probably did not anticipate that Allen would forward a typed copy of his letter to the RAM, as well as one he had received two days earlier from Baron Frankenstein—following up on a conversation the two of them had had at the end of January. After McEwen saw the letters, a chain of events was touched off which drove an even larger wedge between Matthay and his former RAM associates, provoked especially by Frankenstein's comment: "I understand that the plan has met with the approval of Sir John McEwen."[94] About two weeks later, McEwen took it upon himself to write Frankenstein at the Austrian Legation in Belgrave Square. Although his language was unequivocally clear, one might wonder why Parrott's letter to Matthay two months earlier had not spoken with similar clarity:

Dear Baron Frankenstein,

Sir Hugh Allen has told me that on the authority of Mr. Tobias Matthay, you have quoted me as "approving" of the proposal to form a Children's Conservatoire at the Matthay School under Dr. Carner representing the Neue Wiener Conservatorium. I am afraid that Mr. Matthay quite unwarrantably misrepresented the communication directed to him from the Royal Academy of Music. In order that you may judge for yourself, I enclose a copy of the letter sent to Mr. Matthay in reply to his first communication about this suggested Children's Conservatoire.

I may add that the Authorities of the Academy do not regard with equanimity the institution of such a Conservatoire which will undoubtedly compete with and affect the Junior School of the Royal Academy of Music.[95]

On the same day, Parrott sent a curtly formal admonition to Matthay, informing him that the Committee of Management "have the strongest objection to any of their staff being associated with a foreign scheme which must come into direct opposition with the work carried on by the Royal Academy of Music in its Junior Department."[96] A month later, Matthay responded to the Committee as a whole, challenging several points, especially their use of the adjective "foreign," since "The constitution of the scheme itself would be British and not foreign."[97] But the reply offered by Parrott on 21 May merely echoed their previous statements, adding that "They wish me to reiterate that they have the strongest objection to any Professor of the Royal Academy of Music being concerned directly or indirectly with the proposed Children's Conservatoire."[98] The term "indirectly" was new, and it sent such an alarm signal to Matthay that on 4 June, he took the unprecedented step of sending a handwritten letter to his (once) friend Philip Agnew, Chairman of the Committee of Management. His concern with establishing a meeting time almost assumes a tone of desperation.

My dear Agnew,

I wonder whether you could grant me a favor for "Auld Lang Syne?" This matter of the new Children's Class here is assuming a serious aspect, and being quite misunderstood by Sir Hugh Allen, and your Committee in consequence, a few minutes['] talk might clear all this up. Could I come to see you, or could you come to see me here [at Wimpole Street] or at Marley? I return Tuesday morning and could be here by 12.30 or so. Could you have a snack of lunch with us at 1.30? I don't know where you live now? but can you drive over to High Marley (Haslemere) any time Saturday, Sunday, or Monday?—except during 3 to 4.30 when I am usually fast asleep! We could give you a meal—and the country is wonderful just now!

Or, I could make time on Tuesday[,] Thursday or Friday afternoons, after 5, or on Wednesday or Thursday mornings at eleven or after. Do try to arrange something, a few words of explanation would I am sure set things right—and I cannot go to see Mac about it, as you know!

With all heartiest regards
Yours ever
Tobias Matthay[99]

But with a brazen disregard for confidentiality—or even courtesy—Agnew passed Matthay's letter along to the Committee of Management, and Parrott informed him sternly on 12 June that since the issue had been officially settled, the Chairman "regrets he is unable to discuss the matter."[100] Matthay's final piece of correspondence on the subject was addressed to Parrott on 16 June:

Dear Mr. Parrott,

Will you please tell Mr. Agnew that his message conveyed through you very much surprised me? It looks as if he imagined that I wished to go behind the Committee's back? Nothing was further from my thoughts! In their last letter to me the Committee included a line which might be construed into a veiled threat—but quite impossible one. Instead of sending a long explanatory reply, I suppressed it, and instead took the sane, natural, and human course of asking for an interview with "the man at the wheel", and as I could not hope to get one from the Principal, I appealed to the Chairman. I also made the same request to the Principal of the Royal College, and it was promptly granted. I had a most cordial and friendly talk with Sir Hugh over the matter. I was hoping to convert him to my own views but instead, to my surprise, he was able to convince me that some of his fears might be justified and I fear now that I shall have to throw the whole scheme overboard, unless new light is shed upon it. If I do so, it will therefore be on account of certain possibilities of danger to our profession, which, until I heard Sir Hugh's arguments, I confess I had engenuously [sic] overlooked, in my enthusiasm to further what seemed like a good chance of helping our hard-hit profession, and incidentally the depleted Junior Departments of all our Schools. Perhaps you will kindly convey this message to Mr. Agnew.[101]

It is unknown exactly what Allen said to Matthay, but since it is difficult to envision a musical "kindergarten" constituting a "danger to our profession," one can only speculate that they spoke of Hitler and Nazism, and that Matthay shared his aversion to a tainted business relationship in the event of war. Although it was not unreasonable to assume that similar considerations had concerned the RAM, Matthay knew that McEwen's unbridled animosity was still the major determinant in any actions the institution might have taken toward him. But if McEwen sought to minimize connections between the RAM and the TMPS, he had been singularly unsuccessful over the past decade, because by 1935, fully 18 of the 39 piano professors listed in the Academy prospectus had studied at the Matthay School, as well as numerous professors who taught other subjects. In addition, a "second generation" of Matthayites was arising, and younger pianists like, for example, Eric Grant, a devoted pupil of Frederick Moore, were now making names for themselves as Academy teachers. It should also be noted that on 1 January 1936, Myra (just three weeks after having her appendix removed[102]) had been granted a C.B.E. "for services to music," and on that evening McEwen was required to toast her as an honored guest of the Incorporated Society of Musicians at the Hotel Great Central. But his remarks were aimed only at the importance of younger musicians, without whose "vitality, energy, and idealism" the Society could not flourish.

The response was given by the Society's President, Dr. Stanley Marchant, then the Organist at St. Paul's and a long-time supporter of the TMPS,[103] who "expressed the pleasure of the members of the musical profession on learning that Dr. Percy Buck was to receive the honour of knighthood and Miss Myra Hess to be a Commander of the Order of the British Empire."[104] Sir Hugh Allen also paid a respectful acknowledgement to the honored guests. Although all the surrounding circumstances may never be known, it is possible that a critical mass of Academy personnel had finally lost patience with McEwen's vendetta, and that Myra—one of the Academy's most cherished graduates—had now become too important to snub. And it is almost irresistible to posit a connection between the fact that less than three weeks after the Children's Conservatoire episode had concluded, McEwen's retirement was announced "for reasons of health."[105] Surprisingly, there was no interim period of pro-tem governance, because Marchant was named his successor on the same day, suggesting considerable prior deliberations from behind the scenes. He was officially installed as Principal the following September, and Matthay's eleven-year estrangement from the institution to which he had devoted most of his life had finally come to an end. The hatchet was symbolically buried that fall when Marchant asked Matthay for a photograph that was "accepted with thanks" by the Committee of Management, on 27 January 1937.[106]

Marchant was 51 when he assumed his new office, so despite changing aesthetic tastes and fashions, he was old enough to remember a time when most serious British musicians had paid a respectful nod to the TMPS. Not only had Matthay's influence once extended far beyond the British Isles, but scores of famous pianists who never studied with him routinely offered deferential admiration—especially the large community of Russian musicians who had fled to the West by 1918. In April 1923, during her second tour of the States, Myra wrote her manager, John Tillett, that she met Rachmaninoff in New York, who rehearsed his Second Concerto with her in the basement of Steinway's show-room, which she found "very thrilling[,] and he was so nice."[107] For all of her adult life, Benno Moiseiwitsch (who reached England long before the Revolution) also remained one of her closest friends, and since he was a frequent visitor to Wimpole Street—where his niece had studied for several years—Matthay often asked him to judge the School's competitions. For several summers in the mid-1930s, Matthay's American student Clifford Herzer played for Josef and Rosina Lhévinne in Vienna, and each time "they would send me back to wonderful Uncle Tobs as they were so delighted with his work."[108] And on 25 November 1935, Jessie advised Bruce and Rosalind Simonds that "Medtner has come to settle in London and is going to judge the [TMPS] Chopin Prize Competition next week."[109] For over two decades, Matthay had enthusiastically taught Nicolas Medtner's music, but their first meeting probably did not occur until 16 February 1928, the date of his British debut at Aeolian Hall—which *The Times* praised in a somewhat backhanded fashion:

> We have often wondered why his works have attained the reputation they have; when he plays them himself the question is answered. He knows exactly how to present his own work to an audience, how to turn what may look dull in the written notes and sound ordinary in less skillful hands into a thing of perfect grace and well-moulded outline.[110]

Medtner's biographer, Barrie Martyn, reports that Matthay was also in the audience—and profoundly moved:

> Among those who came to pay their respects was the famous piano teacher Tobias Matthay, who not only had instructed all his pupils to go to the recital, but came to the green-room afterwards, and, with tears in his eyes, embraced Medtner and kissed his hand. He invited the Medtners to visit his Surrey home but unfortunately their full timetable did not allow them to do so.[111]

Although Medtner immediately endeared himself to English audiences, he soon wrote Rachmaninoff with bitterness, "Apart from the English and the Russians, no-one wants to know me."[112] In March of 1930, he returned to play his Second Concerto in Bournemouth, a performance he considered a success, even though he fought "a battle of wills" with the "difficult and irascible Sir Dan Godfrey."[113] The following week he went to Queen's Hall to hear Wood conduct the premiere of Bax's Third Symphony, a substantial forty-minute work that *The Times* noted "did not seem long," bearing "witness

Chapter 11

to Mr. Bax's successful manipulation of his chosen material."[114] Knowing Bax had wanted to meet him, Medtner introduced himself at the interval, and soon announced that though he considered the composer a "modernist," he regarded his work as "much better than Stravinsky or even Richard Strauss."[115] After the concert, Medtner and his wife walked back to Wimpole Street, where they spent a "congenial hour" with Matthay and Jessie.[116] For the next several years the two couples socialized only intermittently since the Medtners were living in Paris, but by 1935 financial exigencies had forced them to accept the largesse of friends who offered them a small house in Golders Green just off Finchley Road—to which they relocated by early October. Denise recalled that they soon became frequent visitors to the Wimpole Street sitting room, with Anna Medtner—who had originally opposed a move to the English climate because of "her husband's weak chest"—tending to his every need, as he remained wrapped in scarves and mittens.[117]

Matthay also soon had another broadcast, this time a ten-minute excerpt from his longest solo work, the lengthy *Thirty-one Variations & Derivations from an Original Theme*, Op. 28, heard on the National Service at 8:10 pm on 29 April 1935. A few months later, Jessie also made a BBC appearance, as she eagerly announced to Bruce and Rosalind in June:

> I am getting along fine and looking forward to walking by myself very shortly. It will depend upon wearing carefully adjusted shoes. I am to broadcast on July 31st—not poems—alas—that I love, but a melodrame [sic] that dear old Corder wrote for me 33 years ago, string quartette[,] harp & organ. A veritable resurrection!![118]

Although Jessie had continued to provide support and guidance for the TMPS and its students, her last documented Wigmore Hall recitation was on 17 July 1930,[119] and no doubt this explains her comment to Simonds that she had undergone a "resurrection" when she gave a speech on Matthay's behalf in July of 1934. On 31 July 1935, she broadcast Corder's setting of Wildenbruch's "Das Hexenlied"—which she had premiered at Bechstein Hall on 25 May 1903—at 10:50 in the evening on the National Service. *The Times*'s program log identified it only as "Chamber Music" with Jessie's ten-minute performance receiving support from baritone Dale Smith, harpist John Cockerill, the Leslie Bridgewater String Quintet, and—although Corder's score stipulated a harmonium—Benjamin Dale as organist.[120] Evidently she and Matthay were both experiencing something of a rejuvenation, as she communicated to Bruce and Rosalind in November:

> Uncle Tobs seems to refuse to give up his boyhood—he is as bonnie as ever & the Chopin Preludes & Studies that float upwards while most of us are thinking of falling asleep have a newly-born zing about them. I wish he would broadcast them one day but he enjoys the sport of playing his own pieces. Next time he and I may share the programme. Mrs. Tobias will fill in the gap between his two sections with six sonnets. So you see I'm still jogging along. Next Sunday I am giving a semi-private recital of poems at Bristol![121]

She also took it upon herself to oversee the TMPS "Kaffee Klatches," which were held "whenever we can find a spare evening,"[122] and had been operating with renewed vigor since the new concert hall had opened at No. 96 in the fall of 1929. On 9 December 1931, for example, the students and professors were treated to performances of Beethoven and Schumann—followed by lighter fare:

> After the "Kaffee" has appeared and disappeared we are to have some North American Indian folk songs, sung to a drum accompaniment by Miss Florence Glenn—who hails from Toronto—and will give those who hear her an unforgettable experience.[123]

By this time, folk music was not an unusual event at the TMPS. As early as May of 1915, Bax had written Harriet Cohen: "Last night at Wimpole [Street] there was a singer of Indian music who seemed to have a marvelous technique for that kind of work."[124] Jack's daughter, Elizabeth, had a lifelong interest in folk idioms,

Chapter 11

and on 21 November 1923 the RAM Committee of Management read a letter from her close friend Cecil Sharp, suggesting "Mrs. Kennedy North as a suitable teacher in Folk Dancing & stating that he would take a personal interest in the class," a proposal Matthay enthusiastically supported.[125] Elizabeth's brother, Douglas Kennedy, was also a prominent member of the English Folk Dance and Song Society, and on 20 July 1929, while awaiting completion of their new concert room, Matthay and Jessie were treated to a bagpipe demonstration in Marylebone's Court House. After solos by Myra, followed by Beethoven's Violin Sonata in G (for which she was joined by her friend Jelly d'Aranyi), and some two-piano works which she played with Denise, a supper was served to commemorate the end of the Festival season. Afterwards, "The Northumbrian Pipes" were "explained and introduced" by Elizabeth's husband, Stanley North, before a performance was rendered by Tom Clough.[126]

On 27 June 1932 Jessie wrote Simonds that "Auntie Jessie has been getting on her feet & shuffling along and generally beginning life all over, which is very cheerful."[127] But she was not referring just to occasional improvements in her physical condition, because she was now preoccupied with writing Matthay's biography, a project which had filled her with renewed enthusiasm. A month earlier, after she had roughed out about two-thirds of it, she mapped the plan of the remainder to Simonds:

> The third part I hope will be an amplification of the portrait which I have tried to draw, unvarnishedly. It is to consist of various documents such as reflections from, I have thought four, men and women who have come in contact with him. The four that I have in mind, are yourself, Myra, Mr Forbes Dennis, a very cultured and much traveled musico psychologist and Madam Orlova. I am not sure whether you have met her, but she represents a keen type of Russian intellectuality.
>
> Something in the length of approximately 750 words, is what I have in mind; but it would not matter if it is shorter or longer than that. I am thinking of including a good deal of an article that appeared in the Musical Observer, March 1928 on "The Ten Foremost Pioneers in Piano

Pedagogy". You may already know it. I also think of a lecture delivered by Professor [Friedrich] Niecks on "Some Ideals in Musical Education" in 1910. Also all the Queen's Hall programmes and a miscellaneous group of other interesting happenings. . . .

Myra has promised, so has Mr Forbes Dennis, and I am writing to Madam Orlova.[128]

Eventually, Dennis, Simonds, and Myra all contributed essays to Jessie's book, but nothing appeared from Orlova, and neither Niecks's lecture nor the *Observer* piece was republished. Over the summer, Jessie sent Simonds a draft of what she had so far completed, and after he returned it to her in late August with comments, she informed him of her most recent revisions:

> I tremble to think how you must have choked over the slap-dashery of the biography. I do not think rough drafts are always so ungentlemanly but it was done in a happy hurry to see how the story would shape and now that I have got it even thus far all sorts of possibilities are cropping up. For instance I have enlarged the third chapter [dealing with Matthay's piano studies at the Academy] almost out of recognition—in fact it wasn't a chapter at all but a fragment and now I have gathered all sorts of interesting beginnings such as his first ray of light on progression which came to him when he was quite a youth; then in later chapters there are the beginnings of key-treatment and study of the various piano actions; the American story with Myra's pilgrimage as its centre is better told I think. I hope to concentrate from middle September to Christmas on its later development and surely we ought to have it out by Christmas of 1933.[129]

She must have been running ahead of schedule, because she evidently considered herself finished well before Christmas of 1932. On 20 November she wrote Bruce and Rosalind:

> We packed up the Book yesterday morning and sent it to the Oxford University Press for still further criticism. It is complete except for Mr

Forbes Dennis' article. I am longing to send you the emendated copy. It has developed tremendously. You might like perhaps to see one of the surplus copies early in Jan. when you may happen to have a little leisure.[130]

But no copies of the book were then available, because as she advised Simonds the following March, "It became clear to me that it was such a long way from being anything but a hasty mess."[131] Since Bruce and Rosalind returned to England that summer, they exchanged little correspondence with Jessie over the next several months, and she may have put the book aside for a while, since her lengthy letter to them on 3 December makes no mention of it. Understandably, most of 1934 was taken up with concerns over Matthay's health, so she probably worked on it very little, if at all. The few letters to Simonds that survive from 1935 and 1936 often seem preoccupied with her "resurrection" as an elocutionist, which was understandable since Matthay later confirmed that her arthritis had indeed forced her to withdraw from the stage several years earlier. On 1 October 1936, she wrote Simonds from Wimpole Street, after having returned from a brief "escape" to Scotland:

My Dear Bruce,

I feel as though I have had a birthday when I read your letter. I have been away in Scotland until the day before yesterday, and I have brought your letter back to Matthay as "a present from Edinburgh[.]" I know just how to value it—something very precious indeed. I went off with my Highland nurse to forget domestic tangles that have spun themselves out for close on three months but now, 'Gott sei Dank' I think they are straightening out. So here we are [at Wimpole Street]—not quite all, for Denise is resting at Marley[.] At the end of the second week of the term, Uncle Tobs has given his first lecture (which I witnessed as a humble student) and really seems in top form. He and I have been quite gay this week—twice to the Proms—Myra with the Mozart D min[or] Concerto on Tuesday, and Irene with the Schumann last night. Myra was quite above the earth all the time, and to my joy, so was the orchestra, rather wonderful seeing that it was the last week of a long season....

Uncle Tobs and I are giving a joint broadcast on Nov. 6th[.] He, with bunches of Lyrics [Matthay was playing some or all of his *Lyrics*, Op. 14: seven short pieces that he had dedicated to Jessie in 1893.] and I with 6 Sonnets in between. We always hoped that one day we could do something together—Voila![132]

Although she does not explain the "domestic tangles," they most likely concerned Denise, now 33, whose friends recalled that she had fallen in love with an RAF pilot, a relationship Jessie forced her to break off. If Denise were despondent, it might explain why she remained at Marley in the middle of the week (Jessie's letter was written on a Thursday), avoiding Jessie, and perhaps even missing both Myra and Irene's performances during the last week of the Proms. Matthay and Jessie's thirty-five-minute broadcast went off as scheduled on the National Service at 6:25 pm on Friday, 6 November, and on 19 February—Matthay's seventy-ninth birthday—Jessie recited a total of seven Sonnets at their Wimpole Street celebration. Matthay also played nearly a full program, including Liszt's "Un Sospiro," Chopin's Berceuse, and several Etudes, and no less than five of his own pieces. To round out the evening, Denise reported that "After coffee York Bowen played his [own] Sonata, Op. 72, and Humoreske."[133] By then Jessie had enthusiastically returned to the book, and less than two months later it was nearing completion. On 12 April she informed Matthay that it was "ready for publication."[134]

Three days later, while Denise and Hilda Dederich were taking a brief holiday in Italy, they received a cable from Hilda's husband with a single sentence: "What kind of flowers should I buy for Aunt Jessie's funeral?"[135] Frantic and overwrought, they both hurried home, and Denise remembered that Matthay drove to the station at Haslemere, where he met her on the platform. Jessie's remains were cremated at nearby Woking, where a brief memorial service was held the next day. By the end of the month, Matthay had sent

Chapter 11

engraved messages of thanks to his friends and students throughout the world:

> I thank you all individually and collectively for your deep sympathy with me in my dire distress and that of my family.
>
> Shortly after tea on April 14th my wife had an internal haemorrhage and soon lost consciousness. She passed away without pain at 10.30.
>
> God bless you all.[136]

And within a few weeks, Matthay had penned an eloquent tribute for the *Musical Times*, which read in part:

> She was my inspiration, my helper and adviser in everything all these forty-four years; and I ascribe to her all the success I may have achieved.
>
> She intended to become a singer like the rest of her family, but she was also quite a fine pianist, and musically could have held her own with any of my artists. On my advice, however, she seriously took up verse-speaking, and with her wonderfully sympathetic contralto voice, keen rhythmical sense, and intense love for the beautiful and the true in poetry, she eventually made a great name for herself; probably she was the most subtle artist of her time—the Myra Hess of her profession! Probably, also, she knew more English verse than anyone in this country. She had many fine elocution pupils, and her influence towards the highest in her Art will keep her name imperishable. . . .
>
> Her musical judgment was impeccable, and she intensely resented anything that in the least savoured of the meretricious. The great influence of her taste on my School and upon my artists has been quite incalculable.[137]

Notes

1. MA. Jessie to Bruce and Rosalind Simonds, 22 Mar. 1933.
2. On 21 July 1931, Gerschefski was officially recognized at Queen's Hall as the recipient of the TMPS "Yale University Scholar" Fellowship. On

30 June 1932, Ina Gerschefski played the Haydn F minor Variations at a TMPS concert in Aeolian Hall, and this was not her only recital appearance during her time in London. MA.
3. MA. Jessie to Bruce and Rosalind Simonds, 31 Aug. 1932.
4. MA. Jessie to Bruce and Rosalind Simonds, 20 Nov. 1932.
5. "Miss Gertrude Peppercorn," The *Daily Telegraph*, 16 Nov. 1932, 8, col. 3.
6. MA. Jessie to Bruce and Rosalind Simonds, 22 Mar. 1933.
7. From Book VI of the *Mikrokosmos*, 148-53 (1939).
8. Hallis used the anagrammatic pseudonym "Hal Dolphe" for *Rich and Strange*, while the screen credit for *Number Seventeen* reads "A. Hallis."
9. *MT*, May 1936, 461.
10. Caroline Mears, "Hallis, Adolph," *RNG*.
11. "Mr. Adolph Hallis," *TT*, 19 Feb. 1937, 12, col. D.
12. "Hallis Chamber Concert," *TT*, 17 Apr. 1937, 12, col. C.
13. "Hallis Chamber Concert," *TT*, 17 Jan. 1938, 8, col. G.
14. "Hallis Chamber Concert," *TT*, 16 Feb. 1938, 10, col. E.
15. "Hallis Chamber Concerts[:] New Series Begun ," *TT*, 15 Nov. 1938, 12, col. B.
16. *MT*, 1 July 1931, 656. At the same festival, Mannheimer also performed chamber works of Quincy Porter and Frederick Jacobi.
17. "Mr. Julian de Gray," *TT*, 23 Nov. 1931, 10, col. C.
18. MA. From DeGray's biography prepared for a tour sponsored by the Arts Program of the Association of American Colleges in 1938.
19. MA. Taped interview with DeGray at his home in Warren, Connecticut, conducted by his former student Elizabeth Lauer on 9 April 1984.
20. Interview with DeGray at his studio in New York City on 7 Nov. 1982.
21. Daniel W. Winter, "My Years with Matthay and Schnabel" [An Interview with Eunice Norton], *Clavier*, March, 1962, 55.
22. Ibid., 56.
23. Ibid.
24. See Jennifer Doctor, *The BBC and Ultra-Modern Music, 1922-1936* (Cambridge, 1999).
25. Matthay to Tillett, 4 Jan. 1928, BBCWA.
26. *MT*, 1 Apr. 1928, 368.
27. Matthay to Boult, 24 Sept. 1930, BBCWA.

Chapter 11

28. Ibid. Hutchinson and Wright wrote their comments along the bottom of Matthay's letter to Boult.
29. Hutchinson to Boult internal memo, 11 Oct. 1930, BBCWA.
30. See Doctor, 241.
31. Boult to Hutchinson internal memo, 17 Oct. 1930, BBCWA.
32. Internal memo from Mase to Boult, 31 Oct. 1930, BBCWA.
33. Ibid.
34. Boult to Matthay, 11 Nov. 1930, BBCWA.
35. Matthay to Tillett, 9 May 1931, BBCWA. Matthay even offered to provide program notes to Tillett, but the *Radio Times* had already gone to press.
36. Matthay to Boult, 20 May 1931, BBCWA.
37. Matthay to Boult, 25 Nov. 1931, BBCWA.
38. Matthay to Boult, 30 Jun. 1932, BBCWA.
39. Boult to Matthay, 29 Jul. 1932, BBCWA. Only a draft of Boult's letter exists in the Archives, and it may have been changed somewhat before it reached Matthay.
40. MA. Matthay to Simonds, 7 Oct. 1932.
41. Columbia DX444.
42. *The Gramophone,* March 1933, 395. The magazine's critic noted that his review was written on 19 February, Matthay's birthday.
43. Cited from Columbia's promotional brochure accompanying the recording in February or March of 1933.
44. The Prelude was published in London by Weekes & Co. in 1897, and later re-issued by the AFMC about 1916. Ricordi issued the Intermezzo and "Bravura" in separate editions in 1910. Sometime afterward, Matthay taped his own copies (now in the MA) of the three pieces together, suggesting that he thought in terms of performing them as a suite. Hereafter cited as "Matthay copies."
45. "Matthay copies."
46. Ibid., "Prelude," 2.
47. *The Gramophone*, March 1933, 395.
48. Columbia promotional brochure.
49. "Matthay copies," "Bravura," opposite 1.
50. Ibid., 2.
51. Ibid., 3.

52. See McKenna, *Myra Hess*, 106-08.
53. One of her earliest recordings was the Chopin "Black Key" Etude, Gramophone Co., 05532, reissued on Gemm CD 9978.
54. *MT*, 1 Oct. 1925, 917.
55. Compton Parkenham, "Newly Recorded Music[:] Columbia Issues a Second Album from "The Well-Tempered Clavichord," *NYT*, 7 Dec. 1930, 134.
56. *MT*, Feb. 1934, 134.
57. See Alan Vicat, Notes for a CD Reissuing of Irene Scharrer's recordings, Gemm CD 9978.
58. The Scherzo was from d'Albert's *Klavierstücke*, Op. 16, no. 2. See Richard Davis, *Eileen Joyce[:] A Portrait* (Fremantle, Australia, 2001), 74.
59. *MT*, Oct. 1930, 906.
60. Ibid.
61. Compton Parkenham, "Newly Recorded Music" *NYT*, 19 Oct. 1930, 122.
62. "Programmes," *TT*, 14 Feb. 1928, 20, col. A.
63. "Death of Miss Raie Da Costa[:] Wireless Syncopated Pianist," *TT*, 27 Aug. 1934, 8, col. E.
64. *TT*, 5 Sept. 1928, 10, col. E.
65. "Recent Gramophone Records[:] Old Popular Songs," *TT*, 20 May 1929, 8, col. D.
66. *TT*, 2 Nov., 1933, 17, col. A.
67. "Gramophone Notes by 'Discus,'" *MT*, 1 Nov. 1930, 996. Frederick Lamond's recording of Liszt's transcription of the "Cujus animam" from Rossini's *Stabat Mater* prompted "Discus" to write: "I cannot understand a pianist of Lamond's position playing it." He also called Da Costa's recording of *Rigoletto* "perhaps the worst display of fireworks of the lot."
68. Interview with Jonson at his Hampstead home, 9 June 2006. The program is in the MA, although Humby is listed as the accompanist.
69. Advertisement in *TT*, 6 Jan. 1933, 8, col. F.
70. John Watson, liner notes for *Raie Da Costa—The Parlophone Girl*, Vol. I, Shellwood, SWCD 8, 1998.
71. MA.
72. MA. Jessie recited a scene from Dane's *Will Shakespeare* on 4 July 1922 at a TMPS Wigmore Hall program.
73. David Ades, "Addinsell, Richard (Stewart)," *RNG*.

Chapter 11

74. Ibid.
75. Davis, *Eileen Joyce*, 101.
76. Letter from John Watson, 8 Dec. 2004.
77. MA. Jessie to Bruce and Rosalind Simonds, 17 Jan. 1934.
78. MA. Jessie to Bruce and Rosalind Simonds, 9 Mar. 1934.
79. *AMAJ*, Summer 1934, 4.
80. McKenna (p. 102) claims that Myra sailed for England in June, but she probably arrived by the last week of May.
81. MA. Jessie to Bruce and Rosalind Simonds, 29 May 1934.
82. Ibid.
83. MA. Jessie to Simonds, 7 Jul. 1934.
84. Ibid.
85. Arthur Hice, "A Personal Glimpse of Activities in London Last Summer," *AMAJ*, 1934, 29.
86. Ibid., 30.
87. LI.
88. LI.
89. For example, on 16 July 1936, Matthay's Queen's Hall speech assured his supporters that "Our Studentship remains at much the same level for the last two or three years," but Jessie reported only 27 Americans attending the Summer School "for longer or shorter periods." *JAMA*, 9 and 39.
90. RAMA. Matthay to McEwen, 30 Jan. 1936.
91. RAMA. Parrott to Matthay, 6 Feb. 1936.
92. RAMA. Neville to Parrott, 7 Feb. 1936.
93. RAMA, Copy of a letter from Matthay to Allen, 18 Mar. 1936.
94. RAMA, Copy of a letter from Frankenstein to Allen, 16 Mar. 1936.
95. RAMA. McEwen to Frankenstein, 3 Apr. 1936.
96. RAMA. Parrott to Matthay, 3 Apr. 1936.
97. RAMA. Matthay to the Committee of Management, 9 May 1936.
98. RAMA. Parrott to Matthay, 21 May 1936.
99. RAMA. Matthay to Agnew, 4 Jun. 1936.
100. RAMA. Parrott to Matthay, 12 Jun. 1936.
101. RAMA. Matthay to Parrott, 16 Jun. 1936.
102. See McKenna, 109.

103. In the 1920s, Marchant had taught a twelve-session course for the TMPS Teachers' Training Course called "Training for School Singing Class." Ironically, his was one of the subjects McEwen had most complained of when he declared the Matthay School to be a competitor to the RAM.
104. "Organized Musicians[:] Appeal for the Support of Youth," *TT*, 1 Jan. 1936, 8, col. D.
105. "Royal Academy of Music," *TT*, 2 July 1936, 14, col. G.
106. COMM, 27 Jan. 1937.
107. Letter from Myra to Tillett, 15 April 1923. Reproduced in Christopher Fifield, *Ibbs and Tillett[:] The Rise and Fall of a Musical Empire* (Aldershot, 2005), 550.
108. *AMAEM*, 14.
109. MA. Jessie to Bruce and Rosalind Simonds, 25 Nov. 1925.
110. "Nicholas Medtner. First Appearance in London," *TT*, 17 Feb. 1928, 12, col. D.
111. Barrie Martyn, *Nicholas Medtner[:] His Life and Music* (Aldershot, 1995), 192.
112. Cited Ibid.
113. Ibid., 203.
114. "B.B.C. Concert[:] Mr. Bax's Symphony," *TT*, 15 Mar. 1930, 10, col. D.
115. Martyn, 203.
116. Ibid.
117. Ibid., 218, and LI.
118. MA. Jessie to Bruce and Rosalind Simonds, 17 Jun. 1935.
119. MA. The poems she recited that evening are not identified in the program.
120. "Broadcasting," *TT*, 31 Jul. 1935, 10, col. D.
121. MA. Jessie to Bruce and Rosalind Simonds, 25 Nov. 1935
122. Letter from Jessie Matthay to "American Associates," *JAMA*, Summer 1931, 5.
123. Ibid.
124. BL. Bax to Cohen, 15 May 1915.
125. COMM, 21 Nov. 1923.
126. MA.
127. MA. Jessie to Simonds, 27 Jun. 1932.
128. MA. Jessie to Simonds, 25 May 1932.
129. MA. Jessie to Simonds, 31 Aug. 1932.

130. MA. Jessie to Simonds, 20 Nov. 1932.
131. MA. Jessie to Simonds, 22 Mar. 1933.
132. MA. Jessie to Simonds, 1 Oct. 1936.
133. Denise Lassimonne, letter to Richard McClanahan, 3 Oct. 1937, published in *AMAJ*, 1937, 9.
134. Tobias Matthay, Foreword to Jessie Henderson Matthay, *The Life and Works of Tobias Matthay* (London, 1945), vii.
135. LI.
136. MA.
137. Tobias Matthay, *MT*, May 1937, 464.

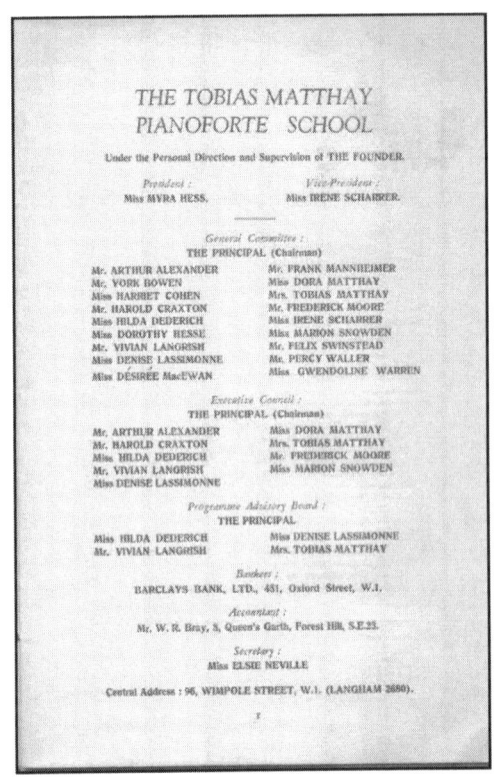

Page from the TMPS prospectus about 1935 listing the School's governing officers

Moura Lympany about 1940

Denise and Myra at Lake Como, Italy, in the summer of 1937

Matthay rowing on Lake Como in the summer of 1937

CHAPTER 12

FINAL DAYS

On 12 January 1942, *Time* magazine ran a feature story entitled "Down With Scales." It began:

> Few youngsters have heard of Tobias Matthay, but many have cause to thank him. Lank, long-jawed, white-maned, "Uncle Tobs" is the man who took the drudgery out of piano lessons. He now lives in the English countryside, nearing 84. In Manhattan last week 50 teacher-members of the American Matthay Association met to discuss Matthay-style teaching.[1]

Accompanied by a photo of Matthay taken by his American pupil Paul Snyder, the article was part factual and part caricature, but it conveyed the message that Matthay ideas were making an impact in America. While conceding that his advocates were still in the minority, it noted that "about one-third of the nation's 1,500,000 piano students are no longer subjected to those scramble-noted exercises composed by [the] implacable Karl Czerny, who is widely believed to have hated children."[2] A half dozen of the "newest piano methods," created by little-known American teachers with no demonstrable Matthay connections, were also cited, and the gist of the story pointed to a new wave, even though "most U.S. piano-moppets must still struggle with Czerny."[3] It remains an open question as to whether Matthay's American popularity, which began to mushroom in the late 1920s, was due more to aesthetic considerations or to a mere fascination with modernity, but in 1984, Julian DeGray recalled that "having a Matthay teacher on your faculty then was the latest thing—a bit like owning a computer today."[4]

Without question, Matthay ranks in the United States and Canada were growing. In 1930 the American Matthay Association reported less than ten AMA members teaching in colleges and conservatories, but by 1939, there were over 70.[5] Although concentrated in the Northeast, they were spread over 23 states and extended as far north as the Halifax Conservatory of Music. Many were attached to liberal arts colleges and even prep schools, but some were also installed in prestigious conservatories and universities. Clarence Burg was Dean of the School of Fine Arts at Oklahoma City University, Cécile Genhart taught at Eastman, Roxy Grove at Baylor, Lura Bailey at Northwestern, Annabelle Wood at Vassar, and Alice Kortschak at the Manhattan School of Music. In 1929, DeGray had joined the faculty of the University of Miami, and three years later he taught the first entering class at Bennington, where he remained for nearly 40 years. Beginning in 1930, Bruce Simonds became one of four permanent jurors for the prestigious Naumburg Competition—which jumpstarted the careers of pianists Dalies Frantz, Jorge Bolet, and Abbey Simon—and by 1940 he had become Chair of Yale's newly created Department of Music, a separate division from its School of Music, designed to "correlate more fully the work in music with that of other departments of the faculty, particularly history and literature."[6] A year later he was appointed Dean of the School of Music, as well as Director of Yale's Norfolk Summer School.

Surprisingly, Simonds maintained an active performing career through all these activities, and for many years he gave annual programs in New York's Town Hall, often to substantial acclaim. In December of 1931 the *New York Times* praised him as a "personal and distinguished talent," performing with "grace, suppleness and a luminous quality of clarity without any of the hardness which is often clarity's step-sister."[7] Although his rendition of Bax's first Sonata—a work the *Times* noted was "not satisfactory in itself"— met with mixed response, he "caught the swift delicacy of Scarlatti, and the many small shades of phrase and tone in the [Pasquini] toccata."[8] Three years later, Olin Downes noted his "wonted sincerity and artistic intelligence" in Beethoven's Opus 109, which was rendered with "a fine sensitiveness and cogency."[9] A few months earlier, he had completed an eight-recital cycle devoted to all 32 Beethoven Sonatas,[10] which he coached with Matthay in the summer of 1933, and in January of 1934, Matthay wrote him that "you must be rushed with all those recitals at hand. I am sure the 'Hammerklavier' will prove to be a <u>memorable</u> performance—probably one of the <u>most perceptive</u> it has <u>ever</u> had!"[11] After extensive nationwide tours for the Arts Program of the Association of American Colleges, DeGray also performed the Beethoven cycle in nine programs at Bennington in the spring of 1938, on mostly consecutive Sundays from 16 April to 4 June.[12] By 1934, Eunice Norton, then living in Pitcairn, Pennsylvania, with her new husband, physicist Bernard Lewis (who commuted to teach at Pittsburgh's Carnegie Tech), had also performed the cycle, a feat she repeated many times over the next several decades. And despite her two years with Schnabel, she remained loyal to Matthay's teachings, as demonstrated by an article she wrote in the spring of 1934:

> To give any kind of correct impression of the spirit of Tobias Matthay's teaching, one can only begin by saying that musical thought is the first and all important aim and ideal of his work. Because of his extraordinary success in relieving students of their technical difficulties, it is often thought by outsiders that Mr. Matthay's training consists only of mastering a method for piano technique. Technical perfection is, of course, of vital importance, but in the training of this master it is considered only a means to a far more important end, the recreating of the greatest works. . . .
>
> It is not difficult for one learning for the first time about relaxation in piano playing to become so absorbed in that phase of the study that he loses sight of the important role played by the fingers. Once free of all tenseness and physical strain, it is the sensitive finger tip which produces the exquisite quality for which one is striving and which one hears in Mr. Matthay's own playing. A vital, crystal clear, bell-like tone is the result when one combines a relaxed arm with fingers that really grip the keys. . . .
>
> This winter in touring from coast to coast I met a great many Matthayites striving hard with their students for these results. It is

thrilling to know that this valuable knowledge is being taught so generally in music schools in this country.[13]

But not all who left Matthay for Schnabel were so generous, especially in England, where he was no longer considered a novelty. Perhaps the harshest indictment came from composer and pianist Alan Bush (1900-95), who—for whatever reason—advised Lewis Foreman years later that Matthay was "the ruination of pianism in England."[14] Bush's wife, Nancy, the sister of composer Michael Head, recalled the first time her brother invited his twenty-year-old classmate to lunch at their home, "having come straight from a lesson with the notoriously unpunctual Tobias Matthay, and we had quite given him up."[15] Bush studied piano with both Matthay and Percy Waller, as well as composition with Corder and John Ireland, and by 1925 he had been appointed to the composition faculty at the Academy. But in the autumn of 1928 he took a year's leave to study piano with Schnabel in Berlin (a sabbatical which McEwen no doubt was happy to approve) and despite the fact that he played for him only six times, he maintained that his life in the German capital was "centered in his lessons with Schnabel."[16] Remarkably, he also admitted that Schnabel had nothing to offer concerning piano technique, as "he seemed to expect a student to do what he did by some mysterious semi-hypnotic process."[17] At his first lesson, Bush performed the Beethoven Sonata, Op. 111, after which Schnabel announced that "You English pianists don't seem to have much heart." But despite technical advice limited to the phrase, "Watch me do it," Bush found the session highly inspirational. Much to his surprise, that afternoon he was followed by another former Matthay pupil, Clifford Curzon, who brought the Schubert C minor Sonata, which he had studied with Matthay, and which Bush thought he played "magnificently."[18]

But though Curzon's admiration for Schnabel seemed boundless (in December of 1951, he even broadcast a lengthy eulogy to him on the BBC[19]), he maintained a respect for Matthay's writings well into the 1970s, admitting that "I constantly go back to those books" for advice and guidance.[20] On 3 January 1920, Curzon entered the

RAM at the age of 12 as a student of Charles Reddie, and on 15 October 1924—when he was only 17—Matthay voted for his appointment to sub-professor at a Committee of Management meeting.[21] But however Curzon may have viewed his long relationship to Reddie, approaching Matthay would have been difficult, since McEwen soon forbade connections between RAM students and the TMPS, and he also kept a tight leash on his sub-professors. Even after Curzon left the Academy in June of 1926, he probably handled his Matthay studies with discretion, because he may not have ruled out a future desire to teach at the RAM.[22] But for a number of years, he was a fixture at the TMPS, adjudicating the Musical Initiative Prize in 1928, and awarding the School's Silver Medals both in 1931 and again in 1933.[23] His first solo appearance under Matthay's guidance was at Wigmore Hall on 13 May 1927, when he performed Schubert's "Wanderer" Fantasy—"boldly" according to *The Times*, and "with force and character."[24] He shared the evening with soprano Dorothy Robson, who was supported by "the beautiful accompanying" of Harold Craxton, another of Matthay's long-time pupils, whose efforts, *The Times* noted, "should be recorded."[25]

The forty-two-year-old Craxton, who had been teaching at the RAM since 1919, was then regarded by many (including Gerald Moore[26]) as the finest accompanist in Britain. He had also enjoyed success as a soloist, at times in unconventional repertoire, and in the early 1920s he even gave a series of Wigmore Hall recitals devoted entirely to the Elizabethan Virginalists. One of his concerts, on 17 February 1923, positioned several of their works between Bach and Chopin, and *The Times* lamented the "puzzle" that "Bach seems to lose nothing, and Byrd, Farnaby, Dowland, and Bull everything, by being played on the wrong instrument, the piano."[27] But the paper did observe that "Mr. Craxton played them tenderly or humorously, as occasion demanded, and always with that live rhythm which is the very soul of them."[28] He was soon receiving similar plaudits for his collaborative work, and by 1924, his extraordinary control of tone and dynamics in both song and chamber recitals was keeping him before the public an average of once per week—with Nellie Melba,

Chapter 12

Clara Butt, and Elena Gerhardt repeatedly requesting his services.[29] Undoubtedly, it was not merely a love of performing which moved him to learn so much repertoire, because by the time he shared an evening with Curzon in May of 1927, he was also the father of five sons. His sixth child, Janet—who later became an internationally acclaimed oboist—was born two years later, and many remembered her proud father quipping to colleagues at the RAM that his family was finally complete, with a "feminine ending."[30] But although Craxton taught to some extent from economic necessity, he took his craft seriously, remaining loyal to both the TMPS and the Academy through the difficult McEwen years. And at the RAM, his students later included some of Britain's most prominent pianists, including Denis Matthews, Peter Katin, and Noel Mewton-Wood.[31]

However, teaching was not a perfect fit for all of Matthay's artist-pupils. Some had gifts so prodigious that they easily lost patience, and Guy Jonson remembered adjudicating Academy students with an increasingly frustrated York Bowen, who frequently offset boredom by producing staff paper from his pocket and sketching entire sonata movements during examinations.[32] And although Bowen remained committed to Matthay principles through his entire career, some of Matthay's pupils had little patience with his verbose explanations. For example, Gertrude Peppercorn once told the father of her teenaged student David Squibb that "Matthay wrote a lot of nonsense," even though she constantly cited his teachings at his lessons. Squibb recalled that at times she demonstrated passages with the explanation, "Matthay knew exactly how to get this sound," and his father often expressed amazement that each lesson made such a demonstrable change in his son's tonal control.[33] Just as Matthay's artists varied in their level of keyboard mastery, his teachers varied in both their commitment and degrees of effectiveness. Denise recalled that Matthay rarely, if ever, dismissed anyone from his staff, but if their pupils continuously fell short of the School's demanding performance standards, he ceased making referrals in their direction.[34]

He also maintained careful oversight of his assignments. Students desiring admission to the School were first required to attend an

"Entrance Hearing," for which the going rate was half a guinea (10s, 6d) through the 1920s.[35] When DeGray arrived for his hearing in 1926, he was stunned at how easily Marion Cole ushered him into Matthay's studio, by contrast to "the inaccessible Cortot hedged about with protective subordinates!"[36] Matthay always made copious notes when prospective students played for him, and his assignments were made with considerable deliberation. He also attentively monitored their progress, as demonstrated by his concern for Marion Fuller, a student of Clarence Hamilton at Wellesley College, and a runner-up in the 1930 AMA Scholarship auditions. When she arrived that summer by courtesy of private funding, Matthay assigned her to Arthur Alexander for additional lessons, but by the spring of 1931 he confided to Simonds that she was unhappy:

> With regard to Fuller, she has made splendid progress—and really plays much better! But—she is down in the dumps, and as she confessed to it at [her] last lesson, I gave her a long talking to, and I think succeeded in dispelling some of her gloom. She says there is "so much to learn and so little time in which to do it." She was quite a star at Wellesley (I think it was Wellesley?) but coming here she finds herself just one of the crowd! As it happens we have a whole row of geniuses here just now, the Chilean, Cabellero, our [AMA] scholar Ray Lev, an Australian genius Eileen Joyce, and Hilda Bor (English Russian) and as they all play like full-blown artists it has made poor Fuller very discouraged—and there are many other fine players here too just now....
>
> Fuller herself has not appeared at the concerts till this term—not having been before "sent in"—I expect Alexander was waiting until she sounded more like one of "ours". But she has now played a piece of Medtner's [*Danza Festiva*] really very finely indeed at the "private" Meetings [on Wimpole Street], and she will therefore play it again at the final Conway Hall Concert next term, and of course at the Summer Festival. [On 7 July, she performed the Medtner piece at Queen's Hall along with Brahms's Capriccio in C-sharp minor from Op. 76.] I myself take her fortnightly, and like her very much indeed, and she comes "up to scratch" on the platform, so I think she will go back not only playing

better, but also with her courage and belief in herself right up again. Alexander is a <u>particularly</u> fine teacher musically, but is rather a pessimist and may not have enthused enough over Fuller's doings—not because he wasn't pleased with her—as a matter of fact I know he is—but just because it is a way he has of appearing <u>undemonstrative</u> even when thoroughly roused. I have also explained that to Fuller, so I think she feels happier now. As a matter of fact during the first term she tried to persuade a friend of hers (Frye) [Margaret Frye was from Buffalo, New York] to leave Dora and also go to Alexander, whereas I chose Dora for Frye as I felt she needed more explanatory minute treatment![37]

Several months after Jessie's death, Matthay administered the TMPS Summer Festival much as usual, except that, as Simonds's pupil Mary Deming poignantly recalled, "It was beautiful to see how Denise, Miss Hess, Miss Scharrer and others were always by his side the evenings of the concerts."[38] A few months later, Denise wrote to McClanahan:

> We had a very lovely holiday [in Italy] on [Lake] Como [Myra and Dora also accompanied Matthay]—three really peaceful weeks, just lazying in the sun, and Uncle Tobs had some magnificent rows on the lake—he even put the sailor to shame, so good was his stroke, with *real* acceleration![39]

On 25 September 1937, Myra and Irene gave a duo-piano recital to a packed house at Wigmore Hall to raise money for a scholarship in Jessie's memory, and *The Times* critic was extremely flattering, noting that their performance of Bax's *Moy Mell* produced "iridescent effects of tone colour."[40] Five months later on 19 February, Matthay celebrated his eightieth birthday in front of 200 guests around the corner from the TMPS at Cowdray Hall on Henrietta Street, an occasion the Bechstein firm commemorated by presenting him with a new studio grand. He made a brief speech expressing gratitude, to which both Myra and Marchant responded, and then he proceeded to play for over 30 minutes on the new instrument. He performed a number of his own pieces, including his early *Walzer Grillen* (Waltz whims, published as "A Waltz-Whim"), which he had dedicated to Sullivan over 50 years earlier. He concluded his own set with "Bravura," before performing the Chopin Berceuse and the "Ocean" Etude in C minor, Op. 25, no. 12. Myra then played "Elves" and "Albumblatt," before joining Irene in some four-hand selections, and Denise ended the program with Mozart's Clarinet Trio in E-flat, K. 498, for which she was joined by clarinetist Reginald Kell and violist Philip Burton.[41] As a further salute, five days later, at 4:15 pm on 24 February, the London Regional Service broadcast fifteen minutes of recorded music by Matthay, Myra, and Irene. To round out the celebration, HMV promptly released Myra's recording of "Elves" and "Albumblatt"—the only Matthay compositions she is known to have committed to disc.[42]

But perhaps an even more gratifying tribute came on the afternoon of 24 April, when at long last the BBC Orchestra under Joseph Lewis performed *In May* on the National Service. Although Matthay had been struggling for over a decade to get his overture broadcast, his most recent campaign succeeded in a matter of months. On 12 February, five days before his birthday celebration, he capitalized on the sentiment it engendered by writing Reginald Thatcher, now the Corporation's Deputy Music Director:

Dear Mr. Thatcher,

I hear that you are going to broadcast my Piano Record on February 24th. It really is very sweet of you to do so. Now I wonder whether you could go a step further still, & at last bring in a performance of my "IN MAY" Overture? Sir Adrian Boult had the score some while ago & i [sic] think did not dislike it, but it was I think turned down on its Mid-Victorian IDIOM. It certainly is in that idiom having been written 50 years ago! But there is quite a formidable mass of very fine music written in that idiom—& in earlier idioms!

After all the idiom does not matter provided there is good in the music! There may or may not be in mine! I have a great affection for this little work, & am sure it is the best piece of music I have written!

If you think it worth looking at, I would gladly send you the score.[43]

Chapter 12

Much to Matthay's surprise, Thatcher requested the score, and a broadcast was scheduled for 24 April. The next day, Matthay sent him a letter of thanks:

My dear Mr. Thatcher,

I had a splendid performance of my Overture "In May" yesterday—the best it has so far had—but for the last previous occasions (in the provinces) I have conducted it myself—when one cannot really hear the effect. Joseph Lewis got the spirit of it perfectly—and all its youthful fire, and I was <u>quite moved by it</u>!!

It has been an immense satisfaction for me to hear it again, and I have written to thank the Committee for giving me the chance of so doing. But I feel that it is probably owing to <u>your good self</u> that I owe this happiness—

Thank you indeed![44]

By now, Matthay had at least some allies at the BBC, because the three-man Programme Committee he referenced included Benjamin Dale. Thatcher passed Matthay's letter along to Lewis, who replied on 27 April with a single sentence: "All this goes to prove that 'there is life in the <u>old dogs</u> yet!!'"[45]

Matthay's pedagogical career was also far from over, for three months later on 19 July, his Queen's Hall program featured the second book of Brahms's Paganini Variations performed by twenty-one-year old Moura Lympany. Born Mary Gertrude Johnstone in Cornwall, her family circumstances were so modest that when she was six she had been sent to a convent school outside Brussels—primarily because it charged only £5 a term. She was sublimely happy in Belgium, and her French soon became so natural that she returned home speaking English with an accent. Almost from infancy, she had been obsessed with the piano, and at the age of 12 she won an Ada Lewis Scholarship to the RAM, where she studied with Ambrose Coviello, a Beringer pupil who often expressed admiration for Matthay's teachings. Shortly before she entered the Academy, she auditioned for conductor Basil Cameron, who was so impressed that he hired her to perform Mendelssohn's G minor Concerto with the Harrogate Municipal Orchestra in Yorkshire. Her mother, who had once lived in St. Petersburg, had always called her "Moura" (the Russian form of "Mary") and Cameron suggested she adopt a simpler spelling of her mother's maiden name—"Limpenny"—for the stage. She left the Academy at 15 for studies with Paul Weingarten in Vienna, and shortly before her seventeenth birthday, perhaps imprudently, she agreed to enter the Liszt Competition in Budapest. Lympany came on the scene just as international competitions were beginning to take hold, but in her words, "I was not yet ready for these 'big guns' of the musical world,"[46] and she was soon eliminated. She quickly re-entered the Academy for more work with Coviello, but remained for only two terms, when her mother insisted she begin studies with Mathilde Verne (1868-1935).

Born in Southampton, Verne had spent considerable time in Germany studying with Clara Schumann, and before the first War, she founded a short-lived piano school in Kensington, where her most notable student was the brilliant prodigy Solomon (1902-88)—whom she virtually adopted when he was nine. She prodded him relentlessly (at times in violation of child labor laws[47]), and his father, Harris Cutner, even briefly considered taking him to Matthay. Matthay was overwhelmed by the youngster's gifts, but he demanded that the family withdraw him from the arduous concert circuit to which Verne was then subjecting him, and Cutner refused. As Denise remembered, this intensified a long-standing rift between Verne and Matthay, who thought she was sacrificing the child to her own aims.[48] Lympany also confirms that Verne subjected her to a demanding regimen: "She was a martinet, adamant that I should play one hour's exercises every day, and practice four hours a day, one hour at a time, with an interval of one hour."[49] Nonetheless, she believed she gained much from her study, and she was saddened when Verne died suddenly in December of 1935. By now, the nineteen-year-old pianist had acquired a reputation for

Chapter 12

versatility, frequently accepting engagements before she had even learned the music, and panic set in when she realized she had no one to teach her Delius's Concerto or d'Indy's *Symphony on a French Mountain Air*, both of which she had agreed to play in Queen's Hall with the British Women's Symphony in March of 1937. Although at times Matthay had been recommended to her, by now she had absorbed so much of London's growing anti-Matthay sentiment that she resisted:

> There was much talk of the 'Matthay Method', and I did not like what I heard of it. Matthay had written nearly twenty books purporting to explain his 'Method'. My old teacher Ambrose Coviello tried to explain Matthay's explanations in *his* book: *What Matthay Meant*. . . . People who went to him for tuition came away exaggerating everything he had told them to do and so I had come to believe that the Matthay Method meant throwing oneself about at the piano, one's arms and hands flying all over the place. He had taught many superb pianists: Myra Hess, whom he called his 'prophetess', twenty-five years older than myself, a deeply serious, profoundly religious pianist; and Irene Scharrer, Eileen Joyce and Harriet Cohen had also gone to Matthay for tuition. So had Clifford Curzon. I obtained his books and tried to read them but could not understand them at all. . . . I did not want to go to Matthay. I felt sure he would want to change my way of playing and I had visions of starting from scratch again. However, I was becoming so nervous about the forthcoming concert I had to do something.
>
> I fell in love with him the moment I saw him. He was so gentle, a darling little white-haired old man with a moustache, his eyes shining behind wire-rimmed spectacles, dressed exquisitely in a frogged black velvet jacket, velvet skull-cap and patent-leather slippers. He smiled sweetly at me, and patiently. His first lesson was a revelation. Seated beside me at the piano he explained more to me in one sentence than I had managed to discover from all his books.[50]

She recalled that the Women's Symphony concert was "a great success" and she remained under Matthay's guidance for the next nine years. Her 1938 performance at Matthay's Summer Festival was preceded a month earlier by a seminal event in her life. For several years, Belgium's Queen Elisabeth had been planning a competition to fulfill the dream of her friend and former teacher, the late Belgian violinist Eugène Ysaÿe (1858-1931). Ysaÿe had wanted to showcase the world's greatest rising stars with an annual Belgian contest that alternated violin with piano entrants, and in June of 1937, Soviet violinist David Oistrakh had been unanimously declared the first winner. The inaugural piano competition was scheduled for June of 1938, and Matthay, fully aware of Lympany's close ties to Belgium and its people, suggested she enter. In her words, "I was convinced I would not stand a chance," but she remembered only that Matthay "gently and quietly" responded with, "On the contrary, I think you will have a very good chance."[51] Because the competition required her to submit a copy of her birth certificate, she was entered as "Mary Johnstone," and she began preparing in earnest. As June approached, she withdrew the remaining £5 from her checking account, made arrangements to lodge with some Brussels friends from her convent school days, and soon found herself competing against 77 pianists from 24 countries. Their numbers were quickly pared to 28, and then to 12. Now the pressure mounted, because a week before the finals they were housed in Laeken, the Royal Palace, where each was given a room with a piano. They were also presented with a new concerto by Belgian composer Jean Absil, which they were required to learn and perform by memory. But surprisingly, Lympany remembered little, if any, of the intense rivalry that seems commonplace on today's competition circuit:

> We were all young, and ambitious I suppose, but we were good-natured too, and when we saw each other at meals every day, we laughed and joked like all young people do. In the evenings we took turns playing the piano yet again, not classical music for the concert hall but dance music. The palace walls rang with our merriment. I loved to dance, and as we were six men and six girls I was never without a partner. One of the contestants was Jacob Flier, a shy young Russian who danced with me a

Chapter 12

lot. I liked him very much but he was so inarticulate, putting all he could not say into his piano-playing. Another was Emil Gilels, who called me 'Mouratscka', which means 'little Moura'—a term of endearment, for I was now twenty-one.[52]

Against the advice of the other contestants, she chose the less bombastic *Variations sérieuse* of Mendelssohn for her final solo work, and the Liszt E-flat for her final concerto, both of which she had carefully prepared with Matthay. And she soon began to draw on all of his counseling to learn and memorize the Absil, studying much of it away from the piano:

'Memory is a series of links,' Uncle Tobs used to say, 'of chains. If you have studied that work well, then you know that once you start, every phrase is a link that will lead on to the very end.' . . .

When it came to my turn, first I played the Absil right through from memory without a fault. This was completely unexpected from a young Englishwoman; someone who had learned the piece by heart and played it within a week.[53]

The twenty-six-member jury included Ignaz Friedman, Walter Gieseking, and Arthur Rubinstein, who had been a close friend of Ysaÿe. When the prizes were announced, Gilels came in first, and "Mary Johnstone"—a name Lympany briefly struggled to identify—came in second. The seventh place was awarded to a seventeen-year-old Italian, Arturo Benedetti Michelangeli, who was nearly disqualified on medical grounds since his hands were "disastrously muscle-bound from too much work."[54] Lympany's fledgling career had now been given an enormous boost throughout Europe, although much of its momentum was curtailed when war broke out in September of 1939. But ironically, the War also brought fresh opportunities. Edward Clark, the BBC's controversial programmer, had resigned in March of 1936, indignant over accusations that he had misused the Corporation's funds,[55] and by 1940 he was working for the Society of Cultural Relations to solidify

Britain's relationship to the USSR. A concert of Soviet works had been scheduled for 13 April at Queen's Hall under the baton of Alan Bush—now a Communist sympathizer—and Clark was soon in search of a pianist to learn Khachaturian's then little-known Piano Concerto. Supposedly, he first offered it to Curzon, who recommended Lympany, since "she learns so quickly."[56] According to Lympany, Clark brought her the score while she was sitting under a hairdryer at a salon, where she began studying it immediately before taking it to Matthay.

One week before the concert, she played the Beethoven Fourth with Cameron and the LPO, and on the following Saturday at 2:30 pm she joined Bush and the same orchestra for the Khachaturian, in a program which also included the Shostakovich Fifth. *The Times* was thrilled with her performance, observing that she played "splendidly," and that she "seemed to know instinctively how to make its points without effort."[57] For a brief time, Lympany virtually owned the Khachaturian Concerto in the West, and the British appetite for the work seemed insatiable. Within a year, she had performed it with three different conductors, and when she broadcast it on 7 February 1942 under Basil Cameron, *The Times* noted that "Miss Moura Lympany brings to it an incisive style that yields, if that were possible, greater brilliance than ever to her playing of the work."[58] The broadcast also enabled Matthay to hear the orchestra part for the first time, and he was so impressed that he sent her a telegram the next day with a single sentence: "BEST CONCERTO SINCE LISZT."[59] At the War's end, she joined Anatole Fistoulari and the LSO to record it for Decca, and William McNaught—who had succeeded his father as editor of the *Musical Times*—was not entirely charitable, noting that Lympany's recording may have celebrated a "popular partnership" rather than noteworthy music. But he did concede that "if the concerto had no attraction of its own to offer not even a Lympany could keep it in the repertory, or would want to."[60]

But the War also brought heartbreak from totally unexpected sources. During a London air raid on 10 May 1941, Lympany spent the entire night under her piano, and the next morning, when she

Chapter 12

arrived to rehearse Franck's *Symphonic Variations* at Queen's Hall, she found only

> a ruin from which rose a thin plume of smoke, for the fire was still smouldering. In dismay I stood there helplessly, to be joined by members of the orchestra and others. . . . Standing crookedly among the ruins was a music-stand bearing sheet music: 'Loveliest of Trees' by Muriel Herbert.[61]

The *Blitz* raid which destroyed Queen's Hall was only the latest in a series of blows inflicted on the TMPS. The first occurred in March of 1939 when the School had been given notice to vacate No. 96, since Debenhams intended to raze the entire block to erect office buildings. By June, the TMPS "pro tem" headquarters had been moved to Marley,[62] but Denise still reported that the Summer School was perhaps the largest ever, since the numbers were significantly swelled by LeRoy Campbell's group of 53—even though they stayed a very short time.[63] At first, the TMPS sought also to maintain permanent offices at the Wigmore Galleries, but a year later Matthay reported, "as there were not enough students, we gave that up, and now only use the studios as required."[64] In fact, by fall the enrollment had dropped to a mere 73 pupils, a number which shrank to 38 a year later, and by the end of 1940 the School was headed for bankruptcy, recording a net loss of £445, 16s, 1d.[65] A decade earlier, Matthay's income from the TMPS alone had averaged £1,200 a year—enhanced by "very substantial" royalties from his publications[66]—but now the impending problems were so severe that on 22 December 1939, he informed Langrish that he was taking preventative action on the advice of counsel:

> My lawyer (who is interested in us) recently discovered that with the old Trust deed [the TMPS corporation charter from 1927] the Trustees might be liable to considerable loss if the School came to grief—so he advised me (if I did not wish to risk anything, and to save my Trustees from any danger) to turn the School into a "limited liability" Co[.] or

Final Days

Association. This will cost me £50 out of my pocket—but I thought that better than having my Trustees in difficulties! So the document is in process of being printed now, and the former Trustees will be converted into a "Council". The process is that the former Trustees "sell" the "goodwill and effects" of the School to the new Company for £500 and the new "Council" of the School in return give the old Trustees (now Council) 500 £1 Shares in the new Company "fully paid up"—(so there is nothing to pay!) Thus you and the other members of the new Body are provided with 500 Shares between you fully paid up—and if there are vast profits they may (perhaps) come to yourselves and all risk and responsibility (momentarily) is completely wiped out—so you can sleep in peace now and I am £50 poorer!

Trust this is clear now?

Allest love from
Uncle Tobs

[P.S.] There are 1000 £1 shares altogether and 500 of them go the old Trustees—£100 each to myself, Myra, Denise, Hilda [Dederich], and yourself—and we have the power of allowing anyone we wish to have any of the remaining shares, but they can't be bought except with our permission, and the old Council are wiped out in favor of this new body who will control the School, and the old General committee will stand as it is. These 500 shares are received by us as fully paid up, so there is no risk of your being called upon for one penny! Please keep this entirely to yourself till after Jan 1st—you understand it is being done just to safeguard the Trustees! Oppenheimer [Herbert Oppenheimer was Matthay's lawyer] in fact strongly recommended this in the first instance [in 1927], but I stood out because I did not like the name "Limited"![67]

On 3 January 1940, The Tobias Matthay Pianoforte School, Limited, officially came into being, and 15 months later—on 20 March 1941 at 6 pm—Matthay, Myra, Denise, Hilda, and Elsie (as recording secretary) convened its first Council meeting at Marley. The minutes record that Matthay was then charging the School

Chapter 12

£84 annually "for Rent, Rates[,] Water, Lighting & Heating," but that he also "irrevocably waived any claim to remuneration for the year-ended 31st December 1940 and also for the period 1st January 1941 to the 5th April 1941."[68] On 25 March 1940, Debenhams had bought out the School's Wimpole Street lease for £400, and it may bear testament to Matthay's financial straits that the Council voted to apply some of the money as reimbursement for the £50, 6s that Oppenheimer (who waived his fee and charged only out-of-pocket expenses) had required for establishing the new company—even though it left only £349, 14s to apply against the School's remaining debt of nearly £450. It should also be noted that Langrish, who was unable to attend, received a typed copy of the minutes from Elsie, in which the following paragraph was marked "<u>confidential</u>:"

> Mr. Matthay reported to the meeting that the secretary had voluntarily offered to accept no salary since last November, in view of the decreased income of the School due to the conditions occasioned by the war. He proposed that a hearty vote of thanks be accorded to Miss Neville for her generosity, and in order to recompense her at some future date, that out of the first profits made by the Company a bonus be paid her. This proposition was seconded by Miss Hess and carried unanimously.[69]

Elsie's husband owned a small electronics factory north of London which by then had been mobilized, and for Langrish's benefit only, she added: "Just for <u>your</u> information Uncle Tobs has given me permission to work part-time at my husband's firm—so that I work one week at Marley & one week at the other place—it works very well."

The new Council strove to uphold TMPS standards as much as possible, and on 25 May 1940, the School's best talent was offered at Haslemere Hall to benefit the Students' Aid Fund. Langrish featured his pupil Olive Cloke, an outstanding performer who rendered Grünfeld's Paraphrase on Strauss's *Fledermaus*, and Matthay presented former AMA scholars Ethel de Gomez and Tessa Bloom (Americans who had married Englishmen) in the Bach C minor

Partita and several Brahms pieces, respectively. Moura Lympany performed Debussy's *Clair de lune* and the Ravel Toccata, and Matthay also featured Vina Barnden—an Australian who held the Jessie Matthay Memorial Scholarship—in several demanding Chopin Preludes. Denise, Hilda, and Irene also presented students, and the program ended with another Australian, Nancy Weir, then studying with both Matthay and Craxton, who offered the Chopin E major Scherzo. Significantly, of the ten performers heard that afternoon, only Irene's student Richard Moulton was male—a pattern that continued for the duration of the War. On a positive note, the anti-German hysteria that had characterized the first War did not yet seem in evidence—at least in Haslemere—since the program freely acknowledged the contribution of "Messrs. T. Andrews," piano dealers from nearby Guildford, who provided the Bechstein used by the performers.[70]

With the enrollment numbers teetering well below what they had once been, the American Summer School soon became an "English" Summer School, moved to the month of August to accommodate the later British term schedule. Although many schools carried on as best they could, children were evacuated from Central London whenever possible, and Hilda's oldest sister, Chris Kahler, was soon living at Marley, teaching a class of East End youngsters every day in a school house at the bottom of the hill. By the spring of 1940, both Hilda and Elsie had joined her, and on 22 October, Hilda advised her American pupil Theresa Coolidge that wartime conditions could often be surprisingly pleasant—allowing for the random intrusions of bombs and artillery:

> First and foremost we are all fit and well, and, as you see, I am still at Marley and at the moment both my sisters are here with me too. Herman [Herman Lindars was Hilda's husband] is up north [in Sheffield] where he has to stay permanently with his works. . . . At the moment I am sitting in my cozy little bedroom at Marley [the smallest bedroom, adjacent to Denise's] with a large slab of toffee and a box of sweets beside me (to stop me smoking). Uncle Tobs, who is marvelously well, is working up

Chapter 12

in his study and Denise is downstairs practicing for a broadcast next week. Elsie is typing away next door [in Jessie's former bedroom]. . . .

So from all this you can see that life is not so abnormal as one might think. It is really quite amazing what one can get used to, and you mustn't believe all that you hear, particularly what the German broadcasts give out. They make us roar with laughter, when they say we are starving!

To give you an example, our menu today has consisted of: an early morning cup of tea. Breakfast: coffee, sausages, toast, marmalade [Eggs were added to the menu after Marley's newly purchased chickens had matured]. Lunch: steak and kidney pie, cauliflower, potatoes, bread, butter, banana custard, and cheese. Tea: scones, cake, strawberry jam. I haven't had dinner yet but I know there are some lovely fresh young runner beans because I grew them myself. (There goes the gong! Will finish this later.)

Since I have been down here the gardener has gone on war work so I have taken over looking after the vegetable garden. It's been rather fun! I have succeeded in keeping the large household, an average of eleven people, in vegetables all summer. We picked two hundred pounds of beans alone, which isn't so bad for a complete amateur!

Just at the moment there are several Jerrys flying about overhead; they go over almost all night. Sometimes they get noisy and drop a few bombs, but most of them try and get nearer London. We get a lot of dog-fights overhead, but no one takes any notice and we calmly go on with whatever we are doing.

The morale of the people is just wonderful and I wouldn't be anywhere else in the world just now. The Londoners are just superb the way everyone carries on in spite of difficulties. I went up to town a few days ago and it is really ghastly to see how they have hit some of our old buildings and irreplaceable churches. They seem to have a passion for churches and hospitals. Don't you believe a word when you hear that they only go for military objectives! They drop them just anywhere. They even dropped one one hundred yards from here, which luckily did no damage and only made my bed feel rather as if it was situated on top of an earthquake. Curiously enough one isn't very frightened and we are all very cheerful.[71]

Final Days

In December of 1940, Hilda's letter was published in the *Journal of the American Matthay Association*, along with letters from Matthay and Denise, and all struck a positive tone. Denise recounted the February celebration of Matthay's eighty-second birthday, "when on a winter's day all his professors came in person to Marley" to hear his hour-long program, "ending with a staggering performance of the Chopin B flat minor Scherzo which led one to believe a very young man was sitting at the piano."[72] Throughout the War years, similar accounts graced the *Journal*'s pages, and although Hilda admitted that bombs and dogfights occasionally marred the calm, few were aware of the Messerschmitt that fired on a terrified Denise one afternoon, as she ran a distance of 30 yards across Marley's south lawn before finally reaching the safety of the house. The next day she and Hilda dug shells out of the yard, grim reminders that Marley's extreme height left it vulnerable to *Luftwaffe* attacks whenever German aircraft traveled between London and the Channel.[73] For over 30 years, Matthay had been so obsessed with the beauty of the landscape that he never allowed anything to obstruct his view, often personally chopping away at many of the trees which grew along the southern face of Moses Hill. But now he allowed them to remain as camouflage, especially since it had been necessary to convert an outlying tool shed on the brow of the hill into a small studio where Denise, Hilda, and even Myra often worked to meet the increased performance demands that Britain's wartime conditions had ironically placed upon them.

The genesis of those demands sprang from a sunny September afternoon a year earlier when Hilda and her advertising-executive friend Ronald Jones, along with Denise and Myra, took tea on the semi-exposed porch at Marley's southern entrance. Myra had just cancelled her November tour of the States (her most elaborate yet, which was to have ended in Australia), and the four of them lamented the plight of London music making, which was already seriously hampered by blackouts. When Myra reiterated her long-standing desire to establish a daytime chamber music series, Denise suggested they try the National Gallery in Trafalgar Square, since over 3,000 of

Chapter 12

its paintings had now been moved to safer locations in Wales. Not to be outdone by her presumed sarcasm, Myra replied, "Why not try St. Paul's, or how about Buckingham Palace?"[74] But Jones, who knew Sir Kenneth Clark, the Gallery's director, volunteered to arrange a meeting, and Myra later reported that she drove back to London "in all states." By fortunate coincidence, at almost the same moment Clark was surveying the Gallery's empty walls, wondering if some scheme could be devised to take people's minds away from this "dreariest spectacle."[75] Within a few days, Jones and Myra appeared at the Gallery, accompanied by Denise, who by prior arrangement did most of the talking, eventually asking if he might allow the museum to be used for an occasional midday concert. Clark's response was an immediate "Why not give one every day?" As he later recalled:

> In a few minutes everything was agreed; that at least was an advantage of war, that one felt no need to ask permission of Trustees or Treasury, although at a later stage this seems to have been done. While Myra began composing programmes the rest of us looked for chairs and a platform and draped the Board Room curtains over the octagon in a hopeless attempt to give the Gallery a vestige of baroque splendour. An old photograph reminds me that we even managed to find some pictures that we had not thought worth evacuating.[76]

But in a 1970 interview, Clark recalled that launching the National Gallery Concerts was more complicated than his earlier account suggests. He was first required to petition the Home Office and the Ministry of Works to set aside the ban on public gatherings, a request facilitated by Marjory's friend Sir Patrick Duff—now the Permanent Secretary of Works. Clark's letter to Duff on 25 September argued convincingly for a waiver:

> The ordinary objections to giving concerts do not apply. The National Gallery has a very large air raid shelter which could accommodate practically the whole audience. In any case the lower rooms in the Gallery are quite as strong as the average air raid refuge. The question of attendants

Final Days

could also easily be solved; there are no pictures here and nothing that anyone could steal. It would therefore be possible to have the concerts staffed by volunteers.[77]

Jones offered to handle advertising and publicity for the series, although he advised against daily concerts, fearing too many logistical complications. But Myra persevered, and to her good fortune, within a week at least some government restrictions on London concert-giving had been rescinded. On 4 October, Duff informed Clark that neither the Home Office nor the Ministry of Works objected to Gallery concerts, provided they be limited to 200 patrons, that they finish by 6 pm, and "if at any time the Gallery should be required for department purposes, the permission to use it for concert purposes may have to be withdrawn, and possibly on short notice."[78] Myra was immediately made chair of an executive committee which voted to offer performances five days a week at 1 pm, a time later changed to 1:30 to accommodate a brass band which soon performed each weekday in Trafalgar Square. The price was one shilling, but on Tuesdays and Fridays the programs were repeated at 4:30 for an entrance fee of 2s, 6d, "to suit the convenience of another section of the public."[79] On Sunday afternoon, 8 October, Myra played the Beethoven Fourth with the LSO at Queen's Hall, and just two days later she gave the first National Gallery Concert, a slightly abridged piano recital which included two Scarlatti Sonatas, two Bach Preludes and Fugues, some Schubert Waltzes, and Beethoven's "Appassionata." *The Times* praised her program as "neatly constructed" and noted that her selections "could be listened to easily and yet attentively in informal conditions," although the critic seemed more concerned about the Gallery's acoustics than about the music's inspirational value:

> The attentiveness of the audience in the quiet building was especially noticeable in view of the number of those who were standing, and the acoustics, which may need to be tested from various angles for different types of programme, [sic] were at any rate sufficiently good to enable all the passage-work in the slow movement of the Appassionata to be

clearly heard from a distance. The piano was set back against a curtain across the far transept so that any confusion from the shape of the dome was avoided and the presence of a large audience absorbed any excess of reverberation from the marble floor.

The audience at the afternoon concert was smaller, though there were enough people present to warrant the belief that the leisured as well as the workers are glad once more to hear music. Miss Hess repeated her programme, and the serenity of Scarlatti and Bach could be better appreciated in the more spacious atmosphere. The acoustics were again proved satisfactory by the clarity of the part-playing in Bach.[80]

For the two Friday concerts three days later, Myra joined her friend violinist Jelly d'Aranyi and Spanish cellist Gaspar Cassado for the Beethoven "Archduke" and Brahms's Trio in C minor, Op. 101. Although *The Times* noted that occasional passages "flitted away from the more remote listeners in an engaging flight around the dome," the artists were praised for their "grand manner" and "utmost nobility."[81] On 31 October she performed violin sonatas with d'Aranyi's older sister, Adila Fachiri, and within weeks her schedule had grown so intense that the forty-nine-year-old pianist was now one of the most visible musicians in the nation. On two consecutive Saturday afternoons, 11 and 18 November, she performed the Schumann Concerto with Henry Wood and the LSO at Queen's Hall, and on 20 November she played the Schumann Quintet at the Gallery with the Menges Quartet. Two days later, she collaborated with Wood and the Boyd Neel Orchestra in Bach's Fifth Brandenburg, and *The Times* rejoiced that "eye and ear alike were refreshed and enchanted in the dimly lit Gallery."[82]

Although Myra was both headliner and impresario, the Gallery schedule was so demanding that she was eager to share the spotlight, and the day after she performed with Fachiri, she even allowed Harriet an engagement with Sidney Griller's Quartet.[83] Griller and his colleagues, all RAM graduates, had formed a highly successful string quartet a decade earlier while still in their teens, and Myra, who called them her "nephews," at times invited them to Marley to

Final Days

rehearse. When they were called up for duty, she even intervened with the RAF to insist they be allowed to remain an ensemble, and during the War they played concerts for troops all over England.[84] Understandably, the pianists who appeared at the Gallery were often Myra's close friends, but by no means was the podium limited to Matthay pupils. Solomon, Moiseiwitsch, and Gerald Moore performed as often as Denise, Irene, and Hilda—who occasionally offered four-hand programs with Matthay's student Ethel de Gomez. Predictably, Craxton appeared frequently, as did Peppercorn, Joyce, and Lympany, but some within the Matthay circle were surprisingly inconspicuous. Although he did use the occasion to premiere a new piano sonata, it seems that Bowen performed only once at the Gallery—on 17 November 1941—and years later Vivian Langrish's widow recalled that her husband was "deeply hurt" that Myra never asked him to appear, despite a close friendship that by then had spanned nearly 40 years.[85]

Myra was also capable of whimsy when the occasion demanded, and the Gallery series was less than three months old when she staged a celebration to welcome New Year's Day 1940—a pastiche involving a substantial cross-section of her friends and associates. The program began with a performance of Schumann's *Carnaval*, a work *The Times* complained was "responsible for more clotted boredom in Wigmore Hall than any other in the repertory."[86] The critic was therefore elated that Myra divided its sections between ten different pianists to make it "positively exciting." A second Steinway was added to the platform and Myra and Moiseiwitsch "led off and finished up on two pianos in order to do justice to the rumbustious [sic] numbers," their ensemble being "synchronized" by conductor Richard Austin. The soloists who followed were Cyril Smith, Kathleen Long, William Murdoch, Eileen Joyce, Lance Dossor, Irene Scharrer, Clifford Curzon, and Matthay's Australian pupil John Simons. Then Myra and Moiseiwitsch returned "for the march against the Philistines, who, needless to say, were routed with heavy losses." Ivor James and Gilbert Vinter then performed Mozart's rarely heard Duet for cello and Bassoon, K. 33b, followed again by Myra and Moiseiwitsch in some four-hand Brahms Waltzes. Finally—in *The Times*'s words—came the *"pièce de résistance,* Haydn's Toy Symphony, in which all the committee and distinguished guests took a hand and an instrument."

> Sir Kenneth Clark, in the spirit of Leonardo . . . added yet another art to his many accomplishments and conducted a spirited performance. The strings were provided by the Menges Quartet, but on this kind of occasion it is the wind and percussion which provide the airs and graces. Miss Irene Scharrer and Miss Myra Hess played the cuckoos with a marked difference of phrasing, Miss Scharrer favouring the legato style, Miss Hess the catch-in-the-throat between Cuck and oo.
>
> Mr. Moiseiwitsch had an airy way with the quail and a firmer touch with the triangle. Those aqueous instruments, the nightingales, poured smooth trills from the lips of Miss Joyce Grenfell and Mr. John Simons. The indefatigable secretary of the concerts, Mr. Ronald Jones, croaked richly on the rattle, while the drums employed a whole galaxy of talent—Mme. [Elena] Gerhardt, Miss Denise Lassimonne, and Mr. Murdoch.[87]

Myra also used the venue to premiere new works, and on 23 April 1940 she gave the first performance of a Sonata by the Ulster-born, thirty-one-year-old Howard Ferguson. Calling it "a work of genuine power," which made a "profound impression," *The Times* seemed enthralled, suggesting that its slow movement evoked images of "Elgar in his meditative mood."[88] Three days later, the paper added that the Sonata deserved "a special place in the small repertory of modern sonatas for the piano."[89] Four years later, Myra also premiered Ferguson's *Five Bagatelles* at the Gallery to marked acclaim, and before the War's end she had recorded both works for HMV. Ferguson was also a fine pianist and was soon appearing frequently at the concerts with Denis Matthews in four-hand and two-piano recitals. He began assisting with more of the administrative details as well, and when *The Times* marked the five-hundredth concert in October of 1944, it identified him as the "chronicler of the concerts."[90]

Final Days

Nearly five years earlier when the concerts were just beginning, *The Times* had run an editorial entitled "A Stock-Taking," which soberly evaluated the effect of war on British music making. While it lamented the fact that choral music had been brought "to an almost complete standstill," it praised Myra for creating a chamber music venue where "one can always be sure of hearing something good." Its concluding sentence even went so far as to argue that "the shock of war has not been all loss if it produces something new and valuable like this series of concerts, which is already developing into an institution."[91] Almost immediately, the Gallery series bred imitators, some of which were even nurtured by Myra. On 5 December 1939, she gave the opening recital for a series sponsored by the Incorporated Society of Musicians, and on 12 January she inaugurated a weekly series of Friday concerts for Birkbeck College near Russell Square, prompting *The Times* to observe that she was "now a kind of fairy god-mother to all such entertainments."[92]

She also showcased younger talent wherever possible, and on 8 July 1940, the Gallery presented a Mozart program by Matthay's student Nina Milkina. Born in Moscow, Milkina had immigrated to Britain with her family in the 1920s, and Guy Jonson remembered that for a number of years her father, Jacques Milkine, eked out a living as a somewhat mediocre piano teacher at their Hampstead home on Belsize Road. For a time he even rented a room to a young Clifford Curzon, whose practicing he barely tolerated since he was convinced that his lodger drilled scales too infrequently to become a successful pianist.[93] At the age of eight, Milkine's daughter began studying with Denise and she made her first TMPS appearance (as Nina Milkin) at a special Wigmore Hall program for gifted children on 26 March 1927. She won the School's Junior Silver Medal in 1928, and she continued her studies at the TMPS with Matthay and Craxton. On 4 November 1935, at the age of 16, she made her debut at Grotrian Hall, and she soon forged a career as one of the most refined miniaturists Matthay produced, specializing in Scarlatti, Haydn, and Mozart.

Two years later, under Beecham's patronage, she became a featured performer in the highly regarded Cambridge Theatre

Concerts, monthly Sunday-night events devoted—at least for the first season—entirely to the music of Mozart. The roster of artists also included Maggie Teyte, Reginald Kell, the Griller and Stratton String Quartets, and an impressive array of pianists, including Curzon, Denise, Hilda Bor, Guy Jonson, Karl Ulrich Schnabel, and William Glock, who first suggested the Theatre as a venue. On 13 March 1938, Milkina shared the podium with Curzon as they performed the Mozart Concerto in G, K. 453, and the "Coronation" Concerto in D, K. 512, respectively. *The Times* critic was generally positive, praising Curzon for showing off the "Coronation" with "great effect, which is not the same thing as showing off his own technique," and noting that Milkina showed "a real feeling for the tenderness of the slow movement and a sparkling gaiety in the Finale."[94] But arguably the finest Mozart pianist involved in the series was its principal organizer, Matthay's twenty-nine-year-old pupil Betty Humby, who was then married to a vicar 17 years her senior. On 14 September 1937, *The Times* dubbed her the "moving spirit" of the Cambridge Concerts, of which Beecham had then been named President, and although this was not their first meeting, their personal and professional relationship was undoubtedly deepening.[95] On 27 April 1940, she performed the Mozart Concerto in C minor, K. 491, with Boult and the LSO at Queen's Hall, and a week later she left her husband to sail for New York with their nine-year-old son on the *Britannic*. They arrived on 11 May with 623 additional "refugees from various European countries,"[96] and she soon allied herself with other evacuees, broadcasting, concertizing, and speaking regularly for British War Relief in New York and other cities.

    A day earlier, the sixty-one-year-old Beecham had arrived on the Italian liner *Rex*, and despite his insistence that he needed a rest, by September he had logged over 60,000 miles guest conducting his way through Canada, Mexico, the United States, and Australia. Beecham had then been estranged from his wife for over three decades, but she steadfastly refused to divorce him, and at some point (some said long before either of them sailed) his affections turned to the blonde, attractive Humby—although she, like he, was still married.[97]

Final Days

On 22 June 1941, he conducted her in Delius's Piano Concerto with the Columbia Symphony in a 3 pm broadcast on New York's station WABC. An Associated Press photo taken that afternoon showing them seated side by side at the piano ran in several newspapers, and as one of Beecham's biographers noted, the couple appeared "twinkling" and "comradely."[98] Soon they were appearing together all over the country, and on New Year's Day 1942 they even collaborated on the Mozart C minor Concerto in Detroit. By now, Beecham had been named Conductor of the Seattle Symphony, and his opening concert on 20 October 1941 created an electric atmosphere, the *Seattle Times* observing that, "Never in the musical history of Seattle has the Seattle Symphony had such an opening!"[99] Three weeks later, when he brought Humby to the stage for the Mozart C minor, the crowd became ecstatic, the *Seattle Star* offering the headline, "Girl Pianist Stars with Orchestra:"

> Near perfection was reached in the Mozart piano Concerto in C Minor, when Betty Humby, famed British pianist, and the orchestra played an exquisite duet. Beecham put everything he had into the Mozart, and during the beautiful larghetto Miss Humby's legato playing stopped almost every breath in the house. Miss Humby, a tall blonde, English girl, took five curtain calls before a packed house.[100]

The *Seattle Times* also commented on Humby's beauty, observing that "she bears more than a slight resemblance to the American screen star, Jean Arthur," while adding that she was a "poet of the keyboard" with "great technical facility."[101] During Beecham's two seasons with the Seattle orchestra, Mozart was the composer most frequently highlighted, and on 27 February 1942 he presented a program featuring the "Haffner" and "Prague" Symphonies, enhanced by Humby's rendition of the G major Concerto, K. 453. The *Star* again praised her performance as "near perfection,"[102] while the *Times* lauded her "facile, deft technique."[103] Up to this point, few of Beecham's American fans knew that he been married for nearly four decades to the former Utica Welles, now Lady Beecham, but in October his flamboyant, bachelor-like lifestyle suddenly became a focus of media interest after he returned from Idaho City—described by the *Seattle Times* as "a 'ghost' mining town, 45 miles northeast of Boise."[104] On 26 August he had taken advantage of Idaho's forty-two-day residency requirement to file a suit for divorce in a town so remote that over a month passed before his actions became generally known. Beecham had now also been appointed Musical Director of the Metropolitan Opera, and on 17 November the *Seattle Post-Intelligencer* reported that he left for New York with Humby (his "secretary" according to railroad officials) "on the same train in an adjoining compartment."[105] The story also reported that she too had "recently" obtained a divorce in Idaho from her clergyman husband, and on 14 January, Beecham's divorce was also granted in Boise. The couple evidently waited a month before formalizing their relationship, and on 24 February the *New York Times* reported that they were married "here a few days ago."[106] It may not be entirely coincidental that two weeks after he was first queried by the press concerning his divorce action (and against the backdrop of an impending "December-May" union), Beecham opened his Seattle concert on 19 October 1942 with Matthay's youthful ode to springtime romance, *In May*—perhaps the most recent performance, at least at this writing, it has received.

Years earlier, while Matthay had been striving to get his overture broadcast by the BBC, he sent Boult a letter on 3 October 1933 offering him "my <u>own</u> score (original MS) very much marked over from my own conducting—but still very readable!" And he also added a post script: "Sir Thomas has the clear copy."[107] Whatever understanding Beecham may have had with Matthay, he almost certainly conducted from the same "clear copy" in Seattle, while the orchestra played from parts copied by one "P. W. Tilbrook."[108] That there were two sets of parts is borne out by the fact that in March of 1938 Matthay provided parts—many copied in Denise's hand—for Lewis's April broadcast, all of which appear to survive at the RAM.[109] Matthay may have been unaware of an impending performance in the States since, as he later told Simonds, he did not learn of it till over two months after it had occurred:

Final Days

> Sir Thomas Beecham produced my Overture "In May" at the first concert of the <u>Seattle</u> season [it was actually the second concert of the season]—so I heard from a message on New Year's evening! He made it a great success it appears!!![110]

It is unknown who conveyed the "message" to Matthay, although it could have been Humby, who by then had relocated with Beecham to New York. Matthay's overture may have been chosen for the October concert to enhance a springtime theme, since Beecham ended the program that evening with Schumann's "Spring" Symphony in B-flat. He conducted to a packed house, many in uniform, but there was little press reaction to *In May*, the *Seattle Times* merely observing that it was "spirited and melodious."[111] However, this was a more positive response than Matthay's music was then being afforded by the BBC. Despite the apparently favorable reception his overture had received in April 1938, Corporation executives were again rallying against his Concert-Piece in A minor, even though BBC Wartime policies mandated that greater attention be paid to British works. On 16 December 1940, Matthay wrote to Arthur Wynn, Head of the Artists' Booking Section, to secure a performance of the work by Moura Lympany, and three days later, Wynn was advised by one of his superiors: "Not a <u>chance</u> to do Matthay's Concerto under Wartime conditions—personally I wouldn't recommend under <u>any</u> conditions!!"[112]

As the War progressed, Matthay's music garnered no more than a lukewarm defense from BBC officials, as evidenced most profoundly by a series of internal memos that circulated on 19 May 1943, three months to the day after his eighty-fifth birthday. The most positive assessment came from the fifty-seven-year-old Benjamin Dale, now in poor health and less than ten weeks away from an untimely death, who advised his Programme Committee colleagues—composers Gordon Jacob and John Ireland—that *In May* was "an attractive piece of the period (1883)." He continued: "A broadcast of the overture would doubtless give much pleasure to the veteran composer, as well as to his considerable 'following'. It should have sufficient entertainment value to justify a broadcast, in my opinion."[113] Jacob

Chapter 12

was also willing to allow sentiment to influence the final decision, so long as *In May* were confined to a less prominent setting:

> Intrinsically the work is not of great interest, but for the many hundreds of old pupils of the composer it would no doubt be welcome for sentimental reasons and it would be a tribute to a well known & aged musician to play it in a not very important programme.[114]

But Ireland was totally unmoved, and his reaction suggests that he regarded Matthay's contributions to be of marginal importance:

> With due respect for the famous teacher, & with all deference to the opinions of my colleagues, I can see no reason why a piece of music of this type should occupy any broadcasting time. His pupils and "following" who would like to hear this work for sentimental reasons constitute only an infinitesimal fraction of the listening public.[115]

On the same day, the Committee issued its report on Matthay's Concert-Piece, which he now wished performed by Langrish's one-time pupil Olive Cloke. Ireland reacted with total negativity: "In an outworn idiom—of no interest to listeners—entirely lacking in distinction."[116] He was supported by Jacob's "There would be no point in resuscitating this work," and Dale's simple: "I agree with the above comments."[117]

But not everyone at the BBC believed that Matthay's day had passed. On 17 November 1941 at 10:50 pm, the Home Service broadcast a thirty-minute play dramatizing "The Life and Work of Tobias Matthay,"[118] which featured Matthay, Myra, Irene, and Ernest Read playing themselves. Although Simonds had attempted to receive the program in America, he was unsuccessful, so Matthay filled him in several weeks later:

> Sorry you missed the Broadcast, you evidently got hold of the wrong wave length for I didn't play [Beethoven's] Op. 78! It was great fun, and Etienne Amyot worked the thing splendidly. It was recorded on disc

Final Days

and film, and was put on the air five times overseas [at least once on the South African Service] and the last one for "Home Service", which I heard myself. It begins with myself, at 16, at my home where I have just returned from hearing Herbert Spencer's lecture, and he insisting that "every effect must have a cause," and this prompted me to seek for "Causes" in Piano playing. The next scene is a conversation between Ernest Read and myself re "The Act of Touch", and I am able to let off steam! Then came the question as to who were my first great pupils, and Irene and Myra are made to play a few bars of the first pieces they ever played to me—Schumann's Schlummerlied and Beethoven's "Moonlight"! We then have a farcical lesson given by someone who contemns [sic] the "Matthay method". After that we are taken to the outside of Queen's Hall, [where] people are being turned away from the doors, from merely "a students' concert". Finally we are taken to Marley with all the family there, and Myra plays my Albumleaf and Irene my Elves, and they make me play my "Bravura" to finish up with. I was also to have played the last two numbers of my "Seven Historiettes", but in the end found time did not allow for it. Everyone says my playing was "terrific"!—Bravura is a very brilliant piece—and that my speaking and Read's were better than the professional actors engaged as Narrator etc.,!! As it was such a success it may be repeated some day later on.[119]

The dramatization had been the brainchild of Etienne Amyot (1909-2004), who both wrote and produced the script. Born in Cape Town of a French father and a Danish-Dutch mother, Amyot's background was highly eclectic, but he had trained seriously as a pianist for two years in Germany before settling in England in the early 1930s. At some point, he began working with Matthay, and he was soon omnipresent throughout London as both chamber musician and soloist, although his reviews suggest that his performances were often subject to an erratic temperament. On 14 January 1935, he collaborated with the Brosa Quartet in Wigmore Hall, and *The Times* complained that he spoiled the piano part to Franck's Violin Sonata by indulging "in a continual *rubato* which, instead of making Franck's music more expressive, merely served to accentuate the short-windedness of the themes."[120] And two years later the review he received for a solo program in the same hall was oddly mixed: "Some over-emphatic accents and a rather erratic control of tone above *mezzo-forte* did not seriously detract from performances which were always lively and intelligent."[121] But he enjoyed enough success that by September of 1939 he was preparing for his third American tour—plans which were abruptly curtailed when he entered the British Army. Within a year, he had been dispatched to Cape Town by British Intelligence to assist with War programming for the BBC, and he soon became Assistant Director of the African Services. As he had injured one of his hands at Dunkirk, he found himself—through circumstances—embarked on a career in broadcasting, albeit for a time in uniform. He was periodically ordered back to London, and the Matthay play, originally conceived for the South African Service, was produced and recorded at Broadcasting House. Amyot was then honing many of the skills he utilized at the War's end, when with Leslie Stokes and George Barnes, he created the Third Programme.[122]

Understandably, Wartime exigencies precluded Matthay from journeying to London with frequency, but he did make an appearance on 19 February 1943—his eighty-fifth birthday—when Myra played his "Albumblatt" and "Elves" at the Gallery. That morning *The Times* ran an extensive, two-column piece by H. C. Colles entitled "A Great Piano Teacher" which, though highly complimentary, was surprisingly vague about the contributions he had made to his art.[123] Colles correctly dismisses the notion of a "Matthay Method," but makes no attempt to articulate any principles defined in *The Act of Touch*: "In that book, published 40 years ago, he collected the sum of his thinking up to date. He went on expanding it in further publications, lectures delivered to societies of teachers, personal conversations, and most conspicuously in his own act of touching keys at the piano."[124] Though the article is laudatory, it suggests that Matthay's importance arose more from his willingness to nurture, than with any revolutionary ideas he may have advanced. And while conceding that his contributions have been influential, his convictions are never identified:

> His has been an influence widely diffused, how widely Matthay himself cannot know, which has brought musical life to whole generations

of young people. Teachers, some of whom would repudiate the "Matthay Method," have profited by it and handed on his lessons to their own pupils after assimilating them into their own teaching. It is that assimilation which is all-important. Bad teachers teach from a book, and just acquire its shibboleths for future use. But whether or not Matthay's dicta are taken for gospel, the fact remains that he has shown, and is still showing at the age of 85, what it is to be a sound teacher, and a teacher in sound.[125]

The article also mentions that Matthay is best known as the man "who taught Dame Myra Hess to play the piano,"[126] for Myra was now being venerated as a Dame of the British Empire. On 12 June 1941, *The Times* announced her title in its list of civilian Birthday Honours, accompanied by a brief editorial comment:

The arts—perhaps it is only to be expected in wartime—contribute only one name, but that is of high distinction. MISS MYRA HESS is honoured not only for her genius as an executant, but because in the daily National Gallery Concerts she has turned the emergency of war itself to account, and has devised a new way of setting chords of music vibrating among the people, which peace, when it comes, must not be allowed to silence.[127]

Dame Myra Hess was now one of the most powerful musicians in Britain, but the economic devastation inflicted by the War had left little musical empire over which to preside. The Tobias Matthay Pianoforte School, Limited, was now an institution largely in name only, staving off total bankruptcy only because its expenses were few. Almost certainly by this point Matthay was living largely on his personal savings, because his income had dwindled to negligible figures. Between September of 1939 and November of 1945 he recorded fewer than 90 Entrance Hearings at Marley, and many of these students never enrolled, often because they could not afford the TMPS fee of nine guineas per term. At times Matthay lowered it, particularly with promising students such as Marion Day, who appeared on 15 September 1939 after studies with Teichmüller in Leipzig. At the bottom of her interview page, he wrote a note to Elsie: "Perhaps Bowen will do it at 6 guineas?"[128] At times, he also lowered his personal lesson fee of three

Chapter 12

guineas, as he did for the Romanian-born Carola Grindea, who first appeared on 18 January 1940, and was to be charged only "1½ guineas for ¾ [hour] lessons." When the family of Jean Harvey, a nine-year-old prodigy, journeyed from Glasgow to purchase a lesson for their daughter, he waived his fee altogether, but later lamented that "they stuck £3, 3- in my pocket! by the brother!" And often he deferred entirely to his staff, whose financial needs were even greater than his own. On 21 September 1939, he heard seventeen-year-old Prudence Gale from nearby Liphook, and after learning that she could afford hour-long lessons, wrote in his record book, "Denise and Hilda <u>tossed</u> for it! Hilda won!" Nor was his remark meant as a joke, for on 31 July 1941 he heard nineteen-year-old Elizabeth Shaw from York, whose parents, though trapped in Greece for the War's duration, sent money for her schooling and living expenses. Matthay was impressed with her talent, and wrote at the bottom of her interview page, "Denise and Hilda better toss for it." And when fourteen-year-old Patricia Carton from Haslemere auditioned, Matthay scrawled, "Hilda's turn to have a paying pupil!"[129]

But the teaching and performance standards were upheld as nearly as possible, and the brief notes Matthay wrote reveal that he was still an instant diagnostician. On 26 July 1940, he heard Gemma Gilmour, a thirty-year-old Canadian pianist he noted was a "friend of Moura's." After she played the Chopin G minor Ballade, he commented,

> Opening all <u>too much broken</u> up, in fact all thro' loses the long lines—not always hand behind finger when it should be. Tries hard to get the musical feeling—<u>has good talent</u>, might do very well[.] Has quite good fingers really—if only she thought more thru' the key. Quite good enough for me to teach myself. Or Denise or Hilda.[130]

But despite Matthay's seeming insistence that his own students be advanced, he was then devoting increasing attention to the fundamentals of his art. In December of 1939, he completed *First Lights on Piano Playing*, a brief "primer" for children issued early in 1942 by Winthrop Rogers, whose firm was by then a division of Boosey and Hawkes. In his brief Preface, Matthay acknowledged the "indefatigable work" of Hilda and Denise, as well as the contributions of Hilda Bor, Mary Lediard, "and other notable actual teachers of children."[131] He also included a lengthy "Forward for the Teacher," which explains much about his concern for laying a proper foundation:

> Much of the faulty technique teachers find with advanced pupils (and even with performers) has arisen from wrong habits contracted during the very first years at the piano. Yet it is just as easy for the child to form right habits as wrong ones. Hence the supreme importance of ensuring that the "First Steps" are the correct ones.
>
> In past days, the First Steps were all upside down....
>
> Instead of first teaching the pupil how to *sound* notes, and then subsequently, teaching him to *read* and write them (as in learning a language), the issue was completely obscured, and it was sought to teach sound-making and note-deciphering as one and the same task. *Easiest-to-read note successions* were therefore chosen instead of those *easiest-to-sound*; and instead of carrying out the educational maxim "From the simple to the complex," the child was expected to grasp two things at once. Thus the *straight-on* five-finger exercise and the *C Major* scale were given first. Because they were the easiest to read; and the fact was quite overlooked that by so doing a child was here expected to provide quite at once complex processes, muscularly![132]

One of the most serious faults likely to ensue from the "upside down" approach was a failure to grasp the "Forearm Rotative Element" that Matthay believed essential for ease in finger passages, and his Foreword continues with an extensive presentation of the subject. The book then includes a discussion of the piano key geared to younger readers, complete with photos to guide experimentation. The student is asked to balance a tablespoon on a matchbox before placing a "dog's light rubber ball" in the bowl of the spoon, thus covering steps "a" through "c:"

> (d) Now use your fist sideways, and bring it down quite gently upon the end of the spoon's handle, but without pushing it down....

(e) Now push the handle down so gently that the ball remains in the spoon.

(f) Then, instead, push it down sharply, and out jumps the ball from the other end. Notice that the quicker your action, the higher jumps the ball.[133]

The same approach is then transferred to adjacent black keys on the piano in a manner very similar to that which Matthay had employed in the *Nine First Steps.* But now he has composed 13 tiny pieces—some involving the teacher's participation—in which actual music is made before the fingers are ever brought into play. The fourth of these, "A Rainy Holiday," extends to 22 measures:

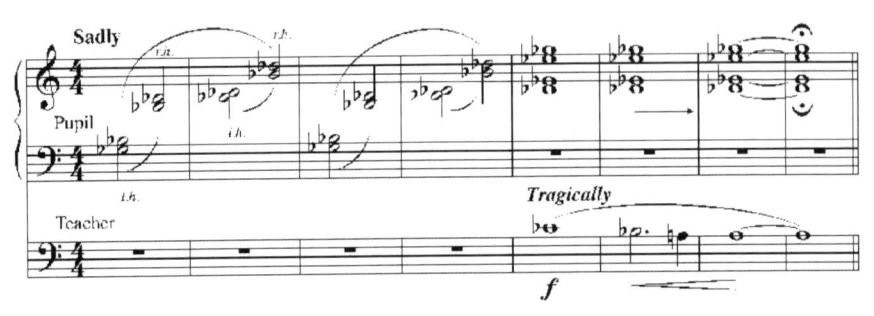

Ex. 12.1 Tobias Matthay: "A Rainy Holiday" from First Lights on Piano Playing, mm. 1-8

Just as the War had decimated Matthay's own teaching schedule, it also brought free time to Craxton and Felix Swinstead, who soon joined him to undertake the publication of a series of graduated repertoire books for children, the Matthay-Craxton-Swinstead *Approach to Music*. Matthay completed the first entry in the series, *"How do you do, Mr. Piano?"* in March of 1940, and in November, Denise wrote McClanahan that the volume was "at press." A year later, she advised him that the complete set had appeared:

> A new and delightful set of five children's books, called "The Approach to Music" have recently been issued by Boosey & Hawkes. As a matter of fact the whole of the first edition has already been sold out. The first of these books . . . is by Uncle Tobs himself—then follow: "First Solo

Book," by Craxton mainly. "First Duets," by Swinstead, "Second Solo Book," by Craxton and Matthay, "Second Duet Book," by Swinstead.[134]

At the beginning of the "First Solo Book," largely by Craxton, Matthay included his own "Fool-proof Five-finger Exercise," which had first appeared nine years earlier in *The Visible and Invisible* to dramatize the importance of rotation. Not surprisingly, it emphasized rotational exertions as a prelude to scale patterns:

Ex. 12.2 Tobias Matthay: Excerpt from "The Fool-proof Five-finger Exercise" from Approach to Music, Vol. II, mm. 1-10

During the War years, Matthay also published a variety of short children's pieces, including the third volume of *Playthings*, which he called "A Miniature Suite for Young and Old." He dedicated it to Hilda Bor (1910-93), by now his most distinguished teacher of children, though under different circumstances her talent and training might have brought her substantial fame as an artist. A Cockney born to Latvian immigrants, she grew up in East London, and by the time she was ten, a photo of her conducting her father's Bexhill orchestra appeared in the *Daily Mail*. She played for Matthay in 1924 and soon entered the RAM, continuing at the Academy with Langrish after Matthay resigned. She made her Wigmore Hall debut on 26 March 1929, and though she was not yet 19, soon became the youngest teacher on the TMPS staff. At a Proms Concert under Wood's baton on 26 August 1930, she performed the Saint-Saëns Fourth Concerto to favorable reviews,[135] and as her successes began to mount, she became engaged to Eric Brough, one of Langrish's most promising students. But while judging for the Associated Royal Board in 1936, he was tragically killed when his seaplane crashed off the coast

Chapter 12

of Trinidad, and soon thereafter her closest remaining male friend, (Dennis) Yelland Richards, died while rock climbing in Wales.[136] Though her personal life was devastated for a time, she continued to perform—often with the Griller Quartet—but she depended heavily on teaching for her income, and the War brought her many hardships.[137]

Matthay's *Playthings*, published by Oxford in 1944, consists of seven short pieces of intermediate difficulty which often show surprising wit and harmonic sophistication. A notable example is the third entry, "Shades of Czerny," which—predictably—demands rotational freedom:

Ex. 12.3 Tobias Matthay: "Shades of Czerny" from Playthings, Book III, Op. 44

Against this backdrop of increased composition and publication, Matthay continued to audition a few students, and on 28 August 1942 he heard Oscar ("Okky") Yerburgh, who had just turned 17. Matthay noted that his tendency to drive the "arm forward needs correcting," but that he was "intelligent" and "certainly" had "excellent talent."[138] Years later, Yerburgh recalled that—perhaps because he was privileged with an upper-class background—his desire to perform professionally had never been well received by those around him. At 13 he entered Eton, and shortly thereafter, its Headmaster, Claude Elliott, advised his aunt that "Music has ruined more people than drink!"[139] Fully expecting to be drafted by the RAF after his eighteenth birthday, Yerburgh decided first to undertake a "trial period" with a distinguished teacher, and several weeks before his audition, he entered the TMPS Summer School. He later wrote that its students "were billeted in a school at the bottom of the hill and each morning we walked together up the little lane to High Marley." He was enchanted with his musical studies and decided to carry them forward, but Eton was "furious" when it discovered his summer activities, and kept him till the end of the term in December. As a final parting gesture, the Headmaster growled, "I hear you are leaving in order to do music. I hope they 'call you up' before you have time for any of that nonsense."[140]

Yerburgh's stepfather was then on duty with the Foreign Service in South Africa, and as the youth temporarily had no home in England, Matthay invited him to stay at Marley. He arrived in January of 1943, and years later, he provided a detailed portrait of the daily life Matthay, Denise, and Hilda were then experiencing:

> When you entered High Marley there was a carpeted staircase on the right which Hillie used to climb on her knees with a duster in each hand to polish the wood on either side, for it was very difficult to get any domestic help during the war. On the right of the entrance hall double doors led down to the drawing room-music room with its two grand pianos and in front of you the hall opened onto a brick floored porch [Marley's southern entrance], and it was here, on summer days, that

Chapter 12

> Uncle Tobs used to take his breakfast. I vividly remember the velvet skull cap which he always wore, and the old, worn-brown dressing-gown. I remember his expression of beaming kindness, and I shall never forget how he was with the chickens . . . [who] would come round to him at his little breakfast table. He would bend down and give them little bits to eat, and he talked to them just as if they were people (even when he was completely alone). He had this quality of treating all life with total attention and respect, and the only things which seemed to irritate him were sloppiness and lack of attention.[141]

Yerburgh also overheard many lessons given at Marley, and on one occasion he verified that even those closest to Matthay could invoke his wrath if he thought they were insufficiently attentive to their musical tasks:

> Only once did I see him (through the music room window) and hear him being really upset. . . . On this occasion he was shouting at Irene Scharrer who had prepared a Chopin broadcast and had come down from London to play the programme to Uncle Tobs. . . . One of the pieces in her programme was the B flat minor Scherzo by Chopin. Irene was so charming and vivacious, and she had such an enormous virtuoso talent and had played the Scherzo so often that it was easy for her not to prepare things with the same deep care and thoroughness of Myra Hess. I heard Uncle Tobs telling her that she should play the piece as if it was being played for the first time, that her playing was slapdash and that she was playing about with the text![142]

Moura Lympany was also a frequent visitor. She was then preparing the Rachmaninoff Third Concerto—which as yet had been rarely performed by female pianists—and Yerburgh recalled how "I used to sit on the hall floor with my ear glued to the music-room door whenever Moura came with her D minor Rachmaninoff." He also vividly remembered Matthay's daily, extremely predictable, habits:

Final Days

He had a nightly routine. Having given several lessons during the day, he would listen after dinner to the 9 o'clock wartime news on the radio and then, wearing his velvet skull cap and a velvet or thick tweed jacket, and usually tweed knee breeches (or 'plus-fours' as they used to be called) he would lie back in his armchair, near the fire, the cat and the pianos, spread a big handkerchief over his face and go to sleep for half an hour. And then, at about 10 pm, his own work began, practicing and composing until 1:30 or 2 o'clock in the morning. One night at about half past one (Hillie and I were sitting in the dining room, still probably discussing Music and the Cosmos!) he came running out of the music-room looking like a boy of 15. He said, "I think I have just discovered how to practice!", and then we went into the kitchen for his pre-bed ritual of eating a grated apple. He grated it because he said it made it taste like strawberries.[143]

During his time at Marley, Yerburgh became especially close to Denise, who turned 40 in May of 1943. The War years seem to have been especially difficult for her, since six months earlier, she wrote McClanahan that Matthay's eighty-fourth birthday party had to be canceled because she required an "enforced rest."[144] Like Myra, she found herself in the grips of a demanding performance schedule under difficult conditions, and it is possible that the strain had been too much for her. On 13 December 1941, Matthay wrote Simonds that Denise "really is smothered with playing work and recording, just now!" And he added that "Decca has just issued her Mozart Fantasia and Fugue in C [K. 394]."[145] But whatever her physical or emotional state, she had every reason to be grateful for the review she received a month later from William McNaught in the *Musical Times*, who wrote that "The value of the record is enhanced by Denise Lassimonne's skillful and intelligent playing."[146] Two months later, McNaught also praised her Decca collaboration with violist Watson Forbes in (his transcription of) Bach's first Gamba Sonata in G, noting that "The playing of both artists is to my mind all that could be desired."[147] And somewhat remarkably, Denise even offered an homage to her one-time composition teacher, when she premiered McEwen's new Viola Sonata with Forbes at the Gallery on 13 April 1943, a performance in honor of the composer's seventy-fifth birthday.[148]

By now, as she apprised McClanahan on 22 November, she had at least some cause for optimism:

> This year much of our news will come to you from Julian DeGray, as I am enclosing a letter from him. He unexpectedly, and much to our pleasure, "turned up" one late summer's day, and we all settled down to an endless exchange of news and views and the lapse of the four war years vanished, and we began to imagine how it would all feel again after the war. . . .
>
> The most important happening for us has been the return of the School to London. The Wigmore Hall Galleries now gives us a roof, and Elsie Neville presides there as she used to in the old Wimpole Street days. This coming back into the midst of things has augured well—many new students have joined the School. The Summer School which numbered 140 on some occasions, gave us the idea of returning to London and it has proved right. Of course Uncle Tobs continues to teach down here, but he went up to Lecture during the Summer School, and many of the local inhabitants around the Wimpole Street Block were thrilled to see his familiar figure back again. He is active and alert as ever, and is still composing.[149]

Elsie, who typed the letter, informed McClanahan that she was also typing Denise's signature, since "she had to go to a rehearsal and unfortunately will not be back in time to sign her letter, before the post is collected."[150] But scarcely any Wartime performance engagements paid well, and Denise neglected to mention that the TMPS had now become the object of charity, since the owners of Wigmore Hall, while charging per-lesson rental fees for their studios, were allowing Elsie the use of an office rent free.[151] And a year later Denise informed McClanahan that the entire 1944 Summer School had been canceled, since "during that time we were being visited by those 'empty-headed' flying bombs [German V-1 missiles] which made all traveling and gatherings a bit difficult and nerve-racking, especially for parents whose children were prospective performers."[152] Denise also wrote that although Matthay's eighty-sixth birthday party had been delayed till the spring, neither age nor the War had diminished his enthusiasm:

> It started off with a recital by the "honoured" one, besides playing his just finished set of little pieces, "Five Miniatures", he gave a memorable three-quarter hour selection from his 31 Variations. Later in the day, after lunch and walks around Marley Woods, Uncle Tobs wound up the party by giving a number of Dumb Crambo [charades] performances. Words acted in dumb show with the audience having to guess, the [syllables] being usually given with atrocious double and triple meanings.[153]

Matthay's *Thirty-One Variations & Derivations from an Original Theme in A minor & major*, Op. 28, is his longest piano work, and during the War he became increasingly interested in performing it for pupils and friends. Dedicated to Corder, it was first written in 1891, and the "final revision" was completed in January 1918. Owing to "the unusual length of this work," Matthay included advice on which variations might be most effectively deleted in performance, and he even suggested taking an interval between Variations 15 and 16. Though rarely played, this is arguably his most significant composition for piano, and its enigmatic, vaguely folk-like theme enables him to shift between tonality and modality at will:

Ex. 12.4 Tobias Matthay: Thirty-One Variations & Derivations from an Original Theme, mm. 8-23 (Theme)

In the first Variation, he begins to toy with the boundaries between major and minor, and although subtle, his harmonic explorations are often engrossing:

Ex. 12.5 Tobias Matthay: Thirty-One Variations & Derivations, Var. 1, mm. 9-16

And as might be expected from the work's Victorian roots, he at times adopts a Wagnerian vocabulary:

Ex. 12.6 Tobias Matthay: Thirty-One Variations & Derivations, Var. 8, mm. 1-8

Not surprisingly, his harmonic adventurousness is also often conjoined to Lisztian brilliance:

Ex. 12.7 Tobias Matthay: Thirty-One Variations & Derivations, Var. 21, mm. 9-18

Denise's November 1943 letter to McClanahan references a visit to Marley from Julian DeGray, who, according to the December *Journal* of the American Matthay Association, was now "attached to the American Legation in Stockholm."[154] Although his fluency in eight languages would no doubt have made him invaluable to the State Department, his service at the Legation was merely a cover, for five months after Pearl Harbor he had been commissioned by the War Department's Military Intelligence Division. His official dates of service were 8 April 1942 to 11 May 1943,[155] and his duties included befriending high-ranking German officers in neutral Stockholm. By summer he had been sent to London for debriefing, and he was soon reassigned to the newly created Office of Strategic Services, which he also served in Stockholm until the War's end, receiving his official discharge on 1 October 1945.[156] Whether or not Matthay and Denise actually believed that DeGray was merely a diplomat on

Chapter 12

holiday is unknown, but they knew better than to ask idle questions, and no doubt they were genuinely glad to see him. He stayed for a weekend, and although he confined his comments to depictions of Marley's activities, he advised McClanahan that he felt he should "take this opportunity of being in London on government business" to give the AMA a "first-hand impression of Marley after four years of war." His comments, written from the converted tool shed where Denise often practiced, offered an optimistic account of what many viewed as a turning point, and a confirmation "that what the future has to offer has been worth fighting for:"

> The train services, which I had been given to understand would be somewhat war-battered, are on the contrary quite as good as ever. Yesterday we even had roast-beef and Yorkshire pudding for dinner; but this involved using up the whole week's meat coupons in honour of the overseas guest....
>
> Uncle Tobs' own Bechstein in the drawing-room has recently been refitted with entirely new hammers and sounds more beautiful than I recall it ever having sounded in the past. At the age of 86, [Matthay was actually only 85] he gave me last night in camera a masterly performance of his A-minor variations, op. 28.[157]

Understandably, Americans did not appear frequently at Marley during the War, but on 29 March 1944, Matthay auditioned Lieutenant Samuel (Sam) Pendleton, then on active duty with the 52nd Replacement Battalion at Camp Stapley near Wellington in Somerset. Born in Malone, Texas, Pendleton was then two days away from his thirty-eighth birthday, and before he had enlisted in 1942, he ran a piano studio in Hibbing, Minnesota. He supervised the food service on the base, practiced on an upright in an unused bank vault (in thirty-minute increments to replenish its oxygen supply), and after he performed Chopin's F-sharp Nocturne, Matthay noted that he was "quite musically disposed."[158] As he had already had a lesson with Hilda, all were grateful when he appeared bearing the sum of four guineas to cover three more lessons at her fee of £1, 8s, and he returned for a lesson with Matthay on 3 May. He also came on 31 August, which no doubt served as small consolation for the cancelled Summer School. In all, Matthay auditioned only 14 students in 1944, a figure which increased merely to 16 in 1945, and although AMA *Journal* reports about the School were always positive, many Americans sensed the underlying realities. Frank Mannheimer, now serving as a professor at Michigan State University, sent clothing to Matthay and Denise,[159] and Marley's residents soon altered Pendleton's nickname to "Spam," in appreciation of the supplies he brought from his base's PX.[160] As early as 27 December 1940 the AMA had voted to assess its active members $5, and its associate members $3, to raise $500 for a "Fifteenth Anniversary Gift,", and it further agreed that if "future events in England create a dire situation for 'Uncle Tobs', whereby he would be in need of financial assistance," $500 would be withdrawn from its Scholarship Fund "for his benefit."[161] Matthay gratefully accepted the AMA anniversary gift to enhance the TMPS Students' Aid Fund, and on 9 February 1943, he also eagerly thanked his American "Nephews and Nieces" for the £50 they sent in honor of his eighty-fifth birthday, noting that the gift "shall go towards several lessons I should otherwise have given without fee."[162] But the School's other financial awards survived mainly through the largesse of its teachers. For example, on 11 October 1943 and again on 22 December 1944, Matthay thanked Langrish for contributing five guineas to maintain the annual TMPS Bach Prize, adding that "[I] only wish you would allow me to announce the donor of it!"[163]

But in counterpoint to their increasingly dire finances, Denise recalled a contented, often serene, home life. In June of 1942, Matthay's terrier, Marco Polo, had been put to sleep at the age of 13, and Myra began searching to replace the loss. In November of 1944, Denise wrote to McClanahan:

> High Marley has a new inmate, he was presented to us by Myra just before last Christmas, and then looked like a small edition of the black and white Panda. Berger (now a year old bobtail English sheep dog and

as big as a Shetland pony) has the house well under his huge white paws and devotedly follows "Master" whenever, and wherever he moves. I hope that by next year he will have learned to keep still long enough so that I may send a picture of him with Uncle Tobs.[164]

If Denise affirmed that Berger was a therapeutic addition to the household, she was also gratified when in early 1945 Boosey and Hawkes—at long last—chose to issue Jessie's biography of Matthay. There was further cause for optimism when the war in Europe finally ended in June, although DeGray recalled that conditions in England were actually worse than he had remembered them two years earlier. After V-E Day, he was offered air passage from Stockholm to Washington via Iceland, and he recalled that his colleagues thought him "utterly mad" when he asked to return instead through London, where "one had to queue up for hours to get a meal of such poor quality that it would have been better to go without it."[165] He stood for hours at Waterloo Station, shoulder to shoulder with eager travelers intent on escaping London's grime, only to find the first three fast (express) trains to Portsmouth commandeered by British detachments. When he finally did reach Marley, he was embarrassed to confess to Matthay that he had been obliged to leave his music behind in Stockholm for later shipping to the States. Moreover, he had practiced so little in the last two years that he had no specific repertoire in mind for a lesson, so Matthay merely handed him a volume of Beethoven Sonatas, and suggested, "Why not start with these?"[166] Although by then DeGray had performed all of the Sonatas, he welcomed the opportunity to play through—however erratically—many that he had never coached with Matthay. The account he later provided undoubtedly serves as the last detailed description of a Matthay lesson:

> We started with the Beethoven Sonatas, and we stopped with them, but the "lesson" continued off and on for the next three days. Denise, cautioning me not to overtax Uncle Tobs' physical strength, had made me promise to call a halt after an hour and a half, but it was just as hopeless to stop Uncle Tobs last summer as it was in the old days when Aunt

Final Days

Jessie used to declare that it took nothing more than the sound of the dinner-gong to set Uncle Tobs off on the Hammerklavier or the Diabelli Variations. . . . On one occasion, prompted not so much by my promise to Denise, as by concern for my own endurance, I tried to explain to Uncle Tobs that I thought he had had enough for that day. His reply was to push me off the bench and, while supper grew cold, to play me his latest compositions, some of which he was still working on.

If in the last years of his life Uncle Tob's [sic] hearing was not as keen as it had been, this was noticeable only when he had difficulty in following a multilateral conversation. Everything addressed directly to him he understood, and, whatever question there may have been of his ability to hear the spoken word, all doubt was dispelled when he got to the piano. He was constantly on the alert for every variety of tone and nuance, and many times he lifted my forearm off the keyboard, admonishing me to "make it sing." . . . Uncle Tobs was as jealous as ever of [his Bechstein's] mellow tone, and when I launched into one or two of the sforzandi in the Appassionata with what must have been too much vehemence, he stopped me with the remonstrance, "Allegro assai e molto appassionata, but *not martellato!*" Taking hold of his arm I countered, "But I want these sforzandi to wrench the listener just as much as I am wrenching your arm." After a moment of quizzical silence, while his eyes danced behind the thick lenses of his glasses, he said, "Have no fear, they will! But you don't have to wrench the piano into the bargain!" Later I was called down for a wrong note high up in the treble on the last page of the Appassionata, where the semiquavers are moving at presto speed. . . . It might be an overstatement to assert that Uncle Tobs could have played all of this music himself by heart, but there is no question that he followed it at every moment in his mind, never once relinquishing the inner image of what he expected me to reproduce in sound. And he gave no quarter when I failed to meet the inner demands of this image. We went back again and again over the passage until the word became flesh—the image, sound.[167]

Even though the TMPS still existed nominally, the War's conclusion led few to believe that it could be easily restored to its previous state. For one thing, it was virtually bankrupt, and for another, Matthay, now 87, no longer had the stamina to conduct the necessary reconstruction without help. Although his health was still generally good, he had been suffering fainting spells for the past two years, and Denise seemed resigned to the fact that these may have signaled a journey that was approaching its end. A few times he fainted at the piano, and once he fainted in his bath, requiring the caretaker to break a window to revive him. His doctor's seeming lack of concern underscored the sense of inevitability. Knowing that Matthay felt most comfortable when he was as active as possible, he strongly advised Denise not to interfere, counseling her to "let him do what he wants." She was relieved that Matthay still relished evening walks, although the outings were briefer in cooler temperatures. Well after 10 or 11, he might take her arm with a persuasive comment such as, "You know, you only get so many full moons in your life, and there's one tonight. Don't you think we should see it?" Their usual pattern was to stroll through the woods around Marley, often losing themselves far from the established footpaths.

Matthay's last recorded Entrance Hearing occurred on 15 November 1945, when he heard thirty-eight-year-old Enid Kayll from Bournemouth play Beethoven's Sonata in D, Op. 10, no. 3, and an unidentified Chopin Nocturne. He wrote that she was "not at all unmusical," and assigned her to 12 weekly lessons in London with Gwendolyn Warren—who most frequently taught younger pianists—at a fee of £12, 12s. But the lessons were never taken, and Elsie returned the money a few months later.[168] In mid-December, she sent Langrish his payment for the TMPS Michaelmas term. He had only two students, each of whom had paid £5, 5s. From one pupil, a Mr. Levett, the School extracted only 25 percent, leaving Langrish a balance of £3, 18s, 6d, and from the other, a Miss McCarthy, its cut was only 15 percent, leaving £4, 9s, 3d. But still, Langrish's compensation for the entire term was only £8, 8s, and after an additional 10 percent administrative deduction, he was left with a balance of only £7, 11s, 3d.[169]

On the morning of Tuesday, 11 December, Denise became worried when her beloved "Panunck" did not come down for breakfast

Final Days

by eleven. She knocked on his door and found him sitting on the edge of the bed. He said he did not have the strength to dress. A doctor was summoned and diagnosed a "minor heart attack." He said there was nothing to be done, and advised Denise simply to let him rest. He also urged her to hire a nurse. When she arrived, Denise asked her to remove her nursing cap, so that she would not alarm Matthay, since he was drifting in and out of consciousness. During his periods of lucidity, he kept wanting to get up to practice, and Denise finally had his Bechstein upright moved from his study into his bedroom, but he did not feel well enough to use it. By Wednesday evening a night nurse had been added. On Thursday, Myra drove down, fearing the end had come. She did not want to have to explain her presence in the event he regained consciousness, so she only watched him slumbering from behind the door. The next day he awoke about tea time and said, "I'm feeling much better now." He actually looked better, he was lucid, and he ate something. For a time Denise thought he might pull through. But that evening, about 11 pm, the night nurse came for her, crying, "He's sinking fast." Denise bolted to his room and found him seemingly asleep, but suddenly to her surprise he reached for her hand and gripped it powerfully—forcefully—with a long squeeze. Then he turned over and was gone.

Denise was surprised at her calmness. The first person she phoned on Saturday morning was Myra, who agreed to handle the "public" details connected with his passing. It was Myra who telephoned the London newspapers and the BBC, and later that evening she gave a tribute to him on the Home Service. Denise attended to the more immediate practical details—the arrangement of the funeral and cremation at St. John's Chapel in nearby Woking, where Jessie's service had been held. On the following Wednesday, the Reverend Greville Cooke, one of Matthay's former students and now a piano professor at the RAM, provided an eloquent eulogy:

> To a precision of mind expressing itself with the exactitude proper to a scientist, he allied a passionate research into the relations of matter and spirit, of muscle and mind, a combination that made of him a very great

Chapter 12

discoverer of Truth. Beauty was his lodestar in life; he was her servant, her interpreter, and her instrument in creation.[170]

Apart from a few professors on the TMPS staff, there were few attendees. Afterward, Myra refused to let Denise return to Marley alone and drove her to London to spend the night at her home on Wildwood Road in St. John's Wood. The two women slept little, sobbing most of the night away. Several days later they conducted a final ceremony on Marley Common, where they mingled the ashes of Jessie and Tobias, letting them float in the breeze.[171]

Notes

1. "Down With Scales," *Time*, 12 Jan. 1942, 37. Hereafter cited as *Time*.
2. *Time*.
3. *Time*.
4. MA. Taped interview with DeGray at his home in Warren, Connecticut, conducted by his former student Elizabeth Lauer on 9 April 1984.
5. See *AMAJ*, 1939, 31-32.
6. "Smith to Quit as Dean of Yale Music School," *NYT*, 28 Apr. 1940, 36.
7. "Concerts[:] Bruce Simonds Applauded," *NYT*, 6 Dec. 1931, 30.
8. *NYT*, 6 Dec. 1931, 30.
9. "Bruce Simonds Gives Varied Piano Recital," *NYT*, 9 Dec. 1934, N6.
10. See *AMAJ*, 1934, 33.
11. MA. Matthay to Simonds, 15 Jan. 1934.
12. MA. Bennington Program. The third concert was on Friday, 23 April, and there was no concert on Sunday, 21 May. The eighth concert occurred on Wednesday, 31 May.
13. Eunice Norton, "The Role Played by the Fingers," *AMAJ*, 1934, 19-20.
14. Lewis Foreman, "Spanning the Century—the Music of Alan Bush," in Nancy Bush, *Alan Bush[:] Music, Politics, and Life* (London, 2000), 100. Hereafter cited as Bush.
15. Bush, 7.

16. Bush, 21.
17. Bush, 21-22.
18. Reprinted in Cesar Saerchinger, *Artur Schnabel[:] A Biography* (New York, 1957), vii-xiii.
19. Interview with Curzon at Denise Lassimonne's home in Buriton, Hampshire, Aug. 1975.
20. COMM, 15 Oct. 1924.
21. Matthay pupils remembered that Curzon was so concerned about McEwen's wrath that he more "publicly" worked with Katherine Goodson for a time after he left Matthay, and it was her suggestion that he go to Schnabel. LI.
22. MA. See TMPS Prospectus for 1935, 7 and 9.
23. "Miss Dorothy Robson's and Mr. C. Curzon's Recital," *TT*, 14 May 1927, 10, col. A.
24. *TT*, 14 May 1927, 10.
25. On 20 February 1967, former EMI executive Walter Legge honored Moore with a "Farewell Recital" at Festival Hall, but the pianist later recalled that "others before me were more worthy to have been similarly flattered," citing both Craxton and Hamilton Harty. See Gerald Moore, *Farewell recital: further memoirs* (New York: Taplinger, 1978), 1.
26. "Mr. Harold Craxton," *TT*, 19 Feb. 1923, 7, col. D.
27. Ibid.
28. Denis Matthews, "Harold Craxton[:] 1885-1971," in program booklet for *Harold Craxton Memorial Concert*, 17 Sept. 1971, 5. The concert was held at Fairfield Hall in Croydon. The performers included Curzon performing the Mozart Concerto, K. 595, Craxton's pupil Nina Milkina (discussed below) who joined Matthews for the Mozart Two-Piano Concerto, K. 365, and Yehudi Menuhin and Vladimir Ashkenazy performing the Beethoven Violin Sonata, Op. 30, no. 2. Gerald Moore gave a eulogy. Booklet provided by courtesy of the Craxton family.
29. Interview with Ruth Harte Langrish at her home in Beckenham, Kent, 4 Jun. 2006.
30. Matthews actually lived with Craxton's family for several years during the War, as he recounts in his engrossing autobiography, *In Pursuit of Music* (London, 1966).
31. Interview with Jonson at his home in Hampstead, 9 Jun. 2006.

32. Interview with Squibb at the RAM, 12 Jun. 2006.
33. LI.
34. MA.
35. Julian DeGray, "Carlos Buhler (April 26, 1897 to September 1, 1976)," *The Matthay News*, Fall 1976, 22.
36. MA. Matthay to Simonds, "Easter Sunday" [5 April 1931].
37. *AMAJ*, 1937, 8. The Association's 1937 issue was "Dedicated to the Memory of Jessie Henderson Matthay."
38. McClanahan was then Editor of the Association Journal, and Denise wrote her 3 October letter with the intent that he publish it.
39. "Two Pianofortes[:] Miss Hess and Miss Scharrer," *TT*, 28 Sept. 1937, 12, col. B.
40. "Tobias Matthay, Octogenarian," *MT*. March 1938, 218.
41. HMV B8758, according to McKenna, 284.
42. BBCWA., Matthay to Thatcher, 12 Feb. 1938.
43. BBCWA. Matthay to Thatcher, 25 Apr. 1938.
44. BBCWA. Lewis to Thatcher, 27 Apr. 1938.
45. Moura Lympany and Margot Strickland, *Moura: Her Autobiography* (London, 1991), 42. Hereafter cited as Lympany.
46. See Mathilde Verne, *Chords of Remembrance* (London: Hutchinson and Co., 1936), 98 ff.
47. LI. Solomon eventually suffered a nervous breakdown, which many blamed on Verne's draconian methods. See Bryan Crimp, *Solo: The biography of Solomon* (Wark, Hexham, Northumberland, 1994), 8 ff.
48. Lympany, 46.
49. Lympany, 51-52.
50. Lympany, 56.
51. Lympany, 57-58.
52. Lympany, 60.
53. Lympany, 58.
54. See Doctor, 395.
55. Lympany, 68.
56. "Soviet Symphonies[;] A Tradition Continued," *TT*, 15 Apr. 1940, 4 col. E.
57. "Russian Programme[:] An Armenian Piano Concerto," *TT*, 9 Feb. 1942, 6, col. B.

Final Days

58. Lympany, 69.
59. W. McNaught, "Gramophone Notes," *MT*, Jan. 1946. 19.
60. Lympany (72-73) incorrectly identifies the year of the bombing as 1940.
61. It may have been coincidental, but the Debenhams news arrived almost exactly as Matthay was to have spoken at a dinner honoring Sir Dan Godfrey, an appearance he was forced to cancel since he was "kept at home by influenza." The event was hosted by the Musicians' Club of London at the Wharncliffe Rooms on 20 March 1939. Myra spoke briefly, and then played, "in spite of an injured finger." See "The Musicians' Club," *TT*, 21 Mar. 1939, 14, col. B.
62. "Miss Lassimonne's Annual Letter," 11 Nov. 1939, *AMAJ*, 1939, 6.
63. MA. Report of the Chairman [Matthay] to the Council of the Tobias Matthay Pianoforte School, Ltd, 29 Mar. 1941.
64. Ibid.
65. Last will of Tobias Augustus Matthay, 11 Jan. 1940, on file at Probate Registry, London.
66. MA. Matthay to Langrish, 2 Dec. 1939.
67. MA. Minutes of the Council of the TMPS, Ltd., 20 Mar. 1941.
68. Ibid.
69. MA.
70. Hilda Dederich to Theresa Coolidge, republished as "Life at High Marley" in *AMAJ*, 1940, 10-11.
71. Denise Lassimonne, "Miss Lassimonne's Annual Letter," *AMAJ*, 1940, 6-7.
72. LI.
73. See McKenna, *Myra Hess*, 122.
74. Ibid.
75. Sir Kenneth Clark, "Music in Place of Pictures," in *Myra Hess by her Friends*, 57.
76. Clark to Duff, 25 Sept. 1939, partially reproduced in McKenna, 123-24. McKenna indicates the letter is in the "National Gallery Concerts" folder no. 1, in the National Gallery Records.
77. Duff to Clark, 4 Oct. 1939 partially reproduced in McKenna, 125-26. McKenna indicates the letter is in the National Gallery Records.
78. See "National Gallery in War-Time[:] Series of Lunch-Hour Concerts," *TT*, 7 Oct. 1939, 4, col. E.

79. "National Gallery Concerts[:] Miss Myra Hess," *TT*, 11 Oct. 1939, 6, col. G. *The Times* also ran a wide-angle photo of the concert audience with a caption identifying Myra as the "artistic director."
80. "National Gallery Concert [:] Chamber Music," *TT*, 14 Oct. 1939, 6, col. G.
81. "National Gallery Concerts[:] Two Innovations," *TT*, 24 Nov. 1939, 6, col. F.
82. See *TT*, 30 Oct. 1939, 4, col. E.
83. See McKenna, 118-20.
84. Interview with Ruth Harte Langrish at her home in Beckenham, Kent, on 4 July 2005.
85. "National Gallery Concerts[:] A Festive New Year Programme," *TT*, 2 Jan. 1940, 6, col. D.
86. Ibid.
87. "National Gallery Concerts[:] A New Piano Sonata," *TT*, 24 Apr. 1940, 4, col. D.
88. "The Piano Sonata[:] Ordinary Mortals," *TT*, 27 Apr. 1940, 4, col. E.
89. "A Birthday and a Moral[:] The National Gallery Concerts," *TT*, 13 Oct. 1944, 6, col. C.
90. "A Stock-Taking[:] National Gallery Concerts," *TT*, 30 Dec. 1939, 4, col. D.
91. "Birkbeck College Concerts," *TT*, 21 Dec. 1939, 6, col. E.
92. Interview with Jonson at his Hampstead home, 9 June 2006.
93. "Cambridge Theatre[:] Two Mozart Concertos," *TT*, 15 Mar. 1938, 12, col. E.
94. See "Sunday Concerts in London[:] Plans for New Series," *TT*, 14 Sept. 1937, 15, col. C. *The Times* also cited "musicians who support the scheme," naming "Sir Hugh Allen, Miss Lilian Baylis, Mr. Tobias Matthay, Herr Artur Schnabel, and Dr. Vaughan Williams."
95. "A Passenger Hears About the Sea," *NYT*, 12 May 1940, 37.
96. A fuller narrative of Beecham's love life, too complex to be conveyed here, is presented in detail in John Lucas's outstanding *Thomas Beecham: An Obsession with Music* (Woodbridge, Suffolk, 2008). Beecham was accompanied on the *Rex* by his long-time mistress, Lady Emerald Cunard, "mistaken by the press for his wife" (242), while—even more improbably—English soprano Dora Labbette, his simultaneous mistress for the previous 13 years (who had borne him a son), sailed for New York on the same liner as Humby. In subsequent months, Beecham continued to live with Labbette in Australia and Canada—and more briefly with Cunard in California.

Final Days

97. Although it may never be known what understandings existed between Beecham and Humby before they left England, Humby confided to Labbette aboard the *Britannic* that an important reason for her sailing to America was to obtain a divorce from her husband so that she could marry a man she did not name. Lucas (269) insists "with confidence" that her intended could not yet have been Beecham, although he also relates a conversation with Humby's son, Jeremy Thomas, who first met Beecham in his mother's New York apartment shortly after they arrived (283). After Humby introduced him as "your Uncle Tom," Beecham took the youngster on his knee and announced, "I'm going to look after you now." It should also be noted however, that both Beecham and Humby were abroad for over a year before they worked together.
98. Charles Reid, *Thomas Beecham: An Independent Biography* (New York: Dutton, 1962), 221.
99. "Drama Rides High at Seattle Symphony Opening," *Seattle Times*, 21 Oct. 1941, 14, cols. 1-8, reproduced in facsimile in J. D. Gilmour, *Sir Thomas Beecham: The Seattle Years* (Aberdeen, Wash., 1978), 20. Hereafter cited as Gilmour.
100. John Randolph, "Girl Pianist Stars with Orchestra," *Seattle Star*, 8 Nov. 1941, 8, col. 2, facsimile in Gilmour, 40.
101. Richard Hays, "Crowd Applauds British Pianist," *Seattle Times*, 8 Nov. 1941, 4, col. 5, facsimile in Gilmour, 40.
102. "Beecham Concludes his Mozart Series," *Seattle Star*, 28 Feb. 1942, 6, cols. 1 and 2, facsimile in Gilmour, 99.
103. N. C. L., "Mozart Concert Finishes Season," *Seattle Times*, 28 Feb. 1942, 4, col. 7, facsimile in Gilmour, 98.
104. "Beecham Files Divorce Suit in Lonely Idaho Ghost Town," *Seattle Times*, 5 Oct. 1942, 1, cols. 7 and 8, facsimile in Gilmour, 108.
105. "Beecham and Miss Humby Leave," *Seattle Post-Intelligencer*, 17 Nov. 1942, 6, cols. 2 and 3, facsimile in Gilmour, 141-42.
106. "Sir Thomas Beecham Weds Young Pianist[:] Recent Marriage of Conductor to Betty Humby Revealed," *NYT*, 24 Feb. 1943, 24.
107. BBCWA, Matthay to Boult, 3 Oct. 1933.
108. The score and the parts are now housed in the Sir Thomas Beecham Library at the University of Sheffield. On 4 June 2007, J. D. Hodgson, the Head of Special Collections, confirmed to me that every hand-copied part bears Tilbrook's signature.

109. RAMRBC MS 1932. Shortly before the broadcast, Matthay noted in ink at the bottom of the score's title page that there were seven copies each for the violins, cellos, and basses, but only three for the viola. He then added: "Ought I to have more copied?" Below that in blue pencil, he later added, "Are there enough Viola and Cello parts?" Though unsigned, the additional string parts are clearly in Denise's hand.
110. MA. Matthay to Simonds, 28 Jan. 1943.
111. Richard E. Hays, "Sir Thomas Brings Spring to Music Hall," *Seattle Times*, 20 Oct. 1942, 18, col. 5, facsimile in Gilmour, 116.
112. BBCWA. Herbert Murrill to Wynn, 19 Dec. 1940.
113. BBCWA. B. J. Dale, Report on "IN MAY" A Symphonic Overture, 19 May 1943.
114. BBCWA. Gordon Jacob, Report on "IN MAY" A Symphonic Overture, 19 May 1943.
115. BBCWA. John Ireland, Report on "IN MAY" A Symphonic Overture, 19 May 1943.
116. BBCWA. John Ireland, Report on "CONCERT-PIECE IN A MINOR," 19 May 1943.
117. BBCWA. Gordon Jacob, Report on "CONCERT-PIECE IN A MINOR," 19 May 1943. Dale simply added his comment to the bottom of Jacob's report.
118. See "Broadcasting," *TT*, 17 Nov. 1941, 8, col. B.
119. MA. Matthay to Simonds, 13 Dec. 1941.
120. "Recitals[:] Pianoforte and Strings," *TT*, 17 Jan. 1935, 10, col. D.
121. "Week-End Concerts[:] M. Etienne Amyot," *TT*, 7 Jun. 1937, 9, col. E.
122. See Humphrey Carpenter, *The Envy of the World* (London: Weidenfeld and Nicolson 1996), 15-ff.
123. *The Times* article is unsigned but the authorship is attributed to Colles in the reprint which appeared in *JAMA*, 1943, 5.
124. "A Great Piano Teacher: First Principles," *TT*, 19 Feb, 1943, 6, cols. C and D.
125. Ibid.
126. Ibid.
127. "Birthday Honours," *TT*, 12 Jun. 1941, 5, col. C.
128. MA. Tobias Matthay lesson record book, begun Sept. 1939.
129. Ibid.
130. Ibid.

131. Tobias Matthay, Preface to *FL* (London, 1942).
132. *FL*, 5.
133. *FL*, 10-11.
134. Denise to McClanahan, 18 Nov. 1941, *AMAJ*, 1941, 7.
135. Her review in *The Times* was positive, but somewhat undercut by the critic's editorial comment: "Is there any music more devoid of significance than that of Saint-Saëns?" See "Promenade Concert," *TT*, 27 Aug. 1930, 8, col. B. I am indebted to Hilda Bor's brother, Edwin, for providing much biographical information about his sister.
136. See "Mr. E. R. Brough," *TT*, 14 Apr. 1936, 12, col. D. Brough and Richards shared an organist's position at the Congregational Church in Lewisham, where a commemorative concert was held in their memories on 7 April 1938. See *MT*, March 1938, 211.
137. Thanks to a letter of recommendation (MA) that Myra wrote to Buckingham Palace in the mid-1950s, Hilda Bor later taught both Prince Charles and Princess Anne.
138. Matthay lesson record book.
139. Oscar Yerburgh, "Reminiscences of Tobias Matthay," *MN*, Fall 1991, 12.
140. Ibid., 13.
141. Ibid., 14.
142. Ibid., 15.
143. Ibid., 20.
144. "Miss Lassimonne's Annual Letter," 19 Nov. 1942, *AMAJ*. 1942, 5.
145. MA. Matthay to Simonds, 13 Dec. 1941.
146. *MT*, Jan. 1942, 17.
147. *MT*, Mar. 1942, 83.
148. See "Birthday Performance of New Sonata," *TT*, 14 Apr. 1943, 6, col. E.
149. "Miss Lassimonne's Annual Letter," 22 Nov. 1943, *AMAJ*. 1942, 7.
150. Ibid., 6.
151. Interview with Oscar Yerburgh at his home in Kensington, 6 July 2005.
152. "Miss Lassimonne's Annual Letter," 17 Nov. 1944, *AMAJ*. 1942, 7.
153. Ibid.
154. *AMAJ*, 1943, 10.
155. MA. On 8 October 1945, he received a certificate from the War Department acknowledging his service, signed by Major General Clayton Bissell.

156. MA. His discharge was signed by Major General William J. Donovan, Director of the OSS.
157. "An Interesting Letter from Julian DeGray," *AMAJ*, 1943, 10.
158. MA. Tobias Matthay lesson record book, begun Sept. 1939.
159. LI.
160. Letter from Pendleton's daughter, Mary, dated 29 Oct. 2006.
161. MA. Minutes of the AMA Annual Meeting held in Steinway Concert Hall, New York, 27 Dec. 1940, submitted 7 Feb. 1941 by Stanley Sprenger, Secretary.
162. Matthay's handwritten letter is reproduced in *AMAJ*, 1943, 3.
163. MA. Matthay to Langrish, 11 Oct. 1943 and 22 Dec. 1944.
164. "Miss Lassimone's Annual Letter," *AMAJ*, 1944, 8.
165. Julian DeGray, "My Last Lesson with Uncle Tobs," *AMAJ*, 1947, 18.
166. Ibid.
167. Ibid, 20-21.
168. MA. Minutes of the Council of TMPS, Ltd., 19 Dec. 1946.
169. MA. TMPS payment record to Vivian Langrish, Esq., for Michaelmas 1945.
170. MA. "Address from Cremation Service[;] 19th December, 1945."
171. LI.

POSTLUDE

At 2:30 pm on 19 December 1946—one year to the day after its founder's funeral—the Council of the Tobias Matthay Pianoforte School, Limited, held its final regular meeting in the London offices of accountants Leonard, Dickinson, and Company. Denise and Hilda were present, and although she was not a Council member, Elsie attended as Myra's legal proxy. George Dickinson was also in attendance to represent his firm, and the three of them immediately voted to place Denise in the chair. Nearly all of the school's few possessions had now been sold, and Elsie reported the income so far received: its typewriter had brought £12, the linotype machine, £7, 5s, and the chairs and "sundry furniture" had fetched £43, 17s. In addition, the School's one remaining Bechstein grand had been sold for £350 to a Miss Shula Doniach, who had already advanced £250, with the balance guaranteed by 21 February. A grand of lesser quality remained as part of its inventory, and plans were discussed to communicate with an Edie Marr of Bournemouth, who promised to sell it for no less than £150, less a 10 percent commission. Since High Marley had now also been sold, the TMPS was legally required to change its address, and with Dickinson's approval, they voted to designate his firm's Victoria Street headquarters as its Registered Office until the liquidation could be finalized. In all—not including the £100 outstanding from the Bechstein sale—the TMPS had cash assets totaling £377, 1s, 1d, against a debt of £168, 10s, 6d. The liabilities included a loan balance of £145, 10s (plus annual interest of £7, 5s, 6d), and storage fees estimated to reach 15 guineas.

Elsie then read a letter from the RAM Committee of Management dated 27 November which endorsed the Council's decision "to wind-up and not to sell the Goodwill" of the School. The Committee was in fact responding to a letter she had sent them, accompanied by a "Solicitor[']s Statement," which it discussed at its 6 November meeting: "The Principal [Stanley Marchant] escplained [sic] that the Academy becomes a beneficiary under a Trust after the winding up of the School (to which he had agreed) subject to the lives of Miss Lassimonne and Mrs Dorothea Kennedy." In fact, Matthay's will—drawn on 11 January 1940, eight days after the reorganized TMPS had come into being—had created a trust to care for Denise and Dora through their lifetimes, but he died with only £127, 2s, 6d in the bank and a mere £2 in currency. Before his debts were paid, the gross value of his estate came to £21,571, 12s, 1d—including a life insurance benefit of £1,151, 13s, 7d—but this amount was reduced to a net of £13,754, 7s, 8d when the will was probated, from which £1,759, 3s was then extracted for Estate Duty. The remaining assets were comprised mostly of property, both real and personal. For example, Marley was assessed at £7,100 for duty purposes, with Matthay's effects being valued at £1,866, and his clothing at £10.

The liquid assets were so minimal that a week after the will was probated, Leonard, Dickinson and Company recorded an annual dividend of only £62, 3d to Denise, and of £33, 1s, 3d to Dora. The payments differed almost by half, thanks to a codicil which Matthay had signed on 13 January 1944 granting his copyright royalties exclusively to Denise through her lifetime, but in subsequent years she rarely received enough to sustain her, even though the royalty payments were combined with interest on some long-term investments. Denise was also one of the estate's four Trustees—Myra, Hilda, and Langrish being the other three—who served as the will's executors, and by careful design, also formed the Council of the TMPS. In addition, Clause 14 of Matthay's will provided for Myra to succeed him as Principal—or Denise, "if for any reason she is unable to accept the Office." Myra promptly accepted the post, but then on New Year's Day of 1946—less than three weeks after Matthay's death and without benefit of counsel—she issued circulars to all of its students declaring the TMPS to be defunct.

Seven months later, at the behest of Matthay's attorney, Herbert Oppenheimer, Myra received a nine-page legal opinion prepared by

Henry Salt, a specialist in corporate law. Salt affirmed the legality of her decision, since Matthay had imbued her with all of his powers except the prerogative to appoint her own successor. However, he also made special mention of Clause 10 from Matthay's will, which read in part:

> If the said capital and income of my residuary estate shall prove more than sufficient to pay the said legacies in full then the surplus shall be paid to the Council of the Tobias Matthay Pianoforte School Limited to be applied for the benefit of said School or if it has ceased to exist then such surplus will be paid to the Royal Academy of Music.

On 22 July, Joseph Magnus, an attorney from Oppenheimer's firm, sent Myra a brief explanation of Salt's concerns:

> Whilst Counsel does not criticise in any way the decision to close the School last Christmas, yet he points out that in theory, the School was property which might have had a value and produced income even after the death of Professor Matthay. . . . He feels, therefore, that the Royal Academy of Music should be approached informally at least, so that they appreciate and concur in the closing of the School last December.

Two days later, Elsie apprised Langrish of a Council meeting Magnus had scheduled at Oppenheimer's offices for 29 July, where "we shall therefore have to consider the best method of dealing" with the RAM question. The legal concerns were largely theoretical, since the Academy only became eligible for benefits after the TMPS had closed, but if it could be demonstrated that reckless governance had diminished its value, the RAM might conceivably have had cause for action. Perhaps as a consequence of these considerations, Myra was soon cultivating a close relationship with the Academy, and on 25 July—four days before the meeting—she distributed its awards on Prize Day. During the same visit, Marchant asked her to preside over the unveiling of three stained glass "thanksgiving" windows, created "as a token of gratitude for the preservation of the Royal Academy of Music during the war." The work of artist Leonard Walker, they were funded by a gift from the late Baron Albert Profumo, and they stood 8'6" high, overlooking the entrance hall over the central stairway between the ground and the first floors. Myra was also advised that Magnus intended to discuss another point raised in Salt's legal opinion:

> Counsel advises some modest form of 'Guild' which in his opinion will allow the Company to be continued as a legal entity and give some fair chance of stopping anyone from misusing the name 'Matthay'. Unless some sort of activity is carried on, Mr. Salt agrees there will be no way of stopping anyone using the name 'Matthay' in any connection. The Professors are clearly interested in this part of the opinion, and you may feel that the details of it should be disclosed to them.

The "branch" locations that had once characterized the TMPS were less prominent after 1940, since none of the outlying operations held shares in the newly organized company, and it is unknown how many may even have sought licensing rights. However, Salt was concerned that after the School was officially dissolved it would be "struck off the register of companies as having ceased to function," and hence it would be legally permissible for anyone to use "Tobias Matthay Pianoforte School" as a trade name. Therefore, he advised maintaining a type of skeleton operation—such as hosting periodic meetings for "the promotion or advancement of musical education"—for an indefinite period "to restrain any person" from holding "himself out to the public (without a licence existing and in force from the Testator or from the Company) as conducting a branch of, or as being a successor to, or as being the proprietor of, the Tobias Matthay Pianoforte School in such a manner as should be calculated to deceive the public."

From a purely legal standpoint, it was proving more complicated to close the TMPS than to allow it to remain open, and since Myra knew all too well that Matthay had never intended his life's work to die with him, her behavior in the few weeks after his death requires some explanation. Clearly, he had always expected the TMPS one day to re-establish itself as a viable enterprise, and even though Denise was realistic about his diminishing energies, a mere month before he died, she was enthusiastically announcing a new appointment:

> The school members are increasing rapidly as everyone is returning to an already full London and our next problem will be accommodation! The one very sad spot in all this is Elsie Neville's relinquishing of the Secretaryship. Personal reasons compelled her to take this step and you can imagine how greatly she will be missed by Uncle Tobs and all of us after thirteen years of wonderful interest and devoted help. I think we can truly say that it is due to her ceaseless and generous efforts that the school continued its existence throughout the war. Her place is being taken by Celia Jackson who has for some time past been assisting Miss Neville, and we feel we are very fortunate in our new secretary.

Fortunately, after the School closed, Elsie returned to her post to facilitate the liquidation, and to act as a go-between for Myra and the other Trustees. It is possible that if the War had not inflicted so many blows precisely as Matthay's physical capacities had begun to ebb, he might have drawn a more detailed, realistic plan for the School's long-term survival. But even before the *Blitz* began, the TMPS had few remaining cash reserves, and it had only avoided bankruptcy by totally withdrawing from London's escalating rents and taxes. On 28 December 1945, 15 days after Matthay's passing, Myra sent letters to each of its remaining professors, assuring them that the decision to disband was supported by the School's four Trustees, and citing the War as the principal source of "insuperable" problems. Confirming that the continued operation of the TMPS would require "a large capital sum," she added:

> Only a few weeks ago, Uncle Tobs spoke to Denise Lassimonne of the many problems concerning the future and expressed his opinion that these difficulties might prove to be insurmountable, in which case, he was fully aware that the School as such, might have to come to an end.

Although her letter does not mention it, the question of succession was also a bit thorny, since Myra had not been abroad for six years, and now—as one of the most marketable pianists in the world—she was understandably intent on resuming her career. When she returned to New York's Town Hall on 12 October 1946, the capacity audience was on its feet before she had even played a note, and Olin Downes seemed as much in awe as the enraptured crowd:

> Miss Hess' musical ministrations in London during the catastrophe, her complete disregard of danger or fatigue or any claims whatever upon her gifts and her strength where it was so badly needed, can never be forgotten.
>
> Add to this her exceptional qualities as a musician! From the standpoint of performance alone she has been too long away. The audience rose when Miss Hess appeared, remaining in the hall to the last note of a long and demanding program, to listen absorbed, to applaud and to cheer.

Although in Myra's absence, Matthay's will also allowed Denise to step in, after his death there was only a nominal institution over which to preside. By 1946, anyone wishing to restore the TMPS to its former stature would have required a substantial investment, and none of Matthay's teachers—not even Myra—had sufficient capital to underwrite such an enterprise, particularly in war-torn London, where undamaged property was now at a premium. But, for whatever reason, it does not appear that the Council ever followed Salt's suggestion to create a TMPS "Guild," or at least none can be documented in the immediate post-War period. However, Myra and Marchant were evidently conferring extensively behind the scenes, because the letter Elsie read from the Committee of Management on 19 December also indicates that the RAM was interested in obtaining the 500 outstanding shares of TMPS stock. In all probability, these shares—by then valued at no more than £200—were being transferred as a symbolic good-faith offering to prod the Academy to initiate the Tobias Matthay Memorial Trust, a proposed fund to assist the careers of deserving pianists, which would incorporate the TMPS residual assets once the School was dissolved. On 25 November 1946, Elsie received a £10 donation from Egerton Tidmarsh, the proceeds from a two-piano recital he had just given with Langrish, and fundraising was pursued far more aggressively through 1947. Langrish and Tidmarsh gave another benefit at the RAM on 14 May which netted £155, 4s, 3d, and less than a month later, on 11 June, Myra offered a recital "In Memory of Tobias Matthay" at the Royal Albert Hall. An elaborate eight-page booklet, complete with program notes by Denis Matthews, accompanied the event, as well as an insert explaining the fund's purpose—coupled to a detachable donation form:

> In answer to a widespread desire to perpetuate the name of Tobias Matthay and as a testimony of appreciation for his great work, it has been decided to form a Trust in his memory. The purpose of this trust will be to endow a Student Fellowship at the Royal Academy of Music, at which Institution he spent so many years of his life. The student fellowship is to be an award to a senior student of exceptional distinction.
>
> A generous donation has already been received from the American Matthay Association and it is hoped that a sum will be realized large enough to provide such an award, which would include maintenance and also assist the young artist in starting his career.
>
> Cheques should be made payable to the Tobias Matthay Memorial Trust and all donations sent to Dame Myra Hess, c/o The Royal Academy of Music, Marylebone Road, London, N. W. 1.

In point of fact, the AMA had never intended its meager resources to subsidize the careers of British pianists. Although the funds collected for Matthay's benefit during the War had long since been transferred to the TMPS Students' Aid Fund, the Association was not apprised of the Memorial Trust's existence until several months after Myra performed, at which time McClanahan merely offered to sell the program booklets she provided for $1 apiece and donate the proceeds. Unquestionably, the Americans also felt a profound sense of loss, for just two weeks after Matthay died, the AMA staged a memorial tribute in New York's Steinway Hall. Ray Lev opened the program with the Funeral March from Beethoven's Sonata, Op. 26, followed by Bruce Simonds, who gave a poignant talk called "Tobias Matthay, Teacher and Friend," before performing Matthay's Prelude in E and his "Elves." Bruce and Rosalind concluded with the Adagio from Bach's Concerto in C minor for two keyboards and Langrish's two-piano transcription of the choral prelude *In der ist Freude* ("In Thee Is Joy"). But ironically, the AMA was also about to disband—at least briefly. Several of its key members agreed with Simonds, who feared "the Association could never receive new blood, as it were, from Mr. Matthay himself (in the shape of personal pupils) and that the personnel of the Association would get progressively more and more remote from Mr. Matthay himself, with the inevitable disagreements about different points in his teaching, which are only emphasized by an organization."

On 14 October 1947, George Dickinson gave notice of the last "extraordinary" meeting of the TMPS Council, to be held in his Victoria Street offices at 11 am on 22 November. This gathering was mandated by Section 236 of the Companies Act of 1929—pursuant to the "Voluntary Winding-Up" of British corporations—in which the Council was to decide "the manner in which the Books, Accounts, and Documents of the Company and of the Liquidator thereof shall be disposed of." Although no minutes of the meeting are known to survive, it should be noted that except for an occasional broadcast, Denise had then largely withdrawn from professional activity, and no doubt this final stage of the liquidation process merely added to a depression that had begun soon after Matthay's death. On 21 February 1946, Elsie advised the TMPS professors that Myra's proposed staff meeting to discuss general concerns was being postponed till April "on account of the illness of Denise Lassimonne . . . as the Doctor has ordered a further few weeks of complete rest." And undoubtedly another contributing factor was the impending sale of High Marley. Even though Matthay had owned his home freehold and absent any liens, the decision was made early on to sell it, as the house was simply too large to be maintained by his surviving assets. Through 1946, its maintenance fees alone came to £209, 8s, 8d, and undoubtedly this was a bare minimum, since most likely its proper stewardship would have required far greater outlays on an ongoing basis.

Postlude

And Marley was not easily sold. Denise wanted to ask £12,000, but although the house sat on nearly six acres, the structure was small by the standards of most affluent buyers, and it needed so many repairs that an appraiser from John D. Wood and Company—one of London's leading estate agencies—advised her that it was worth less than half that amount. His estimate was supported by C. Bruce Durham of Basingstoke, who was retained to sell the property. On 14 June, Durham wrote candidly to Magnus:

> As I think you are aware, Miss Lassimonne, due to personal feelings, was particularly anxious to try and obtain an exceptional price but as Mr. Icke of John D. Wood and Co., and I pointed out to her the house itself, taken out of its position [location], does not merit any expectation of a price much higher than £5,000, or perhaps £6,000 today. The situation [setting] is, of course, unique and unspoilable and it is exceedingly hard to assess how much a purchaser would be prepared to pay for such a unique position in that part of the Country but while we are naturally anxious to obtain the highest possible price, we are far more likely to lose a sale by asking too much for a start, upon the other hand there are purchasers today so desperate to obtain a house that they will pay ridiculous prices. Weighing one thing up with another I consider that for the first month after the advertisement appears we might ask a price of £9,750 and after that time if no purchaser has materialised, I think we shall have to come down to £8,500[,] but I consider that probably the fair value of this property today is nearer £7,500 but in view of the general shortage of this type of property, it is certainly worth trying for the extra.

The Trustees agreed to the £9,750 figure, but even though Durham lowered the price several times, the house remained unsold through the summer. On 16 September, Denise was still living at Marley when she wrote Langrish with some urgency:

> Now comes the matter of Marley which is'nt [sic] sold yet—& it is suggested we should sell it by auction—I enclose the letter from Mr. Magnus to Bruce Durham who is handling the sale—Do you agree to what they

propose—that is auctioning the house with a reserve price of £6,500—If we don't sell it, we may have to let it furnished as we dare not leave it empty <u>one</u> second as it will be requisitioned immediately [because] the [Sussex County] Council here are on the pounce for empty houses!!! Please, Viv, may we hear what you think as soon as possible as we want to proceed quickly, the winter is upon us.

Exactly six weeks later, the firm of Cubitt and West placed an ad in *The Times* announcing its intention to auction Marley in late November 1946, and by mid-December the conveyance had been transferred to London businessman Kenneth John Garle. Precisely what Garle bid for the house is unknown, but it was heartbreaking for Denise to discover that after the various commissions were deducted, the sale netted only £6,345, 4s, 5d. By then she had relocated a few miles away to "Redlands," a small house in Wormley, near Godalming, and by early 1949 she confessed to McClanahan that "I am so much out of things down here—away from Concerts—teaching—all the old group, etc.—it is a little difficult to find anything to say." She continued:

> My life has been so utterly different these past three years with very little musical activity apart from a few concerts and broadcasts which I've given. I have at last found a small flat in London and hope to resume old ties and teaching once again, and I am madly busy trying to find another tiny place in the country for week-ends, as this house is to be sold in March.

One of her few recent performances had included a recital given the previous August under the auspices of the Music Teachers' Association, which sponsored a week-long "Refresher Course" on Matthay principles—perhaps also fulfilling the TMPS "guild" legality that Matthay's attorneys had once recommended. Myra, Irene, Bowen, and Nina Milkina also appeared as recitalists, while Langrish, Craxton, and Read offered daily lectures. All of the participants donated their services, and the course fees were soon turned over to the Matthay Memorial Trust, which was now beginning to accumulate a substantial principal. On 15 November 1949, Elsie informed Langrish that "today I am sending a cheque to the R.A.M. for £3529.12.1. which is the amount we have received from donations for the Tobias Matthay Memorial Fund." She also advised him that three days later she was instructing Magnus to turn over the TMPS Students' Aid Fund as well, which by then held "approximately £2100." By now, the TMPS had also been liquidated, and on 30 November 1949, the RAM Committee of Management read a letter from Oppenheimer's firm acknowledging that all of its remaining assets were to be transferred to the Academy. These included £159, 14s, 7d, in cash, £549, 1s, in War stock (paying 3½ percent interest), and £114, 15s, in consolidated stock.

At the same meeting the Committee acknowledged Elsie's check "on behalf of the Trustees of the late Tobias Matthay," and the Academy's new Principal, Reginald Thatcher (1888-1957), reported on a conversation he had had with Myra outlining the proposed conditions of the Fellowship: 1) It was to pay £200 per annum to a recent RAM graduate, and 2) it would be limited to pianists who were citizens of either the United Kingdom or the United States. At some point it was also decided that the award be conferred at the discretion of the Principal, rather than by jury. Thatcher, who first became acquainted with Matthay when he served as Deputy Director of Music for the BBC, had trained as an organist at the Royal College, and in 1943 he joined the Academy as Warden, owing to the death of Benjamin Dale. He became Principal when Marchant died suddenly in February of 1949, but the change of command may have delayed the Fellowship's momentum, since Marchant and Myra had expected the first award to be given in September of 1950, and it was not conferred for another two years. Thatcher chose Reginald Ham as the first recipient, and although Ham's subsequent performances attracted little attention from the London press, he was followed the next year by the Edinburgh-born Alexander Kelly, who had arrived in 1946 at the age of 17 for studies with Craxton and Lennox Berkeley, and who rapidly became far more visible. The Fellowship promoted a Matthay lineage for a time, as in 1956 when it went to Jamaican pianist Oswald Russell—a pupil of Eric Grant—and especially four years later, when it was awarded to the highly regarded Hamish Milne. Milne, himself an RAM professor, worked extensively with Craxton, and at this writing is arguably Medtner's leading interpreter.

Expanding the award's citizenry status to the United States was no doubt a concession to the American Matthay Association, since Myra was well aware that during the War, AMA monies had been mingled with the TMPS Students' Aid Fund, and Thatcher may even have hoped that the Americans might consider future donations to the Memorial Fund. But although the Association was back on its feet by 1949, no donations were forthcoming. Three years later, Simonds still refused to play any role in the organization, although he graciously offered good wishes to its then President, Pittsburgh pianist and teacher Mae MacKenzie: "I am aware that most of the people in the Association do not agree with me, and if you are making it go, I am very glad." By this time, Denise had also begun a series of summer classes near Petersfield in Hampshire, to which many AMA members happily sent their pupils, but the "guild" that Matthay's attorneys had once so strongly recommended never materialized in Britain. Concurrent with the establishment of the Fellowship, the RAM designated one of its second-floor teaching studios as its "Matthay Room"—eventually filling it with Matthay artifacts—and Craxton and Langrish remained on the Academy staff until their retirements in 1961 and 1968 respectively. But this was insufficient to regenerate substantial British interest in Tobias Matthay, whose presence was rapidly vanishing from the minds of younger pianists and teachers.

One symptom of that fading eminence was a marked decrease in book sales, and in 1975 Oxford University Press advised the Matthay Estate that it was unable to finance another press run of *The Visible and Invisible*. By then, the Estate was being managed by the firm of Shaw, Bickmore, Bishop, and Company, and on 8 October Joseph Shaw wrote department head P. A. Mulgan to ask if Oxford could afford to issue a paperback version, "keeping the cost down to more economic levels for students intending to use this book." Mulgan offered a detailed reply on 30 October, explaining that 800 copies bound in paper—a number believed sufficient to satisfy market demand on both sides of the Atlantic for about three years—would save no more than £100 over binding in boards. But he added that Oxford would proceed if the Estate were willing to advance a subsidy of £300. On 10 November, Shaw answered affirmatively, but six years later the inventory was again exhausted and this time Oxford—perhaps feeling that the risk was unacceptably high—was asking more than £1,000 to help underwrite a run of 1,000 copies. In June 1981, most likely at Denise's behest, Shaw appealed to the Secretary of the Royal Academy of Music:

Dear Sir,
Matthay Trust

We act for the above Trust, which has been in existence for many years, both to perpetuate the teachings of Tobias Matthay on the pianoforte and to provide income for the life tenant of the trust [Denise only. Dora had passed in 1951].

We have just heard from Oxford University Press that the book by Tobias Matthay, entitled as below, is about to go out of print, and your advice and assistance is being sought in this regard. The book is

"The Visible and Invisible in Pianoforte Technique."

According to Oxford University Press, the trust must find the sum of £1,293 in order to reprint 1,000 copies of the book. The future income therefore will be 15% of the new retail price of £4.95—i. e. 0.74p per copy. As the cost to the Trust[,] £1.293 per copy, about 0.55p will be lost on each book sold. Could you let us know please:

1. Whether in your view serious students of the pianoforte require the book and therefore provide the Trustees with an incentive to reprint.
2. Whether the Academy is willing to subsidize a reprint to the extent of say 0.55p per proposed reprint—i. e. £550.42

Postlude

Forty years earlier, the Tobias Matthay Pianoforte School had been forced to accept charity, surviving in its final days only through the generosity of a handful of committed supporters. And now, even the ideas that had nurtured it were foundering—but there was little philanthropy available to sustain them. On 26 June 1981, G. J. C. Hambling, the Principal's Chief Administrator, drafted a sincere, courteous reply, concisely affirming that the teachings of Tobias Matthay were no longer a profitable commodity:

> I have consulted the Principal [Sir Anthony Lewis] and his view is that whilst the book "The Visible and the Invisible" is unlikely to be widely bought by piano students today, it marks an important epoch in the study of pianoforte technique and therefore would be desirable to be kept in print.
>
> I regret that the Academy has no funds from which a reprint could be subsidized.

Hambling scarcely misconstrued the proclivities of British piano students, for on the day he wrote his letter, just 40 miles south of London, Denise was finalizing arrangements for her thirtieth annual Matthay Summer School (the last remaining link to what her attorneys might once have termed a "guild"), and nearly all of her participants were American. By then the American Matthay Association played no small role in encouraging these summer migrations, and in fact had been running its own mini-workshops for over two decades. The first, in Tamworth, New Hampshire, occurred in August of 1958, prompted by the one-hundredth anniversary of Matthay's birth, and although it was merely a three-day affair, its success bred annual festivals which still flourish. Through the 1970s, Matthay's own pupils, the so-called "First Generation," were typically the highlights of these gatherings, and as the years passed, their pupils—a "Second Generation"—assumed leadership roles. But by the 1980s, despite an ongoing presence in American colleges and conservatories, attendance still fell—as Matthay's influence continued to wane on both sides of the Atlantic.

Postlude

But if the flame had diminished, it was never fully extinguished—and today the path may be a bit clearer for those who wish to intensify it.

Notes

1. MA. Minutes of the Council of TMPS, Ltd., 19 Dec. 1946. Hereafter cited as Council Minutes.
2. RAM Committee of Management to Elsie Neville Gunst, 27 Nov. 1946.
3. COMM, 6 Nov. 1946.
4. MA. Estate Account of T. A. Matthay, Deceased, Schedule "A," prepared by Leonard, Dickinson & Co., Certified Accountants, 82 Victoria Street, London, S.W. 1, 19 Jun. 1951. Hereafter cited as Schedule "A."
5. Ibid. See also the Will of Tobias Augustus Matthay, probated on 29 Mar. 1946, on file at the Family Records Office, London. Hereafter cited as Matthay Will.
6. Schedule "A."
7. MA. Balance Sheet from Estate of T. A. Matthay, Deceased, prepared by Leonard, Dickinson & Co., 5 Apr. 1946.
8. Matthay Will.
9. Matthay Will, 9.
10. Matthay Will, 4.
11. MA. Joseph L. Magnus to Dame Myra Hess, 22 Jul. 1946. Hereafter cited as Magnus.
12. MA. Elsie Neville Gunst to Vivian Langrish, 24 Jul. 1946.
13. Magnus.
14. See "Gift to the Royal Academy of Music," *TT*, 25 Jul. 1946, 6, col. E.
15. Magnus.
16. MA. Henry Salt[,] Lincolns Inn "Re. The Tobias Matthay Pianoforte School Limited," 17 July 1946, Opinion prepared for Herbert Oppenheimer Nathan & Vandyk[,] 20 Copthall Avenue, London, E. C. 2, 8, Hereafter cited as Salt, Opinion.
17. Salt, Opinion, 7.

18. Salt, Opinion, 9.
19. Denise Lassimonne to Richard McClanahan, 13 Nov. 1945, *AMAJ Memorial Issue*, 1947, 16.
20. MA. Myra Hess to Guy Jonson, 28 Dec. 1945. The form letters were carboned onto TMPS stationery, but Myra personally signed each one and wrote in the salutations by hand. I am much indebted to Guy belonging to her late father.
21. Olin Downes, "Overflow Throng Cheers Myra Hess," *NYT*, 13 Oct. 1946, 52.
22. Council Minutes.
23. On 21 June 1947, the TMPS Council "agreed that a Return of 7s.2d. be made to each Member of the Company upon each £1 Share held by them," according to a letter (MA) Dickinson sent Langrish on 16 July 1947.
24. MA. Elsie Neville Gunst to Langrish, 25 Nov. 1946.
25. COMM, 12 Jun. 1947.
26. MA. "Myra Hess Recital in Memory of Tobias Matthay and in Aid of the Tobias Matthay Memorial Trust," 11 June 1947.
27. See "The Tobias Matthay Memorial Trust," *AMAJ Memorial Issue*, 1947, 11.
28. The program occurred on 29 Dec. 1945.
29. MA. Bruce Simonds to Mae MacKenzie, 3 Nov. 1952.
30. MA. Notice of meeting issued to TMPS Council by George Dickinson, Liquidator, 14 Oct. 1947.
31. MA. Elsie Neville to Guy Jonson, 21 Feb. 1946.
32. MA. Balance Sheet from Estate of T. A. Matthay, Deceased, prepared by Leonard, Dickinson & Co., 5 Apr. 1947. Hereafter cited as Balance Sheet.
33. MA. C. Bruce Durham to Herbert Oppenheimer, Nathan and Vandyk, 14 June 1946.
34. MA. Denise Lassimonne to Vivian Langrish, 16 Sept. 1946.
35. *TT*, 28 Oct. 1946, 10, col. E.
36. Balance Sheet.
37. "A Letter from Denise Lassimonne," *AMAJ*, 1949, 7.
38. MA. Elsie Neville Gunst to Langrish, 15 Nov. 1949.
39. MA. Bruce Simonds to Mae MacKenzie, 3 Nov. 1952.
40. MA. Joseph Shaw to P. A. Mulgan, 8 Oct. 1975.
41. MA. Mulgan to Shaw, 30 Oct. 1975.
42. RAMA. Joseph Shaw to RAM Secretary, June 1981.
43. RAMA. G. J. C. Hambling to Joseph Shaw, 26 Jun. 1981.

APPENDIX I
SELECTED WRITINGS OF TOBIAS MATTHAY

(Works in Appendices I and II that are discussed extensively in the text are followed by the appropriate chapter number.)

Books

The Act of Touch in all its Diversity; an Analysis and Synthesis of Pianoforte Tone-production. London: Longmans, Green and Co., 1903; reprint ed. London: Bosworth, 1963. (Chapter 6)

The First Principles of Pianoforte Playing; being an extract from the author's "The Act of Touch," designed for school use and including two new chapters; Directions for learners and Advice to teachers. London: Longmans, Green and Co., 1905; reprint ed. London: Bosworth, 1908. (Chapter 6)

Relaxation Studies in the Muscular Discriminations Required for Touch, Agility and Expression in Pianoforte Playing. London: Bosworth, 1908. (Chapter 6)

Musical Interpretation, its Laws and Principles, and their Application in Teaching and Performing. London: Joseph Williams, 1913; Boston: Boston Music Co., 1913. (Chapter 8)

The Visible and Invisible in Pianoforte Technique. London: Oxford University Press, 1932; reprint ed. 1947; 1960; 1976. (Chapter 10)

Pamphlets

"Double-Third Scales. Their Fingering and Practice." London: Joseph Williams, 1911. (Chapter 7)

"The Child's First Steps in Piano-forte Playing." London: Joseph Williams, 1912.

The Problems of Agility: A Summary of the Laws governing Speed in Reiteration and Succession for Wireless Operators, Telegraphists, and Typists, and for Pianoforte and Organ Students. London: Anglo-French Music Co., 1916. (Chapter 8)

"On Method in Teaching." London: Anglo-French Music Co., 1921. (Chapter 8)

"The Nine Steps towards Finger Individualization." London: Anglo-French Music Co., 1923; reprint ed. London: Oxford University Press, 1929. (See Appendix III)

"On Memorizing and Playing from Memory and the Laws of Practice Generally." London: Oxford University Press, 1926. (Chapter 10)

"The Slur or Couplet of Notes in all its Variety, its Interpretation and Execution." London: Oxford University Press, 1928.

"The Act of Musical Concentration, Showing the True Function of Analysis in Playing, Teaching, and Practising, with a Note on the Subconscious." London: Oxford University Press, 1934.

"On Colouring as Distinct from Tone-Inflection, a Lecture." London: Oxford University Press, 1937.

Piano Fallacies of To-day. London: Oxford University Press, 1939. ["The Gospel of Relaxation;" "The Doctrine of Stiffness;" "Weight-Touch and Singing Tone;" "Finger or Agility Technique;" "Forearm Rotation;" "Key Sense and Key Hitting;" "The Psychological Error;" "On Quality of Tone, Again!" "The Scale Spectre: An Examination Crime!"]

An Introduction to Psychology for Music Teachers: Three Lectures. London: Oxford University Press, 1939.

I. "The Scope and Subject-Matter of Psychology"
II "The Working Material of Psychology"
III. "On Attention and Interest—and Inhibition"

"The Gentle Art of Chord Spreading." London: Oxford University Press, 1945.

Pedagogical Works Combining Text with Music

Four Daily Exercises for Advanced Pianists. London: Winthrop Rogers [Boosey & Hawkes], 1939.

Matthay, Tobias, Craxton, Harold, and Swinstead, Felix. *The Approach to Music.* London: Winthrop Rogers [Boosey & Hawkes], 1941. (Chapter 12)

I. Matthay, *How Do You Do, Mr. Piano?*
II. Craxton, *First Solos*
III. Swinstead, *First Duets*
IV. Matthay and Craxton, *Second Solos*
V. Swinstead, *Second Duets*
VI. Matthay, Craxton, and Swinstead, *Third Solos*
VII. Swinstead, *Third Duets*

APPENDIX II

SELECTED PUBLISHED COMPOSITIONS OF TOBIAS MATTHAY

Solo Piano

Moods of a Moment, weary, grave, and gay. London: E. Ascherberg & Co., 1882.

Nocturne, Op. 3. London: Edwin Ashdown, 1883. (Chapter 3)

A Summer Day-Dream, Op. 8**.** London: The London Music Publishing and General Agency, 1885. (Chapter 3)

Love Phases (Minne-Lieder), Op. 12. London: Joseph Williams, 1892; reprint ed. 1912 (Chapter 4)

Mono-themes, Confidences and Confessions. Op. 13. London: Forsyth Brothers, Ltd. 1893. (Chapter 3)

Lyrics, Bk I. [op. 14] Glasgow: Paterson and Sons, [1897]. (Chapter 5)

Scottish Dances and Melodies: *Concert Arrangement for Pianoforte.* [Op. 15] Glasgow: Paterson and Sons, 1897. (Chapter 5)

"Elves" *(Die Elfen)*: Impromptu for Pianoforte. [Op. 17] London: Weelkes & Co., 1898. **(**Chapter 12**)**

Con Imitazione. Preambulo for Pianoforte. [Op. 18] London: Weelkes & Co., 1900.

Romanesque for Pianoforte. [Op. 19] London: Weelkes & Co., 1900. **(**Chapter 8**)**

Prelude in E from *Studies in the Form of a Suite*, Op. 16, no. 1. London: Weelkes & Co., 1900. (Chapter 11)

Stray Fancies, Op. 22. London: Charles Avison, Ltd., 1907.

Intermezzo from *Studies in the Form of a Suite*, Op. 16, no. 7. London: G. Ricordi and Co., 1910. (Chapter 11)

Bravura from *Studies in the Form of a Suite*, Op. 16, no. 8. London: G. Ricordi and Co., 1910. (Chapter 11)

From My Sketch Book, Bk. I., Op. 24. London: Cary & Co., 1914.

Appendix II

From My Sketch Book, Bk. II., Op. 26. London: Cary & Co., 1916.
A Mood-Phantasy (in Late Summer, at Marley), Op. 27. London: Joseph Williams, 1916.
Variations & Derivations: from an Original Theme in A Minor & Major for Pianoforte, Op. 28. London: Augener, Ltd., 1917. (Chapter 12)
On Surrey Hills, Op. 30. London: Anglo-French Music Co., 1919. (Chapter 8)
Summer Twilights, Op. 32. London: Anglo-French Music Co., 1921.
Toccata No. 2 in F (Moto Perpetuo), Op. 34. London: Anglo-French Music Co., 1922.
Ballade in A Minor. London: Oxford University Press, 1926.
Cadenza for Beethoven's Piano Concerto in C, Op. 15. London: Augener, Ltd., 1929. (Chapter 3)
Stray Fancies for Pianoforte, Second Set, Op. 41. London: Oxford University Press, 1939.

Teaching Pieces for Younger Pianists

Five Cameos for Miniature Players, Op. 29. London: Anglo-French Music Co., 1919.
Playthings for Little Players, Ten Little Studies for Pianoforte, Op. 35. London: Anglo-French Music Co., 1924.
Playthings, Bk. III, Op. 44. London: Oxford University Press, 1944. (Chapter 12)

Chamber Work

Quartet, in one movement for Violin, Viola, Violoncello, and Pianoforte. [Op. 20] London: Charles Avison, Ltd., 1906.

Orchestral Work

Concert-Piece in A minor for Pianoforte and Orchestra, Op. 23 [Two-piano score] London: G. Ricordi and Co., 1909. (Chapter 7)

Songs

"The Rose Message" (Thomas Nunn). London: Weelkes & Co., 1896.
"There's nae Lark" (Swinburne). London: G. Ricordi and Co., 1908.
    (Chapter 5)

APPENDIX III

TOBIAS MATTHAY: "THE NINE STEPS TOWARDS FINGER INDIVIDUALIZATION THROUGH FOREARM ROTATION"

A Supplement to the First Book of
The Pianist's First Music Making
and
"The Child's First Steps"

[In 1912, Joseph Williams issued Matthay's twenty-one-page pamphlet "The Child's First Steps," and seven years later the newly formed Anglo-French Music Company published his three-volume companion work, *The Pianist's First Music Making,* to which Felix Swinstead contributed pieces of graduated difficulty. Four years later in 1923, the AFMC offered "The Nine Steps towards Finger Individualization," an extraordinarily brief synopsis of Matthay's teaching principles which he characterized as an "Epitome" to both of the earlier works. Over the years, he had come to regard his views on forearm rotation (which he always insisted should be mostly "invisible") to be the most radical—and fundamental—tenet of his teaching, but he also stressed that its elements were extremely simple and easily mastered. As he became increasingly convinced that the "nine steps" were an essential component of effective piano technique he stressed their importance to his artist-teachers as well as to those who trained children. Reproduced here in near-facsimile, The "Nine Steps" represents Matthay's own assessment of the most important fundamentals of his teaching.]

Appendix III

PREAMBLE.

So-called "Finger-Technique" or "Finger-individualization" is a paramount requirement of the Pianist. As shown elsewhere, this depends, physically, in the first place and mainly on the correct application of the Fore-arm rotational adjustments—that is, upon the correct timing of the exertions and relaxations of the Forearm in its twisting direction. Indeed, we see that in this twisting and untwisting of the Forearm lies the basis of all correct so-called "Finger-technique" and that difference between good and bad "finger passages" etc. therefore depends on the correct or incorrect provisions and application of such forearm-rotational *basis*.* Hence, if any pupil (however advanced) is found to be lacking or unsound in the respect—faulty as to Agility, or faulty as to power and control of "finger"—obviously the correct procedure must be to get this set right at once by making him understand the nature of these requirements there and then. Now the most direct way of doing this is to take him successively through the steps which logically lead to correct understanding and mastery of these matters. These steps have been displayed in the "Pianist's First Music Making," Bks. I. and II. and also in "the Child's First Steps." A more concise statement of these steps, however, is now required, for frequent reference both by student and teacher; hence the issue of the present *Epitome*.

It will be seen that the complete process has been condensed into *nine* steps. These, with a pupil otherwise "advanced," can easily be gone over in a lesson of twenty to thirty minutes; and however bad the pupil's technical habits, and provided he is not below average intelligence, he can hereby *at once* be made to provide perfectly correct and easy technique. To transform such correct Doing in to habit, obviously then depends on the pupil's own subsequent practice. If, however, he is found to revert to old-standing wrong habits, then he himself, or his teacher with him, should again and again repeat the mental-muscular exercise (*or discipline*) implied in rehearsing these nine steps.

Here we begin with the simplest process, alone, and then *add* to it each time a new detail, until *all* those elements are included which, together, form the true process of "finger-touch." For instance, the very first step consists of sounding a couplet of notes solely by "Weight-release", with the hand sideways, and closed as a fist, and *without* the implications of any finger-action or forearm rotational action whatever. The subsequent steps are explained in order—an order or routine which I have found the most effective and practical both for children and adults.

Indeed, I hardly ever now give a "first lesson" without taking the pupil through these steps; since the pupil is nearly always faulty in one or other of these respects—either with regard to lack or inefficiency of attention, or lack of freedom rotationally, hence his exhibition of imperfect technique.

To render all this easier, the following bird's-eye view of these steps is here given in their most logical and therefore easiest order. Indeed, so far as Technique is concerned, these steps form the most *practical* application of my "Method of Teaching". Reference to the text of the two booklets mentioned must be made where amplification of the directions is required.

THE NINE STEPS.

I.—HAND (FIST) SIDEWAYS (OR VERTICAL) ON TWO BLACK KEYS

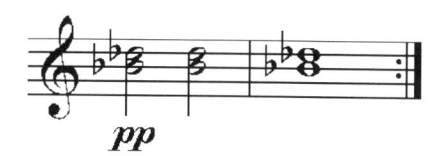

The two sounds must be *equally soft*, and played purely by a slight but sufficient release of the whole arm, accurately timed with the two keys, thus teaching both Key-attention and Weight-release.**

II.—DITTO, BUT WITH HAND HORIZONTAL.

This implies the addition of a slight rotational exertion towards thumb; nevertheless it must feel as *free* as before. *See* page 9 P.F.M.M., or pages 4-5, C.F.S.

III.—NOW ADD ROCKING FROM SIDE TO SIDE, STILL *PP*.

pp

This forms true "passing-on" touch—the weight allowed to rest on keyboard must be no more than for No. I. (*pp*). The sounds must remain equally soft, and the weight must be passed on to each key at surface level—therefore *before* it is allowed to be depressed. See page 12 P.F.M.M.

IV.—REPEAT THE LAST TEST, BUT AT SURFACE OF KEYBOARD.

This is for the more advanced players. The weight rocking from key to key is here executed so lightly that they keys fail to move down—and therefore remain silent. It illustrates the form of *Resting* required for *staccato*, and for light Agility practices.

V.—EXECUTE III. OR IV. BUT NOW ADD A JERK FOR EACH INDIVIDUAL KEY-DESCENT, AND WITH CHANGE OF TONE, THUS:

p ——— *fsf* *p* ——— *fsf*

The hand is still clenched lightly as before, and the jerk is provided by the forearm rotationally, but we now have in combination these two things: (a) the Resting (as in III. and IV.) carried on continuously from note to note, and (b) the "added impetus"—the action individually applied to each key, *solely during its descent*, to provoke tone beyond *pp*. See "Step III.," page 13, P.F.M.M. Play the exercise quite slowly.

Tobias Matthay: "The Nine Steps towards Finger Individualization

NOTE THAT WE HERE HAVE, <u>COMPLETE</u>, THE BASIS OF ALL SO- CALLED <u>FINGER-PASSAGES</u>, THE BASIS OF <u>FINGER INDIVIDUALIZATION</u>, AND THIS WITHOUT ANY FINGER SO FAR BEING CALLED INTO ACTION. THIS POINT IS ONE TO BE WELL DRIVEN HOME AND PONDERED UPON.

After this, still using the fist, *double* the speed of the exercise; and double it again; and once again, thus finally at the tempo of an *ordinary shake* or *tremolo*.

> When applied to an advanced player, who has found difficulty in some "finger-passage" or other, this faulty passage should then at once be referred to, and practiced with this light upon it. Probably it will be found to be cured—and permanently so! If not, repeat the sequence of steps given.

VI.—NOW ADD TWO FINGERS, 1—3, 2—4, AND 3—5.

Note that we here *add* the individually applied *exertions* of the fingers to the previously acquired rotator actions and inactions of the forearm. *See* IV., page 13, P.F.M.M.

VII.—NOW TAKE THE EXTREME FINGERS, PRECEDED BY EACH OTHER FINGER IN TURN.

Appendix III

Do not forget, when playing this exercise with the *notes* in similar motion, that the *rotational effects* required are *opposite* in the two hands. Page 5, Bk. II., P.F.M.M. or page 9, C.F.S.

VIII.—FINALLY, EACH SET OF ADJACENT FINGERS.

In VII. we had the adjacent fingers 4 to 5 and 2 to 1. Next we practice *each* set of adjacent fingers in turn, with its prober rotator complement. Page 12, C.F.S.

IX.—PRACTICE OF COMPLETE FIVE FINGER EXERCISES.

These may now be undertaken—but they can now be properly executed with the forearm rotational conditions correctly applied for each note. At first show, by an actual movement, each time the *direction* in which the rotational element is required, but afterwards apply this element without exhibiting any such movements.

---

* A Basis provided either as *visible* semi-rotational *movements* (always best at first) or as quite *invisible* muscular *changes of state* of the forearm rotationally, and provided for each successive note either in alternate direction or as *repetitions*, as shown later.

** Here we have brought home not only the sense of tone-production by weight-release, but also the necessity of Attention in its two necessary forms: (a) attention to the varying *resistance* offered by the key—through the muscular sense, and (b) attention to the *timing* of the action—through the alertness of ear. Hence this very first step, or exerciser, really includes the two most important elements leading towards correct outlook, both pianistically and musically; and it brings home where precisely is to be found the immediate and most frequent cause of failure. *See* page 7, "Pianist's First Music Making," or page 4, "Child's First Steps." In this first "step," therefore, you really do here play *without* Forearm Rotation!

APPENDIX IV

HISTORICAL REISSUES OF RECORDINGS BY TOBIAS MATTHAY AND HIS PUPILS

Since this book was first published in 2012, practically all the 78 rpms discussed in chapters 11 and 12 have become available on CD, plus a great many additional Matthay-related recordings. Fortunately, this new edition is appearing at a juncture in the piano's history when both the technology and scholarship have reached new heights, and today those with an interest in Matthay and his legacy owe a special debt to two labels in particular: the London-based APR Records, which has released a remarkable seven-part series entitled "The Matthay Pupils," and the Sydney-based Eloquence label—the historical reissue branch of Universal Music—which has recently offered landmark collections devoted to Eileen Joyce and Dame Moura Lympany.

For their continued support and encouragement, special thanks are due to Mike Spring of APR, and to Cyrus Meher-Homji of Universal, who have permitted direct access via the links below to the scholarly and often lavishly illustrated booklets accompanying their collections. And though the support this entire volume has received from the American Matthay Association is obvious, I also want to acknowledge the wonderful three-CD set commemorating the pianistic legacy of artist-teacher Cécile Genhart, which that organization sponsored and released in 2020. Special thanks are also offered to her former pupil (and my former teacher), Stewart Gordon, for permission to link to his enlightening essay which accompanies this set.

What follows is a briefly annotated discography arranged alphabetically by artist. The final entry in APR's "Matthay Pupils" series, *A Matthay Miscellany*—which contains recordings by Matthay and 17 of his pupils—is discussed at the end of this list.

Appendix IV

Bartlett & Robertson: Selected Recordings 1927-1947 (APR 6012), 2 CDs. The two-piano team of Ethel Bartlett and Rae Robertson recorded for Britain's National Gramophonic Society, Homocord, HMV, and Columbia. This collection, part of APR's "Matthay Pupils" series, is especially notable because it includes their 1930 NGS recording of Bax's Sonata for Two Pianos. My liner notes and the complete track listings may be found here: http://pianosage.net/Robertson.PDF

York Bowen: The Complete 78 rpm Solo Recordings (APR 6007), 2 CDs. Most of Bowen's 78s appeared on the Vocalion label, and this set includes the first recorded performance of the Beethoven Fourth (September 1925), with his own highly original cadenza. The complete track listings and liner notes by Jonathan Summers may be found here: http://pianosage.net/Bowen.PDF

Harriet Cohen: The Complete Solo Studio Recordings (APR 7304), 3 CDs. All of Cohen's 78s appeared on the English Columbia label, and this set, part of APR's "Matthay Pupils" series, includes her remarkable performances of the first nine Preludes and Fugues from Book I of *The Well-Tempered Clavier*. My liner notes and the complete track listings may be found here: http://pianosage.net/Cohen.PDF

The Recording Legacy of Artist-Teacher Cécile Genhart (The American Matthay Association for Piano), 3 CDs. The Swiss-born Cécile Genhart (1898-1983), mentioned in passing in chapter 12, taught at the Eastman School of Music for over 40 years, influencing scores of superb artist-teachers, and this collection includes extraordinary live performances of the Beethoven First and Fourth Concertos. At press time, the PDF containing complete track listings and liner notes by Stewart Gordon was not available, but when it appears it may be found by following the link at this site: http://www.matthay.org/newsitems.htm

Myra Hess: The Complete Solo and Concerto Studio Recordings (APR 7504), 5 CDs. Over a thirty-year period, Dame Myra Hess recorded for both Columbia and HMV, and this collection, part of APR's "Matthay Pupils" series, contains her entire solo commercial output drawn from 78s made as early as 1927, and extending to LPs made as late as 1957. My liner notes and the complete track listings may be found here: http://pianosage.net/Hess.PDF

Myra Hess: Live Recordings from the University of Illinois, 1949 (APR 7306), 3 CDs. Many have observed that Dame Myra was at her best in live performance, and these discs contain the only known recordings of her solo recitals, given on 17 and 18 March of 1949 respectively. Her transcendental performance of the Schubert B-flat Sonata, which she never recorded commercially, is especially notable, and her performances of the Mozart Concertos K. 271 and K. 467 with the University of Illinois Sinfonietta are also included. The set also contains a broadcast of her Grieg Concerto with the Detroit Symphony from 7 March 1937. The complete track listings and liner notes by Marshall Izen may be found here: http://pianosage.net/Hess1.PDF

Myra Hess: Historic Broadcast Recordings (APR 5646). Dame Myra's work with the Griller String Quartet is extensively discussed in chapter 12, and this disc contains one of the few surviving recordings—from 25 August 1942—of a live performance during World War II at the National Gallery concerts, as she joins them in the Brahms F minor Quintet, op. 34. Her live BBC broadcast of Schumann's *Carnaval* from 13 October 1950 is also included. The complete track listings and liner notes by Bryan Crimp may be found here: http://pianosage.net/Hess2.PDF

Eileen Joyce: The Complete Parlophone & Columbia Solo Recordings (APR 7502), 5 CDs. The first entry in APR's "Matthay Pupils" series, this title is no longer available, but happily, all these recordings are now included in the larger Eloquence set discussed below. However, many may enjoy the original liner notes by pianist and commentator Bryce Morrison, who knew Joyce well, and which may be found here: http://pianosage.net/Joyce.PDF

Appendix IV

Eileen Joyce: The Complete Studio Recordings (Eloquence 482 6291), 10 CDs. The complete discography of this magnificent, Australian-born pianist is superbly presented in a 10-CD collection containing her Parlophone, Columbia, Decca, HMV, and Saga recordings from 1933 to 1958. Among the highlights is her previously unreleased 1946 Decca recording of the Tchaikovsky Second with the LPO, and the Bach Concerto for Three Harpsichords which she recorded for HMV in 1956 with Thurston Dart and George Malcolm. The set is adorned with an exquisite 56-page booklet containing rare photos and essays by Bryce Morrison, Cyrus Meher-Homji, and Australian scholars David Tunley and Victoria Rogers, which may be accessed here: http://pianosage.net/Joyce2.PDF

Moura Lympany: The HMV Recordings, 1947-1952 (APR 6011), 2 CDs. For over five years, HMV's Walter Legge attempted to lure Lympany away from Decca, and in December 1947 she finally recorded the second book of the Brahms Paganini Variations for him. Part of APR's "Matthay Pupils" series, this set also contains wonderful performances of Liszt's *Feux follets* and Ravel's Toccata. The complete track listings and liner notes by Bryce Morrison may be found here: http://pianosage.net/Lympany.PDF

Moura Lympany: The Decca Legacy (Eloquence 482 9204), 7 CDs. Dame Moura Lympany is not only the first pianist to have recorded all 24 of Rachmaninoff's Preludes, but she is the only pianist to have recorded them on three separate occasions in 78, LP, and CD format. This complete survey of her Decca work extends from 1941 to 1953, and its highlights include both the 78 and LP versions of her Preludes, as well as both recordings of her Khachaturian Concerto, which she made into a signature piece. The collection also contains a marvelous, previously unpublished rendering of the Chopin B minor Sonata, and a breathtaking, live BBC performance of the Barber Sonata from December of 1950—barely 18 months after the work had been completed. The track listings and a 38-page booklet filled with rare photos and documents, including essays by Bryce

Morrison and Stephen Siek, may be accessed here: http://pianosage.net/Lympany2.PDF

Irene Scharrer: The Complete Electric and Selected Acoustic Recordings (APR 6010), 2 CDs. Scharrer's blazing virtuosity and exquisite sensitivity are both well captured in this APR offering, an entry in its "Matthay Pupils" series. These Columbia and HMV recordings range from 1912 to 1933, and highlights include her nearly overpowering accounts of Chopin's double-third and "Winter Wind" Etudes, as well as her Litolff Scherzo from *Concerto symphonique*, one of the best-selling classical recordings of its era. My liner notes and the complete track listings may be found here: http://pianosage.net/Scharrer.PDF

A Matthay Miscellany: Rare and Unissued Recordings by Tobias Matthay and his Pupils (APR 6014), 2 CDs. The final installment in APR's "Matthay Pupils" series, this set contains a potpourri of rare recordings that serious enthusiasts will almost certainly find essential. One of the major highlights is Matthay's beguiling 1932 recording of several of his own pieces, which Columbia released on his seventy-fifth birthday in 1933, and which is discussed extensively in chapter 11. This set also contains recordings by 17 of his pupils, selectively discussed below. My liner notes and the complete track listings may be found here: http://pianosage.net/Matthay.PDF

- The AFMC Series of Recordings: The Anglo-French Music Company, which Matthay and John McEwen founded in 1916 to commission and publish the work of British composers during Wartime, is examined in chapter 8, and as is recounted in chapter 9, the operation continued until 1925, when Matthay's deepening rift with McEwen made its continued existence impossible. But the nearly 80 AFMC recordings made between 1923 and 1926 are not discussed in the main text, primarily because they were pressed in such small numbers that until very recently, scarcely any could be located. After the War, the company embraced

Appendix IV

recorded sound technology to issue artistic performances of ABRSM examination repertoire so that students and their teachers could experience "model" performances. Remarkably, despite their rarity, this set contains 19 separate selections from that series representing seven different artists, including Matthay himself, who recorded some of his own pieces in April 1923. Other AFMC performers represented include Hilda Dederich, Dorothy Howell, Desirée MacEwan, Rae Robertson, and Egerton Tidmarsh, all of whom are discussed in these pages. (It should also be noted that the APR York Bowen disc discussed above contains his AFMC recording of the Capriccio from Bach's C minor Partita, released in October of 1923.)

- Some of Denise Lassimonne's Decca recordings are mentioned in chapter 12, including her performance of Mozart's Prelude and Fugue in C, which is included in this collection. But when this book was first published, there seemed little point in referencing her complete Bach Inventions, recorded at Decca's West Hampstead studios on 23 September 1941, because the set was never released. The likeliest explanation for Decca's reluctance is that it would have required three 12" discs, and Wartime exigencies demanded that shellac, like most other commodities, be carefully rationed. Fortunately, the test records she received are now at the International Piano Archives at the University of Maryland (IPAM), and the digitally enhanced versions taken from the originals represent an extraordinary contribution to modern Bach interpretation on the piano.

- *A Matthay Miscellany* also contains several unpublished recordings by Irene Scharrer, most notably a previously unknown acoustic version of Schumann's G minor Sonata supplied from test discs in the possession of the artist's granddaughter. It is unknown why HMV withheld these discs, recorded on 4 March 1924, but if the intent was to release them the following year, the company may have feared that sales would be harmed by the advent of the newer microphone technology. Since Scharrer never rerecorded the Sonata, the miraculous performance offered here is an especially valuable contribution to this work's discography—despite the fact that the second movement remains lost.

- Other fascinating curiosities contained in this collection include Raie Da Costa's performance of Liszt's *Rigoletto* Paraphrase (HMV, 1930), and Eunice Norton's performance of Honegger's Concertino for Piano and Orchestra with Ormandy and the Minneapolis Symphony (RCA, 1935). Other artists featured include Ethel Bartlett, Harriet Cohen, Adolph Hallis, Ray Lev, Nina Milkina, and Bruce Simonds, all of whom are amply discussed in the preceding pages.

SELECTED BIBLIOGRAPHY

Ades, David. "Addinsell, Richard (Stewart)," *The Revised New Grove Dictionary of Music and Musicians*, ed. S. Sadie and J. Tyrrell. London, 2001.

Aitken, George, "Tobias Matthay and his Teachings." London: *The Queen*, 1907.

Allen, Jean Mary and Ruzena Wood, "Kennedy, David," *The Revised New Grove Dictionary of Music and Musicians*, ed. S. Sadie and J. Tyrrell. London, 2001.

Bach, Carl Philipp Emanuel. *True Essay on the Art of Playing Keyboard Instruments*, trans. and ed. William J. Mitchell. New York: W. W. Norton, 1946.

Barzun, Jacques. *Teacher in America*. Boston: Little, Brown and Co., 1945.

Bax, Arnold. *Farewell, My Youth*. ed. Lewis Foreman. Aldershot: Scolar, 1992.

Bax, Clifford. *Inland Far: A Book of Thoughts and Impressions*. London: L. Dickson, 1933.

Beale, Robert. *Charles Hallé: A Musical Life*. Aldershot: Ashgate, 2007.

Benoliel, Bernard. "McEwen, John (Blackwood)," *The Revised New Grove Dictionary of Music and Musicians*, ed. S. Sadie and J. Tyrrell. London, 2001.

Beringer, Oscar. *Fifty Years' Experience of Pianoforte Teaching and Playing*. London: Bosworth & Co., 1907.

Bookspan, Martin, and Ross Yockey. *André Previn: A Biography*. Garden City, New Jersey: Doubleday, 1981.

Breithaupt, R. M. "The Idea of Weight-Playing—its Value and Practical Application," Pt. I, *The Musician* 26 (January 1911):1.

Breithaupt, Rudolf M. *Natural Piano Technic. Vol II: School of Weight-Touch*. trans. John Bernhoff. Leipzig: C. F. Kahnt Nachfolger, 1909.

Briggs, Asa, ed. *Essays in the history of publishing in celebration of the 250th anniversary of the House of Longman*. London: Longman, 1974.

Bülow, Dr. Hans von, ed., *Sonaten und andere Werke für das Pianoforte von Ludwig van Beethoven in kritischer und instructiver Ausgabe*. Stuttgart: J. G. Cotta'schen, 1882.

Burns, Ken. *Jazz*. Episode 5, "Pure Pleasure," Florentine Films [2000].

Bush, Nancy. *Alan Bush[:] Music, Politics, and Life*. London: Thames, 2000.

Caland, Elisabeth. *Die Deppe'sche Lehre des Klavierspiels* (1893), trans. by Schirmer, G. as *Artistic piano playing as taught by Ludwig Deppe together with practical advice on questions of technique* [New York], 1903.

Carpenter, Humphrey. *The Envy of the World*. London: Weidenfeld and Nicolson, 1996.

Ching, James. *Piano Playing: A Practical Method*. London: Bosworth & Co., Ltd., 1946.

Clodd, Edward. *The Childhood of the World*. London: Macmillan and Co., 1872.

_____. *The Story of Creation*. London: Longmans, Green, and Co., 1894.

Cohen, Harriet, *A Bundle of Time: The Memoirs of Harriet Cohen*. London: Faber and Faber, 1969.

Corder, Frederick. *A History of the Royal Academy of Music, from 1822 to 1922*. London: [Anglo-French Music Company], 1922.

Coviello, Ambrose. *What Matthay Meant: His Musical and Technical Teachings clearly explained and self-indexed*. London: Bosworth & Co., Ltd., [1947].

Crimp, Bryan. *Solo: The biography of Solomon*. Wark, Hexham, Northumberland: Appian Publications & Recordings, 1994.

Czerny, Charles [Karl], *Letters to a Young Lady, on the Art of Playing the Pianoforte, from the Earliest Rudiments to the Highest Stage*

Selected Bibliography

of Cultivation, trans. by J. A. Hamilton. New York: Hewitt & Jacques, 1837[?]; reprint ed., New York: Da Capo Press, 1982.

Darwin, Charles. *The Origin of Species.* ed. Philip Appleman. New York: W. W. Norton, 1975.

Davis, John R., *The Great Exhibition.* Stroud: Sutton, 1999.

Davis, Richard. *Eileen Joyce[:] A Portrait.* Fremantle, Australia: Fremantle Arts Centre Press, 2001.

Dawes, Frank. "Scharrer, Irene," *The Revised New Grove Dictionary of Music and Musicians*, ed. S. Sadie and J. Tyrrell. London, 2001.

DeGray, Julian. "Carlos Buhler (April 26, 1897 to September 1, 1976)," *The Matthay News*, Fall 1976.

Dibble, Jeremy. *C. Hubert Parry: His Life and Music.* Oxford: Clarendon Press, 1992.

_____. "Dannreuther, Edward," *The Revised New Grove Dictionary of Music and Musicians*, ed. S. Sadie and J. Tyrrell. London, 2001.

_____. "McEwen, Sir John Blackwood," *Oxford Dictionary of Biography.*

Doctor, Jennifer. *The BBC and Ultra-Modern Music, 1922-1936.* Cambridge: Cambridge University Press, 1999.

Ehrenfechter, C. A. *Technical Study in the Art of Pianoforte Playing Deppe's Principles.* London: William Reeves, 1895.

Ellsworth, Therese and Susan Wollenberg, eds., *The Piano in Nineteenth-Century British Culture*, Aldershot: Ashgate, 2007.

Fay, Amy, *The Deppe Finger Exercises for Rapidly Developing an Artistic Touch in Piano Playing.* London: W. Reeves., [1900].

_____. *Music-Study in Germany from the Home Correspondence of Amy Fay.* ed. Fay Pierce. New York: MacMillan, 1908; reprint ed., New York: Da Capo Press, 1979.

Fifield, Christopher. "Bülow, Hans (Guido) Freiherr von," *The Revised New Grove Dictionary of Music and Musicians*, ed. S. Sadie and J. Tyrrell. London, 2001.

_____. *Ibbs and Tillett[:] The Rise and Fall of a Musical Empire.* Aldershot: Ashgate, 2005.

Foreman, Lewis, *Bax: A composer and his times*, 3rd ed. Woodbridge, Suffolk: The Boydell Press, 2007.

_____. "Benjamin J. Dale," from *Benjamin Dale[:] Piano music*. Peter Jacobs, piano, Continuum, CCD 1044.

_____. "Dale, Benjamin (James)," *The Revised New Grove Dictionary of Music and Musicians*, ed. S. Sadie and J. Tyrrell. London, 2001.

_____ and Susan Foreman. *London[:] A Musical Gazetteer*. New Haven: Yale University Press, 2005.

Fraser, Norman. "Carreño, (Maria) Teresa," *The Revised New Grove Dictionary of Music and Musicians*, ed. S. Sadie and J. Tyrrell. London, 2001.

Gaburo, Virginia. *Who Is Bruce Simonds?* La Jolla, California: Lingua Press, 1978.

Gerig, Reginald R. *Famous Pianists & Their Technique*. Washington, D.C.: Robert B. Luce, 1974.

Gilmour, J. D. *Sir Thomas Beecham: The Seattle Years*. Aberdeen, Washington: World Press, 1978.

Hall, A. Wilford, and Sedley Taylor. *The "Substantial" and "Wave" Theories of Sound: Two Letters*. London: Macmillan, 1891[.]

Hardy, Lisa. *The British Piano Sonata: 1870-1945*. Woodbridge, Suffolk: Boydell Press, 2001.

Helmholtz, M. D., Hermann L. F. *The Sensations of Tone*, 3rd ed., trans. Alexander J. Ellis. London: Longmans, Green, 1895.

Hice, Arthur. "A Personal Glimpse of Activities in London Last Summer," *Journal of the American Matthay Association*, 1934.

Holland, Frank W., and Arthur W. J. G. Ord-Hume. "Reproducing Piano," *The Revised New Grove Dictionary of Music and Musicians*, ed. S. Sadie and J. Tyrrell. London, 2001.

Horton, Peter, and Bennett Zon, eds. *Nineteenth-Century British Music Studies*, vol. 3. Aldershot: Ashgate, 2005.

Horowitz, Joseph. *Conversations with Arrau*. New York: Alfred Knopf, 1982.

Hughes, Meirion, and Robert Stradling. *The English Musical Renaissance: 1840-1940*, 2nd ed. Manchester: Manchester University Press, 2001.

Jacobs, Arthur. *Arthur Sullivan, a Victorian musician*. Oxford: Oxford University Press, 1984.

_____. *Henry J. Wood[:] Maker of the Proms*. London: Methuen, 1994.

Kennedy Jr., David. *Kennedy's Colonial Travel: A Narrative of a Four Years' Tour through Australia, New Zealand, Canada, &c.* Edinburgh: Edinburgh Publishing Company, 1876.

Kennedy, John H. *Common Sense and Singing*. London: Joseph Williams, Ltd. 1911.

Kennedy[-]Fraser, Marjory. *David Kennedy[,] The Scottish Singer: Reminiscences of his Life and Work*. Paisley: Alexander Gardner, 1887.

_____. *A Life of Song*. London: Oxford University Press, 1929.

Klein, Hermann. *Thirty Years of Musical Life in London*. New York: The Century Co., 1903.

Kullak, Adolph. *The Aesthetics of Pianoforte-Playing*, trans. by Theodore Baker. New York: G. Schirmer, 1893; reprint ed., New York: Da Capo Press, 1972.

Lassimonne, Denise, and Howard Ferguson, eds. *Myra Hess By Her Friends*. New York: The Vanguard Press, 1966.

Leapman, Michael. *The World for a Shilling[:] The Story of the Great Exhibition of 1851*. London: Headline Book Publishing, 2001.

Lebert, Sigismund, and Louis Stark. *Theoretical and Practical Piano School for Systematic Instruction in all Branches of Piano-Playing from the First Elements to the Highest Perfection*, 3 vols. New York: G. Schirmer, [1899].

Legge, Robin H. and Duncan J. Barker. "Niecks, Friedrich [Frederick]," *The Revised New Grove Dictionary of Music and Musicians*, ed. S. Sadie and J. Tyrrell. London, 2001.

Leonard, Florence. "How Breithaupt Teaches," *The Musician* 30 (April 1915):4.

Selected Bibliography

Leuchtmann, Horst. "Kullak; (1) Theodor Kullak," *The Revised New Grove Dictionary of Music and Musicians*, ed. S. Sadie and J. Tyrrell. London, 2001.

Levinskaya, Maria. *The Levinskaya System of Pianoforte Technique and Tone-Colour through Mental and Muscular Control*. London: J. M. Dent and Sons, Ltd., 1930.

Lympany, Moura, and Margot Strickland. *Moura: Her Autobiography*. London: Owen, 1991.

Lucas, John. *Thomas Beecham: An Obsession with Music*. Woodbridge, Suffolk: The Boydell Press, 2008.

Macfarren, Walter. *Memories: An Autobiography*. London: Walter Scott, 1905.

MacGregor, Lynda. "Read, Ernest," *The Revised New Grove Dictionary of Music and Musicians*, ed. S. Sadie and J. Tyrrell. London, 2001.

Mackenzie, Sir Alexander Campbell, K.C.V.O. *A Musician's Narrative*. London: Cassell, and Company, Ltd., 1927.

Martyn, Barrie. *Nicholas Medtner[:] His Life and Music*. Aldershot: Scolar, 1995.

Matthay, Jessie Henderson. *The Life and Works of Tobias Matthay*. London: Boosey & Hawkes, 1945.

_____. Mrs. Tobias. *The Art of the Spoken Word*. Glasgow: Paterson and Son, 1922.

Matthews, Denis. "Harold Craxton[:] 1885-1971," in program booklet for *Harold Craxton Memorial Concert*, 17 September 1971.

McEwen, John B. "Tempo Rubato," Article I, *The Music Teacher* 4 (June 1925): 370.

_____. *In Pursuit of Music*. London: Victor Gollancz, Ltd., reprint ed., 1966.

McKenna, Marian C. *Myra Hess: A Portrait*. London: Hamish Hamilton, 1976.

Moore, Gerald. *Farewell recital: further memoirs*. New York: Taplinger, 1978.

Morrison, Bryce. "Hess, Dame Myra," *The Revised New Grove Dictionary of Music and Musicians*, ed. S. Sadie and J. Tyrrell. London, 2001.

Newman, William S. "On the Special Problems of High-Speed Playing," *Clavier* 2 (May-June 1963): 3.

Norton, Eunice. "A Turning Point," *Enjoy the Music*.

──────. "In Memoriam: Carlos Buhler," *Matthay News*, Fall 1976.

──────. "The Role Played by the Fingers," *Journal of the American Matthay Association*, 1934.

Ortmann, Otto. *The Physical Basis of Piano Touch and Tone*. London: K. Paul, Trench, Trubner & Co. Ltd., 1925.

──────. *The Physiological Mechanics of Piano Technique: An experimental study of the nature of muscular action as used in piano playing, and of the effects thereof upon the piano key and the piano tone*. New York: E. P. Dutton, 1929; reprint ed., New York: Da Capo Press, 1981.

Parker, Louis N. *Several of My Lives*. London: Chapman and Hall, 1928.

Parry, C. Hubert. *College Addresses delivered to Pupils of the Royal College of Music*, ed. H. C. Colles. London: Macmillan, 1920.

Partridge, Michael, *The Royal Naval College Osborne: A History 1903-21*. Phoenix Mill: Sutton, 1999.

Pederson, Sanna. "Marx, (Friedrich Heinrich) Adolf Bernhard [Samuel Moses]," *The Revised New Grove Dictionary of Music and Musicians*, ed. S. Sadie and J. Tyrrell. London, 2001.

Peel, J. D. Y. *Herbert Spencer: the evolution of a sociologist*. New York: Basic Books, 1971.

Pirie, Peter J. *The English Musical Renaissance*. London: Victor Gollancz, Ltd., 1979.

Pott, Francis. Liner notes for *York Bowen: Piano Music*. Stephen Hough, piano. Hyperion CDA86838, Recorded September, 1995.

Read, Ernest. "Tobias Matthay: An Appreciation," *The R. A. M. Magazine* (January 1946) No. 133:2-3.

Selected Bibliography

Reid, Charles. *Thomas Beecham: An Independent Biography*. New York: Dutton, 1962.

Saerchinger, Cesar. *Artur Schnabel[:] A Biography*. New York: Dodd, Mead, 1958.

Schnabel, Artur. *My Life and Music, with an Introduction by Edward Crankshaw*. New York: St. Martin's Press, 1964.

Scholes, Percy A. *The Appreciation of Music by Means of the Duo-Art[:] A Course of Lectures Delivered at Aeolian Hall, London*. New York: Oxford University Press, 1926.

_____. *The Mirror of Music 1844-1944*, 2 vols. Oxford: Oxford University Press, 1947.

Schonberg, Harold C. *The Great Pianists from Mozart to the Present*. New York: Simon and Schuster, 1963.

Schultz, Arnold. *The Riddle of the Pianist's Finger and its Relationship to a Touch-Scheme*. Chicago: Carl Fischer, 1936; reprint ed., 1959.

Schumann, Robert. "William Sterndale Bennett, Drittes Konzert," *Neue Zeitschrift für Musik*, 9:(21 Feb. 1837).

Sietz, Reinhold. "Reinecke, Carl (Heinrich Carsten)," *The Revised New Grove Dictionary of Music and Musicians*, ed. S. Sadie and J. Tyrrell. London, 2001.

Sim, Naomi. *Dance and Skylark: Fifty Years with Alastair Sim*. London: Bloomsbury, 1987.

Smith, W. MacDonald. "The Physiology of Pianoforte Playing, with a Practical Application of a New Theory," *Proceedings of the Musical Association*, 14th Sess. 1887-1888. Oxford University Press.

Spencer, Herbert. *Education: Intellectual, Moral and Physical*. New York: D. Appleton and Company, 1861.

_____. *Literary Style and Music*. New York: Philosophical Library, 1951.

Spry, Walter. "Lessons from Hearing Great Pianists," *The Etude* (June 1935): 378.

Sterndale Bennett, J. R. *The Life of William Sterndale Bennett*. Cambridge: Cambridge University Press, 1907.

Taylor, Sedley. *Sound and music: a non-mathematical treatise on the physical constitution of musical sounds and harmony, including the chief acoustical discoveries of Professor Helmholtz.* London: Macmillan, 1873.

Temperley, Nicholas. "Bennett, William Sterndale," *The Revised New Grove Dictionary of Music and Musicians*, ed. S. Sadie and J. Tyrrell. London, 2001.

⸻. "Macfarren, Sir George (Alexander)," *The Revised New Grove Dictionary of Music and Musicians*, ed. S. Sadie and J. Tyrrell. London, 2001.

⸻, ed. *The London Pianoforte Piano School*, 20 vols. New York and London: Garland Publishing, 1985.

⸻, ed. *Works for Pianoforte Solo by William Sterndale Bennett: from 1834 to 1840*, vols. 17-18 of LPFS.

Todd, R. Larry. *Mendelssohn[:] A Life in Music.* New York: Oxford University Press, 2003.

⸻. "Mendelssohn, Felix," *The Revised New Grove Dictionary of Music and Musicians*, ed. S. Sadie and J. Tyrrell. London, 2001.

Verne, Mathilde. *Chords of Remembrance.* London: Hutchinson and Co., 1936.

Vicat, Alan. Liner notes for a CD Reissuing of Irene Scharrer's recordings, Gemm CD 9978.

Wagner, Richard. *My Life*, New York: Dodd, Mead, 1927.

Walker, Alan. *Franz Liszt: The Final Years[,] 1861-1886.* New York: Alfred Knopf, 1996.

⸻. *Hans von Bülow: A Life and Times.* New York: Oxford University Press, 2010.

Walker, Alfred. "Student Days with Matthay," *Journal of the American Matthay Association*, (Summer 1932).

Warrack, John. "Deppe, Ludwig," *The Revised New Grove Dictionary of Music and Musicians*, ed. S. Sadie and J. Tyrrell. London, 2001.

Warriner, John, ed. *National Portrait Gallery of British Musicians.* London: Sampson, Low, Marston and Company, c.1893.

Selected Bibliography

Watson, John. Liner notes for *Raie Da Costa—The Parlophone Girl*, vol. 1. Shellwood, SWCD 8, 1998.

Wigton, G. M. B. "Your Turn Now, Myra!," letter to *Radio Times* 69 (15 November 1940):10.

Williamson, Rosemary. *Sterndale-Bennett: A Descriptive Thematic Catalogue*. Oxford: Oxford University Press, 1996.

Winter, Daniel W. "My Years with Matthay and Schnabel" [An Interview with Eunice Norton], *Clavier*, March, 1962.

Wood, Henry J. *My Life of Music*. London: Victor Gollancz, Ltd., 1938.

Young, Percy H. *George Grove*. Washington, D. C.: Grove Dictionaries of Music, 1980.

Zagni, Frances. *'Uncle Ernie'—a biography of Ernest Read*. New Malden, Surrey: Ernest Read Music Association, 1989.

INDEX

Act of Touch, The (1903), 244-67
Addinsell, Richard, 503
Aeolian Company. *See* Duo-Art
    Reproducing Piano
Agnew, Philip, 382, 388, 423n, 513-15
Aitken, George, 141, 181
Albanesi, Carlo, 384
Aldrich, Richard, 265, 277n
Alexander, Arthur, 226-27, 235n, 344,
    352, 366, 512, 539-40
Allen, Sir Hugh, 391, 511-513, 515, 590n
Altenmüller, Eckart, 7, 24n
American Matthay Association,
    xi-xvi, 1, 22, 24n, 414,
    440, 457, 478n, 509, 533, 553,
    579, 601, 606, 608, 625-26,
    643
Amyot, Etienne, 564-66
Anderton, Orsmond, 159
Anglo-French (music publishers),
    148n, 355-56, 364, 371, 389,
    402, 425n, 438, 526n, 619,
    629
Antonietti, Aldo, 451
Arrau, Claudio, 19
Arthur Schmidt (publishing house),
    294-95
Avison, Charles. *See* Charles Avison,
    Ltd

Aumonier, Stacy, 460, 479n
Austin, Richard, 557

Bache, Walter, 43-44, 129-130,
    139-140, 144, 150n, 151n,
    319n
Badura-Skoda, Paul, 5
Bailey, Lura, 534
Baldwin, Stanley, 466
Bantock, Granville, 113, 148n, 159,
    180, 369, 388,
Barbirolli, Sir John, 352, 463, 465,
    510,
Barbour, Lyell, 385, 413, 417, 419,
    464
Barnby, Joseph, 156
Barnden, Vina, 551
Barnes, George, 377
Barrère, Georges, 566
Bartlett, Ethel (Mrs. Rae Robertson),
    352, 463-66, 470, 485, 499,
    626, 631
Barzun, Jacques, 2, 23n, 487
Bauer, Harold, 390, 408, 449
Bax, Sir Arnold, xvii, 182, 220-22,
    224, 226, 229, 275n, 296, 302,
    318n, 327, 347-52, 365-66,
    370, 376n, 388, 450-57, 463-64,
    499, 517-19, 534, 540, 626

INDEX

Bechstein Piano Company, 134-35, 144, 182, 223, 235n, 241, 253, 282-83, 285, 289, 291-92, 298, 302-305, 315, 316n, 343-44, 347, 349, 350-52, 358, 406, 453, 519, 540, 551, 580, 583, 585, 595

Bechstein, Carl, 349

Bechstein, Edwin, 349

Beecham, Sir Thomas, 309-310, 473, 559-63, 590n, 591n

Bennett, Sir William Sterndale, 44-55, 58, 61n, 62n, 65-76, 79, 82, 88, 97n, 99n, 100n, 101n, 104, 108, 110, 144, 147n, 152n, 156, 174, 296, 310, 359, 366, 369

Berger, Francesco, 110, 299, 300,

Beringer, Oscar, 8, 24n, 43, 60n, 138-40, 142-43, 152n, 153n, 171, 202-203, 217, 268, 284, 296, 319n, 329, 350, 485, 542

Berkeley, Lennox, 464, 605

Betts, Ida, 144, 182, 319n

Black, Stanley, 503

Bolet, Jorge, 534

Bor, Hilda, 382, 418, 539, 560, 569, 571, 593n

Boult, Sir Adrian, 314, 320n, 490-93, 526n, 541, 560, 562

Bowen, (Edwin) York, xvii, 219-23, 233n, 234n, 275n, 286, 289, 293, 297, 299, 309, 312-14, 320n, 340, 345-46, 348, 352, 359, 366, 370, 384, 388, 472, 490, 495, 498, 523, 538, 557, 568, 604, 626, 630

Bowie, Dulcie, 362

Bowring, Anthea. *See* Skimming, Anthea Bowring

Brand, James, 184

Breithaupt, Rudolf, 4-5, 7, 15-21, 23n, 26n, 140, 256, 434

British Broadcasting Corporation (BBC), xvii, 320n, 391, 485, 489-93, 499-500, 503-505, 541-42, 546, 562-66, 585, 605, 627-28

Broadhurst, Arthur, 442-43

Brough, Eric, 571-72, 593n

Browning, Elizabeth Barrett, 289

Browning, Robert, 105, 243, 299

Buck, Percy, 515

Bülow, Hans von, 15, 103, 131-34, 137, 139, 151n, 155, 248, 459

Buesst, Aylmer, 491

Buhler, Carlos, 407, 411, 413, 417, 487, 488

Burg, Clarence, 534

Burghersh, Lord (John Fane). *See* Westmorland, 10th Earl of

Burns, Robert, 190, 199

Burton, Philip, 541

Bush, Alan, 366, 536, 547

Butler, Antonia, 447, 504

Butt, Clara, 300, 538

Caland, Elisabeth, 12, 25n

Cameron, Basil, 543, 547

Campbell, LeRoy, 416, 507, 548

644

INDEX

Carreño, Teresa, 15-19, 300
Carton, Patricia, 568
Cassado, Gaspar, 556
Chapple, Stanley, 498
Charles Avison, Ltd (music publisher), 234n, 299, 289
Ching, James, 27n, 344, 374n
Christie, Emily, 95, 183, 370
Clark, Edward, 489-91, 546
Clark, Sir Kenneth, 554-55, 558
Clarke, Rebecca, 304, 309, 319n
Clodd, Edward, 114
Cohen, Florence, 304
Cohen, Harriet, 236n, 273, 286, 304-05, 319n, 344, 347, 361, 367, 370, 376n, 448-58, 474, 478n, 485, 498, 519, 544, 556, 626, 631
Cohen, Toni, 319n, 442
Cole, Edward, 287, 292-93, 295, 353
Cole, Hedwig. *See* McEwen, Hedwig Cole
Cole, Sir Henry, 72, 77, 98n, 99n
Cole, Marion White, 353, 399, 412, 442, 474, 508, 539
Coleridge-Taylor, Samuel, 242
Collens, Hilda Hester, 293, 317n
Colles, H. C., 566, 592n,
Compton-Burnett, Judy, 454-55
Compton-Burnett, Katharine ("Topsy"), 454-55
Compton-Burnett, Stephanie Primrose ("Baby"), 454-55
Compton-Burnett, Vera, 454-55
Coolidge, Elizabeth Sprague, 456

Coolidge, Theresa, 551
Corder, Frederick, 57-58, 61n, 67-70, 72, 76, 87, 96-97, 100n, 112-13, 139, 142, 148n, 155, 158-59, 185n, 202-203, 214, 219, 221, 222-29, 241-42, 264, 286, 298, 303, 305, 311, 325-26, 347-48, 350, 362, 367, 371-72, 376n, 388-89, 404, 442, 451, 518-19, 536, 577
Costa, Michael, 103, 147n, 190-91
Coviello, Ambrose, 384, 542-44
Craxton, Harold, 286, 370, 384, 413, 537-38, 551, 557, 559, 570-71, 587n, 604-606
Curwen, Annie (Mrs. Spencer Curwen), 226, 441
Curwen, John, 226
Curzon, Sir Clifford, 359, 385, 464, 499, 536-38, 544, 547, 557, 559-60, 587n
Cutner, Harris, 543
Cutner, Solomon, 543, 557, 588n
Czerny, Carl, 10, 24n, 217, 347, 533

Da Costa, Raie, 417, 500-503, 631
d'Aranyi, Jelly, 520, 556
Dale, Benjamin, 222-25, 234n, 297-98, 369, 385, 388, 404, 519, 542, 563, 605
Dane, Clemence, 503
Dannreuther, Edward, 43-44, 129, 134, 146n
Davey, Henry, 159
Davies, W. R., 466-67

INDEX

Davison, J. W. (James William), 103, 146n, 152n
Dawkin, Evelyn, 345
Day, Marion, 567
de Gomez, Ethel, 550, 557
de Schlözer, Paul, 472
Dederich, Elsie. *See* Neville, Elsie
Dederich, Hilda, 345, 348, 356, 366, 405, 418, 508, 523, 549, 551-53, 557, 568-69, 573, 580, 595-96, 630
DeGray, Julian, 361, 376n, 487-88, 525n, 533-35, 539, 576, 579-80, 582-83, 586n
Deming, Mary, 540
Deppe, Ludwig, 12-15, 19-21, 25n, 166, 246
Dibble, Jeremy, 146n, 389
Dickinson, George, 595-96, 602
Disraeli, Benjamin, 67, 247, 276n
Doctor, Jennifer, 489
Doniach, Shula, 595
Dorrell, William, 79-80, 90, 100n, 135
Dossor, Lance, 557
Downes, Olin, 458-59, 462-63, 465-66, 534, 600
Drinkwater, John, 363
Duff, C. Patrick, 442, 554-55
Duo-Art Reproducing Piano, 387, 390-92, 396, 398, 424n
Durham, C. Bruce, 603

Eccles, C. Yarrow, 444, 477n
Egerton, Lady Alix, 442
Ehlert, Louis, 9

Elgood, George J., 290-91, 402
Elliott, Claude, 573
Ellis, Ashton, 105
Elman, Henry, 406
Elman, Mischa, 300, 451
Erdtsieck, Maria, 508-509
Excelsior Society (Royal Academy of Music), 113, 159, 180-81, 183, 310

Fane, John, Lord Burghersh. *See* Westmorland, 10th Earl of
Farrar, Fannie Judson, 407
Fawcett, P. G., 467-68
Fay, Amy, 9, 12-13, 132
Ferguson, Howard, 558
Fischer, Edwin, 5
Foreman, Lewis, xvii, 222-23, 234n, 235n, 297, 318n, 536,
Fox, Samson, 105, 123n
Frankenstein, Baron Georg, 510, 512
Frantz, Dalies, 534
Friedman, Ignaz, 546
Fuller, Marion, 539-40

Gale, Prudence, 568
Garcia, Manuel, 239-40
Garle, Kenneth John, 604
Geddes, Sir Patrick, 208
Genhart, Cécile, 534, 625-26
Gerhardt, Elena, 312, 538, 558
Gerig, Reginald, 15
Giddins, Gary, 1
Gielgud, Sir John, 362

INDEX

Gieseking, Walter, 449, 459, 499, 546
Gilmour, Gemma, 568
Gladstone, Catherine (Mrs. William), 65-67, 80
Gladstone, Sir William, 65-67, 467
Glock, William, 560
Godfrey, Sir Dan, 314, 320n, 492, 517, 589n
Godowsky, Leopold, 18, 449, 459
Goodman, Alvin, 440
Goodson, Katherine (Kate), 141-43, 202, 587n
Graffman, Gary, 6
Grant, Eric, 515, 606
Grenfell, Joyce, 503, 558
Grindea, Carola, 568
Grinstead, Dorothy, 224, 293, 296, 345
Grove, Roxy, 534
Grove, Sir George, 105, 129, 130, 149n, 157-58, 226
Gunn, Anita, 442, 447
Gunn, Marjorie, 447

Hall, A. Wilford, 177-78,
Hallé, Sir Charles, 41-43, 57
Hallis, Adolph, 366, 485-86, 499, 525n, 631
Hambling, G. J. C., 608
Hambourg, Mark, 297, 304, 459
Hawley, Stanley, 182, 187n, 369
Hely-Hutchinson, Victor, 490-91
Henderson, W. J., 265
Henschel, Sir George, 493
Hess, Dame (Julia) Myra, 2, 223, 228-30, 235n, 236n, 243, 269, 296-98, 300-304, 309-10, 318n, 319n, 320n, 345-48, 360-61, 365, 367-70, 376n, 390, 405, 410, 413-14, 418, 442, 444, 447-459, 463, 471, 473-74, 477n, 495-98, 506-507, 516, 520-24, 528n, 540-41, 544, 549, 553-59, 564-67, 574-75, 581, 585-86, 590n, 593n, 595-601, 606, 626-27
Hess, Dorothy, 407, 505
Heward, Leslie, 499
Hice, Arthur, 412, 507-508
High Marley (Matthay's home). *See* Matthay, Tobias Augustus,
Hofmann, Josef, 449, 459, 462
Holmes, W. H., 79
Hood, Reverend J. C. F., 442
Horowitz, Vladimir, 6, 459
Horszowski, Miecyslaw, 5
Howard-Jones, Evlyn, 234n, 285, 292, 350-51, 498
Howell, Dorthy, 366, 630
Hullah, John, 79, 100n, 247
Humby, Betty (Lady Beecham), 366-67, 382, 385, 502, 527n, 560-63, 590n, 591n
Hutcheson, Ernest, 471
Hutchinson, J. T., 95, 121-22
Hutchinson, Sir Jonathan, 279-80

Ingham, L. W., 293
Ireland, John, 536, 563-64
Irwin, Lord (Edward Wood, 1st Earl of Halifax), 474

647

INDEX

Jacob, Gordon, 563-64, 592n
Jones, Ronald, 553, 558
Jones, Sir Horace, 156
Jonson, Guy, xvii, 151n, 234n, 502,
    527n, 538, 559, 560, 587n,
    610n
Joseph Williams (publishing firm),
    295, 330, 452, 619
Joyce, Eileen, 470-73, 499, 503-504,
    539, 544, 557, 624, 627-28

Karpeles, Maud, 442
Katin, Peter, 538
Kayll, Enid, 584
Kell, Reginald, 541, 560
Kennard, Lily, 345, 348
Kennedy, David Jr., 192, 231n
Kennedy, David, 184, 189-201
Kennedy, Douglas, 520
Kennedy, Elizabeth, 190-93, 201
Kennedy, Helen Henderson, 190
Kennedy, Helen, 191-92, 194-201
Kennedy, James, 192, 194-96
Kennedy, Janet (Jessie) Henderson.
    See Matthay, Jessie
    Henderson,
Kennedy, John (Jack), 192, 300-301,
    330-31, 343-44, 441
Kennedy, Katherine (Kate), 195-96
Kennedy, Margaret, 141, 183, 197, 199,
    200-201, 202-203, 208, 231n,
    343, 441
Kennedy, Robert, 193-98
Kennedy-Fraser, Marjory, 192, 194-
    205, 208-212, 245-46, 286,
    330, 343, 346, 370, 374n,
    440-43, 554
King, Oliver, 109, 147n, 214
Klemperer, Otto, 462
Klindworth, Karl, 103-105, 146n
Knight, Stanley, 108
Kortschak, Alice, 534
Kriehbel, Henry, 266
Kullak, Adolph, 11, 14, 17, 19n

Lamperti, Francesco, 194-95
Land, Edward, 190-91
Langrish, Vivian, xvii, 271-73, 298,
    320n, 344, 347, 352, 356,
    366-68, 370, 383-84, 386-
    87, 405, 411, 413, 417, 423n,
    490-92, 504, 548-50, 557,
    564, 571-72, 581, 584, 596-97,
    600-606
Lassimonne, Denise, xiii-xiv, xvi, 22,
    27n, 235n, 236n, 356-62, 365,
    367, 370, 376n, 384-85, 399,
    401, 404-406, 417, 440-41,
    444-48, 456, 472, 476n, 477n,
    483, 492, 504-505, 508, 518,
    520, 522-23, 538, 540-41,
    543, 548-49, 551-54, 557-60,
    562, 568-70, 573, 575-76,
    579-86, 592n, 595-96,
    598-60, 602-604, 606-608
Lebert, Sigismund, 8-9, 24n
Lediard, Mary, 345, 347-48, 375n, 569
Lehmann, Liza, 175
LeLiévre, Peggy, 406
Leonard, Florence, 17

648

INDEX

Lev, Ray (Rachel), 509, 539, 601, 631
Levinskaya, Maria, 9, 18
Lewis, Bernard, 535
Lewis, Joseph, 491, 541-42

MacDougall, Hamilton, 407, 425n
Macfarren, Sir George, 48, 69-70, 72, 77, 87, 89, 94, 101n, 120, 129, 138, 155-56, 325
Macfarren, Walter, 78, 81-82, 89, 96, 100n, 135, 141, 149n, 221, 285, 295-96, 310, 317n, 329
MacKellar, Mary, 197
Mackenzie, Sir Alexander Campbell, 58, 128-29, 152n, 155-56, 158-59, 202, 211, 219, 236n, 241, 288, 302-303, 305-307, 319n, 325-26, 346, 350, 366-68, 372, 385, 387-88, 391
MacKenzie, Mae, 606
Mackway, Walter, 121, 142, 182, 207
MacLean, Virginia, 248, 282
MacLeod, Kenneth, 346
Maconchy, Elizabeth, 486
Macpherson, Stewart, 310-11, 346
Mannheimer, Frank, 385, 417, 464, 487, 525n, 581
Manns, August, 73, 80, 111, 129, 141, 145, 150n
Marchant, Sir Stanley, 515-16, 529n, 540, 596-97, 600, 605
Marchesi, Mathilde, 197-98, 240
Marr, Edie, 595

Marx, Adolph Bernhard, 10-12, 14-15, 20, 25n, 160-61, 166,
Mase, Owen, 491
Mason, Daniel Gregory, 464
Mason, William, 103, 408
Matthay, Dorothea (Dora) Eleonora (Matthay's sister), 38-39, 90, 92, 97, 113, 121, 141-43, 180-82, 206-208, 213, 241, 284-86, 293, 301, 304, 314, 343-45, 347-48, 384-85, 404-405, 441, 445, 503, 540, 596, 607
Matthay, Dorothea Eleonora Wittich (Matthay's mother), 21-22, 24-25, 58, 144, 192
Matthay, Janet (Jessie) Henderson Kennedy
  Career as dramatic elocutionist, 240-44, 518
  Death of and memorials to, 523-24, 540-41
  Family background with The Singing Kennedys, 192-200
  Health problems, 443-45, 518
  Marriage to Tobias Matthay, 208-213
  Student days at the Royal Academy of Music, 202-207, 239-40
  Writing Matthay's biography, 440, 520-22
Matthay, Tobias Sr. (Matthay's father), 31-33, 35-38, 90-93, 106, 283-84

INDEX

Matthay, Tobias Augustus.
   Birth and childhood, 33-41
   Compositions. See Appendix II
   Early composing and struggle for recognition, 106-112
   Early teaching at the Royal Academy of Music, 83-97
   High Marley construction, 279-84
   Marriage to Jessie Kennedy, 208-213
   Performances on the BBC, 489-94, 541-42
   Provisions of his will, 596-98
   Recognition at the RAM Centenary celebration, 367-72
   Recordings, 495-97
   Resignation from the Royal Academy of Music, 381-90
   Performances on the BBC, 327-31, 360-61, 541-42, 564-65
   Surgery, 504-507
   The Overture articles, 159-80
   World War II and final years, 546-86
   Writings. *See* Appendix I
Matthay Piano School. *See* Tobias Matthay Pianoforte School
Matthews, Denis, 538, 558, 601
Mayerl, Billy, 500-501
McClanahan, Richard, 1, 414-15, 458, 540, 570, 575-76, 579-81, 588n, 601, 604
McEwen, Hedwig Cole, 215, 286, 293, 316n, 345, 385, 399

McEwen, Sir John Blackwood, 214-15, 233, 241, 298, 300, 316n, 345, 355-56, 360, 366, 370, 372, 381-422, 424n, 425n, 509-516, 529n, 531, 536-38, 576, 587n, 629
McNaught, William, 141-42, 263
McNaught, William Jr,. 547, 575
Mears, Caroline, 486
Medtner, Nicolas, 413, 488, 517-18, 539, 606
Melba, Nellie, 197-98, 537
Merrick, Frank, 223
Metcalf, Albion, 414-17, 426n, 487
Mewton-Wood, Noel, 538
Milkina, Nina, 599-60, 587n, 604, 631
Milne, Hamish, 606
Moiseiwitsch, Benno, 223, 345, 451, 516, 557-58
Montagu-Pollock, Sir Montagu Frederick, 118, 370
Moore, Gerald, 537, 557, 587n
Morison, James Cotter, 114
Moscheles, Ignaz, 38, 40, 44, 60n, 73, 139, 264
Moulton, Richard, 551
Mulgan, P. A., 606-607
Murdoch, William, 557-58
Musical Interpretation (1913), 328-44

Nachez, Tivadar, 300
Neville, Elsie, 508, 511, 549-52, 576, 584, 595, 597, 599-600, 602, 605

INDEX

New Philharmonic (Orchestra), 40-41
Newman, William, 5
Niecks, Friedrich, 211-12, 232n, 328, 521
North, Stanley Kennedy, 369-70, 520
Norton, Eunice, 367, 385, 417-19, 488-89, 535-36, 631
Nunn, Cuthbert, 94, 123, 181-82, 215, 241, 285, 293
Nunn, R. Lindley, 88

Oistrakh, David, 545
Oppenheimer, Herbert, 549-50, 596-97, 609n
Ortmann, Otto, 4-8, 164, 431-38
Osborne, Sarah, 213, 282

Paine, John Knowles, 265, 408
Parker, Horatio, 408
Parker, Louis Napoleon, 49-52, 62n, 105-106
Parrott, L. Gurney, 511-14
Parry, C. Hubert, 29-30, 53, 59n, 87, 146n, 493
Pauer, Max, 471
Pendleton, Samuel (Sam), xvi, 580
Peppercorn, Gertrude, xvii, 144-46, 240, 370, 460-61, 484-85, 495, 538, 557
Philharmonic Society of London, 30-31, 40, 46-47, 103, 109-111, 299-300
Philipp, Isidore, 358
Phillipowski, Ivan, 345
Piatti, Alfredo, 42

Pollard, Claude, 141, 285-86, 292-93, 384, 407
Portnoff, Mischa, 464
Potter, Cipriani, 45-46, 54, 79-80, 184n
Powell, Michael, 503
Praeger, Ferdinand, 105
Primrose, William, 463
Profumo, Albert, 598
Prout, Ebenezer, 77-78, 82, 87, 88-89, 110, 139, 149n, 159, 214
Purvis, Edith, 181-82

Radbourne, June, 500
Raff, Joachim, 103, 123, 142, 182
Rawsthorne, Alan, 486-87
Read, Ernest, 215-17, 267, 294, 310, 343, 564-65
Reddie, Charles, 537
Reinecke, Carl, 5, 8-9, 15, 139, 471
Reitler, Joseph, 510
Richter, Hans, 78-79, 105-106, 194
Rietz, Julius, 73
Rihill, Maude, 141-45, 181-83, 202, 319, 370
Robertson, Fanny, 495
Robertson, Rae, 417, 463-66, 470, 485, 499, 626, 630
Robson, Dorothy, 537
Rosenbloom, Sydney, 366
Royal Academy of Music (London), xvi-xvii, 4, 8, 21, 23, 38-40, 43-58, 61n, 62n, 65-97, 99n, 100n, 102n, 106-107, 112-13, 121, 123, 129-30, 138-45,

651

INDEX

147n, 152n, 155-59, 172-84,
184n, 185n, 189, 201-203,
214-15, 219, 222, 227-229,
233n, 234n, 239-40, 244, 262,
284-85, 288, 295-97, 302,
302-312, 315, 325-28, 344,
346-47, 350-51, 362, 366-72,
372n, 381-405, 456, 463, 471,
485, 509-516, 536-38, 543,
595-98, 600-601, 605-608
Royal Albert Hall, 34-35, 66-67, 71, 78, 99n, 156-57, 601
Royal College of Music (London), xvii, 29, 36, 95, 120, 157-58, 219, 275n, 391, 511-12, 514-15, 605
Royal Irish Academy (Dublin), 226
Royal Manchester College of Music, 42
Rubinstein, Anton, 2, 15, 57, 124-28, 130, 150n, 151n, 155, 248-49, 459
Rubinstein, Arthur, 546
Ruggles, Carl, 487
Rummel, Walter, 458
Russell, Oswald, 607

Safonov, Vassily, 18
Sainton, Prosper, 155
Samuel, Maud, 95, 213
Samuel, Moses, 213-14, 236n
Saperton, David, 5
Sauer, Emil von, 12
Scharrer, Ida Samuel, 213-14, 229, 370
Scharrer, Irene, 214, 223, 229, 235n, 236n, 269, 273, 298, 302-304,
309, 365, 367, 370, 405, 413-14, 418, 442-43, 449, 462-63, 498-99, 502, 504, 507, 509, 522, 527n, 540-41, 544, 551, 557-58, 564-65, 574, 604, 629, 630
Schnabel, Artur, 18-19, 488-89, 500, 535n, 536, 587n
Schnabel, Karl Ulrich, 560
Schonberg, Harold, 5
Schultz, Arnold, 3-5, 23n,
Serkin, Rudolf, 5
Sessions, Roger, 487,
Sewell, Oroya, 406
Sharp, Cecil, 442, 520
Sharp, William, 208
Shaw, Elizabeth, 568
Sim, Alastair, 362
Simon, Abbey, 534
Simonds, Bruce, 365, 408-417, 419-421, 426n, 431-32, 437, 441-45, 447-450, 456,460, 468, 472, 479n, 483-84, 487-88, 493-94, 503-504, 506, 517-18, 520-22, 534-35, 539, 562, 564, 575, 601-602, 606, 631
Simonds, Rosalind, 410, 413, 443-44, 446-47, 469, 483, 503-504, 506, 517-19, 521-22, 602
Simons, John, 557-58
Skimming, Anthea Bowring, 418, 426n
Smith, Cyril, 557
Snowden, Lady Ethel
Snyder, Paul, 533
Sokolov, Grigory, 4

INDEX

Somervell, Sir Arthur, 300, 493
Sowerby, Leo, 487
Spencer, Herbert, 115-18, 148n, 149n, 162-63, 172, 226, 246, 249, 285, 565
Spry, Walter, 459-60
Squibb, David, xvii, 538
Stark, Ludwig, 8, 24n,
Steggall, Charles, 53, 214
Stein, Eduard, 155
Steinhausen, Friedrich Adolph, 15, 17, 140
Stoker, Enid, 286
Stokes, Leslie, 566
Sullivan, Sir Arthur, 60n, 72-77, 82, 87, 98n, 99n, 101n, 108-110, 129, 149n, 541
Swinstead, Felix, 242-43, 286, 293, 300, 305, 344, 413, 570-71, 619
Symons, Bernard, 347

Tailleferre, Germaine, 464
Tapia-Caballero, Arnaldo, 509, 539
Taylor, Billy, 1
Taylor, Sedley, 178
Teichmüller, Robert, 471-72, 568
Thatcher, Reginald, 541-42, 605-606
Thompson, Arthur, 520, 239-40
Tidmarsh, Egerton, 345, 347, 366, 370, 384, 411, 600-601, 630
Tillett, John, 516
Tillett, Terrence, 489
Tobias Matthay Pianoforte School, xiv, 284-285, 292-95, 304, 307-310, 316n, 317n, 319-20, 330, 344-45, 347-48, 352-53, 355-56, 359, 361-62, 365-67, 385-86, 399-418, 440, 442, 444, 447, 453, 466-75, 476, 478n, 483, 485, 488-89, 494, 500, 501-502, 506-510, 516-19, 537-38, 540, 548-551, 559, 567, 571, 573, 576, 581, 583-84, 595-608
Turpin, Edmund, 175

Uhlrich, K. W., 155

Vengerova, Isabel, 6
Verne, Mathilde, 543
Victoria, Queen of the United Kingdom, 30, 34, 39, 45, 67-68, 72, 129, 296, 357
The Visible and Invisible (1932), 437-40

Walenn, Gerald, 180-81,
Walenn, Herbert, 509-510
Walker, Alfred, 75, 78-79, 81-82, 88, 96, 115, 138
Walker, Leonard, 597
Waller, Percy, 286, 293, 344, 408, 425n, 536
Warren, Gwendolyn, 584
Weingarten, Paul, 543
Weir, Nancy, 551
West, Lily, 153n, 181-82, 285, 293, 385, 495
Westmorland, 10th Earl of, 39, 47, 61n

INDEX

Wetzler, Hermann Hans, 460, 479n
Weyman, Wesley, 408
White, Marion, *See* Cole, Marion White
Whitehouse, W. E., 181
Whitemore, Cuthbert, 285-86, 384
Wieck, Friedrich, 131
Wigley, Marjorie Middleton, 296
Wigton, G. M. B., 228
Wild, Earl, 499
Williams, G. G., 467, 474-75
Wilson, John (Jock), 189, 191, 200
Wilson, Teddy, 1
Wingham, Thomas, 50-51, 88, 95, 97, 102n

Wood, Annabelle, 534
Wood, S. H., 466-67
Wood, Sir Henry, 215, 301, 303, 312, 314, 320n, 369, 390-91, 472-73, 498-99, 517, 556
Woof, Rowsby, 359
Wright, Kenneth, 490
Wylde, Henry, 39-41, 44, 48, 62n, 129, 150n, 284
Wynn, Arthur, 563

Yerburgh, Oscar, xvii, 376n, 573-75
Ysaÿe, Eugène, 545-46

Zelikhman, Lea, 6

ABOUT THE AUTHOR

Stephen Siek is a Professor Emeritus of piano and music history at Wittenberg University in Springfield, Ohio. He has appeared as recitalist, chamber musician, and lecturer in Britain and throughout North America, and has recorded *The Philadelphia Sonatas* of Alexander Reinagle for the Titanic label. His numerous articles have appeared in such journals as the *American Music Teacher*, the *Piano Quarterly, American Music*, the *Revised New Grove*, and *International Piano*, and from 1998-2002 he served as President of the American Matthay Association. He holds two degrees in piano performance from the University of Maryland, and a Ph. D. in musicology from the College-Conservatory of Music at the University of Cincinnati. He is also the author of *A Dictionary for the Modern Pianist* (Rowman & Littlefield, 2016), and has annotated over a dozen classical CDs for the Decca, Deutsche Grammophon, and Hyperion labels. In May of 2019 he was made an Honorary Associate of the Royal Academy of Music in London. He currently lives in Tempe, Arizona, where he serves as a Faculty Associate at Arizona State University.

Printed in Great Britain
by Amazon